MW00584339

IN PURSUIT OF MILITARY EXCELLENCE

The Cummings Center for Russian and East European Studies
The Cummings Center Series

In Pursuit of Military Excellence
The Evolution of Operational Theory

Shimon Naveh

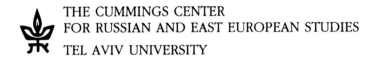

THE CUMMINGS CENTER
FOR RUSSIAN AND EAST EUROPEAN STUDIES
TEL AVIV UNIVERSITY

The Cummings Center is Tel Aviv University's main framework for research, study, documentation and publication relating to the history and current affairs of Russia, the former Soviet republics and Eastern Europe. The Center is committed to pursuing projects which make use of fresh archival sources and to promoting a dialogue with Russian academic circles through joint research, seminars and publications.

THE CUMMINGS CENTER SERIES

The titles published in this series are the product of original research by the Center's faculty, research staff and associated fellows. The Cummings Center Series also serves as a forum for publishing declassified Russian archival material of interest to scholars in the fields of history and political science.

EDITOR-IN-CHIEF
Gabriel Gorodetsky

EDITORIAL BOARD
Michael Confino
Shimon Naveh
Yaacov Ro'i
Nurit Schleifman

MANAGING EDITOR
Deena Leventer

IN PURSUIT OF MILITARY EXCELLENCE

The Evolution of Operational Theory

SHIMON NAVEH

FRANK CASS
LONDON • NEW YORK

First Published in 1997 by
FRANK CASS PUBLISHERS

Reprinted 2004 by Frank Cass
2 Park Square Milton Park Abingdon Oxon OX14 4RN

Transferred to Digital Printing 2006

Frank Cass is an imprint of the Taylor and Francis Group

British Library Cataloguing in Publication Data
Naveh, Shimon
   In pursuit of military excellence : the evolution of
   operational theory. – (The Cummings Center series)
   1. Military art and science   2. Strategy
   I. Title   II. Cummings Center for Russian and East European
   Studies
   355.4

   ISBN 0-7146-4727-6 (cloth)
   ISBN 0-7146-4277-0 (paper)
   ISSN 1365-3733

      Library of Congress Cataloging-in-Publication Data
Naveh, Shimon
   In pursuit of military excellence : the evolution of operational
   theory / Shimon Naveh.
      p.   cm. — (Cummings Center series)
   Includes bibliographical references (p.   ) and index.
   ISBN 0-7146-4727-6 (cloth). — ISBN 0-7146-4277-0 (pbk.)
   1. Operational art (Military science)—History.   I. Title.
   II. Series.
U162.N29   1997   97-14835
355.4—dc21   CIP

Typeset by Regent Typesetting, London

Publisher's Note
The publisher has gone to great lengths to ensure the quality of
this reprint but points out that some imperfections
in the original may be apparent

*To the memory of Richard Simpkin OBE –
a pioneer of operational thinking in the West*

Contents

CONTENTS

Acknowledgements

I would like to thank Professor Itamar Rabinovich whose insightful initiative made this enterprise possible from the start. I am also deeply indebted to Mrs Hedda Ben Shefer for her friendly assistance and good counsel over the years, to the British Council in Tel Aviv for their generous financial support of my work and to Dr Raphael Posner and Deena Leventer, whose penetrating questions and remarks guided me in formulating my ideas into a coherent manuscript. Professor Gabriel Gorodetsky was a driving force in the publication of this volume. I am grateful to him for his careful reading of the manuscript, his enlightening scientific advice and moral support. Finally, special thanks go to Dr Ephraim Karsh whose true benevolence and expository guidance have proved invaluable throughout.

Introduction

The main premise of this book is that for the first time since the French Revolution the phenomenon of war in general, and the domain of military operations in particular, have been characterized by the existence of material system conditions; hence their study must comply with a systemic approach and their examination must be conducted in accordance with systemic criteria. Moreover, the main thesis proposed by this study identifies the basic common denominator of conventional warfare in the course of the last two centuries as its occurrence within the realm – or, rather, level – of operations. Therefore, in those campaigns where a systemic approach was applied, in both planning and management of armed forces, the nature of warfare was marked by sound operational logic and its conduct can be defined as operational art. On the other hand, the longstanding failure to apply a systemic approach to the field of operational conduct throughout the nineteenth century and the first quarter of the twentieth led to the suppression of creative military thinking by a mechanistic mentality of attrition – a trend which has been reflected in the attempt to manipulate tactics on a major scale. In this argument lies the novelty of this book since the majority of Western military historians interpret warfare exclusively from a tactical or strategic point of view.

In an attempt to dissolve the mental fog which has for so long surrounded the sphere of military systems, this work seeks to offer a scientific interpretation of the intermediate field of military knowledge situated between strategy and tactics, better known as operational art, and to trace the evolution of operational awareness and its culmination in a full-fledged theory.

The book combines two approaches: a theoretical analysis and historical research. Using the General System theory as a heuristic framework, this study will clarify the substance of operational art and construct a cognitive framework for its critical analysis. Having done this, it will examine four key landmarks in the evolution of operational theory: nineteenth-century military thought and the roots of operational ignorance; the emergence of the *Blitzkrieg* concept; the evolution of the Soviet Deep Operation theory during the 1920s and

1930s; and the crystallization of the American Airland Battle theory half a century later.

By defining the *levée en masse*, which generated the basic material condition characterizing a military system as the concept initiating the era of modern warfare, the earliest time boundary for our historical discussion is thus set.[1] Moreover, the application of a system approach, based upon the General Systems theory sets an innovative perspective for a coherent examination of both the general course of military thought and operational occurrences.[2]

The material conditions needed for this new province of military endeavour came about through the maturation of a series of historical circumstances towards the end of the eighteenth century: the quantitative increase in the fighting mass of European armies resulting from universal conscription; the institutionalization of a hierarchical linkage between the political, strategic and tactical echelons, deriving from the crystallization of the political and social patterns of the modern state; and the acceleration of the technological development stemming from the Industrial Revolution.

At the beginning of the nineteenth century the convergence of these circumstances introduced, for the first time in the history of war, the logic of systems into the field of warfare. Whether wittingly or unwittingly, both armies and military theoreticians found themselves in a new strategic reality governed by system dynamics.[3] This in turn set warfare in the course of the last 200 years apart from the military activity preceding it, in that, in principle, its application materialized at the intermediate level between tactics and strategy, due to the quantitative, political, and technological changes emerging at the outset of the nineteenth century. At the same time, the new operational layer has been dominated by the complex logic of systems.

Employing system logic for the interpretation of operational art allows a coherent perception of the entire act of war, from abstract thinking and definitions of policy to the mechanical aspects of combat. Here then, the conceptual terms for the definition of the operational level are laid out – and not on the exclusive basis of quantitative aspects.

Through the application of the system approach as a universal framework allowing the explanation of the operational manoeuvre in scientific terms this book aims at attaining two objectives: it aspires to provide students of war, who have not been trained in the military profession, with a solid conceptual framework for understanding the logic of conducting large operations, or, rather, military systems; and to equip field commanders and staff officers with intellectual tools for reviewing military activity, at both the theoretical and practical levels.

Anchoring modern warfare in the operational context, this work sets generic characteristics incorporating the various military activities within a single thematic context distinguishing it from pre-nineteenth-century warfare. This approach is crucial for a systematic examination of the development of military thought in the modern era. A comparative approach to military history research can assist students of war to cope with a whole set of questions deriving almost exclusively from operational complexities such as: How did the obsession with offensive develop before the First World War? How did manoeuvre thinking become dominated by linear patterns? Why, notwithstanding the possession of ample mechanized assets, did the advanced European armies fail to develop operational patterns of manoeuvre in the course of the First World War? Why did the astounding tactical success of the German 1918 Spring offensive ultimately lead to strategic disaster? Why, notwithstanding the Wehrmacht's unique tactical excellence, was the *Blitzkrieg* method defeated? What were the operational factors that generated the succession of Soviet victories after the Summer of 1943? How did the American armed forces manage to rapidly transform their defensive perception into a most effective offensive manoeuvre?

Chapter 1 will provide an academic interpretation of operational art. Employing the essentials of General System theory, which has emerged simultaneously in a number of countries and been applied to various fields since the late 1920s, it will set out a theoretical framework for understanding operational manoeuvre. Thus, surveying the essence of advanced operational theories such as Soviet Deep Operations and American Airland Battle, as well as the modes of reasoning practised in the course of their formulation, the substance of operational art will be revealed. Moreover, by introducing the terms and principles comprising the core of operational art, the reader will be provided with a uniform system of scientific terminology for a critical examination of the development of operational theory.

The other aim is a historical survey of the evolution of operational art. It is governed by a holistic approach which views the development of the theory of modern warfare as a complete historical unit, dominated by the cardinal motive or theme of operational perception. On the other hand, the historical analysis follows Thomas Kuhn's conception that progress in scientific knowledge is achieved through a revolutionary process in which new and advanced theories or paradigms replace archaic, irrelevant ones.[4]

Assuming that operational perception and patterns of conduct capable of producing effective results within the systemic environment which emerged at the beginning of the nineteenth century constitute the main parameters for judging military achievements, both theoretical and practical, the modern era can be divided into two periods: the period of operational ignorance, starting with the Napoleonic wars and ending in the 1920s, characterized by the complete failure of military thought to develop patterns of conduct capable of coping with the material challenges set by the systemic environment; and the period of operational perception which saw the birth of the bastardized concept of *Blitzkrieg* and the rise of the advanced theories of Deep Operations and Airland Battle.

A historical analysis of the evolution – or, rather, degeneration – of military thought in the course of the nineteenth century and the beginning of the twentieth will be presented in the second and third chapters from a new perspective. A study of the 1870 War, the main theoretical works composed during that era, and Clausewitz's *On War* in particular, will attempt to explain from the perspective of systemic criticism why, notwithstanding the prevalence of system material conditions, an operational perception did not develop in that period. Thus, a novel interpretation, explaining not only the failure of the First World War but also the roots of the mental dichotomy characterizing military thought throughout the nineteenth century and first two decades of the present century, is offered. Moreover, viewing European military thought from an operational perspective will disclose an entire chain of cognitive paradoxes, which led to the crystallization of the Clausewitzian paradigm of *Vernichtungsschlacht* (the Integral Battle of Destruction).

The enquiry into the roots of the *Blitzkrieg* concept in Chapter 4 constitutes the most demanding challenge, both historiographically and theoretically. To start with, the idea of *Blitzkrieg* was born and lived without a written theoretical basis. Moreover, the concept is heavily laden with myth and fantasy originating in the historical manipulations and speculative interpretations which arose in the wake of the Second World War. Finally, until the late 1970s very little was known in the West about the operational circumstances under which the Red Army crushed the Wehrmacht.

Applying a system approach in the attempt to explore the roots of the theoretical dynamics guiding the German officer corps in the course of the 1930s reveals that the *Blitzkrieg* concept lacked the true fundamentals of operational thought. The accelerated growth of the armed forces, effectuated by a school of opportunistic technocrats under Hitler's aegis, dictated the suppression of the surviving islands of operational perception that existed in the Wehrmacht. In other words, a fastidious study of the functioning of the Ostheere and Panzer Armee Afrika and the operational conduct of Guderian and Rommel, the spiritual fathers of the *Blitzkrieg*, proves that the bastard concept of *Blitzkrieg* was the product of a hyper-aggressive political ideology and a manipulation of tactical patterns of combat.

Suggesting nothing other than a tactical response to Hitler's incoherent strategic aspirations, the *Blitzkrieg* concept lacked the conceptual framework of a written operational theory; not surprisingly, even a superficial enquiry reveals that no elementary consensus existed within the Wehrmacht high command as to the operational substance of *Blitzkrieg*. Thus, the operational art of *Blitzkrieg*, devoid of system consciousness, was confined to pushing the tactical excellence achieved by the Reichswehr in years of hard work to the extreme limits of human performance.

Consequently, the reconstruction of the original version of the *Blitzkrieg* concept is based on the following resources: personal diaries and autobiographies of Wehrmacht officers, which are rife with retrospective interpretations guided by personal interests; a variety of primary sources, comprising war diaries of Wehrmacht formations and units, battle orders, after-action reports and briefings from the years 1939–45, expressing the distress of the field echelons that resulted from the operational shallowness of the *Blitzkrieg* concept; the post-war enquiries conducted by B.H. Liddell Hart and his interviews with German officers; and some contemporary theoretical material which is dedicated exclusively to tactics.[5]

By way of exploring the circumstances which led to the evolution of the Soviet theory of Deep Operations, Chapters 5 and 6 will present the breakthrough of military perception into the province of system thinking, and the theoretical revolution centring on the shift from the Clausewitzian paradigm of *Vernichtungsschlacht* to the advanced paradigm of operational manoeuvre. In spite of the fact that both chapters constitute a single thematic whole, the range of the subject and its complexity justifies a division in the exposition. Whereas the first discusses the broader context of historical and methodological circumstances characterizing the complex process of the theory's development, the second presents an innovative interpretation of the Deep Operation theory, based upon a critical reading of the ample theoretical material formulated between 1924 and 1937 and the years that followed.

Chapter 5 reconstructs a broad historical picture of the most creative theoretical adventure in the military history of the twentieth century through the illumination of topics such as: the mental impact of the Russian Civil War on the evolution of the operational theory; the professional debate concerning the development of a unified military doctrine in the early 1920s; the methodology of the theoretical process; the confrontation between the veterans of the First Cavalry Army and Mikhail Tukhachevskii's school of operational thought; and the circumstances that led to the composition of tactical Field Service Regulations of Deep Battle in 1936–37.

Chapter 6 will reveal the systemic roots of the theory of Deep Operations. The basic proposition in this chapter in particular and the entire work in general is that the way to defeat a modern military system is not by aiming at its destruction, as was claimed by Clausewitizian philosophy for more than a hundred and twenty years, but rather through the notion of operational shock, defined in Russian as *udar*. This concept, developed by Tukhachevskii and his associates from the school of operational thought as they endeavoured to identify the roots of failure of the First World War, provided the conceptual lever for the abrogation of the *Vernichtungsschlacht* paradigm. Moreover, these theoreticians learned that the effectuation of operational shock implied, first and foremost, the neutralization of the rival system's rationale, i.e. its operational ability to attain the aim or objectives assigned to it by the strategic authority. Rooted in the logic of systems, this unique idea expressed the *raison d'être* for both the operational theory and the concept of the strike manoeuvre, which therefore has also been termed *udar*. By illuminating this aspect of the Deep Operation theory, this study offers an innovative interpretation of the Russian perception of modern manoeuvre.

With this approach in mind, Chapter 6 will unravel the unique notions of simultaneity, momentum and fragmentation, constituting both the cognitive and physical fundamentals of Soviet operational manoeuvre. Later, when attempting to elucidate the Soviet approach to the subject of operational synergy, which is based on a deep interaction among the manoeuvring elements of forward detachment (*peredovoi otriad*), holding echelon (*skovyvaiushchii eshelon*), strike echelon (*eshelon razvitiia proryva/podvizhnaiia gruppa*), and deep airborne echelon (*desant*), the notions of synchronization, coordination and combined arms combat will be interpreted within the relevant operational context. The conceptual analysis of the operational theory, which is based on a study of overt contemporary theoretical material and subsequent references, will be concluded by an exposition of the fundamentals of Soviet operational command philosophy.

On the face of it, the theoretical revolution in American military thought which commenced in the second half of the 1970s resembles that of the Soviet theory of Deep Operations. It, too, emphasizes the shift from a tactical paradigm of destruction to an operational paradigm of advanced manoeuvre. It will be demonstrated that, notwithstanding the emphasis on the dimension of operational mobility as a means for the initial acquisition of depth at the expense of the antagonist, the American conceptual revolution did not bring about significant innovation in the field of operational thought. The innovation thus reflects the dynamics of the revolutionary process, and the methodology of the theory's development. Moreover, since of all Western democratic military establishments it is the United States Army which pioneered the application of the system theory to the field of operational manoeuvre, its success offers a positive model for imitation to states possessing similar political systems and mentality. And finally, the proximity of the Persian Gulf War to the more advanced stages of the American doctrinal process provides a rare opportunity for the examination of the theory's application in practice.

The exploration of the roots of the American operational revolution, the methodology by which the theory developed, and the identification of the elements which initiated the shift of perceptions from the archaic Active Defence to the advanced Airland Battle, are subjects upon which Chapters 7 and 8 will focus.

Employing the essentials of the Soviet theory of operations as perceptional tools for criticism, a comparative analysis of the 1976 Operations Field Manual, and the flow of theoretical literature following its publication with that of 1982, will identify the political, doctrinal and methodological sources of the revolution in American military thought. This approach instigates some of the novel views suggested by Chapters 7 and 8, such as: the roots of failure of the 1976 Active Defence Manual, and the contribution of this failure to the adoption of a system approach by the military; the unique method practised by General Don Starry, who initiated the application of a system approach and the development of the Airland Battle doctrine; the real cognitive sources of the theoretical debate occurring in the United States Army from 1976 to 1983, and their presentation in a broader perspective than the version suggested by TRADOC's official historiography; and finally, disclosing the decisive contribution played by the civilian group of operational reformers in generating the cognitive crisis that led to the development of the operational theory – a matter that official historiography, whether intentionally or not, has spared no effort to conceal.

A comparative examination of the operational manuals of 1982 and 1986 and the corresponding theoretical literature will indicate the conceptual quantum leap accomplished by the United States Army after operational cognition had already been acquired.

The epilogue focuses on the main operational conclusions drawn from the Gulf Campaign and closes the historical-theoretical circle that was initially postulated in this work The recent Gulf Conflict witnessed a vigorous encounter between two military cultures: the first based its professional ethos and strategic credo on system logic, which exemplified the complexities of the post-modern reality; the second derived its rationale from the dynamics of the industrial era. It was a confrontation between a military system which had undergone a conceptual transformation accomplished through the application of the innovative paradigm of operational manoeuvre, and a system locked in the archaic conventions of the nineteenth-century Clausewitzian paradigm.

NOTES

1. Historiographical approaches unaware of the existing identity between mass, systems and the context of operations, tend to identify the advent of modern warfare with events such as the Peace of Westphalia and the end of the Thirty Years' War, the emergence of the genius of Napoleon Bonaparte, or the advent of mechanization. Some of these approaches are reflected in Y. Harkaby, *War and Strategy* (Tel Aviv, 1990, in Hebrew), pp. 117–20; P. Paret, *Understanding War: Essays on Clausewitz and the History of Military Power* (Princeton, 1992), pp. 209–14; idem, 'Napoleon and the Revolution in War', in P. Paret (ed.), *Makers of Modern Strategy* (Princeton, 1991), pp. 123–42; J.F.C. Fuller, *The Conduct of War 1789–1961* (New Brunswick, NJ, 1968), pp. 15–24; D.G. Chandler, *Atlas of Military Strategy* (London, 1980), pp. 19–30; P. Paret, *The Art of Warfare in the Age of Marlborough* (London, 1976), pp. 11–23; R. Aron, *Peace and War* (London, 1966), p. 73; J.U. Nef, *War and Human Progress* (Cambridge, MA, 1950), p. 147; H. Strachan, *European Armies and the Conduct of War* (London, 1983), pp. 8–22; K.N. Waltz, *Man the State and War* (New York, 1970), pp. 2–15; J. Keegan, *The Mask of Command* (London, 1988), pp. 311–15; L. Mumford, *The Condition of Man* (London, 1963), pp. 263–4; T. Ropp, *War in the Modern World* (London, 1962), pp. 17–30; R. Aron, *The Century of Total War* (Boston, 1955), pp. 19–22; M. Howard, *The Causes of Wars* (London, 1985), pp. 17–18; H. von Freytag-Loringhoven, *Die Heerführung Napoleons in ihrer Bedeutung für unsere Zeit* (Berlin, 1910), p. V; H. Camon, *Le Système de Guerre de Napoléon* (Paris, 1923), pp. 1–4; C. Oman, *A History of the Art of War in the Sixteenth Century* (London, 1937), p. 6; H.H. Gerth and C.W. Mills (eds), *From Max Weber: Essays on Sociology,* (New York, 1946), pp. 256–7; H. Nickerson, *The Armed Horde 1793–1939* (New York, 1940), pp. 34–40; H. Delbrück, *Geschichte der Kriegskunst im Rahmen der Politischen Geschichte* (7 Vols.) (Berlin, 1900–1936), Vol. 4, pp. 363, 426; R.A. Leonard (ed.), *A Short Guide to Clausewitz On War* (London, 1967), p. 9.
2. L. von Bertalanffy, *General System Theory* (New York, 1975); M.D. Mesarovic, 'Foundations for a General System Theory', in M.S. Mesarovic (ed.), *Views on General Systems Theory* (New York, 1964), pp. 1–24; A.D. Hall and R.E. Fagen, 'Definition of System', *General Systems*, 1 (1956), pp. 18–29; G.J. Klir, *An Approach to General Systems Theory* (Princeton, 1967); P. Checkland, *Systems Thinking, Systems Practice* (New York, 1981); and D. Kaufman, *Systems 1 : An Introduction to Systems Thinking* (Minneapolis, 1980), provide a general outline for system thinking that has been employed in this study. Both Bertalanffy, *General System Theory*, pp. 197–203, and Bertalanffy, 'Cultures as Systems: Toward a Critique of Historical Reason', in R.H. Garvin (ed.), *Phenomenology, Structuralism, Semiology* (Lewisburg, PA, 1976), pp. 151–61, present

the author's system-theoretical concept of history. P.A. Sorokin, *Contemporary Sociological Theories*, (1928) (New York, 1964); Sorokin, *Sociological Theories of Today* (New York, 1966); W. Buckley, *Sociology and Modern Systems Theory* (Englewood Cliffs, NJ, 1967); and D.A. Hall, *A Methodology for Systems Engineering* (Princeton, 1962), reflect the application of system theory to the field of social science. C.A. McClelland, 'Systems and History in International Relations – Some Perspectives for Empirical Research and Theory', *General Systems*, 3 (1958), pp. 221–47; L.J. Carter, 'Systems Approach: Political Interest Rises', *Science*, 153 (1966), pp. 1222–4; P.M. Boffey, 'Systems Analysis: No Panacea for Nation's Domestic Problems', *Science*, 158 (1967), pp. 1028–30, offer an application of system approach to the field of political sciences; I. Even-Zohar, 'The Nature and Functionalization of the Language of Literature under Diglossia', *Hasifrut* II, 2 (1970), pp. 286–302; idem, 'The Polysystem Hypothesis Revisited', *Hasifrut* VIII, 27 (1978), pp. 1–6; idem, 'On Systemic Universals in Cultural History', in *Papers in Historical Poetics*, The Porter Institute for Poetics and Semiotics (Tel Aviv, 1978), pp. 39–44, suggests the application of the system approach to linguistic and literary research.
3. Clausewitz, *On War*, M. Howard and P. Paret (eds), (Princeton, 1976), B. 8, Ch. 3, pp. 591–2; J.W. Goethe, *Campaign in France in the Year 1792*, trans. R. Farie (London, 1859), pp. 72–3, 77, 81; J.F.C. Fuller, *Military History of the Western World* (3 Vols.) (New York, 1967), Vol. 2, pp. 450–86; A.J.P. Taylor, *From Napoleon to Lenin* (New York, 1952), pp. 14–16; T. Ropp, *War in the Modern World*, p. 98; J.A.H. de Guibert, *Essai générale de tactique* (Liège, 1775), Vol. I, Ch. XIII; Vol. II, p. 65; P. de Bourcet, *Mémoires historiques sur la guerre . . . 1757–1762* (Paris, 1792), p. 88; H. Sargent, *Napoleon Bonaparte's First Campaign* (London, 1895), p. 16; H. Camon, *Quand et comment Napoleon a conçu son système de bataille*, (Paris, 1935), p. 5.
4. T.S. Kuhn, *The Structure of Scientific Revolutions* (Chicago, 1970).
5. In this respect, since it represents a unique attempt to provide a complete theoretical outline of *Blitzkrieg* through the exercise of critical methods of research, F.O. Miksche's book is an exception. F.O. Miksche, *Blitzkrieg* (London, 1941). A Czechoslovak officer, the author attempted to compose a theoretical framework of *Blitzkrieg*, based upon a critical research of events almost as they occurred.

Operational Art and the General Theory of Systems

INTRODUCTION

Since the end of the eighteenth century, the art of war has been based on two traditional levels of conduct. The higher, or abstract level, was concerned with the building of military forces and their preparation for war, as well as with the general planning of armed conflict and its conduct. The lower, or mechanical level, centred on the actual operation of the military forces on the battlefield.[1] Consequently, in the course of time, strategy and tactics crystallized as unique fields of knowledge to cope with the challenges posed at each of these two levels.

The marked increase in the size of armed forces, which began in the early nineteenth century, acquired monstrous dimensions towards its end, and led to the expansion of military operations, both in space and time. This quantitative change created a new problem in the conduct of war, in the intermediate sphere between the traditionally accepted levels of military planning.[2] The establishment of the corps formation and the creation of novel patterns of movement did indeed reflect a positive attempt to respond to the new challenges posed by the increase in the fighting mass. Nevertheless, the theory of war remained confined to the traditional levels of tactics and strategy, while the intermediate level was largely ignored. The semantic effort to bridge the cognitive hiatus by the application of terms such as 'grand tactics', 'grand strategy' or 'strategic manoeuvre', was totally unsuccessful, since it merely amplified the existing obtuseness.[3] In 1965, Henry Kissinger admitted that only trivial progress had been made since the nineteenth century towards comprehending the operational level of war. However, while he identified the problem, he failed to provide a solution:

> In the past, the major problem of strategists was to assemble a

superior strength. In the contemporary period, the problem more frequently is how to discipline the available power into some relationship to the objectives likely to be in dispute.[4]

The abstruseness which clouded the operational substance has not entirely disappeared even in the decade following the formal introduction of an operational doctrine by the US and NATO armed forces. An examination of theoretical military writing since the application of the 'Airland Battle' doctrine reveals the existence of a wide diversity of versions and interpretations regarding the operational level, grave doubts concerning its validity in general, and, in particular, the need for a distinct operational theory.[5]

Any exploration of the operational level raises an inevitable query: Why did it emerge so late? Although the answer lies beyond the scope of the present chapter and will be addressed in detail later, the very introduction of the question elicits a complex of problems which hinder an understanding of the operational level.

The methodological difficulty derives first and foremost from the fact that no serious effort has ever been made in the West to provide a coherent historical framework for the evolution of operational cognition. However, it also results from the fact that the sources for studying the operational level have not been defined and that the cognitive tools for its research have only been vaguely specified. Consequently, the roots of the difficulties in understanding the operational dimension have remained hidden, and its study in the West has suffered from a conspicuous lack of scientific discipline.[6]

A discussion of the operational level must face the following issues: In what distinct aspects does it differ from the strategic and tactical levels? What are the criteria by which an operational problem is to be identified? How should one differentiate between the practical aspects of operational art and the cognitive aspects deriving from the operational level? And, finally: What is the justification for the assertion of a distinctive operational cognition?

The methodological difficulties mentioned above are compounded by the lack of precise terminology and definitions for the specific laws and phenomena within the operational level of war. The severity of this problem is reflected both in the absence of uniformity in the use of terms relating to operational matters, and in their distorted and confused utilization. The absence in the West, until only recently, of a fundamental textbook covering the theoretical aspects of the operational level may have been a contributing factor to this state of affairs. The Russian operational setting has been traditionally characterised by an abundance of meticulous, specific terms, while

2

the identical field in the West still suffers from a scarcity, which is reflected in the inability of Western theoreticians to delineate operational matters accurately.[7]

By offering a thorough analysis of the operational level, its principles and unique phenomena, this chapter will attempt to solve the problems described above. Thus, it will attempt to provide a theoretical and terminological basis to facilitate orientation through the theoretical complexity of the operational level. The theoretical foundation will also provide the relevant cognitive tools for judging and assessing operational occurrences.

The new operational field is not an autonomous entity, detached from the universal wholeness of the phenomenon of war, but is founded, in fact, on war craft and is centred entirely on warfare. Thus, the operational level forms a natural, or rather, integral layer within the experience of modern war. This being so, an independent exposition of the operational level is artificial, and is deliberately intended to indicate the existence of an exclusive operational cognition. Nevertheless, the operational level does differ from the tactical level, both in quantity and in quality, and from the strategic level in substance.

Another fundamental assumption which should be made prior to the theoretical discussion is that the operational experience conforms, in its principles and characteristics, to the universal phenomenon of systems. Thus, the operational theory constitutes the military version of the *Gestalt* philosophy or the theory of general systems.

The systems concept was formulated by the Hungarian scientist, Ludwig von Bertalanffy, whose main contribution was the basic rationale for the interdisciplinary approach to systems.[8] This approach not only explains the various phenomena in a system, but also identifies the laws governing a system and their rationale. Thus, Bertalanffy offers a universal framework for understanding systems, as well as the perceptual tools for their definition and criticism. This last point is of the greatest significance since an operational theory, *per se*, has not yet been devised in the West, and the Russian Deep Operation theory (*glubokaia operatsiia*) is still far from being fully understood by Western military theoreticians. Following a brief description of systems theory, we will turn to an examination of the phenomenon of the military system, or operational level, in particular. With the help of the Russian Deep Operation Theory, the American Airland Battle doctrine, and the work of Richard Simpkin, a pioneer researcher of the operational level in the West, an attempt will be made to demarcate this problematic field, and to specify its

3

general attributes.[9] Thus, we will provide our discussion with the correct and relevant context.

THE UNIVERSAL SYSTEM DIMENSION

In terms of Thomas Kuhn's definition of scientific revolutions, the system concept constituted a theoretical revolution, since it refuted the prevailing mechanistic outlook by means of a novel paradigm or philosophy.[10] Evidence of this revolution was manifest in the natural sciences, exact sciences, social sciences and humanities, as well as in the fields of management, business, industry, commerce, education and military conduct. The cognitive crisis, which generated the theoretical revolution, was born out of growing scepticism regarding the abilities of the prevailing analytical-mechanistic approaches to respond adequately to challenges posed by the complexities of modern society and technology. Consequently, the need for a new understanding, based on holistic and system approaches and of an extensive interdisciplinary nature, was recognized. The essence of this revolution, which was conducted simultaneously by scientists in various fields and in different countries, was characterized by Bertalanffy:

> It is a change in basic categories of thought of which the complexities of modern technology are only one – and possibly not the most important manifestation. In one way or another we are forced to deal with complexities, with 'wholes' or systems, in all fields of knowledge. This implies a basic re-orientation in scientific thinking.[11]

Moreover, the development of a new system cognition raised the legitimate need for a theory, not of systems of a more or less special kind, but rather for one applying to systems in general, based upon universal principles.[12] This, to a certain extent, is the justification for applying the theory of general systems to the field of military operations.

Basically, Bertalanffy defines a system as a complex of interacting elements.[13] Thus, a system's problems, according to Bertalanffy, are problems of the interrelation of a great number of variables, which occur in the fields of politics, economics, industry, commerce and military conduct.[14] Bertalanffy goes on to propose cognitive tools for criticizing and assessing systems, and offers three distinct parameters. The first is the quantitative parameter, which concerns the number of elements composing the system; the second parameter is about matter, since it concerns the species of the elements involved; and the third is a qualitative, or rather substantive, parameter that centres on

4

the attributes of the relations between the various elements within the system.[15] Accordingly, Bertalanffy identifies two basic categories of universal systems, the open and the closed:

> We express this by saying that living systems are basically open systems. An open system is defined as a system in exchange of matter with its environment, presenting import and export, building up and breaking down of its material components . . . Closed systems are systems which are considered to be isolated from their environment.[16]

This definition can serve us well not only by classifying military systems as open systems, but also by demonstrating the striking affinity between open systems in general and the field of military operations, since hierarchical organization constitutes the typical pattern for an open system, and unsurprisingly it reflects the main traits of the universal system:

> Characteristic of organization, whether of a living organism or a society, are notions like those of *wholeness, growth, differentiation, hierarchical order, dominance, control, competition* etc. . . . . System theory is well capable of dealing with these matters.[17]

Clearly, the essence of a system centres on the existence of the interaction between its components more than on anything else and, by applying the universal experience, Bertalanffy identified the main characteristics of this interaction.

Since his basic argument presented the system's interaction as fundamental for its subsistence, Bertalanffy is correct in concluding that amplifying the dynamism of this interaction inevitably leads to an increase in the system's consequential product. However, according to Bertalanffy, attaining such dynamism prescribes that the nature of the interaction be non-linear.[18]

Applying this notion in a military situation requires a deep setting, hierarchical structure and a columnar mode of relation between the system's components, or between the sub-systems within the overall system. Thus, succession and echelonment constitute the first of the interaction's characteristics.

The second characteristic is the absolute dominance of the system's aim. The initial assertion of the aim by the system's brain or directing authority predetermines the comprehensive *whole*, i.e. the all-embracing accomplishment of its future destined action.[19] It also provides the focus of the system's performance since it creates the framework for the interrelations between its various elements and defines the orbit for the system's relations with its environment. In other words, the definition of the aim is the cognitive force that

5

generates the system and determines the directions and patterns of its action.[20] Thus, the deliberate exposition of the entire aim of a system's operation, which is made prior to its occurrence, manifests the holistic approach at its best. Moreover, it is this actual definition of the system's aim that indicates the focus of tension between the system and its rivals and the direction for releasing its internal stresses. And, finally, it is the abstract exposition of the aim that provides the system with its unifying determinant.[21] The acute importance of this cognitive unity derives both from the natural tendency of the elements to split from the system and from the fact that perpetuating cohesiveness within the system guarantees its self-regulating ability, which, in turn, enables the system to overcome the turbulence of external disturbances.[22]

Examining the relationship between the system and its components within the context of the aim reveals a dichotomy which seems to be the most complex aspect characterizing the system's existence. This dichotomy generates a certain tension, which is a crucial condition for the dynamic functioning of consciousness-driven systems. As already mentioned, the cognitive propagation of a system depends upon establishing its aim, which has both holistic and authoritative connotations. However, moving the system from a state of abstract, cognitive commonality to a practical course of positive progress can only be achieved by translating the overall aim into the concrete objectives and missions for the system's individual components. Thus, in order to accomplish its aim and so justify its existence, the system must steer itself as a total whole towards its general aim, and, at the same time, initiate a complex of concrete actions through its various components. In other words, the transformation of the system from a state of static anticipation always implies the existence of an intrinsic dichotomy. Moreover, since it is a dominant characteristic of the system's very nature, the permanent quality of contradictive tension, derives from the intermediary position of system occurrences between the mechanical context of random activity and the context of abstract thinking.[23]

The complexity of this dichotomous phenomenon, as well as its risks and implications, were pointed out by Bertalanffy:

> The positive progress of the system is possible only by passing from a state of undifferentiated wholeness to differentiation of parts. This implies, however, that the parts become fixed with respect to a certain action. Therefore, progressive segregation also means progressive mechanization. Progressive mechanization, however, implies loss of regulability.[24]

In order to harmonize this dichotomy and steer the system towards the achievement of its aim while forestalling the dangers of segregation and mechanization, modes of thinking must be utilized which are entirely different from those exercised in the traditional fields of tactics and strategy. Cognitive tension and a unique intellectual creativity, characteristic of commanders at the various echelons of operational systems, is a prerequisite which can only be acquired through a scientific process of training.[25]

In the military context, this dichotomy requires the preservation of a controlled disequilibrium between the general aim and the specific missions. Tactical missions should correspond to the general aim. Since these objectives are intangibly defined at the strategic level, and the mechanical performance is the domain of tactics, the acute importance of the operational level becomes clear. Only on this level can the abstract and mechanical extremes be fused into a functional formula, through the maintenance of cognitive tension.

The synergetic characteristic derives from the former two. According to Bertalanffy, the system approach demonstrates, in its sheer substance, the tangibility and prominence of wholes, which are dynamic by nature and are not just the sum of basic elements.[26] This notion is based both on the structural attributes of the system and on the nature of the existing interaction between its components. Whereas in linear complexes the result of the interaction can be defined as *summative*, the interaction of deep structured systems invariably results in *constitutive* effects.

The last notion sheds a somewhat different light upon the myth of quality. This myth, which prevails in certain armed forces, claims that quantity is insignificant, and it is only the quality that counts.[27] However, as we have seen, the importance of quantity derives from the basic fact that it constitutes one of the three cardinal factors in the system's efficiency. While it is true that the nature of the interrelations between the quantitative components of the system determines the quality of the final product, this very nature is influenced by the magnitude of the mass. Bertalanffy's summary illuminates this rather vague synergetic phenomenon:

> The meaning of the somewhat mystical expression, 'the whole is more than the sum of its parts' is simply that constitutive characteristics are not explainable from the characteristics of isolated parts. The characteristics of the complex, therefore, compared to those of the elements, appear as *new* or *emergent*.[28]

The last of the interaction's attributes to be described by Bertalanffy concerns its somewhat chaotic nature. System's occurrences are generally conducted towards situations of maximum probability and system's laws are, therefore, essentially 'Laws of Disorder' – the outcome of unordered statistical events.[29] In military operations this last notion becomes immediately apparent. The idea of 'organized chaos' reflects the constant contradiction between the random nature of such operations and the traditional trend to institutionalize their study in scientific patterns.

THE OPERATIONAL DIMENSION

In his revealing book dealing with the broadest aspects of modern strategy, Edward Luttwak not only disclosed the essential problem in the Western perception of the operational level of war, but also rationalized it and put it into a pertinent context:

> It is a peculiarity of English language military terminology that it has no word of its own for what stands between the tactical and strategic, to describe that middle level of thought and action wherein generic methods contend and battles unfold in their totality.[30]

The Western failure to coin a term to cover the operational field indicates, first and foremost, the lack of cognition regarding that field. Once a term was adopted from a foreign setting, cognition followed suit. In Luttwak's definition, the most conspicuous indicator of the operational level concerns its intermediary location. Another identifying mark, noted by Luttwak, relates to its integrative nature.[31] The operational level, not only bridges between the strategic and the tactical levels, but also combines the unique qualities and characteristics of each of these levels, i.e. abstract contemplation and mechanical action. Furthermore, the meeting of the traditional approaches representing tactics and strategy that transpires within the operational level radiates a certain tension. This unique tension was observed and noted by Luttwak.

The introductory attempt of the new American field manual to explain the holistic structure of modern warfare illuminates additional aspects of the operational level:

> War is a national undertaking which must be coordinated from the highest levels of policymaking to the basic levels of execution. Military strategy, operational art, and tactics are the broad divisions of activity in preparing for and conducting war. Successful strategy achieves national and alliance political aims at the lowest possible cost of lives and treasure. Operational art translates those aims into effective military operations and campaigns. Sound tactics win the battles and engagements which produce successful campaigns and operations.[32]

8

This introduction provided the basic terms for the subsequent exposition of the 'Airland Battle' doctrine and rationalized the operational level by anchoring it in the national-political system and in international relations. The clarification of the entire structure of political-military relations highlights the sequential nexus between its various layers and also reveals the means by which the discourse between them is induced through the definition of the aim. But above all, the exposition manifests the dominance of the operational level in modern warfare: it is within this level, and by means of thorough planning and systematic conduct of operations, that abstract definitions are transformed into practical actions. Moreover, it is only through operational insight that the numerous tactical engagements can be assembled into a coherent occurrence, leading to the achievement of the strategic aim.

A brief examination of the Russian definition of the military term, *operation*, will emphasize the identity between the operational level and Bertalanffy's concept of the universal system:

> A totality of battles, strikes and manoeuvres of various types of forces united by mutual aims, missions, location and timing, conducted simultaneously or successively according to a single concept or plan aimed at accomplishing goals in a theatre of military operations, in a strategic direction or operational directions – in a predetermined period of time.[33]

Thus, operation constitutes the entire whole or complex of warlike actions governed by an identical concept, and directed towards attainment of the same aim. The quantitative element of matter is provided by the fighting mass. The physical framework for the operational occurrence is comprised of the factors of time and space. The variety of species is reflected through the diversity of arms and forces, and the system's components are represented by the main formations and combat groupings. The interaction between the components is reflected through the manoeuvre, which is based on a unified plan. The substance of the operational plan consists of the strategic aim, which indicates a predetermined definition of the entire operational accomplishment. The division of this aim into operational objectives and tactical missions creates the cognitive tension that moves the system towards its final objective. And, finally, the linkage between the aim and the combined manoeuvre reflects the synergetic postulate, the coherence of the operational action, and its continuity.

Therefore, one can rightly claim that the operational level is the implementation of the universal system in the military sphere.[34] The essence of this level, as the intermediary field between strategy and tactics, is the preparation, planning, and conduct of military operations in order to attain operational objectives and strategic aims.[35] As stated above, the increase in the fighting mass from the beginning of the nineteenth century precipitated the expansion of warfare, in both space and time. Consequently, the polarization between strategy and tactics became so great that it was almost impossible to conduct war in a dynamic manner. Tactics, focusing entirely on the mechanical dimension of warfare, totally lacked the cognitive tools needed to merge and direct the numerous engagements towards attaining the strategic aims. On the other hand, strategy, leaning primarily on abstract definitions of aims and policies, lacked the ability to translate its intentions into mechanical terms.

An archaic inclination towards perpetuating the misconceptions of the Napoleonic experience, and a simplistic and coercive attempt to solve the problems suggested by modern warfare through a precipitous enlargement of the fighting mass, delayed the emergence of an operational cognition for more than a century. The political, strategic and tactical functions in the Napoleonic Wars were incorporated in a single entity, i.e. in Napoleon himself, and for a while the acuteness of the operational level seemed to decrease. However, after 1806, the dimensions of the armies, as well as the political-strategic complexities, grew to such proportions that the application of operational patterns of thought became imperative.

The significance of the operational dimension was recognized in the Soviet Union as early as the 1920s. In an essay, written in 1926, Mikhail Nikolaevich Tukhachevskii, at the time the Chief of Staff of the RKKA (Red Army of Workers and Peasants) and the dominant figure in the development of the Deep Operation theory, indicated the need for a new cognition, compatible with the challenges of modern warfare:

> Modern tactics are characterized primarily by organization of battle, presuming coordination of various branches of troops. Modern strategy embraces its former meaning: that is the 'tactics of a theatre of military operations'. However, this definition is complicated by the fact that strategy not only prepares for battle, but also participates in and influences the course of battle. Modern operations involve the concentration of forces necessary to deliver a strike, and the infliction of continual and uninterrupted blows of these forces against the enemy throughout an extremely deep area. The nature of modern weapons and modern battle is such that it is impossible to destroy the enemy's manpower by one blow in a one-day battle. Battle in modern operations stretches out into a series of battles not only along the front but also in depth until that time when either the enemy has been struck by

10

a final annihilating blow or the offensive forces are exhausted. In that regard, modern tactics of a theatre of military operations are tremendously more complex than those of Napoleon. And they are made even more complex by the inescapable condition mentioned above that the strategic commander cannot personally organize combat.[36]

Although this early presentation predated Tukhachevskii's theoretical brilliance and perfection that were to emerge in the 1930s, it already recognized the limitations of strategy and tactics in the modern context. Furthermore, in his presentation, Tukhachevskii extracted the idea of 'destruction' (*Vernichtung*), that dominated European military thinking for more than a century, from the operational context, and replaced it with the idea of 'operational shock' (*udar*), or system disruption. And finally, he highlighted the aspects of depth, continuity, synergism and wholeness, and emphasized the crucial need for a new theoretical basis.

It was only in 1982 that Colonels L.D. Holder and H. Wass de Czege confirmed that the cognitive crisis, which must precede any theoretical revolution, had at last transpired in the US armed forces:

> The basic question why doctrine was changed can be answered simply: Army commanders became convinced as a result of their field training and war games that they would be unable to defeat the Soviets using the doctrine of 1976.[37]

Other evidence for the process of disillusionment which the US Army went through was provided by General De Puy, who held the post of Head of TRADOC (Training and Doctrine Command), in the mid-1970s:

> Although 100-5 is called operations, we were thinking tactics. That was a fatal flaw. We were wrong in not grasping that. None of us had studied the military business at the operational level very carefully or thoroughly or well.[38]

Nevertheless, the complete perception of the operational level as a distinct field of knowledge took long to mature. Only after thoroughly comprehending the unique problems of the operational level did the Americans realize that the mere existence of a new field manual did not necessarily supply the cognitive dimensions of the operational level. Four years after the publication of the 1982 edition of *FM 100-5*, L.D. Holder indicated the real turning point, when he realized that the operational level demanded from the commanders performing within its boundaries, cognitive faculties, which differed distinctly from the traditional ones:

> Formally distinguishing operational art from tactics is far more than a

11

semantic exercise . . . As the link between strategy and tactics it governs the way we design operations to meet strategic ends and the way we actually conduct campaigns.[39]

The introduction of the term 'operational art' in the 1986 field manual marked the definite recognition of *creativity*, as the basic quality required from operational commanders.[40] By replacing the term 'operational level', employed in the 1982 manual, with 'operational art', the 1986 manual made a perceptional breakthrough and laid the foundations for a long ensuing debate.

At last the Americans managed to perceive the operational field as a new and distinct cognition, consequently abandoning the artificial and extraneous, categorization of levels of war. The American definition also indicated that despite its theoretical determinants, the operational field remained essentially concerned with practical activities. In its final emphasis, the definition pointed out that the context for expressing operational art was provided by means of theatre and campaign. In other words, despite the fact that the operation stemmed directly from the strategic aim, it still remained autarkic within the scope of that aim.

Basically, the American definitions of campaign and theatre now resemble those of the Russians. Nevertheless, since the Russian definitions reflect the general methodology of perceiving the operation in a more detailed manner, and preceded the American in originality, they should be used as a reference for the discussion.

Since the Russians conceive of theatre as a triangular relationship: warfare – mission – space, strategic aims are realized by means of combined warfare which unfolds within a defined geographical terrain. Thus, the demarcation of the operational theatre is based on two types of parameters: cognitive and geographical. The former are hierarchically structured and comprise a strategic aim (*strategicheskaia tsel'*), strategic missions (*strategicheskie zadachi*), and operational objectives (*operativnye zadachi*).[41] The geographical parameters are structured in an order that corresponds to the cognitive parameters, and they comprise a theatre of military operation (*teatr voennykh deistvii*), strategic directions (*strategicheskie napravleniia*), and operational trends (*operativnye napravleniia*).[42] Thus, the theatre represents a territorial integrity related to a complete aim, a specific period of time, and a defined magnitude of force. Through this integrity the coherence, continuity and independence of the operational command are established.

The campaign (*kampaniia*), lacking a unifying plan, constitutes a more general entity than the operation. The campaign, which occurs within the limits of the theatre, is composed of a complex of operations and actions, aimed at accomplishing a strategic goal. The campaign, like the theatre, is related to a comprehensive aim and a defined framework of time, space and force, and is conducted by an independent strategic command.[43]

Until recently 'operational' commonly described a force grouping, larger than a division or corps. Nowadays, however, this meaning has somewhat lost its relevance because attention tends to focus on the linkage between the action and the strategic aim, and also because of technology's contribution in improving the ability to perform special operations. For example, a patrol sent out to acquire a piece of intelligence of strategic value, or a commando raid aimed at a strategic target might well be regarded as operational, despite the fact that such tasks are performed by small units.

In order to provide a theoretical framework for the examination of operational matters by critical and scientific criteria, an attempt should be made to outline the essence of Bertalanffy's arguments and the universal experience of modern warfare. In this study a concept, plan, or any warlike act will be defined as 'operational', only if it responds positively to the following criteria:

* It must reflect the *cognitive tension*, transpiring from the polarization between the general orientation towards the strategic aim and the adherence to the tactical missions.

* It must be based upon industrious manoeuvre, expressing the dynamic interaction between the various elements within the system, as well as the relationship between the general action and the strategic aim.[44]

* The planned action should be *synergetic*, i.e. throughout its entirety, represented by the initial aim, the system should yield a general product that is significantly greater than the linear arithmetic sum of its components' accomplishments. Moreover, in order to be regarded as operational, the matter must reflect the notion of synthesis, through the aspects of combined arms combat, amalgamation of the various forms of warfare, and the integration of the various forces and formations within several geographical units and different dimensions of time.

* Whereas at the tactical level and in the technological context the mechanism of destruction is prevalent, an operation should aim towards the disruption of its opponent's system.

* It must reflect a contemplative attitude towards the factor of randomness which expresses the chaotic dimension in the interrelation between contentious systems.

13

* An operational plan should be of a non-linear nature, namely, it should be hierarchically structured and express depth.

* An operational act must reflect a deliberate interaction between the notions of manoeuvre and attrition. The importance of this interaction derives from the basic nature of the operational level that embraces erosion, being expressed by tactics, and manoeuvre, which is the method of attaining the strategic aims.

* Since an operational plan or action relies on the strategic definition of aims, restrictions, and the appropriate allocation of resources, it constitutes a completely independent entity and must thus be regarded as autarkic within the scope of its mission or aim.

* Finally, in order to be regarded as operational, a concept, plan or act must be related to a broad and universal theory.

THE AIM – AN ESSENTIAL TRIAD[45]

Even a brief study of the theory of the general system makes it clear that the aim of a system constitutes its brain, its heart, and its self-regulating agency. We will now consider how this essential triad is reflected in the military field of operations.

As has already been observed, the aim is a predetermined definition which reflects the entire accomplishment or effect of the system's endeavour, before its occurrence; in this respect, it is the cognitive compass which provides the manoeuvre with its positive direction. Obviously, foreseeing the consequence prior to the act's materialization requires creative faculties. The formulation of the operational aim, therefore, expresses the art at its best.

The definition of the aim is a complicated process which is reflected in the coherent planning of the entire operation. The conspicuous landmarks along this hierarchic process are:

1. The formulation by the supreme political authority of the political-strategic aims and limitations, which defines the strategic objectives and restrictions and allocates the required resources, through a dialogue involving the strategic authorities.

2. The articulation of the operational concept and the definition of the main operational objectives by the relevant strategic-operational authority, which formulates the operational plans and defines the tactical missions by the various operational commands.

3. The creation of battle plans by the tactical levels of command for the tactical missions.

14

Since the process of developing the operational plan is hierarchic in nature, with each stage dependent on its precursor, the initial aims must be logical, realistic and attainable from the very beginning. Therefore, assuming that the political authority behaves rationally, the formulation of the introductory aim virtually dictates the need for a dialogue at the highest level between the politicians and soldiers.[46] Moreover, in order to preserve consistency between aims, objectives and missions all along the hierarchic ladder, in both the planning and implemental phases, professionalism, operational insight and a conceptual denominator common to all the numerous participators in the operational process becomes imperative. Yet, what is even more obvious is the fact that at the implemental stage it is mainly through the existence of the cognitive tension that the preservation of the above-mentioned consistency is assured.

As has already been noted, the breakdown of the system's aim into concrete objectives and detailed missions provides the system with its essential dynamism. Thus, in this respect the aim resembles the functioning of the heart. In practical terms, the incentive for the cognitive tension is generated through the operational commander's intention and the tactical commander's adherence to the missions they have been assigned. However, the stimulus that provokes the culminating points in this tension is provided by the turbulent and random nature of the operational environment. Out of this context emerges the acute importance of the commander's intention-determined disposition, aimed at curbing the natural inclination of the fighting echelons to over-identify with the tactical mission.[47] But more important, the coherence of the commander's intention or aim is the means for reducing the repercussions of friction.[48]

The self-regulating aptitude of a fighting system (operational entity) can be recognized by its ability to overcome external disturbances and restore its operational equilibrium, a procedure which enables it to adhere to its final objectives. This function is performed by the aim, although in a more intricate manner than seems apparent.

The framework for launching an operation is a violent contest between two belligerent systems, and, naturally, each of the contending systems strives to defeat its rival, and, at the same time, to frustrate the rival's efforts to bring defeat upon it. This means that operational aims uniquely combine two aspects, one positive and the other negative. And since operations constitute the consequence of the performance of military systems, which are goal-oriented in principle, it means that depriving the rival system of its ability to attain its goal reflects the negative aspect of one's own aim. Moreover, separating the system from its brain and heart, both

15

cognitively and physically, will inevitably lead to its disintegration and collapse.

This disposition towards disrupting the system's rationale reflects the notion of *udar* (operational shock) which was developed in Russia during the 1930s, and has only recently been grasped in the West.[49] The effect, or state, of operational shock is inflicted upon the rival system by means of the operational manoeuvre; thus it naturally acquired the appellation *udar*, in Russia, and 'strike', in the West.[50] However, at the same time, the operational manoeuvre provides the system with a vital instrument of self-protection against its opponent's endeavour to disrupt the efforts to attain its own aim. Thus, the responsive manoeuvre that evolves all along the operational occurrence, expresses positively the self-regulation, initiated by the aim.

THE NOTION OF OPERATIONAL SHOCK

The notion of operational shock delineates in practical terms a consequential state of a fighting system which can no longer accomplish its aims. This effect, which derives from physical and psychological factors alike, is developed through a process in which the operational manoeuvre serves as the dominant executing element.[51]

The emergence of the advanced idea of operational shock, which had been delayed for more than a century, resulted in the mental disillusionment that repudiated the prevailing paradigm of the integral 'Battle of Destruction' (*Vernichtungsschlacht*). The origins of this paradigm lie in the Napoleonic experience, enhanced by Clausewitz's doctrine which predominated over military thinking, becoming a universal dogma by 1914. The paradigm claimed that in order to defeat the opponent's massive army, the entire volume of military activity must be initially integrated into a single linear battle in which it would be physically destroyed.[52]

Recognizing that military systems cannot be physically destroyed, Russian theoreticians began to develop an alternative approach for defeating systems effectively in the wake of the First World War.[53] This led to a thorough analysis of the system's characteristics and inherent weaknesses.[54]

As indicated earlier, the military system's primary potential weakness, as well as its main source of strength, is the absolute dominance of the aim. It is the aim which provides the cognitive cement to combine the loose complex of independent formations into a coherent operational unity and the decomposition of that cement will cause these formations to spin away from the common operational context. Moreover, since it is the operational command that secures the adherence of the system to its goal-oriented (operational) course, despite the external obstacles and the particularistic inclinations of the various components, it becomes obvious that separating this command from the system will inevitably lead to disintegration and the abandonment of the operational course.

The military system's second potential source of weakness is its deep structure and its hierarchic logic of action. Every fighting formation (aerial, naval, ground or combined) possesses two obvious dimensions.[55] The frontal or rather linear (horizontal) dimension expresses energy, whether by delivering it against the rival system or by absorbing the rival system's delivered energy; hence, it is essentially static and oriented towards holding actions. The depth (vertical) dimension expresses movement and response, and is, therefore, oriented towards delivering a shock. It follows, therefore, that the quantitative relationship between the front and depth indicates whether the nature of the operational deployment is offensive or defensive.[56] The recognition of the various dimensional deployments clearly leads to echelons. However, more important is the fact that the combination of deployment in depth and a pyramidal structure of hierarchic command determines the nature of the operational mechanism of hierarchical action. It assumes that the operational action always develops from the rear, i.e., depth, towards the front, in an interdependent sequential mode.[57] Therefore, any damage to this mechanism disrupts the entire operational action; it can no longer fulfil the practical functions of generating operational shock dictated by the aim, with the result that the system collapses.

It follows, therefore, that the basic method for exploiting the system's structural and substantive weaknesses is by means of division or fragmentation. This division, executed through slashing strikes which pierce the outer defence and penetrate into the depth, also operates in two dimensions.[58] In the horizontal dimension, the dividing strike damages the front of the operational deployment or layout; its aim is to break the continuity of the operational front and separate the formations from each other, thus preventing co-operation between them. This development naturally undermines the coherence of the system's performance and disrupts the defence of the frontal territory. In the vertical dimension, the dividing strike segregates the rear echelons and operational reserves from those in the front and detaches the operational command from the entire command and control structure. By doing this, the dividing strike disrupts the basic operational mechanism (synergy) and breaks down the system's 'whole' into its independent parts.[59]

Another method of creating operational shock involves the idea of

17

simultaneity, that is, engaging the front and the rear of the rival system at the same time and synchronizing a concurrent operation all along the opponent's depth.[60] The simultaneous operation disrupts the essential interaction between the system's components and creates the possibility of defeating them separately. It is quite obvious that such an attempt dictates the application of fire and troops, by means of combined movement, in the depth of the rival system and requires the formulation of creative solutions to the grave problems implied by space, time and the opponent's resistance. Thus, simultaneity depends on compromising the dichotomy between momentum, which is a prerequisite for its development, and the echeloned structure of the operational deep column.[61]

The importance of depth, within the operational context, is that it expresses in territorial terms the entire scope of the operational function. Moreover, the depth comprises the space containing the deployment of the operational fighting mass. Thus emerges the idea of 'Mass Centre', reflecting the relationship between mass and space, and expressing the statistical average of the force deployment. Similarly, the depth provides the arena in which the operational manoeuvre, that is, the system's interaction, will occur. Therefore, the operational sensitivity of a given space tends to increase in direct relation to the progress one makes towards the rival's depth or rear. This assumption is also valid in the strategic aspect, since the rear usually comprises the strategic infrastructure of a given geopolitical entity, a fact that emphasizes its importance. This leads us to the third method for inflicting operational shock.

If the operational system can mass a critical force beyond the opposing system's mass centre, then the course for inflicting operational shock on the opponent will lie open. In other words, when such conditions are realized, the opposing system is forced into a situation in which it will lose its abilities both to accomplish its original aim, and to regain its operational equilibrium.[62] This advanced effect, which can be best referred to as 'turning over', is defined by the Russians specifically as *obkhod*, while the general term *turning manoeuvre* is employed in the West.[63]

The last method for creating the state of operational shock involves the idea of 'Centre of Gravity'. The origin of the vagueness surrounding this notion derives basically from the ambiguity of Clausewitz's definition of the battle of destruction.[64] The American attempt to explicate the idea in the 1986 field manual is not completely successful, since it compromises an advanced and comprehensive perception of the idea with Clausewitz's own obscure interpretation.[65] On the other hand, the concept of centre of gravity matured, in Russian operational theory, into a very high level of intelligibility, notwithstanding the fact that no explicit reference to it exists.

The concept of the centre of gravity comprises three elements: 1) the identification of the exact points of strength and weakness in the opposing system; 2) the deliberate creation of operational vulnerabilities in it; and 3) the exploitation of such vulnerabilities through contemplated manoeuvring strikes. Thus, the broad concept of the centre of gravity expresses simultaneously the physical sensitivities of objectives, such as an essential resource, battle grouping or terrain feature, the cognitive aspect of operational vulnerabilities, initiated by combining deception and surprise, and the actual occurrence of the mechanical manoeuvre.

As one can see, the cognitive aspect, which centres on deception and surprise, constitutes the axis around which the concept of the centre of gravity is structured, hence its great relevance to the issue of operational shock.

An operational vulnerability is not just a sensitive source, a defined boundary line between operational formations, an essential grouping, or a dominating terrain feature. An operational vulnerability implies the identification of a particular situation, created by the accumulation of certain operational circumstances and inviting the delivery of a strike, which will destroy the defeated system's ability to perform its original mission. The anticipation of such an elaborate situation requires a great deal of creative vision, an efficient military intelligence apparatus, and, above all, the inducement of a specific state of mind or consciousness within the command of the rival system.

The meaning of this specific state of mind implies that the passive system is completely ignorant of its weaknesses, that it is unaware of the fact that its rival has identified its vulnerability, and that it is oblivious to the entire operation that is being conducted against it. Such situations, however, rarely occur of their own accord, and when they do it is because of exceptional ignorance.[66]

In this context, the unique importance of deception becomes clear. Its main role is to create a state of mind which distracts the opponent's attention from both his own operational sensitivities and the efforts conducted by his adversary to take advantage of them, namely to create surprise.[67] The success of deception is therefore measured by the rate of the surprise achieved. The magnitude of surprise is reflected either in the success of the manoeuvre or in the ability of the beaten side to respond effectively to the strike. Therefore, since it is aimed at attaining the highest degree of operational shock, the concept of the centre of gravity must involve cunning, which is the essence of operational art, at its best.

19

THE OPERATIONAL STRIKING MANOEUVRE

As the preceding discussion clearly indicates, a reciprocal relationship exists between the operational manoeuvre, which connotes the interaction between the system's elements, and the strategic or operational aim. The aim generates the manoeuvre, plots its cognitive course, and thus determines its operational nature, whereas the manoeuvre serves as the sole instrument capable of attaining the aim. Moreover, the operational manoeuvre expresses dynamically all three cardinal aspects of the aim. The strike to the rival system reflects the negative or pre-emptive aspect of the aim, while the positive aspect of the aim is reflected in its consistent progress towards attaining the actual objective determined by it. The aspect of self-regulation is presented by the appropriate responses to the negative efforts initiated by the rival system. Most significantly, by possessing the qualities of continuity, sequentiality, consistency and flexibility, the operational manoeuvre bridges over the dichotomy which is inherent in the combination of the holistic nature of the aim and the existential compulsion to translate it into concrete missions. The aim thus provides the principal criterion for evaluating the success and effectiveness of an operational manoeuvre.

In its basic form, the manoeuvre expresses the operational ability of a tactical body to perform its mission, and its success depends on the appropriate combination of three qualities: protection, mobility and firepower. This essential combination derives from the universal nature of warfare, independent of a particular field or terrain.

Fire is effectuated by means of energy aimed at the fighting components of the rival unit. Protection is the collective and individual capabilities to absorb the enemy's fire. Mobility is expressed by the ability to overcome both the forces of nature and the resistance offered by the enemy. It seems, therefore, that tactical combat, being confined to specific units of time and space, is best perceived in physical terms and material values. Therefore, the basic trait characterizing the tactical manoeuvre derives from the combination of the three basic operational qualities, in accordance with both the specific circumstances and the relevant mission.[68] In other words, the idea behind the concept of combined arms combat is that of a tactical synthesis, which involves a variety of components, each possessing a distinctive tactical quality. This integration of various qualities is intended to provide the combined unit with the joint ability to overcome complicated tactical problems which would have proved too great for a homogeneous element to overcome independently. The situation in which a certain dominant tactical trait characterizing a specific arm compensates for an inherent weakness in one of the other components from a different arm produces a type of synergism that can be best termed as operational harmony.[69] This, then, is the simpler aspect of the operational interaction reflected in the manoeuvre. The necessity of cooperation at the operational level is inherent in the structure of systems; all the elements in a system are compelled to interact while pursuing the common goal.

The second reason for the operational cooperation is the specific nature of warfare. That is to say, various elements, representing different forces and arms and possessing qualities characteristic of the operational level, such as effects, dimension, range and duration of action, cooperate in order to overcome jointly operational difficulties and solve the entire operational problem by means of a combined manoeuvre.[70]

However, since we are concerned here with operations, determined by the imperative of accomplishing a definite aim, it becomes obvious that the simultaneous combination of various forms of combat in a unified manoeuvre is as essential as the integration of various arms and forces. Thus, it is entirely possible that a single operation will comprise separate formations or units – raising a defence, setting an ambush, executing deep raids, mounting an operational advance, and launching an attack.[71]

This may be the right context to address a common error which is seemingly semantic but is, in fact, substantive and stems from a mis-perception of the operational dimension. Manoeuvre and fire are often referred to, both verbally and in writing, as two distinct and separate entities. The origin of this error is a simplistic reading of the basic tactical scenario, in which one element serves as the fire base covering the advance of the element assaulting the objective. The operational manoeuvre, however, simultaneously embraces the entire scope of the operational problem, from the defined consequential aim to the line of initial operations, and calls for a combination of fire and movement at different levels and in various magnitudes. Fire is, therefore, an integral part of the operational manoeuvre and not merely a separate act to cover an advancing unit. As such it is per-formed by means of air power, barrelled and rocket artillery, missiles, light weapons and so on.[72]

The third vital reason for operational integration lies in the nature of military systems. We have already seen that the non-linear nature of the interaction between the system's components determines the columnar form of the operational manoeuvre and the patterns of cooperation between the operational echelons.[73] Moreover, accepting the basic notion that any operational deployment must comprise the

21

dimensions of front and depth immediately implies the existence of an interactive cooperation between the holding element and the striking one. Indeed, the dynamic interaction between these elements constitutes the essence of the entire idea of operational manoeuvre.[74] The quantitative relationship between the holding and striking elements determines which of the two basic operational forms has been applied by the system. A superiority in weight and resources on the side of the holding element, as well as a thin and shallow structure of the striking vector, designate a defensive manoeuvre, whereas when the striking element is superior in weight, length, and velocity, an offensive manoeuvre is denoted. However, in both situations the decision, i.e. the accomplishment of the initial aim, will ultimately be attained by the dynamic action of the striking force.

In a defensive manoeuvre the intention of the holding force is to retard or bring to a standstill the momentum gained by the operational edge of the attacker. On the other hand, the disposition of the striking element is to thrust simultaneously at the attacker's sequent echelons and prevent them from exploiting the success gained by their frontal elements. Thus, the attacker's ability to accomplish its aim will be negated, and his system will be thrown into a state of shock.

In an offensive manoeuvre the holding element aims at drawing, binding and pulverizing, frontally, as many as possible of the defender's forces, in a manner which affords the striking element as easy a passage as possible to the defender's rear. The arrival of a sufficiently large striking element in a rear sector, lying beyond the defender's centre of mass, will inevitably bring about the turn-over of the defensive force and generate a state of shock. Therefore, a vigorous holding action will induce the defender to concentrate his formations towards the frontal sector and tempt him to attack the holding efforts. The enticement of a large mass of the defending force towards the front which is offered by the opposing holding force, will open the way for unfolding the striking element's movement, and likewise amplify the turning moment, created by the arrival of this same striking force in the defender's depth.

The energetic combination of the manoeuvre's principal elements reflects yet another interaction, conferring vital dynamism on the operational action, i.e. the interaction between attrition and manoeuvre. The holding element represents an attritional trend, since it erodes the opposing force, and, in the best case, detains or contains it. The holding force's action can never achieve decisive results, since frontal patterns of action maximize friction, leading to stalemate;[75] however, deliberate and controlled employment of the attritional trend is essential for creating conditions for the enhancement of the striking force's operation, since it amplifies the latter's development by means of pulverizing and holding the opponent.[76]

The striking element represents the manoeuvring trend at its best, not just by means of its high degree of mobility, but mainly in the fact that its mission is to generate shock, which guarantees the attainment of the operational aim.[77]

The essential interaction between attrition and the attacking manoeuvre in modern warfare requires a balanced approach towards the issues of quality and quantity. The qualitative dimension, manifested in advanced technologies, tactical proficiency, and creative patterns of manoeuvre, is clearly insufficient on its own to bring about a decision in operational contests. The quantitative dimension, on the other hand, is essential for successful attrition. Yet, it should be remembered that the significance of attrition lies solely in its auxiliary service to the manoeuvre. Therefore attrition, in the operational context, will not defeat the opponent, even if overwhelming quantities of force are concentrated and wasted at a rate lower than that suffered by the opposing force. The deliberate interaction between attrition and manoeuvre, implemented, as it is, in the operational manoeuvre, reflects an articulate balance between the quantitative and qualitative dimensions, since both are governed by limitations and restrictions imposed by the strategic level.[78] Hence, the actual determination of this balance is another particular component of the operational art, since it cannot be based on fixed formulae or system analysis. It is entirely dependent on the commander's own considerations in accordance with the specific circumstances.

NOTES

1. C. von Clausewitz, *On War*, M. Howard and P. Paret (eds) (Princeton, 1976), B. 2, Ch. 1, p. 128.
2. Ibid., B. 8, Ch. 3, pp. 591–3.
3. H. De Jomini, *The Art of War*, G.H. Mendell and W.P. Craighill (trans.) (Philadelphia, 1862), pp. 69–70, 178, 360, and J.F.C. Fuller, *The Foundation of the Science of War* (London, 1925), p. 108, both referred to the intermediate level of conducting war as 'grand tactics'. B.H. Liddell Hart, *Thoughts on War* (London, 1943), pp. 207–14, employed the term 'strategy', when relating to the level of operations, and the term 'grand strategy', when referring to supreme level of conducting war. H.K. Weiss, 'Combat Models and Historical Data: The US Civil War', *Operations Research* (Sept.–Oct.1966), p. 788; D.J. Willard, 'Lanchester as Force in History: An Analysis of Land Battles of the Years 1618–1905', *RAC-TP-74*, Bethesda, MD, Research Analysis Corp. (Nov. 1962); J.J. Schneider, 'The Exponential Decay of Armies in Battle', Theoretical Paper No. 1, Ft. Leavenworth, KS, School of Advanced Military Studies, USACGSC, Feb. 1985.
4. H. Kissinger, *Problems of National Strategy* (New York, 1965), p. 5.
5. J.F. Meehan, 'The Operational Trilogy', *Parameters* XVI, 3 (1986), pp. 12–13; R.L. Allen,

'Piercing the Veil of Operational Art', *Parameters* XVI, 4 (1986), pp. 23, 25; K.G. Carlson, 'Operational Level or Operational Art?', *Military Review* LXVII, 10 (1987), pp. 50–51; M. Farndale, 'The Operational Level of Command', *RUSI Journal* 133, 3 (1988), p. 24. H.H. von Sandrart, 'Defence Concepts and the Application of New Military Thinking', *RUSI Journal* 134, 2 (1989), pp. 24–5; *Ha-Ramah Ha-Ma'arakhatit* (The Operational Level), Training and Doctrine Department, General Headquarters, Israeli Defence Forces (Tel Aviv, 1990), p. 4.

6. Allen, 'Piercing the Veil of Operational Art', is the only essay that discusses thoroughly the methodological aspects of operational research. W.P. Franz, 'Operational Concepts', *Military Review* LXIV, 7 (1984), pp. 2 and 3; and S.W. Richey, 'The Philosophical Basis of the Air Land Battle', *Military Review* LXIV, 5 (1984), pp. 48–53, reflect the lack of scientific discipline mentioned above. Both essays strive to identify traces of modern operational cognition in the German concept of *Blitzkrieg*. However, since *Blitzkrieg* lacked a theoretical basis, and was nothing more than an embryonic concept, their conclusions regarding the origins of the operational cognition tend to differ sharply. W.P. Franz, 'Two Letters on Strategy: Clausewitz's Contribution to the Operational Level of War', in M.I. Handel (ed.), *Clausewitz and Modern Strategy* (London, 1986), p. 183, proves the lack of cognitive criteria in the operational research. The author attempts to deduce some operational implications from an essay, written by Clausewitz, while using the latter's own definitions. Thus, his method of argumentation is uncritical.

7. In Germanic and Romance languages, the noun 'operation' is the only existing term capable of defining military actions above the level of tactics. Moreover, the word 'operation' in general has acquired at least two civilian and three military meanings. In the Russian language, there are no less than five terms that deal specifically, with different aspects of military actions above the tactical level, these are: *srazhenie*, *operatsiia, kampaniia, deistviia,* and *bitva.*

8. L. von Bertalanffy, *General System Theory* (New York, 1975).

9. R. Simpkin, *Race to the Swift* (London, 1985), constitutes the first serious attempt in the West to produce a theoretical basis for a general understanding of the operational level of war. M. Howard, 'The Use and Abuse of Military History', *Parameters* XI, 1 (1981), pp. 9–14, specifies three essential criteria, according to which military history should be explored: The first is *width*, the second is *depth*, and the third is *context*.

10. T. Kuhn, *The Structure of Scientific Revolution* (Chicago, 1971); Bertalanffy, *General System Theory*, pp. XIX, 16.

11. Bertalanffy, *General System Theory*, p. 3.

12. Ibid., p. 31.

13. Ibid., p. 32.

14. Ibid., p. XIX.

15. Ibid., p. 51.

16. Ibid., pp. 38, 149.

17. Ibid., p. 46. Bertalanffy's emphasis added to underscore the various traits of the system.

18. Ibid., pp. 17, 27, 51, 55.

19. Ibid., pp. 2, 76.

20. Ibid., pp. 2, 70, 76.

21. Ibid., p. 68.

22. Ibid., p. 70.

23. Within the context of operational manoeuvre, contradictive tension can be observed in issues such as the following: tactical destruction and operation disruption; attrition and manoeuvre; the column, which expresses depth, and the front, which represents linearity; the forward nature of tactical command and the rearward nature of the operational; defensive and offensive; the culminating point and the centre of gravity; and the inclination towards centralism and the relegation of authority.

24. Bertalanffy, *General System Theory*, p. 70.

25. P.M. Senge, *The Fifth Discipline* (London, 1990), pp. 357–8, identified the same phenomenon and suggested a concept for solution which he calls 'creative tension'.

26. Bertalanffy, *General System Theory*, p. 30.

27. E. Vald, *Hakesher haGordi Mitosim vedilemmot bevitachon Yisrael* (The Gordian knot: myths and dilemmas of Israeli national security) (Tel Aviv, 1991), pp. 42, 56–8; E.N. Luttwak, *The Pentagon and the Art of War* (New York, 1984), pp. 98–111.

28. Bertalanffy, *General System Theory*, p. 54.
29. Ibid., p. 30.
30. E.N. Luttwak, *Strategy: The Logic of War and Peace* (Cambridge, 1987), p. 91.
31. C.E. Saint, 'A CINC's View of Operational Art', *Military Review* LXX, 9 (1990), p. 66, refers to the cognitive process that occurs within the operational level as 'integrative', and describes the operational commanders as 'integrators'.
32. US Department of the Army, *FM 100-5 Operations*, Headquarters (Washington, DC, 1986), p. 9. The present edition, unlike that of 1982, refers to the operational level as art. This difference, which indicates a change towards perceiving the operational level as a new cognition, distinct from its traditional sisters, was adopted from the Soviet definitions of the 1930s.
33. *Voennyi entsiklopedicheskii slovar'* (Military Encyclopaedic Dictionary, hereafter *VES*) (Moscow, 1983), p. 516; M.M. Kirian, 'Operatsiia' (Operation), *Sovetskaia voennaia entsiklopediia* (Soviet Military Encyclopaedia, hereafter *SVE*) (Moscow, 1978), Vol. 6, pp. 64–7.
34. Luttwak, *Strategy*, p. 93; J. Bolt and D. Jablonsky, 'Tactics and the Operational Level of War', *Military Review* LXVII, 2 (1987), p. 16; *FM 100-5*, 1986, p. 28. All the above-mentioned sources explicitly refer to the operational occurrence as a system. In Hebrew the term *ma'arekhet* (system) is used both in reference to a system in general, and to a military operation.
35. D. Jablonsky, 'Strategy and the Operational Level of War Part I', *Military Review* LXVII 1 (1987), p. 65; idem, 'Strategy and the Operational Level of War Part II', *Military Review* LXVII, 2 (1987), pp. 52–3, 60; S.E. Runals, 'A Different Approach' *Military Review* LXVII, 10 (1987), p. 44; C.R. Newell, 'What is Operational Art?', *Military Review* LXX, 9 (1990), pp. 3, 4; E.B. Atkeson, 'The Operational Level of War', *Military Review* LXVII, 3 (1987), p. 30; L.D. Holder, 'Operational Art in the US Army: New Vigor', in *Essays on Strategy* III, (Washington, DC, 1986), p. 116; J.J. Schneider, 'Theoretical Implications of Operational Art', *Military Review* LXX, 9 (1990), p. 25; L.D. Holder, 'Concept of Operation: See Ops Overlay', *Military Review* LXX, 8 (1990), pp. 28–9.
36. M.N. Tukhachevskii, 'Voina' (War), 1926, in A.B. Kadishev (ed.), *Voprosy strategii i operativnogo iskusstva v sovetskikh voennykh trudakh 1917–1940 gg.* (Questions of Strategy and Operational Art in Soviet Military Works 1917–1940) (Moscow, 1965), pp. 104–5.
37. H. Wass de Czege and L.D. Holder, 'The New FM 100-5', *Military Review* LXII, 7 (1982), p. 53. Both officers, who were associated with the reform group that rejected traditional military thought and advocated the application of an advanced operational theory, participated in the actual composition of the new field manual.
38. Interview with General W.E. De Puy, 16 April 1986, in Atkeson, 'The Operational Level of War', p. 29.
39. Holder, 'Operational Art in the U.S. Army; New Vigor', p. 116, as *FM 100-5*, 1986, p. 10 puts it: 'Operational art is the employment of military forces to attain strategic goals in a theatre of war or theatre of operations, through the design, organization, and conduct of campaigns and major operations'.
40. W.P. Franz, 'Maneuver: The Dynamic Element of Combat', *Military Review* LXIII, 5 (1983), p. 4; G.R. Sullivan, 'Learning to Decide at the Operational Level', *Military Review* LXVII, 10 (1987), p. 20. In the late 1920s the Soviets recognized *tvorchestvo* (creativity) as the characteristic quality required from commanders at the operational level. Consequently they replaced the Faculty for Operational Art, then a part of the Frunze Academy, with the independent General Staff Academy (or Academy for Operational Art).
41. In the present stage we will leave the definition of the cognitive parameters as they are, assuming that their significance can be picked up from the text. We will clarify them in detail when discussing the subject of the aim.
42. According to M.M. Kozlov, 'Teatr voennykh deistvii', *SVE*, 1980, Vol. 8, p. 9, and *VES*, p. 732: Theatre of military operations (TVD) constitutes a part of a continent with associated coastal areas, inland water contents and airspace, within whose boundaries strategic groupings of forces (air, sea land) deploy and conduct military operations intending to attain strategic aims. According to: 'Strategicheskoe napravlenie' (Strategic Direction), *SVE*, 1979, Vol. 7, p. 555, and *VES*, p. 711: Strategic directions constitute

extensive areas within the TVD. Within the strategic direction, large groups of combined forces deploy and conduct operations intending to achieve strategic missions. According to: 'Operativnoe napravlenie' (Operational Direction), *SVE*, 1978, Vol. 6, p. 64, and *VES*, p. 516: Operational Direction constitutes a subdivision of the strategic direction and represents a territorial sector which contains significant operational objectives.

43. *FM 100-5*, 1986, p. 10; M.I. Cherednichenko, 'Kampaniia', *SVE*, 1977, Vol. 6, pp. 55–6. R.M. D'amura, 'Campaign: The Essence of Operational Warfare', *Parameters* XVII, 2 (1987), p. 45.

44. Luttwak, *Strategy*, p. 93, refers to the operational manoeuvre as 'Relational Manoeuvre', since he emphasizes its absolute dependence on the strategic aim.

45. The term 'Triad', represents, in science, an atom, element, group, or ion, that has a valence of three.

46. The fact that such a dialogue did not occur prior to 1914 led to the German war plan being totally disconnected from the national-political context. Similarly, the lack of such a dialogue, and the inconsistent definition of the strategic objective exercised by Hitler in the autumns of 1941 and 1942, contributed more than anything else to the loss of operational momentum. Aiming towards unrealistic strategic objectives caused Rommel's collapse in the autumn of 1942, despite his former operational successes. Embarking upon the Vietnamese venture without predefining the political and strategic aims, constituted the main cause of American military failure in that venture. And finally, a nebulous formulation of political and strategic aims by the Israeli government in 1982 brought about the Israeli failure in the Lebanese campaign.

47. In this notion lie the origins for the assertion that tactical victories do not necessarily lead to operational successes. Y. Harkabi, *War and Strategy* (Tel Aviv, 1990), pp. 424, 536, 587–8; Vald, *Hakesher haGordi* (Tel Aviv, 1992), pp. 30, 37, 50, 160, refers to this phenomenon within the context of the Israeli Army, as 'the tactization of strategy'.

48. The term friction refers to a mental mechanism that tends to blur the comprehension of the general context or aim, under conditions of extreme pressure, frequently occurring in combat. This notion originated in Clausewitz, *On War*, B. 1, Ch. 7, pp. 119–21.

49. G. Isserson, 'Razvitie teorii sovetskogo operativnogo iskusstva v 30-e gody' (The Development of the theory of Soviet operational art in the 1930s), *Voenno-istoricheskii zhurnal* (hereafter *VIZh*), 1 (1965), pp. 37–9; P.N. Kurpita, 'Udar', *SVE* Vol. 8, 1980, p. 171.

50. I.M. Anan'ev (ed.), *Tankovye armii v nastuplenii po opytu Otechestvennoi voiny* (Tank Armies on the Offensive and the Lessons of the Great Patriotic War), (Moscow, 1988), pp. 10–37; A.J. Radzievskii, *Tankovyi Udar* (Tank Strike) (Moscow, 1977), pp. 41–4; B.W. Rogers, 'Strike Deep: A New Concept for NATO', *Military Technology* 5 (1983), p. 40. *FM 100-5*, 1986, pp. 11–15, 132–3.

51. Anan'ev, *Tankovye armii v nastuplenii*, pp. 10–37; Radzievskii, *Tankovyi udar*, pp. 41, 42; N. Leites, *Soviet Style in War*, (New York, 1985), pp. 300–302; *FM 100-5*, 1986, pp. 11–13, 15.

52. Clausewitz, *On War*, B. 1, Ch. 2, p. 95; B. 4, Ch. 3, p. 228; B. 4, Ch. 11, p. 258.

53. Isserson, 'Razvitie teorii', pp. 37–9.

54. G. Isserson and F. Gaivoronskii, 'Razvitie sovetskogo operativnogo iskusstva' (The Development of Soviet Operational Art), *VIZh* 2 (1978), pp. 24–5; M. Zakharov, 'O teorii glubokoi operatsii' (On the Theory of Deep Operations), *VIZh* 10 (1970), pp. 10–13; V. Daines, 'Razvitie taktiki obshchevoiskovogo nastupatel'nogo boia v 1929–1941 gg.' (The Development of the Tactics of Combined Arms Offensive Battle in the Years 1929–1941), *VIZh* 10 (1978), p. 96.

55. Isserson, 'Razvitie teorii', p. 41, reveals that the deliberate definition of the operational dimensions of front and depth was made by V.N. Mikulin, in relation to the concept of 'mobile scheme'. The emergence of this concept constituted a significant stage in the development of the theory of deep operation.

56. In the defensive stance, the frontal dimension will always appear significantly longer than the depth, due to the fact that a linear configuration tends to produce more energy and reflects the holding of the territory. In an offensive deployment, the depth will always be significantly longer than the front. The columnar image of the offensive derives, therefore, from this notion.

26

57. R. Savushkin, 'K voprosu istochnika teorii posledovatel'nykh nastupatel'nykh operatsii'(Concerning Questions of Theoretical Origins of Successive Offensive Operations), *VIZh* 5 (1983), p. 78; Isserson, 'Razvitie teorii', p. 36; V.K. Triandafillov, *The Nature of the Operations of Modern Armies* (Kharakter operatsii sovremennykh armii), J.W. Kipp (ed.), (London, 1992), pp. 156–79, describes the idea of operational deep mechanism as a contest between defender and offender in his concept of 'movement differential'. *FM 100-5*, 1986, pp. 16–17, also refers to the same mechanism.

58. A.I. Radzievskii, *Proryv* (breakthrough-penetration) (Moscow, 1977), p. 166; Anan'ev, *Tankovye armii v nastuplenii*, pp. 152–6. Both these publications employ the term, *rassekaiushchii udar*, or *frontal'nye rassekaiushchie udary*, which mean either dividing strike, or frontal dividing strike. The term is used commonly in the operational context when referring to a manoeuvring variant, aiming at dividing between the system's components, and separating them from the mother system. The American *FM 100-5*, 1986, pp. 103–6, refers to the same operational effect as either penetration, infiltration, or frontal attack.

59. Anan'ev, *Tankovye armii v nastuplenii*, pp. 38, 40, 143, 153–60; S.N. Kozlov, *O Sovetskoi voennoi nauke* (On Soviet Military Science) (Moscow, 1964), p. 361; V.E. Savkin, *Osnovnye printsipy operativnogo iskusstva i taktiki* (The Basic Principles of Operational Art and Tactics) (Moscow, 1972), pp. 257–65; A.A. Sidorenko, *Nastuplenie* (The Offensive), (Moscow, 1970), pp. 71, 132; V.G. Reznichenko (ed.), *Taktika* (Tactics), (Moscow, 1986), p. 291; A.Kh. Babadzhanian, *Tanki i tankovye voiska* (Tanks and Tank Forces), (Moscow, 1970), p. 259.

60. Isserson, 'Razvitie Teorii', pp. 37–44.

61. *FM 100-5*, 1986, pp. 16–17, 19–20, 37–8; Isserson, 'Razvitie Teorii', pp. 37–44; Simpkin, *Race to the Swift*, pp. 37, 49, 93–115, 137, 145–8.

62. The term 'critical mass of force' refers to a certain quantity that will allow the deep force to accomplish its mission, i.e. to generate the turning over of the yielding system.

63. *FM 100-5*, 1986, pp. 102–3. Unlike the Americans, the Russians do not recognize envelopment as a form of offensive manoeuvre, at the operational level. For the Russians, envelopment is a purely tactical form of manoeuvre and the higher level consists of the frontal offensive, represented distinctively by *proryv* (breakthrough), and the turning manoeuvre, represented by *obkhod*. Both operational forms aim at achieving the state of operational shock – the first by a progressive fragmentation of the defending system, and the second by means of a bold movement to the defender's depth.

64. Clausewitz, *On War*, B. 8, Ch. 4, pp. 595–7. For Clausewitz, the enemy's armed forces always constituted the centre of gravity, since he assumed that their destruction inevitably leads to the collapse of the opposing state. Thus, according to his definition, the centre of gravity is a fixed and permanent objective, on which all energies should be focused.

65. *FM 100-5*, 1986, pp. 179–80.

66. The Polish preparation for the war of 1939 and the response of the Allies to the German offensive of May 1940 are good examples of such ignorance.

67. In this respect, the Russian approach to deception and their conception of surprise are illuminating. The principal role of *maskirovka* (operational deception), is to amplify the effects of *udar* (operational shock), by means of manipulating surprise. This is attained by a combination of psychological and mechanical acts, aimed at developing within the opposing command a certain state of mind that will both suit and encourage the actual implementation of the striking manoeuvre. Thus, they employ three terms, when referring to surprise. Firstly, there is the term *siurpriz*, representing the abstract idea of surprise, in the universal or rather civilian context. Secondly, there is the term *neozhidannost'* (tactical surprise), pointing towards the occurrence of an unexpected tactical act, like an attack from an unpredicted direction. Then there is the term *vnezapnost'* (operational surprise), implying the materialization of some occurrence, lying beyond the mental threshold of the rival command. Therefore implementing a successful operational surprise always implies the achievement of operational shock.

68. *FM 100-5*, 1986, p. 25, refers by the tactical term 'combined arms' to the same idea. The Russians employ the term *obshchevoiskovoi boi*, in the tactical context, in order to express the notion of integration or combination between the various arms. Whenever

referring to the same tactical notion, the Germans use the terms: *Einheitsprinzip* (combined arms integration and decentralization of control), or *Zusammenwirken*. The British employ the term 'all arms combat', while the Israelis use the term *ha-krav ha-meshulav*, meaning, the combined arms battle.

69. A. Jones, *The Art of War in the Western World* (Urbana, 1987), pp. 186–90, referred to the idea of tactical synthesis, but in a different historical context.

70. This is the reason why operational formations are assigned missions suiting their structure and specific operational capabilities. Combined infantry or mechanized formations are assigned to the mission of breaking through the frontal tactical defensive belt, that is usually saturated with fortifications, obstacles and static defensive systems. Combined armour-oriented formations are designed to exploit the success of the breakthrough, and convey the operational manoeuvre to the depth of the defender's layout. Air forces and long-range artillery are supposed to hit simultaneously the numerous echelons all along the defender's depth. Airborne assault formations are bound to operate simultaneously at the extreme sector of the defender's depth.

71. A.A. Svechin, 'Strategiia' (Strategy), 1927, in Kadishev, *Voprosy strategii*, p. 220, confirms that the Russians arrived very early indeed at the notion of simultaneously integrating various forms of combat in a combined manoeuvre.

72. Today it would be correct to refer to fire, at the strategic level, as a separate entity, due to the unique qualities of nuclear ballistic weapons, and to the fact, that strategy is not concerned with manoeuvre *per se*. The Russian concept of *protivoiadernyi manevr* (anti-nuclear manoeuvre) proves beyond any doubt that at the operational level, despite the existence of nuclear weapons, the fire, as a whole, constitutes an integral part of the combined manoeuvre; see F. Sverdlov, 'K voprosy o manevre v boiu' (Concerning the Question of Manoeuvre in Combat), *Voennyi vestnik* 8 (1972), p. 31. V. Savkin, 'Manevr v boiu' (Manoeuvre in Battle), *Voennyi vestnik*, 4 (1972), p. 23.

73. This idea was expressed through the Russian concept of deep operations, emphasizing the simultaneous cooperation between the various operational echelons, in the context of the combined manoeuvre; see Daines, 'Razvitie taktiki', p. 96, and Isserson, 'Razvitie teorii', pp. 37–40. The Western defensive concept of FOFA suggested the same idea through a negative approach, i.e. imposing a state of shock on the attacking system by means of breaking the operational sequence and the cooperation between the successive echelons.

74. Simpkin, *Race to the Swift*, pp. 19–23, 93–115, refers to holding and mobile elements as the essential components of operational manoeuvre. I find the term mobile somewhat simplistic and implying tactical or rather mechanical directions.

75. The attritional trend or direction of warfare derives from the degrading nature of the tactical battle, see: H.H. von Sandrart, 'Considerations of the Battle in Depth', *Military Review* LXVII, 10 (1987), p. 11.

76. Luttwak, *Strategy*, p. 92. The main reason that Iraqis, during the ground phase of operation Desert Storm, did not show real resistance to the advance of the VII and XVIII corps, should be attributed to this premise. The attrition that was imposed on the Iraqis through the systematic degrading air operation and the efficient holding action, conducted by the three southern operational groupings, allowed the striking force to advance easily.

77. One example for conducting a deliberate interaction of attrition and manoeuvre is offered by the combined operation of Grant's and Sherman's groupings in 1864–65. Conversely, the German failure in the Russian campaign derived, among other causes, from the fact that they were not prepared, mentally and in terms of resources, to conduct an operation demanding the conscious combination of attrition and manoeuvre. Operation Desert Storm is a most instructive example of the relationship between attrition and manoeuvre.

78. A. Kasher, 'Quality and Quantity', in Z. Offer and A. Kover (eds), *Quality and Quantity-Dilemma in Force Building* (Tel Aviv, 1985, in Hebrew), pp. 23–4, 26; F.W. Lanchester, *The Principle of Concentration* (London, 1914), and F.W. Lanchester, *Aircraft in Warfare: The Dawn of the Fourth Arm* (London, 1916). Lanchester developed a mathematical model which determined a scientific relation between quantity and quality. In his linear law he asserts that in linear confrontations between homogeneous tactical units, in order to achieve a 2:1 chance for success one must

establish a 2:1 numerical superiority, assuming that the operational quality of both belligerent contenders is equal. However, in a situation in which one side possesses only half the quantity of its rival, one needs a qualitative edge, four times that of the opponent in order to balance this inequality. The main weakness of the Lanchester model is its lack of operational insight, since it concerns homogeneous tactical units, and disregards the issues of command, motivation, organization and so on.

2

Mass and Operational Art: The Theoretical Dichotomy in Nineteenth-Century Military Thought

THE PHENOMENON OF MASS AND THE ADVENT OF THE OPERATIONAL MILIEU

Notwithstanding the variety of approaches to the phenomenon of mass, contemporary scholars, as well as nineteenth-century military theoreticians, are in agreement regarding its substance and nature. Most of them also agree on the historical circumstances of the emergence and development of the mass phenomenon. Moreover, they unanimously perceive it as one of the most decisive factors shaping the nature of warfare in the course of the nineteenth century and the First World War.

The modern historical approach is best represented by Michael Howard who emphasizes the strategical, tactical and technological aspects of the phenomenon, in the broad context of political and social evolution:

> In the eighteenth century it was generally accepted that there was a strict limit to the size of armies that could usefully be deployed in the field . . . By the end of 1794 Lazare Carnot, the organizer of the French revolutionary armies, had over a million men under arms, and he used them to obtain a crushing numerical superiority on every battlefield . . . these were the ideas, and this the instrument, that Napoleon found to hand, and he used them with a genius that was as much political as military . . . In 1870 the North German confederation deployed against France exactly twice the number of men Napoleon had led into Russia – 1,200,000. By 1914 the German figure had again doubled, to 3,400,000 men: with comparable increases among her neighbours. By the end of the century the security of continental powers was seen to depend primarily if not entirely on the size of the armed forces they

were able to put into the field. This assumption rested very largely on the experiences of the German wars of unification . . .[1]

J.F.C. Fuller and Hoffman Nickerson present an anthropological approach, in referring to the revolution of mass as the advent of 'The Armed Horde'.[2]

Liddell Hart's critical writings of the 1930s represent a third approach. His criticism stemmed from two motives: the first was his abhorrence of the slaughter in the First World War, which he attributed to the predominant mentality of mass. The second was his resolute rejection of the stagnant manner in which warfare was conducted. Liddell Hart perceived the mass phenomenon as a continual process of practical and theoretical regression. He believed that four distinctive landmarks led finally to the total decadence of military competence. The mass phenomenon emerged out of events which followed the French Revolution; Napoleon then developed the new pattern into a most destructive operational system; Clausewitz institutionalized the Napoleonic experience in the form of a universal theory; finally, the German victory of 1870 generated an unrestrained manipulation of the mass concept, which ended in the fiasco of the First World War.[3] Liddell Hart traces the theoretical process from its roots, and his piercing observation of tactical nuances exposes the debilitating effect of mass on mobility. Despite the recent criticism by Jay Luvaas and Azar Gat against his verdict on Clausewitz, Liddell Hart's review of the mass phenomenon remains unique in its originality, its intelligibility and its holistic approach.[4]

However, no attempt has been made to explore the impact of mass on the conduct of operations from a system perspective. In attempting to do this the present chapter will follow the periodization suggested by Liddell Hart.

The First Stage

The decree of the French Convention of 23 August 1793, which put the *levée en masse* on a total footing. Since this was a purely political act, and the conduct of war at that time lacked operational coherence, it is beyond the scope of the present study.[5]

The Second Stage

J. Colin, who explored the transformation which occurred in modern warfare, defined the innovation in the initial stage of the mass phenomenon as quantitative: 'Carnot, as a disciple of Guibert, incessantly recommends the assembly of forces and mass action as indispensable to decisive success.'[6] According to Colin, the transition to the Napoleonic stage was marked by the inclination to institutionalize the achievements of the former: 'Napoleon lays down the principles and shows us the models for modern war. In the war to come we shall assuredly have new weapons, larger masses, more efficient means of transportation.'[7]

Clausewitz was the first theoretician to assemble the entire accumulated empirical experience of the Napoleonic era and mould it into a system of laws and principles. As he saw it, the Napoleonic period marked an historical turning point as far as mass was concerned. From that time:

> . . .war, first among the French and subsequently among their enemies, again became the concern of the people as a whole, took on an entirely different character, or rather closely approached its true character, its absolute perfection.

When referring to the change which the Napoleonic mass-approach brought upon the political culture of Western society, Clausewitz concludes:

> A people of thirty millions, all of whom considered themselves to be citizens, became a participant in war . . . The full weight of the nation was thrown into the balance. The resources and efforts now available for use surpassed all conventional limits . . . The sole aim of war was to overthrow the opponent . . . There seemed no end to the resources mobilized: All limits disappeared in the vigour and enthusiasm shown by the governments and their subjects.[8]

In other words, by relating the emergence of the mass armies to the total mobilization of the state's resources in the service of the armed struggle, Clausewitz suggests a linkage between the phenomenon of mass and nationalism. Moreover, through his observation of the consequential nexus between the phenomenon's motive, purpose and result, he anchored both politics and strategy in the mentality of total war, thus focusing the nature of the interrelation between them on the idea of destruction.

Clausewitz then turns to discuss the implications of the mass phenomenon for the art of war:

> . . . The result was that in 1813–1814 Germany and Russia put about a million men into the field . . . Campaigns were on the whole conducted in the new manner, not in that of the past. In the space of only eight months the theatre of operations changed from the Oder to the Seine.[9]

In the operational context, Clausewitz indicated some significant changes. First, in portraying a million-man foot army he touched on

32

the enormous complexities of command and control posed by the challenge of operating such a monster. Moreover, since raising such a huge army required the efforts of more than one state, the aspect of coalition has been introduced into the conduct of war, thus adding another dimension to the existing complexities. Another aspect of the change implied by the mass phenomenon is the time and space in which this huge army operated. Hence, Clausewitz denoted the continuity and dimensions of the units of time and space. And finally, through the last aspect Clausewitz accentuates the vigorous dynamism of the military operations in his time.

A close examination of Napoleon's principal battles during the years 1796–1813 reveals a consistent trend to increase the number of troops, employed by both belligerents, by a factor of ten. Similarly, the size of the battlefields increased fourfold,[10] indicating compatibility between mass and space. The relevance of the latter phenomenon emerges when one comprehends the mode in which the mass was utilized on the battlefield. During the Napoleonic era and throughout the nineteenth century, troops were deployed and operated in a linear mode.[11] This fact was observed by Clausewitz: '. . . What usually happens in a major battle today? The troops move calmly into position in great masses deployed in line and depth.'[12]

Consequently, the linear pattern of operating the mass created a twofold operational problem. The first, which is rooted in the field of Euclidean geometry, derives from the simple fact that of all existing forms the linear is the greatest consumer of space: the bigger the mass of troops deployed on the battlefield, the wider the space required. Secondly, since the method of command relied totally on the supreme commander's personal conduct of the battle, his ability to respond effectively to changing conditions declined in accordance with the expansion of the line of battle. This conjecture is based on Napoleon's experience in three of his largest battles. In the battle of Wagram, Napoleon deployed 170,500 troops along a line of 12 miles. As a result he was not present in a certain sector of the battlefield, nor could he observe a tactical opportunity to break the Austrian left, which was created by an attack of Davout's corps. Hence, the tactical opportunity remained unexploited and a chance to achieve an operational decision was missed.[13] In the battle of Bautzen, 200,000 French troops were deployed along 12 miles. The length of the line prevented Napoleon from noticing Marshal Ney's grave tactical misconduct, which impaired his entire operational plan.[14]

The last example, the battle of Leipzig in October 1813, is the most cogent for proving this argument. In that battle Napoleon operated 198,000 troops along a line of some 21 miles. The emperor's command post was on the Galgenberg, which had visual communication with the sector of Wachau. During the early afternoon hours of 16 October, General Bordesoulle's Cuirassier division was ordered by the sector commander to charge the flank of Eugen of Württemberg's command. The attack drove away the enemy's flank, broke through the main allied line and almost reached the command post of Tsar Alexander. It was a devastating charge which could have been exploited into operational decision. However, at that crucial moment Napoleon was absent from his command post and the sector commander's reserves were already dry. Yet again a fateful tactical opportunity went unnoticed.[15]

Thus, the combination of the unrestrained increase in the fighting mass and the linear mode of operation on the battlefield revealed the fragility of the traditional method of direct command. Moreover, since the linear configuration of military forces tended to develop the highest friction in case of contiguity, the marginal profit gained from the simultaneous maximization of musket fire was offset by a complete loss of operational manoeuvrability and the application of attrition to tactical combat.[16]

The Third Stage

The third stage in the evolution of the mass phenomenon is that of its theoretical crystallization. This achievement was primarily the handiwork of one man – Clausewitz. Not only did he perceive the historical change which the advent of the mass phenomenon brought about, but he also succeeded in defining its essence in theoretical terms. Clausewitz's analytical treatment of the mass phenomenon and his endeavour to formulate it as a universal principle conform to his general perception of the theory of war.[17] He embraced the entire Napoleonic empirical experience and formed a cognitive tool out of it. This tool was not intended to function as a tactical formula in the practical level of warfare, but rather as a critical instrument for studying war.

Thus, establishing the universality of the quantitative factor, Clausewitz leaves no doubt as to its eminence: '. . . In tactics, as in strategy, superiority in numbers is the most common element in victory . . .'[18] In his analysis, Napoleon's manipulative and innovative exploitation of mass brought him his military achievements. However, when the principle of mass was fully adopted by his adversaries and his method of manipulating military masses was implemented by them even more emphatically, his invincibility was broken. Therefore, Clausewitz concludes that mass may serve as a universal substitution for military genius: '. . . These examples may show that in modern Europe even the most talented general will find it very difficult to defeat an opponent twice his strength.'[19] Such an assertion has always been very attractive to generals, since it equips them with an arithmetic formula which rationalizes warfare and guarantees victory. As we have already noticed, Clausewitz anchors his concept of mass in the two levels of war that were accepted in his time. The essence of the tactical engagement is defined as a quantitative confrontation in which the superior numbers win:

> If we thus strip the engagement of all the variables arising from its purpose and circumstances, and disregard the fighting value of the troops involved, we are left with the bare concept of the engagement, a shapeless battle in which the only distinguishing factor is the number of the troops on either side. These numbers, therefore will determine victory.[20]

Similarly, the cognitive origins of the tactical law of superior numbers derive from the perception of battle's attritional nature:

> This description pictures the order of battle simply as a disposition of troops designed to facilitate their use, and the course of battle as a slow process of mutual attrition that will reveal which side can first exhaust its opponents.[21]

Thus, the mass is the operational remedy to the tactical pulverization, and numerical superiority is the main guarantee for victory.

For Clausewitz, as we shall see later, strategy has no substance of its own; its main purpose is to bring about the occurrence of battle under the most favourable conditions. In other words, strategy must provide the battle with all its essentials, of which mass is the foremost:

> It thus follows that as many troops as possible should be brought into the engagement at the decisive point. Whether these forces prove adequate or not, we will at least have done everything in our power. This is the first principle of strategy.[22]

Hence, the importance of mass at the strategic level derives firstly from the notion that strategy is the servant of tactics. Furthermore, Clausewitz suggests that there are two other sources which accentuate the significance of mass within the context of strategy. The first, is the fact that strategy is governed by a trend of attrition, which originates in the accumulation of tactical attritions, and also in the constant advance towards the adversary's territorial depth or one's own culminating point:

> Consequently, only the direct profit gained in the process of mutual

destruction may be considered as having been the object. This profit is absolute . . . It remains fixed throughout the entire balance sheet of the campaign and in the end will always prove pure again.

The second ingredient of strategy which stresses the importance of mass is its aim. The completion of the destructive aim, as we have noticed, prescribes a quantitative mode of conduct. Thus, the ideal type of the battle of decision (*Hauptschlacht*) is formulated, and war becomes even more quantified: '. . . The massing of troops into a single whole, which happens to some degree in every campaign, indicates a belligerent intention to use this mass in a major blow.'[23]

In short, by rationalizing the mass phenomenon Clausewitz manages to escape the paradoxes inherent in his system, namely: the definition of destruction as a universal aim for war; the idealization of attrition; the arbitrary preference for the tactical level over that of strategy; the justification of the linear mode of action; and the legitimization of thinking exclusively in the dimension of offensive. Furthermore, by describing the factor of mass as a key principle in the conduct of warfare, he bequeathed a distorted doctrine to subsequent generations and paved the way for the German conceptual failure in the First World War.

The Fourth Stage

Commencing with the German wars of unification and culminating in the First World War, the fourth stage in the evolution of the mass phenomenon saw not only the quantitative increase of the European armies from 1,200,000 to 3,400,000, but also the entrenchment of the mass mentality – a trend which is reflected both in theoretical works and in the formulation of operational plans for war. The German victory of 1870 reintroduced the element of mass and the quantitative dimension into the conduct of war with new vigour.[24] Indeed, Moltke the Elder, who was the chief of the general staff during the wars of unification and the war of 1870 attest to it. His military correspondence, memoirs and writings on strategy reveal the significance which he attributed to the mass factor, in the planning of the war.[25] The factor of mass manifested its operational benefits in three aspects of the actual conduct of the war. First, it allowed Moltke a high degree of operational flexibility. This is clearly exemplified in his memorandum to the chiefs of sections in the general staff, and in his decision to operate simultaneously with two army groups, which followed the battle of Gravelotte-St. Privat.[26] Secondly, the marked numerical superiority on the German side was the principal condition which presented them with an operational opportunity to encircle their adversary.[27] And finally, by exploiting their superiority in mass, the Germans managed to turn their opponents' flank in most of the tactical engagements.[28]

The stunning German achievements in the wars of unification were attributed largely to Moltke's conduct. And since he regarded himself as a disciple of Clausewitz, the latter's theoretical accomplishment became the philosophical cornerstone for the military in Germany and France.[29] Armed with a compelling theory and devastating empirical experience, the idea of mass became almost a gospel. Consequently, all European powers, except Britain, adopted universal conscription.[30]

Friedrich von Bernhardy, a leading German theoretician in the decade preceding the First World War, illuminates the numerical aspect of the quantitative competition generated among the European states by the adoption of universal conscription: 'It is right to some extent, to speak of the armies of millions of modern times, the like of which have not been seen before in history.'[31] Moreover, he adopted Clausewitz's quantitative approach literally:

> Of all the features which are destined to influence the conduct of war under present conditions, and cause it to strike new lines, it is the levy of masses above all, which no doubt will give its peculiar stamp to the next war.[32]

On the French side Ferdinand Foch echoed the German theoreticians, in a more prosaic tone, when returning to the Clausewitzian equation: '. . . I have pointed out the nature of modern war: war ever more national; masses ever more considerable.'[33]

The radical trend to employ masses as the ultimate solution to any operational problem reached the proportions of a craze. This addiction to numbers is manifested in Bernhardy's, rather critical, illustration:

> All states of Europe are dominated by the mania of numbers . . . The general tendency is rather to increase the levies to the utmost limit of financial and personal capacity. There is no idea of stopping this for the time being. Numbers seem to the present generation the decisive factor in war.[34]

Count Alfred von Schlieffen, who functioned as the chief of the German general staff from 1891 to 1905, was the indubitable product of the mentality just described. His uniqueness derives from the fact that he took the all-embracing concept of mass and refined it into an operational idea. Upon this idea rested one of the most ambitious operational plans ever to be devised.

For Schlieffen, mass was not just another tactical means to augment the destructive effect of the firing line, but the main source of power which generated the operational manoeuvre. Unlike Foch, Schlieffen's approach to mass was entirely realistic, and his method of administering it was logical and consistent. Schlieffen used the mass to feed the strategic advancing front, and to manipulate this incessant line into an operational sledgehammer, which would crush its opponent. In his great memorandum of December 1905 he delineated this operational effect in plain words:

> By attacks on their left flank we must try at all costs to drive the French eastward against their Moselle fortresses, against the Jura and Switzerland. The French army must be annihilated.[35]

Schlieffen was not seen as a wizard, but rather as a master manipulator of numbers. Freytag-Loringhoven recounts the Schlieffen legacy as such, after the First World War:

> Field Marshal Count Schlieffen, who taught us how to manipulate a massed army, and who, because he was convinced of the great importance of numbers in war, was unwilling to abandon the employment of the older drafts in the front line . . .[36]

Schlieffen's intellectual charisma was so great and his manipulative mode of reasoning carried such an impact on his disciples, that his operational concept continued to be regarded as invincible by the German high command, even after the First World War. The crown prince, who commanded the fifth army in 1914, expressed this explicitly after the war:

> The question arose: was it permissible still to hold to the original plan, aiming at a speedy decision in open field battles along the western front? . . . The answer was an unqualified Yes, if the Schlieffen plan, providing for crushing the enemy by sheer masses concentrated on the German right, was fulfilled.[37]

Schlieffen formulated the strategic and operational aspects of mass in modern war at length in two articles, which were published after his retirement.[38] Nonetheless, the depth of his perception of mass is best exhibited in three short excerpts taken from the documents of the famous plan. In the memorandum of December 1905 he estimates the German army's ability to achieve its operational goals in purely quantitative terms: '. . . Only when twenty five army corps have been available left of the Moselle, for which one cannot be too strong, can one await the result with calm conscience.'[39] The second excerpt is an assertion in his last memorandum of December 1912: '. . . With the fifty one divisions corresponding to the original corps, the whole line

Belfort–Nijmegen can be attacked.'[40] This late expression comprises Schlieffen's entire military credo, and thus constitutes the operational rational of the 1912 plan – an ideal which never materialized. Moreover, here the great master displays the Schlieffenian touch at its best. Of what ingredients does this exemplary formula of operational manoeuvre consist? It is a 500 km continuous line, composed of 51 operational formations all advancing simultaneously. Thus, the attacker imposes on his opponent a linear mode of a uniform offensive, depriving the latter of any type of operational initiative by this immense linear push. Therefore, the only problem that confronts the aggressor is that of quantities, i.e., he must feed the line with ample material and thus, secure its continuance, thickness and weight. All these functions will be accomplished by the mass, and in order to comply more suitably with the challenges of the existing reality, it is manipulated from 36 army corps to 51.

The third excerpt is a comment made by Major Wilhelm von Hahnke, in his notes to Schlieffen's memorandums. As Schlieffen's son-in-law and loyal assistant during the creative years of retirement, von Hahnke was the closest person to him.[41] Therefore, his short comments on certain issues indeed elucidate the thoughts behind Schlieffen's programmatic writings. Illustrating the manner in which von Schlieffen perceived the offensive in metaphoric language:

> Therefore the conquered territory must be completely inundated with our troops. Wave must follow wave in the invasion. After the first line must come the reserves, then the *Ersatz* troops, then the *Ersatz* reserves, finally, if necessary, the mobilized *Landsturm*, so that in fact the whole German population able to bear arms will take part in the operations against France.[42]

THE CULTURAL DICHOTOMY: ABSENCE OF OPERATIONAL COGNITION IN A SYSTEM ENVIRONMENT

It is commonly accepted that mass constitutes an essential element of every existing system.[43] Therefore, once massive armies emerged in the European theatre and the concept of mass matured in military thinking, systemic, or rather operational conditions prevailed. Moreover, the application of the corps system by Napoleon yielded an organizational pattern which explicitly indicated the basic components of the manoeuvring system. This is, however, a necessary but insufficient condition for a system's existence. Unless a proper interaction between the elements comprising the mass develops, the mass can never become an effective system possessing a vitality of its own.[44] Simpkin characterized this interaction, in the military context, by utilizing the values of depth and momentum.[45] However, the application of these values to the context of manoeuvre requires appropriate cognition, and any magnification of the physical element alone, be it troops, fire power, or any other fighting resources, will not generate the indispensable operational dynamism of a system. This is, perhaps, the most important lesson to be learned from the First World War.

In the absence of system thinking the development of operational cognition capable of steering the enormous increase in fighting resources into a comprehensive course of operational manoeuvre could never materialize. Thus the manipulative endeavour to expand the mass remained anchored in archaic patterns of tactical thinking – a trend which ultimately led to the bankruptcy of the conduct of war.

Arguing, therefore, that the generals of the period under discussion understood the real problems of war, and performed as well as possible given the inability of contemporary technology to provide the platforms for a dynamic operational manoeuvre, lead to a simplistic historical interpretation.

By attributing the failure of the First World War to tactical deficiencies, one evades the real problem. This is well demonstrated by the German offensive of March 1918. 'Operation Michael' was based on the competent method of tactical infiltration. However, once the initial tactical successes were achieved, they became irrelevant, and the whole German strategic posture collapsed within a period of five months.[46] To contemporaries, such conclusions seemed absurd, since they denied the universal belief which maintained that tactical victory was the only key to strategic success. But would it be wrong to assume that the errant strategy was the culprit? Such a view does not take most of the intermediary combat occurrences into consideration.

Clausewitz and the theoreticians who succeeded him recognized the existence of an intermediary sphere of military activity, which synthesizes the field of mechanics with that of cerebration. Yet, none of them understood the entire nature or the distinctive problems of the operational level of war. On this subject Clausewitz was guilty of serious distortions, such as would have not occurred had he not dealt with it at all. After 1870 his writings indoctrinated the military intelligentsia in Germany; as a result, not only were his ideas adopted almost literally, some of his distortions were corrupted even further. Although Clausewitz's perception of theory in general and his idea about applying it to the military profession are intellectual achievements which remain unsurpassed, his conception of the operational principle is a labyrinth of paradoxes.

The imposition of a complex of rigid rules and premises on the operational field and its subjugation to the mechanical rules of battle is the most serious of Clausewitz's cognitive failures. By doing so he relegated the operational level to an auxiliary one, designed to provide the tactical battle with some of its technical requirements. Therefore, unconsciously and, perhaps, unintentionally, Clausewitz precipitated a state of affairs in which his followers ignored operational substance. In fact, non-operational patterns developed consistently in the course of a conceptual regression, beginning with Clausewitz and ending in the First World War.[47]

The source of this regression and the dominant factor which shaped it were rooted in a chain of paradoxes stemming from Clausewitz's theory.[48] In light of the operational experience gained in the 1870 war, military theoreticians, such as Colmar von der Goltz, Friedrich Bernhardy, W. von Falkenhausen, Julius von Verdy Du Vernois, Prince Kraft zu Hohenlohe-Ingelfingen, A. Boguslawski, as well as J.L. Lewal, G.A. Bonnal, Jerome Colin and Ferdinand Foch, transformed through their programmatic writings this chain of paradoxes into a tactical dogma detached from the systemic reality of their time.[49] The peak of this dogmatic trend can be recognized in the crystallized formula of the Schlieffen plan.[50] Moreover, through coercive mobilization of technology and infrastructure in the service of military thinking a manipulative effort was made to transfer this dogma from the tactical into the strategic context.[51]

Clausewitz's chain of paradoxes comprises his main ideas – a combination which constitutes both the rationale of his entire theory and the essence of his cognitive failure.[52] The foremost link in this chain and in the entire method of argumentation set by *Vom Kriege* is provided by the principle of destruction (*Vernichtungsprinzip*).[53] According to Clausewitz, since *Vernichtungsprinzip* constitutes the universal aim and objective of all wars and engagements, it expresses the desired uniform accomplishment both at the level of the abstract conduct of war and at that of mechanical warfare.[54] Thus, since the tactical endeavour is instrumental in the achievement of strategic results, *Vernichtungsprinzip* denotes both the end and the means in war. This ambiguity contributes significantly to the abstruseness which characterizes Clausewitz's work. Moreover, by importing, by way of induction, the principle of destruction, which he assimilated through direct tactical experience into the context of operational masses, Clausewitz committed an irrational act, depriving his entire strategic philosophy of its basic coherency. Having realized that the physical destruction of mass armies is impractical even in the limited context of a single battle, Clausewitz defines the optimum tactical achievement as inducing the enemy to break off the fighting by inflicting on him a higher rate of losses than that suffered by one's own force.[55] This somewhat deterministic assumption that destruction is effectuated by a process of mutual attrition is only one of the sources for the absurdity implied in Clausewitz's argumentation. Through a simplistic application of this approach to the strategic context, Clausewitz imposes the logic of unidimensional combat occurrences on the field of the complex political-national system. Moreover, by claiming that strategic destruction is attained by the accumulation of tactical destructions he establishes a direct quantitative linkage between the various levels of conducting war, thus undermining the idea of synergism.[56]

The Clausewitzian idea of destruction is, therefore, totally incompatible with the operational conception of war. First, there is the simple fact that systems can not be physically destroyed, a fact as valid today as it was in Clausewitz's day. Secondly, systems are structured hierarchically and are goal-oriented. The aim or goal is always specified according to the concrete political and operational circumstances, commencing at the supreme political and strategic level and descending towards the tactical. In other words, the operational objectives at the different levels of war derive from a single cognitive source, which determines, through a consistent rational, the general functioning of the system and the quality of the interaction between its components. Thus, the definition of the operational aim represents a cognitive act that initially precedes the actual occurrence of the operation or battle. Moreover, it expresses an accomplishment that is qualitatively greater than the arithmetic sum of achievements, which result from the acts of the numerous components composing the system. Therefore, in installing fixed, universal, identical and permanent aims for war, Clausewitz precluded a certain essential of the operational dynamism from transpiring – the one that is concerned with political-military dialogue which *precedes* war, and with the cognitive tension which regulates its turbulent course.[57]

This dereliction of the basic mechanism for systemic conduct of war at all levels produced an illusionary perception of flexibility, since it simplified one of the most demanding challenges of the conduct of war. Yet, in fact, by ignoring the realities of war, and especially the factor of randomness, which tends to become acute with the increase in mass, the conduct of war became so inflexible that it cracked at the first disruption.

This phenomenon accounts for the fact that no serious dialogue between the German Chief of the General Staff and the Chancellor concerning the issue of the war aims and its strategic conduct, ever occurred. It can be assumed that neither Schlieffen nor von Bülow thought it necessary, since the war aims were traditionally established, and the actual conduct of the war was perceived as the exclusive territory of the supreme soldier of the state.[58] Moreover, in the two memoranda Schlieffen does not seem to mention any explicit aims, except the general one of annihilating the French army.[59] Indeed, Clausewitz himself denies any connection between the political purposes of war and its practical conduct.[60] By doing so he legitimizes the dissociation of the conduct of war from political supervision.

Clausewitz then proceeds to argue that the implementation of destruction is attained through the battle, and due to the latter's linear nature, destruction assumes the pattern of attrition.[61]

A reciprocal relationship exists between destruction and the battle. Destruction is the goal of battle, and the battle is the sole means by which that goal can be attained.[62] In other words, destruction determines an inevitable course for the operational director to follow, namely – the one which leads to battle. And since the tactical battle becomes the factor which governs the operational as well as the strategic levels of war – the second paradox in the cognitive chain is established. Moreover, this unidirectional path becomes even narrower, since it dictates yet another prohibition, that is the predetermined adoption of the operational offensive mode.

The complete essence of this second paradox can be appreciated only after Clausewitz consolidates the quantitative equation between the battle and destruction: major battles lead to major destructions.[63] In other words, the relationship between the goal and the means is a quantitative one, since the road to the perfect or absolute goal passes through the integral battle of destruction (*Vernichtungs-schlacht*). This, in turn, leads to another equation, which in fact constitutes the broad basis of Clausewitz's philosophy of war and his cognitive bequest to his adherents: Destruction is the absolute goal; its attainment is effectuated by a linear grand battle; to guarantee the occurrence of the integral battle the strategy must be both linear and offensive. Clausewitz thus complements the fabrication of the second paradox and lays the foundations for the logical structure of his theory.

The offensive, according to Clausewitz, derives from the very nature of the principle of destruction, since the latter is the positive goal, and the offensive constitutes the means to attain it, positively.[64] The roots of this argument lie in the assumption that in order to achieve the complete form of destruction, one has to conquer.[65] This logic determines that conquest is possible only through the offensive, which is oriented to the ideal grand battle, and ultimately leads to its eventuation.

Thus, although Clausewitz devotes an excellent book to a thorough discussion of defence, he does not advocate its application to his fellow Germans. He defines tactical defence as the stronger form of combat, but specifies the defensive as the inferior operational mode, his conclusion being that the strategic defensive is a necessity to be used by the weak.[66] This view creates operational asymmetry, and thus establishes the third link in the chain of paradoxes. Since the existence of a certain homeostasis evolving between the contra-positive ideas of offence and defence is essential for the development of system dynamics in every field and level of operational activity, the extraction of the latter from the professional consciousness damages the inherent qualities of the operational manoeuvre and destroys its *raison d'être*.

The aspirations to contend with operational predicaments by a tactical approach, and an artificial utilization of operational amounts of force through linear methods merely aggravated those predicaments and represent a futile effort to perpetuate an archaic residue. This is the first reason why the quantitative trend is an absurdity. The second reason is that quantitative superiority was perceived as a magic solution to any existing operational problem. The third reason is that at the beginning of the present century, the craze for mass became too great for even the simplistic linear patterns to bear. Consequently, once the quantitative trend had failed to provide the expected solution, the entire theory collapsed.

The entire logic of Clausewitz's theory can be explicitly identified in the war of 1870, and in the theoretical writings of Moltke, von der Goltz, Boguslawski, Bernhardy, Prince Kraft von Hohenlohe-Ingelfingen, Schlieffen and even in those of Caemmerer and Freytag-Loringhoven.[67] Even broad-minded theoreticians such as Schlichting, who had an advanced inclination for operational thinking, were not able to liberate themselves entirely from the heavy bondage of the Clausewitz obsession.[68]

Clausewitzian logic as a whole was manifested literally in two conceptual pillars which were fixed in the First World War – the Schlieffen Plan and Plan 17. The course of the cognitive regression, which originated with Clausewitz, went through two stages in which its basic logic developed primarily in one direction – that of applying it to the increasing aspects of the mass. The process ended with the First World War, although in France it continued, with some variations, for another two decades of operational ignorance.

The stamp of Clausewitzian logic is reflected in the organization and structuring of the armed forces, in the training systems, in the theoretical debates of the time, and also in a series of notions created by Clausewitz. The latter were either elements that formed a part of his main theme, or were indoctrinated through a secondary subject of his preaching.

The force-building of all the leading armies before the First World War was dictated by an exclusive and absolute preference for infantry. Clausewitz discusses the subject of the optimal composition of armies and his conclusion explicitly prefers an army organized almost entirely on the basis of infantry and artillery, since those arms of the military conform to his logic and tactical perceptions. In other words, since destruction was significantly more important than operational mobility, and in any case the application of cavalry on the battlefield was limited to infrequent opportunities, he preferred an army which would rely entirely on the arms possessing the greater destructive abilities. Moreover, since the cost for establishing a squadron of 150 horsemen equalled that of a battalion of some 800 foot soldiers, or a battery of eight guns, he voluntarily gave up operational mobility for cheaper but less mobile fire power.[69] But if such an approach could have been justified in Clausewitz's time, due to the nature of battle and technological limitations, its existence four generations later must be considered an archaism, bordering on absurdity. The renunciation of mechanization, even by the existing means such as horses and wagons, is the direct outcome of a mentality which evolved out of Clausewitz's theory.[70] Due to this state of mind operational mobility never materialized, and manoeuvre warfare could not be implemented.

The conceptual foundation which led to the cultivation of linear patterns of manoeuvre lay in Clausewitz's personal experience when present during tactical engagements in the course of the Napoleonic wars. The tactical advantages suggested by the linear configuration were obvious – a fact which made it so attractive. On the one hand, the linear pattern facilitated simultaneous expression of maximum fire-power – an advantage that both served the principle of destruction and utilized the quantitive trend; on the other hand, by applying the line to tactical manoeuvre, the impression of continuous command and effective control was created both in the transition from *Aufmarsch* to *Begegnungsgefecht* (encounter battle) and in the attempt to exercise flanking movements. In his own words, Clausewitz's preference for the linear mode and tactical simultaneity meant linear deployments exceeding 15 miles and the absolute negation of operational or strategic reserves.[71]

However, the application of linear patterns of manoeuvre to the operational-strategic level allowed Clausewitz's interpreters to fulfil the main theme of his work literally – namely, the integral battle of destruction. Thus, the real attractions of the linear pattern were revealed. By deploying a continuous strategic front in the initial stages of the war one could effectuate the precondition of offensive screening, by means of which the rival army could be located, brought to battle and destroyed. Moreover, practising an approach manoeuvre in the form of an homogeneous line provided the army with a cognitive common denominator and an operational formation, and created the illusion of absolute control over friendly forces and enemy moves alike. Finally, the strategic-operational offensive front integrated into a monstrous *coup de main* not only the multitude of tactical events prior to their occurrence, but also the approach, the engagement and the consequential effect, thus creating the impression of simplicity. The main challenge posed by the application of the uniform linear manoeuvre as a strategic instrument for accomplishing the integral battle of destruction was the problem of feeding the line with human material. This problem was solved by a manipulative use of the mass.

The forced attempt to import patterns of envelopment and encirclement from the tactical milieu to a spatial setting hundreds of times larger than the battlefields of Cannae and Leuthen reflected one of the reasons why Schlieffen's operational model was illogical. The indifference to the factor of depth and the complete repudiation of strategic reserves are further indicators of the absence of operational thought. However, the peak of absurdity was the assumption that by applying the linear configuration, complete control could be exercised both over the movements of millions of men and over the occurrence of every single random engagement.[72] Thus the last link in the chain of paradoxes was established in the form of a geometrical syllogism.

The dogmatic adoption of linearism contradicted the natural tendency of commanders, at both tactical and operational levels, to avoid frontal attacks, and to apply their troops indirectly. The efforts for escaping this dichotomy and for overcoming the dissonance that it produced, resulted in two patterns. The first was an enormous flow of rhetoric suggesting a tactical method, which seemed to be an envelopment, but in fact was nothing more than a linear engagement developing, in its final stages, into a shallow attempt to get around one of the opposing line's flanks.[73] The second was an attempt to transmute Frederick's tactical method of oblique manoeuvre into the operational context literally–a pattern which was termed: *Flügelschlacht* or the wing grand battle of destruction.[74] This unrealistic and forced magnification of a tactical mode of manoeuvre into strategical dimensions, which was elaborated by Falkenhausen, became the strategic creed of almost every German and French theoretician, and finally developed into the operational rationale around which Schlieffen's 1905 memorandum was structured.[75] During his last years of writing in retirement, Schlieffen relinquished the magnified tactical form of *Flügelschlacht* for the more vigorous tactical form of double envelopment, or encirclement. In the memorandum of December 1912, he converted the tactical formula of Cannae into a gargantuan line, hoping to achieve in this way the perfect effects of destruction.[76] Schlieffen's last memorandum, which is very rarely read or mentioned, demonstrates the most advanced degree of cognitive decadence.

An examination of the operational plans, as well as the theoretical literature which predate the First World War, gives the clear impression that they were the result of ardent indoctrination for applying simplicity and directness at every level of military activity. The logic of this approach assumed that simplicity and lucidity were the key factors in military success. The utilization of these qualities in operational planning dictated, almost inevitably, the application of a direct or rather frontal approach in practical combat. However, since energy is the most common substitute for sophistication, one can always compensate for any apparent lack of insight with physical boldness. Thus, the comprehensive equation of war, as preached by Clausewitz and applied by his disciples, was simple linearity + direct physical vigour = victory.[77] In other words, the cognitive substance of Schlieffen's plan of 1912 derived from a Clausewitzian conceptual origin.[78]

That the Clausewitzian concept of centre of gravity (*Schwerpunkt*) was adopted by the Germans is no surprise – its vitality and addictive simplicity made it a most attractive concept for them. Nevertheless, what made the idea of centre of gravity the core of German military thinking, both in the theoretical and practical fields, was the fact that it combined in its substance the principle of destruction (*Vernichtungsprinzip*) and the concept of the grand battle of destruction (*Hauptschlacht*). Thus, Clausewitz's entire theoretical complex was expressed in a single notion, which disguised its inherent inconsistencies.

By initially subjecting the essence of warfare at all its various levels to the mechanical logic of the duel, Clausewitz assumes that the operational manoeuvre is nothing other than a collision between two strategic masses – one defending and the other attacking.[79] Therefore, presuming that the attack must be guided by the positive principle of destruction, he determines that the attacker should always assemble the greater part of his mass against the defender's principal concentration, in spite of the latter's inclination to deploy his force.[80] By defining the main masses of both belligerents as universal centres of gravity, Clausewitz overcomes the problem of applying the dictum of the integral battle of destruction to the realities of strategic deployment; by linking the definition of *Schwerpunkt* to the concentration of masses on both sides, he subjects the relationship between them to the deterministic nature of destruction.

However, since we are dealing with quantitative entities which are driven towards collision by a deterministic trend, the entire idea of centre of gravity has been deprived of real operational significance. Clausewitz's attempt to attach the idea of *Schwerpunkt* to matters taken from a political-strategic context, such as national cohesion, political interest, or a centre of political power, leaves him inconclusive and drives him back to his basic formula: the centre of gravity consists of a destructive trend aimed and directed towards the main body of the enemy army.[81]

Apart from the lack of perspicuity resulting from confusing mechanical aspects and abstract ideas in the concept of *Schwerpunkt*, its formulation by Clausewitz emphasizes a trend that can be recognized primarily in Schlieffen's brainchild. By employing the *Schwerpunkt* concept as an instrument to overcome the difficulties of interpreting the idea of the integral battle of destruction in the military reality of the late nineteenth century, he almost dictated the adoption of a direct mechanical approach to the operational manoeuvre, thus further increasing the tactization of strategy.

A comparison of Schlieffen's operational perception and the manner in which it was communicated in the Plan's documents with the technical aspects of Clausewitz's concept of the centre of gravity reveals a resemblance, so striking that it borders on plagiarism. This resemblance, noticed by Bernard Brodie, concerns the manner in which Schlieffen perceived war planning at the strategical level, and also the way in which both he and Clausewitz defined France as Germany's main enemy, Paris as the centre of gravity in a case of war, and the space between Brussels and Paris as the strategic vital area.[82] Moreover, a critical analysis of the conceptual process through which the Schlieffen Plan matured, since his takeover from Waldersee in 1891, will reinforce the impression that Schlieffen was not merely a disciple of Clausewitz, but absolutely blinded by his doctrine.[83]

TECHNOLOGY — A CATALYST OF OPERATIONAL IGNORANCE

The fact that creative patterns of operational manoeuvre did not appear until the beginning of the Second World War has been basically attributed by modern historiography to the failure of military technology to provide the prerequisite of mechanization. Under the compelling mechanical impressions created by the *Blitzkrieg* this somewhat anachronistic approach perceives the tank as the catalyst which induced the emergence of modern operational precept, thus reducing military theory to the status of a secondary tool, the value of which can be measured by its ability to respond to the random fluctuations of technological developments.[84] By ignoring the crucial importance of system consciousness as a precondition for the development of modes of warfare capable of coping with the challenges of the operational environment, this approach fails to provide answers to questions such as: Why did the allies fail to employ operational patterns of manoeuvre on the Western front in 1917, although they possessed ample quantities of tanks, aircraft and other forms of mechanization? How did the Americans, in spite of enjoying decisive technical superiority, lose the war in Vietnam?[85]

Moreover, by exclusively examining warfare through the perspective of contemporary tactics, the prevailing approach in military historiography falls short of realizing the complete depth and creativity of operational manoeuvres such as those conducted by the Mongols, Wellington in the Peninsular Campaign, Moltke in the second half of August 1870, the Russian 1877–78 Balkan Campaign, and Allenby's march through Palestine.[86] A critical study of these cases proves beyond doubt that whenever system thinking was applied, dynamic operational manoeuvres transpired notwithstanding the absence of mechanization and other forms of modern technology. Moreover, as disclosed by sagacious thinkers such as Caemmerer and Schlichting, the general absence of operational insight and the prevalence of tactical archaism transformed even the technologies which existed at the end of the nineteenth century into an obstruction, causing further distortion to strategic thought and bringing the operational manoeuvre to complete decadence.[87]

The Peninsular War

The case of the Peninsular War of 1808–14 is an outstanding instance, which not only illuminates the general aspects of conducting war in the operational context, but also confirms that such a challenge could have been contested effectively as early as the beginning of the nineteenth century. Wellington's conduct of the war provides a remarkable example of a creative system approach, demonstrated through his perception of the linkage between aim and operational method, his revolutionary application of operational synergy, and his unique comprehension of the interaction between attrition and manoeuvre and the reciprocal relationship between offence and defence.

On assuming command of the theatre Wellington faced a fourfold difficulty: he had to achieve total goals within the strategic scope of operations, that is the complete expulsion of the French forces from the Peninsula; he was obliged to perform his mission with scarce resources; he was compelled to accomplish all that in cooperation with unreliable allies; and he was significantly inferior to his enemy in numbers of regular troops.[88] A scrupulous examination of the two memorandums he had produced a long time before his nomination as supreme commander, reveals a unique operational insight.[89] Wellington comprehended the strategical and operational context of his mission in its entire depth. He perceived accurately the politicians' expectations of him, was fully aware of his operational limitations, defined his enemy's tactical deficiencies and operational weaknesses with great precision, and, finally, was aware of the nature of his theatre of operation.[90]

Since complex problems tend to be resolved by combined methods, Wellington responded to the imperative of reason and turned to the operational field for solutions. Consequently, he devised an advanced operational plan, which took both his limitations and resources into consideration and combined in its essence manoeuvre and attrition, offensive and defensive, and four types of troops: British regulars, Spanish regulars, Portuguese regulars, and irregulars. The general idea, or rather operational rationale of his plan, was to secure Portugal as a base of operations, draw the French inland, force them to disperse, and pulverize them by a coordinated effort of Spanish troops and irregulars. Then, whenever an opportunity to strike at the enemy's main force occurred, he would operate the British contingent as a conventional element of manoeuvre. Thus, he intended to bleed the French white by a long and multifarious process, and, after attaining a more favourable balance of power, to turn to a general offensive.[91] Even his tactical method, which aimed simultaneously at pulverizing his opponent and preserving his own force, conformed to his operational concept.[92]

Another expression of Wellington's operational insight was his perception of attrition within the context of manoeuvre. By imposing attrition deliberately on his adversaries and at the same time preserving his own force, he managed to harness attrition in the service of manoeuvre, and thus prepare the soil for the materialization of the latter.

Finally, Wellington conceived the idea of combining various operational elements in a common context, and applied it to his theatre by mobilizing the Spanish regulars and guerrillas in the service of the same political cause and operational goals, thus creating a cohesive and dynamic system.

The Balkan Campaign

The operation of Lieutenant General Iu.V. Romeiko-Gurko's forward detachment (*peredovoi otriad*) during the summer 1877 Balkan Campaign demonstrates the entire scope and thorough effects of the operational manoeuvre in depth.[93] Gurko's tactical, operational and strategical achievements are eminent even in today's conditions of high technology and mechanization. Moreover, the 1877 experience and the literature it generated introduced into military thinking a series of ingenious terms, which are rooted deep in contemporary operational theory.

The first term was 'raiding division' (*reidovaia diviziia*) and it referred to a newly grouped cavalry division composed of two Cossack brigades.[94] This term, which expressed at the time the modern concept of mechanized infantry in the context of deep operations, was totally ignored in the West.[95]

The second term was 'forward detachment' (*peredovoi otriad*), and it manifested for the first time the embryonic idea of the deep operational manoeuvre in columnar patterns.[96] This term, which reflected the notions of mobility and combined-arms warfare in the broader context of operational thought, was distorted when translated into other European languages, in a form that demonstrated the entire tactical parochialism that dominated Western military thinking at the time.[97]

The third term, which has no equivalent in other European languages except that of 'operation', is *deistvie*. This term implies a military action deeply anchored in the operational context, since it always refers to a mission, command structure and quantitative dimensions that derive from that level of war.[98]

Gurko's formation during the 1877 summer campaign, was an *ad hoc* grouping meant to perform a concrete operational mission.[99] The numerical strength of the Forward Detachment was that of a modern division, yet, in view of the manoeuvre elements of which it consisted, its structure corresponds more to that of a corps.[100]

The distinct innovation of the Forward Detachment was reflected

51

explicitly in two aspects. The first is that of the mission, which was composed of three ingredients: the physical specifications of the task; the dynamic relationship between the general aim of the campaign and that of the detachment; and the independence of the latter within the extensive context of the war. The second aspect is the genuine pattern of combined-arms warfare. But since its emergence was initiated by tactical as well as operational considerations it expresses the idea of manoeuvre in its refined formula.

In Russian military thought the substance of manoeuvre centres on the idea of shock (*udar*) in such a way that the consequential goal and the means for attaining it are specified by the same term. According to Christopher Donnelly, this mode of thinking existed in Russia as early as the end of the nineteenth century.[101] The case of Gurko's Forward Detachment during the summer campaign of 1877, and his performance during the winter campaign of 1878, when operating with an army detachment, support this assumption.

As far as mobility is concerned, Gurko's forward detachment corresponds literally to all the operational criteria and characteristics which were coined by modern Soviet theoreticians. Gurko's formation was structured in a way that would match the ambitious challenges which confronted it.[102] The forward detachment was launched deliberately to a depth of more than 100 miles and was required to manoeuvre independently during a period of more than a month. These demands conform literally with the basic requirements that have been laid by the *Soviet Military Encyclopedia* and the theoreticians Kiriev and Dovbenko, more than a hundred years later.[103] Moreover, the specific missions which were assigned to the formation were those of a modern forward detachment: it was ordered to secure the main force's advance south of the Danube, to gather operational intelligence, to seize passes in the Balkan ridge for the passage of the main force, to improve the roads in the passes for general use, and to disrupt the Turkish operational rear by raiding their lines of communication and agitating the local population into revolt.

Although the exploitation of Gurko's operational accomplishments was delayed by six months, there is no doubt that the Turkish strategical plan, as well as their operational defensive system of the Balkans, collapsed as a direct result of the forward detachment's performance.[104] Thus, by combining mobility and a bold manoeuvre in depth, the forward detachment did succeed in inflicting operational shock on the Turks.

The initial organization of Gurko's formation required a great deal of daring, innovative thinking and creative imagination – qualities, which were encountered very rarely at that time. Yet, his operational conduct is even more impressive, since it reveals traits, which were totally lacking not just in his time, but even half a century later.

During the month in which the forward detachment operated, it covered several hundred miles, starting from the Danube valley, advancing through the Balkans to the valley of Tundja, and retreating back to the Balkan ridges. During its course of operation it employed every form of combat, recognized not just in its time, but even today.

The Palestine Campaign

The last example to be presented in support of the argument that operational conduct was viable in the course of the nineteenth century and the beginning of the twentieth is Allenby's Palestine campaign.

Although the event under discussion occurred in what can be defined as a marginal theatre, it demonstrates all the positive characteristics and dynamism of a creative operational manoeuvre. Furthermore, the Palestine campaign, which followed the failures of Gaza and coincided with the dark age of operational thought, emerges as a paragon of military reason.

It is particularly impressive as Lord Allenby underwent a significant cognitive transformation while leading the Eastern Expeditionary Force in Palestine. Before taking command in Palestine, and especially, during his command of the Third Army in the Arras offensive, his operational conduct conformed to the accepted patterns of the linear and attritional approach.[105] Yet, after June 1917, his entire operational method changed. Wavell, in his illuminative biography of Allenby, recognizes the transformation, but fails to come to grips with it.[106] Allenby's critics, who possess a simplistic, or perhaps, deterministic attitude, negate the notion that the change was conscious, and attribute Allenby's successes in Palestine to more favourable operational and strategic circumstances. However, they overlook two acute problems. First, they do not provide an explanation for the failures in Gaza, prior to Allenby's arrival. And secondly, they disregard some of the difficulties which characterized the theatre of Palestine, and were non-existent in the Western Front, such as the shortage of water, the absence of roads and scarcity of infrastructure, the nature of the terrain, and the lack of military resources.

In fact, the Palestinian theatre did produce distinctive operational conditions. The strategic independence of the Eastern Command provided a favourable environment for operational creativity.[107] On his arrival in the Palestine theatre Allenby inherited a force consisting of a high number of cavalry formations in relation to the foot; moreover, his cavalry contingent enjoyed a devastating superiority over its adversary, both in quantity and quality.[108] The realization of the high potential of operational mobility, which he possessed and which was his enemy's most significant operational weakness, might have reminded Allenby of Lord Robert's mobile columns in the last phase of the Boer War, and of his personal experience in commanding one of these columns.[109] Thus, the essentials for an operational transformation existed, both in the physical and mental aspects – all that was needed to implement this transformation was a cognitive spark.

The spark was provided by a rare gathering of bright and unconventional minds in Allenby's command. The unique concentration in the theatre of officers like Chetwode, Bartholomew, Dawnay, Barrow, Campbell, Evans, Meinertzhagen and Percy made their intellectual impact so perceptible. No less significant was the open and decentralized method of command that was employed by Allenby in the Palestine campaign. This mode of command and control, which was absent on other fronts, was based on common perceptions and on professional confidence. It emphasized the commander's tactical initiative and thus served as a remarkable primer for the operational dynamism.[110]

From an operational point of view, the uniqueness of the Palestine campaign lies in the fact that it provides us with two instances of operational turning manoeuvre, which is a definite recipe for the infliction of operational shock on any defensive system.

In his two major offensives – that of Gaza–Beersheba–Tel Esh Sheria–Jaffa, and that of Sharon–Megiddo–Nazareth–Tiberias–Damascus – Allenby generated exceptionally dynamic strike manoeuvres by synchronizing the elements combining ingenious operations. Firstly, he employed a holding force as a secondary operational effort. This force tied up frontally the main part of the Turkish linear layout, allowing the mobile element to develop the full potential of its striking power. Secondly, he inserted an operational strike of highly mobile troops, operating in a columnar mode, through a narrow sector, into the enemy's depth, far beyond his centre of mass. By operating this mobile force he created the essential conditions for his adversary's turn over. Finally, he made extensive use of deception, both in its active and passive modes, and by employing orthodox and unconventional methods alike. This aspect of Allenby's performance is of special interest, since it reveals a very advanced degree of comprehension of the idea of centre of gravity, both in its physical and cognitive patterns.[111]

These three examples clearly demonstrate that operational approaches could have been utilized with great effect throughout the nineteenth century, and certainly at the beginning of the twentieth. The reason why they were not adopted lies not in the lack of techno-logical means and abilities, or organizational constraints. All three examples prove beyond doubt that the answer should be sought in the field of cognition.

Moreover, as noted earlier, the technological breakthrough of the nineteenth century not only failed to contribute to the level of opera-tional cognition but rather impeded its attainment. In what follows I will refer to Caemmerer, who claimed that the relationship between technology and the operational level involves four elements, of which three derive from the actual field of technology, and one from the field of general infrastructure.[112] The first, which illustrates the aspect of transportation or mechanization, is the railway. The second, which illustrates the aspect of firepower, is the rifle, machine-gun and the cannon. The third element illustrates the aspect of control and communication, and refers to the electrical telegraph and the last is the European road system.

Rail Transport

The railway was unanimously conceived merely as a strategic means, since it suffered from basic technical deficiencies which hindered its application to the operational level.[113] Thus, although the first deliberate use of rail at the strategic level came as early as 1846, its actual utilization at the operational field – except for a single case in the Franco-Austrian war of 1859 – did not occur until the Russian Civil War.[114] Rail could not meet the challenges of tempo and terrain, which are essential for proper performance at the level of actual operations; as Caemmerer expresses it very clearly, in matters of operational advance, a marching corps would always arrive sooner than one transported by rail.

Therefore, Caemmerer and every contemporary theoretician who analyzed the application of rail transport to military use admits that the advantages of rail could only be exploited at the strategic level. In other words, rail transportation was utilized mainly for the initial con-centration of troops, and the implementation of logistics, that is, the strategical context. Thus, concludes Caemmerer, the main contribu-tion of rail to the military was rendered through the fast and smooth concentration of the strategic mass, once mobilized, in the pre-liminary deployment space, and for the extension of the strategical base of logistics.[115]

As long as the utilization of the railway flowed from a strategic defensive plan, whether executed deliberately or imposed by the adversary, as was demonstrated by the French experience of

September 1914, it could have rendered tangible operational fruits. However, the pretentious effort to harness rail in the service of the strategic offensive produced such a distortion that operational conduct could not be applied at all. The attraction offered by the ability to transfer masses from the mobilization centres to the border in a relatively short time by rail, combined with the predilection for linear patterns, prevented critical observers from realizing the dimensions of the error that had been committed. Thus, the limitations of the rail system were absorbed by the linear mentality in a manner that appeared to be a perfect combination, but in fact was one of the gravest operational mistakes ever knowingly committed.

Following Germany's successful experience in the war of 1870, rail was universally accepted as the primary means for the concentration of the strategical force towards the expected operation. The dominant consideration in the planning of a rapid, secure and smooth act of initial concentration of the strategical force relied first and foremost on the principle that the transportation of the armies by rail should be administered towards the broadest available front. The practical implication of this principle was to extend the destination line into which the mass was conveyed by rail to the maximal frontage, since by so doing the train system was utilized to the utmost.[116] Consequently, a whole network of tracks, stations, loading and unloading facilities and spaces for deploying troops and resources were prepared and constructed.

From an operational perspective, the implications of the phenomenon just described were, as Caemmerer observed, twofold. First, it determined that the physical, as well as the cognitive, point of departure for any offensive operation should inevitably become linear in form as well as in content. The second operational outcome, which derived from the technical limitations of the rail system, was the deployment, from the start, of the manoeuvre formations along the most extensive line allowed by the strategical circumstances. By the establishment of this principle and its application to strategic planning, the operational manoeuvre in depth was doomed. Thus, the uncritical application of rail destroyed any option for operational conduct, by imposing on it broad linear patterns – *ab initio*.[117]

The Schlieffen Plan, which was based on this perception, demonstrates the manner in which technology, combined with operational ignorance, stifled the operational art.

In his conclusion regarding the interaction between technology and the conduct of strategy, Caemmerer makes clear not only the destructive impact of rail on the operational level of war, but also the deep frustration which intellectual soldiers like himself suffered both from the realization of this fact and the fact that there was nothing they could do about it:

> The broad front on which concentration by rail must be effected, and which as a rule is absolutely unavoidable, obliges us to divide the whole army into several independent armies, although the actual number of army corps could still be guided by one commander in chief.[118]

Thus, although he is aware of some of the grave implications that resulted from the application of the rail to the higher level of war, Caemmerer does not condemn the act; all he does is to comfort himself by adopting a deterministic approach – an attitude that became traditional with the more critical of Clausewitz's adherents.

Communications

The story of communication technology, or more specifically, the electrical telegraph, resembles to a large extent that of the railway, and clearly demonstrates the power of ignorance. Caemmerer's approach to communication in general and to the electrical telegraph in particular represents the approach preached by Moltke the Elder, both while in office and in retirement. According to Caemmerer, the telegraph's main contribution was that it significantly reduced the uncertainty in the conduct of operations at the strategic-operational level, simply by abolishing the cognitive separation and isolation of the field formations.[119] Thus, the telegraph served mainly the strategic level of command, affording it a general but reliable system of tracing the field formations' locations and a reasonable vehicle for conveying operational orders.[120]

Moltke's system of command relied basically on the principle of *Auftragstaktik*. The term was not used in Moltke's time, but was coined after the First World War and brought into general use after the Second World War, in order to express his operations system of command. Moltke's command philosophy, which was applied in the course of the Sedan operation (19.8.1870–2.9.1870), realized both the complexity of the operational command system and the crucial importance of cognitive tension for its dynamic functioning. The best translation of the term into English was suggested by Richard Simpkin – 'directive control'.

Moltke saw the telegraph and such-like technology as a means whose sole purpose was to facilitate the command and control system, and palliate the impediments forced upon it by the friction of war.[121] He employed the telegraph in a limited role which conformed with his general and advanced concept of command, for the purpose of laying the general concept of each day's operation, while leaving the tactical conduct entirely in the hands of the operational and tactical commanders.[122] The usage of the telegraph was thus confined by Moltke to constructing a daily picture of the general operational situation, concerning his own formations and not those of the enemy, and as a technical channel for transmitting concise orders to the operational commanders.

Moltke's style and pedagogical activity resulted in the formation of a school of German officers who developed an advanced operational approach to command and also a critical view of its problems and requirements. Moltke's disciples, such as Bernhardy and Schlichting, not only correctly understood the mechanisms and problems of operational command, but also grasped the tendencies which were developing during Schlieffen's era, regarding the subject of command.[123]

Therefore, the fact that the operational insight which existed in this sole aspect developed into a trend of open criticism of the establishment's position, pointed up the difference between the subjects of rail and that of the telegraph. In the final analysis, since this criticism was suppressed by Schlieffen, it had no tangible effect.

Despite the open criticism of his command (*Truppenführung*) perception, Schlieffen applied communication technology in a manipulative manner, in order to implement his grand vision of a modern Alexander the Great.[124] He combined megalomaniac tendencies with a quantitative manipulation of the communication technology in order to make the German command patterns – the only operational element to exist in their military milieu – absolutely autocratic.[125]

Thus, the application of telegraph and later the entire inventory of communication technology generated an illusion of absolute control. The real value of the modern means of communication eluded Schlieffen and his school. They did not understand that by employing an appropriate number of communication facilities and by their proper deployment, the supreme commander could detach himself from the noisy and turbulent environment of the actual battle, receive all the required details from the numerous sources at the relevant time, work out the picture of operations accurately, and transmit all details that would enable the operational and tactical commanders to react effectively. Since the overall operational plan was an individual exploit of the commander-in-chief, it became essential that the conduct of the operation, up to the most diminutive detail, should remain under his personal control in order to guarantee absolute conformity with his plan, and he used the communication facilities to ensure that there should be no deviation from that plan. For Schlieffen, and most unfortunately for his successor, the telegraph, telephone and radio provided the magic agent which was supposed to make their visionary system of command work. The extent to which this belief was a fallacy was proven in the first month of the First World War.

Hence, the communication illusion, which was generated by the devices technology provided, created deceptive faith in an absolute, centralised but effective mode of command. It encouraged the military leadership to ignore the factor of randomness and the principle of the inner-system cognitive tension, and to repress the healthy penchant for tactical initiative.

Firepower

It is beyond the scope of this study to detail all the nuances concerning the technological evolution of firepower. However, to illustrate the general essence of the technological change in this field, it is worthwhile citing Caemmerer's introductory words on the subject:

> Our infantry weapons now, at the close of the nineteenth century, carry about ten times farther than those of Napoleon's time: They can fire at least three times more aimed shots than formerly in the same time, and allow the marksmen to load whilst lying down, and to make use of cover, therefore, which they formerly could not use.[126]

From a cursory reading, it would seem that Caemmerer's aim is to clarify the impact of the technological innovations in both their technical and historical aspects. However, his exposition of the theme is far more revealing. To begin with, Caemmerer is exclusively concerned with infantry and its basic weapon. Furthermore, in a book that has pretensions to outline the evolution of strategic science, he deals exclusively with tactical matters. And finally, his introduction – indeed his entire essay – completely ignores both the machine gun and the field gun. Clearly the strategic insight did not exceed the level of tactics, while that of tactics did not exceed the range of the rifle, among the military theoreticians of the late nineteenth century.

J. F. C. Fuller portrays the problem in both its tactical dimension and operational aspect:

> Today I see no reason to doubt that, had the German armies of 1914 been organized round the field gun and the machine-gun – the two dominant weapons of that period - instead of round the rifle – the dominant weapon of the nineteenth century – they would have over-run France nearly as rapidly as they did by means of two very different dominant weapons – the tank and airplane – in 1940.[127]

Thinking in terms of a gun's range rather than those of the rifle would have enabled the belligerents of 1914 to effectuate a proper organization, and an operational manoeuvre would have transpired.

Caemmerer concludes his operational research on the tactical implications of firepower:

> According to the results of musketry practice the assailant during this procedure (the attack) is exposed to at least twenty times the amount of losses which he himself could inflict upon his covered adversary.[128]

If the trend indicated by Caemmerer's research is applied to the operational field, then according to Lanchester's Square Law, which seems to suit perfectly the situation suggested by Caemmerer, only three logical courses remain open.[129] From the quantitative point of view, the operational implication of such a decision is that in order to establish a 2:1 chance of success, 40 times as many troops will be required, deployed in the firing line. From the point of view of quality, assuming that quantitatively the two forces are equal, a 2:1 chance of success will be achieved only if the quality of one force is 400 times better than the other's. Since both these courses are impractical, even in the terms of 1900, the only logical alternative is a third course, which determines that to compete with tactical challenges, tactics must be revolutionized. In other words, in order to render the attack practical, the linear-frontal tactics must be replaced by other patterns.

Even a cursory reading indicates that Caemmerer perceived the constraint which the impact of firepower imposed upon the existing tactical patterns and chose the third course. He bluntly admitted that 'Owing to the improvements in firearms, the purely frontal attack, or tactical penetration, is almost struck out from the military vocabulary.' Caemmerer visualized the need for the attack to: 'envelop the enemy in order to subdue effectively the enormously increased fire effect of the defense'.[130]

Caemmerer's observations, however, lead to two crucial conclusions. The first is the invalidation of the tactical breakthrough (*Durchbruch*), which was perceived by Caemmerer in mechanical terms of a bayonet charge through a line of human flesh. The second is an act of semantic acrobatics which designates the old pattern of linear attack with the new title of envelopment; while the substance remains unchanged, the caption assumes a new garment. The indoctrination for envelopment and the invention of the term *Flügelschlacht* (wing grand manoeuvre) reflect not only an artificial attempt to idealize Friedrich's oblique manoeuvre in Leuthen. The uncritical application of a tactical concept to a context of strategic manoeuvre in the years 1870–1919 indicates an archaic trend to circumvent the challenges posed by industrial warfare. Moreover, detracting professional criticism from the true problems of modern strategic reality, this trend led to a distortion of operational concepts for two generations.

As long as things were confined to the tactical level, the scale of the damage caused remained tolerable; however, when the last two conclusions concerning the practical implications of the growth of firepower were applied to the operational level, an immense problem arose – one that was insurmountable by any conventional cognitive instruments.

The attempt to invalidate the tangibility of penetration or operational breakthrough at the strategical context is expressed positively by von der Goltz, who was fully aware of the operational advantages flowing from the systematization of the columnar mode of high level manoeuvre.[131] However, despite their appreciation of the unique qualities implied by the operational breakthrough, an entire generation of military theoreticians deliberately renounced it because of tactical prejudices and a deep-rooted belief in linear patterns. Due to tactical preconceptions, which derived directly from the superficial and partisan concept of firepower, the opportunity to apply an advanced concept of operational manoeuvre was wasted.

> But penetration is invested with the specific danger that if the motive power be not great enough, the wedge remains embedded. It also frequently leads to tactical frontal attacks, which in these days of highly developed fire effect are attended with the utmost difficulty.[132]

Roads

The last of the factors to be mentioned in the present context is the development of the European road network. Its expansion in the years 1870–1917 originated in progressive trends to compete with systemic conditions which had been generated by the technological developments of the Industrial Revolution. Nevertheless, like the technical inventions in the fields of firepower, communications and transportations, instead of accelerating the evolution of operational thought, the expansion of the European road network had a degenerative impact on its progress. Providing staff and commanders with ample opportunities to exercise linear methods of manoeuvre, the growing road network strengthened the tendency to adhere to archaic patterns of tactical conduct.

According to Caemmerer, at the beginning of the twentieth century the army corps was unanimously perceived as the basic operational formation, and also as an autonomous logistical entity, possessing a daily axial space of 14 miles.[133] Therefore, the Napoleonic operational conceptions regarding movements, organization and logistics remained unchanged. Moreover, in spite of the fact that the army corps increased in volume during the nineteenth century, the corresponding growth of the road network enabled the preservation of the Napoleonic operational pattern of the advancing line of corps' columns.

Whereas in Napoleon's time this pattern suggested some operational aspects, at the close of the century it became entirely unoperational for several reasons. First, as has already been pointed out, by the end of the nineteenth century the linear pattern of the advancing army (*Aufmarsch*), which, at the operational level, was the result of a strategic determinant, had become a tactical pattern. Second, since the army corps, which constituted the core of this conception, was based almost exclusively on infantry, its advancing tempo could not exceed the daily pace of a foot soldier, while the general pace of strategic advance was even slower than that. And finally, both this pattern and the exclusive dependence on infantry, as the main utilizer of manoeuvre at all levels, made the implementation of the columnar manoeuvre in depth an impossible achievement.

With the growing emphasis on the importance of the factor of fire in warfare, a corresponding growth occurred in the quantities of ammunition, hauled by each division and corps. Consequently, the length and volume of the corps' transport columns became five times as great as those existing in the Napoleonic era.[134] Nonetheless, since the intensive growth of the road network allowed the absorption of all the logistical supplementary weight, no crisis developed, and so the old patterns prevailed.

Thus, the growth in the road network postponed a crisis which could have led to a real change in the patterns of operational movements, on the one hand, while on the other, it contributed to the perpetuation of misconceptions.

NOTES

1. M. Howard, *War in European Society* (Oxford, 1976), pp. 80, 83, 99, 100.
2. J.F.C. Fuller, *The Conduct of War 1789–1961* (London, 1961), pp. 26–41; H. Nickerson, *The Armed Horde 1793–1939* (New York, 1940).
3. B.H. Liddell Hart, *The Ghost of Napoleon* (London, 1933), pp. 101–4, 118, 120, 125, 128; idem, *Thoughts on War*, trans. to Hebrew by J. Wallach (Tel Aviv, 1989), pp. 35, 40–41, 95–99, 271–2.
4. J. Luvaas, 'Clausewitz, Fuller and Liddell Hart'. in M. Handel (ed.), *Clausewitz and Modern Strategy* (London, 1986), pp. 198–9, 207–11. A. Gat, *The Origins of Military Thought from the Enlightenment to Clausewitz* (Oxford, 1989), pp. 209–10.
5. Fuller, *The Conduct of War*, pp. 32–3.

6. J. Colin, *The Transformation of War*, trans. L.H.R. Pope-Hennessy (London, 1912), p. 224.
7. Ibid., p. 226.
8. Clausewitz, *On War*, M. Howard and P. Paret (eds) (Princeton, 1976), B. 8, Ch. 3, pp. 592–3.
9. Ibid., pp. 591–2.
10. D.G. Chandler, *The Campaigns of Napoleon* (London, 1976), pp. 1118–21.
11. M. Howard, *Clausewitz* (Oxford, 1983), p. 15.
12. Clausewitz, *On War*, B. 4, Ch. 2, p. 226.
13. Chandler, *The Campaigns of Napoleon*, pp. 727–30.
14. Ibid., pp. 888–95
15. Ibid., pp. 929–30
16. Ibid., pp. 113–21, 286–97, 413–32, 479–506, 572–84, 1118–21. An examination of Napoleonic battles indicates a direct and consistent linkage between the increase in the fighting mass and the rate of losses suffered. In principle, the losing side suffered a rate of 30–50 per cent, whereas the victor suffered a rate of 10–25 per cent. The increase in mass was generally reflected in a proportionate increase in the rate of relative losses. Only in battles such as Rivoli, Marengo, Ulm, Austerlitz, Jena and Friedland did Napoleon manage to shift the rate of relative losses decisively in his favour through the exercise of creative manoeuvre.
17. Clausewitz, *On War*, B. 2, Ch. 2, p. 141; Ch. 5, p. 157; Ch. 6, p.170; B. 8, Ch. 1, p. 578.
18. Ibid., B. 3, Ch. 8, p. 194.
19. Ibid., p. 195.
20. Ibid., p. 194.
21. Ibid., B. 4, Ch. 9, p. 249.
22. Ibid., B. 3, Ch. 8, p. 195.
23. Ibid., B. 4, Ch. 11, p. 258.
24. H.F.A. von Freytag-Loringhoven, *Deductions from the World War* (London, 1918), p. 24.
25. H.K.B. von Moltke, *The Franco-German War* of 1870–71, trans. C. Bellard and H. Fischer (London, 1891), pp. 10–11; idem, *Strategy: Its Theory and Application: The Wars of German Unification 1866–1871*, H. Bell (trans. and ed.) (Ft. Leavenworth, 1911), extract no. 20, pp. 172–6.
26. Moltke, *The Franco-German War*, pp. 65–76.
27. Ibid., pp. 77–102; H.K.B. von Moltke, *Moltke's Military Correspondence 1870–1871*, published by the Prussian General Staff Department for Military History, précis: S. Wilkinson (Oxford, 1923), extracts no. 189–238, pp. 103–26; A. von Blumenthal, *Journals of Field Marshal Count von Blumenthal for 1866 and 1870–71*, trans. A.D. Gillespie-Addison (London, 1903), p. 87.
28. A. von Boguslawski, *Tactical Deductions from the War of 1870–1871*, trans. L. Graham (London, 1872), p. 59; Prince Friedrich Wilhelm Hohenzollern, *The War Diary of Emperor Frederick the Third*, A. R. Allinson (trans. and ed.) (London, 1927), pp. 33–5.
29. M. Howard, 'The Influence of Clausewitz', in Howard and Paret (eds.), Clausewitz, *On War*, p. 30.
30. Freytag-Loringhoven, *Deductions from the First World War*, p. 24; Quincy Wright, *A Study of War*, (Chicago, 1965), pp. 670–71; Howard, *War in European History*, pp. 99–100; M. van Creveld, *Command in War* (Cambridge, MA, 1985), pp. 148–9.
31. F. von Bernhardy, *How Germany Makes War* (London, 1914), p. 21.
32. Ibid.; A. von Schlieffen, *Briefe*, E. Kessel (ed.) (Göttingen, 1958), pp. 296–7, held the same view with respect to the actual conduct of operations.
33. F. Foch, *The Principles of War*, trans. J. de Morinni (New York, 1918), p. 47; ibid., pp. 44–5; Colin, *The Transformation of War*, p. 326. Perceiving the continuous line as the manoeuvring method expressing mass and the crushing push as its consequential operational effect, both Foch and Colin tend to employ the metaphor of a heavy roller when relating to the strategic manoeuvre.
34. Bernhardy, *How Germany Makes War*, p. 37.
35. A. von Schlieffen, 'Text of the Memorandum of December 1905', in G. Ritter, *The Schlieffen Plan. A Critique of a Myth*, trans. S. Wilson (London, 1958), p. 145.

36. Freytag-Loringhoven, *Deductions from the World War*, p. 39.
37. Crown Prince Wilhelm, 'The Narrative of the Fifth German Army at the Battle of the Marne', in *The Two Battles of the Marne* (London, 1927), p. 96.
38. A. von Schlieffen, 'Der Krieg in der Gegenwart', in *Gesammelte Schriften* (Berlin, 1913), Vol. 1, pp. 11–22. The article was published originally in *Deutschen Revue*, Jan. 1909; 'Uber die Millionenheere', in A. von Schlieffen, 'Der Krieg in der Gegenwart', in *Gesammelte Schriften* pp. 23–35. The article was published originally in *Deutschen Revue*, June 1911.
39. Ritter, *The Schlieffen Plan*, p. 146.
40. Ibid., p. 74.
41. Ibid., pp. 179–81.
42. W. von Hahnke, 'Notes by Major W. von Hahnke', in ibid., p. 180.
43. L. von Bertalanffy, *General System Theory* (London, 1973), pp. 37, 51; R. Simpkin, *Race to the Swift* (London, 1985), pp. 79–92, 112–15, 133–7.
44. Bertalanffy, *General System Theory*, pp. 32, 37, 51, 54–5, 70, 149.
45. Simpkin, *Race to the Swift*, pp. 112–15.
46. Van Creveld, *Command in War*, pp. 168–84.
47. C.G. von Ilseman, 'Das Operative Denken des Alteren Moltke', in H. Boog (ed.), *Operative Denken und Hendeln in Deutschen Streikraften im 19. und 20. Jahrhundert* (Bonn, 1988), pp. 17–44; M. Howard, 'Men Against Fire, Expectations of War in 1914', in S.E. Millet, S.M. Lynn Jones and S. Van Evera (eds), *Military Strategy and the Origin of the First World War* (Princeton, 1990), pp. 3–19. According to Michael Howard, since the First World War stemmed from the same cognitive sources as the regression which preceded it, it should be regarded as its lowest depression. Nevertheless, a full analysis of the First World War is beyond the scope of this research.
48. B. H. Liddell-Hart, *Strategy, the Indirect Approach* (London, 1954), p. 352.
49. J. Luvaas, 'European Military Thought and Doctrine, 1870–1914', in M. Howard (ed.), *The Theory and Practice of War* (London, 1965), pp. 71–93.
50. In spite of the fact that traditional historiography refers to the compilation of documents left by Schlieffen as the 'Schlieffen Plan', there is a growing tendency among recent historians to see it as an assemblage of memorandums, reflecting a crystallized concept at best, and not as an actual operational plan; see H.L. Borfert, 'Grundzuge der Landkriegführung von Schlieffen bis Guderian', in *Handbuch zur Deutschen Militärgeschichte 1648–1939*, Vol. 5 (Munich, 1979), p. 455. Nevertheless, most modern researchers agree that Schlieffen's brainchild expressed the prevailing outlook among European armies. J. Wallach, *Das Dogma der Vernichtungsschlacht* (Frankfurt a. M., 1967), p. 306.
51. A. Bucholtz, *Moltke, Schlieffen and Prussian War Planning* (Oxford, 1991), pp. 188–9.
52. The adoption of the chain metaphor was for two reasons which deserve emphasis. The first is that Clausewitz's ideas are interlinked through a consequential pattern flowing out of a general premise – thus, his entire theory evolves deductively. The second is the consistency which characterized the mental continuity from Clausewitz to Schlieffen.
53. The principle of destruction is discussed repeatedly in *On War*, nevertheless, it is dealt with in detail in B. 1, Chs. 1, 2; B. 4, Chs. 3, 4, 11; B. 7, Ch. 6.
54. Clausewitz, *On War*, B. 1, Ch. 2, pp. 90, 99; B. 4, Ch. 3, pp. 227–9, Ch. 11, p. 258.
55. Ibid., B. 1, Ch. 2, pp. 90–92.
56. Ibid., B. 4, Ch. 4, pp. 230, 231; Ch. 9, p. 249; Ch. 11, p. 258; B. 5, Ch. 3, p. 283; B. 6, Ch. 8, pp. 381–2; B. 7, Ch. 4, p. 527. Simpkin, *Race to the Swift*, pp. 19–23. E. N. Luttwak, *Strategy: The Logic of War and Peace* (Cambridge, MA, 1987), p. 92.
    The modern perception of strategic attrition is an operational pattern, optionally initiated and voluntarily inflicted upon the adversary, by strategic, operational and tactical means. The aims of attrition are defined in modern theoretical literature as the anticipation of the operational manoeuvre by attaining a favourable quantitative balance. Therefore, attrition constitutes a unilateral method, implemented operationally by the initiating belligerent. Moreover, the operational initiator uses every viable means and method to prevent any accretionary effects of the attritional mode from affecting his own forces, whether it be by employing a suitable system at the operational level, or by protecting his resources and utilizing superior fighting

techniques at the tactical level. For Clausewitz and his followers attrition is entirely different. It is essentially an unpremeditated and random outcome endured by both belligerent sides, resulting from the linear patterns of the tactical engagement. Moreover, at the strategic level, attrition is an inevitable consequence of the sole initiative that leads towards the positive aim. In other words, in strategic terms, attrition represents self-inflicted damage, which the aggressor suffers at his own initiative.

57. By the term 'cognitive tension' I refer to the universal dynamism that results from the inevitable tension between the tactical objective, which orientates the fighting formations at any level, and the operational or strategic aim, which directs the system as a whole.

58. Prince von Bülow, *Memoirs 1903–1909* (London, 1931), pp. 74–5. The issue of the dialogue between Schlieffen and von Bülow is discussed at length by L.C.F. Turner in his essay, 'The Significance of the Schlieffen Plan', in P.M. Kennedy (ed.), *The War Plans of the Great Powers 1880–1914* (Boston, 1979), pp. 199–221.

59. Ritter, *The Schlieffen Plan*, pp. 134–92.

60. Clausewitz, *On War*, B. 1, Ch. 2, p. 90.

61. Ibid., B. 1, Ch. 2, p. 95; B. 3, Ch. 15, pp. 214–15; B. 4, Ch. 2, p. 226, Ch. 3, pp. 227–8; Ch. 4, pp. 231–2; Ch. 9, pp. 249–50; Ch. 11, p. 258; B. 5, Ch. 4, p. 285; B. 7, Ch. 6, p. 529.

62. Ibid., B. 1, Ch. 2, p. 97; B. 4, Ch. 3, pp. 227–8.

63. Ibid., Ch. 11, p. 258.

64. Ibid., B. 1, Ch. 2, p. 98.

65. Ibid., pp. 90–92; B. 6, Ch. 7, p. 377; Ch. 8, p. 380.

66. Ibid., B. 1, Ch. 1, p. 84; B. 6, Ch. 5, p. 370; Ch. 8, p. 380; B. 7, Ch. 1, p. 524; Ch. 13, p. 541.

67. Howard, *Clausewitz*, pp. 59–73.

68. R. von Caemmerer, *The Development of Strategical Science During the 19th Century*, trans. K. von Donnat (London, 1905), pp. 248–71.

69. Clausewitz, *On War*, B. 5, Ch. 4, pp. 284–91.

70. In *Tactical Deductions from the War of 1870–1871*, pp. 92–8, Boguslawski discusses the lessons of operating the cavalry arm during the war, and the options for general mechanization of the infantry. The lessons conform with the prevailing concepts of the application of cavalry, and in the second subject he rejects the idea of mechanization. H.K.B. Moltke, *Moltke's Military Correspondence 1870–1871*, Prussian General Staff Department for Military History, précis: S. Wilkinson, (Oxford, 1923), 'Memorandum to the Chiefs of Sections of the Great General Staff', p. 173, suggested transporting an entire infantry division which was grouped with two cavalry divisions, as a part of mobile effort towards the French operational depth. This unique suggestion was revolutionary. Moreover, Moltke's suggestion confirms beyond any doubt that the problem of operational mobility was a conceptual and not a technical one. Bernhardy, *How Germany Makes War*, pp. 83–4, 189, both criticizes the prevailing mode of operating cavalry, and highly recommends the implementation of mounted infantry in the strategic and operational depth. In another book, *Cavalry in War and Peace* (London, 1910), p. 367, he speaks of operating masses of cavalry in the mode of mounted infantry, even in broader and more vigorous terms. On the other hand, sources, such as Prince Kraft zu Hohenlohe-Ingelfingen, *Letters on Cavalry* (London, 1893), pp. 80, 82–4, 86, and C.F. von der Goltz, *The Nation in Arms* (London, 1906), pp. 315–22, who openly prefer the tactical mode of *arme blanche*, and the frequent mention of the Russian mass implementation of mounted infantry, confirm that the subject was debated and that the whole problem was one of cognition and not a technical one.

71. C. von Clausewitz, *Historical and Political Writings*, P. Paret and D. Moran (trans. and eds) (Princeton, 1992), pp. 144–57; Clausewitz, *On War*, B. 3, Ch. 13, pp. 210–11; Ch. 15, p. 215; B. 4, Ch. 2, p. 226; Ch. 11, p. 261; B. 7, Ch. 7, p. 330.

72. Ritter, *The Schlieffen Plan*, pp. 52–6, 61–2, 66; Generalstab des Heeres, Kriegswissenschaftliche Abteilung (ed.), *Der Schlachterfolge mit welchen Mitteln wurden sie ersterbt* (Berlin, 1903). This publication of the German General Staff served as a training manual based on the Schlieffen doctrine.

73. J.A. English, *On Infantry* (New York, 1984), pp. 1–28, deals generally with the linear

tactics of the infantry. M. Howard, *The Franco-Prussian War* (Cambridge, 1961), pp. 5–8, deals with the linear-frontal tactics of the infantry, as well as with the prevailing tendency for tactical envelopment. C.F. von der Goltz, *The Conduct of War* (London, 1899), pp. 181–95, discusses in detail the theoretical aspects of the tactical attack. His dissertation confirms my argument that the preferred tactical pattern was no more than a prolonging linear engagement, which ended in an attempt to execute a movement to the flank of the opposing line. W. Balck, *Tactics*, trans. W. Krueger (Ft. Leavenworth, 1911), Vol. 1, pp. 32–47, confirms the validity of Goltz' generalizations at the junior tactical levels. All the references given below confirm my argument through the empirical reflections of the war of 1870–1871: Boguslawski, *Tactical Deductions from the War of 1870–1871*, pp. 56, 60–61, 66, 75, 80; Moltke, *The Franco-German War*, pp. 16–64, describes the battles of Froeschwiller, Spicheren, Colombey–Nouilly, Vionville–Mars-la-Tour and Gravelotte–St-Privat. Prince Friedrich Wilhelm, *The War Diary of Emperor Frederick the Third*, pp. 31–42. A. Forbes, *My Experience of the War Between France and Germany* (London, 1871), Vol. 1, pp. 142–3, 147, 164, gives civilian and unprejudiced impressions, which also correspond with my argument. Caemmerer, *The Development of Strategical Science during the 19th Century*, pp. 173–6, makes probably the most significant progress in analyzing the problem of the tactical attack, yet, although he uses the terms envelopment and firepower in the method he advocates, he becomes another victim of the old prejudices. And despite the use of analytical semantics, the tactical formula which he lays down remains linear and frontal in essence.

74. Caemmerer, *The Development of Strategical Science*, pp. 220–47, discusses the concept of the operational grand wing manoeuvre, which was developed from Wilhelm Rustow through W. von Scherf and von Falkenhausen to its final formulae in the works of von der Goltz, Lewal and Schlieffen. Colin, *The Transformation of War*, pp. 164–7, describes explicitly the linearity of the operational wing manoeuvre. According to Colin's version, we are dealing with a continuous line comprising 1.5–2 million soldiers. Moreover, this linear human mass, of which one wing is significantly superior in weight, is expected to operate simultaneously – thus creating a gigantic push effect that will simply crush the opposing line. The purpose of the accentuated wing is to produce the certain mechanical conditions for the occurrence of the destructive push.

75. J.L. Lewal, *Stratégie de Combat* (Paris, 1895), Vol. 1, pp. 3, 35; Vol. 2, pp. 31, 39, 182, 189. In this unique dissertation on war at all its levels, Lewal preaches a dogmatic, almost absurd doctrine which dictates a general strategic pattern consisting of four armies deployed in a line of some 68 miles. This linear mass is expected to implement a strategic battle drill, which centres on the wing manoeuvre. Von der Goltz, *The Conduct of War*, pp. 160–66, displays his concept of the strategic wing manoeuvre, which resembles Schlieffen's almost to the letter. One specific principle, which is explicitly discussed by Goltz, and later becomes a cornerstone in Schlieffen's plan of 1905, is the essential push effect that is produced by the advance of the strategic line, and especially by the super-heavy wing; see Schlieffen, 'The December 1905 Great Memorandum', in Ritter, *The Schlieffen Plan*, pp. 134–48. Even a superficial comparison of the works of Schlieffen and Lewal will reveal that the only difference between their operational doctrines is the length of the strategic line.

76. Schlieffen, 'The Memorandum of December 28th 1912', pp. 168–78.

77. Clausewitz, *On War*, B. 4, Ch. 3, pp. 228–9, Ch. 9, pp. 250–51; B. 5, Ch. 5, p. 293; B. 6, Ch. 8, p. 386; Moltke, *The Franco-German War*, pp. 50–64, describes the premature and unauthorized attack by von Steinmetz, who commanded the First Army. This event demonstrates the consequences of the system which educated the German generals at the time. Steinmetz's act was a natural and direct result of this education that indoctrinated a preference for simplicity, directness and boldness to sophistication and cunning. Von der Goltz, *The Conduct of War*, p. 171, admits that the unwieldiness of great masses dictates operational simplicity and a frontal approach. Bernhardy, *How Germany Makes War*, p. 201, defines simplicity in the form of linear action, unswerving energy and quantities as the key elements in the German operational perception. Colin, *The Transformation of War*, p. 239, rejects the ideas of operational reserves and depth, since both prevent an amount of force from operating and

66

assaulting the enemy's line simultaneously, with the rest of their own line – thus, wasting troops and complicating the entire operational conduct.

78. Schlieffen, 'The Memorandum of December 28th 1912', p. 174. In the later memorandum, which was composed in a somewhat conspiratorial context, Schlieffen endeavoured to manipulate 36 army corps into 51. The reason for this was that 51 army corps could have allowed the German Army to develop a simultaneous operational offensive in a continuous line, simplifying the operational conduct and making it physically more energetic.
79. Clausewitz, *On War*, B. 1, Ch. 1, pp. 75, 77; Raymond Aron, Clausewitz, (London, 1983), pp. 157–60.
80. Clausewitz, *On War*, B. 6, Ch. 27, pp. 485–6.
81. Ibid., B. 8, Ch. 4, pp. 595–6.
82. B. Brodie, 'A Guide to the Reading of *On War*', in Clausewitz, *On War*, pp. 710–11; Clausewitz, On War, B. 8, Ch. 9, pp. 617–19, 633, 635.
83. Ritter, *The Schlieffen Plan*, pp. 17–69, describes in a detailed and critical manner the precise evolutionary process of the plan from 1891 till its final maturity in 1905. Ten extracts from the various preliminary drafts, translated and edited by Ritter, are given on pp. 148–60. Through the drafts one can accurately follow the entire cognitive process, through which Schlieffen worked out his plan from the origins to its final form.
84. Caemmerer, *The Development of Strategical Science*, p. 170.
85. Ibid., pp. 168–9.
86. C. Bellamy, 'Heirs of Genghis Khan: The Influence of the Tartar-Mongols on the Imperial Russian and Soviet Armies,' *RUSI Journal*, March 1983, pp. 52–9; B.H. Liddell Hart, 'Jenghis Khan and Sabutai,' in *Great Captains Unveiled* (London, 1927), pp. 1–43.
87. S. von Schlichting, *Taktisch und Strategische Grundsätze der Gegenwart, Teil 2 Truppenführungs* (Berlin, 1897–1899) (3 vols.), Vol. 2, pp. 9–10, 97.
88. D. Gates, *The Spanish Ulcer* (London, 1986), pp. 481–2, 485–7, 512–14, 519–22.
89. J. Gurwood (ed.), *Selections from Dispatches and General Orders of Field Marshal the Duke of Wellington* (London, 1841). The memorandum of 3 March 1809 appears on pp. 248–50, and that of 19 December 1809 appears on pp. 325–36.
90. Ibid., pp. 203–6, 217, 248–50, 273, 305–13, 325–36; J. Gurwood (ed.), *The Dispatches of Field Marshal the Duke of Wellington During his Various Campaigns* (London, 1852), Vol. 4, pp. 176–8; J.W. Fortescue, *A History of the British Army* (London, 1912), Vol. 7, pp. 125, 146–7, 389–90; *General Orders, Spain and Portugal* (London, 1809–1814), Vol. 1, pp. 1, 17, 19, 33, 39, 48, 70, 84, 89, 99, 134; Vol. 2, pp. 230–32.
91. Gurwood, *Selections from Dispatches*, pp. 248–50, 305–13, 325–6; R.B. Asprey, *War in the Shadows the Guerilla in History* (London 1975), pp. 138–9; R. B. Asprey, 'The Peninsular War', *Army Quarterly*, 77 (April 1959), pp. 52–63.
92. C. Oman, *Wellington's Army 1808–1814* (London, 1913), pp. 70–92.
93. *Voennaia entsiklopediia* (Military Encyclopaedia) (St Petersburg, 1911–1915), Vol. 8, p. 543; *Sovetskaia voennaia entsiklopediia* (hereafter SVE) (Moscow, 1978), Vol. 6, pp. 282, 373.
94. N. Epanchin, *Operations of General Gurko's Advance Guard in 1877*, trans. H. Havelock (London, 1900), p. 7. In the English edition the name of the author is incorrectly transliterated as Epauchin instead of Epanchin.
95. R. Simpkin, *Mechanized Infantry* (Oxford, 1980), pp. 9–11; M. Howard, 'Men against Fire', in Millet *et al.* (eds), *Military Strategy and the Origins of the First World War*, pp. 8–9.
96. *SVE* (Moscow, 1978), Vol. 6, p. 547; Vol. 8, p. 72.
97. A. Springer, *Der Russische-Türkische Krieg 1877–1878* (Vienna, 1892), Vol. 2, pp. 35–9, 114–65, 242–76; Vol. 3, pp. 18–27, 184; F.V. Greene, *The Campaign in Bulgaria* (London, 1903), pp. 27–49; A. Horsetzky von Horenthal, *Der Russische Feldzug in Bulgarien und Rumelien 1877–78*, (Vienna, 1878), pp. 122–6, 155–62. All the above-mentioned commentaries refer to Gurko's formation and to the operation conducted by him as Advance-Guard. N. Epanchin, *Voina 1877–78, deistviia General-Adiutanta Gurko* (The War of 1877–78, the Operation of Adjutant-General Gurko), (Moscow, 1895), refers to Gurko's operation and formation as *peredovoi otriad*. Since the term

advance guard (*avangard*) had already existed in Russian military nomenclature of the late nineteenth century, it seems rather peculiar that they did not discern the uniqueness of the material they were dealing with, even without studying the details of the operation itself. Nevertheless, they identified the operational novelty with the tactical concept that was deep-rooted in their military thinking, thus reducing an all-embracing operational concept of manoeuvre to the shallow level of battle-like mechanics.

98. *Kratkii anglo-russkii i russko-angliiskii voennyi slovar'* (Concise English-Russian and Russian-English Military Dictionary) (Moscow, 1963), pp. 324–5.
99. Epanchin, *Operations of General Gurko's Advance Guard*, pp. 3–7.
100. Ibid., pp. 3–4.The Forward Detachment consisted of two infantry brigades, four cavalry brigades, the equivalent of an artillery brigade, an engineering unit and a reconnaissance element. In all, about 10.5 battalions of infantry, 43.5 squadrons, 40 field guns, or some 11,500 men.
101. C. Donnelly, *Red Banner. The Soviet Military System in Peace and War* (Coulsdon, UK, 1988), p. 220.
102. Epanchin, *Operations of General Gurko's Advance Guard*, pp. 3–4.
103. N. Kiriev, and N. Dovbenko, 'Iz opyta boevogo primeneniia peredovykh otriadov tankovykh i mekhanizirovannykh korpusov' (From the Experience of Combat Use of Forward Detachments of Tank and Mechanized Corps), *Voenno-istoricheskii zhurnal*, 9 (1982), pp. 20–21; SVE, Vol. 6, p. 547.
104. This assumption can be proved by the hasty recalling of Suleiman Pasha's army from a different theatre, by the dismissal of the Turkish war minister and commander in chief, by the Sultan's desperate despatch of July 2nd, and by the impressions of some foreign observers. Epanchin, *Operations of General Gurko's Advance Guard*, pp. 297–301.
105. A. P. Wavell, *Allenby. A Study in Greatness* (London, 1940), pp. 171–85.
106. Ibid., pp. 295–301.
107. Ibid., p. 299.
108. A.P. Wavell, *The Palestine Campaigns* (London, 1928), pp. 100–101; C. Falls, *Armageddon 1918* (The Nautical and Aviation Publishing Company of America, 1979), p. 13.
109. Howard, 'Men Against Fire', pp. 8–9; B.J. Bond, 'Doctrine and Training in the British Cavalry 1870–1914', in Howard (ed.), *The Theory and Practice of War*, pp. 110–12; B.H. Liddell Hart, *Through the Fog of War* (London, 1938), p. 96.
110. N. Dixon, *On the Psychology of Military Incompetence* (London, 1976), pp. 340–41.
111. R. Meinertzhagen, *Middle East Diary* (Tel Aviv, 1973, in Hebrew), pp. 14–18; W.T. Massey, *Allenby's Final Triumph* (London, 1920), pp. 95, 97, 111–18, 138, 147–59, 180–87; Falls, *Armageddon 1918*, pp. 35–49, 50–99; C. Falls and A.F. Becke (eds), *Military Operations in Egypt and Palestine*, Vol. 2, (London, 1930), pp. 481–570; C.H.C. Pirie-Gordon (ed.), *Brief Record of the Advance of the Egyptian Expeditionary Force, July 1917 to October 1918* (London, 1919).
112. Caemmerer, *The Development of Strategical Science*, p. 157.
113. Ibid., pp. 167, 169–70; J.F.C. Fuller, *Armament and History* (London, 1946), pp. 116–17; E.A. Pratt, *The Rise of Rail Power in War and Conquest 1833–1914* (London, 1915), pp. 346–7, 352–3.
114. Fuller, *Armament and History*; idem, *The Conduct of War 1789–1961*, pp. 92–3; E.M. Earle, 'Lenin, Trotsky, Stalin: Soviet Concepts of War', in E.M. Earle (ed.), *Makers of Modern Strategy* (Princeton, 1971), pp. 329–35; H. Holborn, 'Moltke and Schlieffen: The Prussian-German School', in ibid., pp. 177, 181, 183, 187, 199–201; E. M. Earle, 'Adam Smith, Alexander Hamilton, Friedrich List: The Economic Foundations of Military Power', in ibid., pp. 148–52.
115. Ibid., pp. 163, 168.
116. Ibid., pp. 168–9.
117. H.B. von Moltke, *Militärische Werke*, Berlin 1892–1912, Vol. 2, part 2, p. 291. Here Moltke determines that an error in operational deployment, once committed, is irreparable. Thus, the initial strategical deployment in a linear front, once concluded, becomes irreversible. The extensive dimensions of the strategical line dictated a single mode movement – the simultaneous advance in a uniform line, parallel to the

enemy's linear front, and producing the effect of a general mechanical push.

118. Ibid., p. 177.
119. Ibid., p. 171.
120. Ibid., p. 172.
121. J.T. Nelson, *Where to Go from Here? Considerations for the Formal Adoption of Auftragstaktik by the U.S. Army*, School of Advanced Military Studies, USACGSC Ft. Leavenworth, KS, 5 Dec. 1986, pp. 6–13.
122. Ibid., pp. 172–3; van Creveld, *Technology and War*, p. 170; idem, *Command in War*, pp. 103–47. Generalstab des Heeres, Kriegswissenschaftliche Abteilung (ed.), *Exerzier-Reglement für die Infanterie* (Berlin, 1906), pp. 78, 90–91; F.E.E.A. Cochenhausen, *Die Truppenführung, Teil I: Mittlere und Untere Führung* (Berlin, 1931), pp. 25–6, 105; *Die Kriegswissenschaftliche Fortbildung des Truppenoffiziers* (Berlin, 1926), pp. 1–30, 50, 91–7, 153–6; Von Bernhardy, *How Germany Makes War*, pp. 213–21; F. Hönig, *Inquiries into the Tactics of the Future*, trans. C. Reichman (Kansas City, MO., 1898), pp. 25–7, 43, 45, 220, 232–4, 267, 311.
123. Bernhardy, *On War of Today*, pp. 163–78; S. von Schlichting (ed.), *Moltke Vermächtnis* (Munich, 1901). Both Bernhardy and Schlichting openly criticized Schlieffen's concept of command, and the direction in which he was going in applying centralized, remote and somewhat autocratic methods of command. Consequently, both were dismissed from the military establishment by Schlieffen.
124. Schlieffen, 'Der Krieg in der Gegenwart,' *Gesammelte Schriften*, Vol. 1, pp. 15–16.
125. Between 1870–1911 telegraph stations multiplied in Germany from 1000 to 637,000.
126. Ibid., pp. 173–4.
127. Fuller, *Armament and History*, p. 136.
128. Caemmerer, The Development of Strategical Science, p. 174.
129. F.W. Lanchester, *The Principle of Concentration* (London, 1914); idem, *Aircraft in Warfare, the Dawn of the Fourth Arm* (London, 1916). In his 'Square Law', which constitutes a part of what has been defined as the Lanchester Equation, he suggested that for combat situations where the units of both combatants can engage each other directly and simultaneously in order to assure a two to one chance of victory, one may need twice as many troops, or a four times greater qualitative advantage. M. Osipov, 'Vliianie chislennosti srazhaiushchikhsia storon na ikh poteri' (The Influence of the Numerical Strength of Engaged Forces on their Casualties), *Voennyi sbornik*, 6 (1915), pp. 59–74; 7 (1915), pp. 25–36; 8 (1915), pp. 31–40; 9 (1915), pp. 25–37; 10 (1915), pp. 93–6. In his seminal work, Osipov, employing similar methods to those used by Lanchester, discovered the Square Law of Attrition independently.
130. Caemmerer, *The Development of Strategical Science*, p. 176.
131. Von der Goltz, *The Conduct of War*, p. 154. The author claims in the reference noted: '[Strategical Penetration], this which forces the enemy's line and separates the several parts of the army attacked. So as afterwards to defeat them one after the other, must if it succeeds, be exceedingly effective and attended with great results.' Thus, von der Goltz suggests in this description what would become accepted in later years as the deep operational slashing manoeuvre. This columnar-low friction mode of manoeuvre, which is executed at the operational level of war, is expected to pierce the defender's layout, and divide the various components of the defending system.
132. Ibid.
133. Caemmerer, *The Development of Strategical Science*, p. 159.
134. Ibid.

3

Destruction and Operational Art:
The Roots of Ignorance

THE PARADOX OF DESTRUCTION

> Destruction of the enemy's forces is the overriding principle of war, and so far as positive action is concerned the principal way to achieve our object.[1]

The principle of destruction is the 'Imperative' and 'Dogma' in the entire logical structure of Clausewitz's theory of war.[2] Michael Howard portrays the effect of Clausewitz's idea of *Vernichtungs-schlacht* on the generations preceding the First World War, as hypnotizing.[3] Indeed, Foch's perception of the principle of destruction sounds almost like a tenuous attempt to evade plagiarism; it definitely betrays his source of inspiration.[4]

The subject of destruction was all-conquering to such an extent that it survived the experience of the war and retained its virility in the minds of the most senior military commanders. This is attested by the verdict of the German Crown Prince:

> Military genius was conspicuously absent in all the three armies during the campaign culminating with the battle of the Marne. Neither the Germans nor the allies possessed a leader sufficiently gifted to effect the complete destruction of the enemy.[5]

However, notwithstanding the absence of 'military genius', both the Crown Prince and a critical soldier like Freytag-Loringhoven name Schlieffen as the person capable of implementing Clausewitz's idea of destruction, since he combined the essential qualities in his personality, and his concept of Cannae constituted the living evidence of it.[6]

Historical research has also failed to grasp the distorting impact of Clausewitz's principle. Gordon Craig and Walter Goerlitz, adopted uncritically the Epigon–Paragon myth, devised by addicts of the Clausewitzian theory after the war, and thus attribute the main cause of the German army's failure to personal incompetence. In doing so they confirm the soundness of the concept of destruction.[7]

When looking at the various examples which illustrate the different approaches to Clausewitz's principle of destruction, one cannot help asking who perpetuated this concept with such an overpowering vitality? What made Clausewitz's brainchild such a magnetic attraction for theoreticians and experienced senior officers, such as Caemmerer, Bernhardy, von der Goltz and Freytag-Loringhoven, Moltke the Elder and Count Alfred von Schlieffen?

The answer, which is the subject of the present section, is that the addictive impact of Clausewitz's idea of destruction derived first and foremost from his unique indoctrinative system of reasoning and his brilliant method of structuring his arguments. The fact that his audience entirely lacked the tools of operational criticism provided the appropriate mental environment for its predominance.

The logical exposition of the subject of destruction, which combines theoretical trends based on abstract elements, with practical tendencies based on empirical experience, and also a method of syllogism that employs deductive as well as inductive approaches, is concentrated in the first and fourth books of Clausewitz's work. It was precisely this combination which made the idea of destruction so firm and attractive – unshakable even by the bitter realities of war, and impregnable to any moral or logical criticism.

Clausewitz attributed both the cognitive and the practical sources for the idea of destruction to the Napoleonic experience.[8] The logical and theoretical frameworks of this idea are anchored in political reality. Since war is a means to impose one's political will on the adversary – an achievement which dictates the immediate neutralization of the adversary's military power – destruction constitutes, in theory, the universal aim of any war.[9]

Clausewitz then progresses a step further by clarifying both the violent nature of war and its totality which derive from the crucial contest for survival between two antagonistic political entities. He concludes this section, almost inevitably, by asserting that the overthrowing of the enemy's military forces is essential; this rule derives from universal political reality.[10] Moreover, Clausewitz assumes that since the imposition of one's political will on the opponent prescribes the obliteration of the latter's power to resist, it is obvious that the military act becomes the essential mechanism for attaining this aim.

In his next step, Clausewitz broadens the logical basis of the theory by defining the three elements which compose the course that leads to the political objective: the enemy's armed forces; his base for survival (or country); and his will.[11] By specifying two of the components as physical elements which interrelate among themselves, he is already implying the conclusion of his next step. Moreover, by introducing the enemy's will, which is a metaphysical element, he creates an opportunity which he will exploit later.[12]

By positively referring, for the first time, to the destruction of the opponent's armed forces as the logical and preferred course to the attainment of the political aim, Clausewitz provides the discussion with its definite logical direction for further development:

> The fighting forces must be destroyed. That is, they must be put in such a condition that they can no longer carry on the fight. Whenever we use the term destruction of the enemy's forces this alone is what we mean.[13]

As can be clearly observed, the method of presenting the arguments by the author creates a coherent structure, which is convincing in its logic. In order to accentuate the validity of his assertions, Clausewitz indifferently asks the question which is of the greatest interest to the common mind: How should one define success in war? In providing the answer, he both emphasizes what he has already claimed and explicitly identifies destruction with success.[14] Since war is perceived by the majority of readers first and foremost in terms of combat or physical fighting, Clausewitz momentarily abandons the theoretical course, which deals with the abstract aspects of destruction, and enters the realm of empirical combat.

He begins by laying down two basic axioms: combat is the sole and most effective force in war, and the purpose of combat is destruction.[15] Both axioms are elementary to an extent that their soundness derives simply from their triviality. Hence, if one pursues this line of logic one can not escape the deduction that since destruction constitutes the purpose of combat, and since combat constitutes the substance of war, then destruction comprises the essence or aim of war, in general. Thus, it becomes obvious that destruction is the factor that governs the entire milieu of military activity, both in the fields of planning and execution.[16] As Clausewitz puts it:

> it is evident that the destruction of the enemy forces, is always the superior, more effective means, with which others can not compete.[17]

After anchoring the idea of destruction in the empirical dimension of actual combat, Clausewitz can return safely to his previous line of reasoning and exploit an opportunity which had been left open. Destruction is not only concerned with annihilating troops and materiel; it also aims at destroying metaphysical resources, namely the enemy's morale.[18]

Thus, the cognitive source for the approaches adopted by Foch's school of thought and by von der Goltz is revealed. The main advantage of this argument is that it enables one to ignore the fact that physical destruction was no longer unattainable at the close of the century. Therefore, von der Goltz could still argue that the destruction of a certain specific mass of troops will inevitably generate the collapse of the enemy's morale and thus result in his destruction.[19] Foch, who develops this idea in two directions, is finally swept away to the province of mysticism. On the one hand, he is determined to inflict upon the enemy something terrible and unexpected, and thus to destroy his morale and bring about his annihilation. On the other hand, however, he claims that the total mobilization of one's spiritual resources and the refusal to concede defeat are a certain formula for victory,[20] which activity he apparently believes is beyond the enemy's ability.

Clausewitz's secondary theme, which appears at first glance to be humanitarian, since it discusses the sacrifice that has to be made for the application of the principle of destruction, is nothing other than deceitful. The last sentence of his argument on this point confirms that Clausewitz's real purpose was merely to reinforce the adherence to the principle of destruction, and to strengthen the resolution and trust in destruction, despite its terrible cost.[21]

Clausewitz further argues that: if destruction is identified with the positive aim of war – then, the war's aim can only be attained by the application of a positive mode of action and by the utilization of positive means of warfare.[22] In this way Clausewitz not only associates destruction with the positive aim, but also paves the way for the unilateral preference of the offensive, since, as will be learned later, he exclusively identifies the operational positive mode of action with the offensive.

Through this method of argumentation, Clausewitz manages to impose the principle of destruction on both the strategic and political levels, and in order to complete his achievement he turns to the operational-tactical level.

According to Clausewitz, the idea of fighting centres at the operational level on the planning, organization and actual conduct of a series of engagements, each engagement constituting the basic tactical occurrence. In other words, since combat can be identified with the engagement, and since we already know that destruction can be interpreted in terms of combat, we can safely equate destruction with the engagement.[23] The way Clausewitz portrays it, the relationship between the engagement and destruction is, however, a reciprocal and complicated one. On the one hand, he argues in the first book:

> Since in the engagement everything is concentrated on the destruction of the enemy, or rather of his armed forces, which is inherent in its very concept, it follows that the destruction of the enemy's forces, is always the means by which the purpose of the engagement is achieved.[24]

On the other hand, he claims in the seventh book: 'The engagement is the only means of destroying the enemy's forces.'[25] Therefore, it follows that destruction constitutes the engagement's aim and vice versa. Clausewitz overcomes this contradiction by establishing that destruction constitutes the ultimate aim of all engagements. By doing so, he subjects the intermediate and lower levels of war to the principle of destruction. In order to remove any doubts from his readers' minds, Clausewitz imposes the following rule: 'The destruction of the enemy forces must be regarded as the main objective: not just in the war generally, but in each individual engagement.'[26]

On the abstract level one more achievement was needed in order to render the entire theoretical structure complete: the establishment of the concept of the integral battle of destruction (*Vernichtungsschlacht*). Clausewitz determines a direct quantitative relation between engagement and success: 'Only major engagements involving all forces lead to major successes . . . The greatest successes are obtained where all engagements coalesce into one great battle.'[27] Since he has already established the equation that destruction is identical to success, he can now easily determine a dual law by again employing a cyclic logical approach:

> These facts lead to a dual law whose principles support each other: destruction of the enemy's forces is generally accomplished by means of great battles and their results: and, the primary object of great battles must be the destruction of the enemy's forces.[28]

The destruction thus appears as the supreme and universal aim of all wars, operations, engagements and battles, and its positive attainment is implemented by applying the offensive, which in its turn leads to the occurrence of the integral battle of destruction.

With the completion of the theoretical structure, the conditions for the emergence of the first ingredient of the paradox of destruction, namely the abolition of the system's cognitive tension, finally matured. Since a permanent, universal, supreme and uniform aim has been formulated for all levels of war, a preliminary dialogue, involving the supreme political and military leadership, which will concern the concrete definition of the aims of the war, becomes entirely unnecessary. Consequently, any further political control pertaining to the military conduct of the war is irrelevant or even damaging. Moreover, as will be shown later, even determining operational goals and tactical objectives in advance becomes superfluous, and owing to the fact that no specific goals are being set, the entire planning process becomes a hollow and redundant business. A simplistic adoption of this view led the military theoreticians in the era preceding the First World War to formulate the paradigm of the strategy of a single point (*strategiia odnoi tochki*), which strove to destroy modern strategic systems and mass armies by tactical means. Moreover, had the military historians bothered to examine both the theory and conduct of war through the perspective of systemic criticism, they would have identified the absurdity of Clausewitz's theory.[29]

Moltke in his statements regarding aims and objectives reveals not only his adherence to Clausewitz's conception but also embraces the implications, which result from the abolition of the operational cognitive tension:

> Strategy cannot but always direct its efforts towards the highest goal attainable with the means at disposal. It thereby serves policy best and only works for the object of policy, but completely independent of policy in its actions . . . It is not the occupation of a slice of territory, or a capture of a fortress, but the destruction of the enemy forces that will decide the outcome of the war.[30]

Moltke, who was, above all, a realist, confined the aim to the existing strategic capability, by determining the dependence of the aim upon the resources of the state. Precisely for this reason he rejected the idea that in a war on two fronts Germany could still achieve absolute decision. Therefore, since he realized that in such a case the destruction of both the enemies would be beyond Germany's ability, he worked out a strategical plan, which corresponded with the resources that the state possessed at the time.[31] Unlike Moltke, Schlieffen, who was an addict of Clausewitz's theory and who pursued the latter's principles to the extreme, refused to adapt the aims to the existing means, and insisted on the literal attainment of the destructive aim. This dichotomy is clearly expressed in one of the preliminary drafts of the 1905 plan. Although he realized that the resources at his disposal were less than required for attaining the total destruction, even of the French Army, he did not change the original definition of the general aim of the war, and performed ardent manipulations in order to maintain the traditional aim intact.[32]

The damage that resulted from Schlieffen's approach, at the operational level is best demonstrated in a statement by the commander of the German Fifth Army in the 1914 offensive. His statement is of special interest, since we already know that the Crown Prince adhered to the ideas propagated by Clausewitz's devotees. Nevertheless, he expresses his natural thoughts and criticism, as an operational commander, without realizing that in fact he was undermining his own perceptive posture:

> The plan of the supreme command was simply to overrun the enemy's country, on as broad a front as possible. No definite detailed goal was held in view.[33]

The abatement of cognitive tension severely impaired the operational-tactical levels. The existence of this tension reflects the dilemma regarding the behaviour of the system's components, which transpires within a system in every dynamic or turbulent situation. In military terms, the components involved are the commanders of the operational formations of tactical units. The field commanders must frequently choose between absolute conformity with the general goal and direct responses to immediate threats or local incidents. Moreover, this tension, which concerns not just the friendly system's components but also takes the enemy's reactions into consideration, generates a certain dynamism. This dynamism expresses the reaction of the system as a whole, both to the cognitive imperatives, laid by the commander's plan, and to the imperatives dictated by the randomness of combat. Thus, the existence of this tension is essential to the evolution of a deliberate systemic manoeuvre, which is both cognitively controlled and responsive. This rare combination comprises the substance of the operational cognitive tension and is based on human intelligence, on common methods of thought and nomenclature, on a clear definition of aims and goals, on an understanding of the factor of randomness, and, above all, on system consciousness.

An examination of the first four major battles of the war of 1870 (Spicheren, Wörth, Colombey and Mars-la-Tour), in light of the above and also against the background of Moltke's initial memorandum to the chiefs of sections of the Great General Staff, dating from 6 May 1870, yields no surprises.[34] The total lack of control, from the supreme level of command down to the tactical one, derives first and foremost from the superficiality of the document which was meant to orientate the operation of the entire German Army. The only conformity which this document demanded was to maintain a general course of advance, to locate the French troops, and to bring them to battle, thus, attaining the destructive goal at every level. The various examples from the war of 1870 illustrate clearly the operational damage that was precipitated, due to the lack of the cognitive tension.

The attempts of Sigismund von Schlichting to institute dynamic patterns of command during the era of Schlieffen manifest the stagnation of the philosophy of command which existed within the German Army, even though it possessed the most advanced mode of command in the world at that time.

Schlichting approached the problem of randomness with his advanced concept of the meeting engagement (*Begegnungsgefecht*). This concept, which combined an aggressive combat technique with Moltke's *Auftragstaktik*, advocated unlimited freedom of tactical action for the field commanders. Schlichting's endeavour, despite its revolutionary approach, remained partial and limited in scope, since it referred both to junior levels of command and to narrow tactical situations.[35]

The incident, which is reported by the commander of the German Third Army, in the war of 1870, and in which the Duke of Mecklenburg-Schwerin, the commanding officer of the Sixth German Cavalry Division, was involved on 1 September, in the vicinity of Mézières, demonstrates in a rather negative manner the real significance of the cognitive tension in the operational context.[36] The unique operational importance of Mézières derived from its being a point which gave the Germans the opportunity to envelop the French from the west and north and thus complete their operational encirclement. Furthermore, since it was the railway junction that led from Sedan westward, it could allow, in the event of its capture by the Germans, the blocking of the only axis through which the French Army could have been rescued. On 31 August, when the encirclement of the French Army in Sedan was approaching its final stages, the commander of the Sixth Cavalry Division arrived at Mézières. In spite of the fact that the division formed a part of the organizational battle order of the Third Army, operationally, it was employed by Moltke, i.e. the strategic level. Upon reaching this north-western tip of the entire operational manoeuvring space of the German Army, the Duke of Mecklenburg-Schwerin was neither acquainted with Moltke's aims nor with his operational plan. Consequently, he did what most junior commanders would have done in such circumstances – he sent for further instructions. The situation in which the Duke of Mecklenburg-Schwerin found himself can best be termed as operational opportunity. Such situations occur rarely, and when they do, they must be quickly exploited. Operational cognitive tension is the only way to guarantee the proper exploitation of such opportunities. In this case the essential element that generates this tension, namely the cognition which is produced by the guidance of the commander in chief, was missing.

Whenever the strategic aim is defined permanently as destruction, which is implemented only through the means of battle, the operational goal inevitably becomes the materialization of this battle, and thus the tactical objective becomes inevitably the attrition of the enemy's force or the occupation of his positions. This absurdity originated with Clausewitz, but matured in the writings and behaviour of his adherents.

By setting forth the following premises in his first book, Clausewitz establishes the logical basis for further discussion: destruction constitutes the universal aim of war; destruction implies rendering the opponent incapable of maintaining resistance; destruction is attained only by means of combat; combat is implemented through battles and engagements.[37]

It is only natural that in the fourth book he examines the idea of destruction in the tactical context. By concentrating on the practical and mechanical aspects he adds intelligibility to the idea of destruction, thus reinforcing the validity of his entire argument.

The elementary model of destruction is based upon the tactical-spectacle, in which two linear masses, composed of multitudes of riflemen, strive to erode each other by the effect of fire. The consequence, according to Clausewitz, is a systematic process of mutual attrition:

> This description [of modern battle] pictures the order of battle simply as a disposition of troops designed to facilitate their use, and the course of battle as a slow process of mutual destruction.[38]

Clausewitz's delineation of the battle communicates a dual message – which in fact is the source of its obscurity. Whereas the impression suggested by the process of fighting implies attrition, the use of the term destruction when referring to the battle's consequence connotes resolution and totality. Since the authenticity of attrition which was rooted in nineteenth-century warfare is beyond doubt, the question of Clausewitz's motive in using the term destruction must be asked. The answer can be found in the analogy Clausewitz makes between a tactical battle and a duel and in von der Goltz's explication on the roots of the rifle's lethality.[39]

Through his analogy between war and a duel, Clausewitz not only convinces himself that the aim of each of the combatants is to destroy his opponent, but also that the attainment of that aim by the victor is indeed feasible. In fact, at the individual level of combat he is right, since one individual can either render his opponent incapable of further fighting, or even kill him, and thus destroy him physically.

Von der Goltz defines the rifle as the most lethal weapon ever to exist. The operational research conducted by Caemmerer and J. de Bloch and many others at the end of the century indeed confirm this assumption, at the basic techno-tactical level.[40] According to von der Goltz, a single rifleman could absolutely destroy, from a relatively long range, another rifleman by a single shot. Since the individual infantryman armed with the rifle was conceived, at the time, as the basic component of any fighting system, and since fighting systems were perceived in linear terms, a simplistic induction could therefore lead one to assume that the characteristic principles of the individual level are also valid at the general one. In other words, the destructive principle, which seemed genuine and valid in an individual context, was applied literally to the context of whole armies.

However, systems do not behave exactly like individual components or even like a quantitative sum of individuals. Moreover, the general performance and functional course of a system always produce results that are significantly different from that of the arithmetical-linear summation of results of the various individual ingredients, which compose it.

Clausewitz disentangles the momentary confusion created by the contradiction by simply redefining the tactical destruction as inflicting on the enemy a punishment greater than that which is suffered by oneself: 'Every engagement is a bloody and destructive test of physical and moral strength. Whoever has the greater sum of both left at the end is the victor.'[41] In other words, the ultimate profit or gain, which constitutes in Clausewitz's own words the tactical objective, is the numerical discrepancy in losses between the victor and the vanquished: 'Consequently, only the direct profit gained in the process of mutual destruction may be considered as having been the object.'[42]

However, due to the linear nature of the fire fight the amounts of losses suffered by both sides roughly correspond, and so it becomes almost an imperative that, in order to acquire an advantage, one has to employ larger quantities of soldiers than the adversary: 'Equal absolute losses will, of course, mean smaller relative losses to the side with the numerical superiority and can therefore be considered an advantage.'[43]

From here, Clausewitz turns to impose the tactical premise, by way of induction, on the operational level. Destruction at the operational level means the total balance, which accumulates the attritional results gained in the various battles and engagements.[44]

It must, therefore, be conceded that the attrition of one's own forces is inevitable. One method to contend with this predicament has already been mentioned – superior quantities. The second method is not materialistic but cognitive – self-indoctrination which will institute a deliberate and resolute assent to accept self-attrition indifferently.

Hence, the absurdity of the deterministic approach to attrition is instituted formally, and the way to guarantee its prevalence is, of course, by educating the military leadership to conform with this view. Therefore, the optimal stereotype of a future general is established:

> We are not interested in generals who win victories without bloodshed. The fact that slaughter is a horrifying spectacle must make us take war more seriously, but not provide an excuse for gradually blunting our swords in the name of humanity.[45]

THE PARADOX OF THE BATTLE'S DOMINANCE

The fact that these days tactics is perceived as the lowest level in the structural process of exercising war, and the battle as the mechanical edge that is inaugurated by the operational level, derives undoubtedly from the logic inherited from the Clausewitzian theory.[46]

In its essence, the paradox of the dominance of battle refers to a certain link within the chain of cognitive failures mentioned earlier. Had Clausewitz been able to foresee the consequences of this specific paradox, he would probably have refrained from instituting it at all, since it precipitated the subjugation of the operational level by a tactical concept. Moreover, this same paradox did real damage to strategic consciousness.

The primacy and vigour of the idea of battle derive, according to Clausewitz, from three sources. The first is the vital tradition of the Napoleonic experience:

> To illustrate briefly what I mean, let us recall that such a general as Bonaparte could ruthlessly cut through all his enemy's strategic plans in search for battle, because he seldom doubted the outcome of battle.[47]

This aspect of Clausewitz's theory was one reason that made it so attractive to the French.[48]

The second source is the fact that the battle is deep-rooted in the reality of war and constitutes the real substance of fighting by means of the engagement:

> It is inherent in the very concept of war that everything that occurs must originally derive from combat . . . Everything that occurs in war results from the existence of armed forces: But whenever armed forces, that is armed individuals, are used, the idea of combat must be present.[49]

According to this argument, both the French and the Germans attributed the German victory in the 1870 war to the tactical superiority of the German army.[50]

The third source is the fixed, complex relationship that exists between the battle and destruction, through the link provided by the engagement:

> Engagements mean fighting. The object of fighting is the destruction or defeat of the enemy. The enemy in the individual engagement is simply the opposing fighting force.[51]

This idea constituted the basis for every military theory at the end of the nineteenth century, both in Germany and in France.[52]

Once the roots of the idea of battle have been clarified and their pertinence has been validated, the road to the further pursuance of the matter is open. Since it has been determined that the battle is both the substance of fighting and the sole means by which the war's aim is attained, and since it has been established that the battle constitutes the essential mechanism that generates the entire enterprise of war, it becomes obvious that it must be regarded as the central element of war:

> But since the essence of war is fighting, and since the battle is the fight of the main force, the battle must be always considered as the true centre of gravity of the war.[53]

The prominence of the idea of battle, its proximity to the ideal aim, as well as the direct interaction existing between the two, transformed the battle, in Clausewitz's opinion, into what is termed in Kantian philosophy as 'The Thing in Itself' (*Ding-an-sich*):

> All in all, therefore, *its distinguishing feature* is that, more than any other type of action, battle exists for its own sake alone.[54]

It is this perception which raises tactics above the other levels of war. Moreover, the acuteness of the conduct of battle, which is reflected through the tactical substance, forces the other levels to conform with the first in a manner that will ensure the proper realization of the battle. This aspect should be anchored in the theory of war.[55] Thus, the precedence of the tactical level over the strategic is declaratively established. In other words, since only tactical success leads directly to the aim, the strategic planning should submit to the determinants established by tactics. According to Clausewitz, therefore, the entire strategic planning 'rests on tactical success alone, and that whether the solution is arrived at in battle or not – this is in all cases the actual fundamental basis for the decision.'[56]

Bernhardy, Lewal and Colin uncritically adopted Clausewitz's dictum that 'strategy must never be anything but the obedient servant of the tactical issue'.[57] By ignoring the principle of synergetic interaction, these thinkers legitimized the 'tactization' of strategy.

Indeed, it was precisely this point in Clausewitz's argumentation which contributed at the end of the nineteenth century to the evolution of the approach that saw the operational art as a mere complex of general movement regulations, meant to ensure the occurrence of battle under the most favourable conditions.[58]

Moreover, since due to tactical considerations the actual implementation of the battle was conceived in linear patterns, and since the ability to predict the specific site of battle did not exist due to the general circumstances, the linear pattern of tactical conduct was transferred to the operational level. The result, which assumed the form of an advancing line of formations in column, was expected to search for the enemy's army on the widest possible front, and force it to accept battle by means of a giant mechanical push or thrust.[59] The best manifestation of the entire concept is probably the one presented by Colin:

> When it comes to moving the masses of troops which a European war would bring into play, one thinks first of deploying them in a continuous homogeneous line of almost continuous equal depth, with which one thinks one would without further combination, be in a situation to give battle.[60]

Schlieffen's Freudian slip of tongue when defining in exact terms the action of the right wing in his memorandum of 1912 is no less illustrative of this artificial and coercive trend, since he copies literally the limited patterns of the battle of Cannae to a context which is a hundred times wider in terms of space and more than two hundred times larger, in terms of quantities:

> The first, second and third German armies, joined by the released corps with strong cavalry on their wings, will follow in a wide arc with the intention of completely encircling the greatest possible part of the enemy army.[61]

Exercising such patterns in a tactical context, even at the beginning of the nineteenth century, when the effective range of the musket did not exceed 100 yards, was still practicable, but transforming it to dimensions of 70, 100, or even 300 miles made the linear pattern a most fragile structure, impossible to command and operate. Moreover, with the application of the tactical linear pattern to the operational level, its greatest deficiency, namely its attritional nature, was maintained and unconsciously applied as well.

Clausewitz's next natural step in developing his argument presents a premise which, in combination with the Napoleonic experience, precipitated the Tactical Imperative:

> If a battle is primarily an end in itself, the elements of its decision must be contained in it. In other words, victory must be pursued so long as it lies within the realm of the possible: Battle must never be abandoned because of particular circumstances, but only when the strength available has quite clearly become inadequate.[62]

Beside the general insinuation, which derives from the consistent argument that battle must be pursued at all costs, this last expression of Clausewitz has two other implications. First, it determines the quantitative factor as an essential condition for the materialization of the battle, which means attaining numerical superiority as early as possible. Second, it indicates the element of uncertainty, that is a characteristic of military activity. Both these implications are the cognitive line of departure for the institution of the Tactical Imperative.

The Tactical Imperative incorporates a principle that is induced by four mechanisms: the realization of the dominance of the battle and its autarky; the pursuance of the 'thunder of the guns', which is a cognitive mechanism; the *Kameradschaft*, or sense of soldiers' solidarity, which is a moral mechanism; and the geometrical mechanism or the line of frontal contact.

This pattern is illustrated explicitly in the German reports of the war of 1870. Generally, the Tactical Imperative operated in the following manner: a junior engagement occurs, where one of the units, whether a battalion, brigade or squadron, which leads the advance guard of a corps or divisional column encounters an enemy unit. Consequently a linear fire fight ensues. To the thunder of guns and noise of musketry which develops, all friendly units and formations in the vicinity change their course of march and hasten to the site of the initial encounter. The sudden diversion from a general course of advance towards a specific occurrence or site, which involves at times a whole corps, and sometimes an entire army, is generated by the Tactical Imperative. Thus, reaching the site of battle, indicated by the sound of fire, and joining the formation that initiated the engagement, suddenly becomes a sacred mission that must be obeyed even by distant formations. The smooth and quick entry into battle by the arriving formation is made possible by employing linear patterns of action. In other words, every newly arriving formation joins the already existing line of battle in the open flank, which is closer to its line of march. This process sometimes lasts an entire day, since the length of a corps column exceeds 14 miles, and the dispersion of the parallel columns can be significantly greater. Thus, the gathering of the friendly forces is a long process and their accumulation takes a great deal of time. Towards the later hours of the day, after accumulating an appropriate mass deployed all along the enemy's entire front, an attempt is made towards one of its flanks.[63] According to Moltke's experience in the 1870 war, these engagements required a tactical decision at their end, but operationally they were far from yielding any significant result. Further, these engagements, which involved considerable operational order of battle, transpired without the deliberate intention of the supreme or even operational command echelons.[64] In most of the cases the relevant operational command did not initiate a general engagement, neither was it ready for one; it was simply drawn into it by the tactical units and formations, which were obeying the Tactical Imperative. Moreover, as can be learned from various German reports, both the operational echelons and the high command forbade any tactical initiatives that would lead to an engagement prior to the battles of Spicheren, Wörth and Colombey, and even expressed their objections in explicit orders. Nevertheless, in all these cases an encounter initiated by a tactical unit or formation set the Tactical Imperative in motion and drew the entire army – despite the objections of the operational or strategic command – into a huge battle under unfavourable conditions. Thus, it can be said that the Tactical Imperative surpassed both operational logic and the mechanism of hierarchical command.[65] On such occasions, the operational commander contributed to the development of the battle not by exercising deliberate direction through the conventional mode of command, but simply by urging and speeding up the advancing formations.[66]

However, the most grievous aspect of these battles was that they commenced at random, without clear direction or guidance; they developed without any firm control and proper command, and consequently critical situations, like that at Vionville, resulted. Ultimately, they always terminated in appalling losses.[67] No less grave is the fact that on some occasions, such as that at Gravelotte, an entire operational plan was ruined by the Tactical Imperative.[68]

According to Clausewitz, the tactical effect of destruction can be assessed by three distinct parameters which develop during an engagement. The first is the rate of destroyed morale suffered by the vanquished; the second is the amount of losses inflicted on him; and the third is the amount of ground he was forced to yield by his opponent's linear push.[69] Since his strategic – or, rather, operational – thinking is governed by linear terms of accumulating sums of destruction, Clausewitz determines that the deliberate assimilation of all the engagements and tactical activities into a single integrated battle of destruction precipitates the materialization of the ideal concept:

> But in general it remains true that great battles are fought only to destroy the enemy's forces, and that the destruction of these forces can be accomplished only by a major battle . . . The major battle is therefore to be regarded as concentrated war, as the centre of gravity of the entire conflict or the campaign.[70]

The integral battle of destruction constitutes the perfect agent that implements the positive aim – the ideal which incorporates both the principles of destruction and that of the dominance of battle.[71] Moreover, Clausewitz is again tempted to reinstitutionalize the stereotype of the optimal general, which he identifies as the one who deliberately prefers the course that leads directly to the integral battle of destruction:

> Therefore, commanders with enough self confidence to go for great decisions have always managed to deploy the great bulk of their forces in a great battle, without seriously neglecting other areas.[72]

Thus, the road from here to the ultimate enthronement of the concept of the integral battle of destruction is short and clear:

> There is then no factor in war that rivals the battle in importance: And the greatest strategic skill will be displayed in creating the right conditions for it, choosing the right place, time and line of advance, and making the fullest use of its results.[73]

Nominating the integral battle of destruction as the ideal type had turned it into a very forceful source of intellectual attraction which totally dominated the minds of the military leadership of both Germany and France.[74] When one examines Schlieffen's seemingly arrogant concluding statement to the final operational war game of 1905 in light of Clausewitz's arguments, its perceptional roots immediately become apparent:

> The theory of the decisive battle has been much talked about, ever since war with France and Russia became a threat to Germany. The theory is roughly this: We go with all our forces into France, fight a

decisive battle, which of course ends in our favour, and on the evening of the battle, or next morning at the latest, the trains are ready and the victors roll eastward to fight a new decisive battle on the Vistula and the Niemen.[75]

THE GEOMETRICAL SYLLOGISM

The geometrical syllogism refers to the deductive process by which Clausewitz and his adherents imposed the geometrical logic that constituted the essence of tactical thinking and deportment upon the strategic-operational level, by means of inference. The first argument they proposed was the premise, already established by Clausewitz, that the battle governs the entire province of war. Their second categorical proposition was that the conduct of battle is dominated by geometrical principles. The result was the imposition of geometrical principles or logic on the context of the operational manoeuvre.

This syllogism, instituted by Clausewitz and transformed by his devotees to colossal proportions, suggested two general categoric implications. Firstly, since the battle, which is the power behind destruction, attains its aim by means of linear firepower of which the infantry is the principal agent, armies should be composed primarily of foot soldiers. Secondly, the operational patterns must be formed in a mode that will guarantee the realization of two essential tactical preconditions, namely: the linear commencing of the battle and an appropriate quantitative superiority.

Clausewitz accomplishes the founding of the syllogism mainly in the third and fifth books. The subject then matured through the interpretations of Moltke, von der Goltz, Bernhardy, Caemmerer, and, on the French side, by Colin, Foch and Lewal, and it reaches its final sophistication in the hands of Schlieffen.

The construction of the geometrical syllogism and its development by Clausewitz and his successors is conducted in four conceptual stages, each corresponding to a certain subject: the consolidation of the geometrical principle at the level of battle; the legitimization of the operational pattern of the line of marching columns, and its final crystallization in the mode of the gigantic rolling-crushing line; the institutionalization of the ideal concept of envelopment at the strategical-operational level; and the annulment of operational mobility, the negation of operational patterns of depth, and the rejection of the operational-strategical reserve.

In his first step Clausewitz specifies the linear phenomenon in battle – a process which results in the confirmation of the identity between the battle and geometry. By exploiting this achievement, Clausewitz manages to establish the precedence of geometry, or linearism in warfare. Moreover, in so doing he accentuates the pre-eminence of envelopment as the most decisive of all geometrical patterns.

In his basic premise Clausewitz claims that geometry represents both the movement and the deployment of troops. Therefore, geometry constitutes the substance of tactics, and its importance increases in the modern era:

> Yet, in today's tactics, where the outflanking of the enemy is the aim of every engagement, the geometrical factor has again achieved great significance.[76]

Both the battle's linear nature and its compactness in time and space made the pattern of envelopment into the ideal tactical manoeuvre in the eyes of Clausewitz and his disciples:

> . . . in tactics time and space are rapidly reduced to their absolute minimum . . . For this reason all tactical arrangements aimed at envelopment are highly effective, and their effectiveness consists largely in the concern they induce about their consequences. That is why the geometrical factor in the disposition of forces is so important.[77]

In other words, tactical envelopment involves two definite advantages.[78] By acknowledging the first of these advantages, Clausewitz identifies the envelopment with initiative, which is a central element in German military consciousness.[79] In specifying the second advantage, he links destruction with envelopment, thus sealing the future addiction of his adherents to the patterns of envelopment and encirclement:

> We have been talking about a total victory – that is not simply a battle won, but the complete defeat of the enemy. Such a victory demands an enveloping attack, or a battle with reversed fronts, either of which will always make the result decisive. It is essential, then, that any plan of operations should provide for this.[80]

Michael Howard illustrates, most convincingly, the spectacle, which probably left its signature on Clausewitz's consciousness regarding the tangibility of the geometrical pattern, as he experienced it in battle:

> In battle the need to develop maximum firepower produced linear tactics – the deployment of troops in thin lines blazing away at each other at point-blank range – which turned battles into murderous set pieces.[81]

J. Colin, who follows Clausewitz's ideas literally, highlights the benefits of simultaneity, which is best expressed through the arrangement of a mass in a line, for the attainment of the destructive aim:

> All those things melt away as soon as one reflects that there is nothing in war but forces brought into play, and that consequently everything which is not an active force cannot be accorded any sort of consideration.[82]

Caemmerer, who witnessed the enormous increase in lethality of fire produced by the line of riflemen, attempts to express an innovative approach by asserting what appears to be a revolutionary expression, but is, in fact, nothing more than an imitation of both Clausewitz's nomenclature and manner of thinking:

> Owing to these improvements in firearms the purely frontal attack, or tactical penetration, is almost struck out from the military vocabulary ... But on the whole, the attack must acknowledge that it is necessary to envelop the enemy in order to subdue effectively the enormously increased fire effect of the defense.[83]

Von der Goltz demonstrates most explicitly the implications of applying Clausewitz's geometrical doctrine literally. He confirms that in substance nothing has changed since the days of Clausewitz. The concept of destruction remains dominant, and its attainment is implemented by means of a linear manipulation of firepower. This is achieved by deploying large masses of riflemen in the firing-line:

> There is therefore only one way of attaining it, viz. by numerical superiority, such that the attacker is always able to make good the losses occurring in the firing line, whereas the defender is finally unable to do so ... Thus, the attacker's superiority in numbers must be very considerable for it to turn the scale.[84]

Boguslawski, who surveyed the tactical lessons of the 1870 war, held the view that the infantry and the tactics of the firing-line constituted the key factor for victory. Yet, through his reports one can detect the practical distortion which originated in the pretentious trend to execute tactical patterns of envelopment through linear techniques, and likewise the falsehood behind the term envelopment. The tactical envelopment, as it was practised in the war of 1870, was nothing more than a linear-frontal assault combined with an ensuing attempt to project the unengaged surplus of mass towards one of the opponent's open flanks – an exertion that was usually executed too late to achieve any substantial results, operationally:

> On the German side, the intention was generally evident of attempting

to turn the enemy. But the fight often developed itself in such a manner that, after preparing the way by artillery fire, the Germans made a vigorous attack upon the French centre without waiting for the effect of the movement on the flanks.[85]

Despite this somewhat naive remark, Boguslawski justifies the dense linear pattern of infantry attack in the shape of *Kolonne-nach-der-Mitte*, since it manifested the full impact of firepower. Another advantage which Boguslawski attributes to the linear dense formation is that it facilitates the arrangements of command and control at the tactical level.[86]
Michael Howard reveals that with the French, matters were even worse, both in aspects of linearity and density:

> The notorious regulations of 1894 laid it down that attacking units should advance elbow to elbow, not breaking formation to take advantage of cover but assaulting *en masses* to the sound of bugles and drums.[87]

This approach resulted in awful mutual slaughter.[88]

The conversation between C. von Alvensleben who commanded the third German corps at Vionville and von Pape who commanded the first division of foot guards is worth citing, since it demonstrates the bitter disillusion that affected those who experienced the real substance of the tactical-geometrical approach:

> On the morning of the 18th of August, the leader of the third army corps expressed himself as follows to the commander of the first division of the foot guards, Major General von Pape: 'The *chassepot* fire has been underestimated, and also to some extent the *mitrailleuse*. It is impossible for us to make any progress as the result of tactics practised on the drilling ground. We must have more manoeuvring: we must develop and make use of even the most insignificant cover in the open country. Above all we must employ our artillery long and continuously . . .'[89]

The model upon which the development of the linear manoeuvre of operational advance was based originates in the concepts of Guibert and de Broglie and in the empirical experience of Napoleon, who established it as the most common pattern allowing a smooth transition from the strategic march to the tactical battle.[90]

Clausewitz adhered fully to this pattern, not only because it facilitated the logistical sustenance of a huge advancing mass, but also because it allowed the mass to systematically traverse the theatre of war, to locate the opposing army and to bring it to battle.[91] Moreover, by combining the linear pattern of the operational march with the

Tactical Imperative it was possible to execute a swift transition to tactical engagement and thus destroy the enemy's operational grouping. However, this was not the logic behind the application of the linear configuration to the level of the operational manoeuvre. Schlieffen and the generation of military theoreticians who preceded the First World War describe this pattern as a geometrical means to integrate the numerous tactical engagements into a single, homogeneous destructive battle.[92] Thus, the assimilation of the linear pattern of the operational advance-march, initiated by Clausewitz, constitutes yet another aspect of the geometrical syllogism.

Clausewitz's point of departure for the rationalization of the pattern lies in his perception that destruction is implemented in battle by the deployment of a superior linear mass.

The need to concentrate a superior mass, according to Clausewitz, is accentuated by the impact produced through the interaction of force with space and time, which is a characteristic of the operational level of war. Thus, one can describe the necessity more specifically as the need to concentrate a superior mass in a specific site and in the shortest time.

This crucial requirement and the acuteness of the time dimension determined, more than anything else, the nature of the pattern of operational marching columns. In this respect the rationale of the pattern derives from the field of mechanics, since the accumulation of a mass on a certain point through a process in which the formations are advancing in a line of parallel columns will always be shorter than that on which the formations follow each other in a unified column. Thus, the linear pattern is a compromise between concentration, which is dictated by command and control requisitions, and dispersion, which is induced by the need to assemble the mass as quickly as possible.[93]

Colin emphasizes the search-thrust operational effect, which is produced by the pattern: 'And from the beginning of operations armies extended in this way press the enemy and push him back into the snare.'[94] He admits that the pattern of the broad and shallow operational line of marching columns in its modern version was adopted from Moltke.[95] Like Caemmerer, Colin attributes the acceleration in adoption of the pattern to the intense development of the European road network.[96] Lewal reduces the dimensions of the entire operational-strategical line, both in length and depth, thus creating a dense-solid-homogeneous-linear front, whose overall length is 68km and depth is 21km.[97] In this linear-gigantic form Lewal condenses four armies, comprising more than one million men, and intends to operate it in the manner in which one operates a rifle company.[98]

Unlike the majority of theoreticians, Schlieffen was not content to fill volumes with figurative terminology and abstract ideas, but forced his crystallized concepts into a functional operational plan. This plan provided the cognitive guide book, according to which the German army was supposed to navigate its track to victory in a future war. The operational logic of this textbook derived from a simplistic application of a Clausewitzian archaic principle. In Schlieffen's adroit hands, that principle was amplified through a quantitative manipulation into a battering ram, linearly shaped, that aimed to roll over the French Army physically, and hammer it to pieces on the Swiss anvil.[99]

By basing their strategic perception of manoeuvre on linear patterns and by their exclusive employment of the foot arm, the military theoreticians of the late nineteenth and early twentieth centuries unconsciously gave up the idea of operational mobility. Consequently the renunciation of operational mobility, which had been introduced by Clausewitz, contributed by the distortions it produced, more than any other element or phenomenon, to the fact that until the end of the First World War, patterns of operational manoeuvre did not materialize.

By ignoring mobility and fanatically advocating a tactical archaism for more than a century, three operational absurdities were produced. Firstly, a perceptional stagnation was institutionalized that obstructed the implementation of options of operational mechanization, both with regard to the horse and the internal combustion engine. By so doing, any aspiration to apply patterns of manoeuvre in depth was frustrated.[100] Secondly, in the strategic context, warfare was dominated by the tactical qualities of the foot arm, namely, over-reliance on firepower, lack of momentum and self-inflicted attrition. Thirdly, the idea of reserve was entirely discarded at the operational-strategical level.

Clausewitz's point of departure for determining this trend assumes that at the operational level destruction is preferable to mobility. Thus, whatever does not serve destruction positively and unswervingly does not deserve any allocation of resources:

> Destruction being a more effective factor than mobility, the complete absence of cavalry would prove to be less debilitating to an army, than the complete absence of artillery.[101]

Therefore, since the foot arm is five times cheaper to establish and maintain than cavalry, and since infantry's contribution to tactical destruction is decisive, armies should be primarily composed of infantry:

1. Infantry is the main branch of the service. The other two are supplementary.

2. It is harder to do without artillery than without cavalry.

3. In general, artillery is the strongest agent of destruction and cavalry the weakest.[102]

This last conclusion undermined any serious attempt to develop options for operational mobility, which is essential for the realization of a dynamic manoeuvre.

Clausewitz's approach to the issue of operational or strategical reserve draws directly on the conclusions he drew regarding mobility. The natural medium for the utilization of the reserve lies exclusively in the province of tactics and serves two distinct purposes: 'to prolong and renew the action' and to 'counter unforeseen threats'. Thus, operating reserves suits the context of tactical battle perfectly, mainly within the scope of time and space while at the strategical level, reserves are considered to be entirely ineffective.[103]

This approach was adopted literally by Colin, and despite some criticism from Bernhardy, it was applied as a leading principle in the formulation of the Schlieffen Plan.[104] In his 1905 memorandum, Schlieffen not only did not allot any reserves for the use of the supreme command, but in fact founded his entire idea of linear manoeuvre on manpower resources, which he did not possess at the time.[105] In the memorandum of 1912 he performs an enormous manipulation to produce the manpower resources that were required to feed an operational line designed to attack simultaneously along the entire strategic front, without leaving a single spare soldier:

> But now that they [the French] are imbued with the offensive spirit, we must assume that the part not attacked will advance offensively. To counter this it would be necessary to hold strong reserves. But it is simpler to gain the initiative by using them in the attack from the very beginning.[106]

The traditional debate, which centres on the origins of the operational rationale behind the Schlieffen Plan, whether they be the Frederickian oblique order of Leuthen, or those of Hannibal's Cannae, manifest the scale of the problem.[107]

It appears that some of the fog surrounding the Schlieffen operational concepts has lifted in the process of tracing its roots, both along the time scale of the nineteenth century and through the thematic domain. It is quite obvious now that Schlieffen, despite his intellectual eminence, should only be evaluated within the broader context of German military theory of the nineteenth century. Schlieffen believed that warfare, at the operational-strategic level, centred on the notion of envelopment, as one can learn from his works and from Freytag-Loringhoven's assessment that 'Flank attack is the essence of the whole history of war.'[108] This adherence to the doctrine of envelopment, which according to Ritter became almost a mystical creed in Schlieffen's later years, derives directly from Clausewitz.[109]

Clausewitz mentions the geometrical envelopment as one of the three key factors in the attainment of tactical decision.[110] Nevertheless, the important point is that following his review of the essential factors at the tactical level, he reiterates when specifying those of the strategic level:

> The main factors in strategic effectiveness – are the following: 1. The advantage of terrain. 2. Surprise. 3. Concentric attack. [All three as in tactics].[111]

By establishing an absolute identity between the patterns of strategic and tactical conduct, Clausewitz formulated yet another absurdity, thus adding a further contribution to mechanization, or rather tactization of strategy. Moreover, later in his discussion, Clausewitz argues that the strategical defender can have no hope against an envelopment conducted by a quantitatively superior strategic attacker. The extent to which this fallacy misled the generals of both the French and the German armies, can be learned from the events of August – September 1914. The definition of envelopment as a dynamic expression of tactical operational initiative in meeting engagements (*recontres*, *Begegnungsgefecht*), in both Germany and France, by leading theoreticians such as Schlichting and Lewal, resulted in a simplistic transformation of the limited notion of envelopment to a global one.[112] This mode of thinking, as well as the rejection of operational mobility, generated a deliberate rejection of columnar patterns of manoeuvre. Thus, though theoretically the option of operational breakthrough did exist, it was practically overruled by purely tactical considerations. It was assumed that penetration implied grave mechanical risks, and that if the driving force were not sufficient, the wedge would remain embedded. Further warnings were made against 'tactical frontal attacks, which in these days of highly developed fire effect are attended with the utmost difficulty.'[113]

Schlieffen's simplistic approach, when attempting to apply tactical patterns to the operational context by means of magnification, is explicitly demonstrated by another of Freytag-Loringhoven's accounts. Freytag-Loringhoven reports that Schlieffen planned to reduce the ratio of infantry soldiers deployed in the strategical line from 15 per frontal yard to three, a decision which he attributed to the growing lethality of firepower. However, he intended to employ the surplus in infantry formations for expansion of his strategical line, thus creating an option for a strategic envelopment.[114]

The strategic-operational wing manoeuvre (*Flügelschlacht*), which became a formal doctrine in Germany and France, constituted the operational rationale behind Schlieffen's Plan of 1905. This mode of manoeuvre, which was crystallized by von Falkenhausen, and advocated with almost religious zeal by Lewal, Colin, von der Goltz, Bernhardy and even Caemmerer, was not a simple amplification of Frederick's tactical pattern of Leuthen.[115]

The rationale of the strategic wing manoeuvre assumes that due to the prevalent operational circumstances, the only effective mode of manoeuvre still viable for a general decision, called for a deliberate accentuation of the weight of one of the wings of the strategic line. Through this asymmetry, the manoeuvre would assume the form of a revolving door that would push the opposing line, roll it towards a solid element of terrain or a defensive layout and physically crush it. The similarity to mechanics, suggested by the metaphor, made the concept even more attractive.

In his book, Bernhardy offered his personal vision of the materialization of the wing manoeuvre in a prospective war. This characterization, which preceded by several years the publication of the essentials of the Schlieffen Plan, was undoubtedly composed by its author when the Schlieffen Plan was kept in total secrecy. However, the striking similarity between Bernhardy's description and the real plan of 1905 confirms the assumption that Schlieffen's brainchild was a natural product of a mentality that was common not just in Germany, but also in France.

> Leaving all political conditions alone, we can very well imagine a German offensive against France, being conducted by the northern wing of the German Army with its extreme right along the sea coast, advancing with the armies echeloned forward through Holland and Belgium, while the German forces in the south evade the blow of the enemy, retiring through Alsace and Lorraine in a north-easterly direction, and leaving south Germany open to their opponent. The advance in echelon of the German attacking wing would force the left wing of the opposing army into making a great change of front . . . Strategically would here be attained what Frederick the Great achieved by his attack in echelon in Leuthen tactically.[116]

However, Schleiffen's 1912 memorandum, which was completed a few days before his death, suggests an entirely different rationale from that given in the 1905 memorandum. It is true that the principle of a continuous strategic line, which advances frontally, prevails in both memoranda, and, indeed, in the 1912 Plan Schlieffen aimed to thin out the line by employing the surplus of mass achieved through structural manipulation. It is obvious that both plans aimed at an identical goal – the destruction of the French army. The difference between the two plans, as Schlieffen himself points out, was due to a different operational effect, which he hoped to achieve. Whereas in the 1905 Plan he intended to roll the French and crush them on their eastern border by a revolving door manoeuvre which was generated by the accentuated weight of the German right wing, in the 1912 Plan he intended to attack simultaneously all along the line, and, by his quantitative superiority, to envelop both French flanks and ultimately to create a grand battle of encirclement (*Kesselschlacht*). According to von Hahnke's reports, the last memorandum was composed in somewhat conspiratorial circumstances.[117] Moreover, one wonders what caused Schlieffen to revise his plan. The new plan was not prompted by a new political situation – a consideration which, in any case, never counted in Schlieffen's opinion – nor was it influenced by the new aggressive doctrine which the French army cultivated. In both plans Schlieffen regarded the French offensive potential as immaterial. Moreover, although the 1912 memorandum refers in its title to a war against France and Russia – a new global reality – the operational part of the document did not mention the Russian or Eastern Front even once.

The motive for composing the new memorandum is provided by von Hahnke. Schlieffen's son-in-law reports that the Field Marshal composed the new plan after concluding his research on Cannae, in October 1912. Thus, the new plan was composed between October and December 1912.[118] During his years of retirement, a study of the battle of Cannae brought about a conceptual transformation. The essence of this transformation was a change from the strategical wing manoeuvre, modelled after Leuthen, to the strategical battle of encirclement, modelled after Cannae, or, rather, its more modern variant – the battle of Sedan. Schlieffen came to believe that in the new form the Germans had better chances of attaining absolute destruction of their enemy. It was the adherence to this new idea of encirclement as the perfect agent of destruction, which motivated the old Field Marshal to revise his plan.[119]

Freytag-Loringhoven, who was a close associate of Schlieffen and as such was familiar with his perceptions, confirms my argument in two expressions:

> The intention was to effect an envelopment from two sides. The envelopment by the left wing of the army, was however, brought to a standstill before the fortifications of the French eastern frontier.[120]

And later in his book, he names Schlieffen's cognitive source for his new plan, and also criticizes the concepts that prevailed before the war:

> The individual armies of the enemy may be enveloped – as happened at Tannenberg and later at Harmannstadt, where the Cannae of Schlieffen was realised. But the envelopment of the whole host of the enemy is a very difficult matter.[121]

THE PARADOX OF OPERATIONAL ASYMMETRY

Broadly speaking, the paradox of operational asymmetry derives from a contradiction between the comprehensive nature of the operational level of war and the actual manner in which this level has been perceived and exercised in the nineteenth century and the beginning of the twentieth. Whereas the operational substance combines inherently the offensive and defensive, the declared position taken by the military establishments in both Germany and France exclusively - preferred the offensive dimension. This trend was expressed unequivocally in theoretical literature as well as in the operational plans.[122]

To develop its essential qualities, which are effectuated through the interaction between a holding element and a mobile element, the operational manoeuvre must combine the defensive and the offensive in a balanced manner corresponding to the strategical circumstances. Owing to a distorted perception which originated in Clausewitz's theory, this notion, as well as the idea of operational defensive, was deliberately removed from military thinking. Moreover, in spite of the growing awareness of the increase in the lethality of firepower, patterns of manoeuvre tended to rely solely on the single dimension of offensive.

The total rejection of the defensive, on the one hand, and the forced application of the offensive, on the other, are explicitly expressed in all the leading military dissertations of the late nineteenth and the early twentieth centuries.[123] According to Gerhard Ritter, Schlieffen was possessed by an anti-defensive obsession. Whereas in the 1905 Plan, due to the realization of objective limitations, he consented to a limited mode of action in the Alsace-Lorraine sector, in 1912 he rejected any restrictions on the offensive and dictated a unilateral course of an all-out, simultaneous attack.[124]

Statements by the German generals, von Meckel and von Blume, both leading military theoreticians belonging to the intermediary generation of the 1870s, demonstrate both the prevailing approach and the logic behind the unilateral preference of the offensive. Von Meckel expresses an approach that rejects the defensive on the basis of moralistic and psychological consideration: 'The resolution to act on the defensive is the first step to irresolution.'[125] On the other hand, von Blume suggests an approach that prefers the form of operational manoeuvre that leads directly and resolutely to the attainment of destruction:

> The strategic offensive is therefore the most effective form of conducting war: it is the form which alone leads to the final aim, whatever may be the political object of the war, whether positive or negative.[126]

The obsessive rejection of the defensive calls for a study of the cognitive motives that shaped it, as well as for the sources of its power and vitality. Many historians tend to attribute to Clausewitz a positive inclination towards the defensive. Their sources are the quality of the sixth book, which is devoted to defence, and certain positive citations, usually taken out of context. To comprehend Clausewitz's true attitude to this subject, and to trace the origin of the indoctrinative power of his theory, it must be examined from a somewhat broader perspective, namely both the sixth and the seventh books of *Vom Kriege*.

Although in the sixth book Clausewitz assumes a premise that could be interpreted as a definite preference for defence, later in that book his initial positive attitude towards defence proves to be nothing more than lip service: 'Defense is simply the stronger form of war, the one that makes the enemy defeat more certain.'[127]

Von der Goltz confirms not only the fact that the Germans were never attracted by Clausewitz's positive statements about the defence, but also that they realized the true message behind the theory as a whole: 'The idea of the greater strength of the defence is, in spite of all, only a delusion . . . To make war means attacking.'[128] Thus, Clausewitz truly prefers the offensive. His positive exposition of the defence served only as an instrument to promote the first, by means of dialectical argumentation.

Clausewitz later installs the first doubts in his readers' minds by claiming that 'the weaker' was 'likely to need the defense',[129] and further argued that, 'Since defense is tied to the idea of waiting, the aim of defeating the enemy will be valid only on the condition that there is an attack'.[130]

Clearly, according to Clausewitz, the defence has no independent right of existence, and operationally, is totally dependent on attack. On the other hand the offensive is entirely independent:

> This does not apply to the attack. The offensive thrust or action is complete in itself. It does not have to be complemented by the defense.[131]

In other words, defence should be regarded as a necessary evil, and should be applied only when the positive alternative does not exist.[132] The offensive, on the other hand, is positive in its nature, since it is characterized by the qualities of manoeuvre: 'While the device of manoeuvre is common to attacker and defender, its nature is more closely related to the attack than to the defense.'[133] Moreover, the offensive expresses both the political and military initiative, insofar as it strives to attain the positive aim:

> Certainly a man who can afford to aim at the enemy's total defeat will rarely have course to the defensive, the immediate aim of which is the retention of what one has.[134]

Clausewitz closes the circle of logic and by assimilating all his ideas in a single notion thus, lays the principle which determined the course of German military thought for the future:

> The offensive should be taken by the side that possesses the political initiative – That is the side that has an active purpose, the aim for which it went to war.[135]

Clausewitz's final words are easily detected as the rationale of the future Schlieffen Plan of 1912:

> Against the enemy who is the target of the main offensive there can therefore be no such thing as a defensive in subsidiary theatres of operations. That offensive consists of the main attack and such subsidiary attacks as circumstances make necessary. This removes all need to defend any point that the offensive itself directly does not cover. The main decision is what matters. It will compensate for any loss.[136]

NOTES

1. C. von Clausewitz, *On War*, M. Howard and P. Paret (eds) (Princeton Univ. Press, 1992), B. 4, Ch. 11, p. 258.
2. A. Gat, *The Origins of Military Thought, from Enlightenment to Clausewitz* (Oxford, 1989), p. 200; J. Wallach, *Das Dogma der Vernichtungsschlacht, Die Lehren von Clausewitz und Schlieffen und ihre Wirkung in Zwei Weltkriegen* (Frankfurt, 1967). 'Misperceptions of Clausewitz's *On War* by the German Military,' in M. Handel (ed.), *Clausewitz and Modern Strategy* (London, 1986), pp. 213–16.
3. M. Howard, *Clausewitz* (Oxford Univ. Press, 1983), p. 63.
4. Foch, *The Principles of War*, trans. J. de Morinni (New York, 1918), p. 311.

5. Crown Prince Wilhelm, 'The Narrative of the Fifth German Army at the Battle of the Marne', p. 104.
6. Ibid., p. 105; Freytag-Loringhoven, *Deductions from the World War*, p. 83; A. von Schlieffen, *Cannae* (Ft. Leavenworth, KS, 1931), p. 305.
7. W. Goerlitz, *History of the German General Staff 1657–1945*, trans. B. Battershaw (New York, 1959), p. 135; G. Craig, *The Politics of the Prussian Army 1640–1945* (Oxford, 1955), pp. 279–80. Both refer to Moltke the Younger as the epigon, and attribute the German failure to crush the French in 1914 to his lack of energy, indecision and incompetence, while they name Schlieffen as the paragon who was the only one capable of executing his plan, crushing the French and deciding the war in the West within a month. This approach is uncritical, since it is based on a myth, and it does not scrutinize the Schlieffen Plan using the proper tools of examination.
8. Clausewitz, *On War*, B. 4, Ch. 11, p. 261.
9. Ibid., B. 1, Ch. 1, p. 75.
10. Ibid., p. 77; Ch. 2, p. 90.
11. Ibid.
12. Ibid., Ch. 2, p. 91. The author defines the three elements of which a political entity consists, and also the rational of the interdependence between them. Since the armed forces represent the state's physical ability to resist, their destruction will inevitably lead to the conquest of its territory, and thus to the final collapse of its moral resistance.
13. Ibid.
14. Ibid., p. 92.
15. Ibid., p. 97.
16. Ibid.
17. Ibid.
18. Ibid.
19. Von der Goltz, *The Conduct of War*, pp. 8–9.
20. Foch, *The Principles of War*, pp. 42, 311, 318, 320, 368; R. Aron, *Clausewitz Philosopher of War*, trans. C. Booker and N. Stone (New York, 1983), pp. 246–9.
21. Clausewitz, *On War*, B. 1, Ch. 2, p. 97.
22. Ibid., p. 99.
23. Ibid., p. 95.
24. Ibid.
25. Ibid., B. 7, Ch. 6, p. 529.
26. Ibid., B. 4, Ch. 3, p. 228.
27. Ibid., Ch. 11, p. 258.
28. Ibid.
29. Bernhardy, *How Germany Makes War*, p. 208, confirms that the deliberate application of destruction as a war aim satisfies both the military high command and the political administration, since it simplifies what can be expected as the most complicated issue to exist at the political-strategical level. Von der Goltz, *The Conduct of War*, pp. 127, 132, 181, refers specifically to the military field and the process of planning. In his opinion, which is based on Clausewitz's conception, the entire operational planning process focuses on the general arrangements for the coordination of movements, *per se*.
30. Cited in Caemmerer, *The Development of Strategical Science*, p. 85; Howard, *Clausewitz*, p. 60.
31. Ritter, *The Schlieffen Plan. A Critique of a Myth*, pp. 17–37; H. Delbrück, *History of the Art of War within the Framework of Political History* (4 vols.), trans. W.J. Renfroe (London, 1985), Vol. 4, p. 436. In his examination of Napoleon's expedition to Russia, the author questions the validity of his strategy of destruction in view of the relationship between his resources and the scope of his aim.
32. Ibid., pp. 17–37, 38–47, 50–51, 61–2, 157–9. In the extracts from Drafts nos. 6, 7, Schlieffen, at a certain point during his attempts to manipulate the forces at his disposal, in order to maintain the aim, admits openly that the task Germany has taken upon itself is beyond its powers. Yet, even then he did not alter the aim. Colin, *The Transformation of War*, pp. 343–4, and Lewal, in Caemmerer, *The Development of*

Strategical Science, pp. 235–9, agree to this assessment, although their formulations are more extreme.

33. Crown Prince Wilhelm, *The Narrative of the Fifth German Army in the Battle of the Marne*, p. 101.

34. Moltke, *Extracts from Moltke's Correspondence Pertaining to the War of 1870–71*, p. 172. The battles are: Spicheren, Wörth, Colombey and Vionville. Moltke, *The Franco-Prussian War*, pp. 16–19, 20–26, 30–35, 36–50; Emperor Frederick the Third, *The War Diary of Crown Prince Friedrich Wilhelm Commanding 3rd Army*, pp. 31–42; von Boguslawski, *Tactical Deductions from the War of 1870–1871*, pp. 67–8; von Blumenthal, *Journals of Field Marshal Count von Blumenthal for 1866, and 1870–71*, p. 87; P. Bronsart von Schellendorf, *Geheimes Kriegstagebuch 1870–71*, P. Rassow (ed.), (Bonn, 1954), pp. 39–42; J. von Verdy du Vernois, *With the Royal Headquarters at the War of 1870–1871* (London, 1898), pp. 45–77. The definite impression one gets from the various descriptions, including Moltke's, is that the higher levels of command neither directed the campaign nor controlled it at this stage of the war. Actually, the course of the campaign was dictated by the tactical levels, which initiated a battle whenever an opportunity arose. These battles developed into general engagements, which, according to reports by Moltke and members of the general staff, diverted the course of the campaign from that which was intended by Moltke. According to the reports offered by Moltke and Verdy, at the battle of Gravelotte, Moltke tried to repair this deficiency. After Gravelotte, Moltke changed his method of conduct and mode of command significantly, by laying out more specifically the goals and tactical objectives, although he himself likes to refrain from admitting this fact. L. Schneider, *Aus dem Leben Kaiser Wilhelms 1873*, 3 vols., (Berlin, 1888), Vol. 2, p. 139, reports that on the eve of leaving Germany for war, the Kaiser, as supreme commander, thought it unnecessary to have maps of France immediately available at royal headquarters. Since the strategic aim of the campaign was clear to all echelons of command and since it was understood that, being a precondition for its destruction, the location of the French army would dictate the initial deployment and *Aufmarsch*, one could legitimately dispense with such technicalities as maps of the theatre of operations. H.K.B. von Moltke, *Militrische Korrespondenz. Aus den Dienstschriften des Krieges 1870–1871* (Berlin, 1897), pp. 195–8. Moltke's recollection of the exchanges between himself and Steinmetz concerning the conduct of operations on 5 August provides further evidence that the common recognition of the universal aim of destruction often left the field commanders without operational guidance.

35. S. von Schlichting, *Taktische und Strategische Grundsatze der Gegenwart, teil 2, Truppenführung* (3 vols.), Berlin, 1897–1899, pp. 94–6. The bottom line of Schlichting's argument consists of two points, both of them avoiding the main operational problem. In the first he claims that in any engagement, the reaction of the tactical commander who is present on the spot constitutes only an immediate resort; matters will always be finally settled with the personal arrival of the operational commander. This of course is a very optimistic view, and in fact in an operational context, the commander in chief can very rarely arrive on every spot in which tactical incidents occur, thus this entire assumption is unoperational. The second point is that Schlichting ignores the factor of initial definition of goals and objectives by the operational command, and thus overlooks the significance of the cognitive tension. In his perception, the tactical commander is deliberately not equipped with his commander's definition of goal, or his concept of battle. Therefore, the tactical commander is supposed to guess his superior's intentions. H.K.B. von Moltke, *Moltkes Taktisch-Strategische Aufsätze aus den Jahren 1857 bis 1871* (Berlin, 1900), pp. 23–4.

36. Emperor Frederick the Third, *The War Diary of the Crown Prince*, p. 87; E. Friedrich, *Das Grosse Hauptquartier und die Deutschen Operationen im Feldzug, 1870* (Munich, 1898), maps describing the operations of 28, 29 and 31 August.

37. Clausewitz, *On War*, B. 4, Ch. 3, p. 227; Ch. 11, p. 258.

38. Ibid., Ch. 9, p. 249; Ch. 11, p. 259.

39. Ibid., B. 1, Ch. 1, p. 75; Ch. 2, p. 95. Clausewitz best discloses his logic when he identifies an army as a gathering of individual fighters: '. . . but whenever armed forces, that is armed individuals, are used, the idea of combat must be present'. Since the duel, for Clausewitz, represents the purified form of fighting, i.e. mechanical

combat, by applying its rules to the mass context, he interprets tactics. Von der Goltz, *The Conduct of War*, p. 190.

40. J. de Bloch, *Modern Weapons and Modern War*, trans. W. T. Stead (London, 1900), pp. xi, xxviii, 41, 63–92, 147–59, 319–46; Caemmerer, *The Development of Strategical Science*, pp. 173–5; T. Miller Maguire, *Notes on the Austro-Prussian War of 1866* (London, 1904), pp. 62–3; Balck, *Tactics*, Vol. 1, pp. 102–5, 173–6, 182; F.N. Maude, *Notes on the Evolution of Infantry Tactics* (London, 1905), pp. 51, 61, 82, 147; A.F. Becke, *An Introduction to the History of Tactics 1740–1905* (London, 1909), pp. 40, 44, 45, 51; D. Reitz, *Commando: A Boer Journal of the Boer War* (London, 1929), pp. 39, 42, 69–81.

41. Clausewitz, *On War*, B. 4, Ch. 4, p. 231.

42. Ibid., p. 230.

43. Ibid., B. 3, Ch. 8, pp. 194–5, 197; B. 4, Ch. 4, p. 230; B. 5, Ch. 3, p. 283.

44. Ibid., B. 4, Ch. 4, p. 230.

45. Ibid., Ch. 11, p. 260.

46. Clausewitz was responsible for the logic that claims that war is an instrument used by policy to attain its goals. *On War*, B. 1, Ch. 1, pp. 75–89; Ch. 2, pp. 90–99; B. 8, Ch. 6, pp. 603–10.

47. Ibid., B. 6, Ch. 8, p. 386.

48. H. de Jomini, *The Art of War*, trans. G.H. Mendell and W.P. Craighill (Westport, CT, 1975), pp. 178–9; Colin, *The Transformation of War*, p. 234; V. Derrecagaix, *Modern War* (Washington, 1888), Vol. 1, pp. 22–3; 232, 290, 660; Vol. 2, p. 490; D. Porch, 'Clausewitz and the French,' in Handel (ed.), *Clausewitz and Modern Strategy*, pp. 287–302.

49. Clausewitz, *On War*, B. 1, Ch. 2, p. 95.

50. Colin, *The Transformation of War*, p. 300; Boguslawski, *Deductions from the War of 1870–71*, pp. 61–3.

51. Clausewitz, *On War*, B. 4, Ch. 3, p. 227.

52. Colin, *The Transformation of War*, p. 178; Foch, *The Principles of War*, p. 311; von der Goltz, *The Conduct of War*, p. 8.

53. Clausewitz, *On War*, B. 4, Ch. 9, p. 248.

54. Ibid.

55. Ibid., B. 5, Ch. 5, p. 293.

56. Ibid., B. 6, Ch. 8, p. 386.

57. Bernhardy, *How Germany Makes War*, p. 197; Foch, *The Principles of War*, pp. 8, 42–3, 45; Lewal, *Strategie de Combat*, Vol. 1, pp. 3, 35; Vol. 2, p. 189. Both Foch and Lewal doubted whether there was any need at all to maintain strategy. This contemptuous attitude towards strategy is in fact expressed in the title of Lewal's book.

58. Colin, *The Transformation of War*, pp. 330, 331; Caemmerer, *The Development of Strategical Science*, p. 264; von der Goltz, *The Conduct of War*, pp. 35, 183, 188; G.A. Bonnal, *Froeschwiller: Récit Commenté des Évènements . . . du 15 Juillet au 12 Août 1870* (Paris, 1899), p. 445.

59. Moltke, 'Extracts from Moltke's Correspondence Pertaining to the War of 1870–71,' Extraction no. 20, 'Memorandum to the Chiefs of Sections of the Great General Staff' pp. 172–6; von der Goltz, *The Conduct of War*, pp. 161–2, 181, 187–8; H.K.B. von Moltke, *Militärische Korrespondenz. Aus den Dienstschriften des Krieges 1870–71* (Berlin, 1897), p. 219; Generalstab, Kriegsgeschichtliche Abteilung (ed.), *Kriegs-geschichtliche Einzelschriften, Heft 17: Truppenfahrzeuge, Kolonnen und Trains bei den Bewegungen der I, und der II Deutschen Armee bis zu den Schlachten Westlich Metz* (Berlin, 1895), pp. 461–3; W. Foerster (ed.), *Prinz Friedrich Karl von Preussen: Denkwürdigkeiten aus Seinem Leben* (2 vols.) (Stuttgart, 1910), Vol. II, pp. 225, 228–9, explains how, according to this logic, the manoeuvres of the entire German army and that of the third army in particular were devised at the battle of Gravelotte-St Privat.

60. Colin, *The Transformation of War*, p. 333.

61. Ritter, *The Schlieffen Plan*, p. 176. In his adherence to the model of Cannae, Schlieffen did not just copy the linear pattern, which he magnified more than a hundred times, but also the mode of deploying the cavalry in the wings. This archaic mode suits tactical situations which are limited in space and volume, but is entirely irrelevant in operational situations on a huge scale.

101

62. Clausewitz, *On War*, B. 4, Ch. 9, p. 248.
63. Caemmerer, *The Development of Strategical Science*, pp. 244–9, cites Schlichting, who describes this entire process at length; W. von Hahnke, *Die Operationen der III Armee* (Berlin, 1873), pp. 48–9; Generalstab, Kriegsgeschichtliche Abteilung (ed.), *Kriegsgeschichtliche Einzelschriften, Heft 18: Das Generalkommando des III Armee Korps bei Spicheren und Vionville* (Berlin, 1895), pp. 579–80.
64. Moltke, *The Franco–German War*, pp. 16–19, 20–26, 30–35, 36–50; Emperor Frederick the Third, *The War Diary of Crown Prince Friedrich Wilhelm Commanding 3rd Army*, pp. 31–42; Verdy du Vernois, *With the Royal Headquarters in the War of 1870–71*, pp. 67–8.
65. G. von Widdern, *Kritische Tage* (5 vols.) (Berlin, 1897–1900), Vol. I, pp. 57–9, 104; Vol. II, p. 134; Vol. III, pp. 112–22; Generalstab Kriegsgeschichtliche Abteilung (ed.), *Der Deutsch-Französische Krieg 1870–71* (5 vols.) (Berlin, 1872–81), pp. 104, 163, 167, 202, 203; Moltke, *Militärische Korrespondenz*, pp. 199–200, 201; P. Bronsart von Schellendorff, *Geheimes Kriegstagebuch 1870–71*, p. 38; C.E. von Schell, *The Operations of the First Army under General von Steinmetz* (London, 1873), pp. 126–131; G. Zernin, *Das Leben des Generals August von Goeben* (2 vols.) (Berlin, 1895–97), Vol. II, p. 56; von Verdy du Vernois, *With the Royal Headquarters in 1870–71*, p. 65.
66. Emperor Frederick the Third, *The War Diary of Crown Prince Friedrich Wilhelm*, pp. 31–42.
67. Forbes, *My Experience of the War between France and Germany*, pp. 142–3; L. Bamberger, *Bismarcks Grosses Spiel. Die Geheime Tagebücher Ludwig Bambergers*, E. Feder (ed.) (Frankfurt a. M., 1932), p. 173; A.T.E. von Roon, *Denkwürdigkeiten aus dem Leben des General-Feldmarschalls Kriegministers Grafen von Roon* (3. vols.) (Breslau, 1897), Vol. 3, p. 193; F. Höning, *Dokumentarische-Kritische Darstellung der Strategie für die Schlacht von Vionville-Mars-la-Tour* (Berlin, 1899), pp. 119–26.
68. Moltke, *The Franco-German War*, pp. 51–60; Verdy du Vernois, *With The Royal Headquarters at the War of 1870–71*, pp. 45–77.
69. Clausewitz, *On War*, B. 4, Ch. 9, p. 259.
70. Ibid., p. 258.
71. Ibid., Ch. 11, pp. 259–60.
72. Ibid., p. 261.
73. Ibid.
74. Colin, *The Transformation of War*, p. 164; Moltke, 'Extractions from Moltke's Correspondence Pertaining to the War of 1870–71,' extract no. 101, p. 183.
75. Ritter, *The Schlieffen Plan*, pp. 67–8; A.D. von Zoellner, 'Schlieffens Vermächtnis', *Militärwissenschaftliche Rundschau* Sonderheft, 4 Jan. 1938, pp. 48–52.
76. Clausewitz, *On War*, B. 3, Ch. 15, p. 215.
77. Ibid.; ibid., B. 4, Ch. 2, p. 215. Caemmerer, *The Development of Strategical Science*, p. 252.
78. Clausewitz, *On War*, B. 7, Ch. 7, p. 330.
79. Ibid., p. 330.
80. Ibid., B. 8, Ch. 9, p. 625; and also, B. 4, Ch. 11 p. 261. This was the logic behind Moltke's manoeuvres at Gravelotte-St. Privat and Sedan. Following the war of 1870, the pattern of encirclement, applied by Moltke in the Sedan operation, came to be identified more and more with destruction.
81. Howard, *Clausewitz*, p. 15.
82. Colin, *The Transformation of War*, p. 231.
83. Caemmerer, *The Development of Strategical Science*, p. 176.
84. Von der Goltz, *The Conduct of War*, p. 188. On p. 190 von der Goltz uses the term manipulation to describe this specific process.
85. Boguslawski, *Tactical Deductions from the War of 1870–71*, pp. 56, 58, 60, 80, 87; Generalstab, Kriegsgeschichtliche Abteilung (ed.), *Studien zur Kriegsgeschichte und Taktik, V: Der 18 August 1870* (Berlin, 1906), pp. 90–91, 148–56, 166; K.C. Zu Hohenlohe-Ingelfingen, *Aus Meinem Leben: Aufzeichnungen aus den Jahren 1848–1871* (Berlin, 1907), p. 267. Moltke, *Militärische Korrespondenz. Aus den Dienstschriften des Krieges 1870–71*, p. 234.
86. Ibid., pp. 75–7.

87. Howard, 'Men Against Fire, Expectations of War in 1914,' p. 12.
88. Reported by Archibald Forbes as he witnessed it at Vionville and by the correspondent of the *Daily News* as he witnessed it at Gravelotte. Forbes, *My Experience of the War Between France and Germany*, Vol. 1, pp. 142–43; *The Daily News Correspondence of the War Between Germany and France 1870-71*, pp. 49–50.
89. Freytag-Loringhoven, *Deduction From The First World War*, p. 71
90. Colin, *The Transformations of War*, p. 207.
91. Von der Goltz, *The Conduct of War*, pp., 34, 45, 151; Bernhardy, *How Germany Makes War*, pp. 189, 197.
92. Caemmerer, *The Development of Strategical Science*, pp. 251–2.
93. Clausewitz, *On War*, B. 5, Ch. 10, p. 314; Colin, *The Transformation of War*, pp. 207, 305
94. Ibid., pp. 210, 326. On p. 326 Colin portrays the advance of the operational linear mass as 'an immense steam roller, which pushes and crushes everything on its way'.
95. Ibid., pp. 304–5
96. Ibid., pp. 327–8. The author determines that a marching corps should occupy a space of 10 sq km.
97. *Stratégie de Combat*, Vol. 2, p. 181. Lewal allocates a front of 6 km to an advancing army corps.
98. Lewal applied his concepts in manoeuvres which he conducted in the Paris area in 1894.
99. Ritter, *The Schlieffen Plan*, 'The Memorandum of 1905', p. 145.
100. P. Kennedy, 'Military Effectiveness in the First World War' in A.R. Millett and W. Murray (eds), *Military Effectiveness in the First World War* (Boston, 1988), Vol. 1, pp. 329–50.
101. Clausewitz, *On War*, B. 5, Ch. 4, p. 285.
102. Ibid., pp. 285–7.
103. Ibid., B. 3, Ch. 13, pp. 210–11.
104. Colin, *The Transformation of War*, p. 239.
105. Ritter, *The Schlieffen Plan*, pp. 134–61.
106. Ibid., p. 174.
107. Fuller, *The Conduct of War 1789-1961*, pp. 155–6; L.C.F. Turner, 'The Significance of the Schlieffen Plan,' in P. Kennedy (ed.), *The War Plans of the Great Powers 1880-1914* (Boston, 1979), pp. 199–227.
108. Schlieffen, *Gesammelte Schriften*, Vol. 1, p. 17; Freytag-Loringhoven's account, based on a letter he received from Schlieffen, was cited by Zoellner, 'Schlieffens Vermächtnis', p. 51.
109. Ritter, *The Schlieffen Plan*, pp. 50–51.
110. Clausewitz, *On War*, B. 6, Ch. 2, p. 360.
111. Ibid., Ch. 3, p. 363.
112. Lewal, *Stratégie de Combat*, Vol. 2, p. 31; Caemmerer, *The Development of Strategical Science*, pp. 220–71.
113. Von der Goltz, *The Conduct of War*, p. 154; the breakthrough, penetration or slashing attack, at the operational level, constitute a typical columnar manoeuvre, based upon mobility and depth. Caemmerer, *Development of Strategical Science*, pp. 256, 263; von Schlichting, *Taktische und Strategisch Grundsätze der Gegenwart, Teil 2, Truppenführung*, Vol. 2, pp. 16, 94.
114. Freytag-Loringhoven, *Deductions from the World War*, pp. 73–4.
115. Colin, *The Transformation of War*, pp. 166–7, 179; von der Goltz, *The Conduct of War*, pp. 161–6; W. von Falkenhausen, *Der Grosse Krieg der Yetzeit* (Berlin, 1909), pp. 171–6; *Flankenbewegung und Massenheer* (Berlin, 1898), pp. 33–7.
116. Bernhardy, *How Germany Makes War*, pp. 190–91.
117. Ritter, *The Schlieffen Plan*, pp. 179–80.
118. Ibid., Hahnke's notes.
119. A. von Schlieffen, *Cannae* (Ft. Leavenworth, KS, 1931), pp. 297–8, 300, 305; H. von Seeckt, *Gedanken Eines Soldaten* (Berlin, 1929), p. 17, refers to Schlieffen's concept of Cannae as most disastrous. L. Freiherr von Gebsattel, *Generalfeldmarschall Karl von Bülow* (Munich, 1929), pp. 14–40, describes von Bülow's objection to Schlieffen's concept of strategic encirclement.

120. Freytag-Loringhoven, *Deductions from the World War*, p. 78.
121. Ibid., p. 80.
122. The Schlieffen Plan and Plan XVII.
123. Colin, *The Transformation of War*, pp. 192, 309, 331, 355; von der Goltz, *The Conduct of War*, pp. 35–41, 42–6, 52–4; Bernhardy, *How Germany Makes War*, pp. 144, 158; Foch, *The Principles of War*, pp. 312–3, 324.
124. Ritter, *The Schlieffen Plan*, pp. 134–148, 168–178.
125. Caemmerer, *The Development of Strategical Science*, p. 95.
126. C.W. von Blume, *Strategie* (Berlin, 1882), p. 201.
127. Clausewitz, *On War*, B. 6, Ch. 8, p. 380.
128. Von der Goltz, *The Conduct of War*, pp. 276, 284.
129. Clausewitz, *On War*, B. 6, Ch. 5, p. 370.
130. Ibid., Ch. 8, p. 380.
131. Ibid., B. 7, Ch. 1, p. 524.
132. Ibid.
133. Ibid., Ch. 13, p. 541.
134. Ibid., B. 8, Ch. 4, p. 600.
135. Ibid., Ch. 5, p. 601.
136. Ibid., Ch. 9, p. 624.

4

The *Blitzkrieg* Concept:
A Mechanized Manipulation of
Tactical Patterns

THE *BLITZKRIEG* MYTH

The German *Blitzkrieg* concept is a typical historical myth. As will be seen, reality and fantasy are interwoven to such an extent that it is often difficult to distinguish between cause and effect. It is, therefore, important to dismantle the myth, thereby further revealing the methodological problems involved in research of the subject.

The basic premise of the present chapter is that the term *Blitzkrieg* is a pretentious title, resulting from a union of opportunistic technocratism and ideological trends, which were entirely alien to professional military management.[1] The rationale behind this synthesis was destruction, and the path to its achievement led through a manipulative mobilization of technology and a simplistic attempt to magnify the tactical patterns of infiltration and encirclement. Thus, at its basis the *Blitzkrieg* not only lacked operational coherence but, as will be seen, its actual formation dictated relinquishing a systemic approach to military conduct.[2] The phenomenon which allowed the *Wehrmacht* to attain such impressive achievements at the beginning of the war and afforded it a breathing space from the winter of 1942 was the manifestation of German tactical excellence at all field echelons, on the one hand, and the poor performance of their opponents, on the other. However, it should be remembered that this tactical excellence crystallized during the long years of pedantic work which preceded both the National Socialists' ascendance to power and the formulation of the *Blitzkrieg* concept.[3]

This chapter presents an elaborate reconstruction of the general historical background that induced the formulation of the *Blitzkrieg* concept, and defines both the nature of the conflict between the conservative school of professionals and the school of opportunistic technocrats, and its immediate consequence, notably the bastardization of strategic management. This analytical method will not only delineate the deliberate destruction of operational cognition – a process that the *Wehrmacht* underwent from 1933 until 1938 – but will also clarify the evolution of the circumstances which prevented it from formulating an operational theory. This will be followed by an elaboration of the cognitive sources of the *Blitzkrieg*. By examining the manipulation of the tactical patterns of infiltration and encirclement, the real substance of *Blitzkrieg* will be exposed. Finally, a critical analysis of the *Blitzkrieg* experience, using various operational criteria will illuminate the results of replacing an operational cognition with an approach of aggressive opportunism, and a coherent theory with magnified patterns of fighting techniques.

An investigation of the origins of the term *Blitzkrieg* sheds little light on its operational substance. *Blitzkrieg* is commonly defined as a hyper-violent offensive pattern, designed to defeat the opposition by means of surprise, speed and superiority of material and fire.[4] Thus the question arises whether this impression reflects an unintelligible interpretation of a coherent concept or the best result of an effort to elucidate the English translation of the figurative term, 'lightning war'.

In his introduction to F.O. Miksche's book, a work that demonstrates the most serious endeavour to pursue the theoretical aspects of *Blitzkrieg*, Tom Wintringham writes:

> This is a textbook of modern warfare. It is the only textbook that I know that deals with war as the Germans have shaped it. It is necessarily incomplete, but I believe it will give in general outline a clear picture to the attentive reader of a pattern of warfare that is logically complete, that hangs together.[5]

What Wintringham's remark implies is not only the fact that even after conducting its two most successful *Blitzkrieg* campaigns the *Wehrmacht* still did not possess a universal textbook for operations, but also that a coherent pattern for conducting modern operations can be formulated without any theoretical basis.[6]

The vagueness surrounding the idea of *Blitzkrieg* tends to increase when one turns to more recent interpretations. Regarding the linguistic derivation of the term, Kenneth Macksey, Guderian's biographer, attributes its invention to Hitler in 1936.[7] L.H. Addington, another expert on the subject, claims that the term was coined by the *London Times* in its 25th September 1939 issue,[8] while B.H. Liddell

Hart credited himself with both the creation of the idea as well as the term, and credited the Germans merely with the translation of the term 'lightning war' into German.[9] Historians fare no better. The majority ascribe the *Blitzkrieg* idea to the British school, consisting of B.H. Liddell Hart and J.F.C. Fuller;[10] others claim that Guderian was its originator;[11] and a few point in other directions such as Schlieffen or even Ludwig Beck who was Guderian's most bitter antagonist.[12] The linguistic origins of the term and its inventor are not within the scope of this chapter, however, the mere existence of the controversy accentuates the obscurity embracing the concept – a fact which in itself contributes to the volume of the *Blitzkrieg* myth.

Aided by a profound knowledge of the history of the *Wehrmacht* and great critical discernment, van Creveld managed to summarize in a single sentence the circumstances which brought about the emergence of the *Blitzkrieg* myth: 'The *Wehrmacht* achieved some triumphs so great and unexpected, that they have become almost legendary'.[13] It was not the *Wehrmacht* itself that promoted the legend, since the same human composition had been defeated by the Allies less than a generation earlier. The significant change that occurred in 1939 derived primarily from the mode in which the *Wehrmacht's* successes were interpreted. The term *Blitzkrieg* became almost a magic word since it provided not only a metaphor denoting the tempo and dimensions of the *Wehrmacht's* performance, but also a means of expressing helplessness and a consciousness of inferiority among Western armies. The proliferation of a myth emphasizing the attachment of a violent and revolutionary type of armoured manoeuvre to the German natural fighting excellence seems obvious because the glorification of the *Wehrmacht* afforded an easy excuse for its defeated adversaries.

Evidence suggested by some of the *Blitzkrieg* originators corroborates the fact that even the *Wehrmacht's* higher echelons of command lost any sense of professional criticism due to the impact of the *Blitzkrieg* myth:

> The *Wehrmacht's* successes especially the recent victory so quickly won in the West had impressed the high command to such an extent that they had deleted the word impossible from their vocabulary.[14]

On 3 July 1941, Colonel-General Franz Halder, the Army Chief of the General Staff, wrote in his diary: 'I am not exaggerating when I say that the campaign against Russia was won within two weeks'.[15] The euphoria of the *Wehrmacht's* operational leaders regarding the tangible potentialities of the *Blitzkrieg* raises second thoughts about the validity of its professional basis and operational motive.

The contemporary vigour of the *Blitzkrieg* myth is best reflected in the American attitude. Four decades after defeating the executors of the *Blitzkrieg*, and amidst the process of formulating an intrinsic operational theory, the Americans tended to dwarf their own achievements and still referred to the *Blitzkrieg* concept as the most creative manoeuvre doctrine ever created.

> German operational art in World War II emphasized manoeuvre, whereas, U.S. operational art, with some notable exceptions, tended to emphasize the application of firepower to achieve the attrition of the enemy forces.[16]

At first sight, the sequence of the German operational defeats, starting in Autumn 1942, posed a serious challenge to the myth of *Blitzkrieg* invincibility. Nevertheless, the entire cadre of the *Wehrmacht's* high ranking officers unanimously attributed the ultimate failure of the brilliant method of *Blitzkrieg* to Hitler's amateurish strategic conduct and his coercive management of military operations.[17] Thus, by employing retrospectively a deceptive mode of argumentation, the German generals harmonized the historical and logical inconsistencies, preserved their professional prestige and added yet another layer to the already existing myth.

Apart from the *Wehrmacht's* stunning operational achievements in the first two years of the war, it was Liddell Hart's magic touch that contributed the main volume to the *Blitzkrieg* myth. Moreover, Liddell Hart in his postwar writings created the professional essence of the *Blitzkrieg* myth and also determined the course of its development.[18] The importance of presenting Michael Geyer's critical stance regarding this issue derives from the fact that it discloses not only Liddell Hart's historical deception, but also the fact that in reality the concept of *Blitzkrieg* lacked any operational qualities:

> It was the opposite of a doctrine. *Blitzkrieg* consisted of an avalanche of actions that were sorted out less by design than by success. In hindsight – and with some help from Liddell Hart – this torrent of action was squeezed into something it never was: an operational design.[19]

Thus, by manipulative contrivance, Liddell Hart caused threefold damage to modern historical and military research. First, by distorting the actual historical circumstances of the *Blitzkrieg* formation he obscured its temporal and cognitive origins. Second, through his indoctrinated idealization of an ostentatious concept he perpetuated a historical and professional error and likewise reinforced the myth of the *Blitzkrieg*. And finally, by imposing retrospectively his own perceptions of mobile warfare upon the shallow concept of *Blitzkrieg*, he created a theoretical imbroglio that has taken more than 40 years to unravel. The early-1950s display of the transformed version of *Blitzkrieg* as a historical fact, carrying the joint signature of Liddell Hart and Guderian, lent it an authentic touch and a professional legitimacy that could not be shaken. Moreover, through this joint manipulation Liddell Hart became the patron of the theoretical realm of manoeuvre warfare, and the *Wehrmacht* generals were accepted as the empirical authority in the operational field and given a free hand in interpreting their own wartime activities.

The main evidence confirming Liddell Hart's deliberate conversion of the amorphous concept of *Blitzkrieg* into an authoritative theory for manoeuvre warfare is provided by the extensive and well-documented correspondence between him, Field Marshal Manstein, Rommel's associates and relatives, and Col. Gen. Heinz Guderian.[20] An exchange of letters between Liddell Hart and Guderian from the summer of 1949, intended to provide a comprehensive interpretation of the *Blitzkrieg* essentials, is particularly enlightening since it discloses the fact that Liddell Hart imposed his own fabricated version of *Blitzkrieg* on the latter and compelled him to proclaim it as the original formula.[21]

Since a secretive *modus operandi* or collusion had been achieved between the purported creator of the *Blitzkrieg* theory and its implementors, modern research was obliged to accept their joint version of *Blitzkrieg* as almost axiomatic, and thus it was deprived of any tools of criticism regarding the *Wehrmacht*'s operational activity. Moreover, since the early 1950s all efforts of scholars or military professionals to discover the authentic formula of *Blitzkrieg* have ended up presenting Liddell Hart's postwar dicta.[22]

The proximity in time of the publication of Liddell Hart's tendentious report on his talks with the German generals and the English edition of Guderian's memoirs not only determined the mythical image of *Blitzkrieg*, but attracted the world's attention to the Rommels, Mansteins and, above all, to Guderian himself as the creators of the German *Panzertruppe* and the moulders of the tactical concept of their utilization.[23]

Due to the apparent scarcity of works dealing with the *Reichswehr*'s operational concepts and the development of the armoured forces prior to the National Socialists' rise to power, the Liddell Hart historical manipulation encouraged further distortions and legitimized additional fabrications. One of these convolutions centred on Guderian's autobiographical account, depicting the creation of the German armoured troops and the invention of their employment conception as his individual venture and private achievement. Guderian, with significant support from Liddell Hart, created this impression by combining literary methods and an instrumental approach to history. He nullified almost completely the intellectual contribution of some highly articulate military theoreticians who were active in the late 1920s, to the development of operational thought in the German armed forces.[24] Guderian further played down the performance and exploits of specialists, staff officers from the Command of Motorized Troops, and General Staff officers in promoting the idea of mechanization and the building of armoured forces.[25] Finally, he deliberately suppressed any evidence that could indicate traces of foreign conceptual influence, except that of the British theoreticians, Liddell Hart and Fuller. This trend is particularly conspicuous in light of the following facts: Germany maintained intensive cooperative connections with the Red Army for more than a decade; the Soviets were a long way ahead of the *Reichswehr* both in the field of operational theory and in the practical field of force building and manoeuvres; and, finally, in both Russia and Austria theoretical evidence had been discovered proving the existence of advanced operational concepts preceding that of the *Blitzkrieg*.[26] On the other hand, Guderian created the impression that his contribution to the creation of the armoured forces and the *Blitzkrieg* theory was essential, by emphasizing his individual activities in a most detailed manner as well as by projecting a paternal image whenever referring to the *Panzertruppen*.[27] However, an examination of Guderian's account of the formulation of operational concepts gives the impression that the entire process lacked intrinsic roots and proceeded in a random manner, involving only junior levels.[28]

The most severe distortion to emerge from Guderian's autobiographical version concerns the exposition of the conflict with the General Staff and mainly with Colonel General Ludwig Beck. This distortion, which was later transformed into a myth on its own account, described the process of forming the German armoured troops as a bitter struggle conducted single-handedly by Guderian against a backward and reactionary opposition. The myth introduces Beck as a defeatist, a mean-spirited and narrow-minded reactionary lacking operational comprehension and technical faculties.[29] The full impact of this myth was manifested when Charles Messenger not only confirmed Guderian's version but also referred to the German operational manual (*HD-300 Truppenführung*), which was composed mainly by Beck himself, as an archaic and insignificant pamphlet.[30]

The retrospective selection of Beck as the representative of the opposition to the armoured progressive avant-garde in Germany reflects Liddell Hart's own perception of his controversy with the traditionalists in the British Defence establishment.[31] Guderian's definition of Beck as his adversary restrained, *ab initio*, any potential dissension to such an argument, since even among his associates Beck was regarded as an acrimonious personality.[32] Moreover, by accentuating the reluctance of the figure who served as chief of the General Staff until 1938, Guderian afforded himself a clear excuse for failures that otherwise could have been attributed to the Command of Mobile Forces (*Kommando der Schnellen Truppen*) which was headed by him since 20 November 1938.[33] And finally, by focusing the reader's attention on a specific persona, representing the entire opposition to progress, Guderian transformed the contest between the conservative professional school of General Staff officers and the school of the opportunistic technocrats from the principle level to a personal level, and thus distracted critical attention from the real confrontation that engulfed the *Wehrmacht* during the 1930s.

The strangest aspect of the myth is that apart from being a demanding perfectionist and an embittered person to some measure, Ludwig Beck was an intellectual soldier, possessing strategic vision and operational inspiration, who had been trained according to the professional standards of the General Staff tradition. The best evidence vindicating Beck's professional qualities is provided by the 1936 command manual.[34] This unique document not only demonstrated operational thinking at its best, a rare phenomenon among the officers of the *Wehrmacht*'s generation, but, in Martin van Creveld's words, it lent the *Wehrmacht* both the cognitive basis and the technical derivation for its wartime tactical excellence:

> The best way to understand the German Army's views as to what really matters in war is to quote directly from the official manual *Truppenführung* (roughly translated as 'command of troops') of 1936. Its two volumes are signed by two successive commanders in chief, Generals Kurt von Hammerstein Equord and Werner von Fritsch.[35]

The practical application of tactical excellence has always been by means of fighting power, or *Kampfkraft* as it is called in German, and this constituted the central theme of both the manual and the *Reichswehr*'s training priorities.[36] As will be observed later, it was the *Wehrmacht*'s tactical excellence which bore the burden of the *Blitzkrieg* myth through the entire course of the war. Moreover, counterpoising the *Blitzkrieg*'s pretensions for operational virtuosity by presenting the *Wehrmacht*'s tactical eminence exposes more than anything the real proportions of the myth. This last point was explicitly manifested in F.O. Miksche's theoretical dissertation on the *Blitzkrieg*:

> Therefore the doctrines of the *Blitzkrieg* should not be considered as

111

novelties, but as the new application of the simple classic theories of military science . . . The secret of the *Blitzkrieg* lies not in German material superiority, but mainly in the allies' tactical inferiority.[37]

THE DECLINE OF OPERATIONAL COGNITION

The great importance of comprehending the evolutionary contest between the two schools of thought in the *Wehrmacht* until 1938, which the *Blitzkrieg* myth has striven to conceal, derives from the fact that it provided both the historical conditions for the destruction of operational cognition and the instrumental approach which led to the rise of the *Blitzkrieg* concept.[38] The present section will analyse the deliberate process, lasting from 1933 until 1938, which completely destroyed the *Wehrmacht's* capability to produce a comprehensive theory of operational manoeuvre; it will prove that the *Blitzkrieg* not only lacked any operational basis, but its very emergence required the precondition of suppressing operational cognition. Moreover, a critical examination of the contest between the schools will refute the part of the myth relating to Beck, which was created jointly by Liddell Hart and Guderian.

The historical conjuncture in which the opportunistic technocratic trend emerged within the armed forces involved the occurrence of two developments in the wake of the First World War in Germany.[39] The exploits of a military avant-garde group, operating in the decade that preceded the National Socialist rise to power, constituted the first phenomenon and produced the ethical and perceptional back-ground.[40] The group, which consisted mainly of members of the Operational Section of the Truppenamt, was led by Werner von Blomberg and Joachim von Stülpnagel. It crystallized in the course of the penetrating debate, which involved the entire defence establish-ment in the late 1920s, regarding the creation of a concept for a quick operational decision in a future war. The group's activity constituted an intellectual centre of gravity to counter the approaches adopted by von Seeckt's conservative group on the questions of the military's role in directing the national strategy and the preferable operational method for attaining decision in a defensive situation. These 'Young Turks' advocated the broadening of the basis of participants in the process of strategic conduct through the integration of the military in the national structure. In their attempts to produce operational solutions to Germany's strategic problems, the group's members suggested radical and creative methods which competed with the prevailing traditional patterns. One typical product of this innovative activity in the theoretical field concerned the formulation of concepts and patterns for combining national guerrilla elements (*Volkskrieg*), operating as a holding or eroding force, with regular forces, which would represent the conventional manoeuvring element. Another subject that attracted much of the group's intellectual energy was the attempts to restore operational mobility to warfare by means of developing advanced manoeuvring concepts for mechanized and armoured formations.[41]

Thus, the precedent set by the stimulative performance of an intellectual group challenging the traditional military establishment provided the perceptional background for a future growth of unconventional approaches to warfare, and likewise produced the organizational and ethical mechanisms that would encourage trends deviating from traditional military professionalism. Moreover, the voluntary association with National Socialist ideology by two of the group's prominent personalities, von Blomberg and Guderian, guaranteed not only a further consistency with the group's conceptual line, but also allowed the amalgamation of its ideas with those of Hitler's, and thus accelerated the imposition of opportunism and a technocratic state of mind in the armed forces.

The ideological stimulus, the political strategic dynamism, and the mental incentive which caused the emergence of opportunistic technocratism yielded the other historical developments, namely the National Socialists' rise to power. Nazi ideology emphasized the militant aspect of the regime as a political system aiming at expansion:

> Thus National Socialist war was radically different from the élite traditions of European land warfare. National Socialist war was war for the sake of social reconstruction through the destruction of conquered societies.[42]

For the cadre of professional officers, the military purports of Nazi ideology constituted the most difficult item to digest in the process of becoming opportunistic technocrats. Nevertheless, it was this same militant ideology that generated the new and rewarding politico-strategic dynamism and provided the aggressive Teutonic literary foundation for the *Blitzkrieg*.

The political-strategic dynamism initiated by Hitler derived its vehemence from a fourfold complex of principles: the reinstatement of Germany's military might; the restoration of the lost territories by exploiting the regained military might; the ingathering of the German-speaking populations dwelling in East and Central Europe under German rule; and the annexation of living space in the East purported to be essential for the growth of the German nation.[43] The German officers could hardly resist such baits, since the basic pre-condition for the entire strategic programme implied rearmament and augmentation of the armed forces, and these promised action, prosperity, glory and the restoration of the armed forces to the centre of the national stage.[44]

At this point, the majority of German officers were thrown into a state of confusion since the attractions offered by Hitler's military aspirations were counterbalanced by a deep resentment of the racial and chauvinistic aspects of Nazi ideology. Nevertheless, Hitler's allure prevailed and a remedy for the embarrassment caused by the vociferous tones of Nazi ideology was found by deliberately dis-regarding them.[45] Ignoring the ideological aspects of Hitler's political agenda would ultimately cost the high command the conduct of strategy.

Hitler's initial promises for rearmament and augmentation of the armed forces instantly triggered a sharp division in the German officer corps. The majority tended to follow the course charted by Hitler, whereas a small group of professional conservatives, possessed of operational cognition, formed an oppositional nucleus around Ludwig Beck. Thus, the professional unity of the German officer corps was broken and, with the emerging schism, the denun-ciation of traditional principles and professional patterns was sanc-tioned. The combination of this last phenomenon with the growing inclination, encouraged by the Nazi temperament, to perform in a dashing, tenacious and prodigious manner contributed the principal mental stimulation inciting the emergence of both opportunistic management and technocratic conduct.

The conservative school of professionals was centred around a small nucleus of General Staff officers who preferred loyalty to their professional consciousness over the benefits and glory offered by Hitler. It was this school that led the *Reichswehr*, until 1933, to the achievement of its unique tactical excellence. The group's pro-fessional and ethical ideas remained a source of admiration even after Hitler's rise to power. Nonetheless, the loss of its physical unity as against the attractions posed by the Nazi regime caused the debilita-tion of its professional authority, leaving its few members with a handful of sublime, but unpopular operational notions.[46] Starting in 1933, the General Staff school's contention, led by Beck, centred on three issues: preserving the army's professional unity and quality, retaining the strategic planning and the operational conduct in the hands of the military high command, and keeping German military strategy anchored in a rational and realistic context.[47] The attempt to

114

apply the professional standards of the *Reichswehr* to the *Wehrmacht* dictated the retention of the older model's quantitative dimensions. However, since this implied the preservation of the old system of harsh selection and tedious promotion, Beck's effort was doomed to failure from the start. The surrender of strategic planning and operational conduct to Hitler gradually became the price the officer corps paid for repressing their aversion to Nazi ideology, whereas rational strategy in the form of operational defensive was interpreted under the growing wave of German chauvinism as pure defeatism.[48] In spite of the fact that neither Guderian nor any other *Wehrmacht* general has ever openly admitted the division of the German officer corps into two opposing factions, the actual existence of a General Staff school is clear from Guderian's own account:

> Since he [i.e. Beck] inevitably chose men with much of his own attitude to fill the more important General Staff posts, and even more so to form his own close circle, as time went on he erected – without wishing to do so – a barrier of reaction at the very centre of the Army.[49]

Defining the nature of the school of opportunistic technocrats is a more difficult task – its obvious lack of homogeneity being only one reason among many. This school, which in the course of time attracted the majority of the *Wehrmacht*'s officer corps, did not possess a common cognitive denominator nor did it have any sort of corroborated operational conception. Its *raison d'être* was based on violent competition to achieve a tactical optimization of Hitler's intentions by means of the pattern perceived as *Blitzkrieg*. Thus, the school entirely lacked the essential mechanism of group consciousness. The German historian Michael Geyer managed, in his penetrating analysis, not only to disclose the opportunistic nature of the *Wehrmacht*'s technocratism, but also to prove its direct linkage to the concept of *Blitzkrieg*:

> This kind of operation [i.e., *Blitzkrieg*] befitted a generation of exceedingly ambitious German commanders who were set free by the Third Reich and who emulated in the military field the mobilizing strategy of Hitler. Not that any of them was a committed National Socialist, but they fitted well into a system that honoured success in the pursuit of conquest.[50]

Both Werner von Fritsch, the Commander in Chief of the army until 1938, and Ludwig Beck, its Chief of the General Staff, defined the characteristics of the opponent school, when referring specifically to Guderian, as: opportunism, lack of professional criticism when obeying Hitler's orders, an inclination to focus on technical issues and tactical matters, improbity, and a penchant for daring performance.[51]

Guderian, who undoubtedly represented beyond any doubt the ideal officer in the school of opportunistic technocrats was evaluated by members of his own school, whose military origin had been more traditional, as a unique technician, excellent tactician, a diligent, aggressive and brave officer, and a loyal general to his troops. However, the same sources noted the absence of general staff qualities and faculties in his personality, mentioning, among others, his lack of operational vision, his lack of professional criticism, and above all his lack of political maturity.[52] Erwin Rommel, another legendary representative of the technocratic school, was assessed by his colleagues and subordinates, who had been disciples of the General Staff tradition, as a daring and aggressive master of junior tactics, yet lacking operational vision or an understanding of the essence of modern war.[53]

The National Socialists' rise to power hampered the *Wehrmacht*'s grasp of the operational conception. The subsequent decline of the General Staff school caused the final loss of operational patterns of planning, thinking and direction. The best evidence confirming the existence of operational cognition prior to the year 1938 was provided by the operational command manual – the *Truppenführung HD-300*. Indeed, the best way to understand the professional credo, the operational logic and the perceptional achievements of the General Staff school is to study its cardinal production: the *Truppenführung*. Composed and published under the jurisdiction of Ludwig Beck as Chief of the General Staff, this manual reflects truisms in the context of their time, unlike later versions and officers' personal accounts that emerged after the war.[54]

The manual was intended to provide a universal formula to serve as a cognitive basis for the training and education of the German officer corps and the preparation of the entire armed forces for any type of future conflict. Moreover, the manual aimed at setting an intellectual framework, in the form of a general theoretical foundation, affording the German officer at any level of command a professional means of criticism. Equipped with these cognitive agents the leader of troops was expected to judge every particular combat event specifically and thus produce the appropriate solution, be it a matter of tactical command, operational conduct, or strategic management.

Moltke's embryonic command concept, based on the principles of *Auftrag* and *Weisung*, was developed by Beck and his school into the most advanced operational theory of command ever created.[55] The command concept formulated in the manual was based on the recognition of the entire German officer corps' professional competence. It emphasized initiative out of mutual trust among all echelons of command, and advocated freedom of action to field commanders at every level. In other words, Beck's command theory reflected the notion of the cognitive tension at its best.

The manual's authors analysed Germany's geostrategic position using a holistic approach and on the basis of a systematic examination of its historical experience. Therefore, despite encouraging the offensive spirit at the tactical level, the manual indoctrinated its users to exercise a multi-dimensional, combined and balanced approach at the operational and strategic levels. Realizing the complexity of Germany's strategic position, Beck and his colleagues apprehended any future European conflict involving Germany as an extended war of attrition, taking place simultaneously along several fronts. Thus they argued that meeting such challenges demanded an operational cognition, or in simpler terms, that the conduct of German strategy in Europe required coherence, systematic knowledge, operational criticism and a unified, professional command authority. Strategic aims and operational objectives should be defined by the military strategic authority, following a thorough analysis based upon universal principles and long-term premises, and not using a particularistic approach guided by options of a manipulative application of military power.

It is true that the authors of the manual did not reject the traditional paradigm of annihilation, a fact which constituted its Achilles' heel. However, they did repudiate the Schlieffenian notion of *Gesamtschlacht*, which aimed at developing the integral battle of destruction to decide the war in a single stroke by means of a predetermined plan of deployment and movement. Beck and his colleagues perceived the novel idea of successive operations and emphasized the sequential and coordinated conduct of these operations in the context of attaining the general aim of the war. Thus, unlike its successor the *Blitzkrieg*, which adhered exclusively to the offensive, the manual reflected a balanced approach to offensive and defensive, seeing both as essential and complementary forms of operational manoeuvre.

The manual demanded from the operational levels of command a penetrating and critical intellectual effort in studying the entire spectrum of modern war, and a creative approach when dealing with the applied aspects of war, such as training, organization, planning and actual combat.

In the tactical context, the manual proposed a broad concept, intending to restore mobility to the battlefield by integrating a dynamic method of command, the existing technological assets, and the appropriate combination of the various tactical elements, such as armour, mechanized troops, infantry, engineers, artillery and aviation. Moreover, the manual perceived the tank in the pertinent operational context defining it as the leading weapon system (*Tonangebend*) on the future battlefield.[56] Nevertheless, the manual made it clear that neither the tank nor any other tactical element could achieve the operational objectives by itself. Attaining these and deciding the war as a whole required operational manoeuvring, which meant combined arms combat at the tactical level and coordinating the combined efforts in the context of the relevant objectives and aims, at the general level.

An examination of the *Truppenführung* reveals that Beck and his associates comprehended the complete depth of modern war and were fully aware of the role technology and mechanization played in it. Thus, what Michael Geyer specified as the 'revival of German strategic idealism' is nothing other than the revelation of the operational approach at its best.[57]

The conflict between the two schools of officers never assumed the form of a direct confrontation. The principal reason for this was that the opportunistic school of technocrats lacked group identification and an accepted leadership, was heterogeneous in its composition, and its coalescence into a concrete group took a long time. Moreover, as long as Fritsch and Beck retained their positions, an organized conspiracy within the armed forces against the conservative establishment was intolerable, due to the ethical discipline prevailing in the German army. The contest was actually conducted between Hitler and the General Staff school, while the Political Office in the Supreme Command under Werner von Blomberg functioned as Hitler's battering ram. Thus, when Hitler drew the majority of the *Wehrmacht*'s officer corps to his side and dismissed Fritsch from office by means of a fabricated provocation, Beck found himself isolated, and the schism became a *fait accompli*.

Hitler kept the initiative in his hands from the start, exercising it in a series of intrigues and manipulations, whereas Beck endeavoured to defend his position by employing methods and arguments that were irrelevant to his opponent's techniques. It is indeed plausible that the struggle had been initiated by Hitler against the General Staff school in order to take over the *Wehrmacht* and transfer the strategic and operational planning into his own hands.[58] The emergence of the *Blitzkrieg*, concept was an inevitable sequel to this process.

The sources of the conflict between Hitler and Beck lay deep in the creeds of both men, and since the course of events brought them into contact, a collision became inevitable. Beck strove to promote ideals that were anathema to Hitler: he believed in an army of excellence led by a professional élite; he endeavoured to retain the conduct of military strategy in the hands of this professional élite; and he advocated a rational and coherent strategic course that would suit both the European political setting and Germany's ability to sustain its own armed forces.

The commencement of the conflict lay in the Force-Building Planning (*Mobilmachungsplanung*) affair, starting in the summer of 1935, and in the subsequent decisions to accelerate rearmament with offensive weapons (*Rustungsbeschleunigung*) resulting in the Directives of 1936 and the military preparations for a confrontation on two fronts.[59] In light of the developing circumstances, Beck argued that until completion of the original rearmament plan scheduled for 1940, the military planners should limit themselves exclusively to defensive operations.[60] When, at the initial stages of implementing the plan, Hitler raised the question of whether Germany would be able to attain a simultaneous superiority over all its adversaries, Beck and his associates shifted the discussion from the quantitative dimension to that of principles. They posed a penetrating question in return: Could Germany ever achieve the necessary might in matériel which would allow it to conduct a war according to the operational principles and professional criteria recommended by the *Truppenfhürung*?[61] Indeed, when Hitler decided arbitrarily to advance the date of Germany's preparedness for war from 1940 to 1938, Beck responded by declaring the political authority irresponsible.[62]

Hitler's counterblow came on 5 November 1937 with the emphatic attacks by the Supreme Command's Political Office against the professional logic used in the argumentation of the General Staff. The Political Office had never had any access to operational planning. Nonetheless, following its attacks on the General Staff it embarked upon an intensive planning process, aimed at producing the results Hitler desired, by means of exercising unconventional approaches and impromptu methods.[63] These plans were basically intended to exploit certain political circumstances by initiating the use of military force for the purpose of taking over the victim states.[64]

Following the blow of 5 November 1937 and the subsequent events, Beck strove to prove that due to the military's objective limitations no coherent conduct of a future war would be able to combine rationally the doctrine laid down by Hitler and the universal principles of operations. Beck concluded with the assertion that the attempt militarily to apply Hitler's intentions would inevitably lead to both the destruction of the professional patterns of strategic planning and operational execution and to a strategic cul-de-sac.[65] Beck's efforts, stemming both from his apprehension of yielding

119

strategic planning and conduct to amateurish elements and from his anxiety about the growing inclination to perpetuate opportunistic approaches and mechanistic patterns of thought in the armed forces, constituted, in fact, a desperate rearguard action to save his perceptional assets. He was forced into this because as early as 1938 the majority of the *Wehrmacht's* officers already stood behind Hitler, and Beck was politically and professionally isolated.

From the time he assumed power, Hitler sought to draw the officer corps to his side by promising the rearmament and augmentation of the armed forces. The combination of nationalistic and aggressive utterance and the opportunity to fulfil a longstanding dream posed a temptation that blurred the officers' judgement and exposed their professional integrity as an archaic fantasy. Moreover, by fostering Guderian and later Rommel, Hitler indicated the ideal of officer he preferred. Thus, he not only posed a contender model to that of the prevailing General Staff, but also dictated new norms of behaviour in the armed forces.[66] Therefore, when Hitler struck on 5 November 1937, Beck was not only isolated: he was confronted by a group that was nurtured by the Führer himself. This group, in spite of its lack of cohesion, obtained its rewards collectively from the Führer, and thus had to obey the new ethos he had dictated.[67]

In the new situation that arose at the beginning of 1938, the professional unity of the army was broken; strategic planning and conduct were extracted from military control and transferred to amateurish and ambitious hands, and manipulative opportunism and improvisation replaced professionalism and systematic creativity as the prevailing norms in military management. Moreover, by transforming military strategy into sheer cunning and basing it on a criminal approach, operational cognition was completely suppressed. The revival of this cognition would occur not out of a sudden awakening of operational rationalism, but as a result of the dimensions and circumstances characterizing the Russian campaign. However, this late revival could not repair the damage inflicted by years of ignorance, and even the Guderians were destined to pay the price of the disillusionment.[68]

Once things had settled, the price extorted by Hitler from the opportunistic school constituted the most severe implication to arise from the new situation. Hitler's strategic logic was motivated by four principles: destruction, speed, aggressiveness and opportunism. This same logic compelled the generals to provide the Führer with operational, behavioural and bureaucratic patterns allowing him to apply his strategic intentions in his own way.[69] The results were the emergence of furious competition in the field of operational planning, aimed at pacifying Hitler's hunger, and the appearance of the *Blitzkrieg* concept:

> Technocratically organised armed forces and soldiers trained in skill-oriented programs were placed under military commanders who had long renounced and were mostly incapable of comprehensive operational thinking and who knew no other principle of war other than the optimization of force at any cost . . . But it was these officers who now became the proponents of *Blitzkrieg*, which was neither an outgrowth of military technology nor of the German doctrine of mobile offence, but operational management.[70]

BLITZKRIEG – THE MECHANIZATION OF DESTRUCTION

The *Blitzkrieg* concept was the brainchild of the school of opportunistic technocrats. However, since this group lacked professional adhesion and perceptional unity, the concept remained largely amorphous. This was demonstrated by the inability of the *Wehrmacht* generals to produce a basic formula or an agreed version defining the essence of the concept, even after the war. Another phenomenon reflecting the *Blitzkrieg*'s lack of substantive focus is the ongoing debate among modern researchers regarding the issue of Hitler's contribution to the formulation of the concept.[71]

As seen above, the very existence of operational cognition prevented the application of Hitler's desires. Hence, its suppression constituted an essential condition for promoting the mentality which incubated the *Blitzkrieg* concept. The first technical obstruction was removed with Hitler's splitting of the officer corps, the transfer of the strategic planning into his own hands, and his attainment of the generals' compliance with the new *modus operandi* dictated by him. The behavioural catalyst for the *Blitzkrieg*'s formulation was set by Hitler when he dictated frenzied competition among the officers attempting to produce the optimal military solution for the realization of his strategic intentions.[72] Hence, the *Blitzkrieg* was not developed through a systematic process, characterizing the formulation of theories, but rather in a random, empirical conjuncture. Moreover, since the various war theatres (Poland, Scandinavia, France, Balkans, the Western Desert, and Russia) differed in their tactical-operational nature the forming of *Blitzkrieg* resulted in a wide variety of local patterns.[73]

Therefore, in order to identify accurately the rational roots and cognitive origins of the *Blitzkrieg* concept, it is necessary, in the first place, to thoroughly explore the perceptional framework set by

Hitler, and then to attempt to specify the essential common denominator of the various operational experiences. The state of mind, which later, under competitive circumstances, absorbed the improvised operational ideas produced by officers of the *Wehrmacht*, was depicted very clearly by Michael Geyer:

> The core of these operations [i.e., *Blitzkrieg*] did not consist in any particular use of the new means of warfare, but in a kind of operational opportunism that knew no pre-set or standardized methods, only the fullest possible exploitation of success with all available means in the pursuit of the ultimate goal of overthrowing the enemy by breaking the will of its leadership. *Blitzkrieg* lived off the destruction of the systematic approach to military command decisions. It was the opposite of a doctrine. *Blitzkrieg* operations consisted of an avalanche of actions that were sorted out less by design than by success.[74]

This state of mind encouraged the German officers at all levels of command to improvise tactical and operational patterns, serving no principle, save that of success. However, since it encompassed the entire range of Hitler's strategic rationale, it posited a whole series of dicta which obliged the military planner and executor. The first and principal dictum determined the strategic goal and operational objective for every campaign and operation as that of annihilating the enemy's armed forces, destroying its will to resist, and taking over his territory. Thus, the traditional Clausewitzian notion of *Vernichtung* was revived. By personally applying political and strategic opportunism as the main instrumental patterns for achieving his aims, Hitler set an example and expected his officers to imitate him. This course of action was translated by his generals into exorbitant techniques of forward command, that were reasonable at the tactical level, yet entirely extraneous at the operational level.[75] The designation of speed as a leading element in planning and conducting operations, another of Hitler's dicta, was communicated through the Hossbach Memorandum (*Hossbach Niederschrift*).[76] The adoption of mechanization by the *Wehrmacht* derived primarily from this demand and mitigated, to a large extent, its application. The last dictum concerned aggressiveness and derived from both Nazi ideology and the tactical tradition of the *Reichswehr*. With the adoption of mechanization and the tactical pattern of operating in columns which resulted from it, the ability to effectuate tactical shock reached its culmination. Thus, aggressiveness was provided with most effective instruments of execution.[77]

The fact that the *Wehrmacht* leadership's path to strategic thinking was barred, and proper operational fundamentals were absent from its intellectual milieu, left it with the single option of turning to the field of tactics as the sole possibility for producing operational solutions to the challenges posed by Hitler. And since tactics represented the *Reichswehr's* field of excellence, the *Wehrmacht* officers could easily identify the necessary conceptual means within this field.

The tactical ideal of both the *Reichswehr* and its massive successor, the *Wehrmacht*, centred on imposing the patterns of envelopment and encirclement on the adversary's defensive layout.[78] The strategic nature and operational dimensions of modern military operations determining the penetration of the opponent's defensive layout are almost universal preconditions for the development of both envelopment and encirclement.[79] Here the tactical patterns of penetration that were developed by Oscar von Hutier towards the spring offensive of 1918, provided the conceptual formula.[80] Nonetheless, adopting the encirclement pattern offered a greater temptation than its availability as a developed tactical technique. In the German military consciousness annihilation and encirclement were traditionally perceived as related ideas belonging to an identical context, that is the encirclement manoeuvre was appreciated not only as the ideal form of combat at all levels, but also as the only form of manoeuvre capable of attaining annihilation. This logical combination produced in a single stroke not only a universal solution to all of the Führer's operational demands, but likewise rekindled old aspirations in the direction of the integral battle of annihilation (*Vernichtungsschlacht*) according to the Cannae tradition.[81] The instrument which presented itself as a means for performing both the operational penetration (*Durchbruch*) and the Schlieffen-sized battle of encirclement (*Kesselschlacht* – Operational Cauldron) was nothing other than mechanization.[82]

In his penetrating analysis, which is free from Liddell Hart's later prejudices, F.O. Miksche points out, in the introductory part of his thematic discussion, the rational origins of the *Blitzkrieg*: the *Blitzkrieg's* fundamentals lay in Schlieffen's traditional notion of Cannae, aimed at attaining the complete encirclement of the opponent.[83] Under modern conditions of war, the perfect encirclement requires a preceding operational irruption, a principle the 1918 spring offensive had ignored.[84] Thus, since the act of penetration constituted the essential condition predetermining the evolution of infiltration and encirclement, one could legitimately argue that the essence of *Blitzkrieg* actually centred on this act.[85] Moreover, the instrumental means which afforded the accomplishment of the operational penetration, and its subsequent development into irruption and encirclement, were three technical elements: an appropriate tactical organization in 'offensive combat grouping' (*Angriffsgruppen*); applying the pattern of 'spaces and gaps tactics' (*Flächen und Lückentaktik*); and mobilizing mechanization in the service of implementing these tactics.[86]

Miksche's critical analysis reveals the complete technical basis of the *Blitzkrieg* and discloses the entire structure of its tactical logic. His work is based on a thorough study of contemporary German publications and on acute observation of contemporary operational experiences. It, therefore, has remained the most comprehensive research ever conducted on the subject of *Blitzkrieg*. His thesis presents the entire concept as a tactical recipe, or an instructive prescription of a battle mega-drill, lacking operational scope. The essence of this battle drill emphasized the tactical execution by illuminating a series of tactical achievements interlinked through a technical dependence. Since it was guided by an obstinate uniform aim extreme in its ambitiousness, it lacked realism, essential flexibility and a systematic definition of operational objectives or priorities. Thus, technical aspects like *Schwerpunkt* and *Aufrollen*, that initiated the tactical performance, were identical to the final result and designed to reflect an operational achievement.[87] The complete logic of this technical formula, turning a means, or a procedure, into an aim, can be summed up in a few sentences:

> Logically the process is this: The aim is Cannae, the method is irruption. Next stage in the argument: The aim is irruption, the method is concentration on a narrow front. But here comes in also a third stage in the argument, which should logically be interposed between concentration and irruption, as the method by which the concentrated forces achieve the piercing of the enemy defences. The aim is to carry the local superiority due to concentration forward: The method is described by the two German words: *Schwerpunkt* and *Aufrollen*. These two words are the two most striking features of German military doctrine.[88]

In other words, a doctrine aspiring to offer an operational framework for conducting a grand war was corrupted into a technical prescription comprising a few sentences and displaying a simplistic chain logic: the application of a grand manoeuvre of encirclement was self-imposed by the military planners since it offered the best method for annihilating the enemy's armed forces, thus promising the accomplishment of the strategic aim.[89] The road to the operational objective or the materialization of the encirclement manoeuvre led through the vital pass of irruption. Attaining this dictated the creation of a corridor, by means of a breakthrough and a roll-out clearing operation.[90] The break-in action, which constituted the initial step in this schematic process required the imposition of tactical shock at the point of penetration – an effect which demanded the maximal concentration of fire and resources at that point.[91]

The first success of the *Blitzkrieg* method derived from an unusual lack of operational competence and clear tactical and technological inferiority on the Polish side. Moreover, a whole series of specific geostrategic conditions encouraged the German mechanization to exploit the potential of the *Blitzkrieg* method in a total manner. Hence, the ultimate strategic effect achieved by the *Wehrmacht* could be justly interpreted as annihilation. During the Balkan campaign, the limited dimensions of the forces involved and the mountainous nature of the terrain allowed the Germans to exercise their tactical supremacy through a chain of brigade- and division-sized *Blitzkrieg* battles.[92]

In the North African and Russian theatres, in spite of the differences in magnitude and ferocity of the struggle, one can observe the prevalence of a synonymous regularity of a dialectical nature. The initial tactical excellence of the Germans led, with the development of the campaigns, to a serious exposure of their operational weaknesses and ignorance. The greater their tactical successes and the deeper their penetration into the adversary's territory, the flimsier their operational position became. The German inclination to grab the largest possible number of enemy troops into the cauldrons created by the deep penetrating armoured blows overstretched their resources, split the mechanized formations from the infantry, and severed the succession of operations, thus bringing complete exhaustion upon themselves.[93] The initial successes in Poland, France and the Balkans induced a state of euphoria among the German strategic and operational leaders and convinced them that their operational method was coherent and invincible. This state of mind led them to make a simplistic analogy between the conditions they had confronted in the west and those awaiting them in the Russian theatre.[94]

Yet the conceptual pattern of the offensive in the West was not *Blitzkrieg*. The validity of this premise derives not only from the fact that Erich von Manstein, the conceiver of the offensive plan in the West, did not belong to the hard nucleus of opportunistic technocrats and, in all probability, was not acquainted with the idea of *Blitzkrieg* at that time.[95] A thorough examination of Manstein's Memorandum reveals operational thinking at its best, since he intended to defeat the combined armies of the Allies (France, Britain, Belgium and Holland) by a purely operational approach.[96] Due to the fact that he had not been provided with a strategic aim, and his main argument against the OKH's plan derived from its lack of a coherent strategic aim, Manstein first defined the strategic aim that would guide the entire logic of his operational plan. His strategic intention was to break up the opposing alliance and inflict a complete defeat on the French armed forces. Thus, he provided the operational planning process with the essential positive guiding mechanism, which was holistic and all-embracing in nature, yet logical and realistic. The cognitive anchors – or operational objectives – forming the framework of his plan of manoeuvre were, therefore, to separate three of the Allied armies and the French mobile contingent from the rest of the French army, which constituted the main mass of the opposing system; to prevent simultaneously both the French and the Allied armies from performing their various defensive aims by means of an initial strike, hence inflicting operational shock upon his numerous adversaries at the opening stage of the campaign; and to defeat the main mass of the French army separately. Both the physical fragmentation of the Allies' operational cohesion and the synchronous prevention of each component from performing its specific mission of defending the integrity of its own country were designed to be effected by means of a single pre-emptive strike. The manoeuvre was intended to develop through a succession of two operational stages. The first combined the operations of a huge holding force, comprising Army Groups B and C, and a striking force that was based on Army Group A, or more accurately, on Panzer Group von Kleist. This combination aimed not only at forcing a shift of the defensive centre of mass forward, but, primarily, at creating a perfect centre of gravity in front of the Ardennes.[97] Along this centre of gravity, Panzer Group von Kleist delivered the blow that effectuated the operational shock.

Thus, the factors which turned the actual penetration of the armoured spearheads into a sort of encirclement were the limited dimensions of the operational space and the drawing forward of the defensive into Flanders and Belgium. Guderian's remarks at the briefing of 20 February confirm beyond any doubt that the initial logic that guided the offensive plan was not that of encirclement.[98] Thus, if one examines the Second World War military events in the light of their operational gist and according to operational criteria, it is more than proper to exclude the case of the Battle of France from the category of *Blitzkrieg*.

Conversely, the basic approach in planning the Russian campaign was flawed and indicated deep operational ignorance. The campaign's strategic framework completely disregarded the existence of depth, space, fighting resources and operational trends.[99] Moreover, the German planners realized that the Russian land mass was too large to be enclosed in a single pincer operation. Thus, the rationale of the German operational planning was guided by the following trends: all three operational components – or army groups – were scheduled to attack simultaneously, in a linear form all along the Russian western border. Each army group was meant to penetrate the frontal line and then, after armoured thrusts into the enemy's rear, to conduct an independent encirclement operation which would destroy the majority of defending forces in its sector.[100] The huge cauldron operations of Minsk, Smolensk, Kiev, Bryansk, and Viaz'ma reflected strict conformity to this principle. Furthermore, the shifting of Guderian's Panzer Group, towards the end of August 1941, from its original course in the direction of Kiev, indicated that opportunities for encirclement held a higher priority over consistent operations guided by scheduled objectives.[101] Even when it was realized at the end of October 1941, that the series of prodigious encirclements had not destroyed the Red Army or broken its ability to fight, the German High Command did not abandon its obsession with encirclement. The conquest of Moscow in November 1941 was planned as a pincer operation, combining the Panzer Armies of Guderian and Hoth. In the summer of 1943, following the Moscow check and the Stalingrad disaster, when the Russians deliberately offered the Germans the Kursk Bulge, the tactical urge for encirclement reappeared, and against all possible logical thinking led the Germans to commit operational suicide.

This phenomenon repeated itself in the Western Desert, with Rommel's attempts to envelop his adversary in May 1942 in the Gazala operation, in July 1942 following the conquest of Marmarica, and finally, in the most extreme operational circumstance, when endeavouring to envelop the British Eighth Army in the Alam Halfa operation.[102]

As can be seen from the few cases described, when the *Blitzkrieg* pattern was applied in intensive conditions of operational warfare, and against armies which possessed even a small degree of knowledge in the discipline of military systems – it failed. Moreover, an analysis of those cases reveals that the source of failure was the distorted logic comprising its basis. The pattern of encirclement had never been a negative ingredient of warfare. On the contrary, it had always reflected the acme of tactical manoeuvre. However, as can be deduced from a study of the Battle of Cannae and Hannibal's subsequent failures in the Italian campaign and the Punic War, the use of penetration, envelopment and encirclement should be confined to the tactical context, as one instrument in the inventory of tactical variations. The pretentious attempt to transform encirclement and its accompanying techniques into an operational theory, and the erroneous approach that strove to link it simplistically to the strategic level, by means of the mechanical effect of destruction, created an unrealistic and illogical distortion.

THE ABSENCE OF OPERATIONAL COGNITION – EMPIRICAL REFLECTIONS

Having explored the rational origins of the *Blitzkrieg* and realizing its lack of operational logic, an examination of additional aspects, which indicate a further lack of operational consciousness, is worthwhile. Our examination will employ a certain number of operational principles to serve as criteria.

The striking feature of the *Blitzkrieg* concept is the complete absence of a coherent theory which should have served as the general cognitive basis for the actual conduct of operations. The absence of a theoretical basis is proven by the fact that even the limited literature, published between 1933 and 1945, is concerned exclusively with techno-tactical aspects of warfare and individual experiences.[103] The majority of the published works tend to concentrate on the technical aspects of operating armour and its supporting elements. In fact, this is quite natural since in the mental environment created by Hitler there was no room for abstract theories. The narrow realm of military perception was governed by a clear demand for products concerning the mechanics of manoeuvre to suit the Führer's intentions and satisfy his operational demands. The relinquishment of operational consciousness allowed the military to content itself with the *Truppenführung* as a cognitive basis, emphasizing the tactical aspects of both command and manoeuvre.

Furthermore, the training of the future officers in the War Academy (*Kriegsakademie*) after 1936 focused primarily on tactics. Out of 45 weekly hours of theoretical studies, during three years, 26 were dedicated to the acquisition of tactical knowledge and the rest were left to studies that concerned the cooperation with specialized arms, such as armour, artillery, engineers, logistics, and aviation. The studies concentrated on the levels of brigade and division and only rarely touched on problems related to the operating of corps. The regulations of the War Academy (*Kriegsakademievorschrift*) deleted operational matters regarding the level of army from the curriculum.[104]

As a result of this enforced orientation towards tactics, the common conceptual and terminological denominator existing in the officer corps became superficial and inconsistent. The various utterances of

German generals, whenever treating circumstances or problems requiring an operational approach and a systematic method of reasoning, give the impression of confusion and conceptual ambiguity. This phenomenon is clear from the generals' perception of the influence exercised by Schlieffen's traditional ideas on the maturation of the *Wehrmacht*'s operational concepts,[105] from their stand on the manner of applying the preferable breakthrough method, during the initial phase of the Russian campaign,[106] and from their opinions on questions such as the optimal structure of the armoured formation[107] and the preferable ratio between the various types of formations in the *Wehrmacht*.[108] Consequently, even a technical subject such as the types of tanks to comprise the core of the Panzer divisions was characterized by a sharp polarization of opinion.[109]

The consequence of this inconsistent and superficial trend was revealed in the course of the Russian campaign. Technical issues, such as unexpected tank inferiority in armour thickness, gun calibre, and so on, emerged under the impact of intensive fighting as acute tactical problems. The increasing number of such problems impeded the German natural talent for improvising *ad hoc* solutions to the graver operational threats which were developing. Thus, through the growing accumulation of system deficiencies, operational flexibility diminished rapidly, and ultimately both the organization and its operating method (*Blitzkrieg*) collapsed.

Patterns of action and systematic operating modes comprise a complex of basic codes designed to assure the smooth eventuation of the technical aspects in the operational process. These patterns do not derive from an artificial predilection for formalities, but from the reality governed by the universal principles of system theory and the operational specifications of the relevant organization.

The nature of operating military systems depends on the existence of a certain number of basic mechanisms. The first is the order mechanism, deriving from the hierarchical structure of the military organization. This mechanism determines the direction of the operation's logic – from the vortex of the organizational pyramid towards its base. The mechanism of mutual confidence emanates from the natural distance existing between the initiator of the operation and its executers, all along the various echelons of the system's structure. This mechanism, which is based on a professional consciousness common to the numerous participants in the process, provides the system with its lubricating device and is reflected in a reciprocal confidence between commander and subordinate – each appreciating the professional competence of the other. The third mechanism, which is anchored in the principle of the cognitive tension, expresses the conscious commitment to the operational aim.

The appropriate combination of these mechanisms determines both the smoothness and the dynamism of the system's operation. In other words, as long as an harmonious equilibrium between the various mechanisms is maintained within the framework of the operating system – compliance with orders, accurate reporting and reciprocal informing, and the mutual expression of criticism and protests within the borders of reason – the system works. Moreover, such harmony not only reduces the level of friction developing at both ends of the system, but also yields the essential freedom of action to the executers. When a system does not recognize the importance of these mechanisms and their interrelations, its technical conduct will often lose its balance and discordant patterns will emerge – leading to the development of coercive management and obsessive command, which inevitably results in gradual disintegration.

The events of August 1941 in Army Group Centre, initiated by the Novyi Borisov commanders' meeting with Hitler, reflect the above assertion remarkably. In the course of the August operations, Guderian implemented a series of grave manipulations which led him to ignore explicit orders and operational directives given by Hitler, by advancing forces of his panzer group towards objectives determined independently by him. Moreover, in doing this he contradicted specific orders given by the High Command, and also convinced Army Group headquarters to adopt his position and support his actions.[110]

All this resulted in operational chaos, characterized by strategic loss of time and a huge waste of troops and fighting resources as a result of the immense repositioning of Guderian's Panzer Army towards the south-west by the OKH's reinforcement of its original orders.[111] However, this was not the only damage. In view of Guderian's deliberate violation of the order and his rejection of the operational strategic aim, the High Command lost its operational confidence in him, began to insist on trivial details and assumed a coercive style of command.[112]

Following these events, Guderian executed yet another harsh manipulation, in that he exploited a personal meeting with Hitler to convince the latter to change an operational order given by the OKH. The order, which concerned Guderian's Panzer Army directly, did not correspond with his own views, and so, after failing to have it rescinded through the official channels, he bypassed the entire military command structure and approached the supreme strategic-political authority directly.[113] The logical conclusion of the irreversible process of operational decline was manifested in the battle at the gates of Moscow in December 1941. With the sharp increase in operational and logistical distress, the field commanders of the *Wehrmacht* began to regard orders given by the High Command as mere recommendations.[114] It is entirely possible that Hitler assumed direct command of military operations and adopted a coercive mode of control over the field command echelons because he sensed a loss of control by his generals at a moment of crisis. However, the transfer of the actual operational conduct into Hitler's hands did not change the situation, which persisted as operational chaos, but aggravated it from the generals' point of view. Guderian, who experienced momentarily an operational revelation, lost his political awareness, disobeyed Hitler's 'No Retreat!' order, and consequently was dismissed from his field command.[115]

Another aspect, demonstrating the prevailing absence of operational working patterns, concerns the process of extracting tactical lessons from former experiences and applying them to the future. The dynamic application of this circular pattern of reaction derives its importance from the fact that it provides the system with the technical and cognitive means which lessen the initial power of shock in future encounters with the opposition. These means entail, among other things, the improvement of weapon systems and the development of appropriate combat techniques – both promising a certain breathing space to the tactical echelons in future engagements. Affording the tactical level this relative composure helps postpone the development of the operational disturbances affecting the system on a much higher scale. A series of technical problems – such as tank gun inferiority, both in range and final ballistics,[116] deficiencies in anti-tank guns,[117] insufficiency of tank armour protection as against British and French recent models,[118] inadequacy of the artillery's mobility,[119] and the apparent lack of both means and combat techniques to overcome obstacles and minefields[120] – were revealed in the fighting experience in the Polish and French campaigns, and were reported by the field formations to the relevant headquarters and staffs. However, this information was not transformed into practical measures in a manner that could have affected the tactical conduct in the Russian campaign. Thus, with the dimensions of the Russian theatre, the overwhelming Russian superiority in fighting resources, and the degree of combat ferocity of the war in Russia, tactical disruptions were not long in emerging and soon assumed the shape of operational disturbances.[121]

The *Wehrmacht*'s operational command problems can best be learned from the experiences of Guderian and Rommel. This is not surprising since they were the most conspicuous officers in the opportunistic school and displayed a hyper-aggressive style of leadership, which was expressed in the application of exorbitant patterns of tactical-like forward command. Since neither of them had been adequately trained to command large formations in a system-oriented environment, their operational cognition suffered noticeable deficiencies and their conduct was action-oriented. Thus, they very often fell short of comprehending the essential linkage between operational problems and suitable command organization. Both adhered to the pattern of 'command from the saddle', although they were not cavalrymen. While it is true that operational command structures may occasionally be affected by the specific conditions of an operational situation, such cases are exceptional. The operational command organization must first and foremost be formed according to the principles characterizing systems in general. And since military systems are structured hierarchically and their operational logic is generated from the rear to the front, it is only natural that the principal location of the operational commander should be in the rear.[122] It goes without saying that this premise does not contradict the tactical principle of command, which is based entirely on leading from the front. On the contrary, the integral process of commanding the system stretches between this pair of pivots, combining their different activities into a harmonious whole. The tactical pivot, which focuses on immediate and local matters, competes under the pressure of combat with unpredictable challenges, while exercising direct command from the front. Conversely, the operational pivot, which centres on holistic and future matters, functions from the rear by means of staffs and procedures, while attempting to initiate the deliberate occurrence of future events. Moreover, the abstract and holistic nature of the operational aim, on the one hand, and the fragmentary and chaotic nature of tactical warfare, on the other, only emphasize the need for operational command from the rear. Therefore, the logic of operational cybernetics rests on three principles. The first argues that navigating the process of realizing the operational aim should be conducted by means of indirect control from a rear position. The second principle makes it necessary to maintain a successive dynamic circuit – bearing forward orders from the rear, and passing back details that are accumulated into a general situation picture. And finally, the entire operational command apparatus should be based on layers and organizational units the functions of which must always correspond positively to the general aim.

Among the numerous cases involving command disturbances recounted by Guderian, there are two that particularly merit a close inspection, since they illustrate the entire gravity of the operational command problem in the *Wehrmacht*. The first case arose in the course of the 14 February 1940 war games, when the question of whether a special operational headquarters should be formed for the purpose of coordinating the various armoured corps that operated under Army Group B's command was brought up.[123] The debate that developed subsequently around the question, and even more so Guderian's objection to the forming of such an organization, indicate both a misunderstanding of the essence of operational cybernetics and a distorted approach to the issue of combining armoured forces in an operational context.[124] The reason for that derived from the main idea of the operational plan. The three armoured corps (Guderian's XIX, Reinhardt's XLI, and Wietersheim's XIV) which were meant to operate ahead of the Army Group's bulk of infantry formation in order to achieve a common operational objective, comprised a distinct operational element within the mother organization.[125] Thus, since they bore the same tactical nature, were aimed at an identical operational objective, and the tempo of their conduct extended the operational space beyond the limits of the ability of Army Group B's headquarters to control operations directly, it became only natural that they should be grouped under a specific unified operational command. Such an organization would not only improve the coordination between the three armoured corps, it would also render a positive service to the Army Group by guaranteeing the achievement of the main objective through a unified effort, and by relieving it of the burden of controlling three remote efforts.

In the second case a need arose, due to operational circumstances, to combine the missions of Guderian's Panzer Group, which was meant to make two armoured thrusts on both flanks of Brest-Litovsk, with that of an infantry corps, operating under the command of the 4th Army (Kluge) and assigned the mission of clearing the city's built-up area.[126] There is no doubt that Army Group Centre's attempt to combine in the same operational sector several efforts belonging to different operational entities, without grouping them under a unified operational command, constituted a severe operational shortcoming. Moreover, the compromise finally worked out by Guderian may have solved a problem of prestige, but at the same time it created a severe organizational and command anomaly. The infantry corps and the operational sector of Brest-Litovsk were indeed put under Guderian's command, but the entire panzer group (an equivalent of an army) was placed under the direct charge of the 4th Army commander. In other words, the Army Group commander relinquished control of the most important operational formation under his command

(Guderian's 2nd Panzer Group) for the trivial purpose of solving a local planning problem and satisfying one of his army commanders.[127] Again, this case discloses basic deficiencies in understanding the essence of operational command problems. Furthermore, it implies a mechanistic trend for deviating armour from infantry operations, and finally, it also denotes narrow minded sectarianism.

Rommel's emphatic penchant to lead from the front, as reflected in his direction of the 7th Panzer Division through the French campaign, is a conspicuous illustration of tactical management.[128] However, his simplistic application of this pattern to the command of an independent strategic theatre against an Allied army over the vast spaces of the Western Desert contradicted the basic principles of operational command. Hence, during the heat of operational crises he frequently found himself totally disconnected from his main headquarters and the general course of events, leading a tactical formation in a marginal affair. He thus lost control of the entire operation.[129] There is no doubt that Rommel's behaviour stemmed from his insufficient training in operational management and from his attempt to transfer the command and working patterns of an infantry battalion commander into an operational context.[130]

The idea of combined arms warfare was not alien to the *Wehrmacht*. The evidence for this is provided by the extensive coverage dedicated to the subject in theoretical writings during the 1930s and in the course of the war.[131] Nevertheless, this consciousness was exclusively confined to the technical aspects of tactical manoeuvre.[132] The deeper implications of synergism in the strategic context were never realized nor was its essential contribution to the realization of the operational manoeuvre. Moreover, the linkage between strategic decision-making, especially with regard to force building, the tangibility of a positive theory for operations, and the actual application of combined arms tactics, was never perceived as essential.

The ability to perform combined-arms warfare at the tactical level is thus a function of several factors, or conditions, among which understanding the matter at its basic level is but the first. The second is that a fighting organization must be formed capable of absorbing the idea of synergism at all levels and in all situations. Thirdly, the viability of a technological and industrial infrastructure capable of backing up the organization with the required equipment and weapon systems must be guaranteed. Thus, it can be rightly assumed that not only is a deliberate linkage between the three levels of conducting war indeed essential for the effectuation of combined-arms combat, but also that the function exercised by the operational level in that linkage is as crucial. Formulating the tactical concept of combined arms undoubtedly requires some sort of operational cognition. The extensive space allotted to this subject in *Truppenführung 1936* confirms this premise. Furthermore, it is obvious that constructing any coherent fighting organization is not possible without a general theory of operations serving as its conceptual framework. And finally, the development and production of the means to conduct combat, in both suitable qualities and quantities, requires a dynamic dialogue between the operational authorities, which define the needs, and the political-strategic level, which mobilizes industry and the scientific community.

On the other hand, the presence of tactical synergy contributes significantly to both the dynamism and the quality of the operational manoeuvre. Energetic cooperation between the various elements at the battlefield level accelerates the accomplishment of the tactical missions, and thus invigorates the operational manoeuvre. Similarly, tactical cooperation supports the operation by affording it the essential tempo by means of operational mobility, the necessary power through the attrition of the opposition, and adaptiveness by means of operational flexibility.

The fact that the German infantry never achieved a reasonable degree of mechanization[133] determined the tactical disunion between the infantry arm and the armour.[134] Moreover, even in cases where tanks and infantry found themselves together in the same tactical sector, the latter could not sustain the intensity of the fight due to a conspicuous lack of protection and anti-tank artillery. Thus, fighting separately without the essential reciprocal support weakened both elements piecemeal.[135] The eventual attrition impaired the operational momentum and ultimately crippled the *Wehrmacht*'s ability to accomplish the encirclement battles (*Kesselschlachten*), which constituted the operational essence of the *Blitzkrieg*.[136]

Since they were neither organized nor equipped in a manner that allowed them to integrate smoothly in the armoured tactical manoeuvre, the *Wehrmacht*'s engineers' combat effectiveness was even less than that of the infantry. Only a third of the armoured engineers' order of battle was mechanized and, therefore, they lacked both the mobility and protection needed to tackle the obstacles in front of their tanks.[137] Furthermore, until late in the Russian campaign the engineers did not possess combat techniques to deal effectively with the challenges posed by this theatre of operations.[138] The virtual inability of the engineers to integrate in the tactical manoeuvre accelerated the erosion of the tank forces since the latter were compelled to wait in front of the obstacles. Thus, operational mobility degenerated almost to a standstill in the winter of 1941.

The huge gaps between the combat units and the logistical elements in the course of the Russian campaign originated both in deficient planning and in the equipping of the logistical units with insufficient and unsuitable motorization.[139] These were the result of optimistic predictions of the campaign's duration and a complete disregard of the difference between the nature of the French and Russian road networks. The failure of the logistical effort to provide the fighting formations with winter clothing, medical equipment, ammunition, fuel and spare parts caused a great loss of human life and fighting resources, and in many cases compromised the ability of the tactical units to perform their missions.[140]

The fact that light cavalry-oriented combined formations barely existed in the *Wehrmacht* undermined its ability to attain and maintain operational mobility on the Russian front. These formations, the establishment of which Guderian, out of a tank-centred approach and sectarian envy, rejected, proved their enormous operational value in the Western Desert, both in mobility and flexibility.[141]

As can be understood, in spite of the fact that the *Wehrmacht* did possess a tactical concept of combined arms warfare, it was applied in reality in such a manner as to allow only the accomplishment of tactical objectives and nothing more. The inability to organize the tactical victories and transform them into operational achievements was determined by the inadequacy of operational mobility – a phenomenon that derived first and foremost from the inutile performance of combined-arms combat. In the final analysis the operational mobility displayed by the *Wehrmacht* barely equalled that of the *Grande Armée* in 1812.[142]

The decline of fire support in the course of the Russian campaign resembled in principle the retardation of the tactical synergy. Both artillery and aviation fire were initially perceived – especially in light of the Polish and French experiences – as an essential element in the application of the tactical manoeuvre.[143] Nonetheless, in the *Wehrmacht's* perception, the value of fire support never transcended the limits of tactics. The consequences of ignoring the essential contribution made by the holding element's eroding effort, to the development of operational manoeuvre, became apparent in the Russian campaign, particularly in light of the size of the theatre and of the Red Army itself. Moreover, the simplistic differentiation between fire and manoeuvre, and the natural German preference for movement, led the Germans to discriminate against the mechanization of artillery, in favour of tank production.[144] In the course of the 1939 and 1940 campaigns, the implications of the problem were not particularly felt; however, with the advance through the Russian expanses and the encountering of intensive operational conditions, the signs of this disability did not take long to emerge. In fact during the winter months of 1941–42, the *Wehrmacht* formations were completely deprived of artillery support.[145] Due to the fact that the *Wehrmacht* neither planned nor initiated the seizure and preparation of infrastructure that would allow the *Luftwaffe* the earliest deployment of fighter and bomber squadrons deep in Russian territory, a conspicuous gap developed between the leading ground elements and the supporting aviation. Eventually air superiority in the forward operational zones was yielded to the Russians, friendly air support almost vanished, and the *Wehrmacht*'s armoured spearheads were left entirely at the mercy of the Red air force.[146] Following Russian initiatives, reflecting their awareness of fire support contribution in eroding the adversary, Russian artillery and air power very soon commanded the skies and the battlefields. With the increase of this trend the measure of erosion suffered by the *Wehrmacht* led to its loss of the operational initiative.[147]

Operational flexibility is attained through planning and implementation which strive to harmonize the available resources and forces with the theatre conditions in a manner which permits the accomplishment of the operational aim despite the opposition. This means that at the general level of planning the combination of various forms of combat – attack, defence, retreat and delay, and pursuit – within the operational manoeuvre becomes almost an imperative. It is quite obvious that unless the troops expected to participate in the operational manoeuvre are initially familiar with these tactical forms, their ability to perform them in reality will remain theoretical. The operational plan of the Russian campaign ignored both this principle and the strategic operational limitations of the *Wehrmacht*. The one-dimensional offensive plan, which initially appeared to be sweeping away all opposition, developed into a complete stalemate with the advance into the Russian depth and the subsequent depletion of resources. Hence, unilateral offensive turned into rigid defensive.[148] The abrupt break in the offensive manoeuvre's momentum dictated a sudden need to apply defensive techniques. However, the reports of the high command and the operational formations indicate confusion, due to the fact that the *Wehrmacht* at its various levels was ignorant of the tactical forms of defence, retreat and delay.[149] Moreover, knowledge of the defensive forms of tactical manoeuvre was not pertinent from a professional perspective, since tactical commanders regarded both defence and retreat as manifestations of defeatism, a phenomenon to be avoided at all costs.[150]

German tactical excellence and operational ignorance represented both sides of the *Blitzkrieg* coin, hence its sum total could only be ultimate defeat. Tactical excellence is only one factor among many in any army's general effectiveness, which depends largely on actions and perceptions that are worked out at the operational level. The absence of a comprehensive operational cognition, on one hand, and an excessive tendency to rely exclusively on tactical excellence, on the other, can be a destructive combination. The essence of Guderian's military *Weltanschauung*, as expressed in the pamphlet *Achtung Panzer* is a graphic example of this argument:

> The most dangerous opponent of a tank is an enemy tank. If it can not be beaten, the breakthrough can be seen as a failure, as the infantry and the artillery will also fail to get through.[151]

This statement reveals not only the narrow-mindedness of Guderian's tank-centred approach, but also the complete parochiality of an entire generation, whose military outlook did not rise above the level of tactics-oriented mechanics. The dangerous opponent of the tank is of course not just another enemy tank, but a combined team including a tank, an infantryman, an engineer, a gun, an aircraft and a variety of anti-tank weapons. Yet in spite of W. Spannenkrebs's earlier warning, Guderian and his associates dictated a mentality that *ab initio* prevented the creation of the basic conditions for a true synergism.[152] Moreover, Guderian's claim not only presented the tank as the exclusive instrument of modern warfare, but also argued that the breakthrough is its substance. Hence, a one-dimensional military concept relying solely on combat techniques, even if supported by tactical excellence, is bound to fail in a true operational test.

THE DISTORTION OF THE OPERATIONAL AIM MECHANISM

The phenomenon, which more than anything else exposes the utter laxity of the *Wehrmacht* generals' operational consciousness is their distortion of the aim mechanism. Michael Geyer was right in arguing that the German strategy under the Third Reich was not guided by coherent principles but rather by a chain of opportunistic gambles on the military's ability to exploit extreme political circumstances for the purpose of effectuating ideological aspirations, and on its ability to exploit the limited resources of the German state.[153] To some extent this premise supports the generals' postwar argument attributing the *Wehrmacht*'s failure to Hitler's irrational strategy and his coercive interference in operational direction.

It is true that the definition of political-strategic aims initiating the systematic process of operational decision-making determines, to a large extent, its image. In this sense, Hitler's approach did indeed lack operational coherence from the start. Yet, Hitler was not only free of pretensions to conform to operational logic, he also had never acquired the professional faculties to allow him to do so. On the other hand, the generals traded their operational cognition and professional integrity for the material benefits that resulted from the expansion of the armed forces. By their mere abstention from participating in strategic planning, the generals deliberately disregarded the importance of the aim mechanism in the operational process and thus sanctioned the creation of distorted norms. Moreover, by consenting to provide the instrument which would serve as the key element in the accomplishment of Hitler's intentions, they abdicated their duty to express their professional opinion on strategic management. In doing so they accelerated the development of operational chaos.

Guderian's retrospective remarks, opening his account of the Russian campaign, disclosed not only the hypocritical position the German generals assumed after the war on the issue of the campaign's conduct, but also their total failure to perceive, at the relevant time, the importance of operational logic:

> Three army groups, each of approximately the same strength, were to attack with diverging objectives. No single clear operational objective seemed to be envisaged. Looking at it from a professional point of view this did not appear at all promising.[154]

It would appear that the discussion of the operational aims could be concluded at this point, since Guderian's criticism reveals the entire failure: the absence of a logical framework in the strategic planning impeded the ability to define the operational objectives clearly, which, in turn, produced an unintelligible plan. Thus, Guderian's remarks imply that due to its deficient operational plan, the enterprise in Russia was doomed to failure from the start. However, assessing Guderian's retrospective remarks in the general context of contemporary events raises a series of questions: Was the plan perceived with similar criticism at the time of its distribution? What were the reactions of the General Staff to Hitler's directive, and what was their role in the final operational plan? And finally, in the context of the broader operational experience accumulated by the *Wehrmacht* prior to the Russian campaign, were the professional failures, described by Guderian, a novelty?

Guderian's own account of both the briefing that preceded the launching of the Western offensive, and the actual conduct of the

French campaign, discloses that there was nothing new in the vague definition of operational objectives by the high command:

> The supreme leadership must decide whether my objective is to be Amiens or Paris . . . I never received any further orders as to what I was to do once the bridgehead over the Meuse was captured. All my decisions until I reached the Atlantic seaboard at Abbeville were taken by me and me alone.[155]

Moreover, Guderian's account gives the impression of an operational jungle, lacking strategic aims and operational objectives to guide the manoeuvring elements, and governed by decisions and *de facto* conduct dictated by field commanders.

As can be learned from accounts of General Staff officers who held key positions in the high command, the operational plan for the Russian campaign was not seen as a certain formula for failure. On the contrary, during the initial period of the campaign the prevailing impression was that events were outpacing expectations and operations seemed to reach their successful conclusions after only a few weeks of fighting.[156]

The operational plan for the Russian campaign provides a remarkable illustration of the shallowness of the *Blitzkrieg* concept. The intention was to destroy the Red Army, and it was based on the assumption that the Russian defensive lacked any operational depth. Consequently, the essence of the plan contemplated a rapid breakthrough of the Russian forward defensive lines, followed by the development of encirclement manoeuvres, and ending ultimately in the destruction of the Red Army.[157] In fact, the nature of the plan was not surprising since it was an elaboration of Hitler's directive carried by the OKH. Thus, rather than criticize the deficient strategic concept or compensate for its blunders by producing a coherent plan of operational manoeuvre, the generals themselves presented it to the executing echelons with its imperspecuities and inconsistencies. In other words, since the General Staff did not add or subtract anything from Hitler's original concept, the operational plan reflected accurately Hitler's strategic outlook and operational logic, as it was originally expressed in Directive No. 21.[158] The political aim of the Russian campaign was to occupy the space of European Russia up to the Volga–Archangelsk Line.[159] The strategic aims followed Clausewitz's logic of annihilation, that is, the destruction of the Russian forces in western Russia and the seizure of this territory by means of military operations.[160] This specification of strategic aims determined the offensive nature of the operation. Moreover, the same logic implied the specific method of the operational manoeuvre to be employed, since the destruction of a mass of ground forces could only be effectuated by means of encirclement. Here, then, was laid the foundation for the first operational drawback. The reason for this was the unintelligibility of the definition of destruction, and the fact that including the entire space of European Russia in a single encirclement operation was impractical. Another operational implication of the strategic specification concerned the territorial dimensions of the operational space. Deploying the German complex of ground forces along the entire space in a uniform offensive mode determined the linear structure of the operation. Here lay the second operational drawback.[161]

The plan envisaged the development of the campaign in two operational stages. The operational objectives for the first stage were: (a) The destruction of the southern group of Russian forces in the area of Kharkov–Kiev by Army Group South (Rundstedt); (b) The destruction of the Russian forces in Belorussia by Army Group Centre (von Bock); (c) The destruction of the northern grouping of Russian forces in the Karelian–Baltic area and the capture of Leningrad and Kronstadt by the joint forces of Army Group North (von Leeb) and Army Group Centre.[162] The designation of objectives for the second stage of operations included Moscow and the Ukraine as general options without specifying priorities or operational methods.[163]

The operational plan, which yielded only the essentials of the first stage, was based on three army groups attacking simultaneously along the entire Russian European border. Each army group was meant to conduct, independently, a series of breakthrough and encirclement manoeuvres that would lead ultimately to the achievement of its operational objective.

The main thrust of the first stage was to combine Army Groups North and Centre in a joint operation in order to destroy the Soviet forces in the north-west sector and seize Leningrad and Kronstadt. From this objective, which was presented with remarkable lucidity by the directive, and from evidence surrendered by Guderian and other field commanders, it is legitimate to assert that not only did the plan provide a clear and distinctive definition of the principal objective for the first stage, it also gave a comprehensive explication of the main effort aimed at accomplishing that same objective.[164] Moreover, from Guderian's varying versions on this issue it can be assumed that either he did not completely understand the logic of the operational planning or that he did not reveal the truth for reasons known only to himself.[165] In fact, the strategic and operational benefits that Germany could have gained from an early seizure of Leningrad, Kronstadt and the north-western sector were enormous. Such a move would have

141

denied the Russians access to the Atlantic; it would have created a continental link with the Finns and Norway; it would have secured the entire north-western strategic flank; and, most important, it would have significantly shortened the extended front line. This last advantage would have yielded great economy of force and thus given the *Wehrmacht* the opportunity to create an echeloned deployment towards the second operational stage. As can be seen, specifying the north-western sector of Russia as the main objective for the first operational stage and assigning to it the appropriate operational effort did indicate logical thinking. In light of these facts one wonders what motivated the group of generals led by Guderian and Halder to claim that Moscow had been the main objective early in August 1941.

The plan suggested that in the course of the initial stage the operation conducted by Army Group South was bound to remain an independent operational element. In other words, Army Group South was expected to accomplish the destruction of the Russian forces in the area of Kharkov–Kiev without the support of any other operational element. Moreover, the text implied that Army Group Centre's termination of its immediate mission constituted a precondition to a later transfer of its forces to the north for the purpose of joining efforts with its northern sister in effectuating the main operational objective of the campaign's first stage.[166]

Thus, logically it can be concluded that the definition of Army Group Centre's initial operational objective was the most crucial prerequisite and the key for the development of the entire campaign. In short, a failure to achieve the destruction of the Russian forces in Belorussia by Army Group Centre would inevitably impair the implementation of the main effort and frustrate the successful conclusion of the operation's first stage – a result which would undermine the further development of the campaign in a positive manner. Clarification of this issue is not just a matter of setting the record straight; it indicates the total ignorance of the campaign's military planner and it comprises the third principal operational drawback. Once it was realized through the exercise of basic logic that Army Group Centre's objective constituted the essential condition for the complete unfolding of the entire operational manoeuvre, the elementary duty of the military planner was to ensure immediate operational ability by allocating appropriate forces and resources. Nonetheless, the plan allotted similar forces to all three army groups for the purpose of accomplishing their varying missions.[167] As was discovered in the course of later events, the definition of all three operational objectives posed an overambitious challenge in relation to the force allocation.[168] This issue further underscores our argument. Therefore, focusing the main operational effort on Leningrad or any other objective save that of Army Group Centre was a serious blunder because the definition of the main effort must logically correspond to the matter representing the essential condition for the evolution of the entire operation. This last premise comprises the essence of the centre of gravity concept. Moreover, the plan to employ all the operational groupings in a simultaneous offensive along the entire length of the Russian theatre overstretched the *Wehrmacht*'s fighting resources and thus prohibited the application of a deep-echeloned manoeuvre. Had the plan determined from the outset one of the army groups' operational mission as defensive, or anything less ambitious than the overall destruction of the forces opposing it, the opportunity would have arisen to create a realistic main effort through the economization of force. However, the term defensive was absent from the *Wehrmacht*'s conceptual inventory and qualifying objectives or missions was out of fashion in 1941.

In this operational issue, more than in anything else, lay the causes for the German failure in the Russian campaign. Therefore, those historians who defined the battle of Moscow as the turning point of the campaign are correct, because the failure to destroy the Soviet forces in Belorussia prevented the successful progression of the entire operation, even in a theoretical context. It was this shortcoming in planning that caused the grave deflection in the manoeuvre's development, and led eventually to the operational vortex in Autumn 1941.[169]

The element that generated the operational vortex, terminating in the collapse of the *Wehrmacht*'s command system in December 1941, was not the lack of clear definitions of operational objectives, as argued by Guderian.[170] In fact, the agent who initiated this operational turbulence was Guderian himself in his decisions and actions following the Novyi Borisov meeting of August 1941. Guderian's decision, supported by von Bock, to initiate a preparatory concentration of troops to serve a subsequent advance on Moscow, commenced the dynamic that led to the ultimate chaos.[171] The deliberate deviation from the concluding remarks of the supreme strategic director and the impertinent disobedience of the high command's explicit orders reflected both the utter contempt for the principles of system dynamics and the shallow understanding of the notion of operational objective in the *Wehrmacht*. Moreover, the events which followed Guderian's decision of 4 August demonstrated the destructiveness of the opportunistic-competitive urge, so common among the *Wehrmacht* generals.

Between 8 August 1941 and mid-September, Guderian as

commandant of Panzer Army 2 perpetrated four independent acts of insubordination against the high command's operational orders.[172] In the course of the same period, both in reaction to his disobedient initiatives, and due to the consequent lack of understanding between the high command and the army group headquarters, Guderian's formation suffered the imposition of no less than six countermanding orders, involving the cessation of operations, repositioning, and extensive countermarches.[173] The clearest illustration of the situation in Army Group Centre is provided by the Desna river bridgehead. In the course of the Kiev operation, early in September 1941, Guderian independently initiated a crossing of the Desna by XLVII Panzer Corps in order to create a bridgehead for further operations on the eastern bank of the river. The operation, which met stiff Russian resistance, lasted for several days of intensive fighting and involved heavy losses. Finally, when the high command found out about the successful conclusion of the operation, in which it had no operational interest, it ordered the immediate evacuation of the bridgehead and countermarched the panzer corps to its starting line. The wastage of resources and the decline in morale were appalling.[174]

The events of summer and autumn 1941 revealed an extreme lack of operational consciousness and a hypofunctioning of the *Wehrmacht* as a system. Ignoring explicit orders, directives, and definitions of objectives by the operational echelons of command became an established norm and the independent undertaking of opportunistic initiatives was a common phenomenon. With the decrease of professional guidance according to long-term and coherent aims, the cognitive basis for the system's functioning became less and less intelligible – a fact that destroyed the mutual confidence between the various command echelons and broke the essential course of successive operations.

Between 21 August and mid-October 1941, the *Wehrmacht* high command deliberately altered its own definitions of the operation's main objective twice, and not because of an unpredicted occurrence of an operational development. Moreover, the changes were made in spite of the fact that not one of the initial preconditions that were supposed to generate the implementation of the joint operation of Army Groups North and Centre did in fact materialize. In other words, the Soviet forces in the Ukraine, Belorussia and the north-western sector were severely beaten, but by no means destroyed, since their opposition remained resolute and even increased. Not only did the alterations maintain the entire length of the original front line, they also overextended the *Wehrmacht*'s and Germany's resources to the point of rupture.[175] The reason was that intensive changes ignored crucial considerations, such as the amount of time consumed by preparatory concentrations of forces for operational moves, the rate of technical and human erosion accentuated by successive moves of huge fighting masses along extensive areas, and finally, the logistical implications deriving from the execution of such moves.[176]

On 21 August Hitler altered his original definition of the main objective from Leningrad in the north to the Ukraine in the south.[177] This change, which implied a joint operation combining the forces of Army Groups Centre and South and an almost complete halt of offensive operations in the remaining sectors of the Russian theatre, actually derived from a single consideration, that is, the emerging opportunity to encircle four Russian armies in the area of Kiev–Cherkassey–Lochvitsa which arose with the random arrival of elements from 2nd Panzer Army in the Pochep–Gomel' sector.[178]

When the Kiev operation came to an end and it was realized that in spite of the devastating[179] results, Russian opposition remained effective, the German high command countermarched the 2nd Panzer Army in the direction of Bryansk–Orel and designated Moscow as the objective for Army Group Centre.[180] It is extremely hard to determine whether the motive for defining Moscow as the objective was the appreciation of its strategic value or whether it was because it offered yet another opportunity for a grand encirclement, which emerged from the combined advance of Panzer Armies 2, and 3 (Hoth) towards the area of Viaz'ma–Bryansk. In any case, the advance on Moscow was delayed until the conclusion of the Viaz'ma-Bryansk encirclement, and resumed in the middle of October.[181]

A tactical unit can sustain the pace of such feverish changes due to its compact dimensions and because it is always backed up by logistics and reserves supplied by the mother formation. Operational groupings or complexes are incapable of sustaining a hectic pace of transition over a long period especially when the resources of the state have been drained. The vigorous advance towards Moscow did not help, and the *Wehrmacht* as an exhausted system collapsed in December 1941.[182] Halder's account of 11 August 1941, a time when even a temporary check of the *Wehrmacht* was inconceivable, reveals the futility of the attempt to enforce aims and objectives such as destruction on the Russian theatre:

> It is becoming more and more obvious that the Russian colossus has been underestimated. We calculated around 200 enemy divisions at the beginning of the war. Now we know of at least 360 . . . And when we destroy a dozen of them, the Russians put another dozen in their place.[183]

In the Russian campaign the *Wehrmacht* learned the cardinal operational principle in a negative way. In the absence of a rational and realistic aim, the operational manoeuvre lacks the essential cognitive focus to guide its coherent course. The sharper the amplitudes of the deviating manoeuvre turn, the greater the self-inflicted effects of attrition become, until the system is thrown into a state of paralysis and disintegration. Here lies the essence of operational logic. Tactical excellence can never be a substitute for operational cognition, and not only because it is unaware of system operating principles. The principal mechanisms which contribute to the formation of tactical excellence, such as aggressiveness, initiative, adhering to missions, and the possession of the technical aspects of warfare, if they are not balanced by a cognitive tension and operational judgement, must eventually lead to the system's disintegration and not to the creation of operational excellence. Accumulating tactical successes, as great as they may be, if not backed by professional operational direction expressed by means of rational and coherent objectives, may end up in a fiasco. The North-African campaign of Rommel explicitly illustrates the purely military aspects of this phenomenon. The need for dispatching a German expeditionary force to North Africa arose from the Italian defeats in the summer and autumn of 1940. A theatre survey conducted by W.R. von Thoma in October 1940 determined a force comprising four panzer divisions as a critical mass if a decision was taken to dispatch a German force.[184] Hitler's ultimate decision not only determined the secondary importance of the African theatre, but even set up the limited proportions of the German adventure.[185] The fact that the Royal Navy dominated the Mediterranean, as well as the fact that following the defeat in France, North Africa became the British main theatre of ground operations, only accentuated the strategic constraints which should have obliged Germany to apply a defensive orientation in its conduct of the African enterprise. The isolation of the theatre, from a German point of view, and, on the other hand, the British resolution to retain control over the southern bank of the Mediterranean basin, emphasized Germany's problem of setting a delicate equilibrium between the strategic constraints, the available resources, and the operational system. The Italian involvement, both in the operational and strategic senses, complicated the situation even further by adding to it the dimension of coalition.

By way of contrast, the qualifications for the selection of the German commander of the expeditionary force were not his experience in operational conduct of an independent command. The man who was selected for the post was the brave and energetic commandant of the 7th Panzer Division in the French campaign.

Erwin Rommel indeed combined in his personality the traits and experience one should beware of when appointing a commander for an isolated and complicated independent theatre. Although he was an excellent and opportunistic tactician, a charismatic leader devoted to his troops, and aggressive by nature, he lacked any experience of independent operational command.

At a meeting before his departure for North Africa, Rommel was briefed by von Brauchitsch, the Army's Commander in Chief. His immediate mission was defined as conducting a fighting reconnaissance for the purpose of clarifying the operational picture in the theatre. He was likewise allocated two divisions, a panzer and a light division.[186] From the start, Rommel chose to ignore both his defined mission and the obvious strategic constraints, and on his arrival decided to initiate a real offensive.[187]

In an additional briefing, presided over by Hitler on 19 March 1941, Rommel was informed by the Army's Commander in Chief that the strategic aim was not to force the British out of Africa, an achievement that was considered to be impractical, but to reinforce the Italians so that their presence in the theatre could be maintained.[188] In the course of this meeting approval was given for initiating a limited offensive operation in the direction of Agedabia. Moreover, the possibility of seizing Benghazi was raised but was made conditional on the arrival of the whole 15th Panzer Division and on the emergence of favourable operational circumstances. Rommel, guided by his simplistic tactical perception, immediately raised the issue that unless the whole of Cyrenaica was taken Benghazi could not be held. Thus, through his tactical aggressiveness and manipulative methods he paved the way for broadening the mission's scope.[189] The reservations expressed by the Commander in Chief were seen by Rommel as an attempt to abandon North Africa, and were therefore brushed aside.

On his arrival in Africa, Rommel did not wait for the accumulation of his entire force. The operation that commenced with the seizure of Benghazi and Agedabia developed rapidly into a general offensive and resulted in the capture of all of Cyrenaica by the end of May 1941.[190] The swift and resolute tactical success not only changed the operational situation but also created unpredicted strategic difficulties. As a result of capturing Cyrenaica, Rommel found himself compelled by the new operational circumstances to perform three missions in order to preserve his recent achievements and secure the safety of his forces. First of all he was obliged to protect his new defensive line, which rested on the Egyptian border, against a possible British offensive. Then, he had to secure the entire length of his communications stretching all along Cyrenaica. And finally, he had to contain the large British force, which he had trapped in Tobruk but was not strong enough to overwhelm.[191]

Following the exhausting Gazala operation of May 1942 and the subsequent race along the spaces of Marmarica, Rommel decided to exploit the momentum and attempt a penetration into the Egyptian rear, using the disorganized line of El Alamein as a starting point.[192] Motivated by his brilliant victories in the summer and assuming that the British Army was on the verge of collapse, he ignored both the enormous losses suffered by his forces in the course of the summer campaign and the potential complications that could arise from his attempt to push his luck too far. Rommel's tactic-oriented thinking can be recognized not only in the way he was tempted by his tactical successes. He perceived his opponent merely in numerical terms and tactical units.[193] Moreover, his whole approach to the conduct of operations resembled that of a divisional commander striving to concentrate on his immediate tactical missions. Basically he was driven by a tactical urge to exploit every foreseeable opportunity to destroy his adversary and so regarded logistical considerations and operational risks as trivial nuisances or superficial gambles. His initial analysis completely ignored the basic strategic equation that should have guided him from the start: although he conducted an independent campaign in an isolated theatre possessing scarce resources, his objective was still clear and limited in nature. Thus, instead of devising an operational method to suit this equation and allow him to attain the strategic aim, he determinedly pursued an uncompromising course which, although it might have appeared promising at certain points, must inevitably lead to his ruin. When his resources of troops, equipment, ammunition and fuel were drained due to his hyper-aggressive initiatives, he expected, almost like a tactical commander, his superior command to provide his needs so that he could resume the fighting, which was his sole interest. By disregarding the apparent asymmetry between the British and German abilities to resupply their forces in the North African theatre, he failed to realize the great advantage in the operational sustaining capacity which the British held over him. Thus, a long series of tactical and operational defeats did not terminate the British strategic presence in Africa, whereas for the Germans a single operational débâcle implied the end of their strategic adventure there.[194]

The July 1942 offensive brought Rommel to the El Alamein line and the culmination of his tactical victories. Nevertheless, at this point Rommel, without realizing it, lost the operational initiative. The range of missions which he was forced to undertake as a result of his recent victories was much too great for his exhausted and enfeebled forces to carry out. The check suffered by the Panzer Army Africa in the 3 July 1942 offensive attempt was a hint of the approaching operational standstill. In early July 1942 Panzer Army Africa's order of battle was at less than 25 per cent of its original strength.[195] And indeed the intensive session of fighting, initiated by the British with the aim of causing further erosion to Rommel's force, terminated with the stabilization of the El Alamein line and a prevailing stalemate on 18 July.[196] However, even the instructive lesson of July failed to persuade Rommel of his strategic limitations and he once again surrendered his operational planning to tactical urges. Against sound operational logic and by way of utterly ignoring his incapacity to perform the elementary mission of defending his forward line, Rommel set out to plan the Alam Halfa offensive at the end of August 1942. The operational method applied conformed with the basics of the *Blitzkrieg* tactical formula. Rommel intended to penetrate the British frontal defensive line in its southern sector, irrupt with the Africa Corps into the layout rear, seize the dominant feature of the Alam Halfa ridge, and thus encircle the main body of the 8th Army and bring about its ultimate destruction.[197] After five days of furious fighting and heavy losses the German advance was brought to a halt and the Africa Corps was forced to retreat to its starting line.

The price of the Alam Halfa failure should not be seen simply in the light of the tactical retreat which ensued. With the Alam Halfa failure, Rommel was not only deprived of his operational ability to initiate offensives; in fact he lost the operational and tactical ability to defend the German base in Africa. The only option remaining open to him was to trade area for time. The operational fate of the African Army's remnants and the future of Germany's strategic aims in Africa were both sealed in Alam Halfa.[198]

Martin van Creveld accurately assesses the main problem of the *Wehrmacht's* generals and puts it in a broad perspective:

> Rommel, Guderian, Model, et al. were exceedingly tough officers who fought as hard and as well as any commanders of equivalent rank in history. Not having commanded forces amounting to more than a few army corps, these men were Germany's Pattons. By no stretch of imagination is it possible to see them take on the mantle of an Eisenhower, a MacArthur or a Nimitz. The only officer on the German side who might conceivably have done well on that level was Field Marshal Gerd von Rundstedt, who not incidentally belonged to an older generation.[199]

The striking majority of the *Wehrmacht's* field commanders and General Staff officers genuinely reflected its true nature, that is, tactical excellence. The officers who executed the *Blitzkrieg* at its best were brave and tenacious warriors, charismatic leaders, and, above all, outstanding tactical commanders. Through their connivance they provided Hitler with an operational pattern that was expected to serve as a principal instrument in implementing an irrational and impossible strategy. By their voluntary adherence to Hitler they not only pushed to the margins the surviving islands of operational cognition, but also exchanged this rare quality for a technocratic ethos. In their unbridled opportunism they promoted the tactical formula *penetration × mechanization × encirclement = destruction* beyond the limits of professional and human logic, attempting to satisfy the frenzied fluctuations of an incoherent strategy. Their success was secure as long as the opposition insisted on competing by exercising their own secret weapon, that is, tactics. However, once the Zhukovs, Montgomerys, and Bradleys appeared, and with them a sort of operational consciousness, the *Wehrmacht's* tactical excellence and the magic formula of *Blitzkrieg* lost their ascendancy.

NOTES

1. M. Geyer, 'German Strategy between 1914–1945', in P. Paret (ed.), *Makers of Modern Strategy* (Oxford, 1988), pp. 573, 584, 586–7, 594.
2. Ibid., pp. 572–3, 585–7. The same approach is expressed in A. Hillgruber, *Der Zweite Weltkrieg 1939–1945, Kriegsziele und Strategie der Grosse Mächte* (Stuttgart, 1982).
3. M. van Creveld, *Fighting Power, German Military Performance* (Washington, DC), 1980, p. 40.
4. *Encyclopedia Britannica*, 15th edn (London, 1976), Vol. II, p. 84; *Jane's Dictionary of Military Terms* (London, 1975), p. 29; *Collins Dictionary of the English Language*, 2nd edn (Glasgow, 1986), p. 164; *The Oxford Dictionary of Current English*, 4th edn (Oxford, 1961), p. 124.
5. F.O. Miksche, *Blitzkrieg* (London, 1941), p. 13.
6. P.H. Vigor, *Soviet Blitzkrieg Theory* (London, 1983), p. 24, has also noted the fact that the Wehrmacht lacked an operational theory as late as 1941.
7. K.J. Macksey, *Guderian: Panzer General* (London, 1975), p. 68.
8. L.H. Addington, *The Blitzkrieg Era and the German General Staff 1865–1941* (New Brunswick, 1971), p. 234.
9. B.H. Liddell Hart, *Memoirs* (New York, 1967), Vol. 1, p. 247.
10. This trend was best expressed by works which lacked both professional and academic criticism such as: R.J. O'Neill, 'Doctrine and Training in the German Army 1919–1939', in M. Howard (ed.), *The Theory and Practice of War* (London, 1965), pp. 151–2; C. Messenger, *The Art of Blitzkrieg* (London, 1991), pp. 37–48, 67–84. It was J.J. Mearsheimer, *Liddell Hart and the Weight of History* (London, 1988), who put an end to this trend by proving that Liddell Hart had neither invented *Blitzkrieg* nor exercised any influence on Guderian before 1945.
11. M. Cooper and J. Lucas, *Panzer the Armoured Force of the Third Reich* (London, 1976), pp. 14–15.
12. R. Simpkin, *Race to the Swift* (Oxford, 1985), p. 29, claimed that Beck, as chief of the general staff from 1933–38, was the main contributor to the creation of the *Blitzkrieg* doctrine.

13. M. van Creveld, 'On Learning from the Wehrmacht and Other Things', *Military Review* LXVIII, 1 (1988), p. 66.
14. H. Guderian, *Erinnerungen Eines Soldaten* (Heidelberg, 1951), p. 12.
15. F. Halder, *Kriegstagebuch: Der Russlandfeldzug bis zum Marsch auf Stalingrad*, H.A. Jacobsen (ed.), Vol. 2, Bd. 3, of 3 Aug. 1941. At a briefing of the chiefs of staff of major operational formations which took place at the OKH on 4 June 1941, Halder assessed that the Soviet defensive would collapse after a few days of fighting. Chef des GemSt der HGr Süd Ia No. 299/41 gkdos Chefsache of 6 June 1991 in Aok 17 Führungsabteilung, Annexe 2 to KTB No. 1 Barbarossa. Operations documents of 4 May–August (BA-MA: RH20-17/23, 24).
16. G.A. Higgins, 'German and U.S. Operational Art: A Contrast in Manoeuvre', *Military Review* LXV, 10 (1985), p. 23. A similar approach is expressed in J.W. Woodmansee, '*Blitzkrieg* and the Airland Battle', *Military Review* LXIV, 8 (1984), p. 21.
17. E. von Manstein, *German Defensive Operations against the Soviets by Army Group South 1943/1944*, Liddell Hart Archive (hereafter LHA), 9/24/124, p. 3; *Notes On the Interrogation of Generaloberst Franz Halder*, CW/Oct/45, CRGG 332, LHA, 9/24/107, p. 4; Talk With General Manteuffel, 10 Dec. 1945, LHA, 9/24/125, p. 8; Talk With General Blumentritt, Dec. 1945, LHA, 9/24/93, p. 22; Talk With General W.R. von Thoma, 1 Nov. 1945, LHA, 9/24/144, pp. 5–6; F. Halder, *Hitler as War Lord*, trans. P. Findlay (London, 1950), p. 23; B.H. Liddell Hart (ed.), *The Other Side of the Hill* (London, 1951), p. 129; E. von Manstein, *Lost Victories*, trans. A.G. Powell (London, 1958), pp. 275–6; van Creveld, 'Learning from the Wehrmacht', p. 66; Geyer, 'German Strategy', p. 585.
18. Mearsheimer, *Liddell Hart and the Weight of History*, pp. 8–9, 12, 13, 34–5, 37, 178, 179–201.
19. Geyer, 'German Strategy', p. 585. Mearsheimer, *Liddell Hart*, pp. 180–201, approached the issue of the linkage between Liddell Hart and the concept of *Blitzkrieg* from a single historical perspective. Thus, he revealed Liddell Hart's manipulative deception, but not the fact that the *Blitzkrieg* concept lacked operational substance. B.R. Kroener, 'Squaring the Circle, *Blitzkrieg* Strategy and Manpower Shortage 1939–1942', in W. Deist (ed.), *The German Military in the Age of Total War* (Leamington Spa, UK, 1985), p. 284, views the *Blitzkrieg* with identical perceptions.
20. Mearsheimer, *Liddell Hart*, pp. 188–201.
21. In a letter to Guderian, dated 30 July 1949, Liddell Hart disclosed his interpretation of the *Blitzkrieg* notion, and also urged the German general to reveal his own ideas on the subject. Guderian's irresolute reply offered an unintelligible definition which Liddell Hart emended to conform with his own views, LHA, 9/24/106.
22. B.R. Posen, *The Sources of Military Doctrine, France, Britain, and Germany between the World Wars* (Ithaca, 1988), p. 206, confirms this argument in a most striking manner. Despite the originality and coherence of his dissertation, Posen failed to define the original substance of the *Blitzkrieg* concept, and ended up presenting, unconsciously, Liddell Hart's ideas in his own words.
23. Liddell Hart, *The Other Side of the Hill*; H. Guderian, *Panzer Leader* (New York, 1952), with foreword by B.H. Liddell Hart.
24. The years 1925–33 were characterized by intense intellectual activity focusing on operational matters such as the nature of modern operations, the operational lessons to be learned from the First World War, the operational approaches Germany should adopt in a future conflict, methods of operational offensive and defensive, future organization of the German armed forces, and application of technology, mechanization and armour in a future war. This activity involved great debates between the traditionalists headed by von Seeckt, and the radicals centring around Werner von Blomberg, Joachim von Manteuffel, and W. Fr. von Rabenau. The more renowned works to be compiled during this period were: W. Fr. von Rabenau, *Entschlusse gegen Einen Zahl Uberlegenen Genger* (Berlin, 1935); W. Groener, *Das Testament des Grafen Schlieffen* (Berlin, 1927); W. Foerster, *Aus der Gedankenwerkstatt des Deutschen Generalstabes* (Berlin, 1931); G. Franz, *Die Vernichtungsschlacht im Kriegsgeschichtlichen Beispielen* (Berlin, 1928); G. Brandt, *Moderne Kavallerie* (Berlin, 1931).
25. Posen, *The Sources of Military Doctrine*, pp. 190–92, argues that as early as the mid-1920s the Reichswehr conducted manoeuvres combining motorized and mobile

formations in order to apply mechanization to von Seeckt's offensive concept of
Attaque Brusque. On 10 Nov. 1926 the Truppenamt published through Inspektorat
6(K) (the Weapons Inspectorate for Motorized Troops) RWM HL IV Nr. 601.26, Geh.
In6(K) BA MA RH 39/V.115. The directive based the operational employment of tank
formations on three principles: it rejected the French concept of dividing tank units
in support of infantry formations; it pointed out that the appropriate method for
operating tank formations would be in combination with troops possessing operational mobility (*Schnell Bewegliche Truppen*); and, finally, it determined that tank formations could be operated quite independently of slow moving infantry formations.
On 5 Dec. 1926, the Operations Section of the Truppenamt published document, Ii
(Operations Section) 762/276 Kdos. II, BA MA II H539, signed by W. von Fritsch, who
was the head of the section. This document defined the tank as the weapon of
decision for future wars (*Schlachtenscheidende Angriffswaffe*) and accordingly
ordered the beginning of a gradual conversion of the motorized unit's assignment
from transportation to combat. On 1 Sept. 1929, the training section of the
Truppenamt distributed a training programme for tank formations, preceded by a
detailed concept of organization, signed by W. von Blomberg, Chef. H1 659/29 Geh.
T4 (Training Section), BA MA II H 540.
26. Guderian, *Panzer Leader*, pp. 20–21, admitted reading the writings of J.F.C. Fuller,
Liddell Hart, and also Fritz Heigel's technical book: *Taschenbuch der Tanks*. Miksche,
Blitzkrieg, pp. 106–7, claimed that the German General Staff was significantly
influenced by the Austrian General Eimannsberg. In his book *Der Kampfwagenkrieg*,
which was published in Germany, Eimannsberg suggested structural formulae for a
panzer and mechanized division. These formulae were later adopted, almost to the
letter by Guderian. In 1935 M.J. Kurtzinski's book, *Taktik Schneller Verbande*, was
published in Germany. This Russian book comprised the operational essentials for
employing mobile formations and had no German equivalent. Thus, there can be no
doubt that the Germans were indeed influenced by Russian tactical and operational
thinking.
27. Guderian, *Panzer Leader*, pp. 20–36. A good example demonstrating the literary technique used by Guderian was the combination, in the same context, of the sceptical
expressions made by his superior Stülpnagel and his own optimistic views, regarding
the future of the armoured troops, ibid. p. 25. Another example was provided by
citing the Chief of the General Staff, when referring to Guderian, at the end of the
1936 manoeuvres, as the father of the Panzertruppen: 'There is only one thing missing. The balloon should have "Guderian's Panzers are best" marked on it'; ibid. p. 36.
28. Ibid., p. 24.
29. Ibid., pp. 32–3; Guderian's letters to Liddell Hart, dated 7 Oct. and 14 Dec. 1948, LHA,
9/24/106; Liddell Hart's talk with von Thoma, dated 1 Nov. 1945, LHA, 9/24/144, p. 1;
E. von Manstein, *Aus Einem Soldatenleben* (Bonn, 1958), pp. 240–41.
30. Messenger, *The Art of Blitzkrieg*, p. 78, not only treated the most notable and the
only operational two-volume dissertation to be composed under the National
Socialist regime as a pamphlet, but even failed to note the proper date of its publication.
31. Mearsheimer, *Liddell Hart*, pp. 53–69.
32. Manstein, *Aus Einem Soldatenleben*, pp. 240–41.
33. The most ostensible of these failures concerned arming the backbone of the panzer
divisions with the PzKW I and PzKW II tanks. Both these very light tanks, based upon
the British Carden Loyd chassis, were not designed for combat, but were meant to
serve as training equipment, thus covering the gap until sufficient quantities of the
two main battle tanks (PzKW III, PzKW IV) would be supplied, Guderian, *Panzer
Leader*, p. 28. Another failure concerned the equipping of the PzKW III (the main
battle tank designed for armour versus armour role) with the 37mm and 50mm L-42
inferior guns, 1 Panzer Division Abteilung Ia, Gefechtsbericht der 1 Panzer Brigade of
12 June 1940, (RH 27-1/17), 7 Panzer Division Abteilung Ia, Nr. 440/40 Geheim, of 14
July 1940, p.3, (RH 27-7/52). The third failure concerned the inappropriate organization and equipment of the mechanized infantry and engineers, F.M. von Senger und
Etterlin, *Die PanzerGrenadiere* (Munich, 1961), pp. 67–77, 1 Panzer Division
Abteilung Ia, Gefechtsbericht der Panzer Jägerabteilung 37, of 10 June 1940, p. 2, and

XIX Panzer Korps Abteilung Ia, Erfahrungsberichte des Pioniere Bataillon 43, of Oct. 1939, (RH 21-2/V.29).
34. Generalstab (ed.), Heeres Dienstvorschrift 300 *Truppenführung*, Vol. 2 (Berlin, 1936).
35. Van Creveld, *Fighting Power*, p. 30.
36. *Truppenführung*, Introduction.
37. Miksche, *Blitzkrieg*, pp. 59, 129.
38. Hillgruber, *Der Zweite Weltkrieg 1939-1945* and Geyer, 'German Strategy', pp. 572–3, refer to the process as the collapse of professional strategy. The term 'professional strategy' is original and accurate when one refers to matters concerning strategic conduct and the interaction between the military high command and the political leadership. However, since we are concerned mainly with operational matters we will use the term operational cognition when referring to the specific qualities that were suppressed by the emergence of the *Blitzkrieg* concept.
39. K.J. Müller (ed.), *General Ludwig Beck: Studien und Dokumenten zur Politisch-Militärischen Vorstellungswelt und tätigkeit des Generalstabschefs des Deutschen Heeres 1933-1938* (Bopard, 1980), pp. 266–70. Beck referred to the opposing school as follows: 'They were simply maximizing the use of weapons in manoeuvre . . . They had never learned to evaluate operations within the context of coherent strategy . . . They were technocrats rather than strategists.'
40. Geyer, 'German Strategy', pp. 555–66, referred to the group as the 'young Turks'.
41. R. Barthel, 'Theorie und Praxis der Heeres Motorisierung im Faschistischen Deutschland bis 1939', Diss. D.Phil. (Leipzig, 1967).
42. Geyer, 'German Strategy', p. 566.
43. Posen, *The Sources of Military Doctrine*, p. 180.
44. E.W. Bennett, *German Armament and the West, 1932-1933* (Princeton, 1979), pp. 235–41, 338–55.
45. M. Geyer, 'National Socialism and the Military in the Weimar Republic', in P. Stachura (ed.), *The Nazi Machtergreifung* (London, 1983), pp. 101–23.
46. Guderian, *Panzer Leader*, pp. 32, 302. Guderian's letters to Liddell Hart from 7 Oct and 14 Dec. 1948, LHA, 9/24/106.
47. Guderian, *Panzer Leader*, p. 32, confirmed the first issue when admitting: 'It was Beck's intention to form a general staff for the new army of the Third Reich of which Moltke would have approved.' Geyer, 'German Strategy', pp. 568–71, discusses the remaining issues at length. Müller, *General Ludwig Beck*, 'The Memorandum of May 20', pp. 503–50 emphasized the third issue.
48. Guderian, *Panzer Leader*, p. 33. Messenger, *The Art of Blitzkrieg*, pp. 79–80.
49. Guderian, *Panzer Leader*, p. 33.
50. Geyer, 'German Strategy', p. 586.
51. Guderian, *Panzer Leader*, pp. 31–3. Müller, *General Ludwig Beck*, pp. 266–70.
52. Hasso von Manteuffel's letter to B.H. Liddell Hart, dated 10 March 1949, LHA, 9/24/125; F.G. von Schweppenburg's letter to Liddell Hart, dated 8 March 1949, LHA, 9/24/206.
53. Liddell Hart's talk with W.R. von Thoma, dated 20 Nov. 1945, LHA, 9/24/144. According to von Thoma's account, Rommel, who had been a devoted infantryman, realized after the Polish campaign that the future of a military career would inevitably lie with the armoured troops. He therefore asked Hitler to be transferred to the armoured troops and be given command of a Panzer formation. This anecdote confirms the opportunistic aspect of Rommel's personality.
54. Geyer, 'German Strategy', pp. 567–8; W. Murray, *The Change in the European Balance of Power 1938-1939: The Path to Ruin* (Princeton, 1984), p. 174.
55. M. Messerschmidt, 'German Military Effectiveness between 1919–1939', in A.R. Millett and W. Murray (eds), *Military Effectiveness in the Interwar Period* (Boston, 1988), p. 243.
56. W. Deist, *The Wehrmacht and German Armament* (London, 1981), p. 43, argues that in fact there was no marked difference between Guderian's perceptions of operating armoured formations and those of L. Beck. Moreover, Beck approached the issue of operational organization with greater flexibility.
57. Geyer, 'German Strategy', p. 567.
58. Ibid., p. 586.

59. Müller, *General Ludwig Beck*, in the essay: 'Observations on the Military Political Situation in May 1938', from 5 May 1938, pp. 502–11.
60. M. Geyer, *Aufrüstung oder Sicherheit: Reichswehr in der Krise der Machtpolitik 1924–1936* (Wiesbaden, 1980), pp. 446–9.
61. Müller, *General Ludwig Beck*, pp. 182–3.
62. Geyer, 'German Strategy', p. 569.
63. This series of plans was titled 'Sondefalle', and it constituted an operational framework for a takeover of Austria and Czechoslovakia in case of emergency.
64. Geyer, *Aufrüstung*, pp. 419–32.
65. Müller, *General Ludwig Beck*, 'The Memorandum of May 20', pp. 503–50.
66. Posen, *The Sources of Military Doctrine*, p. 212.
67. Geyer, 'German Strategy', p. 572.
68. On 26 Dec. Hitler issued the famous order that directed the *Wehrmacht* to conduct a rigid defensive in front of Moscow. Guderian, who strove to maintain operational flexibility, attempted a tactical retreat and was eventually dismissed by Hitler. OKW, W.F. St./Op. Abt.(H), Nr. 442,277/41 Geheim Kommandosache Chefsache of 26 Dec. 1941, RW 19/166.
69. After Beck's fall in 1938, Halder, the new chief of the Army General Staff, complied with Hitler's demand and submitted a plan for Gradual Force Building (Wellen Mobilization System), a document Beck would have totally rejected.
70. Geyer, 'German Strategy', pp. 586, 572.
71. Posen, *The Sources of Military Doctrine*, pp. 212–3; R.J. O'Neill, *The German Army and the Nazi Party 1933–1938* (London, 1966); D. Bradley, *Generaloberst Heinz Guderian und die Entstehungsgeschichte des Modernen Blitzkrieges* (Osnabrück, 1978); and Messenger, *The Art of Blitzkrieg*, are a few examples of the many who attempted to tackle the issue.
72. Geyer, 'German Strategy', p. 587.
73. Miksche, *Blitzkrieg*, pp. 43–9, presented the different versions according to their theatre of origin. Posen, *The Sources of Military Doctrine*, argued, for example, that the Polish campaign reflected an improvisation of *Blitzkrieg*, whereas the French campaign demonstrated the classical *Blitzkrieg*.
74. Geyer, 'German Strategy', p. 585.
75. 10. Panzer Division Abteilung Ia, Nr. 141/39 Geheim, of 31 Oct 1939, p. 4, (RH 27-10/5); 3. Panzer Division Abteilung Ia, Bericht von Gen.Lt. Frhr. Geyr von Schweppenburg, p. 28; Panzer Gruppe von Kleist, Abteilung Ia, Chef des Generalstab, Richtlinien für die Führung Schneller Gruppen, p. 11 outline of 20 Oct. 1940 (RH 21-1/37).
76. F. Hossbach, *Zwischen Wehrmacht und Hitler, 1934–1938* (Göttingen, 1965), pp. 181–9. The Hossbach Memorandum, composed by Col. Friedrich Hossbach, a senior *Wehrmacht* aide to the Führer, abbreviated minutes of the conference in the Reich Chancellery. In the conference, which was presided over by Hitler on 5 Nov. 1937, Hitler laid down the main lines of his strategic policy.
77. Guderian's letter to Liddell Hart, dated 20 Dec. 1949, LHA, 9/24/106, expressed his idea of tactical shock as a central element in the *Blitzkrieg* concept.
78. Posen, *The Sources of Military Doctrine*, p. 183.
79. Guderian's letter to Liddell Hart, dated 1 May 1949, LHA, 9/24/106.
80. K. von Kraft Delmensingen, *Der Durchbruch: Studie an Hand der Vorgange des Weltkrieges 1914–1918* (Hamburg, 1937); W. Balck, *Development of Tactics – World War*, trans. by H. Bell (Ft. Leavenworth, 1922), pp. 62, 81, 91, 266; German General Staff, *Der Angriff im Stellungskrieg, 1.1.1918*, trans. by B.E.F. Intelligence, pp. 3–17; G. Bruchmüller, *The German Artillery in the Breakthrough Battles of the World War*, trans. by J.H. Wallace and H.D. Kehrn (Ft. Sill, OK, 1922), pp. 40–71.
81. A. von Schlieffen, 'Cannae Studien', in *Gesammelte Schriften* (3 Vols.) (Berlin, 1913), Vol. 1, 25–266; idem, *Cannae* (Berlin, 1936).
82. C. von der Goltz, *The Conduct of War* (London, 1898), pp. 159–60, rejected the idea of breakthrough or operational penetration for three reasons. The first derived from the prevailing assumption that operational penetration could not be developed out of a strategic line; the second regarded it impractical due to the infantry's lack of

operational mobility; and the third concerned the attempt to refrain from a frontal attack at the tactical context. Miksche, *Blitzkrieg*, p. 50 confirmed the above argument.
83. Miksche, *Blitzkrieg*, pp. 50–51. This argument was also confirmed by: G. Blumentritt's letter to Liddell Hart, no date, LHA, 9/24/93; W.K. Nehring's letter to Liddell Hart, dated 7 Jan. 1958, LHA, 9/24/206; K. Dittmar's letter to Liddell Hart, dated 6 Dec., LHA, 9/24/206; L.G.F. von Schweppenburg's letter to Liddell Hart, dated 12 Jan. 1958, LHA, 9/24/206; L. Crüwell's letter to Liddell Hart, dated 23 Jan. 1958, LHA, 9/24/206; E. von Manstein's letter to Liddell Hart, dated 25 Jan. 1958, LHA, 9/24/206; K. Liebman's letter to Liddell Hart, dated 8 March 1958, LHA, 9/24/206; R. Steiger, *Armoured Tactics in the Second World War* (Oxford, 1991), p. 34.
84. Miksche, *Blitzkrieg*, p. 50.
85. This exact argument was expressed by H. Guderian, *Achtung Panzer, die Entwicklung der Panzerwaffe ihre Kampftaktik und ihre Operative Möglichkeiten* (Stuttgart, 1937), p. 176, and Panzergruppe von Kleist, Abteilung Ia, Nr. 217/40 Geheim Kommandosache Chefsache of 12 March 1940, (RH 21-1/18). Moreover, in his account of the final briefing, presided over by Hitler on 20 Feb. 1940, for the purpose of examining and coordinating the last details of the offensive plan in the West (Fall Gelb), Guderian admitted, when asked by Hitler about the operational objectives of his panzer corps, that the OKH's plan covered only the phase of advance to the Meuse and the breakthrough and did not refer to any further objectives. Thus, it is clear that the operational planning in the *Wehrmacht* indeed focused solely on the technical aspects of the penetration.
86. Miksche, *Blitzkrieg*, pp. 52, 59, 130. The tactical formula for a mechanized-infantry battalion penetration allotted it a sector of 500 meters. The basic method consisted of infiltration, developing in three stages: The first (*Niederhalten*) involved holding the enemy by fire, destroying the enemy's frontal sources of fire by an initiated fire-fight (*Feuerkampf*), and covering the approach of the penetrating force; in the second stage, the defender was blinded by a smoke-screen while the penetrating force broke into the enemy's defended locality; the third stage concerned the mopping up of the defender's layout and the simultaneous attempt by the penetrating force to outflank the defender (*Aufrollen*).
87. The term *Schwerpunkt* should be translated as Thrust Point, which is a tactical idea, unlike the term 'centre of gravity', which represents an operational idea. The term *Aufrollen* expressed in German the technical notion of 'Roll Out', 'Work Along' or 'Clear'.
88. Miksche, *Blitzkrieg*, p. 51.
89. OKH Richtlinien für die Führung und Einsatz der Panzerdivision of 3 Dec. 1940, (B II 2 D g 66); E. von Manstein's letter to Liddell Hart, dated 25 Jan. 1958, LHA, 9/24/206; G. Heinrici's talk with Liddell Hart, from 3 Jan. 1946, LHA, 9/24/110.
90. H. Guderian, *Panzer Marsch*, trans. M. Michaelis, draft offered to Liddell Hart, p. 14, LHA, 9/24/44; Liddell Hart's talk with R.W. von Thoma from 11 Nov. 1945, p. 1, LHA, 9/24/144.
91. OKH Richtlinien für Führung und Einsatz der Panzerdivision of 3 Dec. 1940, p. 21 (B II 2 D g 66); von Manstein, *Lost Victories*, p. 109.
92. E. Rohricht, *Probleme der Kesselschlacht* (Karlsruhe, 1958), p. 11; F.W. von Mellenthin, *Panzer Battles* (Oklahoma, 1986), pp. 26–39.
93. Steiger, *Armour Tactics*, p. 35; Geyer, 'German Strategy', pp. 574, 591.
94. OKW / Wehrmacht – Führungsstab/L, IV, Chefsachen Barbarossa of 30 April 1941, p. 105.
95. Guderian, *Panzer Leader*, pp. 88–9, 90–92; Manstein, *Lost Victories*, pp. 98–102, 109. Both Guderian and Manstein recorded that after conceiving the offensive plan the latter approached Guderian, who was regarded as the expert in armour tactics and a leading exponent of *Blitzkrieg*, asking for his opinion on the question whether tank formations would be able to negotiate the Ardennes ridge. Guderian rejected the entire plan on the spot, but later, having been briefed in detail by Manstein, became one of its leading advocates. Manstein suggested his plan on his personal initiative and out of conviction that the OKH's offensive plan was a modern repetition of the Schlieffen plan. The resistance to Manstein and his plan in the circles of the High Command was such that after his success in convincing Hitler to adopt his plan, he

was transferred to a marginal post. In spite of Hitler's consent to adopt the plan the majority of the German high-ranking generals were sceptical about its prospects and demonstrated little understanding of its essentials, both in the war games of 14 February and Hitler's final briefing of the 20th.

96. Ibid., pp. 98–102.

97. Unlike the *Blitzkrieg* concept which strove to attain a tactical *Schwerpunkt*, or shock, through a mechanical concentration of fire and a columnar mass, the Manstein plan aimed at creating an operational centre of gravity. In other words, it sought an axis of operation which would allow both the splitting of the defensive into various components, and the development of the campaign in such a manner that the defender would be left with no option but that of resigning his original strategic aim.

98. Guderian, *Panzer Leader*, p. 98, recorded that in the offensive plan the OKH did not specify what should be the operational objective after the crossing of the Meuse. If indeed encirclement was the plan's rationale, then Amiens should have been defined as the operational objective. But according to Guderian, who was well acquainted with the plan's fundamentals since being briefed by Manstein, it was not settled even after the briefing whether the operational objective should be Paris or Amiens. G. Blumentritt, *Strategie und Taktik* (Konstanz, 1957), p. 147 referred to the mode of manoeuvre conducted by Army Group A as *Sichelschnitt*, meaning a slashing attack rather than encirclement. Blumentritt, who served at the time with the operations section of the OKH, made a clear distinction in his book between *Kesselschlacht* and *Sichelschnitt*. And since he was acquainted with the plan, we must regard him as an authority in this respect.

99. H. Guderian, *Die Panzertruppen und ihre Zusammenwirken mit Anderen Waffen* (Berlin, 1943), p. 18, recorded that in a visit to the Soviet Union during 1939 he realized that the Russians possessed more than 10,000 tanks, many of them of recent production, 100,000 military vehicles, and more than 150,000 military tractors, used for towing artillery and logistics. He remarked at the time that the Red Army constituted the best equipped and most advanced mechanized land army in the world. This remark and the Russian industrial potential were ignored at the time of planning Barbarossa. Guderian, *Panzer Leader*, pp. 142, 143, 145, 151, 190, 224, 226, 234, 259, also emphasized the German trend to ignore the element of depth in actual operational matters.

100. OKW /Wehrmachtsführungsstab/Abt. L (I) Nr. 33 408/40g. Kdos. Chefsache Barbarossa; H.R. Trevor-Roper, *Hitler's War Directives 1939–1945* (London, 1966), pp. 93–8.

101. Guderian, *Panzer Leader*, pp. 145–6, recorded the shifting of his Panzer Group from the course it was pursuing towards Moscow in a southerly direction in order to exploit the opportunity for encirclement that occurred in Army Group South's sector. The actual definition of Army Group Centre's objectives (Guderian's superior operational grouping) constituted a total imbroglio, due to Guderian's manipulations and inconsistent reports. According to Directive No. 21, Army Group Centre's immediate objective was the destruction of the Soviet forces in Belorussia, whereas its successive objective was to support Army Group North in a combined operation for annihilating the Russian forces in the Leningrad sector. Guderian, without any basis, tended to argue that Army Group Centre's objective was Moscow, and even managed to convince his superior, von Bock, to adopt his opinion by verbal manipulation. This last argument was confirmed by E. von Kleist in his talk with Liddell Hart on 6 Sept 1945, LHA, 9/24/118.

102. B.H. Liddell Hart (ed.), *The Rommel Papers* (London, 1953), pp. 207–14, 245–9, 251, 257, 277, 283.

103. We will note here the prominent theoretical works, published in the course of the period 1933–45: K. Kraft von Delmensingen, *Der Durchbruch*; K. Justrow, *Feldherr und Kriegstechnik* (Oldenburg, 1933); F.E.E.A., von Kochenhausen, *Taktisches Handbuch für den Truppenführer und Seine Gehilfen* (Berlin, 1936); H. Greiner & J. Degener, *Taktik im Rahmen des Verstarkten Infanterie Battaillons* (Berlin, 1937); M. Borchert, *Der Kampf Gegen Tanks* (Berlin, 1931) (although this book was published prior to the period under discussion, its unique relevance justifies its inclusion in this list); W. Nehring, *Panzerabwehr* (Berlin, 1936); H. Guderian, *Achtung Panzer*

(Guderian's book was not intended originally to serve as a tactical manual. It was published on Lutz' orders, as part of a public-relations campaign conducted by the Headquarters of the Mobile Troops. Nevertheless, it remained the principal tactical manual until the end of the war); G.P. von Zezschwitz, *Der Panzerkampf* (Munich/ Berlin, 1938); W. Spannenkrebs, *Angriff mit Kampfwagen* (Oldenburg, 1939); F. von Senger und Etterlin, *Tanks die Abenteuerliche Eine Kriegsmachine* (Potsdam, 1938); M.J. Kurtzinski, *Taktik Schneller Verbanden* (Potsdam, 1935) (this book was a translation from Russian and emphasized our argument concerning the subjects that occupied the attention of the German officer corps); H. Guderian, *Die Panzertruppen und ihre Zusammenwirken mit Anderen Waffen* (published during Guderian's tenure as General Inspector of Armoured Troops. It demonstrated the main tactical problem which infected the *Wehrmacht* during the war years); H. Allmendinger, 'Panzertaktik', *Die Kraftfahrkampftruppe*, 6 (1938), pp. 217–9; W. Bolckheim, 'Zusammenwirken von Panzertruppen mit Flieger', *Die Kraftfahrkampftruppe*, 4 (1937), pp. 101–4; A. Doege, 'Infanterie und Panzer', *Militärwochenblatt*, 29 (April 1938), cols. 2810-2815; H. Guderian, 'Kraftfahrkampftruppen', *Militärwissenschaftliche Rundschau*, 1 (1939), pp. 52–77.

104. Messerschmidt, 'German Military Effectiveness', p. 244.
105. The generals' letters to Liddell Hart discussing this question indicated a sharp lack of consensus, and a wide variation of interpretations: Blumentritt to Liddell Hart, no date, LHA, 9/24/206; Nehring's letter, dated 7 Jan. 1958, ibid.; Dittmar's letter, dated 6 Dec. 1957, ibid.; Schweppenburg's letter, dated 12 Jan. 1958, ibid.; Crüwell's letter, dated 23 Jan. 1958, ibid.; Manstein's letter, dated 25 Jan. 1958, ibid.; Liebman's letter, dated 8 March 1958, ibid.
106. Guderian, *Panzer Leader*, pp. 146–7, recorded a debate that arose during the final preparations for the Russian campaign. The debate, which concerned the question of a uniform breakthrough method to be applied by the German formation in the initial stage of the offensive, involved two groups of generals. The armoured generals, referring to the French campaign, argued in favour of an assault type breakthrough led by armoured formations. Whereas the infantry generals favoured a conditioned breakthrough led by infantry. The debate reflected sectarianism and tactical parochialism since the selection of a particular method of breakthrough should never be guided by an imposed universal rule but by the specific operational circumstances.
107. Guderian's letter to Liddell Hart, dated 20 Dec. 1949, LHA, 9/24/106; Manteuffel's letter to Liddell Hart, dated 15 May 1949, pp.1–12, 9/24/125; The questionnaire of General B. Müller Hillebrand, dated April 1952 and May 1953, LHA, 9/24/227, 9/24/228.
108. Ibid. Guderian, *Panzer Leader*, pp. 36–7.
109. Guderian's letter of 30 July 1949, LHA, 9/24/106, specified the necessity of three types of tanks in a panzer division, whereas Manteuffel's letter from 27 Aug. 1949 recommended the adoption of a single type of universal main battle tank.
110. Guderian, *Panzer Leader*, pp. 190–94. Von Kleist's talk with Liddell Hart, dated 6 Sept. 1945, LHA, 9/24/118. In his account Guderian claimed that all his actions were performed under the impression that Moscow constituted the operational objective of Army Group Centre. These claims have no factual basis to support them. On the contrary, the clear definition of objectives in Directive No. 21 prove the opposite. Moreover, both Guderian's inconsistent references to the objective, and von Kleist's clear remark on Guderian's manipulative convincing of von Bock confirm the assumption that his conduct was tricky.
111. Guderian, *Panzer Leader*, pp. 194–9.
112. Ibid., p. 268, in a personal conversation with Hitler, when analysing the causes for the December 1941 failure outside Moscow, Guderian complained bitterly about the OKH's and OKW's coercive style of command and control.
113. Ibid., pp. 201–2. The official motive for this conversation, which was initiated by Guderian, Halder and von Bock, was a final attempt to convince Hitler in private to alter his definition of the operational objective to that of Moscow. Nonetheless, prior to the meeting the Army Commander in Chief briefed Guderian and warned him not to bring up the issue of altering the operational objective during the meeting. Thus, the formal reason for the meeting was removed and there was no logic, from

Guderian's point of view, in having it, unless he intended to exploit it for his private purposes.

114. OKH Generalstab d.H. /Operation Abteilung III, Nr. 1736/41 Geheim Kommandosache Chefsache of 18 Dec. 1941, (RH 19 II/136); Panzer ArmeeoberKommando 2, Abteilung Ia, Kriegstagebuch Nr. 1 of 21 Dec. 1941, p. 3, (RH 21-2/v. 756); On 18 Dec. 1941, Hitler ordered all *Wehrmacht* units to stick rigidly to their defensive line, all along the Eastern front. Following this order Guderian called a meeting of his formation commanders and rejected the order, claiming that its execution was operationally illogical since it would cause the collapse of the entire front. The meeting, which was attended by von Kluge, the Army Group commander at the time, confirmed the argument that disobeying orders of the high command was not new to the field commanders of the *Wehrmacht*.

115. Panzer ArmeeoberKommando 2 Abteilung Ia, Kriegstagebuch Nr. 1, of 26 Dec. 1941, (RH 21-2/v.277). On 25 Dec. 1941 Guderian called Field Marshal von Kluge, Chief of Army Group Centre by telephone telling him that unless he was granted operational freedom through the cancelling of the OKH order of 18 Dec., he would act according to his individual conscience. Thus, the next day Hitler, through the OKW, communicated the order which both reinforced the 'No Retreat!' order of 18 Dec., and dismissed Guderian publicly from his field command.

116. 1 Panzer Division Abteilung Ia, Gefechtbericht der 1 Panzer Brigade of 10 July 1940, p. 2, (RH 27-1/17). The Germans experienced this inferiority of their tank guns in engagements like Arras, and cited it in a published collection of lessons learned in battle: Richtlinien für die Führung der Panzerdivision, from Dec. 1940 (B II 2Dg 66). However, examining the battle reports of the tactical and operational formations in the Russian campaign, one realizes that in fact nothing had been done except the mere recording of the former experience in the Western offensive. 4 Panzer Division Abteilung Ia, Nr. 71/42 Geheim, of 12 March 1942, (RH 27/4-37).

117. 1 Panzer Division Abteilung Ia, Gefechtbericht der Panzer Jäger Bataillon 37, from 10 June 1940, p. 2 (RH 27-1/17); Panzer ArmeeoberKommando 2 Abteilung Ic, Meldung der Panzer Jäger Abteilung 42, of 8 July 1941, (RH 21-2/v.647).

118. 7 Panzer Division Abteilung Ia, Nr. 440/40 Geheim of 14 July 1940, p. 3 (RH 27-7/53); 4 Panzer Division Abteilung Ia, Nr. 814/41 Geheim of 22 Oct. 1941 (RH 27/4-37).

119. OKH Richtlinien für Führung und Einsatz der Panzerdivision, of 3 Dec. 1940 (B II 2Dg 66); Panzer Armeeoberkommando 2 Abteilung Ia, Kriegstagebuch Nr. 1, p. 6, from 15 Dec. 1941 (RH 21-2/v. 756).

120. OKH Richtlinien für Führung und Kampf der Panzerdivision, of 3 Dec. 1940, p. 22 (B II 2Dg 66); LVII Panzer Korps Abteilung Ia, Tagesmeldung of 12 July 1941, (15 638/2-6).

121. Steiger, *Armour Tactics*, pp. 53, 144–51.

122. This explains why reserves, which constitute the most characteristic operational resource, are always positioned in the rear of the operational layout. In this way they cover a wider range of operational probabilities, and their control by the operational commander is more effective.

123. Guderian, *Panzer Leader*, p. 91.

124. In the second phase of the French campaign, when an army level (panzergruppe) headquarters was formed around Guderian's former XIX Panzer Corps headquarters for the purpose of directing XXXIX (Schmidt), XXXXI (Reinhardt) Panzer Corps, in correlation with that of von Kleist's, Guderian gave up his former objection.

125. Their objective was to divide the allied group of forces in Belgium from the rest of the French Army by a slashing thrust, and likewise to create an operational centre of gravity for the further development of the campaign.

126. Ibid., p. 147.

127. Army Group Centre order for battle included two panzer groups, the 3rd under H. Hoth's command, and the 2nd under Guderian's. Both panzer groups constituted the main instruments which were bound to initiate the development of the encirclement operations.

128. Liddell Hart, *The Rommel Papers*, pp. 10–13, 21–2, 32.

129. W.R. von Thoma's talk with Liddell Hart, of 20 Nov. 1945, LHA, 9/24/144, p. 1; S. Westphal's talk with Liddell Hart, of 4 Oct. 1950, LHA, 9/24/149, p. 1; Westphal, who

had been Rommel's chief of operations in Africa, recorded that during the Crusader campaign in November 1941, Rommel positioned himself, his chief of staff, Bayerlein, and Crüwell, who commanded the Africa Corps, at the head of the two panzer divisions (15, 21). For four and a half days Westphal was left alone to direct the operation and control the units of the African Army. During that time radio contact with Rommel was lost entirely for more than 24 hours. Meanwhile Westphal, who was located at the natural centre for conducting such an operation, received information concerning the British intentions. Thus, on his own initiative, and without Rommel's knowledge or consent, he stopped the manoeuvre which was conducted by Rommel and withdrew the panzer divisions all the way back to the initial line of operations. Rommel realized the complete course of events only when he later returned to his main headquarters.

130. W.R. von Thoma's talk with Liddell Hart, dated 20 Nov. 1945, LHA, 9/24/144, p. 3, was very critical of Rommel's method of command and of his tendency to perform like a junior tactical commander. In the last phases of the First World War, Rommel commanded an infantry Jäger battalion in the Italian Alps and recorded his unique experience in a book entitled *Infanterie Greift An*. The book was published in the early 1930s and reflects all the special qualities which made German tactical excellence so unique.

131. The great space given to the subject of combined arms tactics in the *Truppenführung 1936* implied that the idea was conceived at a time when operational cognition was still prevalent.

132. H. Franke, *Handbuch der Neuzeitlichen Wehrwissenschaften* (Berlin, 1937), Vol. 2, p. 393, confirms that the tactical cooperation of armour with other arms was the principal problem that interested the *Wehrmacht* since the emergence of the armoured troops. The publication of the OKH Richtlinien für Führung und Einsatz der Panzerdivision of 3 Dec. 1940, which followed the French campaign, indicated the same trend.

133. The term 'mechanization', in the present context indicates a specific tactical quality, that is reflected in performance of modern heavy infantry. This quality is attained through the combination of motorization, protection against light firearms, and light calibre fire power. Unlike the tactical quality defined as armoured, mechanization excels in mobility and flexibility, whereas it lacks in firepower. Steiger, *Armour Tactics*, p. 45, remarks that less than 10 per cent of the order of battle of infantry regiments in the panzer divisions were in fact mechanized. H. von Manteuffel's letter to Liddell Hart, dated 15 May 1949, LHA, 9/24/125, pp. 1–2, gives the same data.

134. Ibid.; 20 Panzer Division Abteilung Ia, Erfahrungsbericht des Schutzen Regiment 59, of 5 Nov. 1941, p. 2 (RH 27-20/99); 4 Panzer Division Abteilung Ia, Anlagen der Gefechtbericht zum Kriegstagebuch Meldung der 5 Panzer Brigade of 6 Sept. 1941 (RH 27/4-37).

135. 7 Panzer Division Abteilung Ia, Kurzbericht of 14 May 1940 (RH 27-7/191); 4 Panzer Division Abteilung Ia, Nr. 71/42 Geheim of 12 March 1942, p. 20 (RH 27/4-37).

136. 7 Panzer Division Abteilung Ia Morgenmeldung des Artillerie Regiment 78 of 26 Aug. 1941, p. 2, (RH 27-7/55); the German panzer divisions hardly initiated night combat because the tank lacked the technical ability to see at night. The development of a pattern combining infantry and tanks in close support action, led by the infantry, would have solved the problem. However, German tankmen were unable to accept the idea of being led by infantry in a slow-moving action, and so such a pattern was not developed. Unlike the Germans, the Russians, who grasped the importance of continuity in operations, did develop such a pattern, and initiated regularly night combat. 7 Panzer Division Abteilung Ia, Meldung der Panzer Abteilung 101, of 23 Aug. 1941 (RH 27-7/55); 4 Panzer Division Abteilung Ia, Anlagen zum Kriegstagebuch Nr. 71/42 Geheim Bentwortung Fragebogen OKH Betr. Erfahrung Ostfeldzug, of 12 March 1942, p. 3 (RH 27/4-37).

137. XIX Panzer Korps Abteilung Ia, Erfahrungsbericht des Pionieren Bataillon 43, of 2 Oct. 1939 (RH 21-2/v.29); 4 Panzer Division Abteilung Ia, 71/42 Geheim, of 12 March 1942, p. 3 (RH 27/4-37); each of the armoured divisions engineer battalions possessed only one mechanized company. Moreover, the division level lacked bridging and crossing equipment.

138. XXIV Panzer Korps Abteilung Ia, Anlagen Nr. 253 zum Kriegstagebuch Nr. 8, of 18 Oct. 1941, p. 4 (RH 24-24/122).

139. XXIV Panzer Korps Abteilung Ia, Anlagen Nr. 247 zum Kriegstagebuch Nr. 8, of 14 Oct. 1941 (RH 24-24/122); H. Guderian., 'Der Vorstoss auf Tula 1941', *Allgemeine Schweizerische Militärzeitschrift*, No. 10, 1949, p. 749.

140. XLVII Panzer Korps Abteilung Ia, Anlagen Nr. 699 zum Kriegstagebuch Nr. 3, of 5 Dec. 1941, p. 3 (RH 24-47/28,29); 4 Panzer Division Abteilung Ia, Gefechtbericht, from 11 Aug. 1941, p. 6 (RH 27/4-37); Heeres Gruppe Mitte Abteilung Ia, Kriegstagebuch Nr. 1, from 22 Aug. 1941 (RH 19 II/119).

141. Guderian, *Panzer Leader*, pp. 36-7. Senger und Etterlin, *Die Panzergrenadiere*, pp. 67-77.

142. H.A. Jacobsen, *1939-1945 Der Zweite Weltkrieg in Chronik und Dokumentation* (Darmstadt, 1961), pp. 39-40.

143. OKH Richtlinien für Führung und Einsatz der Panzerdivision, of 3 Dec. 1940, p. 8 (B II 2Dg 66); Panzer Gruppe von Kleist Abteilung Ia, Nr. 3422/40 Geheim, from 9 Aug. 1940, p. 3 (RH 21-1/36).

144. Guderian, *Panzer Leader*, pp. 294-7, complains about this failure to mechanize the artillery, yet he personally was responsible for creating a state of mind which discounted everything but tanks.

145. Panzer Armeeoberkommando 2 Abteilung Ia, Kriegstagebuch Nr. 1, p. 6, of 15 Dec. 1941 (RH 21-2/v.277).

146. LVII Panzer Korps Abteilung Ia, Tagesmeldung an Panzer Armeeoberkommando 3, of 27 July 1941 (15 683/2-6); XXXXVII Panzer Korps Abteilung Ia, Anlagen Nr. 599 zum Kriegstagebuch Nr. 2, of 30 Aug. 1941 (RH 24-47/8); XXXXVII Panzer Korps Abteilung Ia, Anlagen Nr. 697 zum Kriegstagebuch Nr. 2, of 8 Sept. 1941 (RH 24-47/9).

147. Panzer Armeeoberkommando 3 Abteilung Ia, Zwischenmeldung zum Armeeoberkommando 9, of 4 Oct. 1941 (RH 21-3/v.70).

148. OKH General Stab des Heeres Operation Abteilung III, Nr. 1736/41 Geheim Kommandosache Chefsache, of 18 Dec. 1941.

149. Panzer Armeeoberkommando 3 Abteilung Ia, Nr. 520/42 Geheim, of 10 Feb. 1942, pp. 50-51 (RH 21-3/v.113).

150. Ibid. A.A. Strokov, *Istoriia voennogo iskusstva* (History of Military Art) (Moscow, 1966), pp. 425-9. The opposing Russian approach was reflected clearly in their deliberate decision to conduct the defensive operation of Kursk in Summer 1943. In spite of their notable operational success at Stalingrad, and the subsequent feeling that the operational initiative was finally gained by them, they decided after the German counter-offensive at Kharkov to apply the defensive for yet another stage. In doing so, they hoped to draw the Germans into initiating another encirclement offensive. With their thorough preparation of the Kursk defensive they managed not only to defeat the German offensive, but also to inflict upon the Germans such attrition in manpower and resources that they were unable to regain the initiative. This case illustrates not only the Russian pragmatic approach to operational planning, but also their flexibility in applying the various tactical forms and their awareness of the essential linkage between attrition and manoeuvre at the operational level.

151. Guderian, *Achtung Panzer*, p. 176.

152. Spannenkrebs, *Angriff mit Kampfwagen*, p. 175.

153. Geyer, 'German Strategy', p. 575.

154. Guderian, *Panzer Leader*, p. 142.

155. Ibid.

156. Halder, *Kriegstagebuch*, Bd. 3, 3 Aug. 1941.

157. L. Besymensky, *Sonderakte Barbarossa* (Stuttgart, 1968).

158. H. Greiner, *Die Oberste Wehrmachtführung 1939-1943* (Wiesbaden, 1951), pp. 322ff., presents convincing evidence that the main planning of the Barbarossa operation was done by the Army General Staff (OKH). In fact, the planning began in the course of the final phase of the campaign in the West, in July 1940. On 5 Dec. 1940, the basic plan was submitted to Hitler. On 18 Dec. 1940, after articulation by OKW, the basic concept for the campaign in the East was laid down in Directive No. 21 'Case Barbarossa', OKW WFSt Abt. L (I) Nr. 33408140 Geheim Kommandosache Chefsache F.H. Qu, of 18 Dec. 1940. Trevor-Roper, *Directives*, pp. 93-8.

159. Ibid.
160. Ibid. F. von Paulus, *Ich Stehe Hier auf Befehl! Lebensweg des Generalfeldmarschall Friedrich Paulus. Mit den Aufzeichnungen aus dem Nachlass, Briefen und Dokumenten*, W. Görlitz (ed.) (Frankfurt a. M., 1963), pp. 107–25, reported that in a war game conducted in Autumn 1940, the participants came to the conclusion that the Red Army had to be destroyed west of the Dnieper–Dvina line, otherwise the Wehrmacht would lose the chance to defeat the USSR due to its limited dimensions in relation to the Russian spaces.
161. OKH Bericht des Generalinspekteurs der Panzer Truppen Nr. 3940/44 Geheim Kommandosache Chefsache H. Qu. of Nov. 1944. The linear structure implied two problems. The first concerned the strategic and operational lack of depth. The second concerned the ratio of troops to space, which, as reflected in the above reference, was dangerously low. Initially the Wehrmacht deployed 3,580 tanks for the Russian campaign, i.e., only 1,000 tanks more than were deployed for the French campaign. Yet the overall length of the Russian front was more than ten times larger. Thus, initially the linear deployment of insufficient fighting resources presented a severe drawback which was not taken into consideration.
162. Trevor-Roper, *Hitler's War Directives*, pp. 93–8.
163. Ibid.; OKW/WFSt/Abt L (I.op.) No. 41888/41 gKdos Chefs of 11 Nov. 1941 (BA-MA) RW4/v. 578, pp. 162ff. This document redefined the strategic objectives for the second stage of the Eastern Campaign: 1. Capturing the Caucasus; 2. Developing the offensive beyond the Volga as far as the Astrakhan–Saratov–Gorky line; and 3. Establishing a land link with Finland. Thus only at that late date did the German supreme strategic authority realize that the campaign in the East would be a long and painful affair.
164. Guderian, *Panzer Leader*, pp. 146, 149–50, 189–90, 195. This objective was mentioned indirectly by Guderian on several occasions. Additionally, the main objective was mentioned specifically by Colonel Schmundt, Hitler's adjutant, on his visit of 29 July 1941 to Army Group Centre's headquarters. Hitler himself stuck to this definition of the main objective in his meeting of 4 Aug. 1941 in Novyi Borisov with the senior commanders of Army Group Centre. Finally, Halder mentioned this same definition of the main objective in his briefing to the commanders of Army Group Centre on 23 Aug. 1941. P.E. Schramm, A. Hillgruber, W. Hubatsch and H.A. Jacobsen (eds), *Kriegstagebuch des Oberkommando des Wehrmacht (Wehrmacht Führungsstab) 1940-1945* (KTB OKW) (4 vols.) (Frankfurt a. M.), 1961–65, Vol. 1, p. 1031 (23 July 1941), indeed confirms that Hitler emphasized the capture of Leningrad as the main objective of the entire campaign. On that account he mentioned the crucial importance of the Ukraine and the Donets Basin to Germany's war economy.
165. Ibid., pp. 149–50, 189–90.
166. Trevor-Roper, *Hitler's War Directives*, pp. 93–8.
167. The order of battle of all three army groups was more or less identical except the fact that Army Group Centre was allotted two panzer groups instead of one. The reason for this additional allocation of a mobile element derived from the Army Group's central position, and not, as one might think, from the magnitude of its mission. This particular position could afford the opportunities for cooperation with Army Group North by transferring one of Army Group Centre's panzer groups to its sector.
168. This phenomenon should be attributed to the employment of the term 'destruction' in designating an operational objective: What exactly does 'destruction' mean? How can the effect of 'destruction' be defined in an operational context? How much must be destroyed in order to satisfy the definition of 'destruction'? Unlike the tactical context where the effect of destruction is viable and the term carries actual significance, at the operational level it is completely meaningless.
169. K. Reinhardt, *Moscow the Turning Point. The Failure of Hitler's Strategy in the Winter of 1941-42* (Oxford, 1992), pp. 421–6.
170. Guderian, *Panzer Leader*, p. 149.
171. Von Kleist's talk with Liddell Hart, dated 6 Sept. 1945, LHA, 9/24/118, revealed that von Bock, who was an officer of the old school, was manipulated by Guderian to support his views and actions. Guderian, *Panzer Leader*, pp. 189–94, discloses the same picture.
172. Ibid., pp. 193, 195–6, 199–202; on 8 Aug. the Krichev case took place, on 15 Aug. the

Gomel' case, on 22 Aug. the Roslavl–Shumitch, and on 24 Aug. the meeting with Hitler.

173. Ibid., pp. 194–5, 212. On 11 Aug. the advancing operations of the Panzer Army towards Viaz'ma–Roslavl was halted; on 15 Aug. the Panzer Army was transferred to the Starodub–Novosybkov sector; on 19 Aug. the Panzer Army was forced to advance to the Klinzy Triangle; on 20 Aug. this same advance was stopped by the Army Group headquarters, and in the first week of Sept. the Panzer Army was forced to evacuate its forces from the Desna bridgehead.

174. Ibid., p. 212.

175. Jacobsen, *Der Zweite Weltkrieg in Chronik und Dokumenten*, p. 208. On 1 December the commandant of Army Group Centre reported to the high command that his command stretched along more than 1,000 km, and his only available reserve was a single weakened division.

176. Manstein, *Lost Victories*, attributed these failures to Hitler's lack of understanding of operational matters. However, the general staff, which planned these moves in detail and controlled their execution, was no less responsible.

177. W. Haupt, *Kiev, die Grösste Kesselschlacht der Geschichte* (Bad Nauheim, 1964). The actual objective was the destruction of the Soviet forces in the Ukraine, in preparation for a further takeover of the territory. Since Kiev was the capital of the Ukraine and constituted one of the angular points in the triangle Kiev–Cherkassey–Lochvitsa, which was bound to enclose the trapped Soviet forces, it gave its name to the entire operation, in retrospect. Actually, in early Sept. it was not decided whether Kiev or Kharkov should be the objective. The meeting point between Guderian's 2nd Panzer Army and von Kleist's 1st, which sealed the Russian forces in the immense pocket, was in Lochvitsa.

178. Ibid.

179. Ibid. The length of the eastern wing of the Kiev pocket, which was created by the joint movement of the 1st and 2nd Panzer Armies, measured more than 500km. The enclosed area measured 135,000 square km, and the total number of captured Russians amounted to 700,000.

180. It might have been Hitler's intention at that stage to define Moscow as the general main objective of the entire operation. Nonetheless, the strategic delay that resulted from engaging Army Group Centre in the Kiev operation and the immense dispersion of the *Wehrmacht* formations made the implementation of such an intention meaningless.

181. Blumentritt, *Strategie und Taktik*, p. 149. From an operational point of view the order of the decisions made by the supreme strategic authority in the course of summer–autumn 1941 resembled a devil's dance: 1. In directive No. 33 of 19 July 1941, Hitler ordered a simultaneous move combining three elements operating in three different operational directions, an advance of operational formations to support Army Group South, an armoured manoeuvre in support of Army Group North, and an infantry manoeuvre conducted by Army Group Centre towards Moscow; 2. On 23 July 1941, in an addendum to directive No. 33, he deprived Army Group Centre of its two Panzer groups, allotting the 2nd to Army Group South and the 3rd to Army Group North; 3. On 30 July he cancelled the orders outlined in the addendum by the publication of directive No. 34, calling off the attack on Moscow and leaving both Panzer groups with Army Group Centre, due to their acute need for rest and reorganization. Trevor-Roper (*Directives*, pp. 139ff.); 4. On 25 July 1941, von Bock was briefed by Keitel, who visited his headquarters in Borisov, to the effect that Hitler had decided to stop employing strategic manoeuvres of encirclement because they were consuming too much time and the rate of wear on the armoured troops was too great (Halder, *Kriegstagebuch*, Vol. III, p. 121, 26 July 1941); 5. Nevertheless, through an addendum to directive No. 34 dated 12 Aug., the operation in the Ukraine, which led to the massive encirclement of Kiev, was initiated; 6. On 6 Sept. 1941, by means of directive No. 35, the main objective of the campaign was shifted towards Moscow and the huge encirclement operations of Viaz'ma and Bryansk were initiated. The final date for the offensive was set on 28 Sept. ObKdo d-Hgr MITTE Ia No. 1680/47 gKdos CHEFS of 28 Sept. 1941 (BA-MA: RH20-4/216, 322b).

182. 18 Panzer Division Abteilung Ia, Zustandsbericht des Division Ingenieurs from 4 Nov.

1941, p. 3 (RH 27-18/72). The reports of the mechanical staffs of 18th Panzer Division indicated that during the period 22 June–Nov. 1941 the vehicles of the division covered no less than 4,000 km. Halder, *Kriegstagebuch*, Bd. 3, p. 231, from 14 Sept. 1941, disclosed the following details, concerning the effective (technically fit) strength of tanks in the panzer divisions: 3rd Panzer Division – 20 per cent, 4th Panzer Division – 29 per cent, 17th Panzer Division – 21 per cent, 18th Panzer Division – 31 per cent.
183. Ibid., Bd. 3, of 11 Aug. 1941.
184. Von Thoma's talk with Liddell Hart, dated 1 Nov. 1945, LHA, 9/24/144, p. 5.
185. Ibid. Hitler responded to von Thoma's proposal by admitting that he could spare only one panzer division for North Africa. Thus, von Thoma suggested cancelling the whole idea of German intervention. Eventually, in the course of spring 1941 one light and one panzer division reached North Africa. In the course of events another panzer and another light division were dispatched due to Rommel's initiatives and successes. Thus, through tactical manipulation, Rommel increased the original dimensions of the force allocated to his theatre, almost four times.
186. Liddell Hart, *The Rommel Papers*, p. 93.
187. Ibid., p. 100. Rommel disclosed his intentions to the German military attaché in Rome, von Rintelen, who warned him against such a course of action.
188. Ibid., p. 107.
189. Ibid.
190. Ibid., p. 109.
191. Ibid., p. 139.
192. Armee-Befehl für den Angriff, Panzerarmee Afrika/Abt. Ia, Nr. 58/42g. kdos. Chefs. of 20 May 1942, BA-MA, RH 24-288/54, p. 178ff. According to the operation order, Rommel's initial objective for the 1942 summer campaign was limited: 'The encirclement and destruction of the enemy field army in front of Tobruk'. However, once the western border of Egypt was reached operational considerations were pushed aside by both Rommel and the strategic authorities in favour of the tempting prize in the east. Schlachtbericht der Panzerarmee, BA-MA, RH 19 VIII/2d, p. 73, of 29 June 1942.
   Hitler to Mussolini, 23 June, 1942 (copy) BA-MA, RM 7/235, p. 225ff. Fascinated by Rommel's success, Hitler advised Mussolini to permit Rommel, who was under his strategic command, to advance into Egypt and thus exploit his luck to the limit. Influenced by Hitler's recommendation and by Rommel's dashing temperament, Mussolini, on the night of 23/24 June, 'ordered' Rommel 'to pursue the British deep into Egypt'. Rintelen Nr. 5106/42 Geh. Kdos. Chefs. Urgent, of 24 June 1942, 0030 hours, BA-MA, RH 19 VIII/22, p. 249.
193. Ibid., p. 233. When assessing the British operational potential in the course of planning the July 1942 offensive, Rommel related only to two British divisions as combat worthy.
194. Ibid., p. 257. In the course of summer 1942 the 8th Army received 150,000 tons of provisions, whereas the Axis forces received 25,000 tons, of which the German Panzer Army received only 8,000 tons.
195. Ibid., p. 251. On 5 July 1942 the actual strength of the entire Panzer Army Africa amounted to less than a division.
196. Ibid., p. 257.
197. Ibid., pp. 277–8. R. Stumpf, 'From Tobruk to El Alamein: The Operational Basis of the Decision in North Africa in the Summer and Fall of 1942', in G. Roth (ed.), *Development, Planning and Realization of Operational Conceptions in World Wars I and II*, Militärgeschichtliches Forschungsamt (Freiburg im Breisgau, 1989), p. 59.
198. Von Thoma's talk with Liddell Hart, dated 1 Nov. 1945, p. 6, LHA, 9/24/144, reported that early in Nov. 1942, when Rommel sensed that a British offensive was imminent, he ordered the African Army on 4 Nov. to initiate a deliberate retreat from the El Alamein line towards Gazala. Ultimately this retreat never materialized because Hitler forbade it. However, the interesting point of this incident is that it demonstrated beyond any doubt that Rommel realized at that point that his case in Africa was lost.
199. Van Creveld, 'On Learning from the Wehrmacht', pp. 67–8.

5

The Evolution of Soviet
Operational Thought

An attempt to cover the entire evolutionary course of Soviet operational art would require a volume exceeding the scope of this work. It is therefore essential to dwell on the period of the conceptual breakthrough since it manifested the cognitive revolution in modern military thinking and provides the fundamental tools for understanding the operational theories developed in the USSR and throughout the world. The significance of this revolution derived first and foremost from the fact that it indicated a transformation from a paradigm based on tactical consciousness to a paradigm based on operational consciousness. Moreover, this revolution produced the theoretical framework for the construction and operational handling of the Red Army during the stages of the great offensives and in the years that followed the war. And, finally, when the American armed forces were thrown into the conceptual crisis of the late 1970s – an event which led them to launch their cognitive revolution – it was to the Soviet operational theory that they turned for conceptual assistance.

The two following chapters will, therefore, examine one of the most remarkable cases in the history of military and scientific thinking. The diachronic framework set out in this chapter will afford a better understanding of the general aspects concerning the development of the operational theory. In Chapter 6, the philosophic elements and substantive characteristics of the operational theory will be examined according to the following criteria: the idea of operational shock and strike manoeuvre, the principle of depth and echeloning, the notion of operational synergism, the principles of operational command and control, and the interaction between attrition and manoeuvre.

FROM SUCCESSIVE OPERATIONS TO THE OPERATIONAL MANOEUVRING GROUP

The process that led to the creation of the Deep Operation (*glubokaia operatsiia*) theory is related to the commencement of the conceptual revolution generated by the Russian Civil War. In the course of that revolution the paradigm of the integral battle of annihilation, which had dominated military thought for more than a century, was replaced by the newer paradigm of the operational strike manoeuvre.[1] Thus, apart from presenting a unique innovation of thought, the Deep Operation theory reflects the conceptual change which has taken place in modern warfare, namely – the recognition of an intermediate level between strategy and tactics and the application of system thinking to the military field.[2] Moreover, by providing Soviet military thinking with its theoretical basis and cognitive guidance for more than 60 years, the achievements gained by the school of operational thought in the 1920s and 1930s played a dominant role in forming operational art between 1942 and 1990. Therefore, any attempt to interpret recent variants of Soviet operational theory without a thorough understanding of the conceptual origins must inevitably lead to errors and distortions.

The conceptual breakthrough resulting from the negation of the traditional theories of war, culminated in the mid-1930s in the Deep Operation theory – a doctrine which led to the establishment of airborne and mechanized operational formations, the conduct of large-scale and creative manoeuvres, and the acceleration of technological development.[3]

The theoretical achievements came to an abrupt end in 1937 with the physical extermination of the members of the operational school. A ban was imposed on any theoretical activity concerning operational subjects, the disbandment of the operational formations, and an obsessive obliteration of the relevant theoretical literature.[4]

In the summer of 1942, amidst the appalling defeats and hardships of war, the Red Army regained operational consciousness. Deep Operation was revived, and its swift application in the form of operational and organizational patterns coincided with the war needs of the Soviet Union. It provided the Red Army with the basis for the defeat of the *Wehrmacht* and it destroyed all notions of the *Blitzkrieg*'s invincibility.[5]

While the suppression of the late 1930s was motivated by Stalin's personal obsessions, the deceleration of the theoretical development during the years 1954–64 was rationalized by Khrushchev's unilateral strategy which preferred the nuclear option.[6]

165

Khrushchev's fall in 1964 and the emergence from obscurity of a manoeuvre-oriented school of military thought regenerated the development of the operational theory, and what appeared at first sight as a rehabilitation of Tukhachevskii and his colleagues developed into a conceptual renaissance, lasting well into the 1980s. From the start it was characterized by an emphatic attempt to resuscitate the theory of Deep Operations in its original form for it had been somewhat obscured by the modifications introduced into it during the Second World War. While the plethora of literature engendered by this renaissance offered a variety of novel terms and conceptual variants, its essence adhered to the principles laid down in the original theory. Thus, it can be legitimately argued that the process was evolutionary.

Within this process, which was guided conceptually by the idea of operational shock (*udar*), the paradigm of the operational strike manoeuvre crystallized. This premise can best be illustrated by examining the idea of the operational strike element and its evolution through various stages of the process. Originally the strike element had been perceived by Tukhachevskii and other members of the operational school as an integral component of the entire manoeuvre system, designed to inflict the shock effect on the rival system.[7] Since the conceptual and technological context of the 1920s and 1930s was dominated by the idea of successive operations, the method for achieving the shock effect centred on the development of a tactical breakthrough into an operational breakout. Thus, a certain grouping of armoured and mechanized formations, echeloned behind a holding force, was defined as the means for attaining this goal, and was similarly referred to as the 'echelon for developing the breakthrough' (*eshelon razvitiia proryva* – ERP).[8]

The ability to successfully execute deep operations in 1943 to 1945 was limited by the prevailing strategic context: 1. The absence of an air-mechanized operational echelon which hampered the Red Army in performing *desant* operations,[9] an essential element in the original Deep Operation theory; 2. The Soviet failure throughout the entire war to mechanize the infantry, thereby reducing its dynamic participation in the deeper stages of the operational manoeuvre; 3. The depth and intensity of the German tactical defensive layout, which obliged the Russians to initiate any campaign with a systematic breakthrough operation; 4. The Soviet superiority in fighting resources. Since it combined the qualities of mass and velocity, so crucial to the completion of the breakthrough, as well as to the effectuation of the Soviet version of the turning manoeuvre (*obkhod*), the homogeneous tank army emerged as the principal instrument for attaining the operational shock, and was designated 'the mobile group' (*podvizh-naia gruppa*).[10]

The formulation of the OMG concept (*operativnaia manevrennaia gruppa*) in the early 1980s by Marshal Nikolai Ogarkov stemmed from the realization of the strategic changes in NATO's defensive posture, and a recognition of the significance of the application of a system approach to the field of operations by the American army.[11] Moreover, the necessity to produce an overall solution matching both the limitations imposed by NATO's Strike Deep concept and the operational opportunities presented by its forward and shallow defensive induced the Russians to cultivate a different method for attaining the operational shock. Whereas traditionally the Soviet method of operational manoeuvre sought to neutralize the rival system through the projection of the strike element in succession to the penetration of its tactical layout by the holding element, the Ogarkov school of thought intended to arrive at the same result by employing a pre-emptive approach. In other words, by swiftly infiltrating a group of armoured divisions into NATO's depth, before the latter could complete the deployment of its forces, Ogarkov meant to initiate a deep and dynamic centre of gravity that would turn over the defensive, parallel to the frontal holding action exercised by the main force, and thus create the conditions for the accomplishment of the shock effect in the early stage of the campaign.

This brief description of Ogarkov's plan reinforces the argument that the essence of the operational theory formed in the years preceding the Second World War remains valid even today. The changes in terminology are no more than an attempt to interpret current situations according to the universal principles of the original theory. Equally, the phenomenon of conceptual variants reflects a trend to adjust these same principles to the strategic reality by the formulation of specific operational methods. In brief, any endeavour to explain the concepts of OMG and the mobile group without fully understanding the ideas of operational shock and ERP is misleading because it distorts the meaning of these concepts.[12]

THE CIVIL WAR – THE INCUBATION OF MILITARY SYSTEM THINKING

Soviet military historiography, being guided largely by a professional approach, has seen the evolution of operational art as a continuous and dynamic process which stemmed from the political, mental, social and military changes generated by the Bolshevik Revolution.[13] The Civil War has thus emerged as an historical turning point, representing an experience which differed categorically from the western decadent military tradition. The conceptual change and the critical approach induced by the operational experience of the Civil War provided the basis for setting a scientific framework within which a novel corpus of knowledge and military theory were formed.[14]

According to the theory of scientific revolutions, operational experience accumulated from 1917 to 1921, stimulated by an intellectual trend which questioned the validity of the prevailing theories of war and thus instigated the crisis of consciousness so essential for forming an alternative theory or doctrine.[15]

The fluid and dynamic nature of the military operations in the course of the Civil War derived, to a great extent, from the low ratio between force and space. The fighting, which occurred simultaneously in Karelia, European Russia, the Caucasus, Asiatic Russia and Siberia, compelled fronts, being the highest operational organization, to conduct operations over spaces measuring 700–1,800 km, and to attain objectives some 600–3,000 km deep.[16] This phenomenon discredited completely the linear form as an operational manoeuvring pattern in the eyes of the Soviet revolutionary command, thus encouraging the field commanders to seek decisions by means of bold manoeuvres and deep actions.[17]

Whereas in Western Europe the submission of operational mobility to linear tactics and considerations of firepower brought about the paralysis of manoeuvre, as demonstrated so well in the course of the First World War, during the Civil War the Russians recognized the operational potential of the large number of equestrian troops which they possessed. By forming corps and armies of cavalry, an idea that had never occurred to Western European military thinking, they managed to execute columnar manoeuvres, penetrating into depth and attaining operational and strategic achievements.[18] The combination of fronts conducting campaigns as independent commands on the one hand, and concentrating the strategic control at the political end, on the other, trained senior officers for creative competition with operational challenges, and similarly illuminated the crucial importance of the intermediate level between strategy and tactics.[19]

The absence of military conservatism from the senior echelons of the Red Army constituted yet another characteristic, contributing to the moulding of creative patterns of action in the Civil War, because the old military establishment had been destroyed and the field commanders, who were responsible for the conduct of operations, were very young.[20] The combination of rich empirical experience gained by these young commanders in the course of the war and the revolutionary mentality prevailing in Russia at the time, motivated officers like M.N. Tukhachevskii, G.D. Gai, and V.M. Primakov not only to view the validity of the traditional military patterns of thought with scepticism, but also encouraged them to develop individual solutions to the operational problems which confronted them during the various campaigns.[21]

The formal military theory seemed irrelevant under the grave conditions of the Civil War. The acute threats to the very existence of the Communist regime and the scarcity of economic and military resources forced the Bolshevik leadership to militarize the whole Soviet nation and to shift concentrations of efforts from one crisis to another. Consequently, the armed forces were turned into an heterogeneous organization governed by amateurism, while the recruitment of military specialists (voin-spets) could only provide immediate answers to the most pressing problems posed by the operational conduct.[22] However, despite the lack of a formal theory and a professional tradition, the high command of the Red Army managed to diagnose the principal problems correctly and, by harnessing operational logic and a system approach, to provide the appropriate solutions.

The mechanistic approach prevailing in the West led Europeans to perceive the element of depth in the shallow terms of a limited battlefield. Out of this absurdity grew an inclination to apply the element of depth only when the combat situation demanded the encirclement or outflanking of a tactical entity deployed in linear configuration. Although the futility of this approach had been clearly demonstrated in the opening phases of the First World War, the operational implications of the idea of depth remained alien to western military thinking for many years. On the other hand, Russian military culture, combining eastern and western ideas and influenced by holistic trends, developed an entirely different approach to the element of depth. The experience of 1812 incited philosophers of war, such as Tolstoy, to perceive depth as an idea embodying both the holistic nature of the political-strategic aim and the logical aspects of the military manoeuvre.[23]

The growing awareness of the idea of depth raised the initial doubts concerning the validity of the traditional premises which aimed at annihilating the opposing army in a single linear engagement.[24] The existing polarity between the mechanical level of war and the abstract field of strategic conduct, revealed to the critical eyes of the field commanders and staff officers of the Red Army the entire scope of the military venture. This unique consciousness emphasized the need for a new level that would fill the intermediate space in the hierarchic structure of the military system. On the one hand, the new level was perceived as a means for bridging the gap between the abstract and the mechanical, and, on the other, it was charged with providing the conditions for a deliberate assembling of the numerous tactical incidents into a coherent and continuous occurrence.[25] In other words, apprehending the factor of depth in war, which was sharpened by the strategic circumstances of the Civil War, brought about, for the first time in the history of war, the application of a system approach and thus revealed the operational level of war.

Identifying both front and rear as interacting elements within the framework of a unified strategic entity constituted yet another aspect of thinking in depth, which was applied in the course of the Civil War.[26] Nevertheless, since the Russians fell short of realizing the positive aspects of the depth factor in the context of operational offensive manoeuvre, its primary significance as a principle for defeating military systems remained far from being exploited at that stage. One reason for this was that the volume of activity and the urgency of survival prevented the young Red Army from conducting thorough research into the operational rationale of military systems. Another reason was the disproportion between the linear (infantry formations) and columnar (cavalry and mechanized formations) elements that existed at the time in the Red Army. Consequently, the operational ability of the Red Army was confined exclusively to defensive manoeuvres. The 1920 Polish campaign, directed by M.N. Tukhachevskii, who was the most creative of all Red Army field commanders, confirms this argument. Whereas operational insight was expressed clearly in the defensive manoeuvre that broke the Polish offensive, the advance towards Warsaw reflected basic short-comings in conducting large-scale offensive manoeuvres.[27]

The attempts to implement what was defined at the time as the Echelon or Railway War (*eshelonaia voina*) were, in fact, nothing more than urgent responses to crisis situations which involved shift-ing concentrations of force from inactive or rear areas to the more dangerous sectors. The operational formations and organizations suffered throughout the war from a constant scarcity of manpower and resources in relation to the missions allotted to them. Therefore, fronts and armies operated in most cases in a single echelon, which meant a linear configuration.[28] Although an increase in the nominal order of battle of the field formation could be noticed in the last year of the war, in practice the combat manpower did not change significantly. However, as the threats diminished, the operational sectors could be deliberately narrowed, and thus the field formations could deploy in two echelons and a limited operational reserve or cavalry group.[29]

The application of the depth factor in the course of the Civil War had significant repercussions on tactics. Here, the effectuation of depth in both defence and attack did not result from an initial increase in strategic resources, but rather from a deliberate narrowing of the operational sectors of units and formations.[30] Whereas during the first year of the war the width of rifle division attack sectors was some 50 km, by the end of 1920 it had decreased to 7–15 km.[31] Thus, since the size of the divisions was more than doubled in the later period of the war, it becomes clear that their depth was multiplied by a factor of between 7.5 and 15 at the same time. In other words, the operational configuration of the tactical formations not only turned columnar in nature, but also became shock oriented.[32] The tactical shock, which matured in 1920 as the principal pattern employed by the Red field formations, centred on an initial penetration of the enemy's linear deployment through a succession of blows executed by a group of tactical formations echeloned in depth. These penetrating columns were designated as 'shock groups' (*udarnye gruppy*) and were usually followed by a cavalry group, thrown into the corridor which was created.[33]

Unlike the German experience, which suffered from a lack of operational consciousness and therefore failed to transform the development of columnar patterns of penetration from the tactical level to the operational, the tactical lessons gained by the Russians in the course of the Civil War were employed as miniature models for formulating columnar patterns of action at the operational level. Moreover, the mechanical shock exercised in tactical sub-systems in the Civil War provided the Soviet theoreticians later with the cognitive stimulus that led to the development of a substitute for the idea of destruction in the operational level of war. The operational-strategic conditions prevailing during the Civil War and the unique experience accumulated in its course drew attention to a long list of subjects concerning the functioning of military systems, such as the factor of depth, transformation from linear patterns of action to columnar, methods for attaining tactical shock, the irrelevance of the idea of destruction at the higher levels of war, the hierarchical structure and vertical interaction among the various levels of war, the central role played by the operational level in that context, and the importance of successive operations in the context of accomplishing the strategic goal. However, since the turbulent years of 1917–20 did not allow the development of a scientific environment in which a systematic process of thinking could have materialized, the Russians fell short of identifying the idea of operational shock in the course of the Civil War. Thus, the gathering of minds like Tukhachevskii, Triandafillov, Varfolomeev and Isserson in a brain-storming attempt to break the conceptual deadlock imposed by the authoritarian paradigm of *Vernichtungsschlacht*, could materialize only in the aftermath of the war.

The rich combat experience and the deliberate attention to the tactical level led the Russians to define the essence of battle in advanced terms within the time frame of the Civil War. In light of the observations made by the commanders of the Red Army, it was realized that the nature of the tactical activity was governed by the principle of randomness. The roots of this premise were anchored both in the very nature of ground warfare and in the characteristics of the tactical weapons prevailing on the battlefields. Accordingly, the prevalent mode of combat in the context of tactical fighting was defined as the 'encounter battle' (*vstrechnyi boi*).[34] The conceptual solution worked out by the Russians to meet the problems posed by the factor of randomness and the mode of encounter was embodied in the idea of *aktivnost'*: 'Army tactics have been and would continue to be saturated by *aktivnost'* in the spirit of bold and energetically conducted offensive operations.'[35] The term *aktivnost'* represented a unique idea, constituting one of the fundamentals of Russian military thought. Thus, since its origins lay in a different cultural context, simplistic translations such as 'aggressiveness' or 'activism' are inadequate. Basically, the term *aktivnost'* signifies a style of action corresponding to the very challenges posed by the nature of tactical activity.[36] Therefore, besides its figurative connotations, which were relevant in the tactical context, the Soviet theoreticians who matured in the Civil War identified some broader aspects in the term. One aspect concerned the seizure of initiative – a precondition for the application of a volitional manoeuvre. Another aspect concerned the synergy between the various components of any given tactical entity – an issue constituting the essence of the tactical manoeuvre.

In other words, the Russians intended to achieve decision in the complex environment where the tactical engagements occurred, by deliberately generating a dynamic manoeuvre that would suit both the universal principles of tactical combat and the specific circumstances of the relevant engagement. By employing the universal combination of a linear holding group (*skovyvaiushchaia gruppa*) and a columnar shock group (*udarnaia gruppa*), and an appropriate organization of troops and resources for combat (*boevoi poriadok*), the Red Army managed to create both the right synergy and the proper conditions for executing a coherent manoeuvre.

The difference between the Soviet conceptual and practical achievements in the Civil War and those armies which fought on the Western Front in the course of the First World War lies in the principle of synergism. The combination of a holding element and shock elements within every manoeuvring entity produced a universal formula leading to the penetration of the entire depth of the opponent's linear defensive. The moulding of the shock element in a columnar configuration consisting of several groups, echeloned in depth, guaranteed a succession of actions and contributed both to the lessening of friction between the element meant to force the decision and the enemy's line, and to the mechanical convergence of the main effort on the point of decision. Moreover, the columnar configuration provided a logical basis for systemic synergy among the fighting groups. When the combat support elements were organized in a mobile mode, allowing the progression of fire into the tactical depth, parallel to the advance of the various echelons of the striking column, the Red Army achieved the success of tactical synergy.[37]

The idea of tactical synergy or combined-arms warfare (*obshchevoiskovoi boi*) contributed to the professional setting for the formulation of the *edinonachal'stvo* concept.[38] This concept expressed the Soviet effort to solve the command and control problems posed by the necessity to apply tactical synergy through the exercise of a system approach.[39] Soviet thinking in this context arrived at the conclusion that in complex situations where the tactical grouping combined several combat arm elements (*rod voisk*), the successful conclusion of the action tends to depend on the measure of harmony among the elements involved – a matter dependent entirely on the effectuation of a unity of command by the element directing the manoeuvre.[40] Accordingly, the officer heading the combat arm element, which has been assigned the core of the tactical mission, must immediately become the overall commander of the units and elements participating in the operation, regardless of the fact that some of their commanders may hold higher ranks than his own. Thus, it becomes apparent that the concepts of *obshchevoiskovoi boi* and *edinonachal'stvo*, as they were shaped in the course of the Civil War, fused within the context of tactical manoeuvre the generating elements of a systemic operation: the mission, laid down by the person who held the responsibility for conducting the operation, the manoeuvre expressing the systemic interaction among the various components, and the commander, who was expected to navigate the manoeuvre harmoniously towards its mission. Therefore, despite the

fact that the Civil War generation dealt intuitively with crude sub-
systems, it remains a fact that their thinking was guided by system
logic.

Another conceptional breakthrough achieved by the Russians
during the Civil War concerns the identification of the interaction
between attrition and manoeuvre. The issue of the attritional nature
of war was deeply rooted in European military mentality for many
years prior to the First World War.[41] Deprived of system consciousness, the western armies failed to develop an operational methodology capable of handling the subject rationally. Therefore, traditionally, the phenomenon of attrition had been regarded as a decree
from heaven and the optimal means to cope with its implications
centred on the somewhat magical quantitative formula of 3:1.[42] In
contrast to the western experience, the Russians managed to develop
both a conceptual tool and practical patterns that allowed them to
cope with the problem of attrition through a systemic approach.

The Russians perceived manoeuvre in terms of interaction between
a holding element and striking elements and defined the breakthrough as a tactical decision attained by the columnar striking
element, and thus they were provided with practical means to deal
effectively with the problem of attrition. The novelty of structuring
the striking element in a columnar configuration rendered a dual
benefit: on the one hand it lowered the rate of attrition which the
defender could impose on the attacker, and on the other, it created
the opportunity for a decisive concentration of forces and resources
at the chosen point. Through this focal concentration of fighting
resources and suppressive assets (*sredstva podavleniia*) the Russians
sought to erode the defending force at the point of penetration and
to limit its capability to inflict attrition on the attacking force.[43]
Moreover, by applying the echeloned configuration, they intended to
compensate in advance for the wear and tear caused by the enemy as
well as to generate the dynamics for successive tactical actions.

The concentration of troops and resources within the echeloned
udarnaia gruppa (shock grouping) was planned and effectuated
according to specific parameters.[44] These parameters, which
expressed in definite numerical terms a certain relation between the
absolute factors of resources and space possessed by the initiating
army, were formulated through a systemic analysis of data collected
from various engagements.[45] Thus, by applying this concept the
Russians invented a scientific tool for coherent planning to assist
them in their efforts to overcome the irrationality of the tactical attrition factor.

TOWARDS A UNIFIED MILITARY DOCTRINE

The first disclosure of the historical and perceptional circumstances that led to the creation of the Deep Operation theory was in a series of rehabilitative articles by Isserson and other high-ranking officers in the Soviet military establishment in a magazine for military history and operational art during the mid-1960s.[46] The absence of this subject from general military historiography was the result of the physical extermination of its heroes, the destruction of their literary works and the ban which was put on teaching their ideas in the military academies of the USSR.[47] Yet, whereas in the Soviet Union the military setbacks of 1941–42 led to a renewed application of the Deep Operation theory, the access of western research to the sources of this creative experience was barred because of fundamental differences of mentality and an obsession with the *Blitzkrieg* cult.[48]

The beginning of the creative process which led ultimately to the forming of the Deep Operation theory should be credited first and foremost to the series of reforms conducted by M.V. Frunze in the General Staff of the RKKA in 1924.[49] By assembling in the General Staff two types of officers, Frunze intended to create an intellectual centre of gravity which would provide the Red Army with a conceptual basis to guide it coherently into the future.[50] One group consisted of officers, such as F.F. Novitskii, N.E. Varfolomeev, B.M. Shaposhnikov, A.A. Svechin and A.I. Verkhovskii, who were recruited from among the ranks of the *voin-spetsy* (military specialists). Being qualified as general staff officers (*Genstabisty*) in the Imperial Army, they were expected to integrate the knowledge and critical thinking developed by theoreticians such as A.A. Neznamov, B.V. Gerua, A.M. Zaenchkovsky, and P.I. Izmest'ev into the thinking process initiated by a nascent Red Army. The second group consisted of young officers like M.N. Tukhachevskii, and V.K. Triandafillov who were expected to contribute their operational experience in commanding large formations during the Civil War. The process generated by the combined activity of these two groups in the General Staff at the military academies and in the military districts and field formations attracted the support of senior members of the high cadres of the Communist party as well as that of many Red commanders from among the young military intelligentsia. This evolutionary process, which was not stopped even by Frunze's untimely death in October 1925, matured within 14 years into the theory of Deep Operations – coming to an abrupt end in the summer of 1937 with the great purge.

The historical setting which served as the background for the emergence of the theoretical revolution in military science was the immediate result of the closing stages of the Civil War and the Allied military intervention in the USSR. Bearing the burden of total war for eight years brought about the destruction of traditional infrastructures in the fields of economy, social life and culture. The violent eruption of a new ethos, the extreme change in the political system and the decimation of the population by several millions, brought the USSR to a state of social and cultural chaos and complete economic exhaustion. Moreover, in the course of 1922–41, an era which saw the consolidation of the communist system under Stalin's absolute control, the Soviet state went through a new type of political indoctrination and experienced the monstrous ordeals of collectivization, industrialization, urbanization and Stalinist terror. The impact of these turbulent events, involving the destruction of entire socio-economic groups and the deportation of huge populations within the borders of the Soviet Union, left their marks on the military.[51]

During the two decades that saw the development of the Deep Operation theory the quantitative dimensions of the Red Army experienced acute changes.[52] Whereas at the end of the 1920s the Red Army was the worst equipped of European armies in modern aviation, advanced artillery and motorization, in 1935 it already possessed the largest and the most advanced mechanized-armoured fleet in the world.[53] The great population movements caused by collectivization brought about a drastic change in the human composition of the Red Army[54] and its command cadres.[55]

The moulding of the Red Army's structure and thought were influenced during the first decade of its existence by a shortage of resources, political polarity within the crystallizing Communist establishment, the prevalence of a revolutionary climate and polemical trends, and the abolition of a professional managing tradition of the armed forces. Consequently, restrained on the technological and organizational fronts, the Red Army dedicated itself theoretically and professionally to three issues: the form and structure of the future armed forces, the unique nature of the communist military system, and the character of the future war.

The debate that developed around the first issue centred on the question of the system that the future Red Army should adopt. Should it be a standing army based on professional cadres, as was argued by Frunze and his supporters, or should it be the militia system, favoured by Trotsky's camp.[56] The issue of the military nature of the communist system generated an intense debate focusing on the subject of doctrine. Whereas Frunze, Tukhachevskii and Gusev argued vehemently for the immediate development and application of a unified military doctrine (*edinaia voennaia doktrina*), Trotsky and Svechin rejected the notion that a single obligatory doctrine could serve as a universal framework for military thought and practice.[57] The type of strategy the USSR should adopt in the future constituted yet another question emerging from the discussion of this issue. Once again, the high echelons of the Soviet military establishment were divided into two camps. Frunze, Gusev and Tukhachevskii favoured the adoption of an offensive strategy, while Trotsky, influenced by Svechin's perception of the future war as a total war of attrition, favoured a defensive strategy.[58]

VETERANS OF THE FIRST CAVALRY ARMY AND THE SCHOOL OF OPERATIONAL THOUGHT

Since the future composition of the armed forces as well as the eventual course of technological development were expected to follow the definition of the nature of future war, it was within this realm that the debate concerning the preference for cavalry or mechanization took place in the Red Army. The great relevance of this debate to the present discussion derives mainly from the fact that its true origins lay deeper than what was apparently suggested by its title. The views of the participants in this debate did not centre on the technical question which occupied other military establishments at the time, that is, whether to prefer the traditional horse arm or the new armoured one. Rather, they contemplated whether to base the structure and operating concepts of the future Red Army on a universal theory of operational manoeuvre or on a method providing immediate tactical solutions to the apparent problems. Moreover, this debate revealed some interesting aspects of the dynamics occurring among the leading officials of the Soviet defence establishment. The debate sheds fresh light on the linkage between the development of the operational theory and mechanization in the Red Army.

On the face of it, the debate appears simple and even familiar, since it bears resemblance to similar debates in other armies at the same time. On one side stood Tukhachevskii and the enthusiasts of modernization, and on the other stood the school of the First Cavalry Army (*Pervoi Konnoi Armii*), headed by Voroshilov and Budennyi, who, drawing on their successful experience in the Civil War, unequivocally preferred the mounted arm.[59] The inception of the debate can be related to a lecture given by Tukhachevskii in the annual assembly of the Western Front veterans in 1922, envisioning the decline of the traditional cavalry arm and the rise of armour, mechanization, air power and modern artillery.[60]

Tukhachevskii's positive stand on matters such as military technology and force building stemmed from a systemic approach aimed at linking to the advanced operational manoeuvre, any relevant technological or tactical element that could be utilized in its application. Therefore, he advocated the adoption of mechanization by ground and airborne forces. Moreover, in his conception of the deep operational manoeuvre the element of strategic cavalry had been given the crucial role of conveying the operational shock to the maximum depth. Thus, not only did he not reject the idea of employing cavalry in modern war, but by proposing the application of mechanization he encouraged the adaptation of the cavalry to the conditions of the modern operational manoeuvre and developed it into a new dimension:

> Strategic cavalry with its high mobility, powerful technical equipment and great striking power, is capable of independent action in all phases of war. . . Cavalry is particularly well suited to flank operations (*okhvat*), the development of penetrations (*razvitiia proryva*), actions in the enemy's rear areas, raids and pursuit . . . Attacks by major cavalry units, and especially by higher cavalry formations must have dependable air cover.[61]

The negative nature of Voroshilov's and Budennyi's position in the dispute originated not only from a personal animosity towards Tukhachevskii, but mostly from a deep military ignorance. Thus, beyond rejecting any proposition made by Tukhachevskii or his supporters, their own agenda was confined to the archaic concept of tactical shock produced by assaulting cavalry.[62]

The 1927 and 1930 memorandums written by Tukhachevskii strove to generate a general modernization by means of a systematic process of rearmament and reorganization. This is the main reason why recent historiography has placed exaggerated emphasis on the technological aspects of the dispute. Nevertheless, an examination of Stalin's objections to Tukhachevskii's views in general and to the memorandums in particular, reveals that at the heart of the dispute stood motives much deeper than those suggested by the technological or organizational argument. Well familiar with Tukhachevskii and his school, Stalin regarded his theoretical and organizational premises as a mere façade for developing a Red military élite.[63] It must have been apparent to him that the 1927 proposals reflected an almost fully crystallized operational conception, formed by a military intellectual élite. Moreover, Stalin sensed that the intensive efforts invested by Tukhachevskii and his colleagues in the creation of an advanced military theory could easily lead to the formation of a core of military excellence, which he regarded as a potential threat. Consequently, he banned lectures on strategy in the advanced military schools by members of the operational school and many efforts were made to prevent Tukhachevskii from presenting his ideas in public.[64]

All this indicates that the true roots of the dispute between Voroshilov's group and the Tukhachevskii school centred on the development of the operational concepts by the latter, and the so-called arguments concerning the preference for either mechanization or cavalry served as a pretext employed by Stalin's emissaries. Thus, even after Stalin's recognition of the operational qualities of mechanization and his formal sanctioning of the formation of four independent armoured corps, Voroshilov and Budennyi neither ceased to plot against Tukhachevskii nor changed the manner and content of their attacks on him, until he was executed in 1937.[65]

A critical examination of the debate on the issue of mechanization in the RKKA (the Red Army) may help to shed new light on a misinterpretation that has become rooted in western military historiography. Many historians believe that until the emergence of mechanization a modern theory of operational manoeuvre could not be developed. Therefore, they have tended to associate the birth of theories such as *Blitzkrieg* and Deep Operations with the application of armour in the relevant armies. This view immediately raises a number of problems, deriving from the incoherence of its basic argumentation. One problem concerns the difficulty of providing a satisfactory explanation for the fact that the Germans, who served as the basic positive model in this argumentation, never succeeded in endowing the technical framework of *Blitzkrieg* with real operational content (see above). Another problem concerns the inability of this approach to explain the great time gap between the adoption of mechanization and the development of a mature theory of operational manoeuvre in certain armies, such as that of the United States. The last problem derives from the existing discrepancy between the prevailing historical approach and the case of Soviet operational theory. It is a fact that the theory of Deep Operations crystallized in its final written form only in the first half of the 1930s. Nevertheless, as can be seen from the writings of Tukhachevskii, Triandafillov, Varfolomeev, Vol'pe, Belitskii, Krasil'nikov, Galaktionov and Isserson, the Russians possessed a coherent concept of advanced operational manoeuvre as early as 1928 – a time when the entire tank fleet of the Red Army consisted of less than 90 obsolete machines, the remnants of the Civil War. Moreover, the amazing pace, relative smoothness and advanced quality of weapon systems, which characterized the formation of the Soviet armoured troops, aviation, and combat support arms during the first half of the 1930s, proves beyond any doubt that in the Soviet case the build-up of forces was initiated by a fully formed operational theory.[66]

A closer look at the human composition of the rival school confirms the arguments we have just presented. Tukhachevskii's school included distinguished commanders, such as Bliukher, Iakir, Uborevich, military intellectuals, such as Triandafillov, Isserson, S.M. Belitskii, A.M. Vol'pe, N.E. Varfolomeev, S.N. Krasil'nikov, E.A. Shilovskii and V.A. Melikov, and unique figures such as the cavalry corps commanders G.D. Gai and Vitalii Primakov. Thus, with regard to its members' origin, the group was heterogeneous and its common denominator derived from their intellectual prowess and their operational consciousness.[67] The sole support of the group within the Communist political élite came from Georgii Konstantinovich Ordzhonikidze. Notwithstanding his close association with Stalin, Ordzhonikidze was an enlightened liberal, respected Tukhachevskii and supported his ideas and activities. Serving as the Head of the Supreme Council of the National Economy (VSNKh), and later as the Minister for Heavy Industry, Ordzhonikidze made strenuous efforts, beginning in early 1930, to convince Stalin to restore Tukhachevskii from his exile in the Leningrad military district and appoint him as Head of the Armament Directorate of the RKKA.[68] The definite results of the close cooperation between the two, as well as their proximate execution in summer 1937, confirm the existence of a progressive axis of interests, resisting the orthodox trends exercised by the Stalin–Voroshilov–Buddenyi front.[69]

The recruitment of A. A. Svechin to Voroshilov's reactionary group provides yet another proof for the claim that the roots of the dispute with Tukhachevskii's school were deeper than what was suggested by the title 'mechanization or cavalry'. Svechin, who had been a senior General Staff officer in the Imperial Army and a renowned military intellectual possessing a deep operational consciousness, was recruited as a *voin-spets* by Trotsky in 1918. Throughout his copious writings, starting as early as 1907, he expressed a holistic approach to the conduct of war and a profound understanding of the cognitive aspects of directing operations.[70] Nevertheless, in the light of his perception of the future war as one of static attrition, he tended to reject the idea of the deep operational manoeuvre, developed by Tukhachevskii and his colleagues.[71] The question of cavalry over mechanization was entirely irrelevant from Svechin's point of view. He did not object to mechanization inasmuch as he did not particularly favour cavalry. Svechin, who was the first to define coherently both the operational level and operational art, remained attached in his thinking to the nineteenth-century notions of attrition and limited war, and therefore was unable to transform his abstract definitions into the functional field of operational manoeuvre.[72] His argument with Tukhachevskii and Triandafillov centred on the attempt of the latter to employ mechanization for the implementation of the operational strike manoeuvre, an idea he never appreciated.[73] Thus, in spite of the fact that in his basic thinking Svechin was closer to Tukhachevskii than to Voroshilov, since he rejected the idea of modern manoeuvre, he attached himself to the latter's camp as a means for blocking the operational school.[74]

STRATEGY OF A SINGLE POINT[75]

It was the sense of crisis which accompanied the realization that traditional concepts and patterns were unable to provide appropriate answers to the challenges posed by modern war, which brought the individual members of the future school of operational thinking together. With the emergence of a system consciousness and a common motivation to form an alternative military theory suiting modern conditions of war, a mental group cohesion was achieved.

In practice, the members of the school of operational thought were dispersed in the military academies, the General Staff, the military districts, at the headquarters of the various inspectorates, services, and formations, and their contribution to the creation of the operational theory was voluntary, beyond their formal duties.[76] Moreover, the development of the operational theory, which was disturbed by many external factors, was never declared to be, or conducted as, a formal process. Therefore, the participants lacked not only the basic working conditions but also the formal recognition of being a part of a national enterprise. Nevertheless, in retrospect this experience should be regarded as a process due both to the close relationship existing between its initial intentions and the quality of its results, and the teleological nature of its evolutionary course.

The initial stage of the creative process which led ultimately to the formulation of the operational theory focused entirely on the repudiation of the traditional paradigm of the integral battle of destruction. Proving the absurdity of the idea of annihilation constituted the simplest among the numerous tasks confronting the group at that stage. Despite the embryonic nature of the unique approach to war which motivated the group members, it reflected, already at this early stage, the entire depth of their holistic view:

> In spite of all tactical successes accumulated prior to the engagement, the fate of the campaign will be decided at the very last battle . . . In the warfare of modern huge armies, defeat of the enemy results from the sum of continuous and planned victories on all fronts, successfully completed one after the other and interconnected in time.[77]

The methodical invalidation of the old paradigm commenced with the publication of a series of researches which analyzed the principal campaigns and operations of both the First World War and the Civil War. By employing a system approach, these papers identified the main causes for failure in both wars.[78] The formulation of a positive substitute for the old paradigm focused on the attempt to define a set of principles, which would reflect the practical aspects of the operational consciousness. One of these aspects was the identification of the logic of universal systems at the operational level, specifying the substance of this level within the hierarchical order of the military activity in general, and characterizing the nature of the linkage between the three levels of war:

> Battle, then, is the means of the operation. Tactics are the material of operational art. The operation is the means of strategy, and operational art is the material of strategy. This is the essence of the three part formula given above.[79]

Another issue arising from the attempt to interpret system consciousness into practical military terms concerned the essential role exercised by the strategic aim in generating military systems and in providing cognitive guidance to the operational process. In his definition of the term 'operation', Svechin revealed the entire depth of Soviet system consciousness and profound appreciation of the aim mechanism within this new setting:

> Combat actions are not self-sufficient but rather are the basic materials from which operations are composed. Only on a very few occasions can one depend on one engagement to secure the final objectives of military actions. Normally, the path to final aims is broken up into a series of operations, subdivided in time, by more or less sizeable pauses, different territorial sectors of a theatre of war and differing sharply as a consequence of different intermediate aims . . . We call operation that act of war, during which struggling forces without interruption are directed into a distinct region of the theatre of military operations to achieve distinct intermediate aims.[80]

The last aspect crystallized during the endeavour to provide a principle or a systemic framework for the application of operations in place of the idea of annihilation. Defining the notion of Successive Operations (*posledovatel'nye operatsii*), the think tank originating in the 4th Directorate of the General Staff determined the following principle: 'It is essential to conduct a series of successive operations which are appropriately distributed in space and time'.[81]

The formulation of operational consciousness in coherent patterns of thinking, on the one hand, and the critical research for the causes of failure in the preceding wars, on the other, led the Soviet theoreticians to diagnose the dichotomy which dominated the nature of war until the end of the First World War, namely: tactical archaism in an advanced operational environment. Henceforth, the path to the inevitable breaking of the traditional paradigm lay clear of conceptual obstructions. This was clearly expressed in a series of lectures given by Tukhachevskii in the Military Academy between 7 and 10 February 1922:

> Since it is impossible with the extended fronts of modern times to destroy the enemy's army at a single blow, we are obliged to try to do this gradually by operations which will be more costly to the enemy than to ourselves.[82]

THE IDENTIFICATION OF SYSTEM LOGIC IN MILITARY OPERATIONS

The cognitive course of the theory's evolutionary process and the teleologic link between its subsequent activities were determined by the identification of the universal system logic in the field of modern military systems, that is, the specific characterization of operations.

The discovery of the operational dichotomy generated a recognition of the quality required to bridge the gap between the mechanical and the abstract as the fundamental trait required at the various levels of operational command.[83] Consequently, this step led the Soviet theoreticians to define the operational art as a new and independent field of knowledge, intended to accomplish strategic goals by means of a systemic conduct of warfare:

> Strategy decides questions concerning both the use of the armed forces and all the resources of the state for the achievement of ultimate military aims . . . The material of operational art is tactics and logistics. Operational art, arising from the aim of the operation, generates a series of tactical missions and establishes a series of tasks for the activity of rear area organs. Tactics makes the steps from which operational leaps are assembled. Strategy points out the path.[84]

As the cognitive basis for this new field of knowledge, Tukhachevskii and Svechin suggested forming a coherent theory of operations by means of conducting a critical study of the universal military experience.[85] The recognition of the need for scientific methods of research and teaching to ensure the systematic assimilation of the recently accumulated knowledge along the various echelons of command, led to the establishment of a chair for operational art in the military academy and to the development of an accurate and uniform system of terminology.[86]

Creation of the operational corpus of knowledge also involved specifying the linkage between theory and technology in general, and the correct understanding of the latter in the context of operational thinking. The initiative for this step, coming principally from Tukhachevskii and Triandafillov, rationalized these relations. By determining the precedence of theory over technology, the course of the latter's development became functional since it was guided by a logical evaluation of the fighting methods and a systemic assessment of combat requirements:

> Tactics, operational art and strategy as a whole stem from the materiel and personnel that a state allocates for the conduct of warfare. Military art, torn away from this foundation, is inevitably converted into adventurism and fantasy and can lead to nothing good. But all this has a reverse influence as well. Tactics, operational art and all strategy not only consider the material base and flow from this, but in turn indicate and map out the paths of further development and expansion of this materiel base. They solve problems determining which branches of military and overall civilian technology must be developed in the future. The trends this should follow, the combat arms that require further alteration, and what improvements and upgrades must be carried out within the armed forces system.[87]

In creating the idea of operational shock (*udar*) to be attained by a succession of blows aimed at the rival system's depth, the Soviet theoreticians managed not only to produce a logical substitute to the traditional idea of destruction:[88] this idea, outlining the rationale of military system thinking around which all the resulting ideas were constructed, posed an abstract yet logical formula for defeating modern armies or military systems. It also sought to neutralize the rival system by annulling its practical ability to attain its aim, i.e. make it irrelevant. By combining the positive and negative aspects of the operational act, this approach attacked the cognitive fabric of the rival system's behaviour, thus depriving it of its logic. Moreover, in identifying the operational strike manoeuvre (*udar*) as consisting of a series of successive actions (*posledovatel'nye deistvii*) developing towards depth within the context of a strategic aim, the practical validity of the abstract concept was confirmed, and a coherent linkage between the consequences of the operation and the means for their application was established:

> The art of the attacker is to unleash the entire mass of forces quickly enough to break out to the flank and rear area of the enemy forces, to cut his withdrawal routes and disrupt any new grouping of forces the enemy is preparing.[89]

The operational shock idea generated the subsequent conceptual breakthrough, which concerned the subject of depth. Mikulin's mobile scheme (*podvizhnaia skhema*), being anchored in the political nature of ground warfare, identified the dimensions of front and depth in any existing operational configuration, thus setting up a universal framework for the operational manoeuvre, and emphasizing the crucial importance of depth as the system's principal area of sensitivity.[90] Moreover, the perception of the universal military system in terms of both frontal (linear) and deep (columnar) dimensions was instrumental in combining the idea of interaction between attrition and manoeuvre within the context of operational or strategic occurrence. This last achievement led to the crystallization of the factor of operational massing (*massirovanie*). Whereas the linear front was designed to reduce the rival system's depth and troop density by holding it forward along the longest possible line of contact, the columnar strike aimed to produce the operational shock by forcing a massive penetration into its sensitive depth.[91]

Most of the research conducted at that stage perceived systemic succession not only in the abstract context of attaining the ultimate goal, but also in the practical context of operation in depth. In other words, the columnar configuration, defined as the operational strike, was structured in several functional echelons, expressing operational succession through the relationship between them.[92] Hence, for the first time in the history of military thought, by pointing to the columnar configuration as the subject of operational and tactical synergism, a logical relationship was established between continuity and combined-arms warfare. This achievement made it possible to endow the term mobility with operational validity, by linking it to the strategic aim. Moreover, explaining the triangular relation between mass, time, and space – the materials which combine the systemic operation – by analogizing it to the column, illuminated the idea of momentum as a crucial element in the context of the operational manoeuvre.[93]

The method employed by the members of the operational school when enquiring into the complex aspects of the principle of operational depth commenced with a thorough analysis of modern defensive, which was seen as the simpler form of operational manoeuvre.[94] This approach encouraged the early disclosure of a number of the basic principles and mechanisms which control any military system, such as: the principle of movement differential, the principle of bipolar command, the dynamics of the reciprocal command circle, and the mechanism of the conditioned hierarchical action.[95] Since no other army in the modern era had approached the subject of operational manoeuvre from that fundamental viewpoint or employed such methods, the sharp identification of these principles and mechanisms remained exclusive to the Red Army. Moreover, applying that methodical approach gave the Russians not only a better understanding of the defensive, but also deepened their appreciation of the offensive at the operational level.

The understanding of operational command, which crystallized during that stage of development, derived from deep inquiries into the nature of operational warfare and corresponded to the specific challenges suggested by this systemic research.[96] Since they had specified very clearly the differing nature of the activity at the varying levels of conducting war, the Soviet theoreticians could differentiate, in the next step, between *initsiativa* (initiative), as the quality required from tactical commanders and *tvorchestvo* (creativity), as the quality required from operational commanders. *Tvorchestvo* comprised both the intellectual ability to compete with the challenges posed by the abstract aim, and the faculty to assemble the numerous tactical events into a coherent contingency, leading to achievement of the aim. Moreover, by pointing to the quality of creativity, the operational thinkers suggested a level of consciousness commensurate with the difficulties posed by the random environment of the operational level of war.[97] Finally, by developing the concept of the cognitive tension, the gap between the qualities of *initsiativa* and *tvorchestvo* was bridged and the conflict between the various command poles was harmonized.

The results of the creative stage in the evolution of the Deep Operation theory were expressed completely in Triandafillov's book on the nature of operations of modern armies. Through a critical analysis of the recent military experience, Triandafillov focused the revolution in modern warfare on the emergence of the operational dimension, and likewise summarized the principles and characteristics of that level of war. Moreover, he introduced a universal framework for the understanding of war that has not lost its relevance even today.[98] Summarizing the intellectual effort that took

186

place in the most acute stage of theoretical development, this work laid down the scope – in terms of space and time – for the conduct of modern operations, offered operational and logistical configurations, and provided the appropriate command structures. However, the most important conceptual achievement revealed in the book is an outline of universal rules and principles upon which a method for attaining operational shock could be based. This outline specified *obkhod* as the highest degree in effectuating the operational shock situation, and the principles of simultaneity (*odnovremennost'*), the splitting or fragmenting strike (*rassekaiushchii udar*), and momentum (*momenty*) as the means to achieve that situation.[99]

DEEP BATTLE – THE TACTICAL CIRCLE

In the next stage the main theoretical effort focused on the tactical dimension. The results of this activity could be recognized in the accelerated development of armoured and airborne formations, in the large-scale manoeuvres of the 1930s, and in the formulation of the tactial field manuals, that emphasized the deep battle (*glubokii boi*).[100]

It is probable that this deviation from the main axis of the theoretical development was caused by Stalin's intention to restrict the theoretical activity of the operational school to the tactical field and to matters related directly to the industrial policy of the Five Year Plan.[101] Another reason might have been the theoreticians' desire to encourage the assimilation of their conceptual achievements among the Red Army tactical commanders. The last reason derived from the inherent dynamics of the process. At the close of the 1920s, when the essential elements of the new theory had already been formulated, the leaders of the operational school recognized the need to shift the centre of gravity of their activity to the empirical field. Temporary preoccupation with the field of tactics served this intention well since it provided the opportunities to examine the abstract and broader operational ideas by means of miniature tactical models.[102] By addressing the tactical defence complex, which constituted only one element of the entire defensive system, the deep battle concept intended to produce a basic layout for action at the initial stage of the operation. In practical terms, this meant the penetration of the defensive system's forward tactical belt along its entire depth. And since it was assumed that this sector would naturally be most heavily fortified and obstructed, the execution of the breakthrough stage of the operation was assigned to the infantry.[103] Nevertheless, since the concept of the deep battle perceived the tactical defence layout as a sub-system

in the jurisdiction of the operational holding echelon, it was dominated by the rules and principles of the Deep Operation theory.
Moreover, owing to the fact that the operational objective assigned
to the holding echelon centred on the penetration of the enemy's
tactical defence layout, in a manner allowing the irruption of the
strike echelon into the defender's operational depth, it had been
structured in column configuration combining four elements: a shock
element (*udarnaia gruppa*) comprising about two-thirds of the
formation; a holding group (*skovyvaiushchaia gruppa*) comprising
about a third; a reserve; and an artillery group (*artilleriiskaia gruppa*)
which was designed to reinforce the means of suppression (*sredstva
podavleniia*) along the axis of penetration.[104] The grouping in four
elements, as noted above, prevailed at the levels of regiment, division, and corps. These quantitative relations concerned the offensive
only. In the case of the defensive, the relation between the holding
and the strike group were simply reversed in favour of the first. By
effectuating a complete breakthrough of the tactical defence, an
objective indicating the universal mission of the entire operational
holding echelon, the tactical strike group aimed to prevent the
tactical defender from carrying out his mission, thus inflicting upon
him the state of operational shock. In the defensive, the action of the
strike element intended to restore the initial conditions of the operational situation. Therefore, both in the offensive and defensive, the
grouping of the strike element was based on mechanized-armoured
formations. Unlike the second operational echelon, the reserve,
which comprised a limited part of the entire force (one-ninth), lacked
a set definition of an initial mission, thus it was designed to deal with
problems emerging in the course of the operation, according to the
commander's decision. Since the holding element's mission was
to tie up the defender and erode his force, its organization was
based on infantry formations. Whereas in the defence this mission
was achieved by occupying a fortified line, in the attack it was
implemented by infiltration of such a defensive line. In the Soviet
conception, the artillery reserve constituted an independent element,
possessing unique operational traits. Serving as the principal
suppressive asset, the artillery's main mission was to reinforce the
operational concentration factor in the planned point of decision and
thus accelerate the attrition of the rival force.

The real innovation of the deep battle concept did not derive
merely from the artificial emphasis laid upon the principle of depth.
The application of deep infiltration tactical patterns had already been
manifested by the German Spring offensive of 1918. The Soviet
theoreticians were the first to interpret the idea of combined arms

tactics practically in terms of deep action or column patterns. Triandafillov, who articulated this concept, assumed correctly that the penetration of fortified dispositions would remain an operational mission assigned to the infantry.[105] Since the operational and tactical configurations were transformed from linear to columnar, it became imperative that the application of combined-arms patterns of action should depend not only on the definition of the required combat arms, but also on their organization in a mode enabling a depth-oriented successive action. Triandafillov's memorandum determined three groupings of tanks and three of artillery which were designed to cooperate with the penetrating infantry formations along the entire depth of the tactical layout. The definition of these groupings was not determined according to their differing ranges of action, since they were bound to change in the varying operational circumstance, but rather according to the specific types of the tactical missions, arising from the universal context of the breakthrough operation. The forward tactical echelon of tanks and artillery was organized in combat groupings supporting the infantry in the break-in action (*bresh'*).[106] The tank and artillery groupings, designed to escort the infantry formations performing the mission of breakthrough (*proryv*), were organized in an intermediate tactical echelon.[107] The tank and artillery units designed to cooperate with the infantry formations completing the breakthrough and combating the defender's tactical mobile reserves constituted the third echelon in the tactical column configuration.[108] This idea had never been conceived by the Germans and, therefore, their infantry, lacking the fundamental manoeuvre quality, was never capable of exploiting its true operational potential. The result of this limitation was that the Germans assigned the operational mission of breaking through their opponent's tactical defence to their tank formations which, by performing this mission without real cooperation, were eroded and lost their ability to achieve operational or strategic decision.

The thorough discussions and intensive experiments that concerned the development of tactical patterns of deep action and the formulation of the 1933 provisional version of the Deep Battle theory provided the answers to the principal problems that blocked the way to the final stage of the theoretical process.[109]

With the return to the main course of the theory's development – a trend that was interrupted by the abrupt increase of the wave of terror in the summer of 1937 – the research activity was concentrated once again in the Faculty for Operational Art, which became the General Staff Academy in 1936, and in the military districts of Belorussia (Uborevich), Ukraine (Iakir), and the Far East (Bliukher). The theoretical problems, which were identified in academic circles by means of individual analysis, group discussions and war games, were later examined and put to practical tests in the headquarters of the military districts through exercises and manoeuvres.[110] The essence of the Deep Operation theory, which could not be formalized in the prevailing circumstances in the 1930s, can be gleaned from the 1936 *Field Service Regulations* and from abundant individual works, produced between 1927 and 1937. Although it focused exclusively on the tactical level, the *Field Service Regulations*, written under Tukhachevskii's supervision, succeeded in delivering the essence of the operational theory:

> Modern offensive forces, above all the large-scale employment of tanks, aviation, and *desanty* by mechanized forces open up the possibility of attacking the enemy simultaneously over the entire depth of his field force layout, with a view to isolating him, and completely surrounding him . . . With all arms and forms of support acting in concert, an offensive operation should be based on simultaneous neutralization of the entire depth of the enemy defence. This is achieved by: (1) Air action against reserves and rear areas. (2) Artillery fire on the entire depth of the enemy tactical layout. (3) Deep penetration of the enemy tactical layout by groups of long range tanks (DD). (4) Incursions into the enemy tactical layout by infantry combined with groups of supporting tanks (NPP). (5) Strikes deep into the enemy's rear by mechanized and (operational-strategic) cavalry formations. (6) Extensive use of smoke, both to cover manoeuvres by friendly forces, and on secondary sectors to deceive the enemy.[111]

This brief extract demonstrates the complete structure of the operational strike manoeuvre, conducted in the context of attaining strategic aims, through the infliction of operational shock on the defending system. It emphasizes the elements of simultaneity, deep fragmentation, and momentum, achieved through the combined operation of a breakthrough echelon, an echelon conveying tactical success into the operational depth, and a deep echelon neutralizing the defender's use of his own depth, and acting as a bolstering vector from the defensive rear towards its front. Moreover, this concise definition not only identifies operational shock with the neutralization of the rival system's ability to perform its missions, but likewise accentuates the importance of creating an operational centre of gravity by combining mechanical acts with active deception.

The conceptual formula moulded by the theoreticians of the operational school was so visionary and creative in its content that even 40 years after its creation it has not lost any of its relevance, and all that was needed to make it fully applicable was to mobilize technology, and manufacture the weapon systems the theory had foreseen so long ago.[112]

DEEP SIMULTANEOUS STRIKE – TOWARDS AN OPERATIONAL PARADIGM[113]

The intellectual breakthrough that was generated by the Soviet conception of depth derived from the identification of its systemic implications and from its linkage to the idea of operational shock. Through the essential synergy between the dimensions of depth and front, Mikulin's Mobile Scheme (see above), revealed not only the substance of military system dynamics, but also the essence of the interaction between the political-strategic and the operational levels. Within the first context the front represented the holding echelon – an element whose functional roots lay in the nature of tactical combat relying entirely on attrition. On the other hand, the depth, deriving from the intrinsic nature of systems, expressed both the positive and negative aspects of the principle of *udar*.[114] Therefore, by illuminating the synergy between front and depth a conceptual framework for the formation of an effective operational manoeuvre, either offensive or defensive, was set up. The origins of the second context were identified by Mikulin in the nature of political entities which adhere to territorial assets by means of operating ground forces. In that context, the front represents the territorial integrity, being the basic logic underlying any political or strategic aim, and the depth determines the operational method, guaranteeing the preservation of that integrity.[115] By perceiving the presence of these two elements as a precondition to any operational occurrence at all levels of war, this integrative approach elevated – for the first time in the history of modern military thought – the idea of depth from the narrow level of techno-tactical behaviour to the abstract level of systemic thinking.

Out of this mode of thinking, Tukhachevskii, Triandafillov, Isserson and their colleagues developed the unique idea of *obkhod* (the turning manoeuvre).[116] This idea, having no equivalent in any western military theory or language, reflects the most advanced degree in the imposition of the state of operational shock on the rival system. By the swift accumulation of a manoeuvring mass in the defensive operational depth, the attacking system invalidates the relevance of the defender's strategic aim.[117] Moreover, the presence of an operational mass on the far side of the defensive centre of mass undermines the movement differential and the mechanism of the conditioned hierarchical action, reinforcing the defensive system's resisting effectiveness.[118] Thus, the defender's command structure is damaged, his method of manoeuvre suffers disruption, and his operational ability to attain his objectives and goals is entirely negated.

The systemic thinking deriving from the notions of depth and hierarchy led the theoreticians of the operational school to form the idea of shock as the core of the revolutionary theory of manoeuvre they had created. On the other hand, all their efforts to formulate practical methods for implementing the operational shock terminated in the range of options offered by depth. Even today, a leading figure of the theoretical renaissance of the 1970s, when asked to sum up in practical terms the essence of the idea of *udar*, stated: '*Perevozit' uspekha v glubinu*' (to transfer success to the depth).[119] In other words, the operational theoreticians perceived the application of shock as a dynamic occurrence, possessing the form of a column. In this occurrence, depth determines not only its ultimate objectives, but also the nature of its operating mechanism and the character of its mechanical patterns. Therefore, being a basic mechanism of any system, the concept of successive operations could only have originated in the idea of depth:

> If the mission with which the army is charged is not of local significance, but pursues a decisive goal, if the combat actions contemplated at a given time have in mind achievement of such results as a rout of the enemy that might be reflected decisively during the further course of the war, then a significant penetration into the depth of the enemy disposition, immediate infliction of a second, third and subsequent blows on the heels of the first must be envisioned to bring the enemy to complete defeat. The ideal would have to be to plan the actions of friendly armed forces in such a way that, employing a series of crushing blows carried to their conclusion, they would lead to complete defeat of the enemy.[120]

The application of successive operations, implemented by means of integrating the operational components through patterns such as fragmenting strike, simultaneous paralyzation of the entire depth of the enemy's dispositions (*odnovremennoe podavlenie vsei glubiny nepriatel'skogo raspolozheniia*), and operational by-pass (*okhvat*), produces momentum, which accelerates the neutralization of the rival system's operational mechanisms.

NOTES

1. On this type of process in general, see T.S. Kuhn, *The Structure of Scientific Revolutions* (Chicago, 1973), pp. 37–9, 109, 176.

2. Many military analysts tend to identify the conceptual revolution or revival of manoeuvre in modern warfare with the advent of mechanization. As we have seen, until the development of operational consciousness even the best of armies could only obtain a tactical advantage from mechanization. See, for example, J.F.C. Fuller, *The Conduct of War 1789–1961* (New Brunswick, 1968), pp. 174–7; B.H. Liddell Hart, *The Other Side of the Hill* (London, 1970), p. 120; T.N. Dupuy, *Understanding War History and Theory of Combat* (London, 1992), pp. 16–18; James J. Schneider, *The Structure of Strategic Revolution*, (Novato, CA, 1994), pp. 11–53.
3. G. Martel, *The Russian Outlook* (London, 1947), pp. 14–32; C. Bellamy, 'Red Star in the West: Marshal Tukhachevskii and East-West Exchanges on the Art of War', *RUSI Journal* 132, 4 (1987), pp. 66–7, 68–70.
4. M. Zakharov's Introduction to A.B. Kadishev (ed.), *Voprosy strategii i operativnogo iskusstva v sovetskikh voennykh trudakh 1917–1940* (Moscow, 1965), p. 22; 'Pomnit' uroki istorii vsemerno ukrepliat' boevuiu gotovnost' (Remember the Lessons of History, Strengthen Combat Readiness in Every Possible Way), *Voenno-istoricheskii zhurnal* (hereafter *VIZh*) 6 (1988), p. 6; V.G. Kulakov, 'Operativnoe iskusstvo' (Operational Art), *Sovetskaia voennaia entsiklopediia* (hereafter *SVE*) (Moscow, 1978), Vol. 6, p. 53; G. Isserson, 'Razvitie teorii sovetskogo operativnogo iskusstva v 30-e gody' (The Development of the Theory of Soviet Operational Art in the 30s), *VIZh*, 3 (1965), p. 61; A.I. Todorskii, *Marshal Tukhachevskii* (Moscow, 1963), Vol. 1, pp. 235–6, 238, 241, Vol. 2, p. 560; S.S. Biriuzov, *Sovetskii soldat na Balkanakh* (A Soviet soldier in the Balkans) (Moscow, 1963), pp. 141, 143; J. Erickson, 'The Red Army Before June 1941', *Soviet Affairs* 3 (1962), St. Antony's Papers, No. 12, London, p. 95; idem, *The Soviet High Command* (London, 1962), pp. 504–6; B. Orlov, 'The High Command of the Red Army and the Terror of the 1930s in the USSR', Ph.D., diss., Tel Aviv University, 1986, pp. 273–96, 341–52.
5. I.M. Anan'ev, *Tankovye armii v nastuplenii* (Tank Armies in the Offensive) (Moscow, 1988), p. 33; V.A. Anfilov, *Proval blitskriga* (The Failure of *Blitzkrieg*) (Moscow, 1974); C.N. Donnelly, *Red Banner* (Coulsdon, Surrey, 1988), pp. 85–6.
6. V.D. Sokolovskii, *Voennaia strategiia* (Military Strategy), H.F. Scott (ed.) (Moscow, 1968), pp. 192, 193, 209; V.A. Semenov, *Kratkii ocherk razvitiia sovetskogo operativnogo iskusstva* (A Short Sketch on the Development of Soviet Operational Art) (Moscow, 1960), pp. 290–91; N. Krylov, 'Raketnye voiska strategicheskogo naznacheniia' (Strategic Rocket Forces), *VIZh*, 7 (1967), pp. 15–16; D.M. Glantz, *Soviet Military Operational Art* (London, 1991), pp. 177–80.
7. A.I. Radzievskii, *Tankovyi udar* (Tank Strike) (Moscow, 1977), pp. 2–8; Anan'ev, *Tankovye armii v nastuplenii*, pp. 29–30, 94, 110–11; M.N. Tukhachevskii, 'Voprosy vysshego komandovaniia' (Questions of Higher Command) (1924), in Kadishev (ed.), *Voprosy strategii*, pp. 82, 89; 'Novye voprosy voiny' (New Questions of War) (1931), in ibid., pp. 127–38; A.I. Verkhovskii, 'Manevr i ego formy' (Manoeuvre and its Forms) (1928), in ibid., pp. 277–81; A.M. Vol'pe, 'Frontal'nyi udar' (Frontal Strike) (1931), in ibid., pp. 366–70; N.E. Varfolomeev, 'Operatsii udarnoi armii' (Operations of the Strike Army) (1933), in ibid., pp. 441–4, 456–7.
8. G.S. Isserson, *Evoliutsiia operativnogo iskusstva* (The Evolution of Operational Art) (Moscow, 1937), pp. 60–62.
9. The term *desant* (literally: 'descent') connotes the idea of descending on the enemy's depth by an airborne operational movement.
10. I.E. Krupchenko, 'Primenenie otdel'nykh tankovykh (mekhanizirovannykh) korpusov i tankovykh armii dlia razvitiia uspekha v nastupatel'nykh operatsiiakh' (Operating Homogeneous Tank (Mechanized) Corps and Tank Armies in Successful Offensive Operations), in O.A. Losik (ed.), *Stroitel'stvo i boevoe primenenie sovetskikh tankovykh voisk v gody Velikoi otechestvennoi voiny* (The Building and Combat Handling of Soviet Tank Forces in the Years of the Great Patriotic War) (Moscow, 1979), pp. 113–21; Anan'ev, *Tankovye armii v nastuplenii*, pp. 63–4.
11. I.E. Krupchenko, personal communication, Moscow, 2 Feb. 1993.
12. J.G. Hines and P. A. Petersen, 'The Warsaw Pact Strategic Offensive, the OMG in Context', *International Defense Review* LXII, 10 (1983), pp. 1391–3; 'Thinking Soviet in Defending Europe', *Defence* 9 (1989), pp. 513–15; 'The Soviet Conventional Offensive in Europe', *Military Review* LXIV, 4 (1984), pp. 9–16; W.F. Scott and H.F.

Scott, 'The Historical Development of the Soviet Forward Detachment', *Military Review* LXVII, 11 (1987), pp. 27–34; J.F. Holcomb, 'Soviet Forward Detachment: A Commander's Guide', *International Defense Review* 5 (1989), pp. 551, 553; D.M. Glantz, 'Operational Art and Tactics', *Military Review* LXVIII, 12 (1988), p. 38. All the references cited above interpret the OMG as a modern version of the WWII Forward Detachment (*peredovoi otriad*). The following references relate to the OMG as a modern version of WWII Mobile Group: R.N. Armstrong, 'The Mobile Group Experience: the Russians Appear to be Still Refining their WWII Tactics in Today's OMGs, A *rmor* XCVI, 5 (1987), pp. 24–30; J.R. Burniece, 'The Operational Manoeuvre Group, Concept versus Organization', *Military Technology* 10, (1988), pp. 78–9; B. Brown, 'OMG', *Field Artillery Journal* 1, 53 (1985), pp. 26–7; C.N. Donnelly, 'Operational Manoeuvre Group: A New Challenge to NATO', *International Defence Review* 9 (1982), pp. 1177, 1179, 1181, 1182–6; 'Soviet Fighting Doctrine', *NATO's Sixteen Nations*, 5 (1984), pp. 66–7; H.W. Coyle, 'Tatsinskaya and the Soviet OMG Doctrine', *Armor* XCIV, 1 (1985), pp. 33, 37–8; R. Simpkin, 'Countering the OMG', *Military Technology*, 3 (1984), pp. 82–4; J.A. Herberg, 'Operational Manoeuvre Groups', *US Army Aviation Digest*, 9 (1983), pp. 30–32; J.G. Hines, 'The Operational Manoeuvre Group: the Debate and the Reality', *Review of the Soviet Ground Forces*, 2 (1983), pp. 1–7; H. S. Shields, 'Why the OMG?', *Military Review* LXV, 11 (1985), pp. 5–13; W.A. Brinkley, 'The Cost across the Flot', *Military Review* LXVI, 9 (1986), pp. 30–31; D.L. Smith and A.L. Meier, 'Ogarkov's Revolution – Soviet Military Doctrine for the 1990s', *International Defence Review*, 7 (1987), pp. 870–71; C. J. Dick, 'Soviet Operational Manoeuvre Group: A Closer Look', *International Defence Review*, 6 (1983), pp. 772–6; P. H. Vigor, *Soviet Blitzkrieg Theory*, (London, 1983), pp. 130, 204; B.W. Rogers, 'Follow-On Forces Attack (FOFA): Myths and Realities', *Nato Review*, 12 (1984), p. 2; US Department of Defense, *Soviet Military Power 1985*, Superintendent of Documents, US Government Printing Office, Washington, pp. 63, 70–71. A third group perceives the OMG as a kind of massive operational raid: G.C. Swan, 'Countering the Daring Thrust', *Military Review* LXVI, 9 (1986), pp. 43, 45–6; P.A. Karber, 'Tactical Revolution in Soviet Military Doctrine', *Art of War Colloquium*, US Army War College (Carlisle Barracks, PA, 1983), p. 2; J.C. Murguizur, 'Some Thoughts on Operational Manoeuvre Group', *International Defence Review* 4 (1984), p. 380.
13. I.Kh. Bagramian (ed.), *Istoriia voin i voennogo iskusstva* (History of War and Military Art) (Moscow, 1970), p. 83; A.A. Strokov (ed.), *Istoriia voennogo iskusstva* (History of Military Art) (Moscow, 1966), pp. 299–301; V.G. Kulakov, 'Operativnoe iskusstvo' (Operational art) in *SVE*, 1978, Vol. 6, p. 54; G. V. Kuzmin, *Grazhdanskaia voina i voennaia interventsiia v SSSR* (The Civil War and the Military Intervention in the USSR) (Moscow, 1958).
14. P.D. Korkodinov, 'Operativnoe iskusstvo Krasnoi armii' (The Operational Art of the Red Army), *Morskoi sbornik* 6 (1946), p. 6.
15. Kuhn, *The Structure of Scientific Revolutions*, pp. 62, 92; Bernard Cohen, *Revolution in Science* (Cambridge, MA, 1985), pp. 28–31.
16. Bagramian, *Istoriia voin i voennogo iskusstva*, p. 83; M.M. Kozlov, 'Frontovaia nastupatel'naia operatsiia' (Front Offensive Operation) in *SVE*, 1980, Vol. 8, pp. 336–9. The front operational organization was initially formed in June 1918 for the sake of conducting independent operations and campaigns. The various authors, cited above, mentioned diverse data concerning the spatial dimensions of these operations: 300–600 km, when regarding width of front offensive sectors, and 200–300 when referring to the depth of front offensive sectors. S.S. Kromov (ed.), *Grazhdanskaia voina i voennaia interventsiia v SSSR* (The Civil War and the Military Intervention in the USSR) (Moscow, 1983), pp. 114, 240, 384, 529, 617; A.S. Bubnov, S.S. Kamenev, R.P. Ideman (eds), *Grazhdanskaia voina 1918–1921: Voennoe iskusstvo Krasnoi armii* (The Civil War 1918–1921: The Military Art of the Red Army) (2 vols.) (Moscow, 1928–30), Vol. 2, p. 244, presented cases when the width of front sectors measured 300–800 miles, and their depth some 150–500 miles; the advance from Omsk to Irkutsk, which lasted from November 1918 until March 1920, was mentioned as the largest operation conducted by a single front during the entire course of the war.
17. A.A. Brusilov, *Moi vospominaniia* (My Recollections) (Moscow, 1983), p. 122; N.Ia.

Kapustin, *Operativnoe iskusstvo v pozitsionnoi voine* (Operational Art in Positional War) (Moscow/Leningrad, 1927), p. 14.

18. N.N. Azovtsev, P.N. Dmitriev, V.V. Dushen'kin, P.M. Kevdin, S.F. Naida, L.M. Spirin (eds), *Direktivy komandovaniia frontov Krasnoi armii 1917–1922 gg.* (Directives of the Red Army's Front Commands 1917–22) (Moscow, 1978), Vol. 4, pp. 534–5, 586–95; Anan'ev, *Tankovye armii v nastuplenii*, p. 21; Iu.A. Zotov, 'Boi 1-i konnoi armii v raione Rovno v iiune 1920g.' (Battles of the 1st Cavalry Army in the District of Rovno in June 1920), *Voina i revoliutsiia* 2 (1929), pp. 102–3; G.D. Gai, 'Nedostatki v organizatsii Krasnoi Konnitsy' (Shortcomings in the Organization of the Red Cavalry), *Voina i revoliutsiia* 6 (1921), pp. 49–68; A.I. Soshnikov *et al.*, *Sovetskaia kavaleriia: Voenno-istoricheskii ocherk* (Soviet Cavalry: A Military Historical Study) (Moscow, 1984), pp. 3–24; V.V. Dushen'kin, *Vtoraia konnaia: Voenno-istoricheskii ocherk* (The 2nd Cavalry Army: A Military Historical Study) (Moscow, 1968), pp. 168–206; K. Monigetti, *Sovmestnye deistviia konnitsy i vozdushnogo flota* (Joint Operations of Cavalry and the Air Fleet) (Moscow, 1928), pp. 92–3; I. Babel, 'Konarmiia' (Cavalry Army), in *Izbrannye proizvedeniia* (Selected Works) (Moscow, 1966), pp. 27–58; M. Ryshman, *Reid Mamontova, avgust–sentiabr' 1919 g.* (Mamontov's Raid, Aug.–Sept. 1919) (Moscow, 1926), pp. 16–29; V. Melikov, 'Konnye massy v Grazhdanskoi voine' (Massed Cavalry in the Civil War), *Voina i revoliutsiia* 7–8 (1933), pp. 3–16.

19. N.V. Ogarkov, 'Voennaia strategiia' (Military Strategy) in *SVE*, 1979, Vol. 7, p. 560.

20. In this aspect the case of Tukhachevskii may serve as a clear example proving our argument. Tukhachevskii entered the First World War as a young lieutenant barely graduating from the military academy. In May 1920, at the age of 27 he commanded four armies of infantry and one of cavalry during the Polish campaign.

21. Orlov, *The High Command of the Red Army and the Terror of the 1930s in the USSR*, pp. 166–7, 172–3. Both Vitalii Markovich Primakov and Gaia Dmitrevich Gai (Bazhishkian) who commanded cavalry corps during the Civil War, were famous for their ranging nature and daring creativity as well as for their intellectual talents and command abilities.

22. R.L. Garthoff, *Soviet Military Doctrine* (Rand Corporation, 1953), pp. 44–7; L. D. Trotsky, *Kak vooruzhalas' revoliutsiia* (How the Revolution Was Armed) (3 vols.) (Moscow, 1923–25), Vol. 1, p. 29.

23. N.P. Mikhnevich, *Strategiia* (Strategy), 3rd edn (St Petersburg, 1911), p. 152; L.N. Tolstoi, *Milhama veShalom* (War and peace) (2 vols.) (Tel Aviv, 1977), trans. Leah Goldberg, Vol. 2, pp. 93, 235–7, 408–11, 422, 447, 452, 457–8, 504–14.

24. M.N. Tukhachevskii, 'Voina' (War), in Kadishev (ed.), *Voprosy strategii*, pp. 105–6.

25. S.S. Kamenev, 'Ocherednye voennye zadachi' (Forthcoming Military Objectives) (1926), in Kadishev (ed.), *Voprosy strategii*, pp. 149–52; A.A. Svechin, 'Strategiia' (Strategy) (1927), in ibid., p. 220; V. Mastulenko, 'Razvitie operativnogo iskusstva v nastupatel'nykh operatsiiakh' (The Development of Operational Art in Offensive Operations), *VIZh*, 10 (1967), pp. 39–40; Kozlov, 'Frontovaia nastupatel'naia operatsiia', p. 336.

26. M.V. Frunze, 'Front i tyl v voine budushchego' (Front and Rear in Future War), in Kadishev (ed.), *Voprosy strategii*, pp. 64–5; N.N. Azovtsev and E. I. Rybkin, 'Lenin' in *SVE*, 1977, Vol. 4, pp. 605–7.

27. I. Kravchenko, 'Kharakternye cherty nastupatel'nykh operatsii Krasnoi armii v Grazhdanskoi voine' (The Characteristic Features of Offensive Operations of the Red Army in the Civil War) *VIZh*, 3 (1976), pp. 98–101; M.N. Tukhachevskii, 'Pokhod za Vislu' (The March to the Vistula) (lecture given on 7–10 Feb. 1923 to the advanced course at the military academy), in *Izbrannye proizvedeniia* (Selected works), N.I. Solov'ev (ed.) (Moscow, 1964), Vol. 1, pp. 114–68; 'Iz urokov Grazhdanskoi voiny' (Some Lessons of the Civil War) (1928), in ibid., Vol. 2, pp. 24–7.

28. During 1918–19, 'fronts' (the equivalent of army groups) consisted of 3–6 field armies and 45,000–110,000 fighting soldiers. During the same period, armies' order of battle consisted of 3–6 divisions and 25,000 soldiers. *Direktivy komandovaniia frontov Krasnoi armii*, Vol. 4, pp. 11–243.

29. Bagramian, *Istoriia voin i voennogo iskusstva*, p. 85.

30. Ibid., discloses that there was no uniformity in the structure of units and formations and that their order of battle was in fact dictated by circumstances. Another interest-

ing fact emphasized by the author concerned the identical numbers of combatants and non-combatants in the divisions.

31. Ibid., pp. 86–7.
32. V. Kulikovskii, 'Razvitie taktiki Krasnoi armii v gody Grazhdanskoi voiny' (The Development of Red Army Tactics in the Years of the Civil War), *VIZh*, 12 (1971), pp. 70–73.
33. V. Mastulenko, 'Razvitie taktiki nastupatel'nogo boia' (The Development of Offensive Battle Tactics), *VIZh*, 2 (1968), pp. 28–9. 'Udarnaia gruppa' (Shock group) in *SVE*, 1980, Vol. 8, p. 172; I.N. Vorob'ev, 'Oruzhiia i taktika' (Arms and Tactics), *Krasnaia zvezda* (12 Jan. 1982), p. 2, specified two governing elements in combat: *manevr* (manoeuvre), and *udar* (shock). The shock is the resulting effect of a coherent manoeuvre which is attained through the synergy between the various combat arm elements, participating in the action. I.P. Uborevich, 'Znachenie manevra v Grazhdanskoi voine' (The Significance of Manoeuvre in the Civil War) (1921), in Kadishev (ed.), *Voprosy strategii*, pp. 167–9.
34. *Voennyi entsiklopedicheskii slovar'* (hereafter *VES*) (Moscow, 1983), p. 168; A. I. Verkhovskii, 'Obshchaia taktika dlia normal'noi voennoi shkoly' (General Tactics in Support of Normal Military Schools) (1924), in Kadishev (ed.), *Voprosy strategii*, pp. 33–6.
35. M.V. Frunze, *Izbrannye proizvedeniia* (Selected Works) (Moscow, 1950), p. 206.
36. V.G. Reznichenko, *Taktika* (Tactics) (Moscow, 1966), p. 86; V.E. Savkin, *Osnovnye printsipy operativnogo iskusstva i taktiki* (The Basic Principles of Operational Art and Tactics), trans. under the auspices of the United States Air Force (Washington, 1972), pp. 240–42; V. Tuns, 'Aktivnost' oborony' (Active Defence), *Voennyi vestnik* 3 (1980), p. 38.
37. In this context, the *tachanka*, that combined a machine gun mounted on a light horse-drawn carriage, provided a good example of Russian improvisational abilities and their consistent drive to transfer the fire into depth.
38. The English translation 'one man command' only partially explains the term *edinonachalie*. The problem here derives from the fact that the term represents an entire conception or philosophy of which the technical aspects of command constitute but one element among many. Historians overwhelmingly tend to relate the birth of the concept to the mid-1920s, a time when both the military and the political establishment were engaged in a fiery dispute regarding the future image of Soviet armed forces. The moulding of the concept has been attributed by Soviet historiography to Frunze. It was born out of the Civil War experience and owes its origin to two trends. One trend concerned the professional aspects of command that derived from the problems created by the tactical synergy. The other trend was anchored in political considerations. This trend, which originated in the practice of dividing the command of units between a political and professional authority, reflected the tension that existed during the Civil War between the traditional party leaders and the *voin-spetsy*.
39. *SVE*, 1977, Vol. 3, p. 301; S.N. Kozlov (ed.), *Officer's Handbook*, trans. under the auspices of USAF, Washington, 1971, p. 4; *Dictionary of Basic Military Terms*, trans. under the auspices of USAF, Washington, 1965, p. 74.
40. *VES*, p. 638. This idea demonstrates the existing identity between the concepts of *edinonachal'nik* (sole commander) and that of *obshchevoiskovoi komandir* (combined -arms commander). Both these concepts stemmed from a dialectic way of thinking and express ideas such as: attaining a complete and unified result within a heterogeneous framework of action, unity of command and synergy, and the person who possesses the overall authority of command is exclusively responsible for the planning of the action and its conduct (*otvetstvennyi chelovek*). According to Vorob'ev in 'Oruzhie i taktika', p. 2, the *udar*, which is the resulting effect of any tactical action, is attained through a harmonious combination of resources and combat arm elements utilized solely by the person commanding the relevant tactical entity. Thus, since the manoeuvre aimed at bringing about the effectuation of *udar* hinges on the synergy between the various combat arm elements, it also bears the title *udar*.
41. Clausewitz, *On War*, M. Howard and P. Paret (eds) (Princeton, 1976), B. 4, Ch. 9, p. 249; Ch. 11, p. 259.
42. T. Lyman, *Mead's Headquarters, 1863–1865: Letters of Colonel Theodore Lyman from*

the Wilderness to Appomattox, G.R. Agassiz (ed.) (Boston, 1922), p. 224; T.N. Dupuy, *Understanding War History and Theory of Combat* (London, 1992), pp. 31–7.

43. *VES*, pp. 507–8, interprets *sredstva podavleniia* as: Fire support assets required to create the requisite density of forces in a given sector in order to degrade the defender's tactical capability. F. Zhemaitis, 'Proryv Pol'skogo Fronta 1-i Konnoi Armiei' (The Penetration of the Polish Front by the First Cavalry Army), *VIZh*, 6 (1940), p. 6.

44. These parameters, referred to in Russian as *takticheskaia plotnost'*, meant the concentration of troops and resources required for the effectuation of tactical shock, within specific conditions of combat.

45. Bagramian, *Istoriia voin i voennogo iskusstva*, p. 85; M.N. Tukhachevskii, 'Voina kak problema vooruzhennoi bor'by' (War as a Problem of Armed Struggle), in *Izbrannye proizvedeniia*, Vol. 2, pp. 8–11.

46. G.E. Isserson, 'Zapiski sovremennika o M. N. Tukhachevskom' (Observations of a Contemporary on M.N. Tukhachevskii), *VIZh*, 4 (1963), pp. 64–78; idem, 'Razvitie teorii sovetskogo operativnogo iskusstva v 30-e gody' (The Development of Soviet Operational Art in the 1930s), *VIZh*, 1 (1965), pp. 36–46; No. 3, pp. 48–61; N. Lomov, 'Izbrannye proizvedeniia M.N. Tukhachevskogo' (M.N. Tukhachevskii's selected works – a review article), *VIZh*, 7 (1965), pp. 69–76; M.V. Zakharov, 'O teorii glubokoi operatsii' (On the Theory of Deep Operations), *VIZh*, 10 (1970), pp. 10–20.

47. Semenov, *Kratkii ocherk razvitiia Sovetskogo operativnogo iskusstva*, pp. 118–22; P. Grigorenko, *Memoirs* (New York, 1982), p. 92; the author, who had been a student of G.E. Isserson's in the General Staff Academy, recollected that from 1938 to 1942 operational theory had been taught without referring to the term *glubokaia operatsiia* (deep operation), since it had been absolutely deleted from the military lexicon with Tukhachevskii's execution. V.N. Lobov, 'Aktual'nye voprosy teorii Sovetskoi strategii 20-kh–serediny 30-kh godov' (Current Problems Regarding the Soviet Strategic Theory in the Mid-1920s and 1930s), *VIZh*, 2 (1989), pp. 41–2.

48. J.J. Schneider, 'Introduction', in V.K. Triandafillov, J.W. Kipp (eds), *The Nature of the Operations of Modern Armies* (London, 1992), pp. xxv–xxvi confirmed that the first serious attempt to investigate the theoretical and historical aspects of the evolution of Soviet operational theory occurred as late as the end of the 1970s, with the commencement of the American theoretical enterprise and the setting up of a centre for Soviet military studies in Ft. Leavenworth. A. and J. Seaton, *The Soviet Army: 1918 to the Present* (New York, 1987), is a good example of the extent of western scholars' ignorance of Soviet achievements in the field of operational theory. The authors claim: 'The Soviet Armed Forces at the time of the interwar period had no soldiers of genius or experience and the Red Army was an indifferent imitation of the German Army'. D.M. Glantz, 'Predstavleniia Amerikantsev ob operatsiiakh na vostochnom fronte v gody vtoroi mirovoi voiny' (Conceptions of Americans about operations on the Eastern Front during the Second World War), *Voprosy istorii*, 8 (1987), pp. 29–48, acknowledged the somewhat simplistic trend in the West to attribute the causes for the *Wehrmacht*'s failure in the war with the USSR to the hardships of winter, the Soviet superiority in masses, and to Hitler's interventions in the conduct of operations.

49. A. Ageev, 'Voennyi teoretik i voennyi istorik A.A. Svechin' (A.A. Svechin Military Theoretician and Historian), *VIZh*, 8 (1978), p. 102; M.I. Vladimirov, *et al.*, *M.V. Frunze: Voennaia i politicheskaia deiatel'nost'* (M.V. Frunze: Military and Political Activity) (Moscow, 1984), pp. 58–60.

50. I.A. Korotkov, *Istoriia sovetskoi voennoi mysli: Kratkii ocherk 1917–iiun' 1941* (History of Soviet military thought: A Short Sketch from 1917–June 1941) (Moscow, 1980), pp. 32–4; M.V. Frunze, *Sobranie sochinenii* (Collected Writings) (Moscow, 1926), 2 vols., Vol. 2, p. 343.

51. I. Volin, *A Century of Russian Agriculture* (Cambridge, MA, 1970), p. 221, reports that in the course of the collectivization process, enforced by Stalin's regime, more than 400,000 families were deported to Asian Russia, and more than 5.5 million people perished. A. Orlov, *A Secret History of Stalin's Crimes* (New York, 1953), p. 28, proves that during the years of collectivization 3.5 million people died from hunger alone. W.H. Chamberlin, *Russia's Iron Age* (Boston, 1935), p. 88, and D.G. Darlymple, 'The Soviet Famine 1932– 1934', *Soviet Studies* XV, 3 (1964), pp. 259–60, both claim that during the years under discussion more than 6 million people perished in the Ukraine

exclusively. S. Rosefielde, 'An Assessment of the Sources and Uses of Gulag Forced Labour 1929–1956', *Soviet Studies* XXXIII, 1 (1981), pp. 56, 58–9, reports that during the years 1933–35 more than 6 million people were held as prisoners in labour camps, a number six times bigger than the total of the Red Army at that time.

52. *Istoriia Velikoi otechestvennoi voiny* (The History of the Great Patriotic War) (Moscow, 1963), Vol. 1, p. 90; Ministerstvo oborony SSSR, Institut voennoi istorii, *Istoriia Vtoroi mirovoi voiny* (The History of the Second World War) (Moscow, 1973), Vol. 1, p. 270; M.M. Kirian (ed.), *Voenno-tekhnicheskii progress i vooruzhennye sily SSSR* (Technical Progress and the Armed Forces of the USSR) (Moscow, 1982), p. 66; S.A. Tiushkevits (ed.), *Sovetskie vooruzhennye sily* (Soviet Armed Forces) (Moscow, 1978), pp. 130, 150, 159, 165, 192. In the course of the Civil War the numerical strength of the Red Army rose from 300,000 to 3 million; it dropped to 500,000 in the late 1920s and rose again to 1,433,000 in 1937.

53. *SVE*, 1976, Vol. 1, p. 598; *Istoriia Velikoi otechestvennoi voiny*, Vol. 1, p. 90; H. W. Gatzke, 'Russo German Military Collaboration during the Weimar Republic', *American Historical Review* 3, LXIII (1958), p. 590. In the years 1928–29, a time when the full content of the Deep Operation theory had already been fully developed, the Red Army's arsenal of main weapons systems consisted of some 82 tanks of various origins, 98 armoured cars, 7,000 pieces of artillery, 26,000 machine guns and approximately 1,000 obsolete aircraft. Tiushkevich, *Sovetskie vooruzhennye sily*, pp. 163, 192–3, suggested the number of 92 tanks and 1,400 aircraft. I.B. Berkhin, *Voennaia reforma v SSSR* (Military Reform in the USSR) (Moscow, 1958), pp. 58–9, claimed that in the course of the 1920s the USSR was completely incapable of fighting a modern power, and even cited Frunze expressing the same view in 1924. H. Guderian, *Die Panzertruppen und ihre Zusammenwirken mit den Anderen Waffen* (Berlin, 1943), p. 18, reported that during his visit to the USSR in 1939 he was astonished to find out that the Soviets possessed more than 10,000 advanced main battle tanks, 100,000 military vehicles, and 150,000 gun-towing tractors.

54. *XV S'ezd Vsesoiuznoi Kommunisticheskoi Partii (b). Stenograficheskii otchet* (Minutes of the General Communist Party Conference) (Moscow, 1928), p. 398. The report stated that in 1927 urban workers constituted 18.1 per cent of the Red Army manpower, agrarian population 71.3 per cent, and all the rest some 10.6 per cent. In 1933 the composition changed significantly: the urban workers' rate rose to 43 per cent, that of the agrarian population dropped to 7 per cent.

55. K.E. Voroshilov, *Stat'i i rechi* (Articles and Speeches) (Moscow, 1936), p. 230, described the composition of the Red Army command cadres, in the year 1927 as: 22 per cent urban workers, 50 per cent originated in rural communities, and 28 per cent came from other social strata. *Istoriia Vtoroi mirovoi voiny*, Vol. 1, p. 252, presented the following statistics in regard to the situation in the year 1929: 29.4 per cent industrial workers in urban communities; 34.4 per cent peasants or rural workers; and 36.2 per cent from other strata.

56. The irony of fate in this case is that Trotsky, who initially recognized the importance of professional military knowledge for the Red Army to function properly, found himself preaching the idea of an army based on an amateurish system, while young Red commanders, such as Frunze, Tukhachevskii and Triandafillov, who rose to senior positions in the course of the Civil War supported the idea of a standing professional army. This phenomenon reflected some of the peculiarities and paradoxes of the professional debate; Schneider, *The Structure of Strategic Revolution*, pp. 104–5.

57. L. Trotsky, *Kak vooruzhalas' revoliutsiia*, Vol. 2, pp. 202, 206, 242; idem, 'Voennaia doktrina ili mnimo-voennoe doktrinerstvo' (Military doctrine or pseudo-military doctrinairism), *Voennaia nauka i revoliutsiia* 2 (1921), pp. 204–13; D. Petrovskii, 'Edinaia voennaia doktrina v Akademii General'nogo shtaba' (Unified Military Doctrine in the General Staff Academy), *Voennoe znanie* 14–15 (1921), p. 13, described how the academy was affected by the debate; M.V. Frunze, *Edinaia voennaia doktrina i Krasnaia armiia* (A Unified Military Doctrine and the Red Army) (Moscow, 1921), p. 18; idem, 'Edinaia voennaia doktrina i Krasnaia Armiia' (The Unified Military Doctrine and the Red Army), *Voennaia nauka i revoliutsiia* 2 (1921), pp. 33–9; S.I. Gusev, *Grazhdanskaia voina i Krasnaia armiia* (The Civil War and the Red Army) (Moscow,

1958), pp. 216–21; I.I. Vatsetis, 'O voennoi doktrine budushchego' (On Future Military Doctrine) (1923), in Kadishev (ed.), *Voprosy strategii*, pp. 184–9.

58. Tukhachevskii, 'Voina kak problema vooruzhennoi bor'by' (War as a Problem of Armed Struggle) (1928), in *Izbrannye proizvedeniia*, Vol. 2, pp. 16–17. Tukhachevskii's point of view on this matter was not unequivocal. He favoured an offensive strategy since he believed it would accelerate the build-up of the armed forces and a more positive impact upon its thinking. However, at the level of applying strategy and operations, he regarded a reciprocal relation between offensive and defensive as an essential method for the accomplishing of the strategic goals; Schneider, *The Structure of Strategic Revolution*, pp. 104–5, 174–7, interprets this debate in terms of scientific revolutions, i.e. a conflict between two paradigms regarding the systematization of military knowledge or science.

59. After the Civil War, M. N. Tukhachevskii served as Deputy Chief of the General Staff under Frunze. When the latter died in 1925, he was elected Chief of the General Staff, a position he held until 1928 when relieved under Voroshilov's influence. S. M. Budennyi, who commanded the famous 1st Cavalry Army, was appointed Head of the Cavalry Inspectorate after the Civil War, and held this position until 1941. K. E. Voroshilov was nominated after Frunze's death, Head of RVS (Revoliutsionnei Voennoi Sovet), and later as Commissar for the Navy and Army; V.M. Ivanov, *Marshal M. N. Tukhachevskii* (Moscow, 1990).

60. N.I. Koritsky (ed.), *Marshal Tukhachevskii. Vospominaniia druzei i soratnikov* (Marshal Tukhachevskii's Recollections of Friends and Comrades-in-arms) (Moscow, 1965), pp. 171–2. Tukhachevskii's expressions during his lecture provoked the staff of the Cavalry Inspectorate, who were veterans of the First Cavalry Army, to furious verbal reactions. In one of them, Shchedenko, who was one of Budennyi's lieutenants, contradicted Tukhachevskii and claimed that the war of engines, mechanization and gases was nothing other than a fiction invented by the *voin-spetsy* in order to distract attention from the true determinants of future war, namely the horse and the cavalry arm.

61. Narodnyi Komissariat Oborony Soiuza SSR (NKO), *Vremennyi polevoi ustav RKKA 1936* (Red Army Provisional Field Service Regulations 1936, PU-36) (Moscow, 1937), Ch. 1, Art. 7; Tukhachevskii, 'Voprosy vysshego komandovaniia', p. 87.

62. Koritsky, *Marshal Tukhachevskii. Vospominaniia druzei i soratnikov*, p. 170. The roots of Stalin's and Budennyi's personal hostility towards Tukhachevskii lay in the latter's accusations that the south-western Front, in which Stalin served as political commissar during the 1920 Vistula campaign, failed to support the advance of his Western Front to Warsaw. Voroshilov's animosity, which brought about Tukhachevskii's dismissal from the post of Chief of the General Staff in 1928 and led ultimately to his fall in 1937, originated in the proposal made by Tukhachevskii, following Frunze's death, to appoint Ordzhonikidze as head of the RVS. Isserson, 'Zapiski sovremennika o M.N. Tukhachevskom', p. 66, recollected that Voroshilov's response to Tukhachevskii's 1927 memorandum, suggesting the formation of armoured forces, modern artillery, modern air force, and the mechanization of the cavalry, was to reject the programme as being unrealistic. S. Biriuzov, 'Voenno-teoreticheskoe nasledstvo M.N. Tukhachevskogo' (M.N. Tukhachevskii's Legacy to Military Theory), *VIZh*, 2 (1964), p. 40, noted that Voroshilov's reaction to the modernization programme presented in the 1930 memorandum was one of contemptuous objection. *XVII S'ezd Vsesoiuznoi Kommunisticheskoi Partii (VKP (b)). Stenograficheskii otchet* (Minutes of the 17th General Communist Party Congress) (Moscow, 1934), p. 226, described Voroshilov's unrestrained verbal attack in the conference on Tukhachevskii's sabotaging proposals which intended to substitute the horse for an armoured vehicle and the cavalry assault for a sophisticated yet unpractical manoeuvre. In *Pravda*, 24 May 1936, p. 2, an anonymous writer, authorized by Stalin and Voroshilov, accused Tukhachevskii, who was at the time the Head of the Armament Directorate and second deputy to the defence commissar, of proposing destructive theories aspiring to substitute the horseman for a tank and the patterns of the Civil War for a vague idea. K.E. Voroshilov, *XX let RKKA* (Twenty Years of the Red Army) (Moscow, 1938), p. 14, argued that the mounted arm and the tactical cavalry assault would remain the decisive factor in the future war.

63. Biriuzov, 'Voenno-teoreticheskoe nasledstvo M. N. Tukhachevskogo', p. 40
64. Koritsky, *Marshal Tukhachevskii. Vospominaniia druzei i soratnikov*, p. 175, reports
that in the course of an enlarged plenum of the RVS the Kommandarm, I. Iakir
suggested that Tukhachevskii, being the leading theoretician in the USSR, should
lecture to the forum of district commanders and senior officers on the fundamentals
of the operational theory. Iakir's request was rejected by Voroshilov who claimed that
Tukhachevskii's occupations as Head of the Armament Directorate left him no free
time for other activities. M.V. Zakharov, *Uchenyi i voin. O Marshale Sovetskogo Soiuza
B. M. Shaposhnikove* (Scholar and Warrior, on Marshal of the Soviet Union V. M.
Shaposhnikov), Moscow, 1974, p. 66, mentions a written appeal made on 16 April
1928 by Budennyi, his head of logistics, P.A. Dibenko, and Gorov, the commander of
the Belorussian military district, to Voroshilov, claiming that the General Staff of the
RKKA, headed by Tukhachevskii, was developing trends to assume total leadership in
matters concerning the operational direction of the Red Army. The combined pressure
produced by this letter and the hostile position taken by Voroshilov and Unshlikht
convinced Stalin to relieve Tukhachevskii of his post as Chief of the General Staff. N.
Pavlenko, 'Nekotorye voprosy razvitiia teorii strategii v 1920-kh godakh' (Some
Questions Regarding the Development of Strategic Theory in the 1920s), *VIZh*, 5
(1966), p. 12, notes that following the establishment of the Faculty for Military History
in the Military Academy, the planned course in strategic thinking was removed from
the academy's curriculum by I. A. Shchedenko, who was the academy's deputy
director for political affairs and a veteran of the 1st Cavalry Army, arguing that strategy was an occupation reserved exclusively for Stalin. G. E. Isserson, 'Razvitie teorii
Sovetskogo operativnogo iskusstva v 30-e gody' (The Development of the Theory of
Operational Art in the 30s), *VIZh*, 3 (1965), pp. 49–50, recollects that in the course of
a discussion held in the academy between senior instructors and Egorov, the
commandant, the request to include a course in strategy in the programme of studies
was raised. Nevertheless, Egorov refused, admitting that lectures on strategy had been
banned by Stalin.
65. I.E. Krupchenko, 'Razvitie tankovykh voisk v period mezhdu Pervoi i Vtoroi
mirovymi voinami' (The Development of Tank Forces in the Period between the First
and Second World Wars), *VIZh*, 5 (1968), pp. 41–2; Koritsky, *Marshal Tukhachevskii.
Vospominaniia druzei i soratnikov*, pp. 171–2. On 17 July 1929, following a lecture
given by Triandafillov, who was Tukhachevskii's disciple, close friend and a leading persona in the operational school of thinking, the RVS decided to form the
first experimental tank brigade and to establish an independent directorate for
mechanization and motorization. In 1930, after being convinced by Ordzhonikidze,
Stalin attended an armoured manoeuvre for three days. Following this experience he
formally approved the formation of four tank-mechanized corps.
66. A. Ryzhakov, 'K voprosy o stroitel'stve bronetankovykh voisk Krasnoi armii v 30-e
gody' (Questions of the Build-up of the Red Army Tank Forces in the 1930s), *VIZh*, 8
(1968), pp. 105–11; Anan'ev, *Tankovye armii v nastuplenii*, pp. 24–5; I. G. Andronikov
and W. D. Mostowenko, *Die Roten Panzer, Geschichte der Sowjetischen Panzertruppen 1920-1960* (Munich, 1963), pp. 21–8. Between 1932 and 1934 the Russians
concluded the complete build-up of four armoured-mechanized corps. D. S.
Sukhorukov (ed.), *Sovetskie vozdushno-desantnye voiska* (Soviet Airborne forces),
(Moscow, 1980), p. 34; I.I. Lisov, *Desantniki – vozdushnye desanty* (Paratroops – Air
Landings) (Moscow, 1968), p. 22. Between December 1932 and 1936 the Soviet
formed three airborne brigades, three independent regiments and an entire system of
transportation, combat support and training. M. V. Zakharov (ed.), *50 let
Vooruzhennykh sil SSSR* (50 years of Soviet Armed Forces) (Moscow, 1968), p. 205.
The accelerated formation of the Soviet air forces which began in March 1932
reflected more than any other element the principles of a fully developed operational
theory, both in their organization and diversity, and in their command and control
system. Unlike other armed forces, the Russians organized their aviation in two
separate forces, according to their different operational role. The air defence forces
(PVO) combined fighter aviation, warning systems and anti-aircraft artillery under a
single operational command. The conventional air forces (VVS) were organized in
formations correlating to those of the ground forces. Thus, a front, being the highest

operational formation, could have several combined-arms and tank armies and one or two air armies, which could allot fighter and attack (fighter bomber) corps and divisions to the various ground armies.

67. Except Triandafillov, who was killed in an air crash together with Kalinovskii, the chief of the mechanized troops in 1930, and G. E. Isserson who miraculously survived Stalin's harsh hand, all the other members of the group were exterminated in the 1937–38 purges.

68. I. Dubinskii-Mukhadze, *Ordzhonikidze* (Moscow, 1967), p. 237.

69. Ibid., p. 294; Orlov, *The High Command of the Red Army and the Terror of the 1930s in the USSR*, pp. 32–5. The cooperation between Tukhachevskii, who was responsible for determining the military armament policy, and Ordzhonikidze, who directed the civilian industrial effort, played a vital role in the accelerated modernization of the Red Army during the first half of the 1930s.

70. Generalmaior Aleksandr Andreevich Svechin (1878–1938) lectured on strategy and tactics in the Nikolaevsk Military Academy and was regarded as a leading military scholar and theoretician prior to the First World War. After being recruited to the Red Army, he directed military operations in the Smolensk district, and in August 1918 was appointed Chief of All-Russian Great Staff. In the early 1920s he was transferred by Frunze to the General Staff to help expedite the latter's intended reforms. Until his execution in 1938, he served as a professor of military science in the Military Academy. Among his principal works: 'Strategicheskii ocherk Russko-iaponskoi voiny ot nachala kampanii do srazheniia pod Liaoianom vkluchitel'no' (Strategic Outline of the Russo-Japanese War from the Start of the Campaign until the Battle at Liaoian inclusive), *Voennyi sbornik* 4 (1907), pp. 47–69; *Strategiia* (Strategy) (Moscow, 1923) 1st edn, 1927. He was editor of: *Strategiia v trudakh voennykh klassikov* (Strategy in Classical Military Works) (Moscow, 1925); *Evoliutsiia voennogo iskusstva* (The evolution of military art) (Moscow, 1927); *Klauzevits*, (Moscow, 1935); *Strategiia XX veka na pervom etape* (20th Century Strategy, the First stage) (Moscow, 1937).

71. Svechin, 'Strategiia' in Kadishev (ed.), *Voprosy strategii*, pp. 227–38.

72. N.E. Varfolomeev, 'Strategiia v akademicheskoi podgotovke' (Strategy in Academic Establishment), *Voina i revoliutsiia*, 11 (1928) p. 84, cites Svechin's definition. Svechin, 'Strategiia', in Kadishev (ed.), *Voprosy strategii*, pp. 218–22.

73. M.N. Tukhachevskii, 'Voprosy vysshego komandovaniia' (Questions of Higher Command) (1924), in *Izbrannye proizvedeniia*, Vol. 1, pp. 193–4; 'Predislovie k knige Dzh. Fullera "Reformatsiia Voiny"' (Preface to Gen. Fuller's book *The Reformation of War*) (1931), in ibid., Vol. 2, pp. 151–53; 'Novye voprosy voiny' (New Questions of War) (1931–32), in ibid., pp. 184–7; 'O strategicheskikh vzgliadakh prof. Svechina' (On the Strategic Views of Prof. Svechin), in K. Bocharov, I. Nizhechek and P. Suslov (eds), *Protiv reaktsionnykh teorii na voenno-nauchnom fronte. Kritika strategicheskikh i voennoi-istoricheskikh vzgliadov prof. Svechina* (Against Reactionary Theories on the Military-scientific Front. A Critique of Prof. Svechin's Strategic and Military-Historical Views) (Moscow, 1931), pp. 3–16.

74. C. Rice, 'The Making of Soviet Strategy', in P. Paret (ed.), *Makers of Modern Strategy* (Oxford, 1991), p. 665.

75. Isserson, *Evoliutsiia operativnogo iskusstva*, pp. 96–7, indicates the absurdity of the strategic paradigm that dominated military thought until the end of the First World War by referring to it either as *strategiia odnoi tochki* (Strategy of a Single Point) or *lineinaia strategiia preryvchatogo fronta* (Linear Strategy of a Discontinued Front).

76. The main nucleus of the thinking and writing activities consisted of two groups. A group of instructors at the Frunze Military Academy, that included officers, such as N.Ia. Kotov, K.A. Chaikovskii, P.I. Vakulich, S.N. Krasil'nikov, P.G. Ponedelin, I.P. Kitvitenko and R. S. Tsiffer. Another group centred on the Faculty for Operational Art (from 1936, the General Staff Academy) and included the various heads of the institute, such as N.E. Varfolomeev, G.S. Isserson, A.V. Fedotov, and the instructors A.M. Permytov, E.N. Sergeev, I.I. Trutko (logistics instructor), D.M. Karbyshev (intelligence instructor), A.N. Lapchinskii (aviation instructor) and B.K. Leonardov (instructor in military medicine). The school's activity was supported by high-ranking officers, such as I Z. Iakir, I.P. Uborevich, S.S. Kamenev, and the legendary commander of the Far East Military District, V.K. Bliukher. The school's activity attracted officers such as A.I.

201

Sediakin (Head of the Training Department), M.Ia. Germanovich (Head of the Armour Academy), K.B. Kalinovskii (Chief of the Moto-Mechanized Troops), Ia.M. Fishman (Head of Chemical Troops), and other intellectuals including F.P. Shafalovich, N.N. Shvarts, E.A. Shilovskii, V.D. Grendal, S.N. Bogomiakov, A.I. Gotovtsev, V.K. Mordvinov, B.L. Teplinskii and P.D. Korkodinov. The main works published by the school members were: I. Vatsetis, *O voennoi doktrine budushchego* (On Military Doctrine of the Future) (Moscow, 1923); V.K. Triandafillov, *Kharakter operatsii sovremennykh armii* (The Nature of Operations of Modern Armies) (Moscow, 1929), 1st edn; S.M. Belitskii, *Strategicheskie rezervy* (Strategic Reserves) (Moscow, 1930); A.M. Vol'pe, *Frontal'nyi udar*; G.S. Isserson, *Evoliutsiia operativnogo iskusstva* (The Evolution of Operational Art), (Moscow, 1937); N.E. Varfolomeev, *Udarnaia armiia* (Strike Army) (Moscow, 1933); *Nastupatel'naia operatsiia* (The Offensive Operation) (Moscow, 1937); S.N. Krasil'nikov, *Organizatsiia krupnykh obshchevoiskovykh soedinenii* (The Organization of large all-arms formations) (Moscow, 1933); V.A. Melikov, *Problema strategicheskogo razvertyvaniia po opytu Mirovoi i Grazhdanskoi voiny* (Problems of Strategic Deployment based on the Experience of the World and Civil Wars), Izdatel'stvo Voennoi Akademii RKKA imenii M.V. Frunze (Moscow, 1935); M.R. Galaktionov, *Tempy operatsii* (The Pace of Operations) (Moscow, 1937); A.N. Lapchinskii, *Vozdushnaia armiia* (The Air Army) (Moscow, 1939).

77. S.S. Kamenev, 'Ocherednye voennye zadachi', pp. 149–52. An identical view was offered by V.K. Triandafillov in R. Savushkin, 'K voprosu zarozhdeniia posledovatel'nykh nastupatel'nykh operatsii 1921–1929 gg.' (Concerning Questions of Sources of the Theory of Successive Operations 1921–1929), *VIZh* 5 (1983), p. 78.

78. V.K. Triandafillov, 'Vzaimodeistvie mezhdu Zapadnym i Iugo-zapadnym frontami vo vremia letnego nastupleniia Krasnoi Armii na Vislu v 1920g.' (Cooperation between the Western and South-western Fronts in the course of the Red Army's Offensive on the Vistula in 1920), *Voina i revoliutsiia* 2 (1925), pp. 19–43; idem, 'Perekopskaia operatsiia Krasnoi armii' (The Perekop Operation of the Red Army), in Bubnov, *et al.*, *Grazhdanskaia voina*, pp. 339–57; idem, 'O Volkovyskoi operatsii' (On the Volkovysk Operation), *Krasnaia armiia: Vestnik voenno-nauchnogo obshchestva pri Voennoi Akademii* (The Red Army: Military Scientific Herald to the Audience of the Military Academy) 10–11 (1922), pp. 34–43; N.E. Varfolomeev, 'Manevry na zapfronte' (Manoeuvres on the Western Front), *Revoliutsiia i voina* 19 (1923), pp. 5–26; No. 20, pp. 77–104; A. Bazarskii, *Nastupatel'naia operatsiia 9-i Russkoi Armii v iiune 1916 goda* (The Offensive Operation of the 9th Russian Army in June 1916) (Moscow, 1939); M.N. Tukhachevskii, 'Pervaia Armiia v 1918 godu' (The First Army in 1918), *Revoliutsiia i voina* 4–5 (1921), pp. 190–206. Tukhachevskii, 'Pokhod za Vislu', in *Izbrannye proizvedeniia*, Vol. 1, pp. 114–68; idem, 'Iz urokov Grazhdanskoi voiny' (From the Lessons of the Civil War), in ibid., Vol. 2, pp. 24–7; idem, 'Na Vostochnom fronte' (On the Eastern Front), in ibid., pp. 222–8; N.E. Kakurin, *Strategicheskii ocherk Grazhdanskoi voiny* (Strategic Study of the Civil War), (Moscow, 1926); V. Melikov, 'Srazhenie na Visle v svete opyta maisko–avgustovskoi kampanii 1920g.' (The Engagement on the Vistula in the Light of the Experience of the May–Aug. 1920 Campaign), *Voina i revoliutsiia* 10 (1931), pp. 9–44.

79. Varfolomeev, 'Strategiia v akademicheskoi podgotovke', pp. 83, 84. With his appointment to the Chair for Operational Studies in 1924, Varfolomeev, as the officer directly responsible for formulating the theoretical framework of operational art, presented in his writings the views shared by the other members of the group. P.I. Vakulich, 'Sovremennaia operatsiia' (Contemporary operations), in V.N. Levichev (ed.), *Voina i voennoe delo* (War and Military Activity) (Moscow, 1933), p. 550, expressed an identical view.

80. Svechin, 'Strategiia', p. 220.

81. Cited by Savushkin in 'K voprosu o zarozhdenii teorii posledovatel'nykh nastupatel'nykh operatsii – 1921–1929 gg.', p. 79. The 4th Directorate group that worked on the formulation of a conceptual framework for the conduct of modern operations was headed by M.N. Tukhachevskii, and comprised three other officers: Ia.K. Berezin, A.N. Nikonov, and Ia.M. Zhigur.

82. Cited in, Zakharov, 'Predislovie', p. 12; Isserson, *Evoliutsiia operativnogo iskusstva*, p. 96, indicates the absurdity of the paradigm of the integral battle of destruction when

presenting it as *strategiia odnoi tochki* (strategy of a single point). M.N. Tukha-chevskii, 'Taktika i strategiia' (Tactics and Strategy) (1926), in *Voprosy strategii*, pp. 104–5, combines the idea of successive blows conducted towards depth in the context of attaining the strategic aim with the repudiation of the idea of destruction attained in a single giant linear engagement.

83. A.A. Svechin, *Strategiia*, pp. 14–15, refers to this dichotomy as the Old Tactics-Strategy Dichotomy. Tukhachevskii, 'Novye voprosy voiny', in *Voprosy strategii*, p. 181, delineates the historical and cognitive circumstances which led to development of this dichotomy.

84. Ibid., pp. 15–17; Vakulich, 'Sovremennaia operatsiia', pp. 540–52.

85. Svechin, *Strategiia*, pp. 15–17; Tukhachevskii, 'Novye voprosy voiny', in *Voprosy strategii*, pp. 180–81; Vatsetis, 'O voennoi doktrine budushchego', pp. 181–4.

86. Vatsetis, 'O voennoi doktrine budushchego', pp. 184–89; Semenov, *Kratkii ocherk razvitiia sovetskogo operativnogo iskusstva*, pp. 14–35. Akademiia General'nogo shtaba, *Istoriia voennykh ordenov Lenina i Suvorova i stepeni Akademii General'nogo shtaba Vooruzhennykh sil SSSR imeni K.E. Voroshilova* (The History of the Military Orders of Lenin and Suvorov and the Ranks of the K.E. Voroshilov General Staff Academy of the Armed Forces of the USSR) (Moscow, 1987), 2nd edn, pp. 22–4; Isserson, 'Razvitie teorii operativnogo iskusstva v 30-e gody', No. 1, p. 40, No. 3, p. 49. In 1922, when commanding the Military Academy for a short period, Tukhachevskii established an advanced class for operational studies. In 1924, the Chair for Operational Studies was formed under Varfolomeev, as a part of the academy. This institute was designed to perform, by means of its regular staff, three missions: conducting operational researches, developing the operational theory, and lecturing in operational art. In 1931, the chair was transformed into a faculty under Isserson, but due to organizational considerations it remained attached to the academy. Only in autumn 1936, the General Staff Academy was established as an independent institute responsible for training high-ranking officers for command at the operational level. V. Mastulenko, 'Razvitie operativnogo iskusstva v nastupatel'nykh operatsiiakh', pp. 39–40; idem, 'Razvitie taktiki nastupatel'nogo boia' (The Development of the Tactical Offensive Battle), *VIZh* 2 (1968), pp. 28–9; I. Korotkov, 'Voprosy obshchei taktiki v sovetskoi istoriografii 1918–1941 gg' (Questions of General Tactics in Soviet Military Historiography 1918–41), *VIZh* 12 (1977), p. 89. All these sources describe in detail the enormous literary effort conducted in the course of the development of the operational theory, A. A. Bogdanov, V*seobshchaia organizatsionnaia nauka (tektologiia)* (A Universal Organizational Science (Tectology), Vols. I–III (Moscow/Leningrad, 1925–29) may serve as a striking example confirming the fact that a system approach has been developed and applied simultaneously in military and general sciences in the Soviet Union.

87. V.K. Triandafillov, *The Nature of the Operations of Modern Armies*, J. Kipp (ed.) (London, 1993), p. 170.

88. M.N. Tukhachevskii, 'Voina' (War) (1926), in *Voprosy strategii*, pp. 104–5.

89. Triandafillov, *The Nature of Operations of Modern Armies*, p. 153.

90. Isserson, 'Razvitie teorii operativnogo iskusstva v 30-e gody', No. 1, p. 41. V. I. Mikulin served as an instructor in the faculty for operational art under Isserson. As part of his work he developed a training aid, which utilized the understanding of the abstract idea of depth in the context of the principal forms of operational manoeuvre.

91. Triandafillov, *The Nature of Operations of Modern Armies*, pp. 74, 81, 83, 91, 93, 108–9, 114–15, refers to the linear-frontal element as a holding echelon (*skovyvaiushchii eshelon*), whose mission is to attract maximum enemy forces towards the front and to degrade them. To the deep-columnar element he refers as the striking echelon (*udarnyi eshelon*), whose mission is to penetrate, in succession to the holding echelon's action, to the depth of the rival system and effectuate the operational shock. The same view is expressed by Vol'pe, *Frontal'nyi udar*, pp. 44–7, 212–17; V.A. Melikov, *Problema strategicheskogo razvertyvaniia po opytu Mirovoi i Grazhdanskoi voiny*, pp. 579–95; G.S. Isserson, *Martovskoe nastuplenie germantsev v Pikardii v 1918 godu* (The German March offensive in Picardy in the year 1918) (Moscow, 1926), p. 17.

92. Tukhachevskii, 'Voprosy vysshego komandovaniia', pp. 83–5; Triandafillov, *The*

IN PURSUIT OF MILITARY EXCELLENCE

Nature of Operations of Modern Armies, pp. 81, 104, 107, 108, 109, 113–15, dedicates a significant part of his book to the discussion of the subject of successive operations; *PU-36*, Ch. 5, Arts. 106–10; Savushkin, 'K voprosu o zarozhdenii teorii posledovatel'nykh nastupatel'nykh operatsii – 1921–1929 gg.', pp. 77–83.

93. Ibid., pp. 110–11, 119, 132–38. In order to achieve scientific expression of the idea of operational mobility during the stages of planning the operation, two novel values, deriving from a systemic analysis of operational engagements, were used by the Soviet theoreticians: *maksimal'nye tempy operatsii* or *nastupleniia*, meaning the maximal advancing pace of the entire operation, or offensive, towards achieving its objectives and aim, and *srednesutochnye tempy operatsii*, or *nastupleniia*, meaning the mean daily rate of advance for the operation, or offensive, were formed out of a systemic analysis of operational engagements.

94. Isserson, 'Razvitie teorii operativnogo iskusstva v 30-e gody', No. 1, pp. 37–42. Isserson's recollections give the definite impression that the decision to initiate the enquiry of the operational field with the analysis of the defensive, derived from fundamental assumptions in the methodology of thinking and research.

95. Triandafillov, *The Nature of Operations of Modern Armies*, pp. 110, 151, mentions the principle of movement differential. This principle concerns a common situation in which both the operational defender and attacker compete for the occupation of key positions in the defensive depth by employing bold and continuous movements. In this contest, familiarity with the area of operations, the method of the initial deployment of reserves, and the initially prepared infrastructure all play into the hands of the defender, thus giving him a mechanical advantage. Soviet operational theoreticians refer to this advantage as the movement differential – Tukhachevskii, 'Voprosy vysshego komandovaniia', pp. 195–6. Tukhachevskii, 'Novye voprosy voiny', pp. 193–8, discusses the principle of the bipolar command and the dynamism of the reciprocal command circle. The bipolarity of the operational command apparatus derives both from the nature of the tactical command, which is forward, and from the operational which is rearward. Between these two poles stretch the dynamics of the reciprocal command circle, centring on passing orders from the rear to the front and transferring pieces of cultivated intelligence from the front to rear. The mechanism of the conditioned hierarchical action, derives both from the operational command structure and from the method of deploying reserves in depth, which reflects a compromise between the available force and the predicted risks. According to this mechanism the operating of the reserves is always generated from the rear, where they are naturally deployed, and always in reaction to the development of certain conditions in the front resulting from the attacker's initiative.

96. The unique intellectual effort which was dedicated to studying the problems of operational command and control was reflected in the plethora of literary works referring to the subject throughout the entire process of developing the operational theory. M.N. Tukhachevskii, 'Upravlenie armiei i frontom' (Command of Army and Front), *Voennyi vestnik*, 8 (1922), pp. 46–7, a summary of a lecture given on 3 April 1922 in the Military Academy; idem, 'K voprosu sovremennoi strategii' (On the Question of Modern Strategy), in *Voina i voennoe iskusstvo v svete istoricheskogo materializma* (War and Military Art in the Light of Historical Materialism) (Moscow, 1927), pp. 129–33; idem, 'Voprosy vysshego komandovaniia', pp. 185–97; M. Bonch-Bruevich, 'Nekotorye osnovy operativnogo rukovodstva v sovremennoi voine' (Several Elements of Operational Command in Modern War), *Voina i revoliutsiia* 12 (1927), pp. 46–63; V.K. Triandafillov, 'K voprosu ob ocherednykh zadachakh po usovershenstvovaniiu boevoi podgotovki vysshego komandnogo sostava' (On the Question of Immediate Tasks for Improving Combat Readiness of the Higher Command Staff), *Voina i revoliutsiia* 1 (1927), pp. 31–43. Both Isserson, *Evoliutsiia operativnogo iskusstva*, pp. 90–95, and Varfolomeev, *Udarnaia armiia*, pp. 186–9, discuss the problems of operational command.

97. *VES*, p. 168; *SVE*, 1980, Vol. VII, p. 503, refer to the pattern of *vstrechnoe srazhenie* (meeting engagement), as the reflection of the random environment of the operational level of war.

98. J.J. Schneider, 'Introduction', in Triandafillov, *The Nature of Operations of Modern Armies*, p. XXVI, claims that in the process of setting a curriculum for the School of

204

Advanced Military Studies (SAMS) in 1985 it was agreed among the military and academic staffs of Ft. Leavenworth that Triandafillov's book presented the broadest and most penetrating analysis ever written on the operational level of war and operational art.

99. *SVE*, 1978, Vol. V, p. 675, literally the term *obkhod* can be translated into English as 'turning movement'. Nevertheless, this simplistic translation expresses only a minor part of the broader idea suggested by the term. We will examine the complete purport implied by the term, when discussing the subject of shock. Triandafillov, *The Nature of Operations of Modern Armies*, pp. 74, 81, 110, 113, 115–17, 127–8, 149, 151, 153; Isserson, 'Razvitie teorii operativnogo iskusstva v 30-e gody', No. 1, pp. 37–8, 40, 42–3.

100. Ibid., pp. 36–9. R.A. Savushkin and N.M. Ramanichev, 'Razvitie taktiki obshchevoiskovogo boia v period mezhdu Grazhdanskoi i Velikoi otechestvennoi voinami' (The Development of Combined-Arms Battle Tactics in the Period between the Civil War and the Great Patriotic War), *VIZh* 11 (1985), pp. 21–8; A. Ryzhakov, 'K voprosy stroitel'stva bronetankovykh voisk Krasnoi armii v 30-e gody' (Concerning the Formation of Red Army Armoured Forces in the 1930s), *VIZh* 8 (1968), pp. 105–11. During that stage the principal tactical manuals and regulation books published included the following items: Narodnyi komissariat oborony Soiuza SSR (NKO), *Vremennaia instruktsiia po boevomu primeneniu tankov RKKA* (Interim Instructions on the Combat Use of Tanks of the RKKA) (Moscow, 1928); *Polevoi ustav RKKA* (Field Service Regulations) (Moscow, 1929); *Boevoi ustav mekhanizirovannykh voisk* (Combat Regulations of Mechanized Forces) (Moscow, 1932); *Vozhdenie i boi samostoiatel'nykh mekhanizirovannykh soedinenii* (Leadership and Combat of Independent Mechanized Formations) (Moscow, 1932); *Instruktsii po glubokomu boiu* (Instructions on Deep Battle) (Moscow, 1934); *PU-36*, Chap. 5; *Samostoiatel'nye mekhanizirovannye soedineniia, proekt nastavlenii* (Independent Mechanized Formations, Draft Manual) (Moscow, 1937); *Boevoi ustav konnitsy RKKA (BUK-29, BUK-38)* (RKKA cavalry combat regulations, 1929 edn, 1938 edn) (Moscow, 1929 edn, 1938 edn); *Boevoi ustav pekhoty RKKA (BUP-29, BUP-38)* (Combat Regulations of the Infantry of the RKKA, 1929 edn, 1938 edn) (Moscow, 1929 edn, 1938 edn); *Nastavlenie po polevoi sluzhbe voiskovykh shtabov (Vremennoe)*, (Provisional Manual for Field Service of Troop Staffs) (Moscow/Leningrad, 1935). In addition to the official manuals, numerous works have been published by the group of theoreticians on various tactical subjects. In that context the principal works were: A. Bol'tse, *Nochnoi boi* (Night Combat) (Moscow, 1938); K. Lunaev, *Vzaimodeistvie pekhoty s drugimi rodami voisk* (The Cooperation of Infantry with Other Types of Forces) (Kiev, 1936); S.A. Smirnov, *Taktika* (Tactics) (Moscow, 1935) (this book served as a textbook in the various military schools of the RKKA); M. Tikhonov, *Nochnye deistviia* (Night Actions) (Moscow, 1935); N.A. Morozov, *Obshchaia taktika* (General Tactics) (Moscow, 1928); A.D. Syromiatnikov, *Proryv, ego razvitie i parirovanie* (Penetration, its Development and defence against it) (Moscow/Leningrad, 1928); R.S. Tsiffer, *Taktika pekhoty* (Infantry Tactics) (Moscow, 1935). This work served as the principal textbook in the RKKA infantry schools; V.K. Smyslovskii, *Svedeniia po taktike artillerii* (A Summary of Artillery Tactics) (Moscow, 1930); V.K. Tokarevskii, *Taktika artillerii* (Artillery Tactics) (Moscow, 1931); V.D. Grendal', *Artilleriia v nastupatel'nom boiu strelkovogo korpusa* (Artillery in the Offensive Battle of the Rifle Corps) (Moscow, 1937); P.D. Gladkov, *Taktika bronevykh chastei* (Tactics of Armoured Units) (Moscow, 1930); S.N. Ammosov, *Taktika motomekhsoedinenii* (Tactics of Moto-mechanized Formations) (Moscow, 1932); A.E. Gromychenko, *Ocherki taktiki tankovykh chastei* (A Study of Tank Units Tactics) (Moscow, 1935); A.N. Lapchinskii, *Taktika aviatsii* (Aviation tactics) (Moscow, 1931); *Vozdushnye sily v boiu i operatsii* (Air Forces in Battle and Operation) (Moscow, 1932); A.K. Mednis, *Taktika shturmovoi aviatsii* (Tactics of Attacking Aviation) (Moscow, 1935); E.V. Aleksandrov, *Rabota divizionnogo i korpusnogo inzhenera* (Operating the Division and Corps Engineers) (Moscow, 1933); E.V. Leoshenia, *Forsirovanie reki strelkovym batal'onom i strelkovym polkom* (River Crossing by Rifle Battalion and Rifle Regiment) (Moscow, 1938); A.S. Botvinnik, *Tekhnika i taktika khimbor'by. Kratkie svedeniia* (Techniques and Tactics of Chemical Combat. A Short Summary) (Moscow, 1932); N.A. Zhuravlev, *Taktika razvedyvatel'noi*

aviatsii (Tactics of Reconnaissance Aviation) (Moscow/Leningrad, 1933); I.M. Kirillov-Gubetskii, *Organizatsiia i planirovanie artilleriiskogo ognia* (Organization and Planning of Artillery Fire), (Leningrad, 1935); F.K. Kuzmin, *Vstrechnyi boi strelkovogo korpusa* (Rifle Corps Encounter Battle) (Moscow, 1938); V.I. Mikulin, *Sluzhba razvedyvatel'nogo otriada armeiskoi konnitsy* (The Role of Army Cavalry in Forward Reconnaissance) (Moscow/Leningrad, 1928); S.G. Mikhailov, *Deistviia artillerii vo vstrechnom nastupatel'nom i oboronitel'nom boiu* (The Action of Artillery in Encounter, Offensive and Defensive Battles) (Leningrad, 1931); M.S. Svechnikov, *Reidy konnitsy i oborona zheleznykh dorog* (Cavalry Raids and the Defence of Railways) (Moscow/Leningrad, 1928); M.D. Smirnov, *Aviatsiia i pekhota* (Aviation and Infantry) (Moscow, 1931); A.I. Shtromberg, *Sluzhba tankov v motomekhanizirovannykh chastiakh* (The Role of Tanks in Moto-mechanized Units) (Moscow, 1931).

101. Orlov, 'The High Command of the Red Army and the Terror of the 1930s in the USSR', pp. 16–27, provides a great deal of evidence confirming Stalin's attempts to divert Tukhachevskii's theoretical aspirations from the levels of strategy and operations to that of tactics and mechanics. Zakharov, 'O glubokoi operatsii', p. 14, mentions that in December 1934 Voroshilov rejected an offer made in the RVS to recognize the deep battle as a new form of war, and persisted in claiming that it was nothing other than a technical reflection of modern war. Consenting to such an offer would have legitimized Tukhachevskii's efforts to develop the operational art as an independent cognition.

102. Isserson, 'Razvitie teorii operativnogo iskusstva v 30-e gody', No. 1, pp. 37–40.

103. Bagramian, *Istoriia voin i voennogo iskusstva*, pp. 106–10; Strokov, *Istoriia voennogo iskusstva*, pp. 316–21.

104. V. Daines, 'Razvitie taktik obshchevoiskovogo nastupatel'nogo boia v 1929–1941 gg.' (The Development of the Tactics of Combined-Arms Offensive Battle in 1929–1941), *VIZh* 10 (1978), pp. 96–8; Triandafillov, *The Nature of Operations of Modern Armies*, pp. 74–5, 90–94, 102–6, 115–22, 149–56; M. N. Tukhachevskii, 'O novom polevom ustave RKKA' (Concerning the new Field Regulations of the Red Army), *Bol'shevik*, 9 (1937), pp. 46–50.

105. Isserson, 'Razvitie teorii operativnogo iskusstva v 30-e gody', No. 1, p. 37, indicates that it was Tukhachevskii who defined the necessity to express the idea of tactical synergy through the columnar configuration, and to create tactical combinations applicable to the challenges of operating in the depth. Nevertheless, it was Triandafillov who elaborated this idea, by means of a memorandum written in 1928, into practical patterns.

106. Triandafillov referred to this tank group as *neposredstvennoi podderzhki pekhoty* (*NPP*) (direct infantry support), and to the artillery group as *podderzhki pekhoty* (*PP*) (infantry support).

107. The tank groups designed to escort the infantry formations along the breakthrough were defined as *dal'nei podderzhki pekhoty (DPP)* (long-range infantry support). The artillery fire units supporting the infantry along the breakthrough were referred to as *artillerii razrusheniia (AR)* (artillery destruction), since the breakthrough concerned first and foremost moving through the defensive artillery tactical deployment.

108. Both the artillery and tank groupings, designed to escort the infantry formations advancing towards the defender's tactical depth, were defined as *dal'nego deistviia (DD)* (long-range action).

109. Isserson, 'Razvitie teorii operativnogo iskusstva v 30-e gody', No. 1, pp. 42–3, claims that with the initial transition to the development of the Deep Battle theory the group of theoreticians defined six questions or operational subjects, which were supposed to be answered through the tactical discussions and experiments: (1) The formulation of practical patterns supporting the exploitation of the defender's depth for the purpose of attaining the operational shock, or, more simply, how to implement in practice an operational strike along the defender's entire depth; (2) The specification of the fundamental situations in an operation; (3) Forming organizational frameworks and appropriate command structures for the conduct of operations; (4) Formulating the column configuration for an operational manoeuvre and characterizing the synergy between the various operational elements; (5) How to maintain momentum

within the echeloned manoeuvring column, or more specifically, how to transform a tactical penetration (*takticheskii vzlom*) into an operational breakout (*operativnyi prolom*), and defining the specific timing for the insertion of the echelon for developing the breakthrough; (6) Developing methods for the neutralization of the defender's deliberate use of his depth and patterns for the isolation of the operational space. The results of the issues listed above were summarized in six points, which constituted the essence of the Deep Operation theory: The first point defined the front as the principal organization for the conduct of operations, and specified three basic echelons in the operational column configuration, the holding or breakthrough echelon (*eshelon ataki*), the echelon for the development of the breakthrough (*eshelon razvitiia proryva (ERP)*, and the echelon for holding the rear (*operativnoe skovyvanie tyla*), more commonly referred to as *desant*. The second point summarized the options for cooperation between the holding echelon and the echelon for the development of the breakthrough, and defined the timing for the latter's insertion. The third point indicated practical methods for the utilization of simultaneity (*odnovremennost*), the fragmenting strike (*rassekaiushchii udar*), and the turning manoeuvre (*obkhod*). The fourth point laid down frames of time and space for the conduct of the operation in general, and for the operating of the various components, in detail. The fifth point determined methods for the operating of the front and army aviation, and the last point defined methods for the operating of the *desant*.

110. Ibid., p. 45. No. 3, pp. 52–4. The Uborevich group examined two operational variants that concerned the operating of the strike element (ERP). The short variant regarded situations in which the ERP was required to cooperate with the operational holding element in completing the breakthrough of the tactical defensive belt. The lessons learned in the course of this research were to provide the theoretical basis for the development of the Mobile Group (*podvizhnaia gruppa*) concept in the summer of 1942. The other variant concerned situations dealing with the synchronization of two or more ERPs, from adjacent operational entities cooperating in concentric or turning manoeuvres. The lessons accumulated in this aspect served as a basis for the development of the operational encirclement patterns (*okruzhenie*), employed by the Red Army in the course of its big offensives in the Second World War, due to Stalin's strategy of attrition. Iakir's group examined the cooperation in the operational depth between the ERP and the *desant*. Bliukher's group dealt with the application of Deep Operation theory to the climate and terrain conditions of the Far East. The lessons learned in the course of this research were applied in the 1939 Khalkin-Gol operation, and the Manchurian campaign of 1945.

111. *PU-36*, Ch. 5, Art. 112, Ch. 7, Art. 164. The first extract demonstrates the complete synergy among the operational elements, mechanized infantry in the holding echelon, armoured forces in the strike echelon, and the deep operational echelon, composed of aviation and *desant*. The second extract focuses mainly on tactical issues and therefore it tends to be too technical. Nevertheless, it expresses in a miniature form all the essential rules and principles of the Deep Operation theory.

112. N.V. Ogarkov, 'Glubokaia operatsiia' (Deep Operation) in *SVE*, 1976, Vol. 2, p. 574. The ideas and terms employed by the creator of the OMG concept and a leading figure in the theoretical renaissance of the 1970s, were identical to those employed by Tukhachevskii and his colleagues.

113. Isserson, 'Razvitie teorii operativnogo iskusstva v 30-e gody', No. 1, p. 37.

114. I use the Russian term *udar* in this case since it expresses both the operational shock effect and the operational means of attaining that effect. Thus, from a western point of view the term *udar* connotes a dual meaning: operational shock and operational strike.

115. Isserson, 'Razvitie teorii operativnogo iskusstva v 30-e gody', No. 1, p. 41.

116. *SVE*, 1978, Vol. 5, p. 675. Literally the term can be translated as 'turning manoeuvre', but in fact it represents a broader idea, implying both a physical and cognitive turning of the entire defensive system, due to the attacker's accumulation of a strike mass beyond the defender's centre of mass. In practical terms the defender has been deprived of the ability to achieve the strategic goals dictated to him by the political authority. Moreover, operationally, the only option he has left is to run away and save a part of his operational grouping.

117. Triandafillov, *The Nature of Operations of Modern Armies*, p. 116; *PU-36*, Ch. 5, Art. 112, Ch. 7, Art. 173; Tukhachevskii; 'Novye voprosy voiny', pp. 127–30.
118. Triandafillov, *The Nature of Operations of Modern Armies*, pp. 151, 153; Tukhachevskii, 'Predislovie k knige Dzh. Fullera "Reformatsiia Voiny" ', pp. 155–6.
119. I.E. Krupchenko, personal communication, 2 Feb. 1993, Moscow.
120. Triandafillov, *The Nature of Operations of Modern Armies*, pp. 127–8.

6

The Deep Operation Theory – *Glubokaia operatsiia*

DEPTH AND ECHELONMENT: A FRAMEWORK FOR OPERATIONAL INTERACTION

Their unique understanding of the systemic aspects of the idea of depth led the Soviet analysts to identify three universal components in any comprehensive operational process, and integrate their performance, either mechanically or cognitively, along a unified axis of action. The leading echelon (*eshelon atakii*) was designed to penetrate the entire depth of the tactical defensive layout, thus allowing the insertion of the echelon for the development of the breakthrough (*ERP*) into the operational depth.[1] By introducing an operational manoeuvring echelon into the defence's depth, the opportunity for engaging the defender's operational reserves is precipitated, and the latter's ability to launch his mobile formations in support of his penetrated tactical line is impeded. Moreover, the presence of the attacker's manoeuvring echelon in the defender's operational depth prevents the defender from withdrawing his main forces from the forward defending area to prepared lines of defence in his rear and thus creates the conditions for the effectuation of *obkhod* and *udar*.[2] Nevertheless, it is the echelon of *desant* which expresses most thoroughly the creative approach developed by the Soviet theoreticians towards the idea of depth. By operating this unique element the Russians intended not only to mark the maximum range of depth attained by friendly forces in the course of the relevant operation.[3] The emphasis given in the theory to the idea of air-mechanization (*aviamekhanizatsiia*) allowed them to incorporate in the element of *desant*, an operational manoeuvring potential, giving the ability to avoid physical friction and time consumption, caused by the movement of ground forces to the depth. Moreover, since operational manoeuvring potential was also interpreted as the ability to attain operational objectives by means of conducting combined-arms warfare, the *desant* element was designed, following the accumulation of its force in the enemy's rear, to advance vigorously towards the defender's front-line. Thus, by operating as an additional power vector, moving from the defensive rear towards its front, the *desant* was expected to reduce the depth of the defender's manoeuvring space and to reinforce the momentum of the attacker's advancing main manoeuvring element.[4]

More evidence of the special attitude developed by Soviet theoreticians in regard to the idea of depth can be learned from the manner in which they have treated the subject of the encounter battle (*vstrechnii boi*) and the meeting engagement (*vstrechnoe srazhenie*).[5] Due to the apparent difficulties in predicting the defender's actions in his operational depth, the Russians perceived the meeting engagement as the most characteristic operational pattern.[6] The non-operational conceptions that prevailed in the West until the end of the First World War, approached the random engagement with a method which was completely risk-averse. The result was the linear pattern of *Aufmarsch* – a clear manifestation of a strategic absurdity and an unmanageable operational configuration.[7] In contrast to the European tradition, the Soviet theoreticians, by applying the column configuration to the operational pattern of a meeting engagement, did take a calculated risk that suited the random nature of the situation. Moreover, conforming to their general view of conducting operations, this approach furnished them with a universal formula that would allow them to compete effectively with the operational challenges posed by the uncertainty of the modern battlefield.

The application of the column configuration to the advance of the strike element into the operational depth increased its velocity, thus contributing positively to the maintenance of high operational momentum. The initial deployment of forward detachments (*peredovye otriady*) in front of the main bodies of the advancing operational columns permitted, on the one hand, their smooth and continuous advance, while on the other hand, it produced the appropriate conditions for their transition from march formation to combat, by a whole series of actions, such as intelligence gathering, tracking the main bodies, holding the enemy, and covering the main bodies' deployment for combat.[8] Moreover, this structure prepared the ground for a swift transition from marching pattern to attacking pattern, in the manner of turning manoeuvre (*obkhod*) by combining the forward detachment, which engaged the enemy initially, as a holding element, while the main body was deployed in the following echelons as the strike element.

UDAR: THE RATIONALE OF THE OPERATIONAL THEORY

The Operational Aim

Centring on the integration of destruction, the Western ideal of conducting large-scale operations was traditionally based on increasing the operational mass in terms of rifles, and on the application of this mass in linear patterns. Being entirely alien to system logic, this approach determined the static nature of military operations until the end of the First World War.[9] The origins of the operational shock idea derived from an advanced system approach, from a critical identification of the universal nature of war, and from a thorough apprehension of the limitations imposed by the strategic reality. Therefore, in spite of implying some abstract connotations, the idea of *udar* was dynamic and applicable at the same time. The Soviet theoreticians initially understood that the military system, like any other system, could be recognized, first and foremost, by the dynamic interaction of its various elements. Hence, they approached the tasks of moulding the mass into a systemic fighting organization, and defining appropriate aims, that would generate this interaction and provide it with coherent guidance for the logical conclusion of the operational undertaking. Moreover, recognizing the system's hierarchical nature led almost inevitably to the presumption that the operational configuration under discussion should correspond with this principle. The transformation of the absurd idea that sought to destroy the opposing army in single integral battle into an idea aiming to neutralize the rival system's capability to attain its goals provided the operational school with an abstract, yet logical, framework for the construction of the operational manoeuvre. Turning this conceptual framework into a practical scheme leading to the effectuation of *udar*, required not only the clarification of the *raison d'être* of military systems, but also clarification of the principles of action and various mechanisms that motivate operational entities.

When attempting to define the basic aim for the operation of armed systems in general, the Soviet theoreticians began by analyzing the political-strategic context. Concerning the lowest common denominator, their conclusion in this respect suggested two options for a universal aim in war: seizure of political assets, and the defence of such assets.[10] Since it derived from the political nature of war, this assumption reflected the positive aspect of operating armed systems.

211

Nevertheless, the conceptual innovation did not lie in making these assumptions, but rather in illuminating the fact that attaining the positive objectives, determined by each of the universal aims, implied the simultaneous conduct of a correlative effort, guided by a negative end, that is, preventing the rival system from fulfilling the positive aspects of its own aim in the specific operation. In accordance with this mode of thinking two basic categories of operational situations were determined: Defensive, which centred on the positive end of preserving one's own territorial integrity by forestalling the attacker from attaining the opposite of this same end, and offensive, which centred on the positive end of seizing a certain territory by preventing the defender from attaining the opposite of this end.[11]

In both situations the interaction among the various components comprising the system, in the context of attaining the operational end, constituted the essence of the operation. Moreover, since such an interaction could materialize only within systems structured in depth, one could differentiate between the basic situations by observing the changing relations between the dimensions of depth and front. Whereas in the defensive, which was governed by more sensitive political considerations, the front represented the longer dimension, in the offensive, being characterized by the quality of momentum, the asymmetry became inverted. The artificial discrimination between the negative and positive aspects of the operational end was born of a dialectical approach, and served as a methodological consideration in the course of the theoretical discussion. However, unless the negative aspect of the operational end was identified with precision, the cognitive as well as the practical origins of the *udar* idea could never have been revealed. In simpler terms, when they confronted the task of formulating a universal method for the conduct of operational manoeuvre, the Soviet theoreticians sought to undermine the intrinsic principles and mechanisms that furnish the system with its vitality and cohesiveness and incite it to accomplish the positive aspects of its operational end.[12]

As an operational pattern, *obkhod* demonstrated almost perfectly the negative aspect of the operation's end, thus it reflected the closest degree to the state of operational shock. The idea of *obkhod* expressed inversion, both in mechanical and cognitive terms. Mechanically, it represented the leverage effect, created by the sudden accumulation of a strike mass on the deep end of the penetration axis.[13] Cognitively, it represented the reverse in the defending commander's consciousness, that derived from recognizing his inability to control the situation.

However, it was in the area concerning the systemic aspects of the operation that the principal contribution of the *obkhod* pattern could be most distinctly observed. By the rapid positioning of an operational striking mass beyond the defender's centre of mass, a physical barrier was established between his operational reserves and the rear of his tactical layout. The defender's ability to effect the essential synergy among the various operational components of his system was thus denied by pre-emption.[14] Such a development also disrupted the defender's plan to erode the attacker systematically by conducting a retrograde operation towards his own depth.[15] Furthermore, the accumulation of an operational manoeuvring element in the defender's operational depth, initiating a simultaneous penetration along several parallel axes, created the opportunity to divorce certain tactical elements from the operational context and effectuate their encirclement.[16]

While both the Germans and the Russians referred to the subject of encirclement with similar terms, it is through an examination of this same subject that one can begin to comprehend the immense gap that existed between the theory of *glubokaia operatsiia* and the concept of *Blitzkrieg*.[17] Whereas the German rationale in applying the pattern of encirclement derived from their intention to accomplish maximum destruction in a single engagement and thus determine its operational-strategic dimensions, the Soviet theoreticians approached the subject from an operational standpoint. Therefore, perceiving it as nothing other than a mechanical variant of the *obkhod* pattern, the Russians insisted that the encirclement should never exceed tactical-operational dimensions.[18] The creators of the Deep Operation theory regarded tactical encirclements as a possible development resulting from the turning over of their opponent's defensive system. Moreover, the emphasis on the confinement of the encirclement to tactical dimensions was intended to avoid the diversion of the main strike from its operational course by mechanical attractions.[19] Thus, unlike the Germans who perceived the encirclement as an end in itself, the Russians looked upon it as a mechanical pattern terminating the effects of fragmentation within the broader context of the operational manoeuvre.[20]

Elements of Operational Manoeuvre

1. Fragmenting Strike

When the members of the school of operational thought approached the task of translating the idea of *udar* into practical terms of manoeuvre, the principle of fragmentation was the first to emerge.[21] The immediate reason behind this development derived from a certain similarity between the pattern of breakthrough (*Durchbruch, proryv*), which was known to European armies since the beginning of the nineteenth century, and the mechanical aspects of the principle of fragmentation.[22] The assumption that future wars would be characterized by extremely long and continuous defensive fronts provided yet another reason for the Russians to link conceptually the breakthrough and the fragmentation principle.[23] By initiating superior concentrations of troops, fire and resources, structured in column configuration and aimed at a certain point along the continuous defensive front, it was possible to produce a series of successive tactical shocks along the vertical axis of penetration, create an operational cleavage, and overcome the resistance of the defender's holding force.[24]

Nevertheless, the formulation of the idea of the fragmenting strike stems first and foremost from system logic. Depth and the hierarchical structure are key factors in the operating of defensive systems, therefore the rationale behind them determined the orientation of the fragmenting strike and guided the synergy among the operational components towards the direction of a penetrating column created from succeeding echelons.[25] Thus, through the operational method of the fragmenting strike (*rassekaiushchii udar*), the tactical actions of break-in (*bresh'*), breakthrough (*proryv*), breakout (*razrazitsiia*) and the advance into the operational depth (*presledovanie*) were integrated coherently into a unified operational process, penetrating the entire depth of the defender's tactical layout and cultivating the conditions for the development of the tactical success into an operational one.[26]

The full apprehension of the problems of operational cohesiveness within the context of defensive systems led the group of operational scholars to define the fragmenting strike primarily as an instrument for neutralizing the mechanisms producing this cohesiveness. The deep column strikes were designed to produce separation among the defending tactical and operational formations, and, by preventing the essential synergy from occurring, to accelerate the progressive segregation of the rival system, and effectuate its collapse.[27] Out of this systemic trend evolved two operational patterns: The pattern of *drobiashchii udar* (dividing strike) concerned the severance of a certain operational entity from a broader strategic complex – an objective which has been achieved by breaking the succession of strategic-operational command system, and by hindering the flow of reserves and logistics from the strategic context to the severed system.[28] The pattern of *rassekaiushchii udar* entailed the sundering of the operational system which has already been divided from the parent strategic complex, into compact tactical segments, isolating these segments by encirclement, and bringing about their ensuing destruction.[29]

The penetration of successive columns into the defender's operational depth was expected not only to disrupt the synergy among the system's components: through the creation of long vertical corridors leading from the defensive front to its depth, one could convey the critical manoeuvring mass that was required, both to forestall the redeployment of forces evacuated from the penetrated tactical layout in a new line, and to produce the deep centre of gravity needed for the turning over (*obkhod*) of the defensive system.[30] Thus, unlike the German school of tactical opportunists who turned the technique of *Durchbruch* into an end in itself, on which the entire operational manoeuvre of encirclement hinged, the Soviet theoreticians perceived the fragmenting strike as an integral element in the operational manoeuvring process, and the *proryv* as a technical instrument serving the broader systemic principle of *rassekaiushchii udar*. By preventing the essential synergy within the defending system from materializing, the fragmenting strike reflects the negative aspect of accomplishing the operation's objectives, while the flowing of the main manoeuvring mass into depth by means of the same fragmenting strike, expresses the positive aspect in the evolution of the operational strike manoeuvre.[31]

2. *Simultaneity*

From the point of view of creativity, the formulation of the principle of simultaneity was second only to the creation of the idea of operational shock. Having no equivalent in any other military theory, this principle is still little understood by most Western armies.[32] The concept of simultaneity, arising from the effort to form a system of principles and patterns of action upon which a universal method for operational manoeuvre could be founded, centred on the rationale of system paralysis, thus bringing the group of theoreticians to the nearest degree of accomplishing *udar*.[33]

An examination of the operating logic of manoeuvre entities from the operational perspective revealed to the Soviet theoreticians that the application of simultaneity could yield the highest degree of system synergy.[34] By their attempt to operate simultaneously the various components of the manoeuvring system, Tukhachevskii and his colleagues endeavoured to overcome the restriction imposed by the column configuration. The simultaneous synergy, which combined the actions of a frontal holding echelon, an air-mechanized *desant* echelon, operating at the extreme end of the operational depth, and a mobile manoeuvring echelon, operating in the intermediate space and conveying success into depth, was expected to paralyze the rival system and accelerate the occurrence of *obkhod*.[35] Moreover, the effort to assemble on a single time scale the actions of various operational elements deployed over a vast space increased the degree of common consciousness regarding the accomplishment of the operation's aims.[36]

However, the main contribution made by the principle of simultaneity to the effectuation of the operational shock was the frustration of the opponent's manoeuvring capability. The simultaneous assault by troops, fire, and fighting resources on the entire depth of the defender's layout was designed to disrupt the operational mechanisms of the defensive. In the first instance, the application of simultaneity was intended to impose independent warfare on each of the defensive system's elements, thus denying its operational level the option of manoeuvre, and preventing the conditioned hierarchical synergy between operational-strategic reserves and forward echelons from materializing.[37] Secondly, operating the various echelons of the attacking system simultaneously was meant to forestall the defender from deliberately conducting a retrograde operation, aimed at trading space for time and effectuating the attrition.[38] Thirdly, by engaging the defender simultaneously, both at the front and in depth, the Russians strove to stretch the enemy's fighting resources to the breaking point.[39] And finally, the simultaneous operation meant to interrupt the dynamics of the reciprocal circle of command of the defending system. The entire depth of this mode of thinking, as well as the combat organization concept and operating patterns determined by it, was expressed intelligibly by Tukhachevskii:

> The formation of the deep battle – that is simultaneous disruption of the enemy's tactical layout over its entire depth – demands from tanks to perform two tasks. Firstly, they must support the infantry and escort it in its forward advance. Secondly, they must penetrate into the enemy's rear, to disrupt his defensive system and to isolate his main forces from the reserves at his disposal. This deep penetration by tanks must create in the enemy's rear an obstacle, onto which the defender's forward forces must be forced back and destroyed separately.[40]

Moreover, being shock oriented, the simultaneous approach to the conduct of operations illuminated not only the nature of the synergy between the holding echelon and the strike echelon, but likewise gave birth to the idea of the deep *desant*, based on air-mechanized forces – a concept that anticipated Western military thinking by more than 50 years.[41]

3. *Momentum*

The ideal of mobility in European military thinking developed from the tactical pattern of mounted shock combat, employed by armoured knights in the Middle Ages.[42] This assumption is anchored in the fact that even after the European armies became huge organizations based on infantry and linear firepower, the traditional conception, which judged mobility in mechanical terms of speed applied by compact formations of cavalry for the purpose of attaining tactical shock, had lost none of its validity. Therefore, while the term velocity has been commonly used in literature, operationally, the Western armies failed completely in their efforts to mobilize speed in the service of manoeuvre. While it is true that the adoption of mechanization by the *Wehrmacht* and its manipulative application challenged this tradition to a certain extent, ultimately, the Germans failed in their simplistic attempt to transform tactical terms of velocity into situations that required operational mobility.

The uniqueness of Soviet military thought of the 1920s and 1930s derived from the fact that unlike the other European armies, the Russian army managed to apprehend velocity, not in the mechanical sense, but rather in the broader context of operational mobility. The roots of Russian thinking, in this respect, originated in the Mongolian military tradition of operating huge cavalry formations over vast expanses.[43] Out of this integrative approach, perceiving velocity in terms of depth, time, and mass, sprang the concept of momentum.

Once the cognitive barriers impeding the approach to the field of operational thinking were removed, the members of the school of operational thinking dedicated a great intellectual effort to the clarification of the subject of momentum. Furthermore, from its start, the specification of the operational aspects of the momentum principle focused exclusively on the broader scope of system logic.[44]

From one point of view, momentum expressed the dynamics of accomplishing the operational objectives and attaining the strategic goals.[45] In that respect, the concept of momentum was related by the creators of the Deep Operation theory to the striking power (*udarnyi sil*), produced by the attacking system at every point in time in the course of the operation.[46] The concept that was defined by Trianda-fillov, Galaktionov, Krasil'nikov and their colleagues as the tempo of operational advance (*temp operatsii*) concerned the relation among four elements: the element of depth, which provided the spacial setting for the relevant operation;[47] the resistance of the rival system, which represented the element of attrition, affected the attacker's momentum indirectly, either by decelerating his velocity or by consuming parts of his mass;[48] the element of mass which, through the echeloned structure, guaranteed the succession of the strike and thus, increased the advancing pace of the operation towards the achievement of its objectives;[49] the element of operational mobility, which constitutes a key factor in the preservation of the striking mass, was formed by the combination of tactical velocity, appropriate logistical support and successive operations (*posledovatel'nye operatsii*).[50]

It was in linking the concept of momentum to the idea of *udar* that the full scope of Russian creative thinking is revealed:

> Meanwhile, such mobility [of the type practised in WWI] is absolutely insufficient for the achievement of decisive success. The rate of advance [*temp nastuplenia*] not only must not be less than, but *must* exceed, the possible rate of enemy withdrawal in order to achieve encirclement of the enemy, to deprive him of the chance to slip out from under the *strike*. Normally, an attacker must retain the capability for an offensive with his main forces at an average speed equal to the average rate of movement of the organic mass [*voiskovykh mass*], that is less than 20–25 km. per day. Here individual army units must make up to 35–50 km. in order to retain a position enveloping or threatening enemy deep rear area, to provide the capability for a breakout to his rear areas and a denial of his planned withdrawal. Accomplishment of that mission depends upon solution of the problem of high speed tanks with a large radius of action [quality and quantity] and creation of mechanized units of sufficient size. Motorization of the strategic cavalry must also be added to these measures.[51]

Thus, momentum was perceived as the result of the combined action of the holding element, drawing the main defensive mass to the front, and the strike element, penetrating into its depth. By applying the relative term of momentum, the strike element was designed to neutralize the defender's movement differential, to disrupt his ability to attain his goals, to induce him into focusing his attention on saving his force, and to create the conditions for his turning.[52] The eruption of a kinetic mass in the defensive rear was expected not only to disrupt the system cohesiveness, but also to deprive the defender of his ability to control the operational time factor and coordinate the movement of his organic mass in the operational space.[53] Thus, the defender's ability to offer organized resistance by means of combined operational manoeuvre has been reduced significantly.[54] In practice, the Soviet theoreticians focused the application of momentum on the timely insertion of the strike element (*ERP*) into the breach created by the holding echelon.[55] Through the combination of forwardly stretching the defensive and the sudden ramming of a strike mass into depth, the Soviet theoreticians intended to achieve a quantum leap, changing the mass relations at the deeper end of the penetration axis in their favour – thus producing a break point in the defensive system. In this way, the development of the tactical penetration into an operational eruption was guaranteed, and the continuity of the operation within the context of the strategic goal was preserved. Conditions were thereby produced, which gave the attacking strike element an operational speed advantage over any of the defender's initiatives to avoid the creation of a deep centre of gravity in his rear.

In spite of the fact that technically the Russians do not possess a term covering the literal implications of *Schwerpunkt*, the Deep Operation theory exploited the centre of gravity idea more creatively than any existing military theory.[56] Whereas the German ideas of *Schwerpunkt* and *Schwerpunktbildung* expressed uni-dimensional mechanical trends, the Soviet version of the centre of gravity idea (*napravlenie glavnogo udara*) was deeply rooted in the logic of military systems.[57] Basically, the Soviet idea strove towards a combined effectuation of both aspects of the operational aim: the positive, by means of seizing physically the operational objectives, and the negative, by means of forestalling the opponent from attaining his own operational objectives. Thus, in the Soviet version of the centre of gravity were integrated harmoniously a mechanical element (the strike), a cognitive element (surprise and deception) and an element combining the two (momentum).[58] Having no equivalent in any other Western military theory, the Soviet concept of *vnezapnost'* centred on the necessity to create a certain state of consciousness in the rival's mind.[59] The application of this state of consciousness within the opponent camp required both the creation of an operational weakness, by deliberate actions performed by the initiator, and the concealment of this same vulnerability by a methodical deception operation (*maskirovka*).[60] Ramming into the operational vulnerability, a manoeuvre strike was expected not only to effectuate the state of surprise, but also to attenuate the opponent's operational effectiveness.[61] In that context momentum was perceived by the operational theoreticians as an instrument complementing the reciprocal linkage between surprise, being a matter of perception, and the mechanical blow. By reducing the effectiveness of the rival system's resistance, surprise contributed to the preservation of the friendly system mass. On the other hand, the achievement of a high rate of operational momentum, which normally reinforced surprise, depended acutely on the size of the striking mass.[62]

In order to allow the practical application of the abstract concept of momentum, the operational theoreticians developed during the last phase of its formulation a pair of scientific implements, designed to serve operational commanders, both at the operation planning stage, and in the stage of retrospective analysis. The development of these two conceptual tools by Triandafillov, Galaktionov, and Melikov was based on systemic research of operations, which took into account the relevant parameters, such as quantitative force relation, the nature of the terrain, the character of fortifications, the type of the defensive, and the quality of the troops involved. By offering the tools of *temp operatsii* (the pace of operations) and *plotnost' voisk* (the factor of operational density), Soviet theoreticians provided the scientific means for the perception of the operation under planning, both as a whole and in relation to operations characterized by similar conditions.[63] By employing these data, which were accumulated through systemic research, the Russians could initiate accurate and coherent planning of logistics and command and control in operations. Concerning the subject of operational pace, the relevant data, derived by the theoreticians, laid down realistic categories for a systemic assessment of the maximum range of depth and time that could be attained in the planned operation. The factor of operational density provided valid professional categories for appreciating a formation's ability to perform a given mission. Being based on a quantitative comparison of the competing forces, the Western traditional method of determining a formation's operational capability has been detached from the realistic difficulties of operational planning and thus lacked professional coherence. On the other hand, the Soviet theoreticians founded their method of assessing the operational capabilities of such entities as the quantitative measures of the friendly force and the relevant space – both of which are accessible elements that can be accurately estimated.[64]

Until recently most of the Western armies have not possessed a scientific method of accumulation, documentation and examination of the operational experience. Moreover, due to a traditionally non-systemic approach in the area of learning and assimilation of operational lessons, field commanders and staff officers lacked uniform conventions in both planning and analysis. Thus, one could often notice sharp differences in the way officers from the same army related to identical problems. Another consequence was that in most cases the learning process focused exclusively on the tactical field and technical issues.

In the Soviet case, the conception of *temp operatsii* provided a scientific framework for planning and conducting the operation's rate of advance towards the accomplishment of its goals, while the conception of *operativnaia plotnost'* presented accurate parameters for the coherent allotment of troops and resources to the relevant operational problems. Since the first of these conceptions denoted velocity and the second reflected the relevant mass, their combination, within the general context of the operation, expressed more than anything else the idea of momentum.[65]

OPERATIONAL SYNERGY

Synchronization, Coordination and Combined Arms Combat

Since the Soviet idea of operational synergy constitutes a conceptual anomaly even today, the easiest way to understand its uniqueness is by way of comparison to similar ideas, that were developed within the German concept of *Blitzkrieg*.

'The best use of the mobility of tank formations may be achieved on the condition that they operate in the first echelon of advancing troops.'[66] This statement made by Gen. Hermann Hoth, the officer who commanded the 3rd Panzer Group in the first summer of the war in the East illustrates several elements, characterizing the German approach to the subject of operational synergy: first, a techno-tactical approach to the issue of mobility; second, a conception which entirely neglects the dimension of depth; and third, a tankocentric approach, perceiving the operation by means of tactical terms of performance. Moreover, by a critical examination of Hoth's statement one can track the conceptual roots that led to the wasting of the German infantry, the wearing down of its armour, and the ultimate failure of the *Wehrmacht* to implement a coherent operational manoeuvre. Demonstrated by a distorted structuring of the operational manoeuvre, the lack of operational insight frustrated the enormous efforts exercised by the tactical echelons of the *Wehrmacht* to apply tactical synergy (*Zusammenwirken*).[67]

The basic difference in the Soviet approach to the same subject is manifested in the opening article to the fifth chapter (Principles of Command and Control) of the 1936 Field Regulations:

> Combat formation comprises a strike group and a holding force, echeloned in depth (in two or three echelons). The second (or third) echelon enables the formation to manoeuvre in depth.[68]

The Soviet idea of synergy did not depend upon the organization or operating of a single combat element, but was anchored in system logic. Thus, their concept possessed universal validity, and could be applied to any relevant operational situation according to its specific characteristics. Basically, the Soviet idea of synergy centred on the deliberate interaction between two operational elements: a holding element or echelon, that was made up of various combat arms and tactical entities and was designed to wear down the rival system and produce the appropriate conditions for the operating of its brother element, and a combined strike echelon that was designed to develop successively the operational manoeuvre into depth.[69] Thus, the Soviet theoreticians perceived the systemic interaction between the operational elements as an essential precondition for the implementation of a large-scale, successive, and dynamic manoeuvre, and therefore for them this synergy constituted a principal determinant in the system's ability to achieve its designed objectives and goals.[70] Moreover, since the nature of the operational manoeuvre is determined by the defensive's depth, it is only natural that its configuration assimilates the column configuration.[71]

In his article 'New Questions of War' Tukhachevskii complemented the philosophical aspect of the conception of synergy. By illuminating the opportunities offered by technology in the field of synergetic manoeuvre, and by indicating the command and control challenges raised by the application of such a conception, he touched certain aspects of the subjects that were a long way beyond the degree of operational consciousness, possessed by the German officers of *Blitzkrieg* vintage. By linking the idea of operational synergy to the dynamics of operational mobility in its broader context, he offered his disciples a practical bridge between the operational and tactical levels, thus, leading them safely out of the conceptual labyrinth:

> The development of mobility brought in its wake considerable differences in the speed of controlled movement and tactical actions of the various arms – aviation, mechanized formations, motorized infantry, cavalry and infantry. This factor – the difference in the speed of movement, that is – made matching the speeds of columns a very complex business. Moreover, it complicated tactical cooperation between the various echelons of a strike group and between frontal assault and deep penetration groups, likewise between echelons in the defence.[72]

The synergy reflected the actual aspect of the operational occurrence, hence it comprised the essence of the manoeuvre.[73] Furthermore, through the combined operation of a holding echelon, a strike echelon, and a *desant* echelon along the entire depth of the rival system, the principles of simultaneity, fragmentation, and momentum were implemented *de facto*. Thus, the application of operational synergism paved the way to the materialization of *udar*. In addition, by producing a positive dynamism denoting cohesion (*slazhennost'*), operational synergy served as another mechanism moderating the segregative tendencies of the system's components.

Out of their systemic approach and in the light of the analytical method they employed, the Soviet operational theoreticians defined three essential layers whose combination produced the complete operational synergy: the tactical synthesis, or all-arms combat (*obshchevoiskovoi boi, ob'edinenykh rodov voisk*), which aimed at the achievement of combat efficiency (*boesposobnost'*) in a rather limited sense. In other words, by optimizing the functioning of the various combat arms elements present in a given mechanical context, tactical synthesis offered a universal method for overcoming battlefield complexities – thus smoothing the dynamic conduct of successive operations.[74] The second layer, *vzaimodeistvie*, which can be translated either as synchronization or, more simplistically, as cooperation, derived from a common consciousness shared between the operation's director and the commanders of the system's components. Basically, synchronization aimed towards achieving simultaneity, and therefore expressed the highest degree of operational interaction.[75] The Soviet theoreticians defined synchronization as the deliberate composition of the entire actions of the numerous components, within the operational framework of space and time, in the direction of the main strike (*napravlenie glavnogo udara*), and parallel to the actions initiated by the rival system.[76] The common Soviet tendency to explain the idea of synchronization by way of analogy to the conduct of an orchestra stressed the importance of the synergetic aspect of the system harmony, and likewise revealed the difference between synchronization (*vzaimodeistvie*) and what they referred to as *soglasovannost'* (coordination). Whereas *soglasovannost'*, focusing on the technical aspects of the vocal harmony, strives to attain a smooth melody through the coordination of the technical qualities of each individual instrument, *vzaimodeistvie* is reflected in the complete orchestrated harmony, directed by the conductor's interpretation to the composer's written work.[77] Thus, centring on technical terms and representing the linear aspects of the systemic interaction, the layer of coordination is designed to support the accomplishment of synchronization by means of various methods of communication, briefings, and commanders' meetings and councils.[78]

Since it relates exclusively to combat situations, which were limited either in scope or complexity, the tactical synthesis concerns technical problems that could be solved by concrete coordination, appropriate combat grouping, and harmonious combination of the various combat arms elements. The great difficulty in the application of synchronization stemmed from the challenges posed by the scope of the operational mission, the abstractness of the strategic aim, the complexity of the idea of shock, and the problem of translating the concept of simultaneity into practical patterns of action. Therefore, for the members of the Soviet school of operational thought, simultaneity and synchronization constituted two sides of the same coin, that is, the operational strike manoeuvre. By aiming to neutralize the rival system's operational mechanisms, the simultaneity structured in the striking column expressed the pre-emptive or negative aspect of the operational manoeuvre. On the other hand, through the constant attempt to assemble the interaction among the system's components in the direction of acquiring the operational objectives and the strategic goal, the synchronization exhibited the constructive aspect of the same manoeuvre. Moreover, it was the employment of a vertical structure for the simultaneous attack on the entire depth of the opponent's layout that created the practical framework for the application of synchronization.[79] Therefore, since the concepts of simultaneity and synchronization cannot be understood separately, Guderian's casual mention of simultaneity can only be an act of plagiarism from a Soviet military work, probably Kurtsinskii's.[80]

EA and ERP – The Basic Components of Soviet Operational Manoeuvre

Unlike the Germans, who judged any combat or operational element according to its ability immediately to serve the rather limited tank force, the Soviet theoreticians approached the issue of integrating the various combat arms and operational elements from a much broader view. Since they developed a universal concept of operations, which was logically rooted in both present and future conditions, their assessment of the operational value of each element, whether existing or in the process of development, was realistic and technologically sound at the same time. However, the consideration that dominated their judgement in this respect was first and foremost the contribution each individual component could make to the manoeuvre system as a whole. Therefore, while in quantitative terms it comprised the main body of the *Wehrmacht's* field army, the German infantry spent the first half of the war dragging behind the armoured formations, bogged down, on most occasions, in the siege of the cauldrons they themselves had created.[81] On the other hand, in the Russian case the operational theoreticians founded the employment of the holding echelon (*eshelon ataki, avangardnyi eshelon*) on the mass of infantry formation, thus contributing to the system as a whole in two aspects: first, by implementing an operational break-through they removed the principal obstruction for the development of the operational strike, and second, by so doing, they afforded the preservation of the strike echelon formations until after that break-through had been achieved. The 1936 Field Regulations articulated this idea very clearly:

> If the forward edge of the main defended area lies in difficult tank country, the infantry attack, supported by artillery and infantry support tanks (*PP*), should precede the advance of the long range (*DD*, *ERP*) tanks. In this event the infantry seizes the forward edge of the defended area and opens up gaps in the anti-tank obstacles. The long range tank group, exploiting the success of the infantry, passes through and penetrates deep into the enemy defence.[82]

Aware that the penetration of deep fortified defensive layouts would remain the natural mission of infantry-oriented formations, Tukhachevskii and his associates sought, through their system approach, a method that would integrate the infantry element into the system in a manner allowing it to augment the operational manoeuvre.[83] Moreover, mindful of the natural difference in speeds that existed among the various combat arms and operational elements, Tukhachevskii focused the essence of generalship at that level on the ability to achieve synchronization within the framework of a single operation.[84] These assumptions led to the inevitable conclusion that transforming the mass of infantry into a proper manoeuvre component possessing operational qualities obliged one to furnish it with the necessary striking or shocking power, which meant the ability to penetrate independently the entire depth of the enemy's forward tactical defensive. Thus, the Russians organized tactical groups of tanks and artillery, structured in a deep column configuration, and integrated them in the leading echelon's rifle for-mations.[85]

The definition of the *ERP* (*podvizhnaia gruppa*) as the system's strike element focused the essence of operational synergy on the cooperation between the holding and strike echelons, and likewise, emphasized the novel aspect of successive operations.[86] Among other things, the operational theoreticians attributed the strike element's ability to perform its operational missions to the degree of operational flexibility it possessed. And since this was acquired principally through the proper organization and combat grouping of the relevant force, the strike element comprised heavy tank formations, infantry-oriented mechanized formations, and mechanized cavalry formations.

Thus, through the balanced combination of operational qualities, such as mobility, firepower and protection within the relevant strike force, it gained the abilities to perform effectively in a wide variety of terrains, to shift smoothly from offence to defence, and to overcome unforeseen problems in the operational depth.[87]

Yet the scope of cooperation between the strike and holding echelons, as perceived by Isserson, Ammosov and Favitskii, did exceed the narrow aspect of creating an operational passage or corridor by the latter's breakthrough operation. In cases where the holding echelon failed to achieve a 'clean' penetration of the defender's tactical layout, the heavy armoured formations, comprising the main body of the strike echelon, were planned to be thrown earlier into battle (*vybrasovanie*), in order to renew the declining operational momentum and complete the breakthrough.[88] The irruption of armoured-mobile groups (*ERP*) into the defensive depth was designed to produce the operational leverage required to accelerate the progression of the entire friendly system towards its objectives, in general, and the follow-up advance of the holding echelon, in particular. On the other hand, the early arrival of the holding echelon's formations in the defensive depth behind the strike echelon, could serve the latter's actions by performing the following missions: securing the flanks of the operational manoeuvre space;[89] screening rear enemy concentrations and thus allowing the strike echelon to by-pass them and convey the manoeuvre further into depth;[90] forming a defensive solid base in cases of encountering deep enemy strategic groupings;[91] and creating the inner ring around encircled enemy forces which had been turned-over (*obkhoditsiia*) by the moves of the strike echelon.[92]

Effectuating this interaction, which reflected the Soviet view of the interchangeability between offensive and defensive at the operational level, depended on one's ability to synchronize the activity of the various echelons. Thus, the problems of synchronizing the different speeds of the various operational components, and the initial economization of operational time were treated by the creators of the Deep Operation theory through the reapplication of an old Russian concept. By attaching to the rifle formations (*soedinenie*) tank and artillery units (*podrazdelenie, chast'*) for close support (*NPP,PP*), they provided the elements of the holding echelon with organic combined-arms capability. By combining tank and artillery formations (*soedinenie*) for long-range support actions (*DPP,DD,AR*) in the structure of the combined-arms armies (*ob'edinenie, soedinenie*), an operational pattern that crystallized in the course of the Second World War into the modern version of Forward

Detachment (*peredovoi otriad*), they provided the holding echelon with an operational battering ram, guaranteeing its ability to complete the penetration of the enemy's main defensive layout. Moreover, the initial introduction of the forward detachment into the far end of the tactical defensive depth prior to the insertion of the *ERP* into the operational depth, presented the operational directing authority with an operational liaison element that supported the synchronization of the two echelons by bridging the speed differences existing between them.[93]

Forward Detachment – Spearhead of the Operational Manoeuvre[94]

In spite of its tactical dimensions, that only on rare occasions exceeded those of a reinforced brigade combat group, the Soviet forward detachment constituted an operational element within the column manoeuvring system.[95] The operation of the forward detachment, behaving virtually as a forward sub-echelon both in the strike and holding echelons, intended to serve first and foremost the development of the main operational strike.[96] Deriving from its limited tactical dimensions, the forward detachment's low operational signature facilitated its frictionless intrusion into the rival system's depth, ahead of the parent operational body. In other words, one motive for operating the forward detachment lay in the idea of pre-emption or rather the tendency to deprive the operational rival of certain advantages at the initial stage of the operation. Since possessing the traits of velocity, stealth and independence, allowing it to seize (*zakhvat*) key operational assets and hold them for some time, the forward detachment has been designed to create the essential preconditions that could be exploited by the main body's arrival into the opposing system's operational reverse:

> The mission of the forward detachment is the timely capture of tactically important localities and their retention until the arrival of the first units of the main body. Then the former loses its primary significance and becomes the contact group of the latter. Normally the forward detachment operates at a distance of 15–20 km., on special occasions 80–100 km. in front of the main body. In the latter case the forward detachment is particularly strong, and its composition may amount to one third of the whole force. The forward detachment operating under normal conditions is weaker, but it is required to conduct combat without reinforcements during the course of 3–5 hours in which time the first units arrive in the combat area.[97]

Because the initial attempt to create operational conditions facilitating the action of the principal manoeuvring element saved operational time, and was therefore instrumental in both preserving the integrity of the force and in accelerating the progression of the system towards its objectives, this same conception likewise embraced the idea of synchronization, thus revealing the second motive behind the forward detachment's operation.

The range of missions assigned to the forward detachment only emphasized its importance as an operational instrument. Serving both the parent echelon and the entire manoeuvring system, the launching of an echelon forward detachment through the penetration created by the rifle formation into the tactical depth of defensive, intended, first and foremost, to guarantee the completion of the breakthrough operation.[98] By the deliberate seizure of deep enemy defensive lines the forward detachment aimed both at creating favourable conditions for the operation of the strike echelon and at forestalling the defender from manoeuvring his force according to his initial plan of operations.[99] The forcing of water obstacles and the creation of operational bridgeheads in the course of advancing into the enemy's rear by the forward detachment, saved the strike echelon the arduous mission of breaking through these natural lines of resistance, thus encouraging the swift development of the operational strike into the defensive's depth.[100] By promptly depriving the rival system of the possession of key terrain features in its rear and their retention until the link-up with the main manoeuvring echelon, the forward detachment ensured the continuity of the operation and its coherent course.[101] In spearheading the ERP's advance into the rival system's depth by exercising tactical movement, the forward detachment performed the missions of securing the march of the main operational body and screening the direction of the main strike.[102] Moreover, being deployed in tactical formation ahead of the main body, the forward detachment saved the latter the premature transition into combat formation, thus sparing time and resources and accelerating the operational momentum.[103] And finally, by operating in the extreme end of the strike echelon's column, the forward detachment was expected to cooperate with the echelon of *desant* and deep aviation and thus close the operation's circuit.[104]

Airborne Desant – *The Creative Element of Deep Operations*

It is through the idea of airborne *desant* that the rationale of the Deep Operation theory is reflected at its best. By initiating the unfolding of the operational column to its maximal length, synchronously with the progressive development of the ground manoeuvre, the *desant* echelon sought to carry out the principle of simultaneity in its primary mode.[105] The operational manoeuvring potential, incorporated in the *desant* formations, provided them with the integrated abilities to fix the far limits of the rival system's depth, and to systematically reduce this depth by operating from the rear towards the front – thus, depriving the opponent of the most crucial resource for the conduct of a volitional manoeuvre.[106] Performing these missions, the *desant* indicated the maximal achievement of the operation and accelerated the advance of the strike echelon towards the effectuation of the operational shock, thus becoming the principal element in implementing the operational synchronization.[107] By determining the deep end of the operation's space, the airborne *desant* focused the leading element of the attacking operational column upon the defensive system's turning point, synchronously with the progressive development of the ground manoeuvre.[108] The initial launching into depth of an element possessing unique manoeuvring capability was intended, among other things, to abate the intrinsic limitations of echelonment, which derives from the operation of a system, structured in column configuration. This way, Soviet theoreticians managed to combine harmoniously within the framework of the operational manoeuvre the somewhat contradictory principles of echelonment, so essential for the maintenance of succession and momentum, and simultaneity, so crucial for the effectuation of the operational shock.[109] Moreover, by inventing the integrated quality of air-mechanization (*aviamekhanizatsiia*) the Russians developed to perfection the idea of Airland Battle in the element of *desant*, five decades prior to its emergence in the West.

The Element of Aviation

Unlike the German officers of the *Blitzkrieg* school, who sought to extract within a tactical context the immediate advantages suggested by the operation of military forces and resources in the vertical dimension, the Russian theoreticians perceived their aviation, first and foremost, as an operational element, and, therefore, endeavoured to integrate it in the broader context of operational manoeuvre.[110] In light of their operational perspective, the Russians realized not only the benefits which modern air power derived from being independent of gravitational friction, but also its technical limitations and its inability to 'hold' land assets of tactical importance. However, combining in its nature both offensive and defensive aspects, the modern airforce was perceived by the Soviet operational scholars as an essential partner in the action of each of the operational manoeuvre ground echelons.[111] Hence, they defined the role of air power according to the following order of priorities: synchronization of the operational manoeuvre and assurance of its continuity through simultaneous action linking the actions of the various echelons, deployed along the operation's entire depth, into a coherent occurrence;[112] preservation of the operational momentum by wearing down the rival forces, assuring the integrity of friendly forces, and developing a high rate of activity along the entire depth of the operational space;[113] accelerating the materialization of the operational shock by means of interrupting the function of the rival system, impairing its essential mechanisms, and conducting deep interdiction;[114] finally, assisting the various tactical elements in solving their specific problems by providing them with close support.[115]

The Tactical Synthesis

Originating in the immense changes experienced by Soviet society in the years which followed the Bolshevik revolution, tactical clumsiness constituted an indubitable characteristic of the Red Army in the course of creating the Deep Operation theory. Nevertheless, by application of operational approach, Russian theoreticians succeeded in taking a quantum leap forward in developing the concept of combined-arms warfare.

The first conceptual breakthrough which emerged from the composition of tank, artillery, and infantry groups in a column configuration was the tactical synthesis in a deep structure. The application of the operational principle of depth to the tactical concept of combined-arms warfare gave birth to a momentum-oriented method of tactical manoeuvre, intended not only to penetrate the entire depth of the enemy's tactical defensive layout, but also to produce the operational conditions that would suit the functioning of the following operational element, that is, the strike echelon.[116]

The second breakthrough concerned the definition of the tactical synthesis's consequential effect as a manoeuvring capability, combining the three universal qualities: mobility; protection; and firepower. On the basis of this concept the Russians formed their tank armies, which represented the *ERP* in the course of the Second World War, and their air-mechanized-*desant* formations (*VDV*), in the second half of the 1960s.[117]

The final major innovation, in that respect, involved an assessment of the function of operational mobility in terms of *udar* and the employment of the combat engineer arm. The essence of this concept was expressed by an article dealing with engineer support to the encounter battle in the 1936 Field Service Regulations:

230

> The tasks of the engineers in the encounter battle are to keep the columns moving (route clearance and improvement, and the opening of minor routes), likewise the setting up of defence lines and obstacles, should the need arise.[118]

Thus, striving simultaneously to assure the tactical mobility of friendly forces and deny it to the opponent, engineer tactical units and formations, combined in the nature of their operation offensive and defensive functions alike.[119] Moreover, the action of the engineer force was designed to ensure simultaneously the application of both aspects of the factor of operational mobility: that which concerned the maintenance of the parent system's successive progression, as well as that which involved frustrating the rival system's efforts to interrupt the former trend.[120] The precondition for the effectuation of this complex idea, as it was determined by the members of the school of operational thought, concerned the organization for combat of engineering troops, both in offensive and defensive missions, at the level of division, corps, and army, in two basic groupings: *otriady obespecheniia dvizheniia* (march support detachments – *OOD*), combining the elements of assault breaching, sappers, bridging and road construction, were designed to overcome natural obstacles and artificial obstructions laid by the rival force, thus assisting the parent formation in maintaining continuous action and promoting its operational momentum;[121] *podvizhnye otriady zagrazhdenii* (mobile obstacle detachments – *POZ*), which were composed of tank units, anti-tank elements and engineer troops, were expected to perform the dual mission of interrupting the rival force's successive advance towards its objectives, and denying his efforts to interfere with the parent formation's trend towards the main strike (*napravlenie glavnogo udara*).[122] Notwithstanding the difference in the mechanical nature of operation of the two engineer groupings, their ultimate function served identical operational trends: promoting the operational mobility of the parent system, on the one hand, and denial of the same factor from the rival system, on the other. Thus, the universal organization and structuring of the Soviet engineering forces, as well as their fundamental concept of operation, conformed to the idea of *udar*, which is the essence of the Deep Operation theory.

THE ESSENCE OF OPERATIONAL COMMAND AND CONTROL

The formulation of the operational command and control conception inspired by Tukhachevskii, combined several trends in intellectual activity. One trend, which focused on the examination of both the nature of tactical combat and the characteristics of command at that level, saw its principal objective in defining the cognitive qualities required for conducting various activities within the environment of battle. Another centred on the analysis of the principles of the command and control of military systems. Concentrating on the diagnosis of the Red Army's natural deficiencies and systemic limitations in the area of command and control, the last effort aimed at the formulation of systemic solutions that would compensate for the above shortcomings.

When examining the nature of tactical combat, Tukhachevskii, Triandafillov and Isserson identified attrition and randomness as the principal factors determining the character of command at that level.[123] They came to the conclusion that the attrition factor derived from the mechanical aspects of combat, from the over-saturation of the battlefield with fire assets, and from the linear pattern of their application. Focusing on individuals who have been motivated more by personal impulses than by system imperatives, the behaviour of tactical commanders could hardly be rationally predicted in terms of generalizations or standing principles. Thus, since uncertainty predominated over tactical activity more than over any other level of war, the Soviet theoreticians regarded the randomness as the factor dictating the basic patterns of command and control at that level.[124] These assumptions provided the rationale behind the forward manner of tactical command and the direct method of conduct employed by it.

The definition of the encounter battle (*vstrechnyi boi*) as the prevailing mode of combat at the tactical level, and the effects of physical and mental stress as the most common characteristics of the tactical command environment were the operational conclusions to be deduced from the process of reasoning exercised by Tukhachevskii and his colleagues.[125] In other words, the battlefield environment and its tactical characteristics obliged junior commanders to operate their forces in accordance with the following rules: identify the main operational problem after a concise first-hand study of the relevant situation; then initiate a vigorous yet simple manoeuvre, based on the adaptation of a common tactical formula to the specific battle circumstances, by way of optimizing the actions of the various combat arms elements into a coherent move; and finally, spare no effort in synchronizing that move with the aim of the parent system.[126] The ability of tactical commanders to function properly despite the arduous and chaotic nature of the battle environment was guaranteed by employing the concept of *initsiativa* as the basis for their training, and through the development of a command and control method, which guided their performance along a cognitive axis comprising three points of reference: *operativnaia tsel'* (operational aim or objective), *dal'neishaia zadacha* (subsequent mission), and *blizhaishaia zadacha* (immediate mission).

Reflecting the quality upon which the functioning of the tactical command centred, the unique Soviet concept of *initsiativa* was defined by the school of operational thinking as the ability to select out of the common inventory of tactical precepts a specific formula, and implement it effectively, with *aktivnost'*, in accordance with the operational circumstances.[127]

In combining both immediate and subsequent missions within a universal definition, outlining the framework of action for any unit or formation, the theoreticians set down a practical course that would provide cognitive guidance for tactical commanders in the direction of depth. This trend compromised between the recognition of the importance of the cognitive tension to the dynamic functioning of manoeuvre systems, and the realization of the Soviet tactical command limitations.[128] Tukhachevskii and his colleagues understood that the abstract definition of an operational aim constituted an intellectual hurdle which the average Soviet tactical commander fell short of negotiating. Nevertheless, at one and the same time they realized that relying on a tactical mission as the sole focus attracting the entire attention of commanders at that level would have led to the degeneration of the essential cognitive tension and the decline of the system – or, rather, operation – dynamism. Thus, whereas the definition of an immediate mission determined the minimum line for the achievement of a unit's initial move, that of the subsequent mission set a deeper line which both encouraged the tactical commanders to pursue their dynamic course of action in accordance with the developing situation, and afforded them a better appreciation of the operational aim and general situation.[129]

The uniform view expressed in the works of Tukhachevskii, Triandafillov and Isserson, regarding the difference in the forms of command and control at the two practical levels of conducting war emphasized the positive nature of tactical cybernetics, which derived from the integrity of the mission, the unity of time and space, and the compactness of the force. Thus, assuming that the method of conducting actual combat could not endure any tensions existing within the close loop of the sub-system, they concluded that the tactical synthesis should be based on the principles of *edinonachal'-stvo* (one-man command), uniformity of perception, and physical cohesiveness.[130] On the other hand, since the operational milieu reflected paradoxes such as the division of the operational aim into positive and negative aspects, the passing from a state of holistic aim to that of differentiated missions, the polarity between the forward and rearward echelons of command, and the interaction between attrition and manoeuvre, the Soviet theoreticians recognized the existence of an intrinsic tension or homeostasis as a *sine qua non* to the functioning of the command system in the context of operations.[131]

The theoretical framework for the formulation of the Soviet conception of operational command was laid by M.N. Tukhachevskii in his essay, 'New Questions of War'. In this unique treatise, he analyzed the cybernetic labyrinth of modern war, and even suggested an advanced concept for solving its complicated problems.

The main role of the operational command was defined by Tukhachevskii as synchronization (*vzaimodeistvie*), meaning the dynamic or rather creative conduct of the manoeuvring system in the context of accomplishing its operational objectives and attaining its strategic end.[132] One category of problems deriving from this approach was characterized by Tukhachevskii in the following way:

> Commanding the deep battle and engagements or operations in depth is a very difficult matter – and not just because of the complex communications required. That problem could be solved by radio, aircraft and motor vehicles. What makes operational command complex in practical terms is the synchronization [*vzaimodeistvie*] of such heterogeneous actions as landing by mechanized airborne troops [*aviamotodesant*], tank breakthroughs [*proryv*], air-bombing actions, the artillery battle, infantry actions, and so on. It will take far-reaching training to perfect the apparatus of command and control and prepare it for its new tasks.[133]

In other words, posing the most distinct among the numerous challenges confronting the operational level of command, synchronization centred first and foremost on the effectuation of a dynamic synergy between the various combat elements comprising the system, likewise the neutralization of the cognitive friction deriving from the more perspicuous aspects of the operational manoeuvre.

Another category of problems centred on the less intelligible aspects of the operational manoeuvre:

> One cannot afford to have a plan which does not link the beginning and end. And to link beginning and end one must visualize the sequence of disruption [*porazheniia*] of the enemy's combat dispositions – in other words one must combine the front and the power of the combined arms strike [*obshchevoiskovogo udara*] with the

234

successive movement by bounds and the breakout into the area whose seizure signifies the defeat of the enemy. Synergetic command and control must ensure synchronization between the forces involved at all stages of fighting.[134]

Even though they lacked formal training in the field of operation research and system analysis, Tukhachevskii and his colleagues understood only too well that thinking in the traditional disciplines of strategy and tactics had been governed by the mechanistic logic of optimization. Whereas in the tactical context the combination of the various combat arms elements aimed at guaranteeing the execution of missions at the lowest possible price in matters of time and manpower, in the strategic context, both the appropriate allocation of resources and force building intended to reduce friction and assure smoothness of operation in the course of attaining the planned goals.[135]

Through their dialectical thinking the members of the school of operational thought perceived the idea of homeostasis, reflected in many of the operational level's phenomena, as an inherent trait, essential to their proper functioning. Moreover, it was the exercise of this same approach, which brought them to identify cognitive tension as a crucial instrument, supporting the operational command and control apparatus in its principal role of navigating the system through the arduous course of accomplishing its goals. While throwing some light on the duality of the operational aim and elaborating upon the tension existing between holistic trends and tendencies to focus upon details, Tukhachevskii revealed the entire originality of his approach:

> Battles and operations alike represent the development of a complex process which is formed by the arms and actions of the contending sides. It is from this process that the difficulties of command and control in combat arise. Indeed, if one looks at the matter as a whole, one side, in trying to shape the battle to its plan, is in fact directing its own actions. But because of this complexity, real control of the battle must necessarily imply control of the entire fighting process – that is, not just of one's own actions but also in a certain measure of the enemy's actions, forced on him by one's own. The art of command and control in combat calls for an understanding of this complex process of interplay. The attacker for instance must familiarize himself with the enemy's defence. He must unseat those links in the defence which stand in the way of his advance. And he must build up and deploy his combat layout in such a way that, by combining the efforts of his units and formations, he first accomplishes the disruption of these particular links in the defence, and then goes on to overcome the defensive as a

whole. In exactly the same way the side conducting a meeting offensive [*vstrechnoe nastuplenie*] must know how to match its own fighting deployment to the elements of the enemy's offensive, and how to set about defeating these elements in succession.[136]

In accordance with this logic, Tukhachevskii maintained that the combined-arms mission-oriented tactical formations should be constituted in standard composition and led by means of a uniform command array.[137] Moreover, the success of their action was attributed above all to a clear definition of the operational aim, and then to the coherent formulation of their missions in plain terms.[138]

On the other hand, the operational command, combining in its essence a wide variety of subjects, activities and discrepant dimensions was perceived as instrumental in generating the process which would accomplish the abstract aims laid by the political-strategical authority. Therefore, the principal quality required from the operational director was defined as *tvorchestvo* (creativity), and the setting of the command and control system at the levels of both army and front called for planned improvisation.[139]

CONCLUSION – THE DEEP OPERATION THEORY IN RETROSPECT

Until the emergence of the American Air-Land Battle doctrine in the early 1980s, the Soviet theory of Deep Operations represented the most advanced compilation of ideas ever attained in the history of modern military thought. The theory was developed through a deliberate process, led primarily by Tukhachevskii and a group of close associates. In the course of 14 years, the outdated paradigm of the linear battle of destruction was replaced by the advanced paradigm of the operational strike manoeuvre. Moreover, the perceptional consequences of this process provided not only novel categories of thinking, but also a coherent complex of practical concepts concerning matters such as force building, command and control, officer training, technological research and development, and the actual operation of large military forces. With the advanced maturation of the Deep Operation theory in late 1937, Soviet operational art reached a high state of cognitive cultivation, and thus became the principal platform upon which military science developed.

The poor performance of the Red Army during the Finnish War and in the course of the initial stage of the Second World War reflected the effects of the great purge. The main damage caused by the physical extermination of the members of the school of operational thought, which had been the main core of the operational command echelons, and many of the tactical command cadres, was discernible in the complete loss of the Red Army's grasp of operational cognition. Stalin's obsessive inclinations towards destroying people and infrastructure, and suppressing creative thought, ultimately halted the evolution of the Deep Operation theory, and led to a conceptual regression in military thinking, clearly reflected in Marshal Zakharov's remarks:

> The repression of 1937 and successive years brought to the army, as well as the rest of the country, tremendous harm. It deprived the Red Army and Navy of the most experienced and knowledgeable cadres and the most talented and highly qualified military leaders. It had a negative impact on the further development of military theoretical thought. The thorough study of problems of military science became narrow. Strategy in military academies ceased to be studied as a science and academic discipline. All that resulted from not only unfounded repression but also from an impasse in science, in particular military science. Military theory, in essence, amounted to a mosaic of Stalin's military expressions. The theory of Deep Operations was subject to doubt because Stalin said nothing about it and its creator was exposed as an 'enemy of the people'. Some of the elements like, for example, the independent action of motor-mechanized and cavalry formations in advance of the front and in the depth of the enemy defensive were even called sabotage, and for that foolish reason were rejected. Such measures attested to the about-face in military theory – back to the linear form of combat on an operational scale.[140]

The series of frightening disasters and appalling defeats suffered by the Red Army during the first year of the war revived the theory of Deep Operations and similar conceptual achievements created by Tukhachevskii and his colleagues. In the course of a year of strategic transformation, which was highlighted by the publication of *Stavka* Order No. 325 of 16 October 1942, the operations at Stalingrad and Kursk, the Red Army reapplied Tukhachevskii's main ideas, indoctrinated its command cadres with the essentials of the Deep Operation theory, restructured its forces, and regained the strategic initiative. The last two years of the war saw a succession of strategic-operational manoeuvres, which have no equal in scope, intensity and creativity in the history of modern war. In the course of operations, such as Korsun–Shevchenkovskii, Vitebsk–Orsha, Lvov–Sandomierz, Iasi–Kishinev, Vistula–Oder and Khingan–Mukden, expressing accurately the application of Tukhachevskii's ideas, the *Wehrmacht* and the Japanese Kwantung Army were defeated and the myth of *Blitzkrieg* was broken.

Unlike the Germans – who almost at the same time were developing their own conceptual version of armoured manoeuvre but failed to produce a coherent theory of operational manoeuvre – the Russians, following the application of the system approach, turned their collection of embryonic ideas into an institutionalized theory and uniform nomenclature. This achievement, which derived from Tukhachevskii's grasp of the need for a universal theory for the proper functioning of a massive and dynamic system, was a major factor in crushing the *Wehrmacht*, despite the superior tactical training and background of the German officers.

In the mid-1960s, when the operational perceptions were rehabilitated and restructured, the Russians applied the Deep Operation theory, almost to the letter. Moreover, when the Americans embarked on developing their own operational theory, it was to Tukhachevskii's brainchild that they turned for intellectual inspiration, and the United Nations campaign in Kuwait and Iraq in 1991 represented the latest and most complete application of the theory.

NOTES

1. G.S. Isserson, 'Razvitie teorii operativnogo iskusstva v 30-e gody' (The Development of the Theory of Operational Art in the 1930s), *Voenno-istoricheskii zhurnal* (hereafter *VIZh*), 1 (1965), p. 43.
2. V.K. Triandafillov, *The Nature of Operations of Modern Armies* (London, 1992), p. 116; N.E. Varfolomeev, *Udarnaia armiia* (The Strike Army) (Moscow, 1933), pp. 183–5; *PU-36*, Ch. 1 (general principles), Art. 9.
3. M.N. Tukhachevskii, 'Predislovie k knige Dzh. Fullera "Reformatsiia voiny"' in N.I. Solov'ev (ed.), *Izbrannye proizvedeniia* (Moscow, 1964), pp. 155–6.
4. Tukhachevskii, 'Novye voprosy voiny', in Solov'ev (ed.), *Izbrannye proizvedeniia*, pp. 182–4. The actual formulation of the air mechanization concept and the coining of the term *aviamotomekhanizatsiia* implied an operational vision that preceded those of the West by more than 50 years. The realization in the West of the strategic-operational opportunities offered by this concept and understanding its tactical implications, preoccupied the creative theoreticians Richard Simpkin and F.M. von Senger und Etterlin. See: R. Simpkin, 'Flying Tanks – A Tactical-Technical Analysis of the Main Battle Air Vehicle Concept', *Military Technology*, 8 (1984), pp. 62–82; F.M. von Senger und Etterlin, 'New Operational Dimensions', *RUSI Journal* 8, 128 (1983), pp. 11–15.
5. *Voennyi entsiklopedicheskii slovar'* (hereafter *VES*) (Moscow, 1983), p. 168; *Sovetskaia voennaia entsiklopediia* (hereafter *SVE*), 1979, Vol. 7, p. 503; A.A. Sidorenko, 'Vstrechnyi boi' (The Encounter Battle), *SVE*, 1976, Vol. 2, p. 406; V. Vinnikov, 'O vstrechnom boe' (Concerning the Encounter Battle), *Voennyi vestnik*, 1 (1973), pp. 20–25; I. Bgishev and A. Ignatov, 'Obespechivaia vstrechnii boi' (Protecting an encounter battle), *Voennyi vestnik*, 8 (1974), pp. 101–3; A. Kurasov, 'Vo vstrechnom boiu' (In an Encounter Battle), *Voennyi vestnik*, 8 (1974), pp. 29–32.
6. Triandafillov, *The Nature of Operations of Modern Armies*, pp. 103–4; *PU-36*, Ch. 6 (The Meeting Engagement), Arts. 140–43; N. Varfolomeev, 'Vstrechnaia operatsiia' (The Meeting Operation), *Voina i revoliutsiia* 7 (1930), pp. 11–42; A. Bazarevskii, 'Vstrechnaia operatsiia', *Voennaia mysl'* 3 (1973), pp. 97–118.

7. R. von Caemmerer, *The Development of Strategic Science during the 19th Century* (London, 1905), pp. 235–40, 249–52.
8. V.S. Tamruchi (ed.), 'Taktika tankovykh voisk' (Tactics of tank forces) (1940), in A.B. Kadishev (ed.), *Voprosy taktiki v Sovetskikh voennykh trudakh 1917–1940 gg.* (Questions of Tactics in Soviet Military Studies 1917–40) (Moscow, 1970), pp. 280–81; F. Trukhin, 'Osnovy operativnogo presledovaniia' (The Fundamentals of Operational Pursuit), *Voennaia mysl'*, 11 (1939), p. 94; *PU-29*, pp. 54, 57, 69; Isserson, 'Razvitie teorii operativnogo iskusstva v 30-e gody', No. 3, pp. 53–4; F.O. Sverdlov, *Peredovye otriady v boiu* (Forward Detachments in Combat) (Moscow, 1986), pp. 180–83; Triandafillov, *The Nature of Operations of Modern Armies*, p. 107, noted that a rifle corps column deployed along a depth of 70–75 km. He likewise emphasized the transition from march formation to combat deployment as a principal problem characterizing the initial stage of the meeting engagement. The length of a tank division column (1934–36 tank corps), when deployed along a single axis covered 35–45 km.
9. I.M. Anan'ev, *Tankovye armii v nastuplenii* (Moscow, 1988), pp. 10–11; G.S. Isserson, *Evoliutsiia operativnogo iskusstva* (Moscow, 1937), pp. 58–61, 63–5, 94–6.
10. M.N. Tukhachevskii, 'Voina' (War), *Bol'shaia sovetskaia entsiklopediia* (The Great Soviet Encyclopedia), 1926–47 (30 vols.), Vol. 12 (1928), pp. 576–8.
11. Ibid., p. 577.
12. Tukhachevskii, 'Novye voprosy voiny', in A.B. Kadishev (ed.), *Voprosy strategii i operativnogo iskusstva v sovetskikh voennykh trudakh 1917–1940 gg.* (Moscow, 1965), p. 139; Triandafillov, *The Nature of Operations of Modern Armies*, p. 149, employed the same argumentation when referring to the operational manoeuvre as a strike (*udar*). The operational manoeuvre was designed to accomplish the strategic goals of the campaign or the war by means of preventing the opponent from attaining his own goals, i.e employing the operational strike to attain both the operational objectives and imposing operational shock on the opponent. A.I. Verkhovskii, 'Ogon' manevr i maskirovka' (Fire Manoeuvre and Deception) (1928), in Kadishev (ed.), *Voprosy strategii*, pp. 269–73.
13. Triandafillov, *The Nature of Operations of Modern Armies*, p. 153; I. Vorob'ev, 'Oruzhiia i taktika' (Weapons and Tactics), *Krasnaia Zvezda*, 12 Jan. 1982, p. 2.
14. Tukhachevskii, 'Novye voprosy voiny', in Kadishev (ed.), *Voprosy strategii*, pp. 127–8, 130. *PU-36*, Ch. 1, Art. 9.
15. Triandafillov, *The Nature of Operations of Modern Armies*, p. 116.
16. Ibid.; Tukhachevskii, 'Novye voprosy voiny', in Kadishev (ed.), *Voprosy strategii*, p. 130; *PU-36*, Ch. 5 (Principles of Command and Control), Arts. 110, 112.
17. The root of the Russian term *okruzhenie* (*okruzhit'*) implies a mechanical circling or circuiting. The German term *Kesselschlacht* (cauldron battle) combines a metaphor, implying a circular action, and a term connoting the impression of a grand battle.
18. Triandafillov, *The Nature of Operations of Modern Armies*, p. 152.
19. Tukhachevskii, 'Novye voprosy voiny', in Kadishev (ed.), *Voprosy strategii*, pp. 128–9. *PU-36*, Ch. 7 (The Offensive), Art. 181, stressed clearly that should an opportunity to encircle an enemy tactical grouping arise in the course of an operation, it should be left to a limited or secondary force to exploit it, while the main strike force (ERP or the DD tank grouping) should pursue the course of the main strike (*Napravlenie glavnogo udara*) into the operational depth.
20. E.T. Marchenko (ed.), *Taktika v boevykh primerakh, batal'on* (Tactics by Combat Example, Battalion) (Moscow, 1974), p. 71, argued later that in cases when a tactical act of encirclement interfered with the main course of the operation, it should be abandoned in spite of its attractiveness.
21. S.N. Kozlov, et al., *O Sovetskoi voennoi nauke* (On Soviet Military Science) (Moscow, 1964), p. 361.
22. Until the recent emergence of the American operational theory neither the idea of fragmentation nor a linguistic term expressing it has ever appeared in the context of military thinking. What did exist was the pattern of breakthrough, which was rejected by military theoreticians from the second half of the nineteenth century until the beginning of the First World War on the grounds of interfering with the application of the linear manoeuvre of envelopment, see: C. von der Goltz, *The Conduct of War,*

trans. G.F. Leverson (London, 1899), pp. 159–60. Following the German 1940 offensive in the West, the term *Sickelschnitt* was coined by Churchill as an attempt to elucidate the occurrence of a new military phenomenon. See: G. von Blumentritt, *Strategie und Taktik* (Konstanz, 1960), p. 147. Since their basic approach derived from system logic, the Soviet theoreticians regarded the breakthrough (*proryv*) as a tactical means to achieve the deeper effect of fragmentation. Moreover, in their references to the operational principle of fragmentation they used a whole series of terms like *rassech'*, *rassekat'* (to divide), *raz'edenit'* (to split), *razobshchit'*, *razdrobit'*, *drobit'*, *raschlenit'* (to fraction), and *razryvat'* (to tear to pieces), see Isserson, *Evoliutsiia operativnogo iskusstva*, pp. 74–84; A.D. Syromiatnikov, 'Proryv, ego razvitie i parirovanie' (The Breakthrough and its Countering), in Kadishev, *Voprosy taktiki*, pp. 66–8; A.A. Sidorenko, *Nastuplenie* (The Offensive) (Moscow, 1970), p. 89; V.E. Savkin, *Osnovnye printsipy operativnogo iskusstva i taktiki* (The Basic Principles of Operational Art and Tactics) (Moscow, 1972), pp. 256–7.

23. Triandafillov, *The Nature of Operations of Modern Armies*, pp. 69, 81. *PU-36*, Ch. 7, Art. 174.
24. Triandafillov, *The Nature of Operations of Modern Armies*, p. 74; A.I. Radzievskii, *Proryv* (Breakthrough) (Moscow, 1979), pp. 172–5.
25. Triandafillov, *The Nature of Operations of Modern Armies*, p. 109.
26. Isserson, 'Razvitie teorii operativnogo iskusstva v 30-e gody', No. 1, pp. 42–3; *PU-36*, Ch. 7, Art. 181.
27. *PU-36*, Ch. 5 (Principles of Command and Control), Arts. 112, 113; Triandafillov, *The Nature of Operations of Modern Armies*, p. 81; Isserson, *Evoliutsiia operativnogo iskusstva*, pp. 74–84; A.I. Radzievskii (ed.), *Taktika v boevykh primerakh, polk* (Tactics by Combat Example, Regiment) (Moscow, 1974), p. 248; N.A. Lomov (ed.), *Nauchno-tekhnicheskii progress i revoliutsiia v voennom dele* (Scientific-technical Progress and the Revolution in Military Affairs) (Moscow, 1973), p. 139.
28. Anan'ev, *Tankovye armii v nastuplenie*, pp. 91–2; A.I. Radzievskii, *Tankovyi udar* (Tank Strike) (Moscow, 1977), p. 42; Sidorenko, *Nastuplenie*, p. 89; Savkin, *Osnovnye printsipy operativnogo iskusstva i taktiki*, p. 256.
29. M.R. Galaktionov, 'Tempy operatsii' (The Pace of Operations), in Kadishev (ed.), *Voprosy strategii*, pp. 543–44; Anan'ev, *Tankovye armii v nastuplenie*, pp. 91–2; Radzievskii, *Proryv*, p. 166; Marchenko, *Taktika v boevykh primerakh, batal'on*, p. 71.
30. Triandafillov, *The Nature of Operations of Modern Armies*, p. 116; Tukhachevskii, 'Novye voprosy voiny', in Kadishev (ed.), *Voprosy strategii*, pp. 128–30.
31. Triandafillov, *The Nature of Operations of Modern Armies*, p. 81.
32. R. Simpkin, *Race to the Swift*, London, 1985, pp. 37, 147.
33. Tukhachevskii, 'Novye voprosy voiny' in Kadishev (ed.), *Voprosy strategii*, p. 128; Isserson, 'Razvitie teorii operativnogo iskusstva v 30-e gody', No. 1, p. 37.
34. Ibid., p. 40; M.N. Tukhachevskii, 'O novom polevom ustave RKKA' (Concerning the New Field Service Regulation of the Red Army) (published originally in 6 May 1937 issue of *Krasnaia zvezda*), in Solov'ev (ed.), *Izbrannye proizvedeniia*, pp. 255–6.
35. Triandafillov, *The Nature of Operations of Modern Armies*, pp. 116, 154; Tukhachevskii, 'Novye voprosy voiny' in Kadishev (ed.), *Voprosy strategii*, p. 142; *PU-36*, Ch. 7, Art. 173; N.A. Lomov (ed.), *The Revolution in Military Affairs* (Moscow, 1973), trans. and published under the auspices of US Air Force, p. 149; V.G. Reznichenko (ed.), *Taktika* (Tactics) (Moscow, 1966), p. 297.
36. A.Kh. Babadzhanian, *Tanki i tankovye voiska* (Tanks and Tank Forces) (Moscow, 1970), p. 255.
37. Tukhachevskii, 'O novom polevom ustave RKKA', p. 254.
38. *PU-36*, Ch. 1, Art. 9.
39. Triandafillov, *The Nature of Operations of Modern Armies*, p. 154.
40. Tukhachevskii, 'Novye voprosy voiny' in Kadishev (ed.), *Voprosy strategii*, p. 128
41. Tukhachevskii, 'Novye voprosy voiny' in Solov'ev (ed.), *Izbrannye proizvedeniia*, pp. 182–4.
42. L. White, 'Mounted Shock Combat' in L. White (ed.), *Medieval Society and Social Change* (Oxford, 1962), pp. 28–31.
43. C. Bellamy, 'Heirs of Genghis Khan: The Influence of the Tartar-Mongols on the Imperial Russian and Soviet Armies', *RUSI Journal* 1, 128 (1983), pp. 52, 54.

44. Galaktionov, 'Tempy operatsii', pp. 540–41; S.M. Belitskii, 'Strategicheskie rezervy v sovremennoi voine' (Strategic Reserves in Contemporary War) (1930) in Kadishev (ed.), *Voprosy strategii*, pp. 351–4; Triandafillov, *The Nature of Operations of Modern Armies*, pp. 132–49; M.N. Tukhachevskii, 'Strategiia natsional'naia i klassovaia' (National and Class Strategy) (1920), in Kadishev (ed.), *Voprosy strategii*, pp. 77–8.

45. Triandafillov, *The Nature of Operations of Modern Armies*, p. 132.

46. Unlike the unintelligible term Combat Power, employed by Western theoreticians and analysts, the Russians used the term Striking Power, expressing strength in relative terms of *Mass × Velocity = Operational Goal*. Thus, it indicated the ability of the system to attain its ultimate goals along every point of the operation's progress. Whenever relating to the tactical level, the Soviet theoreticians employed the term *boevaia vozmozhnost'* (mission capability), meaning quantitative and qualitative indicators that characterize the capabilities of tactical formations, units and sub-units to perform specific combat missions in a set time and in specific combat circumstances. See Triandafillov, *The Nature of Operations of Modern Armies*, pp. 83, 90; S.N. Krasil'nikov, *Organizatsiia krupnykh obshchevoiskovykh soedinenii* (The Organization of Principal All-arms Formations) (Moscow, 1933), pp. 264–6.

47. Triandafillov, *The Nature of Operations of Modern Armies*, p. 148.

48. Ibid., p. 78; S.S. Biriuzov, *Surovye gody 1941–1945* (The Rugged Years 1941–45) (Moscow, 1966), pp. 172–3; N.I. Biriukov, *Trudnaia nauka pobezhdat'* (The Complex Science of Winning) (Moscow, 1975), p. 132; A.A. Grechko, *Gody voiny* (The War Years) (Moscow, 1976), p. 473; R.Ia. Malinovskii (ed.), *Budapesht, Vena, Praga* (Moscow, 1966), p. 44.

49. Belitskii, 'Strategicheskie rezervy v sovremennoi voine', pp. 347–8; Isserson, *Evoliutsiia operativnogo iskusstva*, pp. 58–9; The idea that a succession of strikes produces momentum was expressed in Tukhachevskii, 'Voprosy vysshego komandovaniia', in Kadishev (ed.), *Voprosy strategii*, p. 86; Babadzhanian, *Tanki i tankovye voiska*, pp. 257, 286; Reznichenko, *Taktika*, pp. 285, 333; Anan'ev, *Tankovye armii v nastuplenii*, pp. 297–8. Sometimes the maintenance of the operation's continuity necessitated the deliberate combination of offensive and defensive. See I.S. Konev, *Zapiski komanduiushchego frontom 1943–1945* (Memoirs of a Front Commander in Chief 1943–45) (Moscow, 1972), pp. 78, 209.

50. Triandafillov, *The Nature of Operations of Modern Armies*, pp. 128, 137; *PU-36*, Ch. 1, Art. 17. A.E. Gromychenko, 'Ocherki taktiki tankovykh chastei' (Tactical scope for tank units) (1935), in Kadishev (ed.), *Voprosy taktiki*, pp. 260–61; M.N. Tukhachevskii, 'Novoe v razvitii taktiki Krasnoi Armii' (Innovations in the development of tactics of the Red Army), in Solov'ev (ed.), *Izbrannye proizvedeniia*, Vol. 2, pp. 246, 248, 249; A.I. Egorov, 'Goriachii bol'shevitskii privet Voennoi Akademii RKKA imeni M.V. Frunze' (Warm Bolshevist Congratulations to the M.V. Frunze Military Academy), *Voina i revoliutsiia* 1 (1934), p. 6; K.S. Moskalenko, *na iugo-zapadnom napravlenii* (In a South-westerly direction) (Moscow, 1973), (2 vols.), Vol. 2, p. 534; K.V. Krainiukov, *Ot Dnepra do Visly* (From the Dnieper to the Vistula) (Moscow, 1971), p. 182; A.L. Getman, *Tanki idut na Berlin* (The Tanks Go to Berlin) (Moscow, 1973), p. 119. All the above cited references illustrated the dependence of successive operations on logistical support, and explained that tactical velocity, being achieved by *aktivnost'* and attacking from the march (*s khodu*), has been an essential element in producing operational mobility. Anan'ev, *Tankovye armii v nastuplenii*, p. 306, illustrated the Soviet approach to tactical velocity when referring to it as *Zakhvat s Khodu*, namely, seizing from the march.

51. Triandafillov, *The Nature of Operations of Modern Armies*, p. 136.

52. Varfolomeev, *Udarnia armiia*, pp. 184–6; K.K. Rokossovskii, *Soldatskii dolg* (A Soldier's Duty) (Moscow, 1972), pp. 98–9, 334–5, 343; Konev, *Zapiski komanduiushchego frontom*, p. 33; K.N. Galitskii, *V boiakh za vostochnuiu Prussiiu* (Fighting in East Prussia) (Moscow, 1970), p. 466; S.M. Shtemenko, *The Soviet General Staff at War* (Moscow, 1970), p. 100.

53. S.S. Kamenev, 'Ocherednye voennye zadachi' (Forthcoming Military Missions) (1922), in Kadishev (ed.), *Voprosy strategii*, p. 150.

54. I.M. Chistiakov, *Sluzhim otchizne* (Serving the Fatherland) (Moscow, 1975), pp. 169–70.

55. V.P. Kryzhanovskii, 'Legkie mekhanizirovannye soedineniia v armeiskom operatsii' (Light Mechanized Formations in Army Operations) (1931), in Kadishev (ed.), *Voprosy strategii*, pp. 580–82; S.N. Ammosov, 'Tanki v operatsii proryva' (Tanks in breakthrough operations) (1932), in Kadishev (ed.), *Voprosy strategii*, 593–4, 598–9; V.V. Favitskii, 'Rol' mekhvoisk v sovremennoi operatsii' (The role of mechanized forces in contemporary operations) (1933), in Kadishev (ed.), *Voprosy strategii*, pp. 603–5, 610; Anan'ev, *Tankovye armii v nastuplenii*, pp. 95, 116–17, 123, illustrated the principle of momentum in a very picturesque manner: 'The tank army (ERP) was the main mobile ramming force (*glavnaia podvizhnaia tarannaia sila*), which imparted high mobility to a front's offensive operation, and made it deep and effective in its operational consequences

56. A great deal of the confusion surrounding the centre of gravity idea derives from the unintelligible manner in which it was initially introduced by Clausewitz. This is demonstrated by the failure of the Americans to present a clear exposition of the idea in the 1986 manual: Headquarters Department of the Army, *FM 100-5 Operations*, 5 May 1986, Washington DC, appendix B, pp. 179–80.

57. Varfolomeev, *Udarnaia armiia*, pp. 180–82; A.M. Vol'pe, 'Frontal'nyi udar' (Frontal Strike) (1931), in Kadishev (ed.), *Voprosy strategii*, pp. 370–73. Literally, the term *Napravlenie glavnogo udara* can be interpreted as the direction of the main strike. Whereas the German term referred to a specific point or area, the Soviet term implied something less definite. However, since the Soviet term was linked both to the shock effect and to the mechanical strike designed to accomplish it, its cognitive basis is clearer and more definite.

58. Tukhachevskii, 'Voprosy vysshego komandovaniia', p. 82.

59. M.M. Kirian (ed.), *Vnezapnost' v nastupatel'nykh operatsiiakh Velikoi otechestvennoi voiny* (Surprise in Offensive Operations of the Great Patriotic War) (Moscow, 1986). The idea of surprise has been covered in the Russian military nomenclature by three different terms. The term *siurpriz*, which has hardly been employed in professional military literature expresses the general or civilian idea of surprise. The second term *neozhidannost'*, which has been used mainly in the tactical context, is a compound word denoting an unexpected, yet limited, occurrence caused by enemy initiative, ignorance of terrain, or meteorological development. The third term *vnezapnost'* has been used principally in the strategic and operational context. This complex term has been interlinked with the idea of *udar* and refers to matters and occurrences beyond comprehension or understanding. Since it denotes dynamism and activism, it has been assumed that its application required the stunning and paralyzing of the operational opponent by means of active deception (*maskirovka*), bold and swift manoeuvre, high pace of operations, and decisive concentration of fire troops and resources. *SVE*, 1976, Vol. 2, p. 161; N. Varfolomeev, 'Operativnaia vnezapnost' i maskirovka' (Operational Surprise and Deception), *Voina i revoliutsiia* 3 (1927), pp. 96–111.

60. B.M. Shaposhnikov, 'Mozg armii' (The Army's Brain) (1929), in Kadishev (ed.), *Voprosy strategii*, pp. 202–8; Galaktionov, 'Tempy operatsii', p. 541; Anan'ev, *Tankovye armii v nastuplenii*, pp. 212–16.

61. Varfolomeev, *Udarnaia armiia*, pp. 177–8; Galaktionov, 'Tempy operatsii', pp. 540–41; D.F. Loza, *Marsh i vstrechnyi boi* (Marching and Encounter Battle) (Moscow, 1968), p. 178; A.A. Bulatov, and V.G. Prozorov, *Takticheskaia vnezapnost'* (Tactical Surprise) (Moscow, 1965), p. 6.

62. Verkhovskii, 'Ogon', manevr, maskirovka', pp. 269–73. A very perceptive illustration of this idea was suggested by M.E. Katukov, *Na ostrie glavnogo udara* (At the Spearhead of the Main Strike) (Moscow, 1974), p. 193; N.K. Popel', *Tanki povernuli na zapad* (The Tanks Turned Westward) (Moscow, 1960), p. 289.

63. The order of *srednesutochnye tempy nastupleniia km/sutki* (mean daily rate of advance in kms/day) has been derived at each operation (preplanned or analysed after execution) by dividing *obshchaia glubina prodvizheniia* (total depth of advance in km) by *prodolzhitel'nost' deistvii* (total time of action days). The order *maksimal'nye tempy nastupleniia km/sutki* (maximum pace of advance km/days) referred to the highest rate achieved in the course of the operation. The factor of operational density served as a function expressing the relation between the amount of main

weapons (tanks, mortars, guns, rocket launchers) engaged in the specific operation, and the relevant sector of front engaged, usually the breakthrough sector (number of weapons km of front), and the relative number of formations deployed along a sector of km. In the first case the term used was *plotnost' oruzhiia* (density of weapons), and in the second *plotnost' voisk* (density of troops). Triandafillov dedicated a significant portion of his book to the discussion of the factor of operational density, while Galaktionov discussed the subject of operational rate of advance.

64. Triandafillov, *The Nature of Operations of Modern Armies*, pp. 69–84, 90–102, 121, 128, 132–8, 144–9.

65. Since through the dimension of depth the values of speed, continuity and mass density were reflected, it was the value of *obshchaia glubina prodvizheniia* (total depth of operational advance) that expressed the constant interaction between the conceptions of *tempy operatsii* and *operativnaia plotnost'*. Another value that expressed that interaction was *shirina polosy operatsii* (width of operational zone of advance). During the first stage of the operation (breakthrough), which normally required the highest density of the operational mass, the width of the operational sector was the narrowest and the operational rate of advance the lowest. On the other hand, in the advanced stages of the operation (breakout, pursuit or advance in depth), the rate of advance and the width of the operational sector tended to become higher and larger, a development which reduced the density of the operational mass. Thus, one could deduce an operational rule here, arguing that whereas the values of depth, rate of advance (operational speed), and width of operational front maintained among them a positive relation, the factor of operational density related to the values of speed, depth, and width in an opposite manner.

66. H. Hoth, *Panzer Operationen, die Panzergruppe 3 und der Operative Gedanke der Deutschen Führung im Sommer 1941* (Heidelberg, 1956), p. 165.

67. H. Guderian, *Achtung Panzer* (London, 1992), p. 190, revealed identical views to those expressed by Hoth on the subject of operational synergy.

68. *PU-36*, Ch. 5, Art. 106; Tukhachevskii, 'Novye voprosy voiny' in Kadishev (ed.), *Voprosy strategii*, pp. 127–31.

69. Vol'pe, 'Frontal'nyi udar' pp. 370–3; Anan'ev, *Tankovye armii v nastuplenii*, pp. 187, 382; A.A. Lobachev, *Trudnymi dorogami* (Paths of Hardship) (Moscow, 1960), p. 230.

70. I.P. Uborevich, 'Operativnoe ispol'zovanie tankov' (The Operational Employment of Tanks), (1929), in Kadishev (ed.), *Voprosy strategii*, p. 176; Tukhachevskii, 'Novye voprosy voiny', in Kadishev (ed.), *Voprosy strategii*, pp. 120–25; Vol'pe, 'Frontal'nyi udar', p. 370; Galaktionov, 'Tempy operatsii', p. 545; Isserson, *Evoliutsiia operativnogo iskusstva*, pp. 67–8, 70–71; N.E. Varfolomeev, *Nastupatelnaia operatsiia* (The Offensive Operation) (Moscow, 1937), pp. 175–76; *Udarnaia armiia*, pp. 174–5, 184–6; I.I. Fediuninskii, *Podniatye po trevoge* (Answering the Alarm) (Moscow, 1961), p. 30; A.V. Gorbatov, *Years of My Life* (London, 1964), p. 191; Iu.Z. Novikov and F.D. Sverdlov, *Manevr v obshchevoiskovom boiu* (Manoeuvre in All-arms Combat) (Moscow, 1967), p. 72; A.A. Grechko, *Bitva za Kavkaz* (The Battle for the Caucasus) (Moscow, 1973), pp. 89, 272. Biriukov, *Trudnaia nauka pobezhdat'*, p. 251; G.E. Degtiarev, *Taran i shchit* (Ram and Shield) (Moscow, 1966), pp. 140–41.

71. *PU-36*, Ch. 5, Arts. 112–15.

72. Tukhachevskii, 'Novye voprosy voiny' in Kadishev (ed.), *Voprosy strategii*, p. 142; V. Kryzhanovskii, 'Legkie motomekhanizirovannye soedineniia v armeiskoi operatsii' (Light Moto-mechanized Formations in Army Operations), *Voina i revoliutsiia*, 1931, No. 10–11, pp. 45–75, expresses the same idea.

73. Krasil'nikov, 'Organizatsiia krupnykh obshchevoiskovykh soedinenii', pp. 478–84; Tukhachevskii, 'Novye voprosy voiny' in Kadishev (ed.), *Voprosy strategii*, p. 140.

74. N.A. Morozov, 'Obshchaia taktika' (General tactics), in Kadishev (ed.), *Voprosy taktiki*, pp. 50–53; *SVE*, 1976, Vol. 1, p. 544; 1977, Vol. 3, pp. 144–7; A. Vasilevskii, *Delo vsei zhizni* (Life's Work) (Moscow, 1975), pp. 597–8; M.N. Tukhachevskii, 'Novoe v razvitii taktiki Krasnoi Armii' (Innovations in the Tactics of the Red Army), (1937), in Kadishev (ed.), *Voprosy taktiki*, pp. 81–2.

75. *PU-36*, Ch. 7, Art. 164.

76. Tukhachevskii, 'Novye voprosy voiny', in Kadishev (ed.), *Voprosy strategii*, pp. 139–40, 142–3; Varfolomeev, *Nastupatel'naia operatsiia*, pp. 175–6. *Udarnaia armiia*,

pp. 173–4, 184–5; Fediuninskii, *Podniatye po trevoge*, p. 109; A.A. Grechko, *Gody voiny* (The War Years) (Moscow, 1976), p. 44; Anan'ev, *Tankovye armii v nastuplenii*, pp. 187, 396. Following the crystallization of the American operational consciousness in the mid-1980s, the idea of synchronization was adopted and allocated a central place in the 1986 edition of the field manual for operations: Headquarters Department of the Army, *FM 100-5 Operations*, Washington, DC, 5 May 1986, pp. 17–19.

77. The difference between synchronization (*vzaimodeistvie*) and coordination (*soglasovannost'*) is best demonstrated through the contrast between the ideas of harmony and melody. Whereas melody, being linear in nature represents the horizontal structure of the interaction between the various instruments, harmony, represents the vertical structure of this same interaction, and therefore is deep in its nature. Thus, *vzaimodeistvie* has been perceived by the operational theoreticians, and especially by Tukhachevskii who had a broad musical background, as the quality represented by harmony. On the other hand *soglasovannost'* concerned the quality represented by melody.

78. *PU-36*, Ch. 1, Art. 8, Ch. 5, Arts. 114, 115, 121, 128, 134, 135, 137, 138; Varfolomeev, *Nastupatel'naia operatsiia*, p. 175; G.K. Zhukov, *Vospominaniia i razmyshleniia* (Reminiscences and Reflections) (Moscow, 1975) (3 vols.), Vol. 1, pp. 284–5, 405. Grechko, *Gody voiny*, p. 339; A.Kh. Babadzhanian (ed.), *Dorogi pobedy* (Roads to Victory) (Moscow, 1975), p. 151; A.I. Eremenko, *V nachale voiny* (At the Beginning of the War) (Moscow, 1964), pp. 75, 82; idem, *Stalingrad. Zapiski komanduiushchego frontom* (Stalingrad. Reminiscences of a Front Commander-in-chief) (Moscow, 1961), pp. 286–7; idem, *Gody vozmezdiia* (Years of Retaliation) (Moscow, 1969), p. 331; K.S. Moskalenko, *Na iugo-zapadnom napravlenii* (Towards the South-west) (2 vols.) (Moscow, 1973), Vol. 1, pp. 246–7, 275; A.M. Sandalov, *Trudnye rubezhei* (Severe Limits) (Moscow, 1965), p. 14.

79. Isserson, *Evoliutsiia operativnogo iskusstva*, pp. 131–2; Tukhachevskii, 'O novom polevom ustave RKKA', pp. 253–5.

80. Guderian, *Achtung Panzer*, p. 180, used on this single occasion the expression: 'it is therefore of great importance to strive to bring the entire depth of the enemy defence under simultaneous attack'. The translator, C. Duffy noticed and mentioned the striking similarity of this expression to the ideas of Tukhachevskii, which he had read in Simpkin's book, *Deep Battle*. However, it is hardly probable that Guderian had a chance to read or learn directly the ideas of the Soviet Marshal. It is more likely that he picked up this idea from M.I. Kurtsinskii's work, *Taktik Schneller Verbände* (Potsdam, 1935), which had been translated from Russian.

81. J.E. Forster, 'The Dynamics of Volksgemeinschaft: The Effectiveness of the German Military Establishment in the Second World War', in A.R. Millet and W. Murray (eds), *Military Effectiveness, The Second World War* (Boston, 1990), Vol. 3, p. 200.

82. *PU-36*, Ch. 7, Art. 181.

83. Galaktionov, 'Tempy operatsii', pp. 545–6.

84. Tukhachevskii, 'Novye voprosy voiny' in Kadishev (ed.), *Voprosy strategii*, p. 142.

85. Ammosov, 'Tanki v operatsii proryva', pp. 593–600; R.D. Gladkov, 'Taktika bronevykh chastei' (Tactics of Armoured Units) (1930), in Kadishev (ed.), *Voprosy taktiki*, pp. 245–7; K.B. Kalinovskii, 'Tanki v gruppakh DD' (Tanks in the Long-range Penetration Groups), *Mekhanizatsiia i motorizatsiia RKKA* (The Mechanization and Motorization of the Red Army), 1931, No. 2, pp. 7–19; A.E. Gromychenko, 'Ocherki taktiki tankovykh chastei' (A Study of Tank Unit Tactics) (1935), in Kadishev (ed.), *Voprosy taktiki*, pp. 260–62; *PU-36*, Ch. 5, Arts. 112–16; Ch. 7, Arts. 180–92; O.A. Losik (ed.), *Stroitel'stvo i boevoe primenenie Sovetskikh tankovykh voisk v gody Velikoi otechestvennoi voiny* (The Formation and Combat Employment of Soviet Tank Forces in the Years of the Great Patriotic War) (Moscow, 1979), pp. 96–106; 'Prikaz NKO No. 325 ot oktiabria 1942 g.' (Order no. 325 of the People's Defence Commissariat of Oct. 1942) in *VIZh*, 10 (1974), pp. 68–73, provided good confirmation that in autumn 1942 the Red Army readopted the essentials of the Deep Operation theory, concerning the subject of integrating tank and infantry formations.

86. Varfolomeev, *Udarnaia armiia*, pp. 175–7; Isserson, *Evoliutsiia operativnogo iskusstva*, pp. 59–61.

87. Triandafillov, *The Nature of Operations of Modern Armies*, pp. 14–29, 51–61; M.N.

Tukhachevskii, 'O razvitii form upravleniia' (Concerning the Development of Forms of Command and Control) (1934), in Solov'ev (ed.), *Izbrannye proizvedeniia*, Vol. 2, p. 209; Isserson, 'Razvitie teorii operativnogo iskusstva v 30-e gody', No. 1, p. 43; S.N. Ammosov, 'Tanki v operatsii proryva' (Tanks in the Breakthrough Operation), *Voina i revoliutsiia*, 1932, No. 5–6, pp. 81–2; V.V. Favitskii, 'Rol' mekhvoisk v sovremennoi operatsii' (The Role of Mechanized Forces in Contemporary Operations), *Mekhanizatsiia i motorizatsiia RKKA* (Mechanization and Motorization of the Red Army), 1933, No. 2, pp. 63–5, 70–71. According to these theoreticians, the strike echelon's (ERP) operational role, whose performance demanded the synchronized cooperation between itself and the system's other elements (*vzaimodeistvie s drugimi ob'edineniiami fronta i s frontovoi aviatsiei riad raznoobraznykh zadach*), concerned the following points: development of the tactical success into operational dimensions, maintaining operational continuity, determining a high tempo of operations, and producing the operational effect (*operativnyi effekt*) of shock. The same sources determined that interpreting this definition of operational role into practical terms required the execution of tactical missions such as: operational pursuit of the enemy (*operativanoe presledovanie protivnika*), seizing defensive lines hastily occupied by the enemy on the move or penetrating them (*zakhvat s khodu ili proryv pospeshno zaniatykh oboronitel'nykh rubezhei vraga*), forcing water obstacles (*forsirovanie vodnykh pregrad*), encircling and destroying major enemy groupings (*okruzhenie i unichtozhenie krupnykh gruppirovok protivnika*), fighting the enemy's operational reserves (*bor'ba s ego operativnymi rezervami*), and fighting for cities and industrial regions (*bor'ba za goroda i promyshlennye raiony*). V. Kryzhanovskii, 'Samostoiatel'-noe motomekhanizirovannoe soedinenie na otkrytom flange armii v nastupatel'noi operatsii' (Independent Moto-mechanized Formation in the Army's Open Flank during Offensive Operation), *Voina i revoliutsiia* 1 (1932), pp. 13–33.

88. Favitskii, 'Rol' mekhvoisk v sovremennoi operatsii', 63–5, 70–1; E.A. Shilovskii, 'Podgotovka i vedenie operativnogo proryva' (The Preparation and Execution of Operational Penetration), *Voennaia mysl'* 8 (1939), pp. 21–9; *PU-36*, Ch. 7, Art. 181; Narodnyi Komissariat Oborony Soiuza SSR (NKO), *Boevoi ustav bronetankovykh i mekhanizirovannykh voisk Krasnoi Armii 1944g.* (Combat Regulations for Tank and Mechanized Forces of the Red Army 1944) (Moscow, 1944), Ch. 8, Arts. 369–71; Anan'ev, *Tankovye armii v nastuplenii*, pp. 148–54, 264–6.

89. Tukhachevskii, 'Novye voprosy voiny' in Kadishev (ed.), *Voprosy strategii*, pp. 128, 130; Anan'ev, *Tankovye armii v nastuplenii*, pp. 396–7, 400.

90. Tukhachevskii, 'Novye voprosy voiny', in Kadishev (ed.), *Voprosy strategii*, pp. 130, 136; Triandafillov, *The Nature of Operations of Modern Armies*, p. 117; I.E. Krupchenko (ed.), *Sovetskie tankovye voiska 1941–1945* (Soviet Tank Forces 1941–45) (Moscow, 1973), p. 252; V.I. Chuikov, *The End of the Third Reich*, (Moscow, 1985), pp. 101–4, 130–33.

91. Triandafillov, *The Nature of Operations of Modern Armies*, p. 118.

92. Tukhachevskii, 'Novye voprosy voiny' in Kadishev (ed.), *Voprosy strategii*, pp. 127–30; Galaktionov, 'Tempy operatsii', pp. 543–5; I.E. Krupchenko, 'Battle for Berlin', in P.A. Zhilin, et al., *Revue Internationale d'Histoire Militaire* 44 (Moscow,1979), pp. 133–8; 'Podgotovka i vedenie operatsii na okruzhenie i likvidatsiiu gruppirovok protivnika' (The Preparation and Execution of Encirclement and Liquidation Operations of Enemy Groupings), *VIZh*, 2 (1988), pp. 60–63; Anan'ev, *Tankovye armii v nastuplenii*, pp. 398–9.

93. V.S. Tamruchi, 'Taktika tankovykh voisk' (Tactics of Tank Forces) (1940), in Kadishev (ed.), *Voprosy taktiki*, pp. 280–81; Isserson, 'Razvitie teorii operativnogo iskusstva v 30-e gody', No. 3, pp. 53–4; P.A. Rotmistrov, *Istoriia voennogo iskusstva* (The History of Military Art) (2 vols.) (Moscow, 1963), Vol. 1, pp. 487–8; 'Proryv sil'no ukreplennoi polosy ukreplennykh raionov strelkovym korpusom' (Penetration of Strongly Fortified Belts and Regions by Rifle Corps) (1940), in Kadishev (ed.), *Voprosy taktiki*, pp. 297–300; N. Naumov, 'Teoriia proryva oborony protivnika v predvoennye gody' (The Theory of Breaking through an Enemy Defensive in the Pre-war Years), *VIZh*, 1 (1975), p. 62; Anan'ev, *Tankovye armii v nastuplenii*, pp. 274–5, 288–9; I. Kuksha, 'Vzaimodeistvie tankov DDP i DD s aviatsiei i artilleriei pri proryve oboronitel'noi polosy protivnika v manevrennoi voine' (Synchronization of DDP and DD Tanks with

Aviation and Artillery in Penetrating the Enemy Defensive lines in a Manoeuvre War), *Voina i revoliutsiia* 1 (1932), pp. 1–12.

94. D.M. Glantz, *The Soviet Conduct of Tactical Manoeuvre, Spearhead of the Offensive* (London, 1991), pp. 227–39, referred to the forward detachment as the spearhead of tactical manoeuvre. While accepting his use of the term spearhead when referring to the forward detachment, I would challenge his view, categorizing it as tactical.

95. *Polevoi ustav Krasnoi Armii (PU-1936), vremenyi* (Field Service Regulations of the Red Army (1936), tentative), trans. by Translation Section, The Army War College, Washington, DC, 1937, p. 55; Isserson, 'Razvitie teorii operativnogo iskusstva v 30-e gody', No. 3, pp. 53–4; Anan'ev, *Tankovye armii v nastuplenii*, pp. 160–61.

96. F. Trukhin, 'Osnovy operativnogo presledovaniia' (Fundamentals of the Operational Pursuit), *Voennaia mysl'* 11 (1939), p. 94; F.D. Sverdlov, *Peredovye otriady v boiu* (Forward Detachments in Combat) (Moscow, 1986), pp. 42–3; Anan'ev, *Tankovye armii v nastuplenii*, pp. 116–17.

97. M. Cherniakov, 'Tanks and Tankettes in the Forward Detachment of a Division', *Voennyi vestnik*, 3 (1934), cited in Glantz, *The Soviet Conduct of Tactical Manoeuvre*, pp. 83–4. It should be remembered that as early as August 1877 the Russians operated a forward detachment (*peredovoi otriad*). This organization, comprising a force much larger than a modern division, operated more than 200 km ahead of the main Russian Army. In the course of its independent operation. which lasted more than a month, the force had captured the essential Shipka Pass, over the Balkan ridge, and retained it until joined by the main army. Similar ideas, concerning the scope of operations of the forward detachment were presented by: Sverdlov, *Peredovoye otriady v boiu*, p. 35; Tamruchi, 'Taktika tankovykh voisk', pp. 280–81; M.M. Kirian, 'Armeiskaia nastupatel'naia operatsiia' (The Army Offensive Operation), *SVE*, 1976, Vol. 1, p. 243; N. Kiriev and N. Dovbenko, 'Iz opyta boevogo primeneniia peredovykh otriadov tankovykh mekhanizirovannykh korpusov' (Lessons from the Combat Use of Forward Detachments of Tank and Mechanized Corps), *VIZh*, 9 (1982), pp. 20–21.

98. Tukhachevskii, 'Novye voprosy voiny' in Solov'ev (ed.), *Izbrannye proizvedeniia*, p. 196; PU-36, Ch. 7, Arts. 180, 181.

99. K.B. Kalinovskii, 'Problema motorizatsii i mekhanizatsii sovremennykh armii' (The Mechanization and Motorization of Modern Armies), in Kadishev (ed.), *Voprosy strategii*, pp. 563–4; 'Tanki v gruppakh DD' (Tanks in the Long-range Action Groups), *Mekhanizatsiia i motorizatsiia armii*, 2 (1931), pp. 10–12; P.D. Gladkov, *Taktika bronevykh chastei* (Tactics of Tank Units) (Moscow, 1930), p. 12; S.N. Ammosov, 'Taktika motomekhsoedinenii' (Tactics of Motorized-mechanized Formations), in Kadishev (ed.), *Voprosy taktiki*, p. 257; A.M. Zvartsev, *3-ia Gvardeiskaia Tankovaia: Boevoi put' 3-i Gvardeiskoi Tankovoi Armii* (3rd Guards Tank: The Combat Path of 3rd Guards Tank Army) (Moscow, 1982), pp. 86–94; Anan'ev, *Tankovye armii v nastuplenii*, p. 309.

100. *PU-36*, Ch. 7, Art. 221; Sverdlov, *Peredovye otriady v boiu*, pp. 140–52; A. Zheltoukhov, 'Vzaimodeistvie osnova uspekha v boiu' (Synchronization – the Basis of Success in Combat), *Voennyi vestnik*, 9 (1973), pp. 46–50; A. Gusev, 'Peredovoi otriad forsiruet reku' (The forward detachment forces a river), *Voennyi vestnik*, 11 (1979), pp. 32–36; R. Baikeev, 'Peredovoi otriad forsiruet reku' (The Forward Detachment Forces a River), *Voennyi vestnik*, 12 (1983), pp. 58–62; I. Smichenko, 'Peredovoi otriad forsiruet reku' (The Forward Detachment Forces a River), *Voennyi vestnik*, 11 (1985), pp. 72–4; M.M. Kirian, *Fronty nastupali* (The Fronts Attacked) (Moscow, 1987), pp. 137–8; A.Kh. Babadzhanian, N.K. Popel', M.A. Shalin and I.M. Kravchenko, *Liuki otkryli v Berline: Boevoi put' 1-i Gvardeiskoi Tankovoi Armii* (They Opened the Road to Berlin: The Combat Path of 1st Guards Tank Army) (Moscow, 1973), pp. 102–19, 234–5, 239–47; K.P. Korol'kov, *Glubokii reid* (Deep Raid) (Moscow, 1967); I.F. Dremov, *Nastupala groznaia bronia* (The Awesome Armour Attacked) (Kiev, 1981), pp. 58–64.

101. Tamruchi, 'Taktika tankovykh voisk', p. 281; Ammosov, 'Taktika motomekhsoedinenii', p. 258; 'Peredovoi otriad' (Forward detachment), *SVE*, 1978, Vol. 6, p. 282; 'Reid' (The Raid), *SVE*, 1978, Vol. 7, p. 94; Sverdlov, *Peredovye otriady v boiu*, p. 73; Babadzhanian *et al.*, *Liuki otkryli v Berline*, pp. 82–5; I.I. Iakobovskii, *Zemlia v ogne* (The Land on Fire) (Moscow, 1975), pp. 232–42; Anan'ev, *Tankovye armii v*

nastuplenii, p. 381; Isserson, 'Razvitie teorii Sovetskogo operativnogo iskusstva v 30-e gody', No. 3, ibid., pp. 53–4; *Polevoi ustav Krasnoi Armii*, p. 55.

102. Anan'ev, *Tankovye armii v nastuplenii*, pp. 336–7; A.I. Radzievskii, *Tankovyi udar* (Tank Strike) (Moscow, 1974), p. 212.

103. Narodnyi Komissariat Oborony Soiuza SSR (NKO), *Polevoi ustav RKKA 1929* (Field Service Regulations of the Red Army 1929) (Moscow, 1929), trans. JPRS, pp. 54, 57; Anan'ev, *Tankovye armii v nastuplenii*, pp. 287, 388.

104. B.M. Teplinskii, 'Rol' aviatsii v sovremennoi voine' (The Role of Aviation in Contemporary War), in Kadishev (ed.), *Voprosy strategii*, p. 673; A.N. Lapchinskii, 'Vozdushnye desanty' (Airborne *Desant*), in Kadishev (ed.), *Voprosy taktiki*, p. 352; V. Sosnitskii, 'Desantniki v atake' (Airborne Troops in the Attack), *Voennyi vestnik*, 10 (1985), pp. 29–30; N. Kravchenko, 'Rubezhi desantnikov' (Frontiers of the *Desant*), *Voennyi vestnik*, 7 (1986), pp. 25–28; R. Salikov, 'V peredovom otriade' (In the Forward Detachment), *Voennyi vestnik*, 3 (1987), pp. 33–6; Sverdlov, *Peredovye otriady v boiu*, pp. 152–7.

105. *PU-36*, Ch. 1, Art. 7; V.A. Bulatnikov, E.D. Grebish, M.N. Kholodov, 'Desant', *SVE*, 1977, Vol. 3, p. 152–4; 'Desantirovanie' (Assault Landing), ibid., pp. 154–5; 'Desantnyi eshelon' (*Desant* Echelon), ibid., p. 157; 'Vozdushno-desantnaia operatsiia' (Airborne *Desant* Operation), *SVE*, 1976, Vol. 2, pp. 284–5; D.S. Sukhorukov, 'Vozdushno-desantnye voiska' (Airborne *Desant* Forces), *VIZh*, 1 (1982), No. 1, pp. 37–43. The Russian idea of *desant*, which has no equivalent in any other military jargon, implies basically an action intended to descend on the rival system's depth. Such a descent can be performed by air-mechanized troops, special forces, naval infantry, or infantry – elements that are being conveyed to their objectives on non-organic platforms. A. Lapchinskii, 'Vozdushnye desanty' (Airborne *Desants*), *Voina i revoliutsiia* 6 (1930), pp. 81–94.

106. Tukhachevskii, 'Novye voprosy voiny' in Solov'ev (ed.), *Izbrannye proizvedeniia*, pp. 182–4; V.G. Reznichenko, 'Osnovnye napravleniia razvitiia Sovetskoi taktiki v poslevoennye gody' (The Basic Direction of the Development of Soviet Tactics in the Postwar Years), *VIZh*, 8 (1971), p. 36.

107. V.V. Khripin and E.I. Tatarchenko, 'Vozdushnaia voina' (The War in the Air), *Vestnik Vozdushnogo flota*, 4 (1934), pp. 5–6; B.L. Teplinskii, 'Osobennosti vzaimodeistviia aviatsii s nazemnymi voiskami' (Characteristics of Synchronizing Aviation with Ground Forces) (1934), in Kadishev (ed.), *Voprosy strategii*, pp. 666–8; A.N. Lapchinskii, 'Vozdushnye desantny' (Airborne *Desants*), in *Voina i revoliutsiia*, 6 (1930), pp. 89–90; V. Kokhanov, 'By Joint Efforts', *Soviet Military Review*, 12 (1974), pp. 20–21.

108. A.Ia. Ianovskii, 'Vozdushnyi desant i bor'ba s nim na zheleznykh dorogakh' (Air *Desant* and Fighting on Railways), *Voennaia mysl'* 5 (1938), pp. 117–18; V.F. Margelov, I.I. Lisov and V.I. Ivonin, *Sovetskie vozdushno-desantnye* (Soviet Air *Desant*) (Moscow, 1986), p. 42; D.S. Sukhorukov (ed.), *Sovetskie vozdushno-desant-nye* (Soviet Air *Desant*) (Moscow, 1980), pp. 270–72; L.N. Vnotchenko, 'Nekotorye voprosy teorii nastupatel'nykh i oboronitel'nykh operatsii 1945–1954 gg.' (Some Questions on the Theory of Offensive and Defensive Operations 1945–54), *VIZh*, 8 (1970), p. 34.

109. N. Ramanichev, 'Razvitie teorii i praktiki boevogo primeneniia vozdushno-desantnykh voisk v mezhvoennyi period' (The Development of the Theory and Practice of the Combat Use of Airborne-*Desant* Forces in the Interwar Period), *VIZh*, 10 (1982), pp. 72–7; P. Pavlenko, 'Razvitie taktiki vozdushno-desantnykh voisk v poslevoennyi period' (The Development of *Desant* Force Tactics in the Postwar Period), *VIZh*, 1 (1980), pp. 28–33; V. Kostylev, 'Stanovlenie i razvitie vozdushno-desantnykh voisk' (The Growth and Development of Airborne *Desant* Forces), *VIZh*, 9 (1975), pp. 80–82; K. Kurochkin, 'Vozdushno-desantnym voiskam – 50 let' (Airborne *Desant* Forces – 50 Years), *VIZh*, 8 (1980), pp. 94–6.

110. A.N. Lapchinskii, 'Vozdushnye sily v boiu i operatsii' (Air Forces in Battle and Operation) (1932), in Kadishev (ed.), *Voprosy strategii*, pp. 624–25; Khripin, and Tatarchenko, 'Vozdushnaia voina', p. 4; Teplinskii, 'Osobennosti vzaimodeistviia aviatsii s nazemnymi voiskami', pp. 666–71.

111. A.N. Lapchinskii, 'Vozdushnaia armiia' (The Air Army), in Kadishev (ed.), *Voprosy strategii*, pp. 639–44; idem, 'Vozdushnaia voina budushchego' (The Future Air War),

Voina i Revoliutsiia 3 (1931), pp. 4–13; Khripin, and Tatarchenko, 'Vozdushnaia voina', pp. 3–4.

112. Lapchinskii, 'Vozdushnye sily v boiu i operatsii', pp. 629–30. Teplinskii, 'Osobennosti vzaimodeistviia aviatsii s nazemnymi voiskami', pp. 667–9.
113. Khripin and Tatarchenko, 'Vozdushnaia voina', pp. 655–6; P.P. Ionov, *Istrebitel'naia aviatsiia* (Fighter Aviation) (Moscow, 1940), pp. 64–5.
114. Teplinskii, 'Vozdushnaia armiia', pp. 641–4.
115. A.S. Algazin, *Obespechenie vozdushnykh operatsii* (Air Support Operations) (Moscow, 1928), pp. 47–9; A.K. Mednis, 'Taktika shturmovoi aviatsii' (Attack Aviation Tactics), in Kadishev (ed.), *Voprosy taktiki*, pp. 325–32.
116. N.E. Kakurin, 'Sovremennaia taktika' (Contemporary Tactics) (1924), in Kadishev (ed.), *Voprosy taktiki*, pp. 64–5; Isserson, *Evoliutsiia operativnogo iskusstva*, pp. 127–31; Tukhachevskii, 'O novom polevom ustave RKKA', in Solov'ev (ed.), *Izbrannye proizvedeniia*, Vol. 2, pp. 249–52; V.K. Smylovskii, 'Ocherki taktiki artillerii' (An Outline of Artillery Tactics) (1928), in Kadishev (ed.), *Voprosy taktiki*, pp. 202–3; V.K. Tokarevskii, 'Taktika artillerii' (Artillery Tactics) (1931), in Kadishev (ed.), *Voprosy taktiki*, pp. 207–8; V.D. Grendal, *Artilleriia v osnovnykh vidakh boia* (Artillery in the Fundamental Types of Combat) (Moscow, 1940), pp. 228–9; A.K. Sivkov, 'Taktika artillerii' (Artillery Tactics) (1941), in Kadishev (ed.), *Voprosy taktiki*, pp. 231–5; Gladkov, 'Taktika bronevykh chastei' (Tactics of Armoured Units) (1930), in Kadishev (ed.), *Voprosy taktiki*, pp. 245–6, 247–9; Kalinovskii, 'Tanki v gruppakh DD', pp. 10–16; Ammosov, 'Taktika motomekhsoedinenii', p. 257; Rotmistrov, 'Proryv sil'no ukreplennykh polos', pp. 299–300.
117. Anan'ev, *Tankovye armii v nastuplenii*, pp. 54–5; Losik, *Stroitel'stvo i boevoe primenenie Sovetskikh tankovykh voisk*, pp. 107–11, 118–20; Margelov, *et al.*, *Sovetskie vozdushno-desantnye*, pp. 305–10.
118. *PU-36*, Ch. 6 (The Encounter Battle), Art. 150.
119. D.M. Karbyshev, 'Inzhenernoe obespechenie obshchevoiskovogo boia' (Engineer Support in All-Arms Combat) (1939), in Kadishev (ed.), *Voprosy taktiki*, pp. 380–82.
120. N.A. Morozov, 'Obshchaia taktika' (General Tactics) (1928), in Kadishev (ed.), *Voprosy taktiki*, p. 47.
121. 'Otriady obespecheniia dvizheniia' (March Support Detachment), *SVE*, 6 (1978), pp. 169–70.
122. 'Podvizhnye otriady zagrazhdeniia' (Mobile Obstacle Detachments), ibid., p. 374; Anan'ev, *Tankovye armii v nastuplenii*, pp. 180, 183–5.
123. Isserson, *Evoliutsiia operativnogo iskusstva*, pp. 127–31; Tukhachevskii, 'O novom polevom ustave' in Solov'ev (ed.), *Izbrannye proizvedeniia*, Vol. 2, pp. 246–7, 249–50, 257; Triandafillov, *The Nature of Operations of Modern Armies*, pp. 69–71, 74–5, 78, 91; *PU-36*, Ch. 1, Arts. 15, 16.
124. Tukhachevskii, *O novom polevom ustave*, pp. 251–3.
125. Tukhachevskii, 'Novoe v razvitii taktiki Krasnoi Armii', p. 257; 'O novom polevom ustave RKKA' in Solov'ev (ed.), *Izbrannye proizvedeniia*, Vol. 2, pp. 257–8; A.I. Sediakin, 'Blizhnii boi' (The Close Battle), *Voennyi vestnik*, 8 (1936), pp. 1–4; *PU-36*, Ch. 6 (*vstrechnyi boi*), Arts. 140–42.
126. Tukhachevskii, 'O novom polevom ustave' in Solov'ev (ed.), *Izbrannye proizvedeniia*, Vol. 2, pp. 252–3; 'Novoe v razvitii taktiki Krasnoi Armii', in Kadishev (ed.), *Voprosy taktiki*, pp. 80–82.
127. Tukhachevskii, 'Novye voprosy voiny', in Kadishev (ed.), *Voprosy strategii*, pp. 139, 143; idem, 'Voprosy vysshego komandovaniia', in Solov'ev (ed.), *Izbrannye proizvedeniia*, Vol. 1, p. 194; idem, 'O novom polevom ustave RKKA', in ibid., Vol. 2, p. 252; *PU-36*, Ch. 7, Art. 181; *BU-bronetankovykh i mekhanizirovannykh voisk Krasnoi Armii 1944*, Ch. 7 (*vstrechnoe srazhenie*), Art. 300; Triandafillov, *The Nature of Operations of Modern Armies*, p. 165.
128. Tukhachevskii, 'Voprosy vysshego komandovaniia' in Solov'ev (ed.), *Izbrannye proizvedeniia*, Vol. 1, pp. 194, 196; 'Novye voprosy voiny', in Kadishev (ed.), *Voprosy strategii*, p. 141. 'Voprosy upravleniia' (Problems of Command and Control), *Voina i revoliutsiia* 7 (1932), pp. 2–3; Varfolomeev, *Udarnaia armiia*, pp. 187–8; Anan'ev, *Tankovye armii v nastuplenii*, pp. 116–19, 121.

129. Tukhachevskii, 'Voprosy vysshego komandovaniia' in Solov'ev (ed.), *Izbrannye proizvedeniia*, Vol. 1, p. 195; Shtemenko, *The Soviet General Staff at War*, p. 253.
130. Tukhachevskii, 'Voprosy vysshego komandovaniia', p. 194.
131. Ibid; idem, 'Novye voprosy voiny' in Kadishev (ed.), *Voprosy strategii*, p. 140; Triandafillov, *The Nature of Operations of Modern Armies*, pp. 3–4, 167–8; Isserson, *Evoliutsiia operativnogo iskusstva*, pp. 88–90.
132. M.N. Tukhachevskii, 'Novye voprosy voiny', *VIZh*, 2 (1962), pp. 73–5.
133. Ibid.
134. Ibid., p. 74.
135. Tukhachevskii, 'Novye voprosy voiny' in Kadishev (ed.), *Voprosy strategii*, pp. 142–3.
136. Ibid., p. 139.
137. Ibid., p. 143; Triandafillov, *The Nature of Operations of Modern Armies*, p. 165.
138. Tukhachevskii, 'Novye voprosy voiny' in Kadishev (ed.), *Voprosy strategii*, pp. 141–3.
139. Ibid., pp. 140–43. 'O razvitii formy upravleniia' (Development of Forms of Command and Control) (1934), in *Izbrannye proizvedeniia*, Vol. 2, p. 210; Triandafillov, *The Nature of Operations of Modern Armies*, pp. 165–7; Isserson, *Evoliutsiia operativnogo iskusstva*, pp. 88–9; Shtemenko, *The Soviet General Staff at War*, pp. 449, 464; Lomov, *Nauchno-tekhnicheskii progress i revoliutsiia v voennom dele*, pp. 148–9, 173; Rotmistrov, *Vremia i tanki*, p. 191; G.E. Isserson, 'Kharakter upravleniia sovremennym boem' (The Character of Command of Contemporary Combat), *Voina i revoliutsiia*, 1931, No. 5, pp. 56–62.
140. Zakharov, 'Predislovie', in Kadishev (ed.), *Voprosy strategii*, p. 22.

7

From Tactical Destruction to Operational Manoeuvre: The Conceptual Revolution in American Military Thought

INTRODUCTION

In March 1985, three years after the publication of the first American operational field manual, one of the more active members of the group of military reformers used the following words in reference to the mental transformation which the American army underwent in the early 1980s:

> For all practical purposes, the study of operations ended in the US Army after World War II. Perhaps the belief that nuclear weapons meant the end of conventional land warfare was to blame, but whatever the cause, the knowledge of large units operations declined continually even with the object lesson of Korea before us. Three years ago the Army substantially revised its doctrine. FM 100-5, Operations, contained some significant changes and a few of these, chiefly deep attack and manoeuvre-based tactics, stimulated a great deal of debate. Yet a less noted change, the addition of the operational level of war as a separate field of military activity, has generated relatively little discussion although it certainly represents a distinct departure from the familiar. In fact, the adoption of operational art may be the most important change in Army doctrine since World War II. The Army's response to it may determine the force's success in the next war.[1]

For anyone aware of the scope and depth of Soviet operational cognition, the naiveté of the above citation is striking. In fact, even a brief comparison between the theory of Deep Operations and the American Airland Battle doctrine indicates not only the existence of a significant conceptual gap between the Soviet theoreticians and their

Western counterparts, but also the heavy impact of Soviet perceptions on each of the American theoretical advances. Thus, almost naturally the question arises: What innovations has the recent American conceptual endeavour contributed to the universal field of operational thought?

Apart from penetrating self-criticism, which in itself is clear evidence of the degree of open-mindedness reached by the American military establishment in the course of the 1980s, a further examination of Holder's exposition may provide the answer to our question. Holder described the evolution of American military thought after the Second World War as a progression comprising three essential phases: the phase of operational ignorance, the formal application of system approach to the field of military activity, and the acquisition of an exclusive operational cognition. Moreover, by focusing the nature of the conceptual change on the operational approach he emphasized the coherence of this evolution, thus defining it as a systematic process.[2]

The transformation of American military thought in the era following the Vietnam War into a coherent and professional process began with the establishment of the Training and Doctrine Command (TRADOC) under the command of General W.E. Depuy.[3] As a result of both the professional criticism that followed the Vietnam experience and the realization of the new strategic challenges posed by the return of the armoured heavy manoeuvre to the central European theatre, the birth of TRADOC precipitated an evolutionary process, and created the structural framework for its systematic progress.[4]

However, the transition from the technical shallowness of an incoherent tactical doctrine into advanced operational consciousness must be credited exclusively to Don A. Starry's term of office as TRADOC commandant.[5] It was Starry who set the explicit aim of developing an American operational theory by which the various intellectual and empirical efforts could be synchronized into a logical and creative process. Moreover, by the institutionalization of scientific patterns of research, criticism and constant change he determined its dynamic nature for the future.

The transition from the traditional paradigm of attrition by means of superior technology and tactics to one of advanced operational manoeuvre comprises the essence of the evolutionary process in the US armed forces and the community of military theoreticians. From a teleologic perspective, our analysis of the American theoretical experience will focus on the following subjects, which constitute the characteristic stages of the evolutionary process: the formulation of

251

the 1976 field manual and the cognitive crisis induced by it; the application of system approach; the revelation of the operational level of war and the formulation of the 1982 field manual; and the conceptual quantum leap that centred on the formulation of the 1986 field manual, better known as Airland Battle. It should be remembered that operation Desert Storm served as the workshop in which the operational theory of Airland Battle was examined.

Apart from its timeliness, the great relevance of the American theoretical adventure derives from the fact that it represents the first conscious attempt of any Western army to apply a systemic approach to the field of operations. In the course of its new conceptual enterprise, resulting from the post-Vietnam professional perplexity, American military mentality moved from an addiction to attrition based on tactical parochialism and technology, to the adoption of the operational manoeuvre.[6] Centring from its outset on the combined activity of two revolutionary trends, this Kuhnistian venture led ultimately to creative achievements in the fields of theoretical discussion, operational organization and technological development.[7] On the one hand, it was initiated by an intellectual centre of gravity, based on civilian reformers who provided the process with bold conceptual guidelines, a profound discourse and a rich terminological basis;[8] on the other, it was sustained by a professional centre of gravity based upon military reformers who, by contributing their technical knowledge and methodology, managed to translate the abstract ideas of the civilian group into a coherent operational theory and practical patterns of action.[9]

Moreover, the long American journey in the provinces of operational thought, which ultimately took the form of a vigorous offensive-like manoeuvre was, in fact, born out of a defensive mode of thinking under nuclear-shadowed conditions. Thus, providing perspicuous proof for both strategic realism and for the ability to think and act harmoniously in a contradiction-saturated environment, this rare combination constitutes yet another unique aspect of the American experience.

Operational theory and praxis finally were put to a test in the vast experimental laboratory of Desert Storm. A rare opportunity thus arose to examine the validity of the newly born operational theory in light of the existing strategic reality. For the first time in the history of their military thought, the US armed forces were given the opportunity to analyze their operational performance using scientific tools of criticism provided by a coherent theory of war.

252

FORMULATION OF THE 1976 ACTIVE DEFENCE FIELD MANUAL

Although theoretically there are hardly any grounds to support the argument that the American armed forces were indeed beaten on the battlefields of Vietnam, a great number of symptoms characterizing defeated armies were evident at the end of the war.[10] The realization of disharmony in the relations between the political and strategic echelons constituted only one of the indicators which promoted grave doubts as to the ability of the armed forces to assemble their tactical activities into operational achievements in accordance with a coherent national strategy.[11] Military thought fluctuated between an attempt to explain what went wrong in Vietnam and wondering about future trends implied by the application of the conventional aspects of the flexible response strategy.[12] Moreover, the military system's inability to restore its lost confidence in the efficiency of the existing doctrine deepened doubts about the ability of the training system, the command structure and the build-up of the field forces to face future operational challenges effectively.[13]

However, in 1991 the Americans seemed to be confident enough to embark on a large-scale war. They possessed an advanced theory of war, according to which they had trained their commanders, structured their field forces, and developed their military technology. Moreover, by practising their newly acquired operational consciousness, they managed to overcome the unfavourable strategic conditions, neutralize their adversary's quantitative advantage and initiate the operational conditions allowing them to employ their doctrine almost to the letter.[14]

By formulating the 1976 field manual, General Depuy's term of office as TRADOC commandant initiated the first step in this categorical process of change.[15] Apart from the desire to justify its formation, the decision by TRADOC's leadership to formulate a new field manual was governed by two considerations: the awareness of the existence of a professional gap, originating in the transition from an environment dominated by the concept of air mobility to an environment in which conditions of heavy armoured manoeuvre were prevalent, and an inclination to attract the professional consciousness to the new strategic reality by focusing mental resources on research of the present and future.[16]

The principal consideration that guided Depuy in the process of formulating the 1976 field manual was his intention to quickly produce a conceptual product that would suit the new conditions facing the American army. The superficiality of the methodology determined by this logic is apparent from the fact that what started in Fort Leavenworth as an inconsistent effort to produce Training Circulars (TC), developed in the course of 1974 into an independent project of writing the field manual itself. Ultimately, and despite the lack of a basic operational perception, it was decided at the end of that year to transfer the writing effort to TRADOC headquarters and thus separate it from the centres of research and tutoring in Fort Leavenworth.[17]

By employing a metaphor of French *pot pourri* to illustrate his policy for the development of the new doctrine, Depuy in fact legitimitized the preference of speed over systematic research, encouraged sectarianism within the armed forces, confirmed the validity of the traditional approaches as the conceptual basis for the new theory, and established the disparity between the content of the new manual and the operational reality.[18]

The conceptual point of departure of the authors of the manual was based on a shallow interpretation of the strategy of flexible response. Determining the theoretical nature of the new manual, this line of thought assumed that the employment of a tactical defence allowed the American army to overcome the strategic problem of numerical inferiority.[19]

The 1973 war in the Middle East had a profound impact on the substance of the 1976 field manual, and on the nature of the writing process. By supplying the Americans with a plethora of technical and tactical data, the recent Israeli experience touched upon their sensitivity to tactical issues, thus reinforcing both their industrial approach to war and the traditional inclination for operation research.[20] Yet lacking operational thinking, the Israelis failed to contribute to their American colleagues the essential insight required for developing a critical approach to the abundance of material. Thus, the distorted Israeli experience of 1973 was conceived from the outset as a paradigm for modern combat and a model for armoured operations.[21]

This line of thought not only hampered any serious attempt to explore the operational nature of modern combat, but also induced Depuy and many officers of the TRADOC community to perceive the transition to the European theatre of mechanized operations in exclusively technical terms. Therefore, almost naturally, the *raison d'être* of the new field manual was defined as satisfying the immediate needs of the junior tactical echelons.[22] Moreover, failing to comprehend the acute importance of a broad operational concept that would serve as an introductory framework, within which one could construct logical modes of mechanical action, Depuy's over-eagerness to start by solving practical questions of 'how to fight' led to the distorted assumption that by employing sound tactics alone, the strategic objectives could be accomplished.[23]

In terms of the culinary metaphor used by Depuy, the formulation of the 1976 field manual developed along the following lines: into the new pot, representing the new strategic concepts of conventional defence, was transferred, from the blackened and cracked pot of the Vietnam experience, the turbid stew of traditional American tactical thought.[24] Through a series of seminars dedicated principally to technical aspects of warfare, the existing *pot pourri* was thickened by the addition of ideas regarding armoured tactics obtained from the data provided by the 1973 Israeli experience.[25]

The field trials, conducted at Fort Hood during the months of April–December 1975, elicited the first doubts about the ability of the Active Defence tactical concept to provide the appropriate solutions to the operational challenges posed by the Russians in Central Europe. Nevertheless, the precept of Active Defence was institutionalized as a tactical recipe guaranteeing victory under conditions of strategic inferiority.

Thus, due to organizational inconsistencies and methodological misperceptions, Depuy's culinary enterprise went sour. In the case of the 1976 field manual, no initial attempt was made to equip either the doctrine's authors or implementors with a general framework of operational concept that would allow them to interpret the new strategic reality coherently. Thus, lacking a common cognitive denominator, the formulation process assumed an inconsistent course of evolution and the resulting product turned out to be illogical. Moreover, by adhering to the traditional tactical precepts, the deficient nature of the new doctrine was fixed. And finally, by employing methods of operational research for the analysis of the parochial Israeli experience, the doctrine was condemned from the outset to remain embedded in the technical spheres of operating weapon systems.

However, the great efforts invested in the formulation of the 1976 field manual did bear a certain positive benefit to the evolution of the future American operational theory. By presenting the American armed forces with a conceptual product, deficient as it might have been, TRADOC managed to provide, for the first time after many years of intellectual drought, a distinctly theoretical foundation upon which a critical discussion could be based.[26] What was needed now to generate such a discussion was an intellectual mechanism that would sharpen the system consciousness, and encourage an operational-oriented enquiry into the defects of the existing manual. This function was introduced by the activity of civilian reformers.

OPERATIONAL BRAINSTORMING: THE CONTRIBUTION
OF THE CIVILIAN REFORMERS

The publication of *FM 100-5 Operations, 1976*, attracted the attention of a small community of civilian intellectuals who had sought for some time to reform the thought patterns and structure of the armed forces. By exercising bold and creative thinking based upon system consciousness, this group of reformers generated a wave of criticism that exposed not only the archaic elements in the new doctrine, but also its failure to provide appropriate answers to the relevant strategic and operational challenges. Consequently, the most profound professional debate in the modern history of American military thought was ignited, and the conditions for the emergence of the cognitive crisis, which ultimately led to the crystallization of the operational theory, were created.

When referring to the contribution of William Lind, who was a member of the group of civilian reformers, a senior Marines officer, John Studt, described the mentality that prevailed in the American military establishment until the middle of the 1970s:

> But we were still relying on the concentration of superior firepower to win – essentially still practising Grant's attrition warfare. And we were still doing frontal assaults.[27]

According to Studt, the group of civilian reformers intended to change this traditional state of mind by criticizing the prevailing conceptions and by offering a positive alternative for change:

> For the first time I was personally hearing someone advocate an approach to war that was based on intellectual innovation rather than sheer material superiority. Mission-type orders, surfaces and gaps, and *schwerpunkt*, instead of the rigid formulas and checklists that we normally associate with our training and doctrine. It was a stimulating experience! Through Lind's articulation, years of my own reading of military history began to make a lot more sense.[28]

The sum of the arguments presented by the civilian reformers, invalidated the industrial approach of attrition and defied the unquestioned authority of tactical thinking. This attitude induced high- and medium-rank officers to re-examine, on the basis of a new state of consciousness, the foundations of the logic of manoeuvre:

> I served over 31 years active duty with the Marine Corps, saw combat in both Korea and Vietnam, and attended service schools from the basic school to the National War College. Yet only toward the end of my military career did I realize how little I really understood the art of

war . . . For the first time in our history we face a potential enemy with superiority in men and material. Against such an enemy we cannot win with the firepower attrition doctrine we embrace today. In this book Bill Lind offers an alternative.[29]

Examining the universal patterns of evolution of military thought at the present, both John Studt's frank report and Michael Howard's thorough analysis confirm that due to systemic limitations inherent in military establishments, the occurrence of a theoretical revolution was possible only through the bold and creative 'dead reckoning' suggested by civilian thinkers:[30]

But why all this from a civilian instead of a professional soldier? In fact, the entire movement of military reform is driven largely by civilian intellectuals not military officers – one notable exception being retired Air Force Colonel John Boyd. When you think about it, this is not surprising. We have never institutionalized a system that encourages innovative ideas or criticism from subordinates.[31]

According to Senator Gary Hart, the military reform started with the combined initiative of Senator Robert Taft and William Lind to write a White Paper on defence in 1976.[32] In the course of a decade the trend for changing the American armed forces developed from a raw idea shared by a limited group into an established reform movement, possessing a political platform and combining members of the Congress and Senate from both parties, civil servants from the defence establishment, academics from various disciplines, and officers on active service.[33]

The essence of the reform movement has thus been described by Gary Hart as an attempt to discover the root causes of American military failures, develop ideas required for restoring military effectiveness, and transform those ideas into policy:

It has two wings, one composed of civilians, the other of serving military officers. At the core of the civilian wing lies a group of five people: John Boyd, Steven Canby, Bill Lind, Norman Polmar, and Pierre Sprey. These individuals do not in any sense control the movement – it is too loosely organised for anyone to control. Rather these five people provide much of the grist for the reform mill in the form of catalyzing ideas.[34]

Since we are mainly concerned here with the circumstances leading to the development of the American theory of operational manoeuvre, we will focus the discussion on the elements which brought operational cognition to life in the army, specifically the group of five intellectuals which served as the catalyst of the conceptual reform.[35]

Boyd perceived the operational manoeuvre, which he sometimes called the OODA Loop, as a succession of actions guided by the logic of making the rival system irrelevant in the context of its own aim.[36] Thus, he formed the idea of operational shock as the rationale of the functioning of military systems and determined the coherent nature of the linkage between the manoeuvre and its consequence. Offering a cognitive basis for the creation of a future operational paradigm, this revolutionary approach was applied in the written works of the group's members in the course of the 1970s, and in theoretical dissertations later composed by serving officers.[37]

Yet Boyd's main contribution, both to his civilian colleagues and to the military reformers who would formulate the future Airland Battle doctrine, concerned his conception of the operational principles of the relational manoeuvre: disruption of synergy among the elements combining the rival system; simultaneous engagement of the operational components, structured hierarchically along the entire depth of the opposing system; and development of operational momentum, exceeding the relative reaction capability of the rival system.[38] Thus, for the first time in the history of Western armies conceptual tools were created allowing the transformation of military thought from techno-tactical categories into operational ones, centring on manoeuvre warfare. Boyd's ideas were interpreted almost literally into the four basic tenets comprising the conceptual skeleton of the Airland Battle doctrine, namely: initiative, agility, depth and synchronization.[39]

Moreover, Boyd argued that the effectuation of operational shock obliged the director of the manoeuvring system to muster his cognitive and mechanical efforts through a continuous systemic process combining the following functions: a deliberate contrivance of an operational weakness or flaw in the rival system's layout; distortion of the operational rival's consciousness by manipulative deception that would detach his apprehension from the strategic reality; and assemblage of the various mechanical activities into a main strike directed at the rival system's operational weakness.[40] Thus, in his abstract, multi-dimensional perception, Boyd identified the pattern of synchronization as the crucial means for the application of the centre of gravity in its operational version.[41]

Boyd likewise perceived the dynamics of operational cybernetics in systemic terms of an harmonious cycle, unfolding between two command poles, adverse in nature. Thus, he illuminated the extreme importance of the cognitive tension, both as an instrument for maintaining a creative equilibrium between centralism and the need for delegated command, and as a means for the system's self-regulation.[42]

Finally, being based on a systemic analysis of historical cases, Boyd's line of reasoning furnished military theoretical research with a sound methodology.[43]

The foremost contribution of William Lind, the other member of the reform group nucleus, was the translation of Boyd's system of abstract ideas into a theoretical product which could be digested by the more advanced circles of the armed forces.[44] Intending to serve the American armed forces under conditions of modern war, Lind's basic approach to manoeuvre warfare repudiated the traditional paradigm that was based on tactical thinking, on the one hand, and recognized the validity of a new paradigm, centring on operational shock, on the other.[45] Moreover, by discerning the operational level as an intermediate layer within the complete hierarchical structure of military activity, he defined the operational art as a unique field of knowledge, rationally bridging both the mechanical and cognitive gap between tactics and strategy.[46]

In the light of this operational logic, Lind managed to explore the roots of the traditional failure of American military thought, and introduce an alternative paradigm of manoeuvre facilitating success under the strategic limitation of quantitative inferiority:

> Why is operational art important if you are to do manoeuvre warfare? Because it is through excellence in the operational art more than through manoeuvre in the tactical battle (as important as that is) that a smaller force can defeat a larger one. Traditionally American armies have tried to attain their strategic objectives by accumulating tactical victories. They have given battle where and whenever it has been offered, wearing their enemy down engagement after engagement. This is attrition warfare on the operational level . . . Fighting this way, a smaller force can win battle after battle, only to find itself facing yet another battle, but with no force left to fight it.[47]

Armed with these arguments, Lind managed to establish in the heart of the American military caste, which had been traditionally indoctrinated to solve every problem by means of manipulating tactical patterns, a bridgehead of system thinking. Thus, he sowed the initial doubts regarding the ability of the 1976 manual to deliver the operational goods required by the strategic circumstances.

Lind never developed his thoughts into a proper theory of operation, because he lacked both the time and resources required for such an enterprise, and because such an objective lay beyond his ideological aspirations.[48] Realizing both the random nature of warfare and the operational challenges posed by modern war, he stressed the importance of a sound theory of manoeuvre for the effective functioning of military systems.[49] For Lind, the theory moulded in the course of an incessant process of critical research and study reflected the professional cognition upon which the preparation of fighting forces for war had been conducted.[50] His perception of theory was not that of an institutionalized collection of formulae for tactical conduct, bound to dictate one's course of action in a specific warlike situation. By offering a scientific framework for studying the profession of field command, the theory's principal function, according to Lind, was no more than to equip military leaders at all levels with the intellectual tools for the interpretation of the relevant operational reality.[51]

Keenly aware of the political and organizational reality in which he operated, Lind understood his own limitations only too well, and thus perceived his own role as an intellectual catalyst accelerating the institution of operational consciousness which would ultimately lead to the formulation of a new theory of operations.[52] Moreover, since he saw John Boyd's ideas as a philosophical basis for the future manoeuvre theory, he concentrated his own efforts on the translation of the abstract gist of 'Patterns of Conflict' into clear and practical language.[53] To win over officers from all ranks to the school of reform, Lind preferred to deliver the essence of his ideas through a concise handbook, focusing on the actual level of combat. Nevertheless, his employment of tactical parlance served no purpose other than smoothing the mental shock implied by the absorption of more advanced operational concepts.[54]

Since his ideological activity lacked any pretensions to produce a detailed and formal operational theory – a role which he left to the military wing of the reform movement – Lind confined the sum and substance of his conception to three main ideas, or cognitive filters as he termed them: *Auftragstaktik, Schwerpunkt,* and *Lücken und Flächentaktik.*[55]

The term *Schwerpunkt* expressed, within the context of Lind's work, the substance of Boyd's theory, namely, the simultaneous synchronization of the manoeuvring system's various elements, operating along the entire physical and cognitive depth of the opposing system as a *sine qua non* for the effectuation of the desired operational shock.[56]

According to Lind's interpretation, the emergence of the operational situation known as *Schwerpunkt* implied the combination of some mechanical as well as cognitive precepts, such as synergy and fragmentation, successive operations and momentum, deception and surprise, within the systemic manoeuvre.[57] Moreover, Lind's extended version of *Schwerpunkt* emphasized both the logical linkage between concentration of effort and accomplishment of the operational aim, and the principle of directing one's own main strike into the rival system's principal operational weakness.[58] Thus, for the first time in its history, American military thought offered a coherent concept allowing the accomplishment of conventional decision under conditions of numerical inferiority.[59]

The principal innovation in Lind's conception of command derived from a critical approach that identified initially a whole series of systemic contrarieties characterizing military activity in its operational context, such as the universal polarity between tactical and operational command, the intrinsic tension between the abstract aim and the mechanical missions, the permanent contradiction between warfare's chaotic nature and the inclination to rationalize the exercise of centralized conduct, and the divergence between creative thinking and technical activity of the drill mode.[60]

Moreover, through his systematic analysis of the subject of command, Lind identified yet another focus of tension, prompted by the structure of the manoeuvring system and the operational dynamics deriving from it. This tension centres on the different qualities required at various levels of command. Combining a high degree of technical competence, adaptability to changing conditions, aggressiveness, and an aptitude for comprehending the operational context, the quality of initiative has been defined by Lind as the required characteristic for tactical command.[61] On the other hand, he defined creativity, namely, the intellectual ability to interpret simultaneously the strategic and tactical realities, and develop appropriate operational solutions by means of system thinking, as the desired quality for the conduct of operations.[62]

Lind recognized the universal solution to the various challenges posed by a modern system saturated with contrarieties to the numerous levels of command, in the assimilation of an intellectual tension, based on uniform professional apprehension, system approach and manoeuvre consciousness, throughout the armed forces. This abstract concept he assembled under the title of *Auftragstaktik*.[63] Disclosing a striking similarity to the Soviet concept of operational command of the 1930s, this innovative approach provided the bridge between Boyd's concept of 'organic design for command and control' and the command philosophy that is reflected both in the Marines' *FMFM 1* and the Army's *FM 100-5*.[64]

The expression *Lücken und Flächentaktik*, representing the tactical idea of 'thrusts and pockets' in the concept of *Blitzkrieg*, was borrowed by Lind as a means for describing the mechanical aspects of manoeuvre warfare.[65] Under the heading of 'spaces and gaps' he concentrated a series of concepts relating to practical aspects implied by the application of the operational manoeuvre, such as: combined arms combat, operational synergy and the pre-emption of such synergy;[66] development of tactical penetration into operational irruption;[67] combination of holding and striking efforts, and interaction between manoeuvre and attrition;[68] interchangeability of the defensive and offensive basic forms of manoeuvre;[69] and operational mobility as a means for attaining momentum and preserving the continuity of manoeuvre.[70]

Boyd's and Lind's endeavours to interpret modern manoeuvre by means of systemic criteria provided the uniformed reformers with the keys for the development of an advanced conceptual substitution for the traditional paradigm of tactical attrition. Moreover, by innovating new operational ideas and terminology, the two civilians provided the military reform circle not only with conceptual and linguistic patterns that could serve as a basis for a new professional cognition, but also with systemic tools of criticism for the examination of the existing doctrine.

THE COGNITIVE CRISIS AND THE GREAT PROFESSIONAL DEBATE

The critical offensive against the 1976 field manual was initiated by an article published by William Lind in *Military Review*, the magazine which serves as a professional forum for theoretical discussions.[71] The publication of a critical article saturated with convincing operational arguments raised some grave doubts among medium- and high-ranking officers about the ability of the Active Defence doctrine to provide appropriate answers to the problems of the new strategic reality.[72] However, Lind's open criticism almost immediately induced both the TRADOC establishment and a group of civilian analysts to march to the defence of the new manual. This spontaneous response marked, *de facto*, the institution of a school of thought whose participants were committed to the vindication of the Active Defence doctrine.[73] Following this unofficial declaration of polemic war, many active officers, who were attracted by the validity of Lind's arguments, set out to disparage the 1976 field manual by disclosing the deficiencies that were not touched by Lind's critical pen.

Thus, the random emergence of two rival schools of thought,

exercising contrasting views in relation to the operational value of the 1976 field manual, marked the prelude to the longest, most intoxicating and creative professional debate which ever occurred in the history of American military thought. In the course of this debate, the 1976 manual, reflecting the last organized attempt to adhere to the paradigm of tactical attrition, was repudiated and a new operational paradigm was instituted through the publication of the 1982 field manual. Therefore, by striving to confine the debate to the years 1976–78 and to the narrow tactical implications of the Active Defence concept, the TRADOC historian not only oversimplified the actual picture of this complex event but also ignored its more advanced phase.[74]

The conceptual rivalry between the two contending schools is illustrated in detail in TRADOC's official historical monograph. Yet, a thorough inquiry into the huge corpus of professional articles, published between 1977–83 reveals the input of yet another group in the debate.[75] Centring on General Don Starry, the new TRADOC Commandant since July 1977 and a group of close associates, the activity of this group succeeded only in increasing the sense of ambiguity surrounding the issues. Since they were guided by political and methodological considerations exceeding the theoretical context of the debate, the members of Starry's group refrained from criticizing the 1976 manual openly. Moreover, they spared no effort in presenting the proceedings which led to the formulation of the 1982 Airland Battle manual as evolving directly from the 1976 manual.[76] Nonetheless, the concepts and ideas initiated by Starry's group purported trends contrasting with those practised by their predecessors.

Lasting some eight years, the debate developed in two distinct stages: the controversy that centred on the manual of 1976, and the controversy relating to the formulation of the Airland Battle concept. Not surprisingly, the critics of the 1976 manual became the defenders of the 1982 manual, and vice-versa – those who had championed the Active Defence concept challenged the Airland Battle doctrine.

Notwithstanding its excessive detail, stemming from the authors' access to the entirety of relevant documents, the segmental method exercised by the official historiography when referring to the professional debate introduces some grave problems. First of all, it falls short of identifying the sources of the debate. Furthermore, it confines the discussion on the debate to the shallow context of technical issues such as the first battle orientation, the defence emphasis, the issue of tactical reserves, the Soviet breakthrough manoeuvre, the emphasis on firepower, and tactics of concentration.[77] Yet, most importantly, the official historiography failed to establish a logical link between the debate's various stages, thus blurring the distinction between cause and effect.

Whereas the advocates of Active Defence were motivated by the traditional techno-tactical inclinations, the school of military reformers applied a system approach from the start,[78] clearly evidenced by the balanced posture practised by Starry in the course of the debate. Both Starry's operational insight and analytic approach allowed him to observe not only the incoherencies of the 1976 manual but also the political and methodological errors committed by his predecessor in the course of its formulation.[79] The content of the 1982 manual and the structure of the process which led to its composition constitute the best testimony for this assumption. However, since he strove to bequeath to the US Army an operational theory for modern manoeuvre as well as systemic patterns for research, criticism and development of such a theory, Starry abstained from employing the term theoretical revolution when referring to the 1982 conceptual exploit. Moreover, he spared no effort to justify the acts of his predecessor by illuminating the difficulties and limitations which he encountered in the immediate years following the Vietnam War.[80]

Approaching the process of conceptual revolution from a holistic perspective, Starry perceived the debate according to its contribution to the final consequence – the application of the operational theory. Thus, while recognizing the source from which the doctrinal process derived its dynamism, he identified the realization of a need for change as the essential mechanism generating the debate.[81] This mechanism was provided by William Lind's essay – a fact which is confirmed by the official historiography.[82]

Moreover, Lind's essay determined both the main conceptual trend that would guide the operational reformers in their efforts to formulate an advanced theory of manoeuvre and the nature of Romjue's technical classification of the debate's main issues.

Lind's method of reasoning was guided basically by an attempt to invalidate the 1976 manual's rationale through the application of operational criticism originating in systemic logic. In the first place, he intended to raise doubts in the minds of his audience concerning the manual's ability to fulfil the strategic aspiration of defending Europe successfully. Attaining this objective, he assumed that a conceptual reorientation would most certainly follow;[83] without imposing his 'manoeuvre warfare' philosophy upon his audience, he managed to infiltrate some of his operational ideas.

By way of introducing the logical criteria for the manual's examination, Lind discloses the operational aspirations constituting the conceptual framework of the Active Defence doctrine, namely, a manoeuvre approach based upon linear defensive tactics, initiating an integral battle of destruction, and thus attaining strategic decision under conditions of quantitative inferiority.[84]

Proposing a series of penetrating questions anchored in the logic of system thinking, Lind endeavoured to prove the incoherence of these aspirations, likewise indicating the paradoxical nature of the manual. By repudiating the operational rationale of the Active Defence doctrine he intended also to revoke formally the traditional 'can do' approach as an indoctrinating means guaranteeing success.[85]

Basing himself on the prevailing strategic situation in Central Europe, Lind identified the other conceptual source of the 'fight out-numbered and win' statement in the premise linking the rise of modern weapons' lethality to the supremacy of the defensive. Through his brief exploration of Soviet military experience, Lind demonstrated that whenever the application of a modern weapon system had been guided by operational logic of disruption rather than by tactical logic of destruction, it served both offensive and defensive with the same degree of effectiveness. Thus, he rejects the premise which was based on an amateurish study of the 1973 Middle East experience. Moreover, the unfolding of the Egyptian operational method, which integrated tactical defensive weapon systems in the offensive, is used by Lind to illustrate the existing homeostasis or interchangeability between the two basic forms of manoeuvre.[86]

Rejecting the first assumption of the Active Defence doctrine, Lind thus manages both to shatter the manual's entire frame of reference, and to prove the vanity of the 'can do' approach.[87] Moreover, he dismisses out of hand the American myth that superior technology can either compensate for inferiority in masses or be a substitute for the lack of operational insight.[88]

Lind then initiates the invalidation of the 'win the first battle' premise by proposing a pair of questions reflecting both a broad and critical understanding of history and a thorough perception of the nature of modern manoeuvring systems. In the first question he doubts the ability of this premise to cancel *ab initio* the option of a subsequent engagement. Secondly, assuming that a second battle would indeed occur, where would, then, the principle of mechanical concentration, which is listed by the manual as the most essential condition for victory in the first battle, lead the American defender?[89]

The discussion centring on the argument of the first battle served Lind not only for the purpose of manifesting the manual's inherent discrepancies. Pursuing the opportunity created by his method of argumentation in favour of displaying the principles of Soviet deep operations, he illuminates the connection between manoeuvre, successive operations, echeloning, depth and momentum. And since the idea of hierarchical synergy between a holding element and a striking element has already been disclosed, he concludes the examination of the second premise by proving that the tactical concentration aiming to decide the first battle does not provide an appropriate solution to the operational challenge posed by the Soviet method of manoeuvre, but in fact plays into its hands.[90]

Explaining that a deliberate interaction between attrition and manoeuvre constitutes a fundamental of modern operations he starts clarifying the third issue.[91] When later in the course of the discussion he introduces the operational manoeuvre as the means for accomplishing strategic objectives, he offers the notion of disruption, or the Soviet version of operational shock, as its rationale.[92] And since he assumes that the only role of attrition is to produce opportunities for the application of the main strike by fixing the opponent and wearing him down, he attributes its conceptual roots to destruction deriving from fighting *per se*.[93]

Hence, by comparing the 1968 *FM 100-5* with that of 1976, Lind proves that the tactical paradigm of destruction dominated the perceptions which guided the authors of the Active Defence doctrine. Finally, along with his utter rejection of the idea of destruction, he suggests the Soviet ideas of trend of the main strike, momentum and fragmentation as a basis for formulating a theory of a real operational manoeuvre.[94]

Since the design of the mechanical patterns of action occupying most of the 1976 operations manual was not preceded by a tendentious formulation of a more general conception of operations, Lind claims in the concluding part of his article that the tactics of Active Defence constituted an incoherent foresight, detached both from the operational reality and from the Soviet method of manoeuvre.

Lind proves that disregard of the dimension of depth, reflected both in a linear deployment of a forward defensive and in the abso-lute renunciation of reserves, forms a basic characteristic of the manual.[95] Aspiring to assemble mechanized formations from unengaged sectors against the opponent's identified main penetrating effort, the technique constituting the core of the active defence concept is perceived by Lind as a fallacy incapable of contending with a manoeuvring system combining a holding echelon and a strike echelon in succession.[96] By way of conclusion, he reveals the inconsistency of a tactical system aimed at providing effective defence, yet saddled with intrinsic deficiencies that can force it into a state of uncontrolled retreat, and thus deviate from the definitions laid down by the political authority.[97]

Lind does not blame the manual for discriminating against the offensive in favour of the defensive. He rather argues that lacking a broad concept of operations it tended to perceive the tactical defence as an independent pattern, capable of attaining the strategic objectives on its own. Therefore, ignoring basic principles like depth, simultaneous synergy and operational initiative, the Active Defence concept deprived the system both of its dynamic qualities and of the operational ability to attain its strategic goals.

Thus, the official historiography's presentation of the 'defence emphasis' as the prime subject, around which the entire debate centred, is somewhat simplistic.[98] This impression is strengthened whenever one examines the views pronounced by both schools participating in the debate. As a matter of fact, Lind's approach to the issue of defence generated two theoretical trends among the operational reformers which, between 1976 and 1983, concentrated either on criticizing directly the 1976 manual's concept of defence, or on formulating new defensive concepts that would lead ultimately to the crystallization of the operational theory.

Perceiving the complementary interaction between defensive and offensive as an essential condition for the development of a dynamic operation, one trend distinguished between both forms of manoeuvre by the difference in the dimensions of the strike and holding vectors.[99] Aiming to deprive the offensive system of its operational logic, the second trend proposed to integrate in the defensive the principles of interchangeability of forms of manoeuvre, hierarchical synergy among friendly forces and fragmentation of the enemy's operational cohesiveness, simultaneity, momentum, depth and initiative.[100]

The first to sense the operational connotations in Lind's criticism was Philip Karber – a leading analyst among the advocates of the 1976 manual. However, lacking any operational logic, Karber's swift counter-attack distorted Lind's arguments by detaching them from the broader theoretical context. Moreover, by accusing Lind of an unrealistic offensive perception, Karber's simplistic commentary contributed significantly to the fabrication of the phrase the 'defence emphasis' – an expression purporting to be the antithesis to the trends exercised by the manual's advocates.[101]

Karber's colleagues tended to anchor their academic judgement on the superiority of the defensive in the Clausewitzian anachronism. Thus, they idealized the unrealistic scenario of linear defensive by applying literally the essentials of the *Vernichtungsschlacht* to the conditions of the 1970s' European theatre.[102]

The 1976 manual's artificial attempt to integrate the various engagements through the employment of a linear configuration into a monolithic battle of defence is a result, according to Lind, of distorted tactical logic.[103] Being unaware of the operational logic suggested by Lind's critical arguments, the apologetic reactions initiated by the advocates of active defence fell short of realizing the manual's absurdities.

TRADOC's reply pretended to exchange the traditional strategy, which sought decision through a long and gradual process of deployment, for a more ambitious one, which endeavoured to destroy the enemy in a single battle.[104]

Presuming that a failure in the initial battle implied a strategic catastrophe for NATO, Philip Karber linked the operational logic of the first battle argument to the idea that a linear incorporation of friendly tactical entities would allow the allied armies to impose, in the course of this battle, a high rate of attrition on the adversary.[105]

Similarly, historian Archer Jones struck an anachronistic analogy between the tactical context of the eighteenth-century infantry linear battle and the 1970s operational context of the non-linear theatre and mechanized warfare.[106]

Fully aware of political sensitivities, Starry did not openly reject the need to win the first battle. On the contrary, he reinforced this argument. Yet, unlike the 1976 manual and its advocates, who sought to accomplish this objective through the application of a unidimensional, reactive defence, integrating tactical activities along a horizontal axis of operations, Starry ascribed the same consequence to a dynamic defensive manoeuvre, combining simultaneously offence and defence at the front and in depth, in order to disrupt the Soviet rationale of operations.[107]

The criticism initiated by the military reformers against the Active Defence Manual during the years 1981–83 must be seen as a crusade to legitimize the application of the Airland battle operational theory. Demonstrating the systemic vulnerabilities of the preceding doctrine they emphasized the unique logic of the 1982 manual, thus justifying both its formulation and adoption. Therefore, one should look at the later critical references on the subject of the first battle as an instrument for promoting the Airland battle concept, more than as an attempt to criticize Active Defence.[108]

The discrimination by the 1976 manual against mobility and in favour of firepower was instrumental to Lind. Employing this secondary issue as one example among many others for illustrating the addiction of the Active Defence concept to the paradigm of destruction, he determined its attritional nature, likewise indicating the bastardization of operational thought. Moreover, pursuing the issue of attrition versus manoeuvre, Lind suggests the idea of operational shock as a rationale for modern operation and the principles of fragmentation and momentum as practical methods for its application.[109] In other words, from Lind's point of view, the emphasis on firepower constituted a secondary issue within a broader discussion centring both on the logic of manoeuvre systems and on a method for assimilating attrition effectively in the framework of advanced operation.

It is not by chance that the attempt to answer the question whether the 1976 manual was oriented towards attrition or manoeuvre occupies such a central place in the debate. Regarding human life as almost a sacred value, in the era following the First World War, Western military thought viewed attrition as a plague that should be avoided through the exercise of creative manoeuvre. However, the confusion of philosophical and operational aspects when referring to the subjects of manoeuvre and attrition emphasized the existing conceptual gap between the contending schools. On the one hand, repelled by the moral implications of the notion of attrition, the advocates of Active Defence weighed manoeuvre in terms of technology or firepower. On the other hand, the operational reformers, who perceived manoeuvre as the essence of any operational occurrence, strove to augment it by employing attrition instrumentally.

In his reply to Lind, Karber introduces a somewhat rhetorical question: Are not the proliferation and increase in the lethality of the present defensive oriented anti-tank weapon systems a clear indication of the triumph of firepower over manoeuvre?[110] Thus, apart from making an erroneous differentiation between tactical firepower and the broader aspects of operational manoeuvre, Karber manages likewise to provide the official historiographer with the phrase for yet another of the debate's topics.

In order to prove the presence of a manoeuvre approach in the very nature of the 1976 manual, TRADOC's reply confirms that Lind's main message has been indeed understood by the establishment.[111] The problem was that at that stage only few among the TRADOC community were aware of the operational implications of Lind's thought.

Since the main consideration in the composition of the official historiography has been diachronic and not a matter of perception, it did not mention among the list of the debate topics certain subjects implied by the operational theory, despite the fact that some of them provided ample material for discussion for both schools. The most prominent among these subjects is the idea of depth.

Lind opens the discussion on the mechanical aspects of manoeuvre by introducing the idea of depth. He argues that depth provides the area in which the operational manoeuvre unfolds, be it offensive or defensive. Therefore, the calculated control of depth reflects both the friendly system's ability to conduct a volitional manoeuvre, and its capacity to deprive that viability from the rival system. Assuming that manoeuvre forms the door to operational shock, one can legitimately deduce that depth constitutes the key to that door.[112] Employing this method of reasoning, Lind determines that the Active Defence doctrine lacks the logic of manoeuvre, and therefore the tactical concepts suggested by the manual are incoherent.

The rejection of reserves, which has been presented by the Active Defence doctrine as a compulsion more than a principle, serves Lind as evidence indicating both absolute disregard for the depth factor, and a complete distortion of fundamental tactical logic.[113] Therefore, more than asserting a negative posture on the issue of reserves, the manual produces confusion among its readers concerning operational conduct.

The consequences of this confusion can be understood from the views expressed by Karber and Archer Jones. Whereas the former accuses Lind of 'thinking linear' when suggesting the 'two forward one reserve' pattern of deployment, he presents his own oblong unidimensional pattern of 'absolute deployment and engagement forward' as a dynamic formula expressing depth.[114] Relying on the eighteenth-century tactical experience, which regarded any musket not invested in the firing line as a waste, Archer Jones argued that maintaining reserves in the mechanized conditions of the NATO defensive was unnecessary and harmful.[115]

Constituting the first scientific attempt to compare the Active Defence concept with the operational approach, the research conducted by the officers Bryla, Lancaster, and Rennagel, attributed the cognitive source for the disregard of depth to the strategic limitations imposed by the German Federal Government on NATO's operational planners.[116] Moreover, this research showed that the reason behind the adoption of a linear approach was not a shortage in forces and resources, as claimed by Starry, but rather a simplified interpretation of the political echelon's directives into mechanical language of tactical patterns.[117]

The analyst Steven Canby, too, identified the same political circumstances which obliged NATO to apply the cordon defence.[118] Nevertheless, understanding that rejection of depth and reserves implied an erosion of the operational ability to manoeuvre, he suggested a substitute concept for creating dynamic options for manoeuvre in depth by the integration of heavy and light forces.[119]

270

Prior to the emergence of Lind's criticism, the issue of depth had never carried any significant weight in America's military thought. Therefore, it is most likely that it was his writing which aroused professional consciousness in that direction. The perception of the Soviet offensive manoeuvre in terms of a depth-oriented echeloned system indicated the first evidence for this conceptual shift. A thorough study of the Soviet method of deep manoeuvre induced Starry, as a pioneer of operational thinking in the United States Army, to develop a preemptive approach, aimed at neutralizing the rationale of the rival manoeuvring system.[120] From here, Starry and his subordinates turned to developing those principles which comprise the essence of the operational theory. Their discussion of manoeuvre, both in physical and systemic terms of depth, revealed to the Americans for the first time the province of operational sensitivity, that is, the province through which one could deprive offensive and defensive manoeuvring systems of their ability to attain strategic goals.[121] Linking depth to the echeloned mode of operation and to operational shock led almost inevitably to identifying the acute requirement for simultaneity.[122] At this specific point, accelerated by Starry's intellectual generation, American military thought ascended to new heights of abstraction. The simultaneous operation along the rival system's entire depth brought forth the principle of initiative, which in its turn, illuminated the operational idea of synergy or synergy deprivation by means of fragmentation.[123] And finally, the combination of various operational elements, manoeuvring simultaneously along different fields of time and space, emphasized both the principle of momentum and the need for synchronization.[124]

Since at that stage the reformers focused the discussion on the operational aspects of the idea of depth, the opposition became taciturn, and the debate turned to a unilateral spectacle serving exclusively the promotion of the operational theory. However, had it not been for the criticism of the 1976 manual's disregard for the principle of depth, it is doubtful whether the chain of conceptual evolution which led the reformers ultimately to formulate the theory of operational manoeuvre in the shape of the four tenets, could have materialized at all.[125]

Lind's thorough treatment of the Soviet method of manoeuvre, both in the general context of studying operational problems, and in the narrower context of proving the futility of the Active Defence concept, raised that issue high on the debate's agenda. For the advocates of the 1976 manual, the analysis of the Soviet method of manoeuvre became the main platform upon which the confirmation of its coherency could be reconstructed. Their basic line of defence assumed that the most effective methodology for establishing the validity of Active Defence lay not in a presentation of arguments anchored in abstract theories, but rather in the proposition of concrete scenarios of action. Thus, by bringing the discussion to a practical level they managed to form a safe base upon which they could compete with their rivals on equal terms. Moreover, the fact that the leading figures among the advocates of Active Defence were already involved as civilians in intelligence research of Soviet operational methods, afforded them an advantage against their rivals, who were attracting an increasing number of officers to their ranks at that stage. Thus, bringing the debate to its climax in matters such as the extent of literary activity and the level of ardour, the issue of interpreting the Soviet method of manoeuvre reflected the extreme polarity between the approaches of both schools.

Examining the Soviet theory of manoeuvre from an operational perspective, the school of reformers used it as a model for the study of modern operations, as a basis for the formulation of the Airland Battle doctrine, and also as an instrument for demonstrating the distorted logic of the Active Defence concept. On the other hand, to reinforce the authenticity of the tactical patterns suggested by the 1976 manual, the school of Active Defence advocates viewed the Soviet breakthrough manoeuvre from a narrow, mechanistic angle. The controversy over the issue of the Soviet manoeuvre concept did not, as TRADOC's official history claimed, centre on the simple question of the degree to which it derived from Second World War experience.[126] In fact, the manner in which both schools interpreted the Soviet concept of operations constituted a mirror image of their approach to what should have been the American method of manoeuvre. Clear evidence for this argument can be found in Philip Karber's works.

While in his various investigations concerning the Soviet concept of manoeuvre Karber introduces a method of operations which differed categorically from the one presented by the manual, his approach to the subject identifies in many respects with that view. In essence, Karber argues that in the course of 1973–76, the Soviet theory of manoeuvre experienced a conceptual revolution which derived both from tactical lessons of the 1973 Middle East war and from the realization of the formidable increase in the lethality of anti-tank weapons.[127] Nevertheless, assuming that both the formulation of the 1976 US Army manual and the transformation of the Soviet military doctrine had identical roots, Karber fails to explain how the same initial logic led in the former case to the adoption of a defensive approach, whereas in the latter it led to the application of a highly offensive one.[128]

Since it was based on an uncritical study of translated technical essays selected from the tactical journal *Voennyi vestnik*, the essence of Karber's analysis made the following predication: the main consideration which led the Russians to transform their operational method from a mode of echeloned contracted heavy-armoured breakthrough manoeuvre, to pre-emptive multi-pronged linear attack, conducted by armour-reinforced BMP regiments along the entire battle front, stemmed from their concern over the susceptibility of the infantry fighting vehicle (IFV/BMP) to the threat of anti-tank weapons.[129]

Lacking a systematic basis of historical research, Karber's thesis sometimes leads to speculative assertions, bordering on the absurd. Karber completely ignores the fact that during the second half of the 1960s, a conceptual renaissance occurred in the Soviet Union, in the course of which the 1930s' Deep Operation theory was readopted almost to the letter. Moreover, he fails to realize that this operational renaissance provided the mental and technological framework for the development of the tactical concepts and weapon systems which were later employed so successfully in the 1973 Middle East war. In other words, whereas the Americans were astounded by the quantitative and tactical aspects of armoured warfare, as revealed in the 1973 War, for the Russians, this same event constituted an empirical laboratory confirming the validity of the concepts they had developed in the course of the late 1960s. And finally, Karber fails to notice that both the wide deployment of anti-tank weapons in the infantry formations, and the concept of the infantry fighting vehicle as a platform expressing the quality of tactical synergy at its best, were initiated by the Russians in the course of that renaissance.[130]

Since he spent no time in exploring the fundamentals of the Deep Operation theory, Karber misinterpreted the term *smelyi reid*, connoting a daring raid performed by a junior tactical unit, the size of a battalion or regiment (*podrazdelenie, chast'*) for an operational idea implying a daring thrust. Moreover, he tends to attribute to the Russians certain trends contradicting the nature of their operational thinking such as an attempt to solve strategic problems by means of tactical patterns, or an inclination towards applying a linear manoeuvre at the operational level.[131]

Comprising talented scholars like C. Donnelly, P. Vigor, C.J. Dick, and John Erickson, the British research group, concentrated in the Centre for Soviet Studies in the Royal Military Academy, Sandhurst, exercised great impact on the perception of Soviet operational theory held by the American school of reformers.[132] Being far ahead of their American colleagues in the study of Soviet deep operations, the British analysts managed to illuminate essential issues such as echeloning, operational breakthrough, simultaneous deep strike, momentum, deception and surprise.[133] Moreover, aware of the conditions characterizing the Central European theatre, they managed to translate the abstract principles of the Deep Operation theory into operational scenarios understood by the military planner.

The organizational form and the patterns of work that were developed by the British group later served their American counterparts as a model for both the establishment of the Soviet Army Study Office (SASO) in Fort Leavenworth, and the training of a talented generation of analysts who successfully researched Soviet operational theory.

Steven Canby pioneered the systemic research of Soviet theory of operations in America. In a study he conducted for the International Institute for Strategic Studies in London in 1974, he identified the operational fundamentals of the Soviet theory of manoeuvre: operational shock as a consequential effect expressing the inability of the beaten system to function effectively; the sequence of operations developing in the direction of the rival system's depth by combining the actions of holding and striking echelons; and the integration of mechanical and cognitive activities within the scope of the operational manoeuvre.[134]

Since his approach to the Soviet theory of operations was initially characterized by system thinking, Canby was able to contribute to the debate in three respects. Firstly, he bequeathed to both his civilian reformer colleagues and to military commanders of the European theatre the exact essence of the Soviet theory of operations.[135] He provided the members of the reform school with cognitive tools for criticizing the Active Defence concept both in the fields of interpreting the Soviet method of manoeuvre and the tactics of defence.[136] Thirdly, he developed and promoted the concept of light forces as an operational element allowing both the application of simultaneity and new values of mobility within a new method of defence.[137]

Introducing the Soviet method of manoeuvre in the light of operational criticism, Canby's perception generated a polemic within the armed forces. The reformer officers charged that the 1976 manual presented an archaic and simplistic interpretation of the theory of manoeuvre in depth. The detachment of the theory from the Soviet theory of operations and from the strategic reality, they argued, had resulted in the formulation of a distorted doctrine, which could lead to severe operational failure.[138]

The publication of Starry's revolutionary article in 1981 reveals the level of maturity acquired by American military thought under the

274

influence of Lind and Canby. The article confirms that the evolving American operational theory derived, in more than one respect, from a thorough study of Soviet concepts. In addition, Starry perceives the combined action of holding and strike echelons as the essence of the Soviet method of operational manoeuvre. Drawing the defensive into an over-inclined forward posture, and decimating its fighting mass, the holding echelon, which is composed of all-arms formations, intends to produce the operational conditions for the eventuation of the deep strike. Relying on the achievements of the holding echelon, the strike echelon aims to convey into the defensive rear an armoured mass, and thus bring about its inversion. In other words, in the effect of momentum, which results from the sequential action, combining both operational echelons, Starry identifies the essential condition for the materialization of operational shock. Therefore, through the application of a simultaneous manoeuvre, integrating the initial decimation of the rival's strike mass, in depth, with the containment of his breakthrough echelon at the front, Starry intends to disrupt the sequence of enemy operations, impair its momentum, and undermine its offensive rationale.[139]

The voluminous work produced by the operational reformers in the course of 1979–83 unanimously endorsed Starry's interpretation of the Soviet method of manoeuvre. Adopting this approach, the reformers employed it as a central argument for rejecting the Active Defence concept and reinforcing the Airland Battle doctrine, at the same time.[140]

In autumn 1982 the opposition to the operational reform mounted a desperate rearguard action. They raised questions which cast doubt on the recent interpretation of the deep operations manoeuvre, in order to impede the assimilation of the new Airland Battle doctrine. Both T.N. Depuy, and M. Stewart argued that if the Soviet rival was capable of defeating the NATO defensive only on the basis of the leading operational echelon attacking, the following echelon became entirely insignificant. Pursuing this line of reasoning, both analysts pushed their argument to the limits of the absurd when they claimed that if NATO was strong enough to stop the first echelon from breaking through, it would indubitably jeopardize this ability if it assigned troops and resources for the engagement of the second echelon.[141]

The most intensive debate in the history of American military thought centred, in the final analysis, on the painful and complicated process of shifting from an archaic paradigm to a more competent one, capable of competing successfully with the challenges posed by the changing strategic reality. What commenced as a cognitive crisis initiated by Lind's critical attack on the 1976 manual, developed into a deep and penetrating discussion which led to the evolution of the Airland Battle doctrine. Leading this unique process along its various stages, Starry identified in the debate a vehicle for generating creative military thought and maintaining its virility. Therefore, he institutionalized the dynamism of self-criticism as a positive instrument for constant progression – a trend that would prove its effectiveness in the future transition from the manual of 1982 to the more advanced one of 1986.

NOTES

1. L.D. Holder, 'A New Day for Operational Art', in R.L. Allen (ed.), *Operational Level of War – Its Art*, US Army War College (Carlisle Barracks, PA, Aug. 1985), pp. 4-1, 4-2.
2. D.A. Starry, 'A Tactical Evolution – FM 100-5', *Military Review*, 8 (1978), pp. 3, 10; 'To Change an Army', *Military Review*, 3 (1983), pp. 22–3, 26, 27; A.W. Chapman, *The Army's Training Revolution 1973–1990, An Overview*, TRADOC Historical Study Series (Fort Monroe, VA, 1991), pp. 1, 3–4, 11, 47; J.C. Romjue, 'Airland Battle: The Historical Background', *Military Review*, 3 (1986), pp. 52–4; L.D. Holder, 'Doctrinal Developments 1975–1985', *Military Review*, 5 (1985), pp. 50–52. All the above-cited references consider the evolution of the operational doctrine to be a systematic, continual process which started in 1973 with the withdrawal from Vietnam and the establishment of TRADOC in July of the same year.
3. Chapman, *The Army's Training Revolution*, pp. 1, 4, 5; J.L. Romjue, *From Active Defense to Airland Battle: The Development of Army Doctrine 1973–1982*, US Training and Doctrine Command (Fort Monroe, VA, 1984), pp. 1–2.
4. H.G. Summers, *On Strategy: A Critical Analysis of the Vietnam War* (Novato, CA, 1982), p. XIII; B. Palmer, *The 25 Year War – America's Military Role in Vietnam* (Kentucky, 1984), pp. 46–7; Romjue, *From Active Defense to Airland Battle*, pp. 2–3; Starry, 'A Tactical Evolution', pp. 3–4; idem, 'To Change an Army', p. 24; H. Wass de Czege, 'Toward a New American Approach to Warfare', in W.P. Franz (ed.), *The Art of War Quarterly*, US Army War College, Carlisle Barracks, PA, II (Sept. 1983), pp. 43, 50.
5. D.A. Starry, 'Operational Concepts and Doctrine', *Commander's Notes No. 3*, Headquarters, TRADOC, Fort Monroe, VA (20 Feb. 1979), pp. 1–5; Starry, 'To Change an Army', pp. 22–3, 25–6; D.R. Morelli and M.M. Ferguson, 'Low Intensity Conflict: An Operational Perspective', *Military Review*, 11 (1984), p. 3; Romjue, *From Active Defense to Airland Battle*, p. 23; idem, 'Airland Battle: The Historical Background', p. 52.
6. Department of the Navy, Headquarters Marine Corps, *FMFM 1 Warfighting* (Washington DC, 6 March 1989), pp. 28–9; J.M. Oseth, 'An Overview of the Reform Debate', in A.A. Clark, *et al.* (eds.), *The Defense Reform Debate, Issues and Analysis* (Baltimore, 1984), pp. 45–8.
7. M. Howard, 'Military Science in the Age of Peace', *RUSI Journal*, 1 (1974), p. 4, argues that the combined activity of both military and civilian theoreticians is essential for the dynamic development of modern military thought: 'Navigation by dead reckoning in an age of peace requires a cooperative effort between the military professional and the occasional outstanding thinker who can short circuit the patient studies of the professionals.'
8. G. Hart, with W. Lind, *America Can Win, the Case for Military Reform* (Bethesda, MD, 1986), pp. 4–11; J.J. Fialka, 'Matters of Defense: Congressional Military Reform Caucus Lacks a Budget but Has Power to Provoke the Pentagon', *The Wall Street Journal*, 13 April 1982, p. 52; N. Gingrich and J.W. Reed, 'Guiding the Reform Impulse', in Clark *et al.*, *The Defense Reform Debate*, pp. 33–4; R.K. Betts, 'Dubious Reform: Strategic versus Managerialism', ibid., pp. 67–8; H. Wass de Czege, 'Army Doctrinal Reform', ibid., p. 102; W.S. Lind, 'Defense Reform: A Reappraisal', ibid., p. 49.

9. W.E. Depuy, 'The Case for Synchronization, Toward a Balanced Doctrine', in R.L. Allen (ed.), *Operational Level of War – Its Art* (special text) (Carlisle Barracks, PA, Aug. 1985), p. 5–114, mentions explicitly the group of young officers who led the conceptual reform that led to the application of the operational manoeuvre doctrine; Starry, 'To Change an Army', p. 26, refers to a group of creative officers, who led the conceptual change and formulated the new operational theory as 'reformers'; Hart, *America Can Win*, pp. 11–12, refers to the group of military reformers as the: 'uniformed reformers'.

10. D.R. Palmer, *Summons to the Trumpet: US–Vietnam in Perspective* (San Raphael, CA, 1978), pp. 103, 110, 254; M.D. Taylor, *Precarious Security* (New York, 1976), p. 48.

11. R.F. Weigley, *The American Way of War: A History of the United States Strategy and Policy* (New York, 1973), p. 418; H. Kissinger, *The White House Years* (Boston, 1979), pp. 34–6, 238, 276; H.W. Baldwin, *Strategy for Tomorrow* (New York, 1970), pp. 13–15; R. Haas, 'Congressional Power: Implications for American Security Policy', *Adelphi Papers* 153 (1979), p. 16; G. Palmer, *The MacNamara Strategy and the Vietnam War: Program Budgeting in the Pentagon 1960–1968* (Westport, CT, 1978), pp. 99–100; W.C. Westmoreland, *A Soldier Reports* (New York, 1976), p. 57; D. Kinkaid, *The War Managers* (New England University Press, 1977), p. 25. H. Ngoc Lung, *Strategy and Tactics* (Washington, DC: US Center of Military History, 1980), p. 71; Palmer, *Summons to the Trumpet*, pp. 75–6; H.Y. Schandler, *The Unmaking of the President: Lyndon Johnson and Vietnam* (Princeton, 1977), pp. 34–5; W.W. Momyer, *Air Power in Three Wars* (Washington, DC: USAF Office for History, 1978), p. 70; W.S. Thompson and D.D. Frizzell (eds), *The Lessons of Vietnam* (New York, 1977), p. 108; E.N. Luttwak, *The Pentagon and the Art of War* (New York, 1985), p. 32; L.E. Grinter and P.M. Dunn, *The American War in Vietnam: Lessons, Legacies, and Implications for Future Conflicts* (New York, 1987), pp. 139–48; D.M. Drew and D.M. Snow, *The Eagle's Talons: The American Experience in War* (Maxwell AFB, AL, 1988), pp. 381–4. J.L. Gaddis, *Strategies of Containment: A Critical Appraisal of Postwar American National Security Policy* (Oxford, 1982), pp. 238–71.

12. Thompson and Frizzell, *The Lessons of Vietnam*, p. 279; N.B. Hannah, 'Vietnam: Now We Know', in A.T. Bouscaren (ed.), *All Quiet on the Eastern Front* (New York, 1977), pp. 146, 149; C. Johnson, *Autopsy on People's War* (Berkeley, 1973), pp. 46–8; S.L. Stanton, *The Rise and Fall of an American Army: US Ground Forces in Vietnam 1965–1973* (Novato, CA, 1985), pp. 346–8; J.R. Galvin, 'The Continuing Validity of Flexible Response and Forward Defense', *RUSI Journal*, 2 (1988), pp. 5, 7, 8, 9; C.M. Minich, 'The Ultimate Deterrent', *Military Review*, 1 (1979), pp. 65–6.

13. Summers, *On Strategy*, pp. 63–4, 93; Luttwak, 'The Decline of American Military Leadership', *Parameters* 4 (1980), pp. 82–8; A.C. Enthoven and K.W. Smith, *How Much Is Enough: Shaping the Defense Program 1961–1969* (New York, 1971), pp. 89–92; US Department of the Army, *FM 100-5 Operations of Army Forces in the Field* (hereafter *FM 100-5 Operations)* (Washington, DC, Sept. 1968), p. 5-1.

14. United States Department of Defense, *Conduct of the Persian Gulf War: Final Report to Congress* (Washington, DC, April 1992), Vol. I, pp. 329–30.

15. Romjue, *From Active Defense to Airland Battle*, p. 3.

16. *FM 100-5 Operations*, July 1976, pp. 1-1, 1-2, 1-5; W.E. Depuy, 'The US Army: Are We Ready for the Future?', *Army*, 9 (1978), pp. 22–4; 'FM 100-5 Revisited' (editorial), *Army*, 11 (1980), pp. 12–14; W.E. Depuy, 'Letter to General F.C. Weyand', Headquarters TRADOC, Fort Monroe, VA, 18 Feb. 1976, p. 3; Starry, 'A Tactical Evolution', pp. 3, 4.

17. E.A. Bryla, M.S. Lancaster and W.C. Rennagel, *Contending Concepts: Tactics and Operational Art* (Newport, Center for Advanced Research, Naval War College, June 1979), pp. 33–4; Starry, 'To Change an Army', p. 25; Romjue, *From Active Defense to Airland Battle*, p. 5; A dynamic system for the formulation of operational military theory can be attained only through the combination, under one institutionalized roof, of three essential functions: research, teaching and writing. Moreover, all three functions must be performed by a unified group of specialists. The writing derives its conceptual basis from the research, and prior to its publication the raw theory must be tested, through lecturing in the General Staff and Command College. The officers and civilians who taught theory in Fort Leavenworth conducted their research within the Combat Studies Institute, which was located also in Leavenworth. Thus, the

deliberate transfer of the writing functionaries from Leavenworth to Fort Monroe severed the research and lecturing functions from the writing and therefore deprived the last function of a sound theoretical basis.

18. W.E. Depuy, 'Letter to TRADOC's Centers and School Commanders', Fort Monroe, 23 July 1974, p. 1; Starry, 'To Change an Army', p. 26; Bryla *et al.*, *Contending Concepts: Tactics and Operational Art*, pp. XXIII–XXIV, 34; Wass de Czege and Holder, 'The New FM 100-5', p. 53.

19. Romjue, *From Active Defense to Airland Battle*, pp. 13, 14–15; *FM 100-5*, 1976, pp. 1-2, 6-2, 13-6; R.A. Doughty, *The Evolution of US Army Tactical Doctrine 1946-1976* (Fort Leavenworth, Combat Studies Institute, 1979), p. 93, argues that the American policy-making system moulded the army's tactical doctrine in nearly a case by case/and *ad hoc* manner, which concentrated naturally on specific operational conditions induced by a concrete theatre of war. Thus, thinking basically in tactical terms implied by a specific theatre, the military theoreticians failed to produce a broad conceptual basis for universal action. This traditional trend, which was practised in the case of the 1976 field manual resulted in the recognized phenomenon that the American Army possessed the wrong operational concept for most of the strategic cases it confronted. R.P. Haffa, *Rational Methods, Prudent Choices: Planning US Forces* (Washington DC, 1988), p. 52, proves the absurdity of this line of logic, employing a convincing analysis based on the Lanchester Equation.

20. W.S. Lind, 'FM 100-5, Some Doctrinal Questions for the US Army', *Military Review* LVII, 3 (1977), pp. 54–5.

21. Bryla *et al.*, *Contending Concepts: Tactics and Operational Art*, p. 32.

22. Depuy, 'Letter to General Weyand', pp. 2–4.

23. Romjue, *From Active Defense to Airland Battle*, p. 6.

24. Depuy, 'Letter to TRADOC's Centres and Schools Commanders', p. 1.

25. Most of the theoretical activity that accompanied the formulation of the 1976 field manual was conducted in discussions or seminars initiated by TRADOC. These seminars concentrated exclusively on the techno-tactical aspects of operating company-sized units, and on the tactical issues implied by the operating of a mechanized-armoured battalion-sized combat team. The first of these sessions was conducted during 1–2 October 1974 in Fort Knox, and named Octoberfest. Comprising two and three star rank officers from TRADOC and FORSCOM, the seminar focused on two main issues: presentation of the technical lessons obtained from the research of the 1973 Israeli tactical experience, and designing methods for the application of these lessons in the new tactical doctrine in a manner that would suit the company-battery level, see: Depuy, 'Letter to General Weyand', p. 2. On 11–12 Dec. 1974, 30 April–2 May 1975, and 20–21 Nov. 1975, respectively, the TRADOC community conducted in Fort Hill concentrated seminars that intended to discuss the lessons of 1973, and decide upon a framework of tactical patterns for the company-battalion level, upon which the formulation of the new tactical doctrine could be based; see, Romjue, *From Active Defense to Airland Battle*, pp. 5, 116. In the course of April–Dec. 1975, both the 1st Cavalry Division and the 2nd Armoured Division tested the new tactical concepts in a series of manoeuvres conducted in Fort Hood, Texas. During 8–9 Nov. 1975 a seminar combining field and school commanders from TRADOC and FORSCOM took place with the intention of clarifying problems of mechanized-armoured warfare. 10–11 Dec. 1975 saw an assembly of army commanders, centring on clearing up last details before the publication of the new field manual. Finally, in the course of the last week of January 1976, a general gathering of company and battalion commanders approved the tactical patterns suggested by the new manual, see: Depuy, 'Letter to General Weyand', p. 3. Headquarters, Training and Doctrine Command, *Combined Arms Test Activity Historical Report, July 1975–Sept. 1976* (Fort Monroe, KS, 1976), pp. 46–7.

26. W.S. Lind, 'The Case for Maneuver Doctrine', in Clark *et al.*, *The Defense Reform Debate*, p. 88.

27. J.C. Studt (Colonel USMC), 'Forward', in W.S. Lind, *Maneuver Warfare Handbook* (Boulder, CO, 1985), p. XI.

28. Ibid.

29. Ibid., p. XII. The opinion expressed here by John Studt constitutes the formal

approach of the Marine Corps establishment which is manifested explicitly in *FMFM 1 Warfighting*, pp. 27–30.

30. Howard, 'Military Science in the Age of Peace', p. 4.
31. Studt, 'Forward', pp. XI–XII.
32. R. Taft, with W.S. Lind, 'White Paper on Defense: A Modern Military Strategy for the United States', in *The Congressional Record*, 25 March 1976, Vol. 22, No. 43; Hart, *America Can Win*, pp. XI–XI.
33. The reform movement included politicians such as Robert Taft, Gary Hart and Republican member of Congress from Virginia, G.W. Whitehurst. Attracting support in both houses from members of both parties, the Congressional Military Reform Caucus was established in 1981. The prominent reformers within the Defense Department were: Franklin C. 'Chuck' Spinney and A. Ernest Fitzgerald. The more notable civilian reformers provided by the defence establishment were: Dr. Jeffry Record – a specialist on defence issues and a former assistant to Senator Sam Nunn, Dina Rasor, Paul Hoven, Joe Burniece and also Dr. Richard Gabriel and Dr. Paul Savage from St. Anselm College. Within the armed forces the movement included a significant number of junior and medium rank officers, and also a number of officers with the rank of Admiral and General. 'Reform Caucus Challenges Pentagon Judgement', *Congressional Quarterly Weekly Report*, 17 April 1982, p. 867; J.W. Reed, 'Congress and Politics of Defense Reform', in Clark *et al.*, *The Defense Reform Debate*, pp. 242–3; A broader historical overview of the Defense Reform Caucus can be found in J. Record, 'The Military Reform Caucus', *Washington Quarterly*, 6 (Spring 1983), pp. 125–9.
34. Hart, *America Can Win*, pp. 4–5.
35. John Boyd, a retired Air Force Colonel, was in many respects the intellectual leader of the group. As a captain he developed the tactics constituting the basis for the Air Force approach toward air to air combat. Later, as a major, he developed the energy manoeuvrability theory of air combat, which quantified the characteristics of manoeuvre in a mode which served tacticians, aeronautical engineers and combat pilots, alike. The main theme of his unique thought is condensed in a briefing termed 'Patterns of Conflict'. This concept, sometimes referred to as the 'Boyd Cycle' (observation-orientation-decision-action – OODA) was developed on the basis of Boyd's thorough analysis of the air war in Korea, in which the Americans attained a 10:1 killing ratio, in relation to their rivals. Comprising the substance for a manoeuvre approach, Boyd applied this system in the mid-1970s to the field of ground manoeuvre. See also: D. Smith, 'The Roots and Future of Modern Day Military Reform', *Air University Review*, 9 (1985), p. 33. Graduating from West Point, Dr Steven Canby embarked on a military career – a course which he later decided to abandon, due to the fact that the Army rejected a revolutionary tactical manual for junior units, which he had composed. After completing a doctoral dissertation at Harvard, he worked for some time as a defence analyst for the Rand Corporation. Later his work centred on operational and tactical advice which he provided for NATO's military forces. Within the framework of this trend he interpreted the Soviet operational theory, and formulated with the *Bundeswehr* Generals Franz Uhle-Wettler and Franz-Joseph Schutze the concept of modern light infantry, see: F. Uhle-Wettler, *Gefechtsfeld Mitteleuropa, Gefahr der Übertechnisierung von Streitkraften* (Bonn, 1980); S. Canby, *Classic Light Infantry and the Defense of Europe* (Washington, DC, 1982). Norman Polmar is a specialist in naval affairs, both the theoretical and technological aspects. He participated in composing *Jane's Fighting Ships*, from 1967 to 1977, and contributed to *Guide to the Soviet Navy*. In the mid-1980s he was employed as adviser by the Defense Nuclear Agency and by the Office of the Secretary of Defense. Pierre Sprey came from the field of engineering and technology. In the late 1960s he led the planning of the A-10 design concept for the Office of the Secretary of Defense. Later, in combination with John Boyd he initiated the planning of the F-16. In the course of the 1970s he worked intensively on the improvement of the combat effectiveness of tanks, anti-tank weapons, air defence weapon systems, and APC. He strove to establish a rational linkage between weapons development and acquisition and their concepts of operating, and lobbied for the anchoring of the technological effort in a framework of operational theory.
36. J.R. Boyd, *Briefing on the Boyd Theory – Competitive-Observation-Decision-Action*

Cycles (Introduction by W. Lind), TRADOC, 1 Aug. 1978; idem, 'Patterns of Conflict', unpublished paper, Oct. 1980, pp. 33–4.

37. Lind, 'FM 100-5 Operations, Some Doctrinal Questions', p. 58; D.A. Starry, 'Extending the Battlefield', *Military Review* LXI, 3 (1981), p. 32; Wass de Czege, 'Toward a New American Approach to Warfare', p. 55; Wass de Czege and Holder, 'The New FM 100-5', pp. 58–9; J.A. Machos, 'Airland Battles or Airland Battle', *Military Review* LXIII, 7 (1983), p. 37; US Army, Training and Doctrine Command, *Airland Battle Doctrine*, briefing given by Major General M.G. Kelly at Fort Monroe, 7 Nov. 1983, pp. 47–8; US Army, TRADOC, Combined Arms Center, *Airland Battle* (special text prepared for the exclusive use of students of the Army War College) (Carlisle Barracks, PA, 29 Aug. 1983), pp. 54, 56; *FM 100-5 Operations*, 20 Aug. 1982, p. 2-1; Air Force Manual 1-1, *Basic Aerospace Doctrine of the United States Air Force* (Air Power Research Institute, Maxwell AFB, AL, 16 March 1984), pp. 3-3–3-4; *FM 100-5 Operations*, May 1986, pp. 132–3.

38. Boyd, 'Patterns of Conflict'; P. T. Devries, 'Maneuver and the Operational Level of War', *Military Review*, 2 (1983), pp. 17–19, 24–5; A.M. Coroalles, 'Maneuver to Win: A Realistic Alternative', *Military Review*, 9 (1981), p. 39; TRADOC, *Airland Battle Doctrine*, briefing given by Major General M.G. Kelly at Fort Monroe 7 Nov. 1983, p. 20; Combined Arms Center, *Airland Battle*, p. 58.

39. *FM 100-5 Operations*, 1982, pp. 2-2–2-3; 1986, pp. 14–18; Oseth, 'An Overview of the Reform Debate', p. 48.

40. Boyd, 'Patterns of Conflict'; Oseth, 'An Overview of the Reform Debate', p. 46.

41. Boyd's profound impact of bequeathing the operational notions of synchronization and centre of gravity can be recognized explicitly in the following references: G.K. Otis, (Commandant of TRADOC), 'The Airland Battle' (message to distribution), 23651, TRADOC, Headquarters, Fort Monroe, VA, Aug. 1981, p. 1; Combined Arms Center, Airland Battle, pp. 31, 33, 35, 62, 64; *FM 100-5 Operations*, 1982, p. 2-3; (1986), pp. 10, 15–16, 110, 179; US Command and General Staff College, *FC 100-11 Force Integration Corps/Division* (Fort Leavenworth, KS, July 1985), pp. 2-10–2-11; Headquarters, Department of the Army, *FM 90-2 Battlefield Deception* (Washington, DC, Oct. 1988), pp. 2-1, 2-4, 2-5, 2-9; *FMFM 1 Warfighting*, p. 29; Holder, 'A New Day for Operational Art', pp. 4-3, 4-4.

42. Boyd, 'Patterns of Conflict'; Lind, *Maneuver Warfare Handbook*, pp. 4–5, 6, 7, 13–14.

43. Ibid., pp. 15–24.

44. Deriving both from the need to conduct combined operations in the global context, and from the permanent constraint of fighting outnumbered, the openmindedness of the Marine Corps drove its leadership to pioneer the application of the ideas of Boyd and Lind. The close cooperation between the Marine Corps and the civilian reform group had, likewise, a personal dimension. Major General A. M. Gray, who commanded the 2nd Marine Division in the late 1970s voluntarily adopted the reformer's theory of manoeuvre warfare as the official doctrine of his formation, and made every effort to introduce it into the various schools and exercises. Later, when he became Commandant of the Marine Corps, he adopted the theory as the formal doctrine of the entire corps, and guaranteed its publication as *FMFM 1 Warfighting*. Naturally, the military nuclei supporting the civilian reformers developed from the start in the command and training centres of the armed forces. Being based on the highest echelon of command, one of these nuclei included senior officers like Air Force General David C. Jones, who served as Chairman of the Joint Chiefs of Staff in 1978–82, Army General P. E. Gorman, who served in the late 1970s as Assistant Chairman of the Joint Chiefs of Staff and later as Commander in Chief, Southern Command. Another nucleus, centred on the tutorial staff of the Military Academy, and comprised officers like A.A. Clark, T.W. Fagan, and J.M. Oseth. The third nucleus developed in the backyard of the Command and General Staff College, and included officers like L.D. Holder, and Huba Wass de Czege.

45. Lind, 'The Case for Maneuver Doctrine', pp. 89, 92.

46. Lind, *Maneuver Warfare Handbook*, pp. 23–4.

47. Ibid., p. 24.

48. Ibid., pp. 2, 49–51; W.S. Lind, 'Defense Reform: A Reappraisal', in Clark *et al.*, *The Defense Reform Debate*, p. 330, argued that civilian analysts and thinkers may provide

the armed forces with ideas and concepts. Yet, the development of a formal theory for operations remains the exclusive responsibility of the armed forces. Therefore, being enriched by civilian specialists' conceptual guidance, the actual operational theory should be formulated by those bound to implement it, in a dynamic process combining systematic research, empirical tests and writing.

49. Lind, *Maneuver Warfare Handbook*, pp. 7, 23–4.
50. Ibid., pp. 12–13, 42.
51. Ibid., pp. 23, 42, 47.
52. Ibid., pp. 24, 42–3; idem, 'Defense Reform: A Reappraisal', p. 331; Hart, *America Can Win*, pp. 4–5.
53. Lind, *Maneuver Warfare Theory*, pp. 5–8; idem 'Defense Reform: A Reappraisal', p. 330.
54. Lind, *Maneuver Warfare Handbook*, pp. 1–2, 23–4, 42, 71–2.
55. Ibid., pp. 12–13; idem 'The Case for Maneuver Doctrine', pp. 94–5. Borrowed from the experience of the *Wehrmacht*, these terms were not used in their traditional meaning but as titles representing deeper and more complex ideas than those conceived by the *Wehrmacht*.
56. Lind, *Maneuver Warfare Handbook*, pp. 1, 17–18, 20; idem, 'The Case for Maneuver Doctrine', pp. 89, 92. In both cases referred to in the note Lind employed the term *Schwerpunkt* not in the meaning of creating a tactical shock by assembling a high concentration of resources and fire in the break-in point but rather as an operational situation implying the complete disruption of the rival system.
57. Ibid., 93–5; idem, *Maneuver Warfare Handbook*, pp. 1, 5, 6, 9, 12, 18–22.
58. Ibid., p. 18.
59. Ibid., pp. 2, 18; idem, 'The Case for Maneuver Doctrine', p. 92.
60. Ibid., pp. 89, 93–4; idem, *Maneuver Warfare Handbook*, pp. 7, 9, 12–13, 22, 28–30, 42.
61. Ibid., pp. 7, 12–14.
62. Idem, 'The Case for Maneuver Doctrine', pp. 93, 96–7.
63. Ibid., p. 94; idem, *Maneuver Warfare Handbook*, p. 13.
64. *FM 100-5 Operations*, 1982, pp. 2-2, 2-5–2-7, 7-3–7-8; *FMFM 1 Warfighting*, pp. 61–5, 85. The Marine's manual not only reiterated accurately Lind's concepts but also pointed towards Boyd as the conceptual source of its command philosophy.
65. Lind, *Maneuver Warfare Handbook*, p. 18; idem, 'The Case for Maneuver Doctrine', p. 94.
66. Lind, *Maneuver Warfare Handbook*, pp. 20–21, 25, 28.
67. Ibid., p. 19; idem, 'The Case for Maneuver Doctrine', 89, 93–4.
68. Lind, *Maneuver Warfare Handbook*, pp. 19, 26–7, 31.
69. Ibid., p. 21.
70. Idem, 'The Case for Maneuver Doctrine', p. 89.
71. Idem, 'FM 100-5 Operations: Some Doctrinal Questions for the United States Army', *Military Review*, 3 (1977), pp. 54–65. The formal publication of Lind's article followed that of the field manual by six months. Nevertheless, the gist of Lind's critical article has been circulating in Army circles as early as the actual publication of the field manual. This fact can be learned from an editorial essay initiated by TRADOC, in September 1976, as a direct response to Lind's criticism, see: 'TRADOC's Reply', *Armed Forces Journal*, 9 (1976), p. 27; Romjue, *From Active Defense to Airland Battle*, pp. 13–14. As TRADOC's formal historian it seems only natural that Romjue attached little weight to the conceptual contribution yielded by Lind to the evolution of the Airland Battle doctrine. Nevertheless, in his historical monograph, which was entirely dedicated to TRADOC's endeavour to develop its operational doctrine, he could not avoid the admission that it was Lind's critical article which initiated the great professional debate.
72. R.E. Wagner, 'Active Defense and All That', pp. 4–5; Holder, 'Doctrinal Development 1976–1986', p. 51; Wass de Czege, 'Toward a New American Approach to Warfare', p. 51; Wass de Czege and Holder, 'The New FM 100-5', p. 53; Romjue, 'Airland Battle: The Historical Background', p. 53; Personal Interview with General D.A. Starry, Tel Aviv, 5 June 1994. The General confirmed that these doubts became apparent at the level of regiment and above in the course of manoeuvres he conducted with the V Corps in Germany at the end of 1976 and in early 1977.

73. P.A. Karber, 'Dynamic Doctrine for Dynamic Defense', *Armed Forces Journal*, 9 (1976), p. 28, referred to the publication of the 1976 field manual as a 'doctrinal renaissance'; D.G. Loomis, 'FM 100-5 Operations: A Review', *Military Review*, 3 (1977), pp. 66–9, defined the new manual as an essential stage in the evolution of American military strategic thought; Archer Jones, 'The New FM 100-5: A View from the Ivory Tower', *Military Review*, 2 (1978), pp. 27–36, noted that by reaffirming the principle of concentration, the new manual re-established the old truth of the defence's supremacy, and thus provided the Army with a relevant doctrinal basis. C.S. Gray, 'Force Planning, Political Guidance, and the Decision to Fight', *Military Review*, 4 (1978), pp. 5–16, referred to the new manual as 'an excellent new master operations manual for the army'.

74. Romjue, *From Active Defense to Airland Battle*, pp. 13–21.

75. Starry, 'A Tactical Evolution – FM 100-5', pp. 2–11. 'To Change an Army', p. 24; 'The Principles of War', *Military Review*, 9 (1981), pp. 2–4; Wass de Czege, 'Toward a New American Approach to Warfare', p. 35.

76. Wass de Czege, 'Army Doctrinal Reform', p. 106; Starry, 'A Tactical Evolution – FM 100-5', p. 2; W.G. Hanne, 'Airland Battle Doctrine Not Dogma', *Military Review*, 6 (1983), p. 18.

77. Romjue, *From Active Defense to Airland Battle*, pp. 13–21.

78. R.K. Betts, 'Dubious Reform: Strategism Versus Managerialism', in Clark *et al.*, *The Defense Reform Debate*, pp. 74–7. In spite of the fact that he criticizes the military reformers, the author identifies the roots of the debate as the application or rejection of the system approach to the field of operational manoeuvre.

79. Starry, 'The Principles of War', pp. 2–4; 'To Change an Army', pp. 25–6. A striking example reflecting Starry's positive approach can be found in his attitude to the issue of the principles of war. Realizing the unique importance of the principles of war as a critical framework for the construction of a coherent theory of war, there is no doubt that he identified their absence from the 1976 manual. Yet he never mentioned this deficiency even once. In 1978, he initiated the publication of *FM 100-1 The Army*, which included an appendix of the principles of war.

80. Starry, 'A Tactical Evolution FM 100-5', pp. 2, 5–6, 9, 11; 'A Perspective on American Military Thought', pp. 2, 8.

81. Starry, 'To Change an Army', p. 23.

82. Romjue, *From Active Defense to Airland Battle*, p. 13; Lind, 'FM 100-5 Some Doctrinal Questions', pp. 64–5 confirms this argument, leaving no doubt concerning the author's initial motives: 'In summary, it appears that there are serious questions which can be raised about the new doctrine. Some of these questions suggest that no examination of the possibility of reform is being undertaken in key areas such as the "can do" mentality and the adherence to an attrition/firepower rather than a manoeuvre doctrine. Other questions can be raised as to whether new assumptions, such as that the new battlefield technology works solely to the advantage of the defender, are fully justified. Still others suggest that the genuine change in some areas may be in the wrong direction: the proposed doctrine of "win the first battle" is a case in point. These questions must raise a serious doubt as to whether FM 100-5 and the basic doctrinal outlook FM 100-5 represents, constitute doctrinal progress.'

83. Ibid., pp. 54, 56; J.A. Barker, *Paradigms, the Business of Discovering the Future* (New York, 1993), p. 40, discusses the question: 'What kind of person is a paradigm shifter?' His definition exactly covers Lind's perceptional exploits.

84. Lind, 'FM 100-5 Some Doctrinal Questions', p. 54. In the introduction to his article Lind challenged the operational logic of the manual by proposing four aspects of criticism: fight outnumbered and win; win the first battle; attrition or manoeuvre doctrine; tactics.

85. Ibid., p. 56.

86. Ibid., p. 55.

87. Ibid.

88. Ibid., pp. 55–6.

89. When posing this question to representatives of the TRADOC community in the course of an official briefing, confusion prevailed, and the only answer Lind could get in return was: 'It is something of a Chinese fire drill at that point'.

90. Ibid., p. 57.
91. Ibid.
92. Ibid., pp. 58, 61.
93. Ibid., p. 58. Both R. Simpkin, *Race to the Swift* (Oxford, 1985), pp. 19–23, 93–115, and E.N. Luttwak, *Strategy: The Logic of War and Peace* (Cambridge, MA, 1987), p. 93, express the same idea.
94. Lind, 'FM 100-5 Some Doctrinal Questions', pp. 58–61.
95. Ibid., pp. 61–2, 64–5.
96. Ibid., pp. 62–4.
97. Ibid., pp. 62–5.
98. Romjue, *From Active Defense to Airland Battle*, pp. 14–15.
99. Wass de Czege, 'Toward a New American Approach to Warfare', pp. 51–2, 55; Starry, 'Extending the Battlefield', pp. 34–6, 38; Wass de Czege and Holder, 'The New FM 100-5', pp. 55, 61–63; J.M. Dubik, 'FM 100-5: Comparing the Operational Concept and Defense', *Military Review*, 12 (1982), pp. 13–14; TRADOC, *Airland Battle Doctrine* (Gen. Kelly's briefing), p. 36; Bryla *et al.*, *Contending Concepts Tactics and Operational Art*, pp. XVIII–XXIV; Doughty, *The Evolution of the Army Tactical Doctrine 1946–1976*, pp. 29, 33.
100. Wass de Czege, 'Army Doctrinal Reform', p. 101; 'Toward a New American Approach to Warfare', pp. 50–1; C.J. Tate and L.D. Holder, 'New Doctrine for the Defense', *Military Review*, 3 (1981), pp. 2–9; Wass de Czege and Holder, 'The New FM 100-5', pp. 53–4; J.C. Barbara and R.F. Brown, 'Deep Thrust on the Extended Battlefield', *Military Review*, 10 (1982), p. 22; Bryla *et al.*, *Contending Concepts Tactics and Operational Art*, pp. XXIV, 32; B.R. Mccaffrey, 'Infantry on the High Intensity Battlefield of Central Europe', *Military Review*, 1 (1978), pp. 3–6; R.H. Sinnereich, 'Tactical Doctrine or Dogma', *Army*, 9 (1979), pp. 16–19.
101. P. A. Karber, 'Dynamic Doctrine for Dynamic Defense', *Armed Forces Journal* (Oct. 1976), p. 29.
102. Archer Jones, 'The New FM 100-5: A View from the Ivory Tower', pp. 27, 30–31, 35–6; idem, 'FM 100-5: A View from the Ivory Tower', *Military Review*, 5 (1984), pp. 18–20. By providing an historical analysis based on the tactical experience of the 18th–19th centuries, Jones' first essay explicitly defended the linear approach of the active defence concept. In his more recent essay he accused the formulators of the Airland battle doctrine of abandoning the linear approach to the defensive; R.A. Doughty and L.D. Holder, 'Images of the Future Battlefield', *Military Review*, 1 (1978), pp. 56–9. Basing their arguments on Clausewitz' axiom, both authors claimed, in a somewhat naive manner, that in the foreseeable future, the defensive would overcome the offensive. Shortly afterwards, both Holder and Doughty became enthusiastic members of the operational school.
103. Lind, 'FM 100-5 Some Doctrinal Questions', pp. 61–5; *FM 100-5 Operations*, 1976, p. 1-1.
104. 'TRADOC's Reply', p. 27.
105. Karber, 'Dynamic Doctrine for Dynamic Defense', p. 29.
106. Jones, 'The New FM 100-5: A View from the Ivory Tower', 1978, pp. 34–6.
107. Starry, 'A Tactical Evolution – FM 100-5', pp. 5–6; 'Keynote Address', *Armor*, 4 (1978), pp. 32–3.
108. Wass de Czege, 'Toward a New American Approach to Warfare', p. 52; Wass de Czege and Holder, 'The New FM 100-5', pp. 54, 66.
109. Lind, 'FM 100-5 Some Doctrinal Questions', pp. 58, 60–1. The following references prove that Lind's ideas were accurately understood by the operational reformers already at that early stage: Doughty, *The Evolution of US Army Tactical Doctrine 1946–1976*, p. 43; Wass de Czege and Holder, 'The New FM 100-5', pp. 54, 67; J.S. Doerfel, 'The Operational Art of Airland Battle', *Military Review*, 5 (1982), p. 4; Barbara, and Brown, 'Deep Thrust on the Extended Battlefield', p. 22; D.A. Starry, 'Extending the Battlefield', *Military Review*, 3 (1981), pp. 32, 38, 45; Devries, 'Maneuver and the Operational Level of War', pp. 54–6; Miller, 'Winning Through Maneuver', p. 63; A.M. Coroalles, 'Implementing Maneuver Style of War', *Military Review*, 12 (1982), pp. 20, 21; J.T. Westwood, 'Maneuver: A Broadened Concept', *Military Review*, 3 (1983), pp. 15–17.

110. Karber, 'Dynamic Doctrine for Dynamic Defense', p. 29.
111. 'TRADOC's Reply', p. 27.
112. Lind, 'FM 100-5 Operations Some Doctrinal Questions', pp. 62–3.
113. *FM 100-5 Operations*, 1976, pp. 5-2, 5-3, 5-13–5-14, demonstrates the entire absurdity of its posture on tactics, its complete lack of operational thought, and some of its intrinsic paradoxes: 'In fact, the defender has every advantage but one – he does not have the initiative. To gain the initiative he must attack . . . A defender which spreads two brigades thinly across a wide area and holds one brigade in reserve for counter attack will be defeated by a breakthrough attack . . . If the active defense can maintain coherence along the line of the FEBA or in the tactical zone just behind it, the easier coordination on the flanks will be, and the more successful the total defense will be . . . Counter attacks should be conducted only when the gains to be achieved are worth the risks involved in surrendering the innate advantages of the defense.'
114. Karber, 'Dynamic Doctrine for Dynamic Defense', p. 29.
115. Jones, 'FM 100-5: A View from the Ivory Tower', 1978, pp. 34–6.
116. Bryla, *et al.*, *Contending Concepts – Tactics and Operational Art*, Vol. 1, p. 27.
117. Ibid., pp. 26–8; Starry, 'A Tactical Evolution – FM 100-5', p. 9.
118. Canby, 'Military Reform and the Art of War', in Clark, *The Defense Reform Debate*, pp. 128, 130–31, 137.
119. Ibid., pp. 130–36.
120. D.A. Starry, Personal Communication, 5 June 1994, Tel Aviv. 'Extending the Battlefield', pp. 34–5; Wass de Czege, and Holder, 'The New FM 100-5', pp. 53–4.
121. Ibid; TRADOC, *Airland Battle Doctrine* (Gen. Kelly's briefing), pp. 47–8; Richardson, 'Winning on the Extended Battlefield', pp. 35, 37, 41–2.
122. Wass de Czege and Holder, 'The New FM 100-5', pp. 54, 59–61; Starry, 'Extending the Battlefield', pp. 32, 33, 35, 38, 42; L.D. Holder, 'Maneuver in the Deep Battle', *Military Review*, 5 (1982), pp. 55, 57; Combined Arms Center, *Airland Battle*, p. 60.
123. Combined Arms Center, *Airland Battle*, pp. 57, 58; Starry, 'Extending the Battlefield', pp. 32, 33, 34, 35, 38, 39; Wass de Czege and Holder, 'The New FM 100-5', p. 55; T.A. Cardwell, 'One Step Beyond – Airland Battle Doctrine Not Dogma', p. 46; Report Number AV–AWC 82–036, *Command Structure for Theater Warfare: The Quest for Unity of Command*, p. 213. Department of the Army, *Field Manual (FM) 100-1 The Army*, p. 22; Department of the Air Force, *Air Force Manual (AFM) 1–1 Basic Aerospace Doctrine of the United States Air Force* (Air Power Research Institute, Maxwell AFB, AL, 16 March 1984), pp. 1-4v, 2-5, 2-6.
124. Dubik, 'FM 100-5: Comparing The Operational Concept and the Defense', p. 18; A.M. Coroalles, 'Maneuver to Win: A Realistic Alternative', p. 39; Starry, 'Extending the Battlefield', p. 34; Wass de Czege and Holder, 'The New FM 100-5', pp. 63–4.
125. Wass de Czege, 'Toward a New American Approach to Warfare', pp. 53–54; 'Army Doctrinal Reform', pp. 109–10; Wass de Czege and Holder, 'The New FM 100-5', pp. 55–6.
126. Romjue, *From Active Defense to Airland Battle*, p. 16.
127. P.A. Karber, 'Soviet Lessons of Middle East War', in 15th Annual Army Operations Research Symposium, *Army Research and Development*, Nov.–Dec. 1976, pp. 11–15; idem, 'The Tactical Revolution in Soviet Military Doctrine', *Military Review*, 11 (1977), pp. 83–5; 12 (1977), pp. 33–4; idem, *Daring Thrust – The Tactical Revolution in Soviet Doctrine*, BDM (Virginia, 1977), pp. 4, 6–13, 83–4.
128. Ibid., pp. 20–25, 27–29; idem, 'Anti Tank Weapons and the Future of Armor', *Armed Forces Journal*, 11 (1976), pp. 52–3; idem, 'Dynamic Doctrine for Dynamic Defense', pp. 27–9.
129. Karber, *Daring Thrust*, pp. 13–19; 'The Soviet Anti Tank Debate', *Military Review*, 11 (1976), pp. 67–76.
130. *Boevaia Mashina Pekhoty* (BMP/infantry fighting vehicle) is a concept expressing the quality of tactical synergy. By carrying a rifle squad, a 73mm smoothbore gun, a machine gun, and an anti-tank missile launcher, this light-armoured, tracked vehicle combined in a perfect balance, both the principles of mobility, firepower and protection, reflecting tactical manoeuvre, and the various qualities representing the principal combat arms of the ground forces. The Americans adopted this concept only with the development of the Bradley series of combat vehicles.

131. Notwithstanding the fact that he touches upon the issue of pre-emptive offensive, an idea rooted deep in the nature of the Soviet military thought, his manner of introducing the subject is entirely alien to the logic of deep operations.

132. Later, the close circle of British analysts has been joined by Richard Simpkin. Through his profound operational insight and unique analytical ability, Simpkin contributed significantly to the evolving American operational cognition.

133. C.N. Donnelly, 'The Soviet Concept of Desant', *RUSI Journal* 663 (Jan. 1971), pp. 52–3; idem, 'Soviet Reconnaissance', *RUSI Journal* 121 1 (1976), pp. 68–70; idem, 'The March in Soviet Tactical Doctrine', *RUSI Journal* 119, 3 (1974), pp. 77–90; idem, 'The Development of Soviet Military Doctrine', *International Defence Review* (hereafter *IDR*), 12 (1981), pp. 1593–6; idem, 'Operations in Enemy Rear, Soviet Doctrine and Tactics', *IDR*, 1 (1980), pp. 35–41; idem, 'Soviet Tactics for Overcoming NATO Anti Tank Defense', *IDR*, 6 (1978), pp. 1099–106; idem, 'Tactical Problems Facing the Soviet Army Recent Debates', *IDR*, 9 (1978), pp. 1405–7; idem, 'The Development of the Soviet Concept of Echeloning', *NATO Review*, 6 (1984), pp. 9–17; idem, 'The Soviet Operational Manoeuvre Group – A New Challenge to NATO', *IDR*, 9 (1982), pp. 1177–86; J. Erickson, 'Soviet Breakthrough Operations: Resources and Restraints', *RUSI Journal*, 9 (1976), pp. 74–9; idem, 'Some Developments in Soviet Tactical Aviation – *Frontovaia aviatsiia*', *RUSI Journal* 20, 3 (1975), pp. 70–72; idem, 'The Northern Theatre – TVD – Soviet Capabilities and Concepts', *RUSI Journal* 21, 4 (1976), pp. 16–17; P.H. Vigor, 'Soviet Reconnaissance', *RUSI Journal* (Dec. 1975), pp. 41–5; idem, 'Soviet Army Wave Attack Philosophy', *IDR*, 1 (1979), pp. 43–7; idem, 'Doubts and Difficulties Confronting a Would-be Soviet Attacker', *RUSI Journal* 125, 2 (1980), pp. 32–8.

134. S.L. Canby, *The Alliance and Europe: Part IV, Military Doctrine and Technology – Adelphi Papers* (The International Institute for Strategic Studies, London, 1974), p. 16.

135. Ibid.; Canby, 'NATO Reassessing the Conventional Wisdoms', *Survival*, 4 (1977), pp. 164–8; idem, 'Mutual Forces Reduction: A Military Perspective', *International Security* 2, 3 (1978), pp. 123–8.

136. S.L. Canby, *Defense Concepts and Short War Responses* (final report prepared for the assistant secretary of defence program analysis and evaluation) (Silver Springs, MD, 22 Sept. 1978), pp. 15–23; idem, 'NATO Defense: The Problem Is Not More Money', in R. Harkavy and E. Kolodjiez (eds), *American Security Policy Making* (Lexington, KY, 1980), pp. 85–99; idem, *NATO Corps Battle Tactics* (Washington, DC, 1978), pp. 8–17; idem, 'Military Reform and the Art of War', pp. 128, 131–4.

137. S.L. Canby, 'Territorial Defense in Central Europe', *Armed Forces and Society* (Fall, 1980), pp. 51–67; idem, *Classic Light Infantry and the Defense of Europe*.

138. G.F. Steger, 'More Dilemmas in Studying Soviet Tactics', *Military Review* LVIII, 2 (1978), pp. 88–91; G. Fontenot and M.D. Roberts, 'Plugging Holes and Mending Fences', *Infantry*, 5 (1978), pp. 32–6; D.K. Griffin, 'If the Soviets Don't Mass', *Military Review* LIX, 2 (1979), pp. 2–13; A. Carlson, 'A Revisionist's View', *Infantry*, 3 (1978), pp. 37–9.

139. Starry, 'Extending the Battlefield', pp. 31–50.

140. Wass de Czege, 'Toward a New American Approach to Warfare', p. 51; Wass de Czege and Holder, 'The New FM 100-5', pp. 52–4; Barbara and Brown, 'Deep Thrust on the Extended Battlefield', pp. 23–4; Bryla *et al.*, *Contending Concepts, Operational Art and Tactics*, pp. XXIII, 34; Holder, 'Maneuver in Deep Battle', p. 55; Doerfel, 'The Operational Art of Airland Battle', pp. 4–6, 8–9; Frantz, 'Maneuver: The Dynamic Element of War', pp. 4–5, 7; Hanne, 'Airland Battle Doctrine not Dogma', p. 18; R. Armstrong, 'Fighting the Threat: Advance Guard', *Armor*, 3 (1982), pp. 35–8; E.H. Cabaniss, 'Ground Soviet Tactics', *Military Review*, 12 (1979), pp. 37–45; J.H. Haynes, 'Patterns, Plain and Fancy', *Military Review*, 7 (1979), pp. 2–10; R. Peters, 'Attacking the Attacker', *Armor*, 3 (1983), pp. 31–3; C. Wertman, 'Attack – Soviet Style', *Marine Corps Gazette*, 7 (1982), pp. 46–9; G.R. Wright, 'The 20x20 Threat', *Infantry*, 2 (1981), pp. 15–17; W.P. Baxter, 'Soviet Communications Bare Bones but Secure', *Army*, 8 (1982), pp. 30–33; idem, 'Soviet Echelonment: Tactic for Depth and Flexibility', *Army*, 11 (1981), pp. 39–40; idem, 'Soviet Doctrine Responds to Anti-tank Missile Threat', *Army*, 6 (1980), pp. 29–32; idem, 'A Lesson in Tank Tactics – River Crossing Soviet Style', *Army*, 7 (1980), pp. 39–41; idem, 'What Ivan Knows about Us', *Army*, 5 (1980),

pp. 33–5; idem, Soviet Economy of Massed Fires', *Army*, 6 (1982), pp. 61–3; 'Soviet Exploitation of Western Technology and Military Art', *Military Review*, 7 (1983), pp. 41–53; D.M. Glantz, 'Soviet Operational Formation for Battle', *Military Review*, 2 (1983), pp. 2–12.

141. T.N. Depuy, 'The Soviet Second Echelon: Is This a Red Herring?', *Armed Forces Journal*, 8 (1982), pp. 60, 62–4; M. Stewart, 'Second Echelon Attack: Is the Debate Joined?', *Armed Forces Journal*, 9 (1982), p. 113.

8

From Central Battle to Airland Battle

THE CENTRAL BATTLE – AN INITIAL STEP INTO OPERATIONAL COGNITION

If it can be argued that it was the activity of the civilian reformers which ignited the cognitive crisis and set in motion the professional debate of the late 1970s, it is equally valid to argue that Starry's individual experience in commanding the V Corps in Germany constituted the first positive step in the development of the operational manoeuvre paradigm within the Army.[1] Leaving for his new field command equipped with the doubts raised by Lind's arguments and deeply impressed by the beginning of the debate, Starry's tenure in the V Corps was a period of incubation for his operational perception, during which the absurd concept of the First Battle was transformed into the operational concept of the Central Battle. He thus anchored the future doctrinal developments in the context of system thinking, and by doing so determined the methodological direction of the process.[2]

Thus it happened that with the appointment of Starry as the new head of TRADOC in July 1977, all the necessary conditions for the development of the operational theory matured. The ongoing debate paved the way for a change in perception. Having crystallized in Germany, Starry's systemic approach provided the operational content, while his methodological foresight determined the evolutionary direction for the process.

Notwithstanding the fact that the fundamentals of the Central Battle concept, unlike those of its predecessor, lay within the realm of system thinking, it would still be a mistake to view it as a theoretical framework for the conduct of operational manoeuvre. Developed by Starry and the V Corps' staff, this embryonic concept offered a variety of principles, terms and other cognitive tools by which to assess

287

operational as well as tactical capabilities in a corps manoeuvring system.[3]

In an address to American field commanders in July 1978 Starry referred to the complex of ideas comprising the conceptual skeleton of the Central Battle concept: the interaction between the front and depth as the main areas of activity and comprehension reflecting the entirety of the corps manoeuvre; the operational entity, as an inter-mediary level, which allowed a logical assemblage of various tactical activities into preconceived strategic ideas; the simultaneous integra-tion of the operations of the various elements combining the corps system as a basic condition for the achievement of synergetic results; the dynamic linkage between the levels of tactics and operations in terms of interaction between attrition and manoeuvre; the unique quality of operational command as a capability to combine the various elements of the system in a manner that would render syner-getic results; and finally, the principles of mass, momentum, succes-sive operations, and disruption as fundamentals of the Soviet method of manoeuvre.[4]

Basing the formulation of the concept on an analysis of 150 cases of armoured combat, both simulated and genuine, Starry and his colleagues in the V Corps determined scientifically, for the first time, quantitative criteria for the evaluation of the corps' fighting capability in areas such as: the dimensions of the corps' operational space, the duration of a corps operation, the unfolding pace of a modern corps operation, the scale of destruction that can be exchanged in the course of a corps-sized duel, and so on. Reflecting an unprecedented attempt to replace the archaic 1:3 force ratio magic formula, rooted in impressionistic convictions (a throwback to the mid-nineteenth century), with a systemic approach based on operational research, the quantitative conclusions of this unique study were assembled in the concept of battle calculus.[5]

In the conceptual laboratory of the V Corps, Starry visualized the tension resulting from the combination of activities governed by the random nature of actual combat, on the one hand, and the challenges of thought and management, implicit in the systemic nature of opera-tions, on the other.[6] Through the application of the Central Battle concept, Starry strove to render a conceptual as well as a structural framework which would allow the harmonization of random combat activities, initiated by tactical authorities, with the general logic of the operation. This was the first step in a broader trend aiming to correct the distortions of tactical particularism, that had been dictated by the active defence linear approach.

Nevertheless, the initial framework of the Central Battle concept lacked some of the dynamic elements characteristic of the operational manoeuvre. The operational implications of the idea of depth, from the defender's point of view, were fully realized once the concept of the Central Battle and the operational estimate of the Soviet echeloned manoeuvre were juxtaposed. At that point Starry and his staff appreciated, for the first time, the notion that the corps' manoeuvring room inherently comprises two dimensions of space, that is, front and depth, and two categories of operational time – the present and the future. Thus was born the concept of force generation centring on the need to convey deliberately offensive activity into the depth or rear of the attacking system, that is the area containing the force elements intended consequentially to exploit the success of the leading breakthrough echelon.

By redefining the corps' areas of operation, two correlating trends of study were in fact determined. The first concentrated on the analysis of the Central Battle's tactical aspects, and examined the issue of integrating the various fighting elements at the levels of battalion and brigade, with the intention of producing a true defensive capability within the area of the close-in battle. The second trend concerned the study of the force generation concept and focused on identifying needs and developing methods for the acquisition of an operational capability by which one could disrupt the attacking system and neutralize its logic.[7] In other words, through the application of a system approach, the Central Battle concept supported the tactical defence with operational logic. In itself, this achievement indicated a conceptual quantum leap from the concept of active defence. Yet, the road to the real intellectual breakthrough was paved by the force generation study.

Focusing the unique functions of the corps level in the province of the enemy's depth, the force generation study discovered new operational qualities in the manoeuvre in areas such as tempo, mobility, continuity and succession, fire, surveillance and coordination. Moreover, by linking the manoeuvre in depth to the notion of neutralizing the operational rationale of the rival system, it transformed the consciousness of the American senior military echelons from thinking in terms of branch organization and capabilities into abstract thinking in systemic terms.[8] And finally, despite the fact that both the force generation and Central Battle concepts focused on different areas of time, space, and fighting problems, the acute necessity to integrate them by means of simultaneous operations into a complete and harmonious manoeuvre was appreciated already at that early stage.

Starry identified the main reason for the failure of the 1976 manual as its lack of a theoretical framework based on operational perception.[9] This deficiency led not only to the application of an inconsistent doctrinal process based on distorted methodology, but also to the emergence of an incoherent tactical doctrine. Therefore, as soon as he assumed his new position as commandant of TRADOC, Starry made it clear that the application and successful assimilation of an operational doctrine constituted a basic condition for the four main challenges that confronted the Army: training the force and educating its commanders for modern warfare; developing and acquiring the appropriate technologies; restructuring the force to meet its global-wide missions; and operating the force successfully in the event of conflict.

One of the first steps initiated by Starry when assuming office was to assign to TRADOC's Chief of the Combat Development Analysis Directorate, A.G. Pokorny, the dual mission of developing, on the basis of the existing concepts of force generation and Central Battle, a framework for perceiving an operation, and engineering a methodology for a doctrinal process. Unlike his predecessor, whose interest focused on immediate problems, Starry set a time limit of eight years for the work of the analytical planners. Constituting a compromise between the inclination of the field tactical elements to concentrate on the immediate, and the tendency of academic researchers to predict the future, Starry's time definition provided a point of reference for the doctrine formulators, force designers and the engineers representing the various technologies.

In accordance with Starry's definition, the enterprise known as the Battlefield Development Plan (BDP) began by identifying the operational implications of the Central Battle and force generation concepts. The research group employed the multi-attribute utility modelling analytical method in order to perform the following functions: definition of the main capacities of the areas of depth and front; exploration of the qualitative differences between the close-in battle and the deep battle; suggestions for integrating both areas of interest into a unified operational manoeuvre.

By synthesizing the conceptions of the future battlefield and the Soviet method of manoeuvre, the battlefield development plan identified the operational opportunities presented by technology, while recommending preferred directions of development and priorities for acquisition. Moreover, the conclusions reached by BDP were swiftly transformed into a language of operational force designing. Setting the conceptual framework for the Army Study 86, BDP in fact determined the structure of the future light division, heavy division, the corps and the echelons above, and also the nature of their operation within an advanced manoeuvring system.[10]

Since the army already possessed a satisfactory conception for an advanced operation at the beginning of 1979, Starry sensed that the basic condition for generating the new doctrinal process had indeed materialized. Therefore, in an effort to guarantee favourable conditions for the continuation of the process, he published a policy document expressing his vision of the doctrine's future development.[11] Starry's basic assumption was that the operational thought, temporarily named Central Battle, would provide the theoretical framework for the development of terms, precepts and operational concepts in the future.[12] Through the selection and composition of these ideas into a systemic critical process, the future operational doctrine would be created, and this would serve as a theoretical derivative for a coherent tactical doctrine, a compatible organizational doctrine, a dynamic training doctrine, and a realistic policy of technological development.[13]

Defining the fundamental terms, operational concept and doctrine in the document, Starry introduced a uniform basis for thought and a common language, shared not only by a limited group of doctrine formulators within TRADOC, but by the entire professional community of the American armed forces.[14] The operational concept was defined as a universal tool, accessible to any unit, individual or authority in the armed forces, suggesting operational ideas which were not covered by the existing conceptual system. On the other hand, doctrine was specified as the unified set of operational notions or concepts that were tested critically and found to be coherent by the official authority.[15]

Starry encouraged creative independent thinking and dynamic production of operational ideas at all levels of the existing services and combat arms. At the same time he provided the system with the authority to judge and the tools to select and assemble the various concepts into a complete and logical doctrine. Since he managed both to maximize the circle of active participants contributing to the intellectual process and to maintain effective control in the hands of the central doctrinal authority, Starry struck a healthy balance between conflicting trends that tended to neutralize each other in the past.[16] In characterizing the dynamics of the constant process of doctrine development, Starry lays down three essential cornerstones. First, the formulation of operational concepts can be initiated by any field or staff echelon in the US armed forces or NATO, as a consequence of a threat, a mission, emerging technological opportunities, or a relevant historical context. Second, examining the concepts, articulating and integrating them within the net of ideas constituting the fabric upon which the complete doctrine is supposed to rest, should be conducted by TRADOC's Deputy Chief of Staff for Combat Development (DCSCD) through the various schools and centres, an integration centre and the Tactics Development Office (TDO). The final stage of writing the relevant doctrine must be performed by the Combined Arms Center, forming a part of the Department of Tactics (DTAC) in Fort Leavenworth.[17] Thus, between May 1979 and the summer of 1980, combining the lessons of the 1976 failure and Starry's systemic approach, the various organizations and patterns of work that would promise a smooth and coherent process of development were institutionalized.[18]

Another important lesson learned by Starry from the formulation of the 1976 field manual was that the spiritual fathers of the Active Defense concept failed to attain a broad consensus prior to its publication.[19] Seeking to win support for the operational philosophy, he practised a diverse constructive approach. From the start he presented his initiative as an evolutionary trend succeeding the achievements of his predecessor. By initially involving the various field echelons in the doctrinal process, he guaranteed their backing. By deliberately bringing together the highest echelon of command of both Army and Air Force to participate in the development of the new operational doctrine, he secured their endorsement of the process from the outset.[20]

THE INTEGRATED BATTLEFIELD – A DEEP
CONFIGURATION FOR OPERATIONAL SYNERGY

Apart from its being an intermediate evolutionary stage between the basic concept of the Central Battle and the advanced concept of the Extended Battlefield, the concept of the Integrated Battlefield merits mentioning because in the course of its formulation the close-in battle and the deep battle were integrated into a unified operational entity. Moreover, the substance of the Integrated Battlefield centred on the transformation of synergy among the elements of the manoeuvring system from a tactical context to an operational one. Finally, one of the concept's basic assumptions repudiated the prevailing convention among NATO members that one would not combine nuclear weapons with ground operations, unless forced to do so by the other side's initiative.

The delay in replacing the Central Battle concept with the more advanced Integrated Battlefield was caused by the revival of the interdiction idea in operational patterns. Considered the exclusive province of air forces, the interdiction traditionally derived its logic from two main sources: the attrition approach, which sought to impair the opponent's strategic capabilities, dictated a course of action depending on initial bombing of his logistic layout, command and control installations, lines of communication, deep reserves and other crucial resources.[21] On the other hand, by manipulating fire-power mobility, the preventive approach strove to isolate the battle-field and freeze the tactical situation.

Since it was conducted from an operational point of view, the renewed discussion approached the question of interdiction from different angles. Firstly, recognizing the echeloned structure of the Soviet operational manoeuvre, the revisionists of interdiction aspired to slow down its momentum, and thus bring about its disruption.[22] Secondly, with the crystallization of deep operations consciousness, Starry's disciples sought to exploit the operational mobility of the air force in order to acquire space for deep manoeuvre on the expanse of the opponent's territory, without violating the strategic limitations set by NATO's political echelons. And thirdly, by operating simul-taneously a deep oriented group of forces and a front oriented group-ing, Starry and his subordinates aimed at generating a new type of synergy, relating to the operational manoeuvre as a unified whole.

In other words, this was not the traditional approach to interdiction endeavouring to dispose the results of the tactical battle by exploiting the service of propelling firepower. Through the integration of various elements, differing in velocity, an attempt was made to generate operational initiative that would unfold a continuous manoeuvre from the opponent's depth to one's forward line of troops, and thus defeat the rationale of the attacking system.[23]

In the traditional interdiction approach the operation of the air force was meant to support the ground forces by preventing the aggressor from mechanically penetrating the defensive, but by adding an offensive dimension to the defence, the new approach aimed to exploit dynamically the intrinsic vulnerabilities in the Soviet method of manoeuvre, and thus confound the attacking system as a whole.[24] Therefore, the interdiction in its operational context should not be perceived as a responsive act supporting the mechanical effort of depriving the opponent of territorial gain, but rather as an attempt to harmonize the activities at the front and in depth into an integrated manoeuvre.[25]

Aiming to emphasize both the systemic connotations of the renewed employment of interdiction and the principle of synergism as a conceptual catalyst for the combination of additional elements in the operation, the new concept was named 'The Integrated Battle-field'.[26] In addition to the name given to the concept, the human composition of the research group indicates even further the theoretical objectives to which Starry aspired.[27]

The rationale of the Integrated Battlefield was to produce the synergetic effect of operational shock by means of a strike manoeuvre, and it centred on integrating simultaneously, along the entire depth of the Soviet system's offensive, an oriented echeloned configuration and a variety of elements such as heavy armoured forces, light forces, army aviation, tactical air forces, artillery assets, operational fire and nuclear weapons.[28] The threat of attacking the depth of the Soviet offensive layout with a nuclear tactical strike was intended, first and foremost, to force the opponent to increase the intervals between the various echelons. An opportunity would thus be created to effectuate a split between the breakthrough and strike echelons, to fracture the attacking system's operational cohesiveness, and break the continuity of the manoeuvre. Coinciding with the mechanized battle at the front, which required tactical mobility, the exploitation of such opportunities was initially assigned to forces characterized by operational mobility.[29] Therefore, it can be assumed correctly that the deliberate application of a vertical or columnar synergy aiming to fragment the rival system, constituted the basic principle of the integrated battlefield concept.[30]

Combining the simultaneous operation of the friendly system's various elements along the entire depth of the rival system, the Integrated Battlefield concept sought to neutralize the occurrence of the essential hierarchical interaction among the elements of the offensive, and thus impart to the defensive the rare qualities of a dynamic manoeuvre. Hence, exploiting the contrary aspects of the systemic synergy phenomenon, the principle of simultaneity aspired to augment the striking capability of the defensive system, whereas on the other side it aimed to bring the rival system into a state of paralysis.[31]

The third principle of the Integrated Battlefield concept centred on halting the attacking system's momentum. The initial projection of forces and fire into the depth of the aggressor's territory intended to provide the defensive with the operational time and conditions for the pulverization of the strike echelon's mass. Moreover, exploiting the effects of attrition yielded by a synchronized manoeuvre combining holding and striking elements, allowed the defender to interrupt the succession of the offensive, disrupt its momentum, and thus decide the operation in its own favour.[32]

Apart from elevating the conception of operational manoeuvre a further notch, the concept of the integrated battlefield accelerated the development of operational thinking in other areas as well. The attempt to synchronize the initiation of tactical nuclear weapons with the operational manoeuvre entrusted the field command echelons with higher responsibilities, thus shortening the lines of decision-making. Moreover, the combination of tactical weapons, both at the stages of planning and actual operations obliged the operational commanders to apply a holistic approach which perceived the operation in a broader strategic context rather than as a series of battles developing randomly. This progress reflected a categorical change in the mentality of senior commanders. It improved significantly the quality of command at the operational and strategic levels and accelerated the development of technological means for the acquisition of deep intelligence.[33]

THE EXTENDED BATTLEFIELD

The concept of the Extended Battlefield marked the crystallization of a new paradigm, formulated from 1976 onwards, into a comprehensive guideline for operational manoeuvre. Therefore, the transition from the Extended Battlefield concept to the Airland Battle doctrine may be regarded as a technical change, deriving from the need to translate an abstract idea into practical patterns applicable to the framework of a field manual.[34] Moreover, the fact that both the development of the new concept and the composition of the revised edition of the field manual were conducted simultaneously from the middle of 1980, only reinforces this argument.[35]

In March 1981 Starry published a personal article, unequalled both in the quality of writing and in the depth of its ideas in the history of modern American military thought.[36] Apart from presenting the philosophical essence of the theory of operational manoeuvre in a most thorough and creative manner, the article, like the works of the Soviet theoreticians, Tukhachevskii, Triandafillov, Varfolomeev and Galaktionov, reflected the trend to initiate the formulation of the operational theory by the higher echelons of command, combining empirical experience with abstract thinking.

Like the members of the Soviet deep operations school, Starry set as the basic assumption for the concept, the premise that the defensive should be regarded as one of the two forms of manoeuvre existing at the operational level. And since he interpreted the manoeuvre as the military manifestation of the systemic interaction, he realized that unless it strove to overwhelm the rival system, in place of the traditional approach which had been content with the aim of slowing down its mechanical advance towards its territorial objectives, the defensive would remain deprived of the positive dimension capable of turning it into a dynamic operation.[37]

As a result, for the first time since the end of the Second World War, American military thought managed to infuse the linkage between strategic conduct and operational manoeuvre with system logic. Moreover, by applying patterns of system thinking into the field of operational manoeuvre, Starry succeeded in liberating Western military thought from the oppressive domination of the Clausewitzian prejudice of the strategic impotence of the defensive.[38] From now on, the defensive would cease to be regarded as an inferior method lacking capability of decision, but would be seen, rather, as a dynamic form of manoeuvre bound to serve strategy with the same level of effectiveness as the offensive. By abrogating the last of the Clausewitzian dogmas which guided the Western concepts of manoeuvre for more than a century, the emergence of the Extended Battlefield concept indicated, more than any other event, the maturation of the American operational theory.

Another breakthrough generated by the formulation of the Extended Battlefield concept concerned the detection of the systemic implications deriving from the existing tension between the mechanical aspects of combat and the intellectual aspects of operational conduct. Unlike its predecessors, the Central Battle and the Integrated Battlefield, the advanced concept of the Extended Battlefield not only identified the qualitative differences between the tactical and operational fields of warfare, but also suggested a general method for harmonizing the inherent contradictions that exist between them.[39] In other words, the concept of the Extended Battlefield offered patterns of thought, and command and control, which permitted the user to assemble dynamically a wide variety of local events into a multidimensional manoeuvre guided by operational logic.[40] Thus the road was paved for the articulation of the idea of synchronization, and for the release of the theory of manoeuvre from the conceptual bonds imposed by the mechanistic concept of the centre of gravity.[41]

The broadening of the definition of depth from the narrow aspect of space to include time and resources, allowed tactical combat to be perceived as one pole within a system of complementary contradictions.[42] And since Starry assumes that the framework of physical combat rests on the dimensions of front and present, which means a unity of time and space, he defines the consequential effects of tactical occurrences in limited terms of focal points. In other words, the idea of concentrating superior combat power, by means of mechanization and combined arms fighting, at a certain breaking point along the opponent's front line, embraces the entire logic of tactics.[43]

From studying the echeloned nature of the Soviet manoeuvring system Starry realized the need to engage the entire depth of the offensive structure as a basic condition to achieve its disruption.[44] When the members of the Extended Battlefield Contact Team examined this new assumption in the light of the prevailing convention of tactical concentration, they encountered what appeared to be, at first sight, a paradox – for the idea of deliberately deploying a given complex of fighting resources along the rival system's entire depth seemed to contradict the tactical principle of concentration.[45] Moreover, the definition of simultaneous operations as a means to neutralize the interaction among the rival system's components, only emphasized the impression of a paradox.[46]

The solution to the paradox involved a thorough study of the inter-relations between tactics and operations. Thus, whereas tactics were defined as the field concerned with the solution of limited mechanical problems through the optimal combination of fighting resources, the conduct of operations was specified as the province centring on the anticipation of complex situations and their implementation through combined manoeuvre.[47] Therefore, it is the general framework of the operational manoeuvre which produces favourable opportunities for tactical engagements.[48] Moreover, the synchronized assemblage of the consequences of these engagements produces the operational situation paving the road to the accomplishment of the strategic aims: since tactics are restricted to unified cells of time and space, they are dominated by mechanical logic. On the other hand, centring on simultaneous conduct of various fighting activities at the front and in depth, at the present time and in future, the operational field combines the cognitive dimension in addition to mechanical aspects – thus, it is dominated by the systemic logic of homeostasis.

The method of attaining creative equilibrium among the contrarieties of mechanical concentration at the level of tactical occurrences, and the simultaneous deployment of the various elements along the rival system's entire depth in the context of accomplishing operational objectives, has been defined as synchronization.[49] By generating a sequence of actions and contemplating the relationship unfolding between the present-front and future-depth, Starry intended to guarantee the existence of a synchronized operation.[50] Combining in its essence both a holistic approach and a deep appreciation of the significance of intelligence in modern operations, the advantage of that method derived from its simplicity and practicality.

In order to understand the systemic implications of the 'see and attack in depth' method, which expresses the operational version of John Boyd's OODA pattern, we shall have to examine Starry's approach to the issue of operational conduct, in contrast to the approach of the 1976 field manual.

By attempting to organize the operation according to artificial categories, it separated cognitive and mechanical functions, thus disrupting the continuity of military activity.

> In the division of responsibilities on the battlefield, generals commanding corps and divisions *concentrate the force.* Colonels and lieutenant colonels of brigade and battalions *control and direct the battle.* Captains and their companies, troops and batteries *fight the battle.*[51]

By initially ruling out the ability to integrate harmoniously the various activities into a synergetic operation, this definition institutionalized the dichotomy between thinking and acting.

Referring to the operation as an integrity developing out of a dynamic interaction between two rival systems, Starry intended to produce a simultaneous continuity of anticipation, action and cogitation oriented towards the future.[52] The entire depth of the operational space, which can be recognized according to the defensive and offensive deployment of both rival systems, was classified into fields of anticipation or premonition – called areas of interest – and fields of action – called areas of influence. The logic of this classification was based on the definition of time sectors relating to the operational structures of both systems.[53] Since assuming that the awareness gained through observation and surveillance would always surpass the capacity of action due to technological limitations, Starry ascribed to each of the friendly system's operational elements an area of interest exceeding the area of action by an operational order of magnitude.

In the specific case of defensive against a possible Soviet attack in Central Europe, the various areas of interest and influence were defined as follows: the brigade area of influence concerned the battle against the leading regiments of the first echelon divisions, whereas its area of interest concerned the follow-on regiments of the first echelon divisions deployed at a distance of 10–15 hours from direct contact with the front. The division's area of influence was identical to the brigade's area of interest, whereas its area of interest focused on the second echelon divisions deployed at a distance of 16–48 hours from contact with the front line. The corps' area of influence corresponded with the division's area of interest, whereas its area of interest concerned the Soviet second echelon armies which were supposed to be present at a distance of 72 hours from the close-in battle.[54]

By simultaneously transforming combinations of striking

capabilities with beams of apprehension into two areas of time and operational problems, a systemic network was created guaranteeing synergy, continuity and maintenance of manoeuvre initiative. Moreover, like the Soviet command system that integrated a succession of immediate and follow-on missions into a cognitive axis preserving the coherence of the various tactical activities, the Extended Battlefield concept stretched the consciousness of each operational element beyond the area of its immediate tactical capability and so served as a lever for the simultaneous synchronization of the numerous random combat activities in the direction of a unified operational aim.[55]

The last conceptual quantum leap generated by the formulation of the Extended Battlefield concept concerns the institutionalization of the linkage between manoeuvre and attrition. Being limited to thinking in tactical patterns, the American traditional approach had tended to interpret the operational reality in terms of attrition engagements. Therefore, despite the effort to indoctrinate the senior echelons of command with manoeuvre thinking, the operational conduct in the United States Army developed into nothing more than a trend to amplify tactical patterns of attrition into industrial dimensions.[56] Reinforced by the enormous national technological capabilities, the American *materialschlacht* approach perceived attrition not only as the essence of the operation but also as being inevitable.

From the identification of momentum as the rationale of the Soviet manoeuvring system the American operational reformers learned to perceive mass, first and foremost, as the element generating the manoeuvre's velocity and maintaining its continuity. This mode of thinking induced the operational reformers to define the deliberate pulverization of the second echelon's mass as a means to deprive the rival system of its operational manoeuvring capability. Moreover, viewing the defensive as a systemic process, combining simultaneously defence at the front with offence in depth only emphasized the instrumental contribution yielded by attrition to the preparation of future manoeuvring opportunities that would preserve the integrity of the NATO territory.[57]

For the first time since the days of the Civil War, attrition was portrayed in a new light, and the deliberate interaction between manoeuvre and attrition has become one of the fundamentals of advanced operations.[58]

FM 100-5 1982

Keen to provide operational guidance to commanders and instructors at all levels, the architects of the Airland Battle field manual attempted to translate the abstract ideas of the Extended Battlefield concept into a comprehensive framework of concepts, principles and rules of action applicable at any level, under any conditions, and in any theatre of operations.[59]

The results of this aspiration, which implied a certain compromise of the philosophical qualities of the Extended Battlefield concept, can be recognized in a series of inconsistencies such as: over-emphasis on the mechanical principle of all-arms combat at the expense of operational synergy;[60] an artificial differentiation between manoeuvre and fire;[61] confusing tactical destruction with operational disruption;[62] and an indiscriminate employment of sets of tenets, principles, fundamentals and imperatives, aiming to guide thinking in specific areas of activity.[63]

Since their approach was dominated by system thinking, the architects of the 1982 field manual, unlike their predecessors from the 1976 manual, emphasized the uniqueness of the operational level of war. Therefore, they spared no effort in demonstrating the linkage between the manual's conceptual derivation and NATO's strategy, the accepted set of universal principles of war, and the historical experience of war. Moreover, starting with the definition of challenges, levels of war and fundamentals of operations – moving later to display the forms of operational manoeuvre – and concluding by presenting the various combat tactics and techniques, the manual's methodological structure aimed at anchoring tactics within a broader conception of warfare.

The accurate definition of the operational level supplied by the 1982 field manual established the conceptual framework for a theory of manoeuvre. The manual clarified the fundamentals upon which modern operations rest; it determined the nature of the linkage between this intermediate level and its traditional sisters; it defined the key principles of operational manoeuvre; and it also determined the various occupations, characteristic to the new field of knowledge:

> The operational level of war uses available military resources to attain strategic goals within a theater of war. Most simply, it is the theory of larger unit operations. It also involves planning and conducting campaigns. Campaigns are sustained operations designed to defeat an enemy force in a specified space and time with simultaneous and sequential battles. The disposition of forces, selection of objectives, and actions taken to weaken or to outmaneuver the enemy all set the

terms of the next battle and exploit tactical gains. They are all part of the operational level of war. In Airland Battle doctrine, this level includes the marshalling of forces and logistical support, providing direction to ground and air maneuver, applying conventional and nuclear fires in depth, and employing unconventional and psychological warfare.[64]

In order to create a conceptual common denominator and provide the wide community of users with the cognitive means to interpret any operational reality, the essence of the manoeuvre theory was condensed into four comprehensive cornerstones: initiative, depth, synchronization, and agility.

Intending to satisfy first and foremost the theoretical needs of the junior tactical echelons, the manual opens with a somewhat simplistic explanation of the morale aspects of the tenet of initiative: 'Initiative implies an offensive spirit in the conduct of all operations. The underlying purpose of every encounter with the enemy is to seize or to retain independence of action.'[65]

The transition to the operational context is exercised by harnessing John Boyd's OODA argumentation, which is interpreted here, both as tactical patterns of action, and as operational effects: 'To do this we must make decisions and act more quickly than the enemy, to disorganize his forces and to keep him off balance.'[66]

Nevertheless, as can be learned from the paragraph concluding the discussion on the tenet of initiative, its essence concerns mainly the philosophy of operational command, which is based on a deliberate generation of a cognitive tension through the apprehension of the inherent contrarieties within the manoeuvring system:

> To preserve the initiative subordinates must act independently within the context of an overall plan. They must exploit successes boldly and take advantage of unforeseen opportunities. They must deviate from the expected course of battle without hesitation when opportunities arise to expedite the overall mission of the higher force. They will take risks, and the command must support them.[67]

Since the issue of depth is entirely irrelevant to the tactical level, the discussion on this tenet centres from first to last on the operational context.

Unlike the traditional approach which related the idea of depth exclusively to the dimension of space, the Airland Battle manual extends its meaning to the dimensions of time and resources. It defines depth as the physical framework for the operational interaction and anchors the discussion at that level.[68] Moreover, by identifying depth as the origin for both momentum and elasticity, it

301

manages to establish a harmony between offensive and defensive.[69] Like their Soviet counterparts from the 1930s the authors of the manual paved the way to the definition of depth as the source for operational shock:

> Commanders need to use the entire depth of the battlefield to strike the enemy and to prevent him from concentrating his firepower or manoeuvering his forces to a point of his choice.

Finally, discussion of the tenet of depth is almost naturally concluded by reinstating the employment of reserves as an essential element for the application of operational manoeuvre, whether offensive or defensive.[70] In an effort to explain the tactical context of warfare, the discussion of the tenet of agility starts by reducing the logic of combat to its basics, that is, the swift creation of a relative advantage in fighting power by means of combining a mental edge and tactical adaptation. But even this modest beginning serves to develop the discussion in operational directions. The combination of avoiding the rival's strength, on the one hand, and attacking his vulnerabilities by anticipating his acts, on the other, leaves no doubt that Boyd's theory constitutes the conceptual derivation of this tenet. Emphasizing the continual exercise of this logic along the entire course of the operation, as a condition for accomplishing the disruption of the rival system, brings American military thought very close to the Soviet idea of *napravlenie glavnogo udara* (trend of the main strike). Ultimately, the manual links the ability to apply agility to the appropriate structuring and organization of the manoeuvring system.[71]

The abundance of critical writing attempting to reinterpret the idea of synchronization in the period following the publication of the first Airland Battle doctrine, indicates that the manual failed to present a clear explanation of the last tenet:

> Airland Battle doctrine identifies four basic tenets: Agility, depth, initiative, and synchronization. A close examination of the discussion of synchronization in the 1982 field manual (*FM 100-5 Operations*) reveals why this tenet is perhaps the least understood by practitioners in the field. The manual described and characterized synchronization, but it did not provide a clear definition. This resulted in confusion on the part of many commanders and staff planners in the development of their concepts and plans.[72]

Synchronization means a deliberate and dynamic combination of various activities integrating simultaneously the friendly system's components along the entire depth of the rival system for the purpose of producing the operational circumstances to induce the latter's collapse.[73] Reflecting the most advanced level of synergy, synchronization orchestrates numerous types of forces and weapon systems, various forms of tactical manoeuvre and other activities in a vertical configuration deployed along several categories of time and space with the intention of outmanoeuvring the rival system into an impossible operational posture. Moreover, as an abstract idea synchronization allows the operational planner and practitioner to bridge the paradox emerging from the combination of the tactical imperative of concentrating superior combat power at a certain point, with the operational principle of simultaneous dispersion of the system's elements along spacious depth. Thus, the idea of synchronization cannot be relevant unless related to an operational context.

However, in its explanation of the idea of synchronization, the 1982 manual focuses on the mechanical aspects of tactics. It defines synchronization as a method for the application of mechanical concentration – an effect confined to unified cells of time and space. Thus, almost naturally, it identifies synchronization with the tactical principle of combined arms combat.[74]

The exposition of the idea becomes even more confused when the manual, on the one hand, emphasizes reservations concerning the integration of nuclear weapons, operational fires and aviation, deep intelligence and special forces in the operational manoeuvre; while on the other, it attempts to augment the validity of its mechanistic arguments by presenting phrases aimed at indoctrination and lacking any practical significance, such as: 'Synchronized, violent execution is the essence of decisive combat'.[75]

Attempting in a final effort to repair the damage by illuminating the operational aspects of the idea, the authors of the manual reveal their own confusion, thereby formalizing the ambiguity embracing the tenet of synchronization:

> Forceful and rapid operations achieve at least local surprise and shock effect. Commanders must look beyond these immediate effects when they plan operations. They must make special provisions in advance to exploit the opportunities that tactical success will create.[76]

A critical examination of the Airland Battle's initial version confirms not only the fact that at the time of its publication the operational theory lacked maturity, but also creates the impression that it was formulated in haste.

An official letter – The Airland Battle – distributed by Starry in January 1981 to the community of TRADOC commanders, and the publication of an articulated version of the Airland Battle concept in March indicate a transition in trends from the loose development of concepts, to institutionalization of the conceptual achievements accumulated in the course of the doctrinal process.[77]

Three months prior to the official publication of the 1982 manual, when trying to introduce the essentials of the Airland Battle doctrine to the entire population of the American armed forces, General Glenn Otis pointed out the two main challenges implied by the application of the operational theory: breaking away from the traditional inclination to concentrate on immediate tactics and extension of the commander's consciousness to the realm of depth; and discontinuation of the traditional trend of non-collaboration among the various services in implementing the operational manoeuvre:

> Airland Battle is now the doctrine of the United States Army. It states that the battle against the second echelon forces is equal in importance to the fight with the forces at the front. Thus, the traditional concern of the ground commander with the close-in fight at the forward line of own troops (FLOT) is now inseparable from the deep attack against the enemy follow-on forces. To be able to fight these simultaneous battles, all of the armed services must work in close cooperation and harmony with each other. If we are to find, to delay, to disrupt and to kill the total enemy force, we will need the combined efforts of the Air-Army team.[78]

Constituting the primary means for overcoming the cultural challenges that the American armed forces were facing at that moment, the assimilation of the new theory, according to the head of TRADOC, demanded a dynamic professional discourse that would engage the various command echelons at that sensitive transition period.[79] Moreover, as proved by the experience of the 1976 manual, such a discourse could materialize only on the basis of an existing official doctrine. This may well have been the reason for the urgency in the publication of the 1982 manual. The abundance of theoretical writing initiated by officers from the TRADOC community in association with the publication of the manual indeed confirms this assumption.[80]

As the father of the Army's conceptual revolution, Starry's departure from TRADOC in August 1981, prior to the consolidation of the operational theory, might have caused much concern among the operational reformers – and may have been the reason for the accelerated formulation of a new manual.

Like the Soviet Deep Battle Field Regulations of 1936 (*PU-36 Glubokii Boi*) which focused on the tactical context in an attempt to swiftly impose operational logic throughout the armed forces, the 1982 publication of the Airland Battle manual reflected a compromise between two trends: the perfectionist trend that aspired to bring the development of the operational theory to completion, prior to its publication, and the realistic trend, which sought to strengthen the basis of officers supporting the operational theory through the institutionalization of the existing conceptual gains, and thus create better conditions for further development.[81] A close inspection of the theoretical trends that led to the reformulation of the original version of the Airland Battle manual in the advanced version of 1986 reinforces this argument.[82]

A QUANTUM LEAP IN OPERATIONAL COGNITION: FM 100-5 1986

The emergence of the 1986 advanced Airland Battle manual occurred as a natural consequence of the evolutionary doctrinal process initiated by Starry. The actual formulation of the new manual was the natural result of objective factors such as the successful assimilation of the operational theory between 1982–86, the application of a systemic approach to the development of the Army doctrine, and the institutionalization of a critical discourse in professional matters. It was further facilitated by the presence of William Richardson, who had served as Starry's right-hand man in the crucial years 1977–81, and who commanded TRADOC from 1983 onwards, which afforded the completion of the operational theory's development and the publication of an advanced manual.

Loyal both to the prevailing operational approach and to the methodology of doctrine development set by Starry, Richardson permitted himself certain criticism of the 1982 manual, when justifying the publication of the new 1986 manual.[83]

Since we are concerned here mainly with understanding the conceptual motives of the development of the American theory of manoeuvre, we will focus in the following section on the operational trends as reflected both in the theoretical works which followed the publication of the 1982 manual, and in the new manual of 1986. Accepting Richardson's explanations of the deficiencies of the 1982 manual, we will avoid issues such as the inconsistency of the 1982 manual with NATO's tactical doctrine, the integration of nuclear weapons in the operational manoeuvre, and the 1982 manual's neglect of certain political sensitivities.[84]

Like its predecessor, the new manual perceives the practice of war as a holistic notion reflected simultaneously in three areas of activity: strategy, operations and tactics.[85] Yet, unlike the original version of the Airland Battle doctrine which emphasized the tactical level and therefore sometimes perceived destruction as the operation's objective, the advanced version defines the universal objectives of an operation in the following manner:

> The principal task of theatre commanders and their subordinate commanders is to concentrate superior strength against enemy vulnerabilities at the decisive time and place to achieve strategic and policy aims.[86]

This statement implies a categorical change in the approach to operations. Firstly, the idea of destruction, as a universal aim guiding all operations, is substituted here with the idea of a concrete aim, defined specifically by the political-strategic authorities.[87] Secondly, the purpose of the manoeuvre is defined as the initiation of a complex operational situation to take advantage of the opponent's principal systemic vulnerability. It is the consistent exploitation of this vulnerability by a physical strike that leads ultimately to the accomplishment of the strategic objectives.

Thus, expressing the rationale of the operational manoeuvre, the convergence of one's main strike against the opposing system's inherent weakness portrays dialectic thinking as the crucial cognitive quality required at the operational command echelons. Moreover, the practical application of this mode of thinking to the operation can be exercised exclusively through the method of synchronization.[88]

In other words, the mechanistic approach that perceived the operational context as a distinctive level of activity is replaced by a new approach.[89] The characterization of the operational context as an 'art' derived, as in the Soviet case, from its identification as a unique cognition, bridging abstract definitions of aims, capabilities and limitations, and mechanical performances like movements, launches of fires and other energies, maintenance or seizure of space, and so on:

> Operational art is the employment of military forces to attain strategic goals in a theater of war or a theater of operations through the design, organisation and conduct of campaigns and major operations.[90]

Thus, whereas military strategy and tactics strive, through the calculated investment of resources and optimization of their employment, to support the politician's intention to produce a new reality, the operational art interprets, through dialectical thinking, the military implications resulting from the political decisions, and initiates future situations to lead to the materialization of the desired reality:

> Operational art thus involves fundamental decisions about when and where to fight and whether to accept or decline battle. Its essence is

the identification of the enemy's operational center of gravity – his source of strength or balance – and the concentration of superior combat power against that point to achieve decisive success.[91]

Characterizing a novel field of knowledge, this definition introduces intellectual challenges unrecognized before by the traditional military disciplines, such as '. . . broad vision, the ability to anticipate, and a careful understanding of the relationship of means to ends, and effective joint and combined operations'. Operational art thus requires the commander to answer three questions: '(1) What military conditions must be produced in a theatre of war or operations to achieve the strategic goal? (2) What sequence of actions is most likely to produce that condition? (3) How should the resources of the force be applied to accomplish that sequence of actions?'[92] Moreover, in spite of the fact that one could, through the exercise of definitions such as campaign, operation and theatre, link the new quality to quantitative aspects of space and force size, its application, as a principle, is not confined to a specific echelon.

Reflecting the main aspect of the conceptual quantum leap introduced by the formulation of the 1986 manual, the appreciation of operational cognition as a novel corpus of knowledge requiring new intellectual faculties, generated a whole line of theoretical trends persisting to the present time.

The effort to explore the complex nature of operational art and reveal the fundamentals of the new cognition reflected only one of these theoretical trends. On the one hand, this trend aspired to illuminate the intellectual problems implied by the nature of the advanced operational manoeuvre. On the other hand, it sought through the assimilation of tools of abstract thinking, dialectical perception, and multi-dimensional understanding to promote the ability to develop creative solutions among the medium and higher command echelons of the armed forces.[93]

Another trend, reflected in both official publications of doctrinal literature and in theoretical works of senior experienced officers, centred on the efforts to translate the ideas of operational art into practical principles, methods of action, and patterns of behaviour for the operational commander.[94]

The cognitive approach to the domain of operational command emphasized the acute need for accurate and comprehensive definitions of doctrinal matters. Thus, the third trend concentrated on reinterpreting the substance of doctrine in the context of the changing strategic circumstances, on the cultivation of cognitive and practical links among the doctrines of the various armed services, and

307

on the inspection of the doctrine's impact on the application of warfare at the various levels of war.[95]

The last trend which arose out of the appreciation of operational
cognition concerned the development of training and educating
systems that would produce the intellectual qualities required from
commanders and staff functioning in operational environments.[96]

Of all the innovative ideas introduced by the original Airland Battle
manual, the exposition of the tenet of synchronization required the
deepest insight. Yet, due to the urgent circumstances which led to the
final formulation of the 1982 manual, the cultivation of the notion of
synchronization was left incomplete – a fact that contributed to errors
and distortions in its subsequent interpretation. And since it constituted a central layer in the conception of the operational manoeuvre,
it became almost imperative that the re-examination of this tenet
should occupy a key place in the advanced stage of the theoretical
development. Thus, both the thorough exposition of the operational
contents and definitions, and the exercise of an advanced method of
reasoning turn the enquiry of the tenet of synchronization in the 1986
new manual into a most remarkable achievement.[97] Putting forward
a statement, employing the 1982 terminology, the discussion of the
idea of synchronization opens by creating a misleading impression of
conceptual continuity:

> Synchronization is the arrangement of battlefield activities in time,
> space and purpose to produce maximum reactive combat power at the
> decisive point. Synchronization is both a process and result. Com-
> manders synchronize activities: they thereby produce synchronized
> operations.[98]

Later, the 1986 manual corrects the original mechanistic interpretation of synchronization. Discarding the simplistic approach which
identified synchronization with concentration of fire and troops at the
decisive point, the authors of the new manual manage to broaden the
theoretical framework of the idea.[99] Consequently, the numerous
analysts and commentators relating to the subject are inspired to
define synchronization – without creating a paradox – as the simultaneous combination of various elements and systemic activities
along the entire depth of the operational space with the aim of inflicting disruption on the rival system.[100] Thus, Tukhachevskii's conception, which, as early as 1931, related the ability to perform
synchronization to the existence of elements possessing various capabilities of operational mobility within the manoeuvring system, has
been applied in practice.[101]

This approach generated extensive theoretical scrutiny of issues such as operational mobility, methods for the application of simultaneous operations, and the design and integration of light forces, in addition to the prevailing heavy-mechanized ones, within the operational manoeuvre.[102]

The authors of the advanced 1986 manual correct yet another conceptual distortion created by the ambiguity of its predecessor, when expressing their reservations regarding the identification of synchronization with coordination:

> By itself, however, such coordination is no guarantee of synchronization, unless the commander first visualizes the consequences to be produced and how activities must be sequenced to produce them.[103]

By the irrevocable linkage of synchronization with the ability of the operational commander to anticipate the consequence of the operational occurrence, the *aim* has been determined as the generator of the manoeuvre and the derivation for the synchronization's logic. Synchronization is perceived to take place primarily 'in the mind of the commander and then in the actual planning and coordination of movements, fires and supporting activities'.[104] Associating the idea of synchronization within the province of abstract thinking, the manual turns to discuss the issue of cognitive tension and its essential contribution to the maintenance of synchronization within the operational manoeuvre. Since the aim serves as the cognitive propulsion to the manoeuvre for both contending systems, by intending to disrupt the friendly system's operation, the antagonistic trend of the rival system expresses a contrapositive element which can be negotiated only through the dynamic method of synchronization:

> Synchronization need not depend on explicit coordination if all forces involved fully understand the intent of the commander, and if they have developed and rehearsed well-conceived standard responses to anticipated contingencies. In the chaos of battle, when communications fail and face to face coordination is impossible, such implicit coordination may make the difference between victory and defeat. The enemy for his part will do everything in his power to disrupt the synchronization of friendly operations. The less that synchronization depends on active communication, the less vulnerable it will be.[105]

The cognitive tension provides the element which synchronizes the succession of random encounters along the entire battlefield and the preconceived operational effect – in other words, the intellectual capacity of the commanders of the friendly system to interpret a relevant tactical situation according to the abstract terms of the operational aim, and consequently devise a concrete dynamic solution promoting its accomplishment.[106]

The rigorous discussion on the subject of synchronization concludes with a list of the intellectual qualities required from operational commanders and their subordinates in order to apply synchronization:

> To achieve this [synchronization] requires anticipation, mastery of time–space relationship, and a complete understanding of the ways in which friendly and enemy capabilities interact. Most of all, it requires unambiguous unity of purpose throughout the force.[107]

Synchronization expresses the essence of the operational art and as such it reflects both the rare ability to think and act simultaneously at two different categories of time, and the unique apprehension of the antithetical nature of the systemic environment. Finally, and perhaps unwittingly, since even at this advanced stage the Americans still declared their adherence to the archaic and incoherent idea of *schwerpunkt*, the authors of the 1986 manual appeared in this last extract to have adopted the Soviet idea of the trend of the main strike.[108]

The profound journey into the nature of the large scale manoeuvre led the authors of the 1986 manual almost naturally to recognize three distinct areas of time, space, and activity, upon which the modern operation is structured. Through the synchronized integration of these various areas unfolds the entirety of the operation. Defined here as close operations, the immediate area includes the tactical combination of a series of combined arms-mechanized acts, occurring concurrently, and designed to accomplish the physical aspects of the operational aim.[109] Defined in the post-1982 literature as deep operations, the deep area includes the simultaneous combination of manoeuvring elements operating in a future context of time, and designed to accomplish the negative aspects of the operational aim, that is, infliction of operational shock or disruption.[110] The area of friendly rear, which was not mentioned in the 1982 manual, is defined in 1986 as rear operations:

> Rear operations at any echelon comprise activities rearward of elements in conflict designed to assure freedom of maneuver and continuity of operations, including continuity of sustainment and command and control. Rear operations may have little immediate impact on close ground operations, but are critical to subsequent operations, whether in exploiting success or recouping failure. At the operational level, rear operations focus on preparing for the next phase of the campaign or major operation.[111]

Thus, to provide the complete operational manoeuvre with continuity and the ability to reach depth with sufficient combat power, rear operations are perceived in the 1986 manual as the main source for momentum. The definition of this area as an operational element to all intents and purposes indicates a conceptual breakthrough. Whereas in the 1982 manual logistics were perceived as a secondary element supporting manoeuvre, and thus were presented only in a narrow technical aspect, in the 1986 advanced manual logistics are portrayed as an element whose absence will deprive the operational manoeuvre of its systemic qualities, thus inducing its decline.[112] Moreover, constituting a mirror image of the rival system's depth, rear operations seek to prevent the opponent from accomplishing the same effects assigned to friendly deep operations.[113] Adding to the operation an entire dimension of warfare, the aspect of rear operations was completely neglected in the original version of the Airland Battle doctrine.

Through the application of the operational logic to the field of sustainment of the fighting elements the authors of the 1986 manual manage to broaden the scope of activities combined in rear operations:

> Four rearward activities in particular must be conducted as a part of rear operations: assembly and movement of reserves, redeployment of fire support, maintenance and protection of sustainment effort, and maintenance of command and control . . . In addition to these critical activities, others relevant to rear operations include – establishment and maintenance of lines of communications, traffic regulation and control, medical and field services, refugee control and maintenance of civil order.[114]

Traditionally, special operations have been attributed by the Americans to the province of strategy. The traditional negligence of depth, which constitutes the natural operating area for special forces, served as the main factor extending the conceptual rift between special operations and the operational manoeuvre. Moreover, since it lacked conceptual maturity when the original Airland Battle doctrine was formulated, the operational theory failed to integrate special operations in the operational manoeuvre.[115]

Following the extension of operational consciousness onto the areas of depth and rear, the advanced manual of 1986 surveys not only the domains of High Intensity Conflict (HIC) and Medium Intensity Conflict (MIC), but also the domain of Low Intensity Conflict (LIC) as a relevant area upon which the operational logic of Airland Battle can be applied.[116] Moreover, the failure of the 1979 hostage

311

rescue operation in Iran generated a renewal of interest in special operations, placing the organization, training and command and control of special forces high on the defence agenda. The combination of all these circumstances led not only to profound modifications of the entire array of special forces, but also to their intimate association with the operational manoeuvre.[117]

Apart from the strategic aspects concerning the application of special operations and special operations forces, both the 1986 manual and the theoretical literature following the publication of the initial Airland Battle version assessed their possible contribution to the operational manoeuvre in the following manner:

> Special forces elements can deploy unilaterally into the enemy's rear area to assist in the attack of uncommitted enemy forces by locating, identifying, and destroying targets of operational value. Special forces detachments may have the following missions: intelligence collection; target acquisition; terminal guidance for strike aircraft and missile systems; interdiction of critical transportation targets; destruction of nuclear storage sites and command and control facilities; personnel recovery.[118]

Thus, being fully integrated in the operation's framework, special forces add yet another dynamic element to the operational system serving the operational manoeuvre, whether offensive or defensive according to the systemic logic, by providing deep intelligence and extending the scope of consciousness among friendly command circles, initiating deception and distorting the apprehension of the opposing command system, inflicting accurate strikes upon essential elements of the rival system and disrupting its operational functioning, supporting the deep strike effort and augmenting the operational effectiveness of its main components.[119]

The amalgamation, within the operation of special forces as a prolific element augmenting the operational synergy, provided yet another indication of the conceptual quantum leap which created the advanced version of the Airland Battle doctrine. The results of this enormous progression were evident in the Desert Storm campaign.

During the second half of the 1980s the conceptual revolution in the United States Army reached a climax with the assimilation of the theoretical achievements indicated by the 1986 quantum leap. At the outset of the 1990s the Army possessed a unified doctrine for the conduct of advanced operational manoeuvres. Thus, for the first time in their history, the American armed forces acquired not only a common theory of operations but also a uniform basis of comprehensive terminology. Absorbed at every command echelon, the operational doctrine provided the rationale for the training and education of the military forces, for force design, for technological development, and for the actual conduct of troops in war. Due to its systemic nature, the Airland Battle doctrine induced a healthy and dynamic interlocution among the various command echelons in the entire defence establishment. Moreover, its validity and compatibility with the strategic conditions have been constantly examined through a systematic process of research and criticism.

On the basis of the operational doctrine, patterns for effective cooperation were developed between the Army and the Air Force, the Marine Corps, the Special Forces, and between the various manoeuvring elements and combat arms within the ground forces.

As a central characteristic of the conceptual evolution, the awareness of depth induced an accelerated build-up of light and air-mechanized formations excelling in operational mobility. The thorough development of operational thought gave birth to coherent command structures and effective patterns for the conduct of complex and lasting operations in remote theatres.

Thus, when thrown into a strategic conflict, not only did the US armed forces manage to transcend the patterns of industrial thinking and the tradition of attrition, they also rapidly transformed a defence-oriented doctrine into a most creative offensive manoeuvre.

NOTES

1. J.L. Romjue, *From Active Defense to Airland Battle: The Development of Army Doctrine 1973–1982*, United States Training and Doctrine Command (Fort Monroe, VA, June 1984), p. 23; D.A. Starry, personal communication, Tel Aviv, 5 June 1994; 'A Tactical Evolution – FM 100-5', *Military Review*, 8 (1978), p. 7; idem, *Commander's Notes No. 3 – Operational Concepts and Doctrine* (Fort Monroe, VA, 20 Feb. 1979), pp. 1, 3.
2. D.A. Starry, 'To Change an Army', *Military Review*, 3 (1983), p. 25. Prior to the formulation of the Central Battle concept in Germany, Starry and his staff developed an embryonic concept which they naturally named 'The Corps Battle'.
3. D.A. Starry, 'Comments', in *Analysis: Selected Papers*, ODCSCD Anl. Ofc (Fort Monroe, VA, 1 Aug. 1977), p. 1, defined the essence of the Central Battle in the following manner: 'Central Battle – the place where all the combat systems interact on the battlefield'. D.A. Starry, 'Keynote Address', *Armor*, 4 (1978), p. 32, defined the concept in a more abstract manner, while emphasizing its limitations: 'On both sides (the US and the USSR), the concepts are independent: one is not sufficient to a military system without the others. For they all relate to one another. Let's look at that interdependence as a capability, a system's capability – interdependence of concept, interdependence of weapon systems, of tactics, or organization and structure'. Starry, *Commander's Notes No. 3*, p. 1, referred later to the concept of Central Battle as: 'When the Central Battle idea was first conceived, I made the point that operational concepts had to be the driving force for describing interactions that were to occur on the most intense part of the battlefield'.
4. Starry, 'Keynote Address', pp. 32–6.
5. T.N. Dupuy, *Understanding War – History and Theory of Combat* (London, 1992), pp. 31–7; J.F.C. Fuller, *Grant and Lee – A Study in Personality and Generalship*

(Bloomington, 1982) pp. 45–6; T. Lyman, *Mead's Headquarters 1863–1865* (Boston, 1922), p. 224; Starry, 'Keynote Address', pp. 33, 35; Romjue, *From Active Defense to Airland Battle*, p. 24.

6. D.A. Starry, 'Integrated Operations' (letter, AIG 7573 091530Z to distribution), Headquarters TRADOC, Fort Monroe, VA, July 1980, p. 1; idem, *Commander's Notes No. 3*, p. 3.

7. Headquarters Training and Doctrine Command, *Division 86: Blueprint of the Battlefield* (Fort Monroe, VA, April 1979); H. Wass de Czege, 'Army Doctrinal Reform', in A. Clark, *et al.* (eds), *The Defense Reform Debate* (Baltimore, 1984), p. 106.

8. Starry, *Commander's Notes No. 3*, pp. 1, 3; Romjue, *From Active Defense to Airland Battle*, p. 27.

9. Starry, 'To Change an Army', p. 26; 'Keynote Address', p. 32.

10. J.L. Romjue, *A History of Army 86*, Vol. I: *Division 86: The Development of the Heavy Division September 1978–October 1979*, Vol. II: *The Development of the Light Division, the Corps, and Echelons Above Corps November 1979–December 1980*, Headquarters TRADOC (Fort Monroe, VA, June 1983).

11. Starry, *Commander's Notes No. 3*, pp. 1–9.

12. Ibid., p. 1; 'To Change an Army', p. 26; 'Keynote Address', p. 32.

13. D.A. Starry, 'A Perspective on American Military Thought', *Military Review*, 7 (1989), p. 3. *Commander's Notes No. 3*, p. 1.

14. Ibid., pp. 1–2.

15. Ibid., pp. 1–3.

16. Ibid., pp. 3–9.

17. Starry, *Commander's Notes No. 3*, encs. 1, 2, 3.

18. TRADOC, Historical Office, *Annual Historical Review: FY 1979* (Fort Monroe, VA, 1980), p. 60 ff. The Office Deputy Chief of Staff for Doctrine (ODCSDOC), established in October 1979, was the heart of the system. In December 1979, an officer carrying the rank of General was nominated to command this organization, which since has been responsible for the following functions: development of concept papers: adjustment of the concepts to the general operational conception: articulation of the operational conception: and control of the doctrinal process. E.G. Scribner, *Doctrine Development by TRADOC May 1973–December 1979* (Fort Monroe, VA, 20 Feb. 1980) (special paper), notes that in January 1980 a Doctrine Management Office was established inside ODCSDOC with the aim of developing and conducting of a management system for doctrinal plans, and running the administrative and technical aspects of the process. TRADOC Regulation 11-7, *Operational Concepts and Army Doctrine* (Fort Monroe, VA, 29 Dec. 1980). D.A. Starry, 'The TRADOC Doctrinal Literature Program' (letter to distribution), 282000Z, Fort Monroe, VA, April 1980. 'The Writing of Doctrine' (letter to distribution), 292030Z, Fort Monroe, VA, April 1980, confirms that late in 1979 Starry transferred the review of the 1976 manual and the composition of the new manual to DTAC in Fort Leavenworth, and assigned this mission to the theory instructors and researchers in the Combined Arms Center.

19. Starry, 'To Change an Army', p. 26.

20. A good example to confirm this argument is provided by Starry's initiation of the '20 Stars Meeting'. In the course of this meeting, which was attended by the Chiefs of Staff of the Army and Air Force, the Army Deputy Chief of Staff (Lt. General Vessey, later to become Chairman of the Joint Chiefs of Staff), Commander in Chief USAF Tactical Air Command (General W. Creech), and General Starry himself, operational issues concerning the cooperation of Air Force elements and Army formations in attacking the Soviet second echelon were discussed, as a part of the formulation of the deep operations concept.

21. E.A. Dinges & R.H. Sinnereich, 'Battlefield Interdiction: Old Term New Problem', *Field Artillery Journal* (Jan.–Feb. 1980), p. 14.

22. Ibid., p. 15.

23. Ibid.

24. D.A. Starry, 'Extending the Battlefield', *Military Review*, 3 (1981), pp. 34, 37, 45.

25. Ibid., pp. 39, 43, 45.

26. The term was actually coined by Colonel John P. Stewart who was a member of the concept development nucleus in Fort Sill in October–December 1979. Stewart, who

served as a staff officer in V Corps under Starry, worked in the early 1970s in the Army Combat Development Command on a concept research called 'Integrated Battlefield Control System'. Thus, possessing a system approach, he adopted from a previous experience a term expressing clearly the operational rationale of the new concept.

27. The team comprised the following members: Mr. James Struve of Sandia Laboratories, Livermore, who had been involved in the examination of V Corps defensive plan; Colonel (Ret.) Art Winn, from BDM Corporation who had served as G-2 in V Corps under Starry, contributed to the development of the intelligence aspects of the concept; Lieutenant Colonel Howard Clark who had functioned as G-3 in V Corps, contributed in the field of operational planning; Mr. Reed Stone from TRADOC Combined Arms Test Activity, who had conducted formerly a study on command and control for V Corps, contributed in this field. The rest of the team consisted of people who shared no former common experience with Starry: Majors R.W. Zawilskii and H.H. Rubin from the artillery school, and Mr. D.P. Porreca, an analyst from R. & D. Associates of Marina del Rey, California.

28. J.S. Doerfel, 'An Operational Concept for the Integrated Battlefield', briefing presented at Fort Sill, OK, 18 Dec. 1979; idem, 'The Operational Art of the Airland Battle', *Military Review* LXII, 5 (1982), p. 6.

29. Ibid., p. 9; L.D. Holder, 'Maneuver in Deep Battle', *Military Review*, 5 (1982), pp. 55–6. The characteristic qualities of operational mobility, as expressed in air mechanization have been explored by: F.M. von Senger und Etterlin, 'New Operational Dimensions', *RUSI Journal*, 2 (1983), p. 11, and R.E. Simpkin, *Race to the Swift Thoughts on Twenty First Century Warfare* (Oxford, 1985), pp. 93–115, 117–32. Tactical mobility represents the mechanical ability of a fighting unit to cover a limited space within a defined unit of time. Therefore, since mechanization, which expresses tactical mobility, can be achieved by combined arms warfare, it is this last quality which characterizes tactics at its best. Operational mobility concerns, both the ability of the system to operate simultaneously along the entire operational space and to initiate a succession of actions which render the reactions of the rival system completely ineffective. Therefore, allowing certain elements within the system to overcome the problem of physical friction with space, air mechanization constitutes the method expressing operational mobility. This concept was initially formulated by Tukhachevskii in the late 1920s: M.N. Tukhachevskii, 'Novye voprosy voiny' in *Izbrannye proizvedeniia*, V.B. Kuznetsov (ed.) (Moscow, 1964), Vol. 2, pp. 180–84.

30. The idea of initiating operational conditions invigorating the synergy among elements of the friendly system in order to deprive the rival system of the ability to synergize its elements, represents the typical Russian approach to operations. This mode of thought gave birth to the pattern of fragmenting strike.

31. Starry, 'Extending the Battlefield', pp. 33–5, 39, 42; Doerfel, 'The Operational Art of the Airland Battle', p. 9; W.G. Hanne, 'The Integrated Battlefield', *Military Review*, 6 (1982), pp. 34–44; T.A. Cardwell, 'Extending the Battlefield: An Airman's Point of View', *Air University Review* (March–April 1983), pp. 86–93; C. Lanier Deal, 'BAI: The Key to the Deep Battle', *Military Review*, 3 (1982), pp. 51–4.

32. Ibid.

33. Romjue, *From Active Defense to Airland Battle*, p. 37.

34. The name 'Extended Battlefield' was suggested by the architects of the Extended Battlefield Contact Team, who worked on the development of the concept under Lieutenant General William Richardson in the Combined Arms Center. They argued that the name 'Integrated Battlefield', had become too clearly identified with the issue of nuclear and chemical weapons and had ceased to reflect the full depth of the maturing operational theory. Therefore, they suggested a new name.

35. Romjue, *From Active Defense to Airland Battle*, pp. 42–4.

36. Starry, 'Extending the Battlefield', pp. 31–50.

37. Ibid., pp. 32, 34.

38. C. von Clausewitz, *On War*, M. Howard and P. Paret (eds.) (Princeton, 1976), B. 6, Ch. 5, p. 370; B. 7, Ch. 1, p. 524, Ch. 13, p. 541, B. 8, Ch. 4, p. 600, Ch. 9, p. 624; C.W. von Blume, *Strategie* (Berlin, 1882), p. 201; C. Freiher von der Goltz, *The Conduct of War* (London, 1809), pp. 276, 284; D.A. Starry, 'Running Things', *Parameters*, 3 (1987), pp. 18–19.

39. Starry, 'Extending the Battlefield', p. 42; W.R. Richardson, 'Winning on the Extended Battlefield', *Army*, 6 (1981), pp. 36–7.
40. Ibid., p. 37; Starry, 'Extending the Battlefield', pp. 38–9.
41. J.J. Schneider and L.L. Izzo, 'Clausewitz's Elusive Center of Gravity', *Parameters*, 3 (1987), pp. 56–7.
42. Starry, 'Extending the Battlefield', p. 32; Richardson, 'Winning on the Extended Battlefield', pp. 37, 41.
43. Starry, 'Extending the Battlefield', p. 37.
44. Ibid., p. 34; Richardson, 'Winning on the Extended Battlefield', pp. 41–2.
45. This research and concept development team comprised the following members: Lieutenant Colonel L.D. Holder, and Major Dennis Long from the Combined Arms Center, and Major J.R. Zawilskii from the Field Artillery School.
46. Being unaware of the contradictive nature of the operational manoeuvring system, T.N. Dupuy, 'The Soviet Second Echelon: Is this a Red Herring?', *Armed Forces Journal*, 8 (1982), p. 63, falls into this conceptual trap.
47. Starry, 'Running Things', p. 14.
48. Starry, 'Extending the Battlefield', pp. 38–9; Richardson, 'Winning on the Extended Battlefield', p. 37; H. Wass de Czege and L.D. Holder, 'The New FM 100–5', *Military Review*, 6 (1982), pp. 59–60.
49. Starry, 'Extending the Battlefield', p. 39.
50. Ibid., pp. 36–7.
51. Headquarters Department of the Army, *FM 100-5 Operations* (hereafter *FM 100-5 Operations*) (Washington, DC, 1 July 1976), p. 3-4.
52. Starry, 'Extending the Battlefield', pp. 32, 39–40, 46; Richardson, 'Winning on the Extended Battlefield', pp. 37, 41.
53. Starry, 'Extending the Battlefield', pp. 36–7; Richardson, 'Winning on the Extended Battlefield', pp. 37, 41, the last reference translated the definitions of time into terms of space.
54. Starry, 'Extending the Battlefield', pp. 35–44.
55. *Blizhaishaia zadacha* represents in the Soviet system of command and control the immediate mission or objective assigned to each tactical entity, whereas the term *posleduiushchaia zadacha* represents the follow-on mission or objective. The follow-on mission of each junior tactical unit or formation forms a part or is identical with the mother formation's immediate mission. Moreover, whereas the first serves as a guide for immediate mechanical action the second orientates one's consciousness into deeper areas of time, space and interest.
56. Department of the Navy, Headquarters United States Marine Corps, *FMFM 1 Warfighting* (Washington, DC, 6 March 1989), pp. 28–9.
57. Starry, 'Extending the Battlefield', pp. 34, 37, 38.
58. Starry, 'A Perspective on American Military Thought', pp. 4–11; A. Badeau, *Military History of U.S. Grant* (New York, 1882) (3 vols.), Vol. III, p. 644; R.F. Weigley, *The American Way of War* (New York, 1973), p. XXII.
59. *FM 100-5 Operations*, p. i.
60. Ibid., pp. 1-4–1-5.
61. Ibid., p. 7-1.
62. Ibid., pp. 2-1, 2-2.
63. Ibid., pp. 2-1–2-3, lists the four basic tenets of the Airland Battle doctrine: initiative, depth, agility and synchronization. Ibid., pp. 2-6–2-10, links success in battle to the exercise of seven imperatives of combat: insure unity of effort, direct friendly strength against enemy weakness, designate and sustain the main effort, move fast – strike hard – finish rapidly, use terrain and weather, protect the force. Ibid., p. 7-2, lists yet another seven fundamentals of Airland Battle that guarantee victory: indirect approaches, speed and violence, flexibility and the reliance on the initiative of junior leaders, rapid decision making, clearly defined objectives and operational concepts, a clearly designated main effort, deep attack. Ibid. lists five fundamentals which are essential to success in offensive operations: concentration of effort, surprise of the enemy, speed – the attack must move rapidly, the attack must be flexible, audacious. Ibid., pp. b-1–b-5 presents in conclusion a list of the principles of war: objective, offensive, mass, maneuver, unity of command, security, surprise, simplicity.

64. *FM 100-5 Operations*, 1982, p. 2-3.
65. Ibid., p. 2-2.
66. Ibid.
67. Ibid.
68. Ibid., p. 2-3.
69. Ibid., p. 2-2.
70. Ibid.
71. Ibid. Harnessing technology and operational organization for the application of operational mobility, simultaneity and operational shock seem like an accurate copy of M.N. Tukhachevskii, 'O novom polevom ustave RKKA' (1936) (The Red Army's new field service regulations), in V.B. Kuznetsov (ed.), *Izbrannye proizvedeniia* (Moscow, 1964), Vol. 1, pp. 255–66: 'But modern combat resources allow the attack to be mounted in such a way as to strike the enemy simultaneously over his whole depth and to delay movement of reserves to the threatened sector'.
72. J.B. Rogers, 'Synchronizing the Airland Battle', *Military Review*, 4 (1984), pp. 61–2.
73. M.N. Tukhachevskii, 'Novye voprosy voiny', (1931), in A.B. Kadishev (ed.), *Voprosy strategii i operativnogo iskusstva v sovetskikh voennykh trudakh 1917-1940* (Moscow, 1965), pp. 139–44.
74. *FM 100-5 Operations*, 1982, p. 2-3.
75. Ibid.
76. Ibid.
77. D.A. Starry, 'The Airland Battle' (letter to distribution), 0291245Z, Fort Monroe, VA, Jan. 1981 (02 291305Z); United States Army, Training and Doctrine Command, *Pam 525-5 Military Operations: Operational Concepts for the Airland Battle and Corps Operations 1986* (Fort Monroe, VA, 25 March 1981).
78. G.K. Otis, 'The Airland Battle' (letter for distribution), *Military Review*, 5 (1982), p. 2.
79. Ibid.
80. M.C. Baur, 'Airland Battle's Power Punch', *Armor*, 5 (1982), pp. 38–41; B. Case, 'Air Defense for Airland Battle: Coming of Age in High Tech', *Army*, 11 (1983), pp. 34–7, 41, 46–8; J.D. Colanto, 'Intelligence Preparation of the Battlefield for the Airland Battle', *Military Intelligence* (June 1983), pp. 4–6; F.T. Curry, 'EW for the Airland Battle', in ibid., pp. 15–16; J.S. Doerfel, 'The Operational Art of the Airland Battle', *Military Review*, 5 (1982), pp. 3–10; D.E. Grange, 'Infantry and Air Defense in the Airland Battle', *Air Defense Magazine*, 4 (1981), pp. 24–5; J. Griffis, K. Pierce and E. Sherwood, 'The Mechanized Infantry Battalion Task Force in the Airland Battle', *Infantry*, 4 (1982), pp. 21–4; W.G. Hanne, 'Airland Battle: Doctrine not Dogma', *Military Review*, 6 (1983), pp. 11–25; Infantry School's Experts, 'New Clout for Mech-Infantry: The M-2 and Airland Battle 2000 Tactics', *Army*, 8 (1983), 18–22, 25–7, 29; M. Lancaster, 'The Armor Force in the Airland Battle', *Armor*, 1 (1982), pp. 26–32; S. Lancaster and J. Clemens, 'Airland Battle Defeat Mechanisms', in ibid., pp. 35–7; E.C. Ludvigsen, 'Modernization: Readiness for Airland Battle 2000', *Army*, 5 (1983), pp. 38–44; J.A. Machos, 'Airland Battles or Airland Battle?', *Military Review*, 7 (1983), pp. 33–40; C.H. McNair and J. Reinsprecht, 'Army Aviation Forces in the Airland Battle', *US Army Aviation Digest* (July 1981), pp. 6–13; J.B. Oblinger, 'Air Defense in the Airland Battle', *Air Defense Magazine* (Part II), 1 (1982), pp. 35–8; J. Schultz, 'Airland Battle 200: The Force Multiplier', *Defense Electronics*, 12 (1983), pp. 48–67; R. Sennewald, 'Tailoring Airland Battle Doctrine to Threat in Korea', *Army*, 10 (1983), pp. 92–104; J.M. Sollinger, 'Airland Battle – Implications for the Infantry', *Infantry*, 2 (1982), pp. 22–5; T. Velocci, Battle Doctrine for the 21st Century', *National Defense* 11 (1982), pp. 11–14; A.M. Coroalles, 'Implementing a Maneuver Style of War', *Military Review*, 12 (1982), pp. 20–25; J.M. Dubik, 'FM 100-5 and Counterinsurgency Warfare', *Military Review*, 11 (1983), pp. 41–8; H. Wass de Czege and L.D. Holder, 'The New FM 100-5', *Military Review*, 7 (1982), pp. 53–70; P.T. Devries, 'Maneuver and the Operational Level of War', *Military Review*, 2 (1983), pp. 13–34; J.C. Barbara and R.F. Brown, 'Deep Thrust on the Extended Battlefield', *Military Review*, 10 (1982), pp. 21–32; L.D. Holder, 'Maneuver in the Deep Battle', *Military Review*, 5 (1982), pp. 54–61.
81. Romjue, *From Active Defense to Airland Battle*, pp. 57–61, 65–6; A.W. Chapman, *The Army's Training Revolution 1973–1990: An Overview*, Office of the Command

Historian, United States Army Training and Doctrine Command (Fort Monroe, VA, 1991), p. 17.
82. W.R. Richardson, 'FM 100-5: The Airland Battle in 1986', *Military Review*, 3 (1986), pp. 7–8.
83. Ibid., pp. 5–10.
84. Ibid., pp. 8–10.
85. *FM 100-5 Operations*, 1986, p. 9; *FM 100-5 Operations*, 1982, p. 2-3.
86. *FM 100-5 Operations*, 1986, p. 27; *FM 100-5 Operations*, 1982, p. 2-1, defined it as follows: 'The object of all operations is to destroy the opposing force'.
87. *FM 100-5 Operations*, 1986, p. 29, lists destruction as the worst possibility for the guidance of operational planners and directors.
88. Ibid., pp. 27–8.
89. Ibid., p. 9; *FM 100-5 Operations*, 1982, p. 2-3.
90. *FM 100-5 Operations*, 1986, p. 10.
91. Ibid. A similar view is presented by K.G. Carlson, 'Operational Level or Operational Art?', *Military Review*, 10 (1987), pp. 52–4; C.R. Newell, 'What is Operational Art?', *Military Review*, 9 (1990), pp. 4, 6–8.
92. *FM 100-5 Operations*, 1986, p. 10.
93. J.A. Cope, 'Doctrinal Credibility: A Problem of Focus with FM 100-5', *Military Review*, 8 (1984), p. 71; R.L. Maginnis, 'Harnessing Creativity', *Military Review*, 3 (1986), pp. 13, 14, 16; C.G. Sutten, 'Command and Control at the Operational Level, *Parameters*, 4 (1986), pp. 18–19; R.L. Allen, 'Piercing the Veil of Operational Art', *Parameters*, 4 (1986), pp. 23–27; W.A. Downing, 'Training to Fight', *Military Review*, 5 (1986), pp. 19, 26–27; J.F. Meehan, 'The Operational Trilogy', *Parameters*, 3 (1986), pp. 9–12; C.R. Newell, 'Exploring the Operational Perspective', *Parameters*, 3 (1986), p. 21; 'Fog and Friction: Challenges to Command and Control', *Military Review*, 8 (1987), pp. 19, 20; T. Roszak, *The Cult of Information: The Folklore of Computers and the True Art of Thinking* (New York, 1986), p. 88; D. Jablonsky, 'Strategy and the Operational Level of War', *Parameters*, 1 (1987), Part I, pp. 73–4; 2 (1987), Part II, p. 54; L.V. Buel, 'Intelligence Preparation of the Battlefield', *Military Review*, 10 (1987), pp. 25–7; J.J. Schneider, 'Theoretical Implications of Operational Art', *Military Review*, 9 (1990), pp. 21, 24–6; S. Silvasy, 'Airland Battle Future: The Tactical Battlefield', *Military Review*, 2 (1991), pp. 5–7, 9; J.F. Antal, 'Maneuver Versus Attrition: A Historical Perspective', *Military Review*, 10 (1992), p. 26; United States Air Force, Air Command and Staff College, *Conventional Warfare* (Maxwell AFB, AL, Jan. 1991), pp. 1–2; United States Naval War College Operations Department, *Joint Military Operations Syllabus 1993*, College of Naval Warfare, pp. VII, 14; Department of the Navy, Headquarters United States Marine Corps, *FMFM 1-1 Campaigning* (Washington, DC, Feb. 1990), pp. 2–15; D.L. Adams and C.R. Newell, 'Operational Art in the Joint and Combined Arenas', *Parameters*, 2 (1988), pp. 33–9; D.A. Macgregor, 'Future Battle: The Merging Levels of War', *Parameters*, 4 (1992), pp. 33–46; J.E. Turlington, 'Truly Learning the Operational Art', *Parameters*, 1 (1987), pp. 51–64; Joint Chiefs of Staff, Joint Pub O-1 (proposed final publication), *Basic National Defense Doctrine* (Washington, DC, 7 May 1991), p. IV, 5–11; E.R. Snoke, *The Operational Level Of War* (Fort Leavenworth, KS, US Command and General Staff College, Combat Studies Institute, 1985), pp. 9–30; Strategic Studies Institute, *The Operational Art of Warfare Across the Spectrum of Conflict* (Carlisle Barracks, PA, US Army War College, 1987), pp. 14–26; J.J. Schneider, 'The Loose Marble and the Origins of Operational Art', *Parameters*, 1 (1989), pp. 85–99; R.M. D'Amura, 'Campaigns: The Essence of Operational Art', *Parameters*, 2 (1987), pp. 44–6; E.B. Atkeson, 'The Operational Level of War', *Military Review*, 3 (1987), pp. 29–32; W.M. Hall, 'A Theoretical Perspective of Airland Battle Doctrine', *Military Review*, 3 (1986), p. 35.
94. Headquarters Department of the Army, *FM 101-5 Staff Organization and Operations* (Washington, DC, 25 May 1984), pp. 1-2-1-5, 2-5-2-16, 7-1-7-5, 8-1-8-4; S.E. Runals, 'A Different Approach', *Military Review* LXVII, 10 (1987), pp. 46–7; G.R. Sullivan, 'Learning to Decide at the Operational Level of War', ibid., pp. 18–20; C.E. Saint, A CINC's View of Operational Art', *Military Review* LXX, 9 (1990), pp. 66–9; C.L. Donnelly, 'An Air Commander's View of Operational Art', ibid., pp. 80–84; Joint Chiefs of Staff Publication O-2, *Unified Action Armed Forces* (Washington, DC, 1 Dec. 1986),

318

pp. 1-1–2-14, 3-1–3-11, 3-12–3-18, 3-26; Joint Chief of Staff Publication 3-O, *Doctrine for Unified and Joint Operations* (Washington, DC, Jan. 1990); Headquarters Department of the Army, *FM 63–5 Combat Service Support Operations– Theater Army* (Washington, DC, 22 Jan. 1985); Headquarters Department of the Army, *FM 100–6 Large Unit Operations* (Washington, DC, 30 Sept. 1987); Headquarters Department of the Army, *FM 22–103 Leadership and Command at Senior Levels* (Washington, DC, June 1987); Joint Chiefs of Staff, Joint Publication 5–00.1., *Doctrine for Joint Campaign Planning* (Washington, DC, June 1992), Chs.I, II; Headquarters Department of the Army, *FM 100–15 Corps Operations* (Washington, DC, 13 Sept. 1989); Combined Arms and Services Staff School, *E 104/8 Military Decision Making* (Fort Leavenworth, KS, Feb. 1987), pp. 1–13; J.J. Yeosock, 'Army Operations in the Gulf Theater', *Military Review* LXXI, 9 (1991), pp. 3–8; US Army War College, *Forces Capabilities Handbook Vol. I* (Carlisle Barracks, PA, academic year 1993), pp. 2-18–2-29; Joint Chiefs of Staff Publication 1, *Joint Warfare of the US Armed Forces* (Washington, DC, 11 Nov. 1991), pp. 45–8, 49–61; Joint Chiefs of Staff Publication 0-1, *Basic National Defense Doctrine*, pp. II-44–II-49, IV-43–IV-46; W.D. Freeman, 'The Challenges of Combined Operations', *Military Review* LXXII, 11 (1992), pp. 2–11; *FM 100-5 Operations*, 1986, pp. 27–40, 139–41, 161–4; Headquarters Department of the Army, *FM 100–7 The Army in Theater Operations* (Washington, DC, 4 Oct. 1993) (edited DRAG version), pp. 1-8–1-22, 1-46–1-52, 2-1–2-14, 3-1–3-31, 4-1–4-41; Headquarters Department of the Army, *FM 100-5 Operations* (Washington, DC, June 1993), pp. 4-1–4-5, 5-1–5-3, 6-0–6-23.

95. J.J. Redden, *Airland Battle – The Global Doctrine*, US Army War College (Carlisle Barracks, PA. 18 May 1983), p. 2; US Army Command and General Staff College, *FC 100-11 Force Integration Corps/Division* (Fort Leavenworth, KS, July 1985), pp. 2-1–2-14; R.L. Schmidt, 'A Doctrine for Command', *Military Review*, 11 (1985), p. 46; US Army War College, *Strategic and Operational Capabilities Planning* (Carlisle Barracks, PA, academic year 1986), Vol. I, p. 7-7; Joint Pub 1, *Joint Warfare of the US Armed Forces*, pp. 5–7; G.R. Sullivan, 'Doctrine: A Guide to the Future', *Military Review*, 2 (1992), pp. 3–4; J.R. Mcdonough, 'Building the New FM 100-5: Process and Product', *Military Review*, 10 (1991), pp. 11–15; US Army Training and Doctrine Command, Deputy Chief of Staff for Doctrine, 'Doctrine Overview' (a briefing given by LTC Troutman), Fort Monroe, VA, April 1993, pp. 3, 12–13, 21–5; US Army Training and Doctrine Command, Deputy Chief of Staff for Concepts and Doctrine Development, 'Doctrine Overview' (a briefing given by Col.D. Ferezan), Fort Monroe, VA, April 1993, pp. 20, 22, 26, 38, 40; US Air Force Air Command and Staff College, 'The Doctrine Strategy Link', in *Military History and Doctrine* (Maxwell AFB, AL, Sept. 1990), p. 10; G.M. Hall, 'Culminating Points', *Military Review*, 7 (1989), pp. 79–86; H.P. Wayne, *Fleet Tactics: Theory and Practice* (Annapolis, 1986), pp. 140–54, 290–97; Department of the Air Force, *USAF Manual 1-1 Basic Aerospace Doctrine of the United States Air Force* (Washington, DC, March 1992), Vol. I, pp. 5–16, Vol. II, pp. 9–15, 71–86, 125–34; *FM 100-5 Operations*, 1986, pp. 14, 15; *FM 100-5 Operations*, 1993, p. 1-1; Richardson, 'FM 100-5: The Airland Battle in 1986', pp. 10–11.

96. J.A. Lecuyer, 'Force Integration', *Military Review*, 2 (1984), p. 24; J.L. Bates and J.B. Quinn, 'T2S=V', *Military Review*, 3 (1986), p. 29; G.C. Mallory, 'Combat Training Center: Training the Force to Fight', *Military Review*, 10 (1987), pp. 3–6; J.M. Vermillion, 'The Pillars of Generalship', *Parameters*, 2 (1987), pp. 13–15; L.D. Holder, 'Educating and Training for Theater Warfare', *Military Review*, 9 (1990), pp. 85–99; 'Offensive Tactical Operations', *Military Review*, 12 (1993), pp. 54–6; US Army Command and General Staff College, 'School of Advanced Military Studies' (a briefing), Fort Leavenworth, KS, 1993, pp. 7, 10, 15, 28, 29; *FM 100-5 Operations*, 1986, pp. 6–7; *FMFM 1 Warfighting*, pp. 49–51.

97. *FM 100-5 Operations*, 1986, pp. 17–19, 28–32.

98. Ibid., p. 17.

99. Ibid.

100. Ibid., pp. 17, 29, 35; W.P. Franz, 'Operational Concepts', *Military Review*, 7 (1984), pp. 3, 14–15; Headquarters US Readiness Command, US Army TRADOC, USAF Tactical Air Command, *General Operating Procedures for Joint Attack of the Second Echelon (J-SAK)* (USREDCOM Pam 525-8, TRADOC Pam 525-45, TACP 50-29) (Macdill AFB,

FL; Fort Monroe, VA.; Langley AFB, VA., 31 Dec. 1984), pp. 2–7; Headquarters Department of the Army, *FM 6-20-2J Division Artillery, Field Artillery Brigade, and Corps Artillery Headquarters* (Washington, DC, 10 Sept. 1984), pp. 3-2–3-3, 4-4; J.W. Montcastle, 'On the Move: Command and Control of Armor Units in Combat', *Military Review*, 11 (1985), pp. 35, 38; T.A. Cardwell, 'Airland Battle Revisited', *Military Review*, 9 (1985), pp. 7–9; US Army Command and General Staff College, *Field Circular (FC) 100-26 Air Ground Operations* (Fort Leavenworth, KS, 31 July 1984), pp. 2-1, 2-2, 2-3, 2-6, 2-30, 3-4; Headquarters Department of the Army, *FM 63-2-2 Combat Service Support Operations – Armored, Mechanized and Motorized Divisions* (Washington, DC, 29 Oct. 1985), p. 1-6; Rogers, 'Synchronizing the Airland Battle', pp. 68–9; W.T. Mariott, 'Force Integration's Next Big Challenge', *Military Review*, 4 (1986), pp. 8–12; J.J. Snow, 'Airland Battle Doctrine: Tenets in Opposition', *Military Review*, 10 (1987), pp. 63–4; T.A. Cimral, 'Moving the Heavy Corps', *Military Review*, 7 (1988), p. 31; B.R. McCaffrey, 'Airland Battle' (briefing presented to US Marine Corps Command and Staff College), Quantico, VA, 14 April 1987, pp. 5–6, 13; W.J. Bolt and D. Jablonsky, 'Tactics and the Operational Level of War', *Military Review*, 2 (1987), pp. 10–14; C.E. Saint, 'Attack Helicopter Operations in the Airland Battle: Close Operations', *Military Review*, 6 (1988), pp. 4–5; P. T. Bingham, 'Ground Maneuver and Air Interdiction in the Operational Art', *Parameters*, 1 (1989), pp. 17–19, 28–9; D.R. Anderson, 'Modernizing Army Command and Control', *Military Review*, 7 (1990), pp. 6–8; Dynamic Research Corporation, System's Division, *Blueprint of the Battlefield* (draft) (Wilmington, MD, 21 May 1992), pp. 58–73, L1–L22; *FM 100-5 Operations*, 1993, pp. 2-8–2-9; *FM 100-7 The Army in Theater Operations*, 1993, pp. 2-9–2-10; H.H. Shelton and K.C. Benson, 'Depth and Simultaneity: Half the Battle', *Military Review*, 12 (1993), pp. 58, 60, 62; US Army TRADOC, USAF Tactical Air Command, USAF Europe, US Pacific Air Forces, US Alaskan Air Command, *Rear Security Operations Army-Tactical Air Forces Procedures for Rear Security Operations at Echelon Above Corps* (FM 90-23, TACP 50-49, USAFEP 50-49, PACAFP 50-49, AACP 50-49 (Fort Monroe, VA; Langley AFB, VA; Ramstein AFB, Germany; Hickam AFB, Hawaii; Elmendorf AFB, Alaska, 14 Nov. 1989), p. 1-12.

101. Tukhachevskii, 'Novye Voprosy Voiny', in Kuznetsov (ed.), *Izbrannye Proizvedeniia*, p. 196.

102. C.L. Barry, 'Planning Aviation Cross-FLOT Operations', *Military Review*, 1 (1984), pp. 34, 36, 37–39, 42–4; D.H. Petraeus, 'Light Infantry in Europe: Strategic Flexibility and Conventional Deterrence', *Military Review*, 12 (1984), pp. 38–47; W.B. Moore and G.M. Harned, 'Air Assault in the Desert: How to Fight?', *Military Review*, 1 (1985), p. 60; J.E. Thompson, 'Heavy-Light Operations in the Desert', *Military Review*, 5 (1985), pp. 56–61; D.A. Fastband, and R.H. Graves, 'Maneuver, Synchronization and Obstacle Operations', *Military Review*, 2 (1986), pp. 37, 43; W.A. Downing, 'Light Infantry Integration in Central Europe', *Military Review*, 9 (1986), pp. 19–22; K.N. Lewis and P.A. Wilson, ' A Follow-on US Echelon for NATO Defense', *Military Review*, 6 (1986), pp. 17–20; R. Lungerich, 'US Rapid Deployment Forces – US CENTCOM – What is It? Can It Do the Job?', *Armed Forces Journal International* (Oct. 1984), pp. 88–103; E.W. Besch, 'Are Our Light Divisions Too Light?', *Army*, 2 (1985), pp. 43–9; R.S. Rush, 'Comparing Light Divisions', *Military Review*, 1 (1987), pp. 68–9; W.W. Harzog and J.D. Howard, 'Heavy Operations', *Military Review*, 4 (1987), pp. 26–33; R.F. Dees, 'Battle Rhythm', *Military Review*, 4 (1987), pp. 63–4; A.L. Cooley, 'Quick Thunder: True Multi-Echelon Training', *Military Review*, 5 (1987), pp. 4–7; L.D. Holder, 'Moving the Heavy Division', *Military Review*, 7 (1988), pp. 47–8; K.D. Stubbs, 'Beyond the Army of Excellence', *Military Review*, 8 (1988), pp. 26–34; J.C. Bahnsen and R.C. Stack, 'A Mobile Division for Future War', *Military Review*, 6 (1989), pp. 30–36; M.J. Dugan, 'Air Power: Concentration, Responsibilities, and the Operational Art', *Military Review*, 7 (1989), pp. 15–18; M.K. Robel, 'Operational Mobility for the Light Division', ibid., pp. 42–5; S.H. Watkins and M.J. Barron, 'Air Maneuver on the Modern Battlefield', ibid., pp. 49–51; Center for Army Lessons Learned, '89–2 Heavy-Light Lessons Learned', pp. 9–10; L.W. Carr, 'Mobility Differential – Army Aviation Branch's Challenge', *US Army Aviation Digest* (Nov.–Dec. 1989), pp. 14–15; C.P. Otstott, C.A. Hagan and M.E. Richmond, ' Battle Rhythm – Division Command and Control', *Military Review*, 6 (1990), pp. 15–18, 23–6; P. J. Boylan, 'Complementary Force Operations', *Military Review*, 6 (1990), pp. 28, 33–6; US Department of the Army, *FM 71-100 Division*

Operations (Washington, DC, 15 Nov. 1988), p. 1-7; P.J. Bodelson and K.B. Smith, 'Design for Tempo', *US Army Aviation Digest* (March–April 1991), pp. 9–15; C.B. Whelden, 'Light Cavalry: Strategic Force for the Future', *Military Review*, 4 (1993), pp. 17–20; C.M. Burke and D.C. Presgraves, 'US Army Concept for Aviation', *US Army Aviation Digest* (Sept.–Oct. 1993), pp. 8–13; L.G. Nowak, 'Synchronizing Deep Attack Support – The Corps Troops Operational Cell', *Military Review*, 7 (1988), pp. 21, 24; US Army Command and General Staff College, *Student Text 100-9 Techniques and Procedures for Tactical Decision Making* (Fort Leavenworth, KS, July 1991), pp. 4-3, 4-6, 4-7.

103. *FM 100-5 Operations*, 1986, p. 17.
104. Ibid.
105. Ibid., pp. 17–18.
106. Ibid., pp. 17–18, 30, 32, 35; an identical view is presented by: D.A. Fastband, 'The Application of the Commander's intent', *Military Review*, 8 (1987), pp. 61, 64; L.D. Holder, 'Concept of Operation: See Ops Overlay', *Military Review*, 8 (1990), pp. 30–32; Center for Army Lessons Learned, *90-1 Fire Support for the Maneuver Commander* (Fort Leavenworth, KS, Feb. 1990), p. 3; Center for Army Lessons Learned, *Company Team Synchronization Training Battle Book*, pp. D-1–D-7; Headquarters Department of the Army, *FM 25-100 Training the Force* (Washington, DC, Nov. 1988), p. 2-9; W.K. Maynard, 'The New American Way of War', *Military Review*, 11 (1993), p. 15.
107. *FM 100-5 Operations*, 1986, p. 18.
108. S. Metz and F.M. Downey, 'Centers of Gravity and Strategic Planning', *Military Review*, 4 (1988), pp. 24–5; L.L. Izzo, 'The Center of Gravity is not an Achilles Heel', *Military Review*, 1 (1988), pp. 76–7; Headquarters Department of the Army, *FM 90-2 Battlefield Deception* (Washington, DC, Oct. 1988), pp. 2-1-2-2.
109. *FM 100-5 Operations*, 1982, pp. 7-14–7-17, referred to the immediate area of operations as the close battle; *FM 100-5 Operations*, 1986, p. 19; Mobile Armored Corps Phantom, 'Employment of the Modern Heavy Corps' (unpublished briefing), AO 710 – Sept. 1992 – 0027, pp. 20–21, 29, 40, 51.
110. Ibid., pp. 19–20; *FM 100-5 Operations*, 1982, pp. 7-13–7-18. Like their Soviet counterparts, the Americans referred at the initial stage of the development of the operational theory to the remote area of operations as deep battle. Later, with the evolving theory, both armies changed the term 'deep battle' for that of 'deep operations'.
111. *FM 100-5 Operations*, 1986, p. 20.
112. Ibid., pp. 59–74; *FM 100-5 Operations*, 1982, pp. 5-1–5-11.
113. *FM 100-5 Operations*, 1986, pp. 10–107.
114. Ibid., pp. 20–21. This same view is held by: K.E. Lewi and J.D. Dellinger, 'Training the CSS', *Military Review*, 11 (1989), pp. 34–42; G.T. Raach, 'The Logistic Estimate – A New Approach', *Military Review*, 7 (1985), pp. 66–72; C.E. Saint and W.H. Yates, 'Attack Helicopter Operations in the Airland Battle: Rear Operations', *Military Review*, 10 (1988), pp. 2–10; B.D. Sullivan, 'Logistical Support for the Airland Battle', *Military Review*, 2 (1984), pp. 2–16; A.G. Wheeler, 'Operational Logistics in Support of the Deep Attack', *Military Review*, 2 (1986), pp. 13, 14; G.M. Harned, 'Offensive Real Battle', *Military Review*, 2 (1986), pp. 30–36; M.F. Montero, 'Supporting Remote Operations', *Army Logistician* (May–June 1984), pp. 3–5; J.M. Vann, 'The Forgotten Forces', *Military Review*, 8 (1987), pp. 4–7; Headquarters Department of the Army, *FM 100-16 Army Operational Logistics* (Washington, DC, 5 Oct. 1993), pp. 1-7-1-17; Center for Army Lessons Learned, *Logistics Preparation of the Battlefield* (Fort Leavenworth, KS, Nov. 1992, pp. 10–11, 14).
115. *FM 100-5 Operations*, 1982, pp. 7-22–7-24, touches upon the issues of unconventional warfare, psychological operations and Ranger operations. Of all three, only the issue of psychological warfare is linked to the operational level, more by definitions of staff responsibilities for planning than by contents of manoeuvre. The other two issues are portrayed according to the traditional approach. Strategic Studies Institute, *Organization, Missions, and Command and Control of Special Forces and Ranger Units in the 1980s* (unclassified) (US Army War College, Carlisle Barracks, PA, 1979), discusses mainly the strategic aspects of employing special forces. Headquarters Department of the Army, *Army Training and Evaluation Program 31-101, Special*

Forces, pp. IV, 1-3-1, 4-1, guides the training of SOF towards the context of strategic missions and functions. Headquarters Department of the Army, *FM 31-22 Command Control and Support of Special Forces Operations* (Washington, DC, 23 Dec. 1981), focuses like its predecessors on the strategic aspects of operating special forces.

116. *FM 100-5 Operations*, 1986, pp. 2–5; H.S. Summers, 'Principles of War and Low Intensity Conflict', *Military Review*, 3 (1985), pp. 43–9; whereas: Headquarters Department of the Army, *FM 100-20 Low Intensity Conflict* (Washington, DC, 16 Jan. 1981), pp. 12–20, 24, 125–29, while examining the operating of SOF in LIC remains confined to the strategic context, exclusively.

117. *FM 100-5 Operations*, 1986, pp. 17, 49, 57–59; US Army John F. Kennedy Special Warfare Center, *Special Operations Mission Area Analysis* (unclassified) (Fort Bragg, NC, May 1983), p. 7-6.

118. *FM 100-5 Operations*, 1986, p. 57.

119. D.J. Baratto, 'Special Forces in the 1980s: A Strategic Reorientation', *Military Review*, 3 (1983), pp. 9–11; D.R. Morelli and M.M. Ferguson, 'Low Intensity Conflict: An Operational Perspective', *Military Review*, 11 (1984), pp. 3–5, 8–11; G.M. Harned, 'Special Operations and the Airland Battle', *Military Review*, 9 (1985), pp. 79–80; W.P. Johnson and E.N. Russel, 'An Army Strategy and Structure', *Military Review*, 8 (1986), p. 69; W.J. Olson, 'Organizational Requirements for LIC', *Military Review*, 1 (1988), p. 9; US Army John F. Kennedy Special Warfare Center, 'Special Forces RISTA in support of the Corps', Fort Bragg, NC (briefing), 12 Nov. 1989, pp. 2–5, 7–8; W.D. Kutter, 'Deep Behind Enemy Lines', *Military Review*, 6 (1990), pp. 40–41, 45–8; Center for Army Lessons Learned, *90-9 Operation 'Just Cause' Lessons Learned* (Vol. II) (Fort Leavenworth, KS, Oct. 1990), p. 4; R.B. Adolph, 'Strategic Rationale for SOF', *Military Review*, 4 (1992), pp. 39–40, 44–6; Office of the Assistant Secretary of Defense for Special Operations and Low Intensity Conflict, The Joint Staff and US Special Operations Command, *US Special Operations Forces – Status Report* (Washington, DC, June 1990), pp. 12–30; C.W. Steiner, 'The Strategic Employment of Special Operations Forces', *Military Review*, 6 (1991), pp. 2–13; J.T. Scott, 'Special Operations Forces – the Future is the Focus', *Army* (1993–94 Green Book) (Oct. 1993), pp. 180–84; C.W. Steiner, 'Special Operations Forces', *Parameters*, 2 (1992), pp. 2–11; C.L. Lambeth and N. Chen, 'C3I for Special Operations Forces: On War's Threshold', *Army*, 4 (1990), pp. 49–52, 55–6; W.H. Burgess, 'Toward a More Complete Doctrine – SOF in Airland Battle Future', *Military Review*, 2 (1991), pp. 30–37.

Afterword:
Operation Desert Storm

As a major war in the closing years of a century of total conflict, and occurring after 200 years of systemic war, Operation Desert Storm can serve as a suitable case study for the main arguments presented in this volume.

The Gulf War brought two schools of military thought into collision. On the one side stood the attrition-oriented, anachronistic school, adhering almost habitually to the nineteenth-century Clausewitzian conception. This school of thought, which crystallized in the prolonged Iran–Iraq War, tended to view warfare through the mechanistic perspective of linear confrontations of masses and resources. It was confronted by a manoeuvre-oriented operational school of thought that had developed during 15 years of vigorous theoretical work.

Many military analysts tend to attribute the allied victory to Saddam Hussein's strategic ignorance and to the clear American technological superiority and in so doing give a simplistic interpretation to a very complex series of events. Moreover, in keeping with the traditional European prejudice, which assumes that combat can only be regarded as serious if it involves a great deal of bloodshed on both sides, the inclination to discredit the operational value of the event, due to the poor Iraqi combat performance, confuses cause and effect and ignores the ingenuity of the United States Central Command.

Since, at least on the part of the allies, this conflict has been referred to in terms of theatre and campaign, it must be examined according to operational criteria.[1] Apart from the abundance of techno-tactical lessons to be learned from the occurrence of actual combat, such an examination will yield a series of illustrations pertinent to our discussion.

In the broader context of war, the Gulf conflict has proved, contrary to the predictions by some analysts of the end of conventional wars, that unless our political perception changes, the following strategic conventions will remain valid: territory is the clearest expression of a state's political sovereignty, and the state's armed forces are the main instrument for securing this value. The strategic-political objectives, guiding the military operations will, in most cases, be defined in territorial terms. Ground forces will remain the dominant asset within the military system's inventory to accomplish these objectives. The combined operational manoeuvre will remain the most relevant method in effecting this accomplishment.

Despite the remoteness of the theatre of operations from the mother bases, the fact that the strategic objectives could be defined *ab initio* in territorial terms, implying a coherent method of action, contributed significantly to the success of the coalition. Moreover, despite the apparent asymmetry between the time allotted to the air operation and the ground manoeuvre, it was the latter which accomplished the strategic objectives and brought the campaign to its successful conclusion.

In other words, since modern armies are, to all intents and purposes, systems, the conduct of modern wars centres first and foremost on the application of an operational mode of thought. Therefore, those who are slow to appreciate this fact are doomed to failure, or, at best, destined to pay a disproportionately high price for attaining their political objectives.

In the light of the precarious circumstances that prevailed at the outset of the campaign, the casualty ratio of victor to vanquished and the rate of advance of the ground manoeuvre, which have no equal in the history of modern warfare, reflect both the conceptual gap between the rival armies, and the contribution of a coherent operational theory to the ability of a modern military system to adapt to the gravest strategic conditions.[2]

The political objectives which the United States' National Command Authority sought to attain through the application of military force were initially interpreted by the theatre commander-in-chief in terms of territory. This made it clear from the start that the ground element would play a major role in the ability of the combined forces to attain the strategic objectives.

Since the third US national policy objective was the preservation of security and stability of friendly states within the Persian Gulf region, the rationale of Operation Desert Shield focused on the defence of the Saudi Arabian mainland, either by deterrence or by applying operational methods of defence corresponding to the rate of accumulating a reasonable mass of ground forces.[3] Viewing Operation Desert Shield from a systemic perspective, the theatre commander realized that his ability to perform his defensive mission depended on a developing process. Similarly he understood that the initial lack of heavy formations was his main operational weakness, and accordingly defined the period of time needed to assemble a defending critical mass as a window of vulnerability.[4]

On the other hand, realizing that the restoration of Kuwait's legitimate government would require forcing the Iraqi ground forces to withdraw from the occupied territory, General Schwarzkopf assumed in the early stages of the campaign that the attainment of this objective depended mainly on the application of a large-scale ground offensive manoeuvre.[5]

Moreover, unlike senior officials within the United States defence establishment who thought the matter could be decided by the Air Force exclusively, the theatre commander saw its Air Force activity as a contribution to the preparation of favourable strategic and operational conditions for the initiation of a ground manoeuvre.[6]

The great sensitivity of the theatre command echelon to the dominance of the aim as the cognitive generator of the hierarchical process of planning and execution is revealed not only through its ability to translate abstract definitions of policy and military directives into the language of action. Once the accumulation of a reasonable defensive mass was completed, and the strategic assumption that the Iraqis would stick to the defensive option had crystallized, certain trends emerged within the American political-strategic echelons pushing towards a shift of planning emphasis from defensive to offensive.[7] The theatre commander realized that this redefinition of strategic guidance not only required a change in the operational planning, but was also a commitment on the part of the National Command Authority to allot the appropriate resources to the operation as a result of the change in strategic circumstances. Consequently, Schwarzkopf exerted pressure on the Joint Chiefs of Staff to convince the National Command Authority to redefine its strategic guidance to the theatre level precisely, and once that was done, the allocation of an offensive order of battle followed.[8]

Furthermore, Schwarzkopf's behaviour illuminates an issue which Rommel, as commander of an independent strategic theatre, never understood. Whereas at the level of actual operations, the difference between offensive and defensive centres on the reversed relations between the holding and striking efforts, at the level of theatre command this difference has quantitative implications. Hence the level responsible for the allocation of strategic resources must be aware of this delicate logic.

The operational mentality prevailing among the American commanders engaged in the Gulf War can best be depicted from the Final Report to Congress, when referring to the Airland Battle doctrine:

> The basis for ARCENT operations was Airland Battle doctrine. The essence of Airland Battle is to defeat the enemy by conducting simultaneous offensive over the full breadth and depth of the battlefield. It is the intellectual road map for operations, conducted at corps and above, and tactics conducted below corps. This doctrine places tremendous demand on combat leaders. Commanders must fight concurrently what is known as close, deep and rear operations, all as interrelated parts of one battle. Commanders fight close – to destroy enemy forces where the battle is joined. They fight deep – to delay or attack enemy reserves. These operations are intended to disrupt the enemy's plan and create opportunities for success in close operations. They fight rear, behind forward units, to protect CSS assets and to retain freedom of action for friendly sustainment and movement of reserve forces. Airland Battle doctrine is centered on the combined arms team, fully integrating the capabilities of all land, sea and air combat systems, and envisions rapidly shifting and concentrating decisive combat power, both fire and maneuver, at the proper time and place on the battlefield . . . Evolving joint operations doctrine guided the planning and conduct of the ground offensive. The basic principles of initiative, depth, agility, synchronization and combined arms are understood and practiced by all services. Forces are trained to fight using common principles and techniques to ensure battlefield interoperability.[9]

The main elements in the extract quoted above are: depth, simultaneous operations, synergy, disruption, intellectual tension between the tactical and operational poles of command, and synchronization.

When exploring the diplomatic-strategic and tactical aspects of the Gulf War, it is quite probable that future military historians will expend great effort trying to answer the intriguing question: Who was the genius whose ideas served as the basis for the Desert Storm offensive plan?

Suggesting a remarkably articulated operational concept, a chart introducing Commander in Chief, Central Command (CINCCENT), Schwarzkopf's intent from 25 August 1990, provides not only a definite answer to the above question, but also proves beyond doubt that the conceptual framework for the offensive operation was clearly defined as early as three weeks after the Iraqi invasion of Kuwait – a time when only two and a half light American divisions were present on Saudi Arabian soil:

> We will offset the imbalance of ground combat power by using our strength against his weakness. Initially execute deception operations to focus his attention on defense and cause incorrect organisation of

326

forces. We will initially attack into Iraqi homeland using air power to decapitate his leadership, command and control, and eliminate his ability to reinforce Iraqi forces in Kuwait and Southern Iraq. We will then gain undisputed air superiority over Kuwait so that we can subsequently and selectively attack Iraqi ground forces with air power in order to reduce his combat power and destroy reinforcing units. Finally, we will fix Iraqi forces in place by feints and limited objectives attacks followed by armored force penetration and exploitation to seize key lines of communication nodes, which will put us in a position to interdict resupply and remaining reinforcements from Iraq and eliminate forces in Kuwait.[10]

Combining the initiation of an inherent operational vulnerability within the rival system, the creation of a distorted perception, detached from the actual operational reality in the mind of the rival system's strategic leadership and the infliction of a massive strike combined with an effective holding attack, CINCCENT's operational conception demonstrated an advanced approach – very close to the Soviet notion of *napravlenie glavnogo udara*.

Inducing the Iraqis to move the main mass of their ground forces into the Kuwait theatre of operations yielded the operational vulnerability that could be exploited through the application of a strike manoeuvre to induce a state of operational shock. The assemblage of the Iraqi principal source of military strength into a well-defined unit of space detached from the strategic rear afforded the coalition the operational opportunity to split the defending mass from its centralistic command authority, from its main logistical bases, from its supporting air power and from friendly reinforcements. Thus, through the consolidation of the Iraqi fighting mass inside Kuwait the actual theatre of operations was sundered *de facto* from its general strategic context. Reflecting the quantitative advantage enjoyed by them, the deliberate Iraqi concentration of ground forces within a limited space, under the condition of absolute rival air superiority offered the coalition a killing zone dominated by their own source of strength. Under such circumstances, the mass of Iraqi ground forces could be pulverized systematically and the entire campaign could be decided by a single operational manoeuvre, aiming to turn over the isolated defending system.

The confinement of the Iraqi mass to the restricted area of Kuwait opened a free strategic corridor, allowing the coalition to convey its striking mass swiftly beyond the centre of the defensive mass without the precondition of breaking through a deeply echeloned, heavily fortified defensive layout. Whereas at the actual level of manoeuvre, the combination of a holding element, attacking the main Iraqi defensive line head-on with the movement of a highly mobile striking mass through the Western corridor introduced a mobility differential, allowing the turning element to attack simultaneously the flanks of the various echelons of the defending system.[11]

In other words, by manipulating a certain operational advantage, this concept deliberately employed attrition in the service of creating opportunities for the acceleration of the ground manoeuvre.

Striving to prevent the synergy among the operational elements of the enemy from transpiring, the coalition's concept of operation applied the principle of fragmentation at all three levels of conducting war. At the strategic level the operational theatre was sundered from the strategic context by means of air power and projection of elements from the XVIII Corps to the line of Al Basra–An Nasiriyah–As Samawah. At the operational level, the emergence of a heavy and light corps, respectively, in the flank of the system that had been fixed to the front, allowed the employment of eight manoeuvring bodies with the aim of imposing division among the various Iraqi deeper echelons comprising mechanized formations. At the tactical level, the operational groupings of Joint Forces Command East, Joint Forces Command (JFC) North, and especially the Marine Corps (MarCent), while attacking frontally from South to North fragmented the Iraqi tactical defensive layout throughout its depth.

This combination produced an exemplary interaction between an operational holding effort, based on the elements of JFC North, JFC East and MarCent, an operational striking effort comprising the formations of VII Armoured Heavy Corps, and a deep operational effort centring upon the XVIII Airborne Corps.

Moreover, to prevent the essential synergy among the operational element of the Iraqi system from transpiring, the coalition manoeuvring method implemented, through the simultaneous operation of its various elements along the entire depth of the defensive layout, a perfect synergy.

The main condition upon which the application of this operational method rested was the initiation of a distorted perception within the entire Iraqi command system – imposing a multi-dimensional deception on the Iraqi system and suppressing its ability to acquire operational intelligence. At the political-strategic level the aggressive American disinformation campaign led the Iraqis to misinterpret the strategic reality and the coalition's intentions – consequently inducing them to concentrate the mass of their ground forces within Kuwait in a defensive posture. At the operational level, the American deception led the Iraqi planners both to anticipate an amphibious operation on Kuwaiti soil, and to believe that the coalition's five operational corps groupings were deployed south of the Saudi Arabian–Kuwaiti border with the intention of mounting a direct attack into the occupied territory.[12]

Thus, intensifying their rival's strategic misconception, the American deception induced the Iraqis to construct a deep echeloned defensive layout, heading south and aiming to frustrate a ground offensive or to impose upon the attacker a long and systematic attrition operation.[13] Moreover, whereas the Iraqis were persuaded that the VII and XVIII allied Corps lay with the mass of coalition ground forces opposite the Kuwaiti border, the blinding effect of the suppressive air operation deprived them of the ability to identify the colossal operation of shifting both formations 150–250 miles to the west all along their defensive front, three weeks prior to the commencement of operation Desert Storm.[14] Therefore, when the offensive manoeuvre was finally launched the Iraqis were entirely unaware of the fact that the coalition's main striking mass had been positioned to the west of Wadi Al Batin and opposite a free corridor leading to the defensive depth.[15] At the tactical level, the 1st Cavalry feint attack towards Wadi Al Batin and the deliberate delay of the VII Corps' initial movement was intended to distract the defender's attention from the main striking effort, while ensuring the success of the southern holding effort in fixing the Iraqis to their positions.[16]

Through the exercise of advanced operational perception and deep understanding of the nature of modern warfare, the theatre commander managed to interpret the operational reality accurately and thus define coherent objectives corresponding with the strategic aims set by the National Command Authority. Moreover, keenly aware of the logic of modern operations, he managed not only to effectively translate a defensive concept into a creative method of offensive manoeuvre, but also to anticipate the consequential situation bearing the systemic elements of his rival's defeat.

With the Airland battle doctrine's baptism of fire, the initial stage in the development of the American theory of operations was brought to completion. However, occurring 200 years after the decree of the *levée en masse*, that is, the event which generated the initial characteristic of systemic or modern warfare, Operation Desert Storm indicates the closure of a broader historical circle. The validity of the operational paradigm which emerged in the United States in the late 1970s was proven, while the traditional dominance of the *Vernichtungsschlacht* paradigm was completely invalidated. Moreover, for the first time in the history of modern warfare, the deterministic predisposition toward self-attrition, so common in Western military culture, was replaced by a manoeuvre approach.[17]

The operational methods exercised by both contenders in the course of the Persian Gulf War reflect the main approaches that have dominated warfare since the advent of the Industrial Revolution. One approach, that flourished in the USSR during the years following the First World War, interpreted modern warfare in accordance with system logic; defining armies as systems and identifying manoeuvre as the military method for accomplishing strategic objectives, it emphasized the operational dimension. The other approach, having monopolized universal military thought since the beginning of the nineteenth century has not ceased to impose on modern warfare quantitative patterns and archaic ideas borrowed from the tactical context.

The systemic nature of the modern environment of conflict derives from political patterns of thought, formulated in the course of the nineteenth century from the technological dynamism generated by the Industrial Revolution and from the quantitative basis determined by Napoleonic warfare. Thus, the mental effort required to address the challenges posed by this environment through the application of system thinking and operational patterns of conduct, constitutes the true substance of the development of modern military thought. When, due to general historical circumstances, a conceptual revolution occurred and a system approach prevailed, warfare assumed a dynamic nature which has been referred to as the indirect approach, or manoeuvre warfare. Nevertheless, as can be learned from the military experience of the last 200 years, in general, and from the Iraqi approach to the conduct of operations as reflected in the Gulf War, in particular, the archaic paradigm of *Vernichtungsschlacht* is still very much in evidence.

NOTES

1. Department of Defense, *Conduct of the Persian Gulf War: Final Report to Congress* (Washington, DC, April 1992), pp. VI–IX; J.W. Foss, 'Building the United States Army for the Twenty-First Century', *RUSI Journal*, 1 (1991), pp. 13–15; R. Smith, 'The Gulf War: The Land Battle', *RUSI Journal*, 1 (1992), pp. 1–2, 4.
2. *Conduct of the Persian Gulf War*, pp. II–III
3. Ibid., pp. 38–46; H.N. Schwarzkopf, *It Doesn't Take a Hero* (New York, 1992), pp. 298–9, 301, 333, 350, 352.
4. *Conduct of the Persian Gulf War*, pp. 46–51.
5. Ibid., pp. 38, 84–88; P. de la Billière, *Storm Command: A Personal Account of the Gulf War* (London, 1992), p. 85; Schwarzkopf, *It Doesn't Take a Hero*, pp. 315, 319–20.
6. Ibid., pp. 318–19 mentions the officers of Curtis LeMay School of Air Force planners as: 'Guys who think strategic bombing can do it all and armies are obsolete'; De la Billière, *Storm Command*, p. 86, mentions Brent Scowcroft, President Bush's National Security Adviser, as one who recommended the independent air option. *Conduct of the Persian Gulf War*, pp. 84, 87.
7. Schwarzkopf, *It Doesn't Take a Hero*, pp. 367–9; *Conduct of the Persian Gulf War*, pp. 83–8.

8. Ibid., pp. 87, 90; Schwarzkopf, *It Doesn't Take a Hero*, pp. 370, 386–7; De la Billière, *Storm Command*, p. 85.
9. *Conduct of the Persian Gulf War*, p. 329.
10. Ibid., p. 84.
11. Central Intelligence Agency, Directorate of Intelligence, *Operation Desert Storm: A Snapshot of the Battlefield* (Washington, DC, Sept 1993), IA 9–10022, illustrates clearly how the following engagements occurred almost simultaneously along the entire depth of the Iraqi defensive layout: US 24th Mechanized Division against elements from the Republican Guard Hammurabi Armoured Division: US ACR 2, US 3rd Armoured Division, US 1st Armoured Division, US 1st Infantry Division against the RG Tawakalna Mechanized and 12th Armoured Divisions: US 1st and 2nd Marine Divisions and US 2nd Tiger Brigade against the Iraqi 3rd Armoured and 1st and 5th Mechanized Divisions.
12. *Conduct of the Persian Gulf War*, pp. 322–4, 344. The amphibious deception was conducted by Marine ATF and 13th Marine Expeditionary Unit both through the raid on Umm Al Maradin Island and actual conduct of preparations for landing to the east of Kuwait. Task Force Troy, consisting of infantry, armour, reconnaissance, engineers, Seabees and Army PSYOPS created the impression that both the VII and XVIII Corps were located opposite the Kuwaiti border with the main mass of allied ground forces.
13. Ibid., p. 112.
14. Ibid., pp. 341–3.
15. Ibid., pp. 356–8.
16. Ibid., pp. 344, 358–72.
17. J.R. Galvin, 'Foreword', in R.D. Hooker (ed.), *Maneuver Warfare – An Anthology* (Novato, CA, 1993), pp. VIII–IX.

Bibliography

1. PRIMARY SOURCES

A. Documents

Bundesarchiv Militärarchiv, Freiburg im Breisgau

Oberkommando der Wehrmacht
RW19/166, W.F., St/OP. Abt.(H), Nr. 442,277/41, Geheim Kommandosache (26.12.1941).
RW4/v. 575, 577, 578 Chefsachen Barbarossa (3.2–28.11.1941).

Oberkommando des Heeres
BII 2Dg66, Richtlinien für Führung und Einsatz der Panzerdivision (3.12.1940).
RH19II/136, Generalstab d. H./Operation Abteilung III, Nr. 1736/41 Geheim Kommandosache Chefsache (18.12.1941).

Heeres Gruppe Mitte
RH19II/119, 120, 121, 122D, Kriegstagebuch Nr. 1 (1.8–31.12.1941).
RH20-4/216, 322b, Abteilung Ia, Nr. 1680/41g, Kommandosache Chefsache (28.9.1941).

Heeres Gruppe Nord
RH19III/579, Führungsabteilung Kriegstagebuch Tätigkeitbericht II, Barbarossa (1.8–31.12.1941).

Heeres Gruppe Süd
17 236/11;16u. Führungsabteilung 21 Kriegstagebuch (20.10–1.12.1941).

Armee Oberkommando 4
RH20-4/337 Studie: Die Kämpfe der 4 Armee im Ersten Kriegsjahr gegen die Sowjets.

Armee Oberkommando 9
RH20-9/22, Abteilung Ia, Anlagen zum Kriegstagebuch HGr. Befehle (25.6–31.12.1941).

Panzergruppe von Kleist
RH21-1/18, Abteilung Ia, Nr. 217/40 Geheim Kommandosache Chefsache (3.12.1940).
RH21-1/36, Abteilung Ia, Nr. 3422/40 Geheim (9.8.1940).

Panzer Armee Oberkommando 2
RH21-2/v.756, Abteilung Ia, Kriegstagebuch Nr. 1 (21.12.1941).
RH21-2/v.277, Abteilung Ia, Kriegstagebuch Nr. 1 (26.12.1941).
RH21-2/v.647, Abteilung Ic, Meldung der Panzerjäger Abteilung 42 (8.7.1941).
RH21-2/v.756, Abteilung Ia, Kriegstagebuch Nr. 1 (15.12.1941).
RH21-2/v.277, Abteilung Ia, Kriegstagebuch Nr. 1 (15.12.1941).
RH21-2/v.244, 876, 877D, Kriegstagebuch PzAOK 2 vom 1.11.1941–31.3.1942.

Panzer Armee Oberkommando 3
RH21-3/v.70, Abteilung Ia, Zwischenmeldung zum Armeeoberkommando 9 (4.10.1941).
RH21-3/v.113, Abteilung Ia, Nr. 520/42 (10.2.1942).
RH21-3/v.611, Abteilung O. Qu. Kriegstagebuch (10.6–31.12.1941).

Panzer Armee Oberkommando 4
RH21-4/50D, 51D, Abteilung Ia, Kriegstagebuch Russlandfeldzug (6.12.1941–27.4.1942).
RH21-4/31, Abteilung Ia, Anlagen zum Kriegstagebuch 'Befehle von Oben' (20.9–14.10.1941).

Panzer Armee Afrika
RH24-288/54, Abteilung Ia, Armee Befehl für den Angriff Nr. 58/42, Geheim Kommandosache Chefsache (20.5.1942).
RH19VIII/2d, Abteilung Ia, Schlachtbericht der PanzerArmee (29.6.1942).
RH19VIII/22, Rinteln Nr. 5106/42 Geheim Kommandosache Chefsache (24.6.1942).

PanzerKorps XIX
RH21-2/v.29, Abteilung Ia, Erfahrungsberichte des Pioniere Bataillon 43 (2.10.1939).

PanzerKorps XXIV
RH24-24/122, Abteilung Ia, Anlagen Nr. 253 zum Kriegstagebuch Nr. 8 (18.10.1941).
RH24-24/122, Abteilung Ia, Anlagen 247 zum Kriegstagebuch Nr. 8 (14.10.1941).

PanzerKorps XXXXVII
RH24-47/28, 29, Abteilung Ia, Anlagen Nr. 699 zum Kriegstagebuch Nr. 3 (5.12.1941).
RH24-47/8, Abteilung Ia, Anlagen Nr. 599 zum Kriegstagebuch Nr. 2 (30.8.1941).
RH24-47/9, Abteilung Ia, Anlagen Nr. 697, zum Kriegstagebuch Nr. 2 (8.9.1941).

PanzerKorps LVII
15 638/2–6, Abteilung Ia, Tagesmeldung (12.7.1941).
15 638/2–6, Abteilung Ia, Tagesmeldung an PanzerArmeeoberKommando 3 (27.7.1941).

PanzerDivision 1
RH27-1/17, Abteilung la, Gefechtbericht der 1 PanzerBrigade (12.6.1940).
RH27-1/17, Abteilung la, Gefechtbericht der PanzerJäger Abteilung 37 (10.6.1940).
RH27-1/17, Abteilung la, Gefechtbericht der 1 PanzerBrigade (10.7.1940).

PanzerDivision 4
RH27/4-37, Abteilung la, Nr. 814/41 Geheim (22.9.1941).
RH27/4-37, Abteilung la, Nr. 71/42 Geheim (12.3.1942).
RH27/4-37, Abteilung la, Anlagen der Gefechtbericht zum Kriegstagebuch Meldung der 5 PanzerBrigade (6.9.1941).
RH27/4–37, Abteilung la, Anlagen zum Kriegstagebuch Nr. 71/42, Geheim Bentwortung Fragebogen OKH Betr. Erfahrung Ostfeldzug (12.3.1942).
RH27/4-37, Abteilung la, Gefechtbericht (11.8.1941).

PanzerDivision 7
RH27-7/52, Abteilung la, Nr. 440/40 Geheim (14.7.1940).
RH27-7/53, Abteilung la, Nr. 440/40 Geheim (14.7.1940).
RH27-7/191, Abteilung la, Kurzbericht (14.5.1940).
RH27-7/55, Abteilung la, Morgenmeldung der Artillerie Regiment 78 (26.8.1941).
RH27-7/55, Abteilung la, Meldung des PanzerAbteilung 101 (23.8.1941).

PanzerDivision 18
RH27-18/72, Abteilung la, Zustandbericht des Division Ingenieurs (4.11.1941).

PanzerDivision 20
RH27-20/99, Abteilung la, Erfahrungsbericht der Schützen Regiment 59 (5.11.1941).

Miscellaneous
RM7/235, Hitler to Mussolini (23.6.1942).

Studies
IIIH(A)20, Liebenstein, Frhr. von, 'Die Operationen der 2 PzArmee in der Doppelschlacht von Bryansk und Wyazma und beim Vorstoss auf der Moskau (20.9–5.12.1941)' (typed manuscript, no specific date).

Liddell Hart Archive
9/24/44
Guderian, H., *Panzer Marsch*, ed. Michaelis, M., draft offered to Liddell Hart.

9/24/93
G. von Blumentritt: Interview with Liddell Hart, Dec., 1945.
G. von Blumentritt. Letter to Liddell Hart (no date).

9/24/106
Liddell Hart: Letter to Guderian, 30 July 1949.
H. Guderian: Letter to Liddell Hart, 7 Oct. 1948.
H. Guderian: Letter to Liddell Hart, 14 Dec. 1948.
H. Guderian: Letter to Liddell Hart, 20 Dec. 1949.

9/24/107
Notes on the Interrogation of Generaloberst Franz Halder C.W/Oct/45, CRGG 332.

9/24/110
G. Heinrici: Interview with Liddell Hart, 3 Jan. 1946.

9/24/118
E. von Kleist: Interview with Liddell Hart, 6 Sept. 1945.

9/24/124
E. von Manstein, 'German Defensive Operations against the Soviets by Army Group South 1943/1944' (typed manuscript, no definition of specific date).

9/24/125
H. von Manteuffel: Interview with Liddell Hart, 10 Dec. 1945.
H. von Manteuffel: Letter to Liddell Hart, 10 March 1949.
H. von Manteuffel: Letter to Liddell Hart, 15 May 1949.

9/24/144
W.R. von Thoma: Interview with Liddell Hart, 1 Nov. 1945.
W.R. von Thoma: Interview with Liddell Hart, 11 Nov. 1945.
W.R. von Thoma: Interview with Liddell Hart, 20 Nov. 1945.

9/24/149
S. Westphal: Interview with Liddell Hart, 4 Oct. 1950.

9/24/206
G. Frhr. von Schweppenburg: Letter to Liddell Hart, 8 March 1949.
G.Frhr. von Schweppenburg: Letter to Liddell Hart, 12 Jan. 1958.
W.K. Nehring: Letter to Liddell Hart, 7 Jan. 1958.
K. Dittmar: Letter to Liddell Hart, 6 Dec. 1957.
L. Crüwell: Letter to Liddell Hart, 23 Jan. 1958.
E. von Manstein: Letter to Liddell Hart, 25 Jan. 1958.
K. Liebman: Letter to Liddell Hart, 8 March 1958.

9/24/227
Questionnaire of B. Müller-Hillebrand, April 1952.

TRADOC Historical Office
Boyd, J.R., *Briefing on the Boyd Theory – Competitive-Observation-Decision-Action Cycles* (introduction by W. Lind), 1 Aug. 1978.
—, 'Patterns of Conflict' (unpublished paper), Oct. 1980.
Central Intelligence Agency, Directorate of Intelligence, *Operation Desert Storm: A Snapshot of the Battlefield* (Washington, DC, Sept. 1993), IA 93–10022.
Doerfel, J.S., 'An Operational Concept for the Integrated Battlefield' (briefing given by Major J.S. Doerfel), Fort Sill, OK, 18 Dec. 1979.
General W.E. DePuy, CG TRADOC, Letter to Centers' Commanders and School Commandants, Fort Monroe, VA, 23 July 1974.

—, Letter to General F.C. Weyand, Army Chief of Staff, Fort Monroe, VA, 18 Feb. 1976.

General D.A. Starry, CG TRADOC, *Commander's Notes No.3, Operational Concepts and Doctrine*, Fort Monroe, VA, 20 Feb. 1979.

—, 'Comments', in: *Analysis: Selected Papers*, ODCSCD Anl.Ofc., Fort Monroe, VA, 1 Aug. 1977.

—, 'The TRADOC Doctrinal Literature Program' (letter for distribution), 282000Z, Fort Monroe, VA, April 1980.

—, 'The Writing of Doctrine' (letter for distribution), 292030Z, Fort Monroe, VA, April 1980.

—, 'Integrated Operations' (letter for distribution), 091530Z, Fort Monroe, VA, July 1980.

—, 'The Airland Battle' (letter for distribution), 0291245Z, Fort Monroe, VA, Jan. 1981 (02 291305Z).

General G.K. Otis, CG TRADOC, 'Doctrinal Perspectives of War', Fort Monroe, VA, Sept. 1981.

—, 'The Airland Battle' (message for distribution), 23651, Fort Monroe, VA, Aug. 1981. TRADOC Headquarters, 'Airland Battle Doctrine' (published briefing given by Major General G.M. Kelly), Fort Monroe, VA, 7 Nov. 1983.

Brigadier General B.R. McCaffrey, 'Airland Battle' (briefing presented to US Marine Corps Command and General Staff College), Quantico, VA, 14 April 1987.

US Army John F. Kennedy Special Warfare Center, 'Special Forces RISTA in Support of the Corps' (unpublished briefing), Fort Bragg, NC, 12 Nov. 1989.

Mobile Armored Corps Phantom, 'Employment of the Modern Heavy Corps' (unpublished briefing), AO 710 – Sept. 1992 – 0027.

US Army Command and General Staff College, 'School of Advanced Military Studies' (briefing), Fort Leavenworth, KS, Feb. 1993.

B. Military Manuals

German

Generalstab des Heeres, Kriegswissenschaftliche Abteilung, *Der Schlachterfolge mit Welchen Mitteln Wurden Sie Ersterbt*, (Berlin, 1903).

—, *Exerzir – Reglement für die Infanterie*, (Berlin, 1906).

—, *Der Angriff im Stellungskrieg* (Berlin, 1 Jan. 1918) (trans. by the BEF Intelligence).

—, *Dienstvorschrift 300 Truppenführung* (2 vols.), (Berlin, 1936).

—, *Begegnungsstate. Studien zur Kriegsgeschichte und Taktik* (Berlin, 1939).

—, *Dienstvorschrift G.151 – Mobilmachungsplan für das Heer: Erhaltung des Heeres im Kriegszustand* (Berlin, 1939).

—, *Dienstvorschrift 81/15 Wehrersatz Bestimmungen be Besonderen Einsatz* (Berlin, 1942).

—, *Dienstvorschrift 299/1b, Ausbildungsvorschrift für die Panzertruppen* (Berlin, 1943).

Soviet

Narodnyi Komissariat Oborony Soiuza SSR (NKO), *Vremennaia instruktsiia po boevomu primeneniu tankov RKKA* (Interim Instructions on the Combat Use of Tanks of the RKKA) (Moscow, 1928).

—, *Polevoi ustav RKKA* (Field Service Regulations of the RKKA) (Moscow, 1929).

—, *Boevoi ustav konnitsy RKKA (BUK–29)* (The RKKA 1929 Cavalry Combat Regulations) (Moscow, 1929).

—, *Boevoi ustav pekhoty RKKA (BUP–29)* (The RKKA 1929 Infantry Combat Regulations) (Moscow, 1929).

—, *Boevoi ustav mekhanizirovannykh voisk* (Combat Regulations of Mechanized Forces) (Moscow, 1932).

—, *Vozhdenie i boi samostoiatel'nykh mekhanizirovannykh soedinenii* (Leadership and Combat of Independent Mechanized Formations) (Moscow, 1932).

—, *Instruktsii po glubokomu boiu* (Instructions on Deep Battle) (Moscow, 1934).

—, *Nastavlenie po polevoi sluzhbe voiskovykh shtabov* (Provisional Manual for Field Service of Troop Staffs) (Moscow/Leningrad, 1935).

—, *Samostoiatel'nye mekhanizirovannye soedineniia, proekt nastavlenii* (Independent Mechanized Formations, draft manual) (Moscow, 1937).

—, *Vremennyi polevoi ustav RKKA 1936 (PU–36)* (RKKA Provisional Field Service Regulations 1936) (Moscow, 1937).

—, *Boevoi ustav konnitsy RKKA (BUK–38)* (The RKKA Cavalry Combat Regulations) (Moscow, 1938).

—, *Boevoi ustav pekhoty RKKA (BUP–38)* (The RKKA Infantry Combat Regulations) (Moscow, 1938).

—, *Boevoi ustav bronetankovykh i mekhanizirovannykh voisk Krasnoi Armii 1944g.* (The 1944 Combat Regulations for Tank and Mechanized Forces of the Red Army) (Moscow, 1944).

United States

Department of the Navy, Headquarters Marine Corps, *FMFM 1 Warfighting* (Washington, DC, 6 March 1989).

—, *FMFM 1–1 Campaigning* (Washington, DC, 25 Feb. 1990).

Department of the Army, *FM 100–5 Operations of Army Forces in the Field* (Washington, DC, Sept. 1968).

—, *FM 100–5 Operations* (Washington, DC, July 1976).

—, *FM 100–5 Operations* (Washington, DC, 20 Aug. 1982).

—, *FM 100–5 Operations* (Washington, DC, May 1986).

—, *FM 100–5 Operations* (Washington, DC, June 1993).

—, *FM 100–1 The Army* (Washington, DC, 14 Aug. 1981).

—, *FM 101–5 Staff Organization and Operations,* (Washington, DC, 25 May 1984).

—, *FM 63–5 Combat Service Support Operations – Theater Army* (Washington, DC, 22 Jan. 1985).

—, *FM 100–6 Large Unit Operations* (Washington, DC, 30 Sept. 1987).

—, *FM 100–15 Corps Operations* (Washington, DC, 13 Sept. 1989).

—, *FM 100–7 The Army in Theater Operations* (Washington, DC, 4 Oct. 1993) (edited DRAG version).

—, *FM 6–20–2J, Division Artillery*, Field Artillery Brigade, and Corps Artillery Headquarters (Washington, DC, 10 Sept. 1984).

—, *FM 63–2–2 Combat Service Support Operations – Armored, Mechanized and Motorized Divisions* (Washington, DC, 29 Oct. 1985).

—, *FM 71–100 Division Operations* (Washington, DC, 15 Nov. 1988).

—, *FM 25–100 Training the Force* (Washington, DC, Nov. 1988).

—, *FM 90–2 Battlefield Deception* (Washington, DC, Oct. 1988).

—, *FM 100–16 Army Operational Logistics* (Washington, DC, 5 Oct. 1993).

—, *Army Training and Evaluation Program 31–101, Special Forces* (Washington, DC, 1980).

—, *FM 31–22 Command, Control and Support of Special Forces Operations* (Washington, DC, 23 Dec. 1981).

—, *FM 100–20 Low Intensity Conflict* (Washington, DC, 16 Jan. 1981).

Department of the Air Force, *Air Force Manual (AFM) 1–1 Basic Aerospace Doctrine of the United States Air Force* (Air Power Research Institute, Maxwell AFB, AL, 16 March 1984).

—, *US Air Force Manual 1–1 Basic Aerospace Doctrine of the US Air Force* (Washington, DC, March 1992).

Joint Chiefs of Staff, *Joint Pub O-1, Basic National Defense Doctrine* (Washington, DC, 7 May 1991) (proposed final publication).

—, *Joint Pub O-2, Unified Action Armed Forces* (Washington, DC, 1 Dec. 1986).

—, *Joint Pub 3-O, Doctrine for Unified and Joint Operations* (Washington, DC, Jan. 1990).

—, *Joint Pub 5–00.1, Doctrine for Joint Campaign Planning* (Washington, DC, June 1992).

—, *Joint Pub 1 Joint Warfare of the US Armed Forces* (Washington, DC, 11 Nov. 1991).

—, *Joint Pub 2-0 Joint Doctrine for Intelligence Support to Operations* (Washington, DC, 12 Oct. 1993).

—, *Joint Pub 3–05 Doctrine for Joint Special Operations* (Washington, DC, 28 Oct. 1992).

US Army Training and Doctrine Command *TRADOC Regulation 11–7, Operational Concepts and Army Doctrine* (Fort Monroe, VA, 29 Dec. 1980).

—, *Pam 525–5 Military Operations: Operational Concepts for the Airland Battle and Corps Operations 1986* (Fort Monroe, VA, 25 March 1981).

—, USAF Tactical Air Command, USAF Europe, US Pacific Air Forces, US Alaskan Air Command, *Rear Security Operations – Army-Tactical Air Forces Procedures for Rear Security Operations at Echelon Above Corps* (FM 90–23, TACP 50–49, USAFEP 50–49, PACAFP 50–49, AACP 50–49)

(Fort Monroe, VA, Langley AFB, VA, Ramstein AFB Germany, Hickam AFB, Hawaii, Elmendorf AFB, AK, 14 Nov. 1989).

US Command and General Staff College, *FC 100–11 Force Integration Corps/Division* (Fort Leavenworth, KS, July 1985).

—, *FC 100–26 Air Ground Operations* (Fort Leavenworth, KS, 31 July 1984).

—, *Student Text 100–9 Techniques and Procedures for Tactical Decision Making* (Fort Leavenworth, KS, July 1991).

Combined Arms and Services Staff School, *E 104/8 Military Decision Making* (Fort Leavenworth, KS, Feb. 1987).

Headquarters US Readiness Command, US Army TRADOC, USAF Tactical Air Command, *General Operating Procedures for Joint Attack of the Second Echelon (J – SAK)* (USREDCOM Pam 525–8, TRADOC Pam 525–45, TACP 50–29) (Macdill AFB, FL, Fort Monroe, VA, Langley AFB, VA, 31 Dec. 1987).

2. SECONDARY SOURCES

A. Books

Abelson, R.P., Aronson, E., Mcguire, W.J., Newcomb, J.M., Rosenberg, N.J. and Tennenbaum, P.M., *Theories of Cognitive Consistency: A Sourcebook* (Chicago, 1968).

Addington, L.H., *The Blitzkrieg Era and the German General Staff* (New Brunswick, 1971).

Aganov, S.Kh. (ed.), *Inzhenernye voiska Sovetskoi Armii 1918–1945* (The Engineer Forces of the Soviet Army 1918–1945) (Moscow, 1985).

Akademiia General'nogo Shtaba im. K.E. Voroshilova, *Istoriia voennykh ordenov Lenina i Suvorova i stepeni Akademii General'nogo Shtaba Vooruzhennykh Sil SSSR im. K.E. Voroshilova* (The History of the Military Orders of Lenin and Suvorov and the Importance of the K.E. Voroshilov General Staff Academy of the Armed Forces of the USSR), 2nd edn (Moscow, 1987).

Alexandrov, E.V., *Rabota divizionnogo i korpusnogo inzhenera* (Operating the Division's and Corps' Engineers) (Moscow, 1933).

Algazin, A.S., *Obespechenie vozdushnykh operatsii* (Air Support Operations) (Moscow, 1928).

Allen, R.L. (ed.), *Operational Level of War – Its Art* (special text) (US Army War College, Carlisle Barracks, PA, 28 Aug. 1985).

Ammosov, S.N., *Taktika motomekhsoedinenii* (Tactics of Moto-mechanized Formations) (Moscow, 1932).

Anan'ev, I.M., *Tankovye armii v nastuplenii po opytu Velikoi otechestvennoi voiny* (Tank Armies in the Offensive According to the Experience of the Great Patriotic War) (Moscow, 1988).

Andronikov, I.G. and Mostowenko, W.D., *Die Roten Panzer. Geschichte der Sowjetischen Panzertruppen 1920–1960* (Munich, 1963).

Anfilov, V.A., *Proval blitskriga* (The Failure of the Blitzkrieg) (Moscow, 1974).

Ardant du Picq, C.J.J., *Battle Studies* (New York).

Aron, R., *Clausewitz* (London, 1983).

Asprey, R.B., *War in the Shadows, The Guerilla in History* (London, 1975).

Azovtsev, N.N., Dmitriev, P.N., Dushenkin, V.V., Kevdin, P.M., Naida, S.F. and Spirin, L.M. (eds), *Direktivy komandovaniia frontov Krasnoi Armii 1917–1922gg.* (Directives of the Red Army's Front Commands 1917–1922) (Moscow, 1971–78).

Babadzhanian, A.Kh. (ed.), *Dorogi pobedy* (Roads of Victory) (Moscow, 1975).

—, Popel', N.K., Shaplin, M.A., Kravchenko, I.M., *Liuki otkryli v Berline: boevoi put' 1-i Gvardeiskoi Tankovoi Armii* (The Turrets were Opened in Berlin: The Combat Path of the 1st Guards Tank Army) (Moscow, 1973).

—, *Tanki i tankovye voiska* (Tanks and Tank Forces) (Moscow, 1970).

Babel', I., *Izbrannye proizvedeniia* (Selected Works) (Moscow, 1966).

Badeau, A., *Military History of U.S. Grant* (New York, 1882).

Bagramian, I.Kh. (ed.), *Istoriia voin i voennogo iskusstva* (History of War and Military Art) (Moscow, 1970).

—(ed.), *Voennaia istoriia* (Military History) (Moscow, 1971).

Balck, W., *Development of Tactics – World War*, trans. Bell, H. (Fort Leavenworth, KS, 1922).

—, *Tactics*, trans. Krueger, W. (Fort Leavenworth, KS, 1911) (2 vols.).

Bald, D., *Der Deutsche Offizier* (Munich, 1984).

Baldwin, H.W., *Strategy for Tomorrow* (New York, 1970).

Bamberger, L., *Bismarcks Grosses Spiel. Die Geheim Tagebücher Ludwig Bambergers*, ed. Feder, E. (Frankfurt a.M., 1932).

Barker, J.A., *Paradigms, The Business of Discovering the Future* (New York, 1993).

Bartov, O., *Hitler's Army* (Oxford University Press, 1992).

—, *The Eastern Front 1941–1945, German Troops and the Barbarization of Warfare* (London, 1985).

Bauer, E., *Der Panzerkrieg. Die Wichtigsten Panzeroperationen des Zweiten Weltkrieges in Europa und Afrika*, Vol. I: *Vorstoss und Rückzug der Deutschen Panzerverbande* (Bonn, 1965).

Beck, L., *Studien* (Stuttgart, 1955).

Becke, A.F., *An Introduction to the History of Tactics 1740–1905* (London, 1909).

Beinhauer, E., *Artillerie im Osten* (Berlin, 1944).

Belitskii, S.M., *Strategicheskie rezervy* (Strategic Reserves) (Moscow, 1930).

Bellamy, C., *The Evolution of Modern Warfare* (London, 1990).

Bennett, E.W., *German Armament and the West 1932–1933* (Princeton University Press, 1979).

Berkhin, I.B., *Voennaia reforma v SSSR* (Military Reform in the USSR) (Moscow, 1958).

Bernhardy, Frhr. von, *Cavalry in War and Peace* (London, 1910).

—, *How Germany Makes War* (London, 1914).

—, *On War of Today* (London, 1912).

Bertalanffy, L. von, *General System Theory* (New York, 1968), 1st edn, 1973, Penguin University Press edn, 1975, 5th edn.

Besymensky, L., *Sonderakte Barbarossa* (Stuttgart, 1968).

Bidwell, S. and Graham, D., *Fire Power: British Army Weapons and Theories 1904–1945* (London, 1982).

Billière, P. de la, *Storm Command – A Personal Account of the Gulf War* (London, 1992).

Biriukov, N.I., *Trudnaia nauka pobezhdat'* (The Difficult Science of Winning) (Moscow, 1975).

Biriukov, S.S., *Sovetskii soldat na Balkanakh* (A Soviet Soldier in the Balkans) (Moscow, 1963).

—, *Surovye gody 1941–1945* (Severe Years 1941–1945) (Moscow, 1966).

Blau, G.E., *The German Campaigns in Russia – Planning and Operations 1940–1942* (Washington, 1953).

Bloch, J. de, *Modern Weapons and Modern War*, trans. Stead, W.T. (London, 1900).

Blume, C.W. von, *Strategie* (Berlin, 1882).

Blumenthal, A.C.C. von, *Journals of Field Marshal Count von Blumenthal for 1866 and 1870–71*, trans. Gillespie-Addison, A.D. (London, 1903).

Blumentritt, G., *Strategie und Taktik* (Konstanz, 1957).

Bocharov, K., Nizhechek, I. and Suslov, P. (eds), *Protiv reaktsionnykh teorii na voenno-nauchnom fronte. Kritika strategicheskikh i voenno-istoricheskikh vzgliadov prof. Svechina* (Against Reactionary Theories on the Military Front. A Critique of Prof. Svechin's Strategic and Military Historical Views) (Moscow, 1931).

Boerner, H., *Mit Stukas und Panzern nach Frankreich Hinein* (Berlin, 1943).

Boguslawski, A. von, *Tactical Deductions from the War of 1870–1871*, trans. Graham, L. (London, 1872).

Bol'shaia Sovetskaia Entsiklopediia (The Great Soviet Encyclopedia) (Moscow, 1926–47) (30 vols.).

Bol'shaia Sovetskaia Entsiklopediia (The Great Soviet Encyclopedia) (Moscow, 1969–78) (3rd edn).

Bol'tse, A., *Nochnoi boi* (Night Combat) (Moscow, 1938).

Bond, B.J., *Liddell Hart: A Study of His Military Thought* (London, 1977).

Bonnal, G.A., *Froeschwiller: Récit Commenté des évènements du 15 Juillet au 12 Août 1870* (Paris, 1899).

Boog, H., et al., *Der Angriff auf die Sowjet Union* (Stuttgart, 1983).

—(ed.), *Operative Denken und Handeln in Deutschen Streitkräften im 19. und 20. Jahrhundert* (Bonn, 1988).

Bor, P., *Gespräch mit Halder* (Wiesbaden, 1950).

Bourcet, P. de, *Mémoires Historiques sur la Guerre 1757–1762* (Paris, 1762).

Borchert, H.W., *Panzerkampf im Westen* (Berlin, 1940).

Borchert, M., *Der Kampf gegen Tanks* (Berlin, 1931).

Botvinnik, A.S., *Tekhnika i taktika khimbor'by, kratkie svedeniia* (Techniques and Tactics of Chemical Combat, a Short Summary) (Moscow, 1932).

341

Boulding, K.E., *Conflict and Defense* (New York, 1962).

Bouscaren, A.T. (ed.), *All Quiet on the Eastern Front* (New York, 1977).

Bradford, K.E. and Brown, F.J., *The US Army in Transition* (Beverly Hills, 1973).

Bradley, D., *Generaloberst Heinz Guderian und die Entstehungsgeschichte des Modernen Blitzkrieges* (Osnabruck, 1978).

Brandt, G., *Moderne Kavallerie* (Berlin, 1931).

Brehm, W., *Mein Kriegstagebuch 1939–1945, mit der 7 Panzerdivision, Fünf Jahre in West und Ost* (Kassel, 1953).

Bronsart von Schellendorff, P., *Geheimes Kriegstagebuch 1870–1871*, ed. Rassow, P. (Bonn, 1954).

Bruchmüller, G., *The German Artillery in the Breakthrough Battles of the World War*, trans. Wallace, J.H. and Kehrn, H.D. (Fort Sill, OK, 1922).

Brusilov, A.A., *Moi vospominaniia* (My Recollections) (Moscow, 1983).

Bryla, E.A., Lancaster, M.S. and Rennagel, W.C., *Contending Concepts: Tactics and Operational Art* (Newport, Center for Advanced Research, Naval War College, June 1979).

Bubnov, A.S., Kamenev, S.S., and Ideman, R.P. (eds), *Grazhdanskaia voina 1918–1921: Voennoe iskusstvo Krasnoi Armii* (The Civil War 1918–1921: The Military Art of the Red Army) (Moscow, 1928–30).

Buchholtz, A., *Moltke, Schlieffen and Prussian War Planning* (Oxford, 1991).

Buckley, W., *Sociology and Modern Systems Theory* (Englewood Cliffs, NJ, 1967).

Budennyi, S.M., *Proidennyi put'* (The Road Travelled) (Moscow, 1958–73).

Bulatov, A.A. and Prozorov, V.G., *Takticheskaia vnezapnost'* (Tactical Surprise) (Moscow, 1965).

Bulgakov, T.P. (ed.), *Akademiia generalnogo shtaba* (The General Staff Academy) (Moscow, 1987).

Bülow, Prince von, *Memoirs 1903–1909* (London, 1931).

Bundesministerium für Landesverteidigung, Militärwissenschaftliche Abteilung (ed.), *Gliederungen der Panzertruppen im 2. Weltkrieg* (Vienna, 1962).

Burleigh, M., *Germany Turns Eastwards. A Study of Ostforschung in the Third Reich* (Cambridge, 1989) (2nd edn).

Caemmerer, R. von, *The Development of Strategical Science during the 19th Century*, trans. Donnat, K. von (London, 1905).

Camon, H., *Le Système de Guerre de Napoléon* (Paris, 1923).

—, *Quand et Comment Napoléon a Conçu son Système de Bataille* (Paris, 1935).

Canby, S., *Classic Light Infantry and the Defense of Europe* (Washington, DC, 1982).

—, *Defense Concepts and Short War Responses (Final Report prepared for the Assistant Secretary of Defense, Program Analysis and Evaluation)*, (Silver Springs, MD, 22 Sept. 1978).

—, *NATO Corps Battle Tactics* (Washington, DC, Nov. 1978).

—, *The Alliance and Europe: Part IV, Military Doctrine and Technology –*

Adelphi Papers (London, (IISS), 1974).

Carrel, P., *Unternehmen Barbarossa. Der Marsch nach Russland* (Berlin, 1963).

Carver, M., *The Apostles of Mobility, the Theory and Practice of Armoured Warfare* (London, 1979).

Center for Army Lessons Learned, *89-2 Heavy-Light Lessons Learned* (Fort Leavenworth, KS, 22 Aug. 1989).

—, *89-4 Corps – Division Lessons Learned* (Fort Leavenworth, KS, Nov. 1989).

—, *90-6 Company Team Synchronization Training Battle Book* (Fort Leavenworth, KS, 1990).

—, *90-1 Fire Support for the Maneuver Commander* (Fort Leavenworth, KS, Feb. 1990).

—, *90-9 Operations 'Just Cause', Lessons Learned* (Fort Leavenworth, KS, Oct. 1990).

—, *Logistics Preparation of the Battlefield* (Fort Leavenworth, KS, Nov. 1992).

Chales de Beaulieu, W., *Der Vorstoss der Panzergruppe 4 auf Leningrad 1941* (Neckargemünd, 1963).

—, *Generaloberst Erich Hoepner, Militärisches Porträt eines Panzerführers* (Neckargemünd, 1961).

Chamberlin, W.H., *Russia's Iron Age* (Boston, 1935).

Chandler, D.G., *Atlas of Military Strategy* (London, 1980).

—, *The Campaigns of Napoleon* (London, 1976).

—, *The Art of War in the Age of Marlborough* (London, 1976).

Chapman, A.W., *The Army's Training Revolution 1973–1990, An Overview* (US Army Training and Doctrine Command, Fort Monroe, VA, 1991).

Checkland, P., *Systems Thinking, Systems Practice* (New York, 1981).

Chistiakov, I.M., *Sluzhim otchizne* (Serving the Fatherland) (Moscow, 1975).

Chuikov, V.I., *The End of the Third Reich* (Moscow, 1985).

Clark, A.A., Chiarelli, P.W., Mckitrick, J.S. and Reed, J.W. (eds), *The Defense Reform Debate – Issues and Analysis* (Johns Hopkins University Press, 1984).

Clausewitz, C. von, *Historical and Political Writings*, trans. and ed., Paret, P. and Moran, D. (Princeton University Press, 1992).

—, *On War*, ed. Howard, M. and Paret, P. (Princeton, University Press, 1976).

Cochenhausen, F.E.E.A., *Die Truppenführung, Teil I: Mittlere und Untere Führung* (Berlin, 1931).

—, *Die Kriegswissenschaftliche Fortbildung des Truppenoffiziers* (Berlin, 1926).

—, *Taktisches Handbuch für den Truppenführer und seine Gehilfen* (Berlin, 1936).

Colin, J., *The Transformation of War*, trans. Pope-Hennessey, L.H.R. (London, 1912).

Conquest, R., *The Great Terror. Stalin's Purge of the Thirties* (London, 1968).

—, *The Harvest of Sorrow. Soviet Collectivization and the Terror Famine* (London, 1986).

343

Cooper, M. and Lucas, J., *Panzer: The Armoured Force of the Third Reich* (London, 1976).

Craig, G., *The Politics of the Prussian Army 1640–1945* (Oxford, 1955).

Creveld, M. van, *Command in War* (Harvard University Press, 1985).

—, *Fighting Power: German Military Performance 1914–1945* (US Department of Defense, Washington, DC, 1980).

—, *Supplying War* (Cambridge, 1977).

—, *Technology and War from 2000 B.C. to the Present* (London, 1989).

Curti, P., *Umfassung und Durchbruch* (Frauenfeld, 1955).

Degtiarev, G.E., *Taran i shchit* (Ram and Shield) (Moscow, 1966).

Deist, W. (ed.), *The German Military in the Age of Total War* (Leamington Spa, UK, 1985).

—, *The Wehrmacht and German Armament* (London, 1981).

Delbrück, H., *History of the Art of War within the Framework of Political History* (4 vols.), trans. Renfroe, W.J. (London, 1985).

—, *Geschichte der Kriegskunst im Rahmen der Politischen Geschichte* (Berlin, 1900).

Delmensingen, K. Kraft von, *Der Durchbruch: Studie an Hand der Vorgänge des Weltkrieges 1914–1918* (Hamburg, 1937).

Demerath, N.J. and Peterson, R.A., *System Change and Conflict. A Reader on Contemporary Theory and the Debate over Functionalism* (New York, 1967).

Demeter, K., *Das Deutsche Offizierkorps* (Berlin, 1965).

Department of Defense, *Conduct of the Persian Gulf War: Final Report to Congress* (Washington, DC, April 1992).

Derrecagaix, V., *Modern War* (2 vols.) (Washington, 1888).

Dictionary of Basic Military Terms, trans. under the auspices of US Air Force, Washington, DC, 1965.

Dixon, N., *On the Psychology of Military Incompetence* (London, 1976).

Donnelly, C., *Red Banner – The Soviet Military System in Peace and War* (Coulsdon, Surrey, 1988).

Doughty, R.A., *The Evolution of US Army Tactical Doctrine 1946–1976* (Fort Leavenworth, Combat Studies Institute, 1979).

Dremov, I.F., *Nastupala groznaia bronia* (The Terrible Armour Attacked) (Kiev, 1981).

Drew, D.M. and Snow, D.M., *The Eagle's Talons: The American Experience in War* (Maxwell AFB, AL, 1988).

Dubinskii-Mukhadze, I., *Ordzhonikidze* (Moscow, 1967).

Dupuy, T.N., *A Genius for War: The German Army and General Staff 1807–1945* (New York, 1977).

—, *Numbers, Predictions and War* (Fairfax, VA, 1984).

—, *Options of Command* (New York, 1984).

—, et al., *Opposed Rates of Advance of Large Forces in Europe* (Dunn Loring, VA, 1972).

—, et al., *Effects of Combat Losses and Fatigue on Operational Performance* (Dunn Loring, VA, 1978).

—, *The Evolution of Weapons and Warfare* (Fairfax, VA, 1984).

—, *Understanding War, History and Theory of Combat* (London, 1992).

Dunshenkin, V.V., *Vtoraia Konnaia: voenno-istoricheskii ocherk* (The Second Cavalry: A Military Historical Outline) (Moscow, 1968).

Dwinger, E., *Panzerführer. Tagebuchblatter vom Frankreichfeldzug* (Jena, 1941).

Dynamic Research Corporation, System's Division, *Blueprint of the Battlefield* (draft) (Wilmington, DE, 21 May 1992).

Earle, E.M., *Makers of Modern Strategy* (Princeton University Press, 1971).

Egorov, A.I., *L'vov–Varshava. 1920 god, vzaimodeistvie frontov* (Lvov–Warsaw. The Year 1920, Cooperation among Fronts) (Moscow, Leningrad, 1928).

English, J.A., *On Infantry* (New York, 1984).

Enthoven, A.C. and Smith, K.W., *How Much Is Enough: Shaping the Defense Program 1961–1969* (New York, 1971).

Epanchin, N., *Operations of General Gurko's Advance Guard in 1877*, trans. Havelock, H. (London, 1900).

—, *Voina 1877–1878, deistviia General Adiutanta Gurko* (The War of 1877–1878, the Operation of General Adjutant Gurko) (Moscow, 1895).

Eremenko, A.I., *Gody vozmezdiia* (Years of Retaliation) (Moscow, 1969).

—, *Stalingrad, zapiski komanduiushchego frontom* (Stalingrad, Reminiscences of a Front Commander in Chief) (Moscow, 1961).

—, *V nachale voiny* (The Beginning of the War) (Moscow, 1964).

Erickson, J., *The Road to Stalingrad* (London, 1985) (2nd edn).

—, *The Soviet High Command* (London, 1962).

Essays on Strategy III (National Defense University, Washington, DC, 1986).

Ewell, J. and Hunt, I.A., *Sharpening the Combat Edge: The Use of Analysis to Reinforce Military Judgement* (Washington, DC, 1974).

Falkenhausen, W. von, *Der Grosse Krieg der Jetztzeit* (Berlin, 1909).

—, *Flankenbewegung und Massenheer* (Berlin, 1898).

Falls, C., *Armageddon 1918* (The Nautical and Aviation Publishing Company of America, 1979).

— and Becke, A.F. (eds), *Military Operations in Egypt and Palestine* (London, 1930).

Fediuninskii, I.I., *Podniatie po trevoge* (Answering the Alarm) (Moscow, 1961).

Fedotov-White, D., *The Growth of the Red Army* (Princeton University Press, 1944).

Fervers, H.K., *Der Vernichtungskrieg* (Frankfurt a.M., 1956).

Foch, F., *The Principles of War*, trans. Morinni, J. de (New York, 1918).

Foerster, W. (ed.), *Prinz Friedrich Karl von Preussen: Denkwürdikeiten aus seinem Leben* (2 vols.) (Stuttgart, 1910).

—, *Aus der Gedankenwerkstatt des Deutschen Generalstabes* (Berlin, 1931).

Forbes, A., *My Experience of the War between France and Germany* (London, 1871) (2 vols.).

—, *The Daily News Correspondence of the War between Germany and France 1870–1871* (London, 1871).

Förster, G., *Totaler Krieg und Blitzkrieg. Die Theorie des Totalen Krieges und des Blitzkrieges in der Militärdoktrin des Faschistischen Deutschland am Vorabend des Zweiten Weltkrieges* (Berlin, 1967).

Fortescue, J.W., *A History of the British Army* (London, 1912) (12 vols.).

Frank, W.C. and Gillette, P.S. (eds), *Soviet Military Doctrine from Lenin to Gorbachev* (Westport, CT, 1991).

Franke, H., *Handbuch der Neuzeitlichen Wehrwissenschaften* (Berlin, 1937) (2 vols.).

Franz, G., *Die Vernichtungsschlacht im Kriegsgeschichtlichen Beispielen* (Berlin, 1928).

Franz, W.P. (ed.), *The Art of War Quarterly Vol. II* (US Army War College, Carlisle Barracks, PA, Sept. 1983).

Fretter-Pico, M., *Verlassen von des Sieges Göttern* (Wiesbaden, 1969).

Freytag-Loringhoven, F. von, *Deductions from the World War* (London, 1918).

—, *The Power of Personality in War*, trans. Spaulding, O.L. (Harrisburg, PA, 1938).

—, *Heerführung Napoleons in Ihrer Bedeutung für Unsere Zeit* (Berlin, 1918).

Friedrich, E., *Das Grosse Hauptquartier und die Deutschen Operationen im Feldzug 1870* (Munich, 1898).

Frunze, M.V., *Edinaia voennaia doktrina i Krasnaia Armiia* (Unified Military Doctrine and the Red Army) (Moscow, 1921).

—, *Izbrannye proizvedeniia* (Selected Works) (Moscow, 1950).

—, *Sobranie sochinenii* (Collected Writings) (Moscow, 1926).

Fuchs, K.H. and Kolper, F.W., *Militärisches Taschenlexikon* (Frankfurt a.M., 1961).

Fuller, J.F.C., *A Military History of the Western World* (3 vols.) (New York, 1954).

—, *Armament and History* (London, 1946).

—, *Armoured Warfare* (London, 1943).

—, *Generalship, Its Diseases and Their Cure* (London, 1937).

—, *Grant and Lee, A Study in Personality and Generalship* (Indiana University Press, 1982).

—, *Machine Warfare* (Washington, 1943).

—, *On Future Warfare* (London, 1928).

—, *The Conduct of War 1789–1961* (Rutgers University Press, 1968).

—, *The Foundation of the Science of War* (London, 1925).

Gabriel, R.A. and Savage, P.L., *Crisis in Command: Mismanagement in the Army* (New York, 1978).

Gaddis, J.L., *Strategies of Containment: A Critical Appraisal of Post War American National Security Policy* (Oxford University Press, 1982).

Galaktionov, M., *Tempy operatsii* (The Pace of Operations) (Moscow, 1936).

Galbraith, J., *Designing Complex Organizations* (Reading, MA, 1978).

Galitskii, K.N., *V boiakh v Vostochnoi Prussii* (Fighting in East Prussia) (Moscow, 1970).

Gardner, H., *The Mind's New Science: A History of the Cognitive Revolution* (New York, 1985).

Garthoff, R.L., *Soviet Military Doctrine* (Rand Corporation, 1953).

Garvin, R.H. (ed.), *Phenomenology, Structuralism, Semiology* (Bucknell University Press, 1976).

Gat, A., *The Origins of Military Thought from Enlightenment to Clausewitz* (Oxford University Press, 1989).

Gates, D., *The Spanish Ulcer* (London, 1986).

Gebsattel, L.F. von, *Generalfeldmarschal Karl von Bülow* (Munchen, 1929).

General Orders Spain and Portugal (6 vols.) (London, 1809–14).

Generalstab, Kriegsgeschichtliche Abteilung (ed.), *Der Deutsch-Französische Krieg 1870–1871* (5 vols.) (Berlin, 1872–81).

—, *Kriegsgeschichtliche Einzelschriften, Heft 17: Truppenfahrzeuge, Kolonnen und Trains bei den Bewegungen der I und II Deutschen Armee bis zu den Schlachten Westlich Metz* (Berlin, 1895).

—, *Kriegsgeschichtliche Einzelschriften, Heft 18: Das Generalkommando des III Armee Korps bei Spicheren und Vionville* (Berlin, 1895).

—, *Studien zur Kriegsgeschichte und Taktik V: Der 18 August 1870* (Berlin, 1906).

Gerth, H.H. and Mills, C.W. (eds), *From Max Weber: Essays on Sociology* (New York, 1946).

Getman, A.L., *Tanki idut na Berlin* (The Tanks Go to Berlin) (Moscow, 1973).

Geyer, M., *Aufrüstung oder Sicherheit: Reichswehr in der Krise der Machtpolitik 1924–1936* (Wiesbaden, 1980).

—, *Military Work, Civil Order, Military Politics: The German Military Experience 1914–1945* (Woodrow Wilson Center ISSP, Working Paper No. 39, Washington, DC, 1982).

Gladkov, P.D., *Taktika bronevykh chastei* (Tactics of Armoured Units/ Regiments) (Moscow, 1930).

Glantz, D.M., *Soviet Conduct of Tactical Maneuver, Spearhead of the Offensive* (London, 1991).

—, *Soviet Military Operational Art* (London, 1991).

Glazunov, N.K. and Nikitin, N.S., *Operatsiia i boi* (Operation and Battle) (Moscow, 1983).

Goerlitz, W., *History of the German General Staff 1657–1945*, trans. Battershaw, B. (New York, 1959).

Goethe, J.W., *Campaign in France in the Year 1792*, trans. Farie, R. (London, 1859).

Goltz, C. Frhr. von, *The Conduct of War* (London, 1899).

—, *The Nation in Arms* (London, 1906).

Gorbatov, A.V., *Years of My Life* (London, 1964).

Grams, R., *Die 14. Panzerdivision 1940–1945* (Bad-Nauheim, 1957).

Grechko, A.A., *Bitva za Kavkaz* (The Battle for the Caucasus) (Moscow, 1973).

—, *Gody voiny* (The War Years) (Moscow, 1976).

Greene, F.V., *The Campaign in Bulgaria* (London, 1903).

Greiner, H., *Die Oberste Wehrmachtführung 1939–1943* (Wiesbaden, 1951).

— and Degener, J., *Taktik im Rahmen des Verstärkten Infanterie Battalions* (Berlin, 1937).

Grendal', V.D., *Artilleriia v nastupatel'nom boiu strelkovogo korpusa* (Artillery in the Offensive Battle of a Rifle Corps) (Moscow, 1937).

—, *Artilleriia v osnovnykh vidakh boia* (Artillery as the Basis of Combat) (Moscow, 1940).

Grigorenko, P., *Memoirs* (New York, 1982).

Grinter, L.E. and Dunn, P.M., *The American War in Vietnam: Lessons, Legacies and Implications for Future Conflict* (New York, 1987).

Groener, W., *Das Testament des Graffen Schlieffen* (Berlin, 1927).

Gromychenko, A.E., *Ocherki taktiki tankovykh chastei* (An Outline of Tactics for Tank Units) (Moscow, 1935).

Guderian, H., *Achtung Panzer! Die Entwicklung der Panzerwaffe, ihre Kampftaktik und ihrer Operative Möglichkeiten* (Stuttgart, 1937).

—, *Achtung Panzer! The Development of Armoured Forces, their Tactics and their Operational Potential*, trans. Duffy, C. (London, 1992).

—, *Die Panzertruppen und ihre Zusammenwirken mit Andern Waffen* (Berlin, 1943).

—, *Erinnerungen Eines Soldaten* (Heidelberg, 1951).

—, *Panzer Leader* (New York, 1952).

Guibert, J.A.H. de, *Essai Générale de Tactique* (Liège, 1775) (2 vols.).

Gurwood, J. (ed.), *Selections from Dispatches and General Orders of Field Marshal the Duke of Wellington* (London, 1841).

—, *The Dispatches of Field Marshal the Duke of Wellington during his Various Campaigns* (London, 1852) (6 vols.).

Gusev, S.I., *Grazhdanskaia voina i Krasnaia Armiia* (The Civil War and the Red Army) (Moscow, 1958).

Hackett, J., *The Profession of Arms* (London, 1983).

Haffa, R.P., *Rational Methods, Prudent Choices: Planning US Forces* (Washington, DC: National Defense University Press, 1988).

Halder, F., *Hitler as Warlord*, trans. Findlay, P. (London, 1950).

—, *Kriegstagebuch* Vol. I: *Vom Polenfeldzug bis zum Ende der Westoffensive*, Vol. II: *Der Russlandfeldzug bis zum Marsch auf Stalingrad*, ed. Jacobsen, H.A. (Stuttgart, 1964).

Hall, D.A., *A Methodology for Systems Engineering* (Princeton University Press, 1962).

Handel, M. (ed.), *Clausewitz and Modern Strategy* (London, 1986).

Harkaby, Y., *War and Strategy* (Tel Aviv, 1990).

Harkavy, R. and Kolodjiez, E. (eds.), *American Security Policy Making* (Lexington, KY, 1980).

Hart, G., with Lind, W., *America Can Win, The Case for Military Reform* (Bethesda, MD, 1986).

Haas, R., *Congressional Power: Implications for American Security Policy,*

Adelphi Paper No. 153 (London: IISS, 1979).

Haupt, W., *Heeresgruppe Mitte 1941–1943* (Dosheim, 1968).

—, *Kiev, die Grosste Kesselschlacht der Geschichte* (Bad-Nauheim, 1964).

Hayward, P.H.C. (ed.), *Jane's Dictionary of Military Terms* (London, 1975).

Headquarters, US Army Training and Doctrine Command, *Combined Arms Test Activity Historical Report July 1975–September 1976* (Fort Monroe, KS, 1976).

—, *Division 86: Blueprint of the Battlefield* (Fort Monroe, VA, April 1979).

—, *Historical Office, Annual Historical Review: FY 1979* (Fort Monroe, VA, 1980).

Hemsley, J., *Soviet Troop Control* (Oxford, 1982).

Hillgruber, A., *Der Zweite Weltkrieg 1939–1945, Kriegsziele und Strategie der Grosse Mächte* (Stuttgart, 1982).

—, *Hitlers Strategie. Politik und Kriegsführung 1940–1941* (Frankfurt, 1965).

Hittle, J.D., *The Military Staff: its History and Development* (Harrisburg, PA, 1961).

Hohenlohe-Ingelfingen, Kraft, C. zu, *Aus Meinem Leben: Aufzeichnungen aus dem Jahren 1848–1871* (Berlin, 1907).

—, *Letters on Cavalry*, trans. Walford, N.L. (London, 1889).

Hohenzollern, W.F., *The War Diary of Emperor Frederick the Third*, trans. Allinson, A.R. (London, 1927).

Höning, F., *Dokumentarische–Kritische Darstellung der Strategie für die Schlacht von Vionville – Mars la Tour* (Berlin, 1899).

—, *Inquiries Into the Tactics of the Future*, trans. Reichman, C. (Kansas City, MO, 1898).

Hooker, R.D. (ed.), *Maneuver Warfare – An Anthology* (Novato, CA, 1993).

Horsetzky von Horenthal, A., *Der Russische Feldzug in Bulgarien und Rumelien 1877–1878* (Wien, 1878).

Hossbach, F., *Zwischen Wehrmacht und Hitler 1834–1938* (Göttingen, 1965).

Hoth, H., *Panzer Operationen, die Panzergruppe 3 und der Operativ Gedanke der Deutschen Führung im Sommer 1941* (Heidelberg, 1956).

House, J.M., *Towards Combined Arms Warfare: A Survey of Tactics, Doctrine and Organization in the Twentieth Century* (Combat Studies Institute, US Army Command and General Staff College, Fort Leavenworth, KS, 1986).

Howard, M., *Clausewitz* (Oxford, 1983).

—, *The Franco-Prussian War* (Cambridge, 1961).

— (ed.), *The Theory and Practice of War* (London, 1965).

—, *War in European Society* (Oxford, 1976).

—, *The Causes of War* (London, 1985).

Hubatsch, W., *Hitlers Weisungen für die Kriegsführung 1939–1945, Dokumente des OKW* (Frankfurt a.M., 1962).

Iakobovskii, I.I., *Zemlia v ogne* (The Land on Fire) (Moscow, 1975).

Imhoff, C. von, *Sturm durch Frankreich* (Berlin, 1941).

Ionov, P.P., *Istrebitel'naia aviatsiia* (Fighter Aviation) (Moscow, 1940).

Isserson, G.S., *Evoliutsiia operativnogo iskusstva* (The Evolution of

Operational Art) (Moscow, 1937) (2nd edn).

—, *Lektsii po glubokoi taktike* (Lectures on Deep Tactics) (Moscow, 1933).

—, *Martovskoe nastuplenie Germantsev v Pikardii v 1918 godu* (The German March Offensive in Picardy in 1918) (Moscow, 1926).

Ivanov, V.M., *Marshal M.N. Tukhachevskii* (Moscow, 1990).

Ivanov, S.P., *Lektsii o voennom iskusstve v Kievskoi, Balatonskoi, i Venskoi operatsiiakh* (Lectures on the Military Art in the Kiev, Balaton, and Vienna Operations) Voennaia Akademiia General'nogo Shtaba Vooruzhenykh Sil SSSR im. K.E. Voroshilova, 1972), 72 pp.

—, *Shtab armeiskii shtab fronta* (The Army Staff and the Front Staff) (Moscow, 1990).

Jacobsen, H.A., *Deutsche Kriegsführung 1939–1945* (Hanover, 1961).

—, *Dokumenten zum Westfeldzug 1940* (Göttingen, 1956).

—, *Fall Gelb: Der Kampf und den Deutschen Operationplan zur West-offensive 1940* (Wiesbaden, 1957).

—, *1939–1945 Der Zweite Weltkrieg im Chronik und Dokumentation* (Darmstadt, 1961).

—and Rohwer, I. (eds), *Decisive Battles of World War II: The German View* (New York, 1965).

Johnson, C., *Autopsy on People's War* (University of California Press, 1973).

Jomini, A.H. de, *Tableau Analytique des Principales Combinaisons de la Guerre* (Paris, 1830).

—, *The Art of War*, trans. Mendell, G.H. and Craighill, W.P. (Westport, CT, 1975).

—, *Traité des Grandes Operations Militaires* (4 vols.) (Paris, 1852).

Jungenfeld, E. Frhr. von, *So Kämpften Panzer* (Berlin, 1941).

Justrow, K., *Feldherr und Kriegstechnik* (Oldenburg, 1933).

Kadishev, A.B. (ed.), *Voprosy strategii i operativnogo iskusstva v Sovetskikh voennykh trudakh 1917–1940 gg.* (Questions of Strategy and Operational Art in Soviet Military Works 1917–1940) (Moscow, 1965).

—, *Voprosy taktiki v Sovetskikh voennykh trudakh 1917–1940 gg.* (Questions of Tactics in Soviet Military Works 1917–1940) (Moscow, 1970).

Kapustin, N.Ia., *Operativnoe iskusstvo v pozitsionnoi voine* (Operational Art in Positional Warfare) (Moscow/Leningrad, 1927).

Karber, P.A., *Daring Thrust – The Tactical Revolution In Soviet Doctrine* (BDM: VA, 1977).

Katukov, M.E., *Na ostrie glavnogo udara* (At the Spearhead of the Main Strike) (Moscow, 1974).

Kaufman, D., *System 1: An Introduction to Systems Thinking* (Minneapolis, 1980).

Kavtaradze, A.G., *Voennye spetsialisty na sluzhbe Respubliki Sovetov 1917–1920gg.* (Military Specialists in the Service of the Soviet Republic 1917–1920) (Moscow, 1988).

Keegan, J., *The Mask of Command* (London, 1987).

Keep, J.W., *Mass Mobility and the Red Army's Road to Operational Art 1918–1936* (Fort Leavenworth, KS, 1987).

Kennedy, P.M. (ed.), *The War Plans of the Great Powers 1880–1914* (Boston, 1979).

Kesselring, A., *Kesselring: A Soldier's Record* (New York, 1954).

Kielmannsegg, J.A. von, *Panzer Zwischen Warschau und Atlantik* (Berlin, 1941).

Kinkaid, D., *The War Managers* (Hanover, NH, 1977).

Kir'ian, M.M. (ed.), *Fronty nastupali po opytu Velikoi otechestvennoi voiny* (The Fronts Attacked according to the Experience of the Great Patriotic War) (Moscow, 1987).

—, *Vnezapnost' v nastupatel'nykh operatsiiakh Velikoi otechestvennoi voiny* (Surprise in Offensive Operations of the Great Patriotic War) (Moscow, 1986).

—, *Voenno-tekhnicheskii progress i Vooruzhennye Sily SSSR* (Military Technical Progress and the Armed Forces of the USSR) (Moscow, 1982).

Kirillov-Gubetskii, I.M., *Organizatsiia i planirovanie artilleriiskogo ognia* (Organization and Planning of Artillery Fire) (Leningrad, 1935).

Kissinger, H., *Problems of National Strategy* (New York, 1965).

—, *The White House Years* (Boston, 1979).

Kitson, F., *Warfare as a Whole* (London, 1986).

Klir, G.I., *An Approach to General System Theory* (New York, 1968).

Kollenkovskii, A., *O nastupatel'noi operatsii armii vkhodiashchei v sostav fronta* (On the Army Offensive Operations as Part of a Front) (Moscow, 1929).

Konev, I.S., *Zapiskii komanduiushchego frontom 1943–1945* (Memoirs of a Front Commander in Chief 1943–1945) (Moscow, 1972).

Koritskii, N.I. (ed.), *Marshal Tukhachevskii, vospominaniia druzei i soratnikov* (Marshal Tukhachevskii, Recollections of Friends and Comrades-in-Arms) (Moscow, 1965).

Korol'kov, K.P., *Glubokii reid* (Deep Raid) (Moscow, 1967).

Korotkov, I.A., *Istoriia Sovetskoi voennoi mysli: kratkii ocherk 1917–iiun' 1941* (History of Soviet Military Thought: A Short Sketch 1917–June 1941) (Moscow, 1980).

Kozlov, S.N. (ed.), *Officer's Handbook*, trans. under the auspices of US Air Force (Washington, DC, 1971).

—, *et al.*, *O Sovetskoi voennoi nauke* (On Soviet Military Science) (Moscow, 1964).

Krainiukov, K.V., *Ot Dnepra do Visly* (From the Dnieper to the Vistula) (Moscow, 1971).

Krasil'nikov, S.N., *Organizatsiia krupnykh obshchevoiskovykh soedinenii* (The Organization of Combined Arms Formations) (Moscow, 1933).

Kratkii slovar' operativno-takticheskikh obshchevoiskovykh slov (terminov) (A Concise Dictionary of Operational-tactical and Military Terms) (Moscow, 1958).

Kratkii anglo-russkii i russko-angliiskii voennyi slovar' (Concise English–Russian and Russian–English Dictionary) (Moscow, 1963).

Kreipe, W., Blumentritt, G., *et al.*, *The Fatal Decisions* (London, 1956).

Kromov, S.S. (ed.), *Grazhdanskaia voina i voennaia interventsiia v SSSR* (The Civil War and the Military Intervention in the USSR) (Moscow, 1983).

Krupchenko, I.E., *Sovetskie tankovye voiska, 1941–1945* (Soviet Tank Forces, 1941–1945) (Moscow, 1973).

Kuhn, T.S., *The Structure of Scientific Revolutions* (Chicago, 1973; Penguin, 1971).

Kulikov, V.G. (ed.), *Akademiia general'nogo shtaba* (The General Staff Academy) (Moscow, 1976).

Kurochkin, P.A. (ed.), *Obshchevoiskovaia armiia v nastuplenii* (The Combined-Arms Army in the Offensive) (Moscow, 1966).

Kurtzinskii, M.J., *Taktik Schneller Verbänden* (Potsdam, 1935).

Kuzmin, F.K., *Vstrechnyi boi strelkovogo korpusa* (Encounter Battle of a Rifle Corps) (Moscow, 1938).

Kuzmin, G.V., *Grazhdanskaia voina i voennaia interventsiia v SSSR* (The Civil War and Military Intervention in the USSR) (Moscow, 1958).

Lanchester, F.W., *Aircraft in Warfare: The Dawn of the Fourth Arm* (London, 1916).

Lapchinskii, A.N., *Bombardirovochnaia aviatsiia* (Bomber Aviation) (Moscow, 1937).

—, *Taktika aviatsii* (Aviation Tactics) (Moscow, 1931) (3rd edn).

—, *Vozdushnaia armiia* (The Air Army) (Moscow, 1939).

—, *Vozdushnye sily v boiu i operatsii* (Air Forces in Battle and Operation) (Moscow, 1938).

Leach, B., *German Strategy against Russia 1939–1949* (Oxford, 1973).

Leeb, W. von, *Defense* (Harrisburg, PA, 1943).

Leliushenko, D.D., *Moskva–Stalingrad–Berlin–Praga, zapiski komandarmiia* (Moscow–Stalingrad–Berlin–Prague, Reminiscences of an Army Commander) (Moscow, 1973).

Leonard, R.A., *A Short Guide to Clausewitz' 'On War'* (London, 1967).

Leosheniia, E.V., *Forsirovanie reki strelkovym batal'onom i strelkovym polkom* (River Crossing by a Rifle Battalion and a Rifle Regiment) (Moscow, 1938).

Levichev, V.N. (ed.), *Voina i voennoe delo* (War and Military Matters) (Moscow, 1933).

Lewal, J.L., *Stratégie de Combat* (Paris, 1895) (2 vols.).

Lewin, R., *Rommel as Military Commander* (London, 1968).

Liddell Hart, B.H., *Great Captains Unveiled* (London, 1927).

—, *Memoirs* (New York, 1967).

—, *Strategy: The Indirect Approach* (London, 1954).

—, *The Ghost of Napoleon* (London, 1933).

—, *The Other Side of the Hill* (London, 1951).

—, *The Revolution in Warfare* (London, 1946).

—(ed.), *The Rommel Papers* (London, 1953).

—, *Thoughts on War*, trans. Wallach, J. (Tel Aviv, 1989).

—, *Through the Fog of War* (London, 1938).

Lind, W.S., *Maneuver Warfare Handbook* (Boulder, CO, 1985).

Lisov, I.I., *Desantniki–vozdushnye desanty* (Paratroops–Air Landings) (Moscow, 1968).

Lomov, N.A. (ed.), *Nauchno-tekhnicheskii progress i revoliutsiia v voennom dele* (Scientific-technical Progress and the Revolution in Military Affairs) (Moscow, 1973).

—, *The Revolution in Military Affairs*, trans. and publ. under the auspices of US Air Force (Washington, DC, 1973).

Losik, O.A. (ed.), *Stroitel'stvo i boevoe primenenie Sovetskikh tankovykh voisk v gody Velikoi otechestvennoi voiny* (The Building and Combat Handling of Soviet Tank Forces in the Years of the Great Patriotic War) (Moscow, 1979).

Loza, D.F., *Marsh i vstrechnyi boi* (Marching and Encounter Battle) (Moscow, 1968).

Lunaev, K., *Vzaimodeistvie pekhoty s drugimi rodami voisk* (The Cooperation of Infantry with Other Friendly Forces) (Kiev, 1936).

Luttwak, E.N., *Strategy, the Logic of War and Peace* (Cambridge, MA, 1987).

—, *Strategy and History: Collected Essays* (New Brunswick, 1985).

—, *The Pentagon and the Art of War* (New York, 1984).

Lyman, T., *Mead's Headquarters 1863–1865: Letters of Colonel Theodor Lyman from the Wilderness to Appomattox*, ed. Agassiz, G.R. (Boston, 1922).

Machiavelli Niccolo, *The Chief Works and Others*, ed. Gilbert, A. (Durham, 1965).

Mackensen, E. von, *Von Bug bis zum Kaukasus. Das III Panzerkorps im Feldzug gegen Sowjetrussland 1941–1942* (Neckagemünd, 1967).

Mackintosh, M., *Juggernaut, A History of the Soviet Armed Forces* (New York, 1967).

Macksey, K.J., *Guderian: Panzer Leader* (London, 1975).

Mahlman, P., *Die Planübung* (Berlin, 1942).

Malinovskii, R.Ia., *Budapesht, Vena, Praga* (Budapest, Vienna, Prague) (Moscow, 1966).

Manstein, E. von, *Aus Einem Soldatenleben* (Bonn, 1958).

—, *Lost Victories*, trans. Powell, A.G. (London, 1958).

Manteuffel, H. von, *Die 7. Panzerdivision im Zweiten Weltkrieg. Einsatz und Kampf der Gespenster Division 1939–1945* (Urdingen am Rhein, 1965).

Marchenko, E.T. (ed.), *Taktika v boevykh primerakh, batal'on* (Tactics by Combat Example, Battalion) (Moscow, 1974).

Margelov, V.F., Lisov, I.I., Ivonin, V.I., *Sovetskie vozdushno-desantnye* (Soviet Airborne *Desant*) (Moscow, 1980).

Martel, G., *The Russian Outlook* (London, 1947).

Massey, W.T., *Allenby's Final Triumph* (London, 1920).

Maude, F.N., *Notes on the Evolution of Infantry Tactics* (London, 1905).

Mearsheimer, J.J., *Liddell Hart and the Weight of History* (London, 1988).

Mednis, A.K., *Taktika shturmovoi aviatsii* (Tactics of Attack Aviation) (Moscow, 1935).

Meinertzhagen, R., *Middle East Diary* (Tel Aviv, 1973).

Melikov, V.A., *Marna–1914 goda, Visla–1920 goda, Smirna–1922 goda* (The Marne–1914, the Vistula–1920, Smyrna–1922) (Moscow/Leningrad, 1928).

—, *Problema strategicheskogo razvertyvaniia po opytu Mirovoi i Grazhdanskoi voiny* (Problems of Strategic Deployment according to the Experience of the World and Civil Wars) (Izdatel'stvo Voennoi Akademii RKKA im. M.V. Frunze, 1935).

Mellenthin, F.W. von, *Panzer Battles* (University of Oklahoma Press, 1986).

Mesarovic, M.S. (ed.), *Views on General System Theory* (New York, 1964).

Messenger, C., *The Art of Blitzkrieg* (London, 1991).

Methe, S., *Vom Geist Deutscher Feldherren Genie und Technik* (Zurich, 1938).

Middeldorf, E., *Taktik im Russlandfeldzug: Erfahrungen und Folgerungen* (Darmstadt / Dortmund, 1956).

Mikailov, S.G., *Deistviia artillerii vo vstrechnom nastupatel'nom i oboronitel'nom boiu* (The Action of Artillery in the Encounter Offensive and Defensive Battle) (Leningrad, 1931).

Mikhnevich, N.P., *Strategiia* (Strategy) (St Petersburg, 1911) (3rd edn).

Miksche, F.O., *Blitzkrieg* (London, 1941).

Mikulin, V.I., *Sluzhba razvedyvatel'nogo otriada armeiskoi konnitsy* (The Role of the Special Army Cavalry Intelligence Unit) (Moscow/Leningrad, 1928).

Miller-Maguire, T., *Notes on the Austro-Prussian War of 1866* (London, 1904).

Millet, S.E., Lynn-Jones, S.M. and Van Evera, S. (eds), *Military Strategy and the Origins of the First World War* (Princeton, 1990).

Millett, A.R. and Murray, W. (eds), *Military Effectiveness*: Vol. I: *The First World War*, Vol. II: *The Interwar Period*, Vol. III: *The Second World War* (Boston, 1988).

Model, H.H., *Der Deutsche Generalstaboffizier* (Frankfurt a. M., 1968).

Moltke, H.K.B., *Militärische Werke* (Berlin, 1892–1912).

—, *Militärische Korrespondenz. Aus dem Dienstschriften des Krieges 1870–71* (Berlin, 1897).

—, *Moltkes Taktisch–Strategische Aufsätze aus den Jahren 1857 bis 1871* (Berlin, 1900).

—, *Moltke's Military Correspondence 1870–71*, publ. by the Prussian General Staff Dept. for Military History, précis: Wilkinson, S. (Oxford, 1923).

—, *Strategy: its Theory and Application: The Wars of German Unification 1866–1871*, trans. Bell, H. (Fort Leavenworth, KS, 1911).

—, *The Franco-German War 1870–1871*, trans. Bellard, C. and Fischer, H. (London, 1891).

Momyer, W.W., *Air Power in Three Wars* (Washington, DC: USAF Office for History, 1978).

Monigetti, K., *Sovmestnye deistviia konnitsy i vozdushnogo flota* (Joint Operations of the Cavalry and Air Fleet) (Moscow, 1928).

Morozov, N.A., *Obshchaia taktika* (General Tactics) (Moscow, 1928).

Moskalenko, K.S., *Na iugo-zapadnom napravlenii* (In a South-westerly Direction) (Moscow, 1973) (2 vols.).

Movchin, N.N., *Posledovatel'nye operatsii po opytu Marny i Visly* (Successive Operations According to the Experience of the Marne and the Vistula) (Moscow/Leningrad, 1928).

Müller, K.J., *General Ludwig Beck: Studien und Dokumente zur Politisch-Militärischen Vorstellungswelt und Tätigkeit des Generalstabschefs des Deutschen Heeres 1933–1939* (Boppard, 1980).

Müller-Hillebrand, B., *Das Heer* (3 vols.) (Darmstadt, 1954).

Mumford, L., *The Condition of Man* (London, 1963).

Munzel, O., *Panzertaktik. Raids Gepanzerte Verbande im Ostfeldzug 1941–1942* (Neckargemünd, 1959).

—, *Die Deutschen Gepanzerten Truppen bis 1945* (Neckargemünd, 1959).

Murray, W., *Strategy for Defeat: The Luftwaffe 1939–1945* (Maxwell AFB, AL, 1983).

—, *The Change in the European Balance of Power 1938–1939: The Path to Ruin* (Princeton, 1984).

Nef, J.U., *War and Human Progress* (Cambridge, MA, 1950).

Nehring, W., *Die Geschichte der Deutschen Panzerwaffen 1916 bis 1945* (Berlin, 1969).

—, *Panzerabwehr* (Berlin, 1936).

Nelsen, J.T., *Where to go from Here? Considerations for the Formal Adoption of Auftragstaktik by the US Army* (School of Advanced Military Studies, US Army Command and General Staff College, Fort Leavenworth, KS, 5 Dec., 1986).

Newell, C.R., *The Framework of Operational Warfare* (New York, 1991).

Nickerson, H., *The Armed Horde 1793–1937* (New York, 1940).

Ngoc Lung, H., *Strategy and Tactics* (Washington, DC, US Center of Military History, 1980).

Novikov, Iu.Z., Sverdlov, F.D., *Manevr v obshchevoiskovom boiu* (Manoeuvre in All-arms Combat) (Moscow, 1967).

Oberkommando der Wehrmacht (OKW), *Der Sieg in Polen* (Berlin, 1940).

Offer, Z. and Kover, A., *Quality and Quantity Dilemma in Military Force Building* (Tel Aviv, 1985).

Ogarkov, A., *Vsegda v gotovnosti k zashchite otechestva* (Always Ready to Defend the Fatherland), (Moscow, 1982).

Oman, C., *Wellington's Army 1808–1814* (London, 1913).

—, *History of the Art of War in the Sixteenth Century* (London, 1937).

O'Neill, R.J., *The German Army and the Nazi Party 1933–1938* (London, 1966).

Orlov, A., *A Secret History of Stalin's Crimes* (New York, 1953).

Osborn, R.N., Hunt, J.G and Jauch, L.K., *Organization Theory: An Integrated Approach* (New York, 1980).

Palmer, B., *The 25 Year War–America's Military Role in Vietnam* (Lexington, KY, 1984)

Palmer, D.R., *Summons to the Trumpet: US–Vietnam in Perspective* (San Raphael, CA, 1978).

Palmer, G., *The MacNamara Strategy and the Vietnam War: Program*

355

Budgeting in the Pentagon 1960–1968 (Westport, CT, 1978).

Paret, P. (ed.), *Makers of Modern Strategy* (Oxford, 1988).

—, *Understanding War: Essays on Clausewitz and the History of Military Power* (Princeton, 1992)

Paulus, F. von, *Ich Stehe Hier auf Befehl! Lebensweg des Generalfeldmarschal Friedrich Paulus. Mit dem aufzeichnungen aus dem Nachlass, Briefen und Dokumente*, d. Gorlitz, W. (Frankfurt a.M., 1963).

Perrett, B., *A History of Blitzkrieg* (London, 1985).

Philippi, A. and Heim, F., *Der Feldzug gegen die Sowjetunion 1941–1945. Ein Operativer Überlick* (Stuttgart, 1962).

Pirie-Gordon, C.H.L. (ed.), *Brief Record of the Advance of the Egyptian Expeditionary Force July 1917 to October 1918* (London, 1919).

Plekhov, A.M., *Slovar' voennykh terminov* (Dictionary of Military Terms) (Moscow, 1988).

Popel', N.K., *Tanki povernuti na zapad* (Tanks Turned Westward), (Moscow, 1960).

Posen, B.R., *The Sources of Military Doctrine, France, Britain and Germany between the World Wars* (Ithaca, 1988).

Pospelov, P.N., *et al.* (eds), *Istoriia Velikoi Otechestvennoi Voiny Sovetskogo Soiuza 1941–1945* (The History of the Great Patriotic War of the Soviet Union 1941–1945) (Moscow, 1960–65).

—, *Velikaia Otechestvennaia Voina Sovetskogo Soiuza 1941–1945, kratkaia istorii* (The Great Patriotic War of the Soviet Union 1941–1945, a Short History) (Moscow, 1965).

Post, G., *The Civil Military Fabric of Weimar Foreign Policy* (Princeton, 1973).

Pratt, E.A., *The Rise of Rail Power in War and Conquest 1833–1914* (London, 1915).

Putna, V.K., *K Visle i obratno* (To the Vistula and back) (Moscow, 1927).

Rabenau, W. Frhr. von, *Entschlusse gegen Einen Zahl Überlegenen Genger* (Berlin, 1935).

Radzievskii, A.I. (ed.), *Akademiia imeni M.V. Frunze* (The M.V. Frunze Academy) (Moscow, 1973).

—, *Armeiskie operatsii* (The Army Operation) (Moscow, 1977).

—, *Dictionary of Basic Military Terms*, trans. DGIS Ottawa (Washington, DC, 1977).

—, *Proryv* (Breakthrough) (Moscow, 1979).

—, (ed.), *Taktika v boevykh primerakh, polk* (Tactics through Combat Experience, Regiment) (Moscow, 1974).

—, *Tankovyi udar* (Tank Strike) (Moscow, 1977).

Rapoport, A., *Fights, Games and Debates* (Ann Arbor, MI, 1960).

Reinhardt, K., *Moscow the Turning Point. The Failure of Hitler's Strategy in the Winter of 1941–1942* (Oxford, 1992).

Reitz, D., *Commando: A Boer Journal of the Boer War* (London, 1929).

Report Number AV–AWC 82–036, *Command Structure for Theater Warfare: The Quest for Unity of Command* (Airpower Research Institute, Maxwell

AFB, AL, May 1982).

Reznichenko, V.G., *Taktika* (Tactics) (Moscow, 1986) (1966, 1st edn).

Rhona, T.P., *Weapon Systems and Information War* (Seattle, 1976).

Ritter, G., *The Schlieffen Plan: A Critique of a Myth*, trans. Wilson, S., (London, 1958).

Robertson, E.M., *Hitler's Pre-War Policy and Military Plans 1933–1939* (London, 1963).

Röhricht, T.F., *Problem der Kesselschlacht* (Karlsruhe, 1958).

Rokossovskii, K.K., *Soldatskii dolg* (A Soldier's Duty) (Moscow, 1972).

Romjue, J.L., *From Active Defense to Airland Battle: The Development of Army Doctrine 1973–1982* (US Army Training and Doctrine Command, Fort Monroe, VA, 1984).

—, *A History of Army 86*: Vol. I: *Division 86: The Development of the Heavy Division September 1978–October 1979*, Vol. II: *The Development of the Light Division, The Corps, and Echelons Above Corps November 1979–December 1980* (Fort Monroe, VA, June 1983).

Roon, A.T.E. von, *Denkwürdigkeiten aus dem Leben des General-Feldmarschalls Kriegsminister Graffen von Roon* (3 vols.) (Breslau, 1897).

Ropp, T., *War in the Modern World* (London, 1962).

Roszak, T., *The Cult of Information: The Folklore of Computers and the True Art of Thinking* (New York, 1986).

Roth, G. (ed.), *Development, Planning and Realization of Operational Conception in World Wars I and II* (Militärgeschichtliches Forschungsamt, Freiburg im Breisgau, 1989).

—, *Operatives Denken und Handeln in Deutschen Streitkräften im 19. und 20. Jahrhundert* (Bonn, 1988).

Rotmistrov, P.A. (ed.), *Istoriia voennogo iskusstva* (History of Military Art) (Moscow, 1963) (2 vols.).

—, *Vremia i tanki* (The Time and the Tanks) (Moscow, 1972).

Ryshman, M., *Reid Mamontova, avgust–sentiabr' 1919g.* (Mamontov's Raid August–September 1919) (Moscow, 1926).

Saaty, T.L., *Mathematical Methods of OR* (New York, 1959).

Sandalov, A.M., *Trudnye rubezhi* (Strict Limits) (Moscow, 1965).

Sargent, H., *Napoleon Bonaparte's First Campaign* (London, 1895).

Sargent, W., *Battle for the Mind* (London, 1957).

Savkin, V.E., *Osnovnye printsipy operativnogo iskusstva i taktiki* (Basic Principles of Operational Art and Tactics) (Moscow, 1972).

—, *Tempy nastupleniia* (The Pace of the Offensive) (Moscow, 1965).

—, *The Basic Principles of Operational Art and Tactics*, trans. under the auspices of the US Air Force (Washington, DC, 1972).

Savushkin, R.A., *Razvitie Sovetskikh Vooruzhennykh Sil i voennogo iskusstva v mezhvoennyi period 1921–1941* (The Development of the Soviet Armed Forces and Military Art in the Interwar Period 1921–1941) (Moscow, 1989).

Schandler, H.Y., *The Unmaking of the President: Lyndon Johnson and Vietnam* (Princeton, 1977).

Schell, C.E. von, *The Operations of the First Army Under General Steinmetz*

(London, 1873).

Schlichting, S. von (ed.), *Moltke Vermächtniss* (Munich, 1901).

—, *Taktisch und Strategische Grundsätze der Gegenwart*, Vol. 2: *Truppen-führungs* (Berlin, 1897–99) (3 vols.).

Schlieffen, A. von, *Briefe*, ed. Kessel, E. (Göttingen, 1958).

—, *Cannae* (Berlin, 1936).

—, *Cannae* (Fort Leavenworth, KS, 1931).

—, *Gesammelte Schriften* (3 vols.) (Berlin, 1913).

Schneider, L., *Aus dem Leben Kaiser Wilhelms 1873* (3 vols.) (Berlin, 1888).

Schramm, P.E., Hillgruber, A., Hubatsch, W. and Jacobsen, H.A. (eds.), *Kriegstagebuch des Oberkommando des Wehrmacht (Wehrmacht Führungsstab) 1940–1945* (Frankfurt a.M., 1961–65).

Schwarzkopf, H.N., *It Does Not Take a Hero* (New York, 1992).

Scott, H.F and W.F., *The Armed Forces of the USSR* (Boulder, CO, 1979).

Scribner, E.G., *Doctrine Development by TRADOC May 1973–December 1979* (Fort Monroe, VA, 20 Feb. 1980).

Seaton, A and J., *The Soviet Army: 1918 to the Present* (New York, 1987).

Seeckt, H. von, *Gedanken Eines Soldaten* (Berlin, 1929).

Semenov, V.A., *Kratkii ocherk razvitiia Sovetskogo operativnogo iskusstva* (A Short Outline of the Development of Soviet Operational Art) (Moscow, 1960).

Senff, H., *Die Entwicklung der Panzerwaffen im Deutschen Heer zwischen dem Beiden Weltkriegen* (Frankfurt a.M., 1969).

Senge, P.M., *The Fifth Discipline – The Art and Practice of the Learning Organization* (London, 1993).

Senger und Etterlin, F.M. von, *Die Panzergrenadiere* (Munich, 1961).

—, *Tanks Abenteurliche Eine Kriegsmachine* (Potsdam, 1938).

Shaposhnikov, B.M., *Mozg armii* (The Brain of the Army) (Moscow, 1927–29).

Shestrin, F.I., *Voennoe iskusstvo nastupatel'noi operatsii Sovetskikh voisk pod Leningradom i Novgorodom 14.1–1.3.1944 (Lektsiia)* (Military Art of Offensive Operations of Soviet Forces in Leningrad and Novgorod 14.1–1.3.1944 (Lecture)) (Voennaia Akademiia GS VS SSSR im. K.E. Voroshilova, 1974) (30 pages).

Shtemenko, S.M., *The Soviet General Staff at War* (Moscow, 1970).

Shtromberg, A.I., *Sluzhba tankov v motomekhanizirovannykh chastiakh* (The Role of Tanks in Motomechanized Units) (Moscow, 1931).

Sidorenko, A.A., *Nastuplenie* (The Offensive) (Moscow, 1970).

Simpkin, R., *Deep Battle: The Brainchild of Marshal M.N. Tukhachevskii* (London, 1987).

—, *Mechanized Infantry* (Oxford, 1980).

—, *Race to the Swift* (London/Oxford, 1985).

—, *Red Armour* (London, 1984).

Smirnov, M.D., *Aviatsiia i pekhota* (Aviation and Infantry) (Moscow, 1931).

Smirnov, S.A., *Taktika* (Tactics) (Moscow, 1935).

Smylovskii, V.K., *Svedeniia po taktike artillerii* (A Summary of Artillery

Tactics) (Moscow, 1930).

Snoke, E.R., *The Operational Level of War* (Fort Leavenworth, KS: US Command and General Staff College, Combat Studies Institute, 1987).

Sokolovskii, V.D., *Voennaia strategiia* (Military Strategy) (Moscow, 1968).

—, *Military Strategy*, ed. Scott, H.F. (Stanford Research Institute, 1975).

Sorokin, P.A., *Contemporary Sociological Theories* (New York, 1964).

—, *Sociological Theories of Today* (New York, 1966).

Soshnikov, A.I., et al., *Sovetskaia kavaleriia. voenno-istoricheskii ocherk* (Soviet Cavalry: A Military Historical Outline) (Moscow, 1984).

Sovetskaia Voennaia Entsiklopediia (Soviet Military Encyclopedia) (Moscow, 1976–80) (8 vols.).

Spannenkrebs, W., *Angriff mit Kampfwagen* (Oldenburg, 1939).

Springer, A., *Der Russische – Turkische Krieg 1877–1878* (Wien, 1892) (7 vols.).

Stachura, P. (ed.), *The Nazi Machtergreifung* (London, 1983).

Stalin, I.V., *Sochineniia* (Works) (Moscow, 1946–52).

Stanton, S.L., *The Rise and Fall of an American Army: US Ground Forces in Vietnam 1965–1973* (Novato, CA, 1985).

Starry, D.A., *Commander's Notes No. 3*, Headquarters US Training and Doctrine Command, Fort Monroe, VA, 20 Feb. 1979.

—, *Vietnam Studies: Mounted Combat in Vietnam* (Washington, DC, 1978).

Steiger, R., *Armoured Tactics in the Second World War* (Oxford, 1991).

Steinbruner, J.D., *The Cybernetic Theory of Decision: New Dimensions of Political Analysis* (Princeton, 1974).

Strachen, H., *European Armies and the Conduct of War* (London, 1983).

Strategic Studies Institute, *Organization, Missions and Command and Control of Special Forces and Ranger Units in the 1980s* (unclassified) (US Army War College, Carlisle Barracks, PA 1979).

—, *The Operational Art of Warfare across the Spectrum of Conflict* (Carlisle Barracks, PA 1987).

Strokov, A.A., *Istoriia voennogo iskusstva* (History of Military Art) (Moscow, 1966).

Stumpf, R., *Die Wehrmacht Elite: Rang und Herkunfts – Struktur der Deutsche Generale und Admirale 1933–1945* (Boppard, 1982).

Sukhorukov, D.S., *Sovetskie vozdushno-desantnie voiska* (Soviet Airborne *Desant* Forces) (Moscow, 1980).

Summers, H.G., *On Strategy: A Critical Analysis of the Vietnam War* (Novato, CA, 1982).

Svechin, A.A., *Evoliutsiia voennogo iskusstva* (The Evolution of Military Art) (Moscow/Leningrad, 1927–28).

—, *Strategiia* (Strategy) (Moscow, 1927).

Svechnikov, M.S., *Reidy konnitsy i oborona zheleznykh dorog* (Cavalry Raids and the Defense of Railways) (Moscow/Leningrad, 1928).

Syromiatnikov, A.D., *Proryv, ego razvitie i parirovanie* (Penetration, Its Development and Parrying) (Moscow/Leningrad, 1928).

Sywottek, J., *Mobilmachung für den Krieg* (Opladen, 1976).

359

Taylor, A.J.P., *From Napoleon to Lenin* (New York, 1952).

The Joint Staff and US Special Operations Command, *US Special Operations Forces – Status Report* (Washington, DC, June 1990).

Thompson, W.S. and Frizzel, D.D. (eds), *The Lessons of Vietnam* (New York, 1977).

Tikhonov, M., *Nochnye deistviia* (Night Actions) (Moscow, 1935).

Tiushkevits, S.A. (ed.), *Sovetskie Vooruzhennykh Sily* (Soviet Armed Forces) (Moscow, 1978).

Todorskii, A.I., *Marshal Tukhachevskii* (Moscow, 1963).

Tokarevskii, N., *Taktika artillerii* (Artillery Tactics) (Moscow, 1931).

Tolstoi, L.N., *War and Peace*, Hebrew trans. Goldberg. L. (Tel Aviv, 1977).

Tovstikha, P.P. and Portugal'skii, R.M., *Upravlenie voiskami v nastuplenii po opytu Velikoi otechestvennoi voiny* (The Command of Troops in the Offensive according to the Experience of the Great Patriotic War) (Moscow, 1981).

Traditionverband der 3. Panzerdivision (ed.), *Geschichte der 3. Panzerdivision Berlin – Brandenburg 1935–1945* (Berlin, 1967).

Trevor-Roper, H.R., *Hitler's War Directives 1939–1945* (London, 1966).

Triandafillov, V.K., *Kharakter operatsii sovremennykh armii* (The Nature of Operations of Modern Armies) (Moscow, 1932, 1937).

—, *Razmakh operatsii sovremennykh armii* (The Scope of Operations of Modern Armies) (Moscow, 1926).

—, *The Nature of Operations of Modern Armies*, ed. Kipp, J.W. (London, 1992).

Trotsky, L.D., *Kak vooruzhalas' revoliutsiia* (How the Revolution Was Armed) (Moscow, 1923–25).

Tsiffer, R.S., *Taktika pekhoty* (Infantry Tactics) (Moscow, 1935).

Tukhachevskii, M.N., *Izbrannye proizvedeniia* (Selected Works), ed. Solov'ev, N.I. (Moscow, 1964) (2 vols.).

Turney, A.W., *Disaster at Moscow: Von Bock's Campaigns 1941–1942* (Albuquerque, 1970).

Uhle-Wettler, F., *Gefechtsfeld Mittleuropa, Gefahr der Übertechnisierung von Streitkräften* (Bonn, 1980).

US Air Force, Air Command and Staff College, *Conventional Warfare* (Maxwell AFB, AL, Jan. 1991).

—, *Military History and Doctrine* (Maxwell AFB, AL, Sept. 1990).

US Army John F. Kennedy Special Warfare Center, *Special Operations Mission Area Analysis* (unclassified) (Fort Bragg, NC, May 1983).

US Army Training and Doctrine Command, Combined Arms Center, *Airland Battle* (special text prepared for the exclusive use of students of the Army War College) (Carlisle Barracks, PA, 29 Aug. 1983).

US Army War College, *Forces Capabilities Handbook*, Vol. 1 (Carlisle Barracks, PA, Academic Year 1993).

—, *Strategic and Operational Capabilities Planning* (Carlisle Barracks, PA, Academic Year 1986).

US Department of Defense, *Soviet Military Power 1985* (Washington, DC,

1985).

—, *Conduct of the Persian Gulf War: Final Report to Congress* (Washington, DC, April 1992).

US Naval War College, Operations Department, *Joint Military Operations Syllabus 1993* (College of Naval Warfare, 1993).

Vald, E., *Hakesher haGordi – Mitosim vedilemmot bevitachon Yisrael* (The Gordian Knot – Myths and Dilemmas of Israeli National Security) (Tel Aviv, 1991).

Varfolomeev, N.E., *Nastupatel'naia operatsiia* (The Offensive Operation) (Moscow, 1937).

—, *Udarnaia armiia* (The Strike Army) (Moscow, 1933).

Vasilevskii, A.M., *Delo vsei zhizni* (Life's Work) (Moscow, 1975).

Vatsetis, I., *O voennoi doktrine budushchego* (On Future Military Doctrine) (Moscow, 1923).

Verdy du Vernois, J. von, *With the Royal Headquarters at the War of 1870–1871* (London, 1898).

Verkhovskii, A.I., *Na trudnom perevale* (A Hazardous Passage) (Moscow, 1959).

—, *Osnovy nashei taktiki – ogon', manevr, maskirovka* (The Fundamentals of our Tactics – Fire, Manoeuvre, Deception) (Moscow, 1928).

Vigor, P.H., *Soviet Blitzkrieg Theory* (London, 1983).

Vladimirov, M.I., *et al.*, *M.V. Frunze: voennaia i politicheskaia deiatel'nost* (M.V. Frunze: Military and Political Activity) (Moscow, 1984).

Voennaia Entsiklopediia (Military Encyclopedia) (St Petersburg, 1911–15).

Voennyi Entsiklopedicheskii Slovar' (Military Encyclopedic Dictionary) (Moscow, 1983).

Volin, I., *A Century of Russian Agriculture* (Cambridge, MA, 1970).

Vol'pe, A., *Frontal'nyi udar* (Frontal Strike) (Moscow, 1931).

Vorob'ev, F.D., *et al.*, *Poslednii shturm, Berlinskaia operatsiia 1945g.* (The Last Storm, the Berlin Operation 1945) (Moscow 1975).

Voroshilov, K.E., *Stat'i i rechi* (Articles and Speeches) (Moscow, 1936).

—, *XX let RKKA* (20 Years of the Red Army) (Moscow, 1938).

Wallach, J., *Das Dogma der Vernichtungsschlacht* (Frankfurt a. M., 1967).

Waltz, K.N., *Man, the State and War* (New York, 1970).

Warlimont, T.W., *Im Hauptquartier der Deutschen Wehrmacht 1939–1945* (Frankfurt, 1962).

Wavell, A.P., *The Palestine Campaigns* (London, 1928).

Wayne, H.P., *Fleet Tactics: Theory and Practice* (Annapolis, 1986).

Wegner, R., *Wehrmachtserziehung und Kriegsfahrung* (Berlin, 1938).

Weigly, R.F., *The American Way of War: A History of the United States Strategy and Policy* (New York, 1973).

Westmoreland, W.C., *A Soldier Reports* (New York, 1976).

Westphal, S., *Heer in Fesseln* (Bonn, 1950).

White, L. (ed.), *Medieval Society and Social Change* (Oxford, 1962).

Widdern, G. von, *Kritische Tage* (5 vols.) (Berlin, 1897–1900).

Wright, Q., *A Study of War* (Chicago, 1965).

Wust, H. and Himburg, L.F., *Das Militarische Führungssystem* (Frankfurt, 1974).

XV S'ezd Vsesoiuznoi Kommunisticheskoi Partii(b) stenograficheskii otchet (A Stenographic Report of the 15th General Communist Party Congress) (Moscow, 1928).

XVII S'ezd Vsesoiuznoi Kommunisticheskoi Partii (VKP [b]) stenograficheskii otchet (A Stenographic Report of the 17th General Communist Party Congress) (Moscow, 1934).

Zakharov, M.V., *General'nyi shtab v predvoennye gody* (The General Staff in the Prewar Years) (Moscow, 1989).

—, *50 let Vooruzhennykh sil SSSR* (50 Years of the USSR Armed Forces) (Moscow, 1968).

—, *Uchenyi i voin, o marshale Sovetskogo Soiuza B.M. Shaposhnikove* (Scholar and Warrior, on Marshal of the Soviet Union B.M. Shaposhnikov) (Moscow, 1974).

Zernin, G., *Das Leben von Generals August von Goeben* (2 vols.) (Berlin, 1895–97).

Zezschwitz, G.P. von, *Der Panzerkampf* (Munich/Berlin, 1938).

Zhilin, P.A., *et al.* (eds), *Revue Internationale d'Histoire Militaire* (Moscow, 1979).

Zhukov, G.K., *Vospominaniia i razmyshleniia* (Reminiscences and Reflections (Moscow, 1975) (3 vols).

Zhuravlev, N.A., *Taktika razvedyvatel'noi aviatsii* (Tactics of Reconnaissance Aviation) (Moscow/Leningrad, 1933).

B. Articles

Ageev, A., 'Kontrnastuplenie Krasnoi Armii na Vostochnom fronte osen'iu 1918 goda' (The Red Army's 1918 Fall Counter-offensive on the Eastern Front), *Voenno-Istoricheskii zhurnal*, 1982, No. 11, pp. 66–73.

—, 'Pervaia frontovaia operatsiia Krasnoi Armii' (The Red Army's First Front Operation), *Voenno-istoricheskii zhurnal*, 1979, No. 8, pp. 62–7.

Alferov, S., 'Peregruppirovka 3-i Gvardeiskoi Tankovoi Armii v bitve za Dnepr, oktiabr' 1943g.' (Regrouping of 3rd Guards Tank Army in the Battle of Dnieper, October 1943), *Voenno-istoricheskii zhurnal*, 1980, No. 3, pp. 16–22.

Algazin, A., 'Primenenie i organizatsiia vozdushnoi armii' (The Employment and Organization of an Air Army), *Voennaia mysl'*, 1937, No. 2, pp. 116–40.

Allen, R.L., 'Piercing the Veil of Operational Art', *Parameters*, 1986, Vol. XVI, No. 4, pp. 23–9.

Allmendinger, H., 'Panzertaktik', *Die Kraftfahrkampftruppe*, 1938, No. 6, pp. 217–19.

Ammosov, S., 'Reidy motomekhsoedineniia' (Moto-mechanized Formation Raids), *Voina i revoliutsiia*, 1931, No. 6, pp. 42–58.

—, 'Tanki v operatsii proryva' (Tanks in Breakthrough Operations), *Voina i revoliutsiia*, 1932, No. 5–6, pp. 81–91.

Anderson, D.R. 'Modernizing Army Command and Control', *Military Review*, 1990, Vol. LXX, No. 7, pp. 2–10.

Anisov, A., 'Armeiskaia oboronitel'naia operatsiia' (The Army Defensive Operation), *Voina i revoliutsiia*, 1934, No. 11–12, pp. 40–50.

Antal, J.F., 'Maneuver Versus Attrition: A Historical Perspective', *Military Review*, 1992, Vol. LXXII, No. 10, pp. 21–33.

—, 'Thoughts About Maneuver Warfare', in Hooker, R.D. (ed.), *Maneuver Warfare – An Anthology* (Novato, CA, 1993), pp. 57–75.

—, 'The Wehrmacht Approach to Maneuver Warfare', in *idem.*, pp. 347–59.

Anuchin, V.V. and Zdorov, O.N., 'Zarozhdenie i razvitie teorii boevogo primeneniia VVS 1917–1938gg.' (The Origin and Development of the Theory of Combat Employment of the Air Force 1917–1938), *Voenno-istoricheskii zhurnal*, 1988, No. 8, pp. 19–26.

Apanasenko, I., 'Pervaia Konnaia' (The First Cavalry Army), *Voenno-istoricheskii zhurnal*, 1939, No. 4, pp. 35–42.

Armstrong, R.N., 'Fighting The Threat: Advance Guard', *Armor*, 1982, No. 3, pp. 35–8.

—, 'The Mobile Group Experience: The Soviets Appear To Be Still Refining Their WWII Tactics in Today's OMG', *Armor*, 1987, Vol. XLVI, No. 5, pp. 24–30.

Asprey, R.B., 'The Peninsular War', *Army Quarterly*, April 1959, Vol. 77, pp. 52–63.

Atkeson, E.B., 'The Operational Level of War', *Military Review*, 1987, Vol. LXVII, No. 3, pp. 28–36.

Babadzhanian, A., 'Bronetankovye i mekhanizirovannye voiska' (Tank and Mechanized Forces), *Voenno-istoricheskii zhurnal*, 1977, No. 11, pp. 38–44.

Bahnsen, J.C. and Stack, R.C., 'A Mobile Division for Future War', *Military Review*, 1989, Vol. LXIX, No. 6, pp. 30–36.

Baikeev, R., 'Peredovoi otriad forsiruet reku' (The Forward Detachment Forces a River), *Voennyi vesnik*, 1983, No. 12, pp. 58–62.

Baratto, D.J., 'Special Forces in the 1980s: A Strategic Reorientation', *Military Review*, 1983, Vol. LXIII, No. 3, pp. 2–14.

Barbara, J.C. and Brown, R.F., 'Deep Thrust on the Extended Battlefield', *Military Review*, 1982, Vol. LXII, No. 10, pp. 21–32.

Barry, C.L., 'Planning Aviation Cross-FLOT Operations', *Military Review*, 1984, Vol. LXIV, No. 1, pp. 34–45.

Barthel, R., 'Theorie und Praxis der Heeres Motorisierung im Faschistischen Deutschland bis 1939', Ph.D. diss., Leipzig, 1967.

Bartov, O., 'Blitzkrieg', *Zmanim* (Tel Aviv University), 1985, No. 18/19, pp. 76–85.

Bates, J.L. and Quinn, J.B., 'T2S = V', *Military Review*, 1986, Vol. LXVI, No. 3, pp. 21–31.

Baur, M.C., 'Airland Battle's Power Punch', *Armor*, 1982, No. 5, pp. 38–41.

Baxter, W.P., 'A Lesson in Tank Tactics – River Crossing Soviet Style', *Army*, 1980, No. 7, pp. 39–41.

—, 'Soviet Communications – Bare Bones but Secure', *Army*, 1982, No. 8, pp. 30–33.

—, 'Soviet Echelonment: Tactics for Depth and Flexibility', *Army*, 1981, No. 11, pp. 39–40.

—, 'Soviet Doctrine Responds to Anti-Tank Missile Threat', *Army*, 1980, No. 6, pp. 29–32.

—, 'Soviet Economy of Massed Fires', *Army*, 1982, No. 6, pp. 61–3.

—, 'Soviet Exploitation of Western Technology and Military Art', *Military Review*, 1983, Vol. LXIII, No. 7, pp. 41–53.

—, 'What Ivan Knows about Us', *Army*, 1980, No. 7, pp. 39–41.

Bazarevskii, A., 'Vstrechnaia operatsiia' (The Meeting Operation), *Voennaia mysl'*, 1937, No. 3, pp. 97–118.

Beaumont, R.A., 'On the Wehrmacht Mystique', *Military Review*, 1986, Vol. LXVI, No. 7, pp. 44–56.

Belitskii, S., 'Eshelonnaia voina' (The Rail War), *Voina i revoliutsiia*, 1927, No. 10–11, pp. 197–207.

—, 'K voprosu o strategicheskikh rezervakh' (On the Question of Strategic Reserves), *Voina i revoliutsiia*, 1925, No. 2, pp. 14–20.

—, 'Podvizhnost' sovremennykh armii (The Mobility of Contemporary Armies), *Voina i revoliutsiia*, 1930, No. 11, pp. 3–9.

Bellamy, C., 'Antecedents of the Modern Soviet Operational Manoeuvre Group (OMG)', *RUSI Journal*, Sept. 1984, Vol. 129, pp. 50–58.

—, 'Heirs of Genghis Khan: The Influence of the Tartar-Mongols on the Imperial Russian and Soviet Armies', *RUSI Journal*, March 1983, Vol. 128, pp. 52–60.

—, 'Red Star in the West: Marshal Tukhachevskiy and East–West Exchanges on the Art of War', *RUSI Journal*, Dec. 1987, Vol. 132, pp. 63–73.

—, 'Seventy Years on: Similarities between the Modern Soviet Army and its Tsarist Predecessor', *RUSI Journal*, Sept. 1979, Vol. 124, pp. 29–38.

Besch, E.W., 'Are Our Light Divisions Too Light?', *Army*, 1985, No. 2, pp. 43–9.

Betts, R.K., 'Dubious Reform: Strategism versus Managerialism', in Clark, A.A., *et al.* (eds), *The Defense Reform Debate – Issues and Analysis* (Baltimore, 1984), pp. 62–84.

Bgishev, I. and Ignatov, A., 'Obespechenie vstrechnogo boia' (Protecting an Encounter Battle), *Voennyi vestnik*, 1974, No. 8, pp. 101–3.

Bingham, P.T., 'Ground Maneuver and Air Interdiction in the Operational Art', *Parameters*, 1989, Vol. XIX, No. 1, pp. 16–31.

Biriuzov, S., 'Voennoe teoreticheskoe nasledstvo M.N. Tukhachevskogo' (M.N. Tukhachevskii's Military Theory Legacy), *Voenno-istoricheskii zhurnal*, 1964, No. 2, pp. 37–49.

Blockheim, W., 'Zusammenwirken von Panzertruppen mit Flieger', *Die Kraftfahrkampftruppe*, 1937, No. 4, pp. 101–4.

Bodelson, P.J. and Smith, K.B., 'Design for Tempo', *US Army Aviation Digest*, 1991, No. 2, pp. 9–15.

Boffey, P.M., 'Systems Analysis: No Panacea for Nation's Domestic Problems',

Science, 1967, No. 158, pp. 1028–30.

Bolger, D.P., 'Maneuver Warfare Reconsidered', in Hooker, R.D. (ed.), *Maneuver Warfare – An Anthology* (Novato, CA, 1993), pp. 19–41.

Bolt, J. and Jablonsky, D., 'Tactics and the Operational Level of War', *Military Review*, 1987, Vol. LXVII, No. 2, pp. 2–19.

Bonch-Bruevich, M., 'Nekotorye osnovy operativnogo rukovodstva v sovremennoi voine' (Several Elements of Operational Management in Contemporary War), *Voina i revoliutsiia*, 1927, No. 12, pp. 46–63.

—, 'Nekotorye problemy budushchei voiny' (Several Problems of Future War), *Voina i revoliutsiia*, 1929, No. 5, pp. 60–4.

Bond, B.J., 'Doctrine and Training in the British Cavalry 1870–1914', in Howard, M. (ed.), *The Theory and Practice of War* (London, 1965), pp. 95–128.

—, 'Liddell Hart and the German Generals', *Military Affairs*, 1977, No. 41, pp. 16–20.

Boylan, P.J., 'Complementary Force Operations', *Military Review*, 1990, Vol. LXX, No. 6, pp. 27–37.

Brinkley, W.A., 'The Cost across the FLOT', *Military Review*, 1986, Vol. LXVI, No. 9, pp. 30–41.

Brodie, B., 'A Guide to the Reading of *On War*', in Clausewitz, C. von, *On War*, eds Howard, M. and Paret, P. (Princeton, 1976), pp. 641–711.

Brown, B., 'OMG', *Field Artillery Journal*, 1985, Vol. 53, No. 1, pp. 26–7.

Buel, L.V., 'Intelligence Preparation of the Battlefield', *Military Review*, 1987, Vol. LXVII, No. 10, pp. 24–33.

Burgess, W.H., 'Toward a More Complete Doctrine – SOF in Airland Battle Future', *Military Review*, 1991, Vol. LXXI, No. 2, pp. 30–37.

Burke, C.M. and Presgraves, D.C., 'US Army Concept for Aviation', *US Army Aviation Digest*, 1993, No. 5, pp. 8–13.

Burniece, J.R., 'The Operational Maneuver Group: Concept versus Organization', *Military Technology*, 1988, No. 10, pp. 65–79.

Busse, H., 'Das Scheitern des Operationplanes "Barbarossa" im Sommer 1941 und die Militärische Legende von der Führungskrise', *Zeitschrift für Militärgeschichte*, 1962, No. 1, pp. 62–84.

Cabaniss, E.H., 'Ground Soviet Tactics', *Military Review*, 1979, Vol. LIX, No. 12, pp. 37–45.

Canby, S.L., 'Military Reform and the Art of War', in Clark, A.A., *et al.*, *The Defense Reform Debate*, pp. 126–46.

—, 'Mutual Forces Reduction: A Military Perspective', *International Security*, 1978, Vol. 2, No. 3, pp. 123–8.

—, 'NATO Defense: The Problem Is Not More Money', in Harkavy, R. and Kolodjiez, E. (eds), *American Security Policy Making* (Lexington, KY, 1980), pp. 85–99.

—, 'NATO Reassessing the Conventional Wisdoms', *Survival*, 1977, Vol. XIX, No. 4, pp. 164–8.

—, 'Territorial Defense in Central Europe', *Armed Forces and Society*, Fall 1980, pp. 51–67.

Cardwell, T.A., 'Airland Battle Revisited', *Military Review*, 1985, Vol. LXV, No. 9, pp. 4–13.

—, 'Extending the Battlefield: An Airman's Point of View', *Air University Review*, 1983, No. 2, pp. 86–93.

—, 'Follow-On Forces Attack: Joint Interdiction by Another Name', *Military Review*, 1986, Vol. LXVI, No. 2, pp. 4–11.

—, 'Managing Theater Air Assets', *Military Review*, 1983, Vol. LXIII, No. 5, pp. 40–45.

—, 'One Step Beyond – Airland Battle, Doctrine Not Dogma', *Military Review*, 1984, Vol. LXIV, No. 4, pp. 45–53.

Carlson, A., 'A Revisionist's View', *Infantry*, 1978, No. 3, pp. 37–9.

Carlson, K.G., 'Operational Level or Operational Art', *Military Review*, 1987, Vol. LXVII, No. 10, pp. 50–54.

Carr, L.W., 'Mobility Differential – Army Aviation Branch's Challenge', *Army Aviation Digest*, 1989, No. 6. pp. 14–15.

Carter, L.J., 'Systems Approach: Political Interest Rises', *Science*, 1966, No. 153, pp. 1222–4.

Case, B., 'Air Defense for Airland Battle: Coming of Age in High Tech', *Army*, 1983, No. 11, pp. 34–7, 41, 46–8.

Chales de Beaulieu, W., 'Sturm bis vor Modkaus Tore. Der Einsatz der Panzergruppe 4', *Wehrwissenschaftliche Rundschau*, 1956, No. 7, pp. 349–65, No. 8, pp. 423–39.

Cherednichenko, M., 'Razvitie teorii strategicheskoi nastupatel'noi operatsii v 1945–1953gg.' (The Development of the Theory of Strategic Offensive Operations 1945–1953), *Voenno-istoricheskii zhurnal*, 1976, No. 8, pp. 38–45.

Chikalin, S., 'Ob osnovakh primeneniia organizatsii operativnykh tankovykh soedinenii' (On the Fundamentals of Employing and Organizing Operational Tank Formations), *Voina i revoliutsiia*, 1930, No. 4, pp. 25–35.

—, 'Organizatsiia i ispol'zovanie takticheskikh tankovykh soedinenii' (The Organization and Employment of Armoured Tactical Formations), *Voina i revoliutsiia*, 1930, No. 3, pp. 12–28.

Cimral, T.A., 'Moving the Heavy Corps', *Military Review*, 1988, Vol. LXVIII, No. 7, pp. 28–34.

Colanto, J.D., 'Intelligence Preparation of the Battlefield for the Airland Battle', *Military Intelligence*, 1983, No. 3, pp. 4–6.

Cooley, A.L., 'Quick Thunder: True Multi-Echelon Training', *Military Review*, 1987, Vol. LXVII, No. 5, pp. 2–7.

Cope, J.A., 'Doctrinal Credibility: A Problem of Focus with FM 100–5', *Military Review*, 1984, Vol. LXIV, No. 8, pp. 66–73.

Coroalles, A.M., 'Implementing Maneuver Style of War', *Military Review*, 1982, Vol. LXII, No. 12, pp. 20–26.

—, 'Maneuver to Win: A Realistic Alternative', *Military Review*, 1981, Vol. LXI, No. 9, pp. 35–46.

Coyle, H.W., 'Tatsinskaia and the Soviet OMG Doctrine', *Armor*, 1985, Vol.

XCIV, No. 1, pp. 33–8.

Creveld, M. van, 'On Learning from the Wehrmacht and Other Things', *Military Review*, 1988, Vol. LXVIII, No. 1, pp. 62–71.

—, 'War Lord Hitler: Some Points Reconsidered', *European Studies Review*, 1974, No. 4, pp. 57–79.

Curry, F.T., 'EW for the Airland Battle', *Military Intelligence*, 1983, No. 3, pp. 15–16.

Daines, V., 'Razvitie taktiki obshchevoiskovogo nastupatel'nogo boia v 1929–1941gg.' (The Development of the Tactics of Combined Arms Offensive Battle in 1929–1941), *Voenno-istoricheskii zhurnal*, 1978, No. 10, pp. 96–101.

Danilov, F. and Kravchenko, I., 'U istokov Sovetskoi teorii operativnogo iskusstva 1921–1930gg.' (The Sources of the Soviet Theory of Operational Art 1921–1930), *Voenno-istoricheskii zhurnal*, 1973, No. 11, pp. 38–45.

Danilov, V., 'Organizatsiia strategicheskogo rukovodstva Sovetskimi Vooruzhennymi Silami 1917–1920gg.' (The Organization of Strategic Control of the Soviet Armed Forces 1917–1920), *Voenno-istoricheskii zhurnal*, 1988, No. 3, pp. 17–25.

D'amura, R.M., 'Campaign: The Essence of Operational Warfare', *Parameters*, 1987, Vol. XVII, No. 3, pp. 42–51.

Dees, R.F., 'Battle Rhythm', *Military Review*, 1987, Vol. LXVII, No. 4, pp. 59–64.

Dement'ev, V., 'Nauchno-tekhnicheskii progress i razvitie voennogo dela' (Scientific-technical Progress and the Development of Military Affairs), *Voenno-istoricheskii zhurnal*, 1979, No. 3, pp. 8–15.

DePuy, W.E., 'The US Army: Are We Ready for the Future?', *Army*, 1978, No. 9, pp. 22–4.

—, 'The Case for Synchronization, Toward a Balanced Doctrine', in Allen, R.L. (ed.), *Operational Level of War – its Art* (special text) (US Army War College, Carlisle Barracks, PA, Aug. 1985), pp. 5-14–5.121.

Devries, P.T., 'Maneuver and the Operational Level of War', *Military Review*, 1983, Vol. LXIII, No. 2, pp. 13–34.

Dick, C.J., 'Catching NATO Unaware – Soviet Army Surprise and Deception Techniques', *International Defense Review*, 1986, No. 1, pp. 21–6.

—, 'Soviet Doctrine: Equipment Design and Organization', *International Defense Review*, 1983, No. 12, 99.1715–22.

—, 'Soviet Operational Concepts', *Military Review*, 1985, Vol. LXV, No. 9, pp. 29–45, No. 10, pp. 4–19.

—, 'Soviet Operational Manoeuvre Group – A Closer Look', *International Defense Review*, 1983, No. 6, pp. 772–6.

Dinges, E.A. and Sinnereich, R.H., 'Battlefield Interdiction: Old Term New Problem', *Field Artillery Journal*, 1980, No. 1, pp. 14–17.

Doege, A., 'Infanterie und Panzer', *Militärwochenblatt*, 29 April 1938, cols. 2810–15.

Doerfel, J.S. 'The Operational Art of the Airland Battle', *Military Review*, 1982, Vol. LXII, No. 5, pp. 3–10.

Donnelly, C.L., 'An Air Commander's View of Operational Art', *Military Review*, 1990, Vol. LXX, No. 9, pp. 79–84.

Donnelly, C.N., 'Fighting in Built-Up Areas: A Soviet View', *RUSI Journal*, 1977, Vol. 122, No. 3, pp. 63–7.

—, 'Operational Manoeuvre Group: A New Challenge to NATO', *International Defense Review*, 1982, No. 9, pp. 1177–86.

—, 'Operations in Enemy Rear. Soviet Doctrine and Tactics', *International Defense Review*, 1980, No. 1, pp. 35–41.

—, 'Soviet Fighting Doctrine', *NATO's Sixteen Nations*, 1984, No. 5, pp. 65–9.

—, 'Soviet Reconnaissance', *RUSI Journal*, 1976, Vol. 121, No. 1, pp. 68–75.

—, 'Soviet Tactics for Overcoming NATO Anti-Tank Defense', *International Defense Review*, 1978, No. 6, pp. 1099–106.

—, 'Tactical Problems Facing the Soviet Army Recent Debates', *International Defense Review*, 1978, No. 9, pp. 1405–7.

—, 'The Soviet Concept of Desant', *RUSI Journal*, 1971, Vol. 116, No. 3, pp. 52–5.

—, 'The "March" in Soviet Tactical Doctrine', *RUSI Journal*, 1974, Vol. 119, No. 3, pp. 77–80.

—, 'The Development of the Soviet Concept of Echeloning', *NATO Review*, 1984, No. 6, pp. 9–17.

—, 'The Development of Soviet Military Doctrine', *International Defense Review*, 1981, No. 12, pp. 1593–6.

Doughty, R.A., 'From the *Offensive à Outrance* to the Methodical Battle', in Hooker, R.D. (ed.), *Maneuver Warfare – An Anthology* (Novato, CA, 1993), pp. 294–315.

— and Holder, L.D., 'Images of the Future Battlefield', *Military Review*, 1978, Vol. LVIII, No. 1, pp. 56–9.

Downing, W.A., 'Light Infantry Integration in Central Europe', *Military Review*, 1986, Vol. LXVI, No. 9, pp. 18–29.

—, 'Training To Fight', *Military Review*, 1986, Vol. LXVI, No. 5, pp. 18–27.

—, 'US Army Operations Doctrine: A Challenge for the 1980s and Beyond', *Military Review*, 1981, Vol. LXI, No. 1, pp. 64–73.

Dubik, J.M., 'FM 100–5: Comparing the Operational Concepts and Defense', *Military Review*, 1982, Vol. LXII, No. 12, pp. 13–19.

—, 'FM 100–5 and Counterinsurgency Warfare', *Military Review*, 1983, Vol. LXIII, No. 11, pp. 41–8.

— and Montano, J.J., 'FM 100–5: Conceptual Models and Force Design', *Military Review*, 1984, Vol. LXIV, No. 7, pp. 16–26.

Dugan, M.J., 'Air Power: Concentration, Responsibilities and Operational Art', *Military Review*, 1989, Vol. LXIX, No. 7, pp. 12–21.

Dupuy, T.N., 'The Soviet Second Echelon: Is This a Red Herring?', *Armed Forces Journal*, 1982, No. 8, pp. 60, 62–4.

Earle, E.M., 'Adam Smith, Alexander Hamilton, Friedrich List: The Economic Foundations of Military Power', in Earle, E.M. (ed.), *Makers of Modern Strategy* (Princeton, 1971), pp. 117–54.

—, 'Lenin, Trotsky, Stalin: Soviet Concepts of War', in *idem*, pp. 322–64.

Egorov, A., 'Goriachii bol'shevitskii privet Voennoi Akademii RKKA imeni M.V. Frunze' (Warmest Bolshevist Greetings to the RKKA Frunze Military Academy), *Voina i revoliutsiia*, 1934, No. 1, pp. 3–7.

—, 'Taktika i operativnoe iskusstvo RKKA na novom etape' (Tactics and Operational Art of the RKKA at a New Stage), *Voenno-istoricheskii zhurnal*, 1963, No. 10, pp. 30–9.

Eideman, R., 'K izucheniiu istorii Grazhdanskoi voiny' (On Learning the History of the Civil War), *Voina i revoliutsiia*, 1932, No. 2, pp. 90–99.

Erickson, J., 'Some Developments in Soviet Tactical Aviation – Frontovaia Aviatsiia', *RUSI Journal*, 1975, Vol. 120, No. 3, pp. 70–72.

—, 'Soviet Breakthrough Operations: Resources and Restraints', *RUSI Journal*, 1976, Vol. 121, No. 3, pp. 74–9.

—, 'The Northern Theatre – TVD – Soviet Capabilities and Concepts', *RUSI Journal*, 1976, Vol. 121, No. 4, pp. 16–17.

Even-Zohar, I., 'The Nature and Function of the Language of Literature under Diglossia', *Hasifrut/Literature*, 1970, Vol. II, No. 2, pp. 286–302.

—, 'The Polysystem Hypothesis Revisited', *Hasifrut/Literature*, 1978, Vol. III, No. 27, pp. 1–6.

—, 'On Systemic Universals in Cultural History', in *Papers in Historical Poetics* (The Porter Institute for Poetics and Semiotics, Tel Aviv University, 1978), pp. 39–44.

Farndale, M., 'The Operational Level of Command', *RUSI Journal*, 1988, Vol. 133, No. 3, pp. 23–9.

Fastband, D.A., 'The Application of the Commander's Intent', *Military Review*, 1987, Vol. LXVII, No. 8, pp. 60–68.

— and Graves, R.H., 'Maneuver, Synchronization and Obstacle Operations', *Military Review*, 1986, Vol. LXVI, No. 2, pp. 36–48.

Favitskii, V.K., 'Podvizhnaia oborona' (Mobile Defence), *Voina i revoliutsiia*, 1932, No. 3, pp. 28–42.

—, 'Rol' mekhvoisk v sovremennoi operatsii' (The Role of Mechanized Forces in Contemporary War), *Mekhanizatsiia i motorizatsiia RKKA*, 1933, No. 2, pp. 63–71.

Fedde, E., 'Airlandbattle and S2 – Airland Battle: No Longer Theory, but a Doctrine', *Military Intelligence*, 1983, No. 3, pp. 12–13.

Fedorenko, V.S., 'Tankovye i mekhanizirovannye korpusa v nastupatel'nykh operatsiiakh' (Tank and Mechanized Corps in Offensive Operations), *Voennaia mysl'*, 1965, No. 4, pp. 54–67.

Fedorenko, L., 'K voprosu o konnykh massakh' (On the Problems of Massed Cavalry), *Voina i revoliutsiia*, 1930, No. 6, pp. 24–43.

Fedotov, A., 'Isopol'zovanie sredstv podavleniia v proryve' (Employing Suppression Assets in the Breakthrough), *Voina i revoliutsiia*, 1932, No. 8–9, pp. 44–63.

Fialka, J.J., 'Matters of Defense: Congressional Military Reform Caucus Lacks a Budget but Has Power to Provoke the Pentagon', *The Wall Street Journal*, 13 April 1982, p. 52.

Fitton, R.A., 'A Perspective on Doctrine: Dispelling the Mystery', *Military*

Review, 1985, Vol. LXV, No. 2, pp. 63–74.

Flyd, B.O., 'The Airland Composite Wing', *Field Artillery Journal*, 1993, No. 5, pp. 9–11.

Foerster, J.E., 'The Dynamics of *Volksgemeinschaft*: The Effectiveness of the German Military Establishment in the Second World War', in Millett, A.R. and Murray, W. (eds), *Military Effectiveness*, Vol. III: *The Second World War* (Boston, 1990), pp. 180–220.

Fontenot, G. and Roberts, M.D., 'Plugging Holes and Mending Fences', *Infantry*, 1978, No. 5, pp. 32–6.

Foss, J.W., 'Advent of Non-Linear Battlefield', *Army*, 1991, No. 2, pp. 20–24, 33–7.

—, 'Building the United States Army for the Twenty-First Century', *RUSI Journal*, 1991, Vol. 136, No. 4, pp. 13–17.

—, 'The Evolving Airland Battle Future Concept', *Field Artillery Journal*, 1990, No. 4, pp. 9–11.

Franks, F.M., 'Continuity and Change: Discussing Our Evolving Doctrine', *Military Review*, 1991, Vol. LXX, No. 10, p. 1.

—, 'Full-Dimensional Operations: A Doctrine for an Era of Change', *Military Review*, 1993, Vol. LXXIII, No. 12, pp. 5–10.

Franz, W.P., 'Maneuver: The Dynamic Element of Combat', *Military Review*, 1983, Vol. LXIII, No. 5, pp. 2–12.

—, 'Operational Concepts', *Military Review*, 1984, Vol. LXIV, No. 7, pp. 2–15.

—, 'Two Letters on Strategy: Clausewitz' Contribution to the Operational Level of War', in Handel, M. (ed.), *Clausewitz and Modern Strategy* (London, 1986), pp. 171–94.

Freeman, W.D., 'The Challenges of Combined Operations', *Military Review*, 1992, Vol. LXXII, No. 11, pp. 2–11.

Freiser, K.H., 'Der Vorstoss der Panzergruppe Kleist zur Kanalküste (10 bis 21 Mai 1940)', in Boog, H. (ed.), *Operatives Denken und Handeln in Deutschen Streitkräften im 19. und 20. Jahrhundert* (Bonn, 1988), pp. 123–48.

—, 'Blitzkrieg ohne "Blitzkrieg"–Konzept–Der Westfeldzug 194', *Militärgeschichte*, 1991, No. 1, pp. 4–14.

Frolov, B., 'Vstrechnye srazheniia tankovykh armii v nastupatel'nykh operatsiiakh' (Meeting Engagements of Tank Armies in Offensive Operations), *Voenno-istoricheskii zhurnal*, 1977, No. 9, pp. 24–33.

Frunze, M.V., 'Edinaia voennaia doktrinai Krasnaia Armiia' (Unified Military Doctrine and the Red Army) *Voennaia nauka i revoliutsiia*, 1921, No. 2, pp. 33–9.

Fugate, B., 'Thunder on the Dnieper: The End of the Blitzkrieg Era Summer 1941', Ph.D. diss. (University of Texas, Austin, 1976).

Gai, G.D., 'Nedostatki v organizatsii Krasnoi konnitsy' (Shortcomings in the Organization of the Red Cavalry), *Voina i revoliutsiia*, 1921, No. 6, pp. 49–68.

Gaivoronskii, F., 'Razvitie Sovetskogo operativnogo iskusstva' (The Development of Soviet Operational Art), *Voenno-istoricheskii zhurnal*,

1978, No. 2, pp. 23–9.

Galaktionov, M., 'Artilleriia i tanki' (Artillery and Tanks), *Voina i revoliutsiia*, 1932, No. 12, pp. 38–64.

—, 'Moto-mekhsily i aviatsiia v operatsii "Kanny"' (Moto-mechanized Forces and Aviation in a "Cannae" Operation), *Voina i revoliutsiia*, 1934, No. 7–8, pp. 26–41.

Galvin, J.R., 'The Continuing Validity of Flexible Response and Forward Defense', *RUSI Journal*, 1988, Vol. 133, No. 2, pp. 4–9.

Gerasimov, I.A., 'Upravlenie Vooruzhennymi Silami v operatsiiakh Velikoi otechestvennoi voiny' (Command of Armed Forces in Operations of the Great Patriotic War), *Voennaia mysl'*, 1985, No. 4, pp. 44–57.

Geyer, M., 'German Strategy between 1914–1945', in Paret, P. (ed.), *Makers of Modern Strategy* (Oxford, 1986), pp. 527–97.

—, 'National Socialism and the Military in Weimar Republic', in Stachura, P.D. (ed.), *The Nazi Machtergreifung* (London, 1983), pp. 101–23.

Gingrich, N. and Reed, J.W., 'Guiding the Reform Impulse', in Clark, A.A., *et al.* (eds), *The Defense Reform Debate*, pp. 33–43.

Gladysh, S.A., 'K voprosu o razgrome kontrudarnykh gruppirovok protivnika' (Concerning Questions of Defeating Counterstrikes of Enemy Groupings), *Voennaia mysl'*, 1975, No. 8, pp. 58–60.

Glantz, D.M., 'Force Structure – Meeting Contemporary Requirements', *Military Review*, 1988, Vol. LXVIII, No. 12, pp. 58–70.

—, 'Operational Art and Tactics', *Military Review*, 1988, Vol. LXVIII, No. 12, pp. 32–40.

—, 'Predstavleniia Amerikantsev ob operatsiiakh na Vostochnom fronte v gody Vtoroi mirovoi voiny' (Conceptions of Americans about Operations on the Eastern Front during the Second World War), *Voprosy istorii*, 1987, No. 8, pp. 29–48.

—, 'Soviet Operational Formation for Battle: A Perspective', *Military Review*, 1983, Vol. LXIII, No. 2, pp. 2–12.

—, 'Soviet Operational Maneuver in a Period of Reform', *Military Review*, 1989, Vol. LXIX, No. 12, pp. 31–43.

—, 'Soviet Military Strategy after CFE: Historical Models and Future Prospects', *Journal of Soviet Military Studies*, 1990, No. 2, pp. 254–95.

—, 'Soviet Military Art: Challenges and Change in the 1990s', *Journal of Soviet Military Studies*, 1991, No. 4, pp. 547–93.

—, 'Soviet Mobilization in Peace and War, 1924–1942: A Survey', *Journal of Soviet Military Studies*, 1992, No. 3, pp. 323–62.

—, 'Surprise and Maskirovka in Contemporary War', *Military Review*, 1988, Vol. LXVIII, No. 12, pp. 50–58.

—, 'The Nature of Soviet Operational Art', *Parameters*, 1985, Vol. XV, No. 1, pp. 2–12.

Grange, D.E. 'Infantry and Air Defense in the Airland Battle', *Air Defense Magazine*, 1981, No. 4, pp. 24–5.

Gray, C.S., 'Force Planning, Political Guidance and the Decision to Fight', *Military Review*, 1978, Vol. LVIII, No. 4, pp. 5–16.

371

Griffin, D.K., 'If the Soviets Don't Mass', *Military Review*, 1979, Vol. LIX, No. 2, pp. 2–13.

Griffis, J., Pierce, K. and Sherwood, E., 'The Mechanized Infantry Battalion Task Force in the Airland Battle', *Infantry*, 1982, No. 4, pp. 21–4.

Grossman, D.A., 'Maneuver Warfare in the Light Infantry: The Rommel Model', in Hooker, R.D. (ed.), *Maneuver Warfare – An Anthology* (Novato, CA, 1993), pp. 316–35.

Guderian, H., 'Armored Warfare', *Armored Cavalry Journal*, 1949, No. 1, pp. 2–7.

—, 'Erfahrungen im Russlandkrieg', *Bilanz des Zweiten Weltkrieges*, Oldenburg/Hamburg, 1953, pp. 81–98.

—, 'Kraftfahrkampftruppen', *Militärwissenschaftliche Rundschau*, 1939, No. 1, pp. 52–77.

—, 'Schnelle Truppen Eins und Jetzt', *Militärwissenschaftliche Rundschau*, 1939, No. 2, pp. 229–43.

Gudmundsson, B.I., 'Maneuver Warfare: The German Tradition', in Hooker, R.D. (ed.), *Maneuver Warfare – An Anthology* (Novato, CA, 1993), pp. 273–93.

Gureev, M., 'Soviet Military Doctrine: Current and Future Development', *RUSI Journal*, 1988, Vol. 133, No. 4, pp. 5–10.

Gusev, A., 'Peredovoi otriad forsiruet reku' (The Forward Detachment Forces a River), *Voennyi vestnik*, 1979, No. 11, pp. 32–6.

Hall, A.D. and Fagen, R.D., 'Definition of System', *General Systems*, 1951, No. 1, pp. 18–29.

Hall, G.M., 'Culminating Points', *Military Review*, 1989, Vol. LXIX, No. 7, pp. 79–86.

Hall, W., 'A Theoretical Perspective of Airland Battle Doctrine', *Military Review*, 1986, Vol. LXVI, No. 3, pp. 32–43.

Hanne, W.G., 'Airland Battle: Doctrine Not Dogma', *Military Review*, 1983, Vol. LXIII, No. 6, pp. 11–25.

—, 'The Integrated Battlefield', *Military Review*, 1982, Vol. LXII, No. 6, pp. 34–44.

Hansen, J.H., 'Countering NATO's New Weapons – Soviet Concepts for War in Europe', in Allen, R.L. (ed.), *The Operational Level of War – its Art* (US Army War College, Carlisle Barracks, PA, 28 Aug. 1985), pp. 7-17-7-22.

Harned, G.M., 'Offensive Real Battle', *Military Review*, 1986, Vol. LXVI, No. 2, pp. 30–36.

—, 'Special Operations and the Airland Battle' *Military Review*, 1985, Vol. LXV, No. 9, pp. 72–83.

Harzog, W.W. and Howard, J.D., 'Heavy Operations', *Military Review*, 1987, Vol. LXVII, No. 4, pp. 24–33.

Haynes, J.H., 'Patterns, Plain and Fancy', *Military Review*, 1979, Vol. LIX, No. 7, pp. 2–10.

Heiber, H., 'Der Generalplan Ost', *Vierteljahreshefte für Zeitgeschichte*, 1958, pp. 281–325.

Hemsley, J., 'Command Technology: Voennaia Sistemotekhnika. An

Algorithmic Approach', *RUSI Journal*, 1980, Vol. 125, No. 3, pp. 58–64.

—, 'The Influence of Technology upon Soviet Operational Doctrine', *RUSI Journal*, 1986, Vol. 131, No. 2, pp. 21–8.

Herberg, J.A., 'Operational Manoeuvre Groups', *US Army Aviation Digest*, 1983, No. 9, pp. 30–32.

Herman, M., 'Reflections on the Study of Soviet Military Literature', *RUSI Journal*, 1988, Vol. 133, No. 2, pp. 79–84.

Higgins, G.A., 'German and US Operational Art: A Contrast in Manoeuvre', *Military Review*, 1985, Vol. LXV, No. 10, pp. 22–9.

Hill, J.C., 'Shaping the Battlefield – Deep Operations in V Corps', *Field Artillery Journal*, 1993, No. 2, pp. 7–10.

Hines, J.G., 'The Operational Manoeuvre Group: The Debate and the Reality', *Review of the Soviet Ground Forces*, 1983, No. 2, pp. 1–7.

— and Petersen, P.A., 'The Warsaw Pact Strategic Offensive: The OMG in Context', *International Defense Review*, 1983, No. 10, pp. 1391–5.

—, 'Thinking Soviet in Defending Europe', *Defence*, 1989, No. 9, pp. 511–20.

Hohenzollern, W. (Crown Prince), 'The Narrative of the Fifth German Army at the Battle of the Marne', in (no author indicated) *The Two Battles of the Marne* (London, 1927), pp. 91–130.

Holborn, H., 'Moltke and Schlieffen: The Prussian–German School' in Earle, E.M. (ed.), *Makers of Modern Strategy* (Princeton, 1971), pp. 172–205.

Holder, L.D., 'A New Day for Operational Art', in Allen, R.L. (ed.), *Operational Level of War – its Art* (US Army War College, Carlisle Barracks, PA, 28 Aug. 1985), pp. 4-1–4-9.

—, 'Concept of Operations: See Ops Overlay', *Military Review*, 1990, Vol. LXX, No. 8, pp. 27–34.

—, 'Doctrinal Developments 1975–1985', *Military Review*, 1985, Vol. LXV, No. 5, pp. 50–52.

—, 'Educating and Training for Theater Warfare', *Military Review*, 1990, Vol. LXX, No. 9, pp. 85–99.

—, 'Maneuver in the Deep Battle', *Military Review*, 1982, Vol. LXII, No. 5, pp. 54–61.

—, 'Moving the Heavy Division', *Military Review*, 1988, Vol. LXVIII, No. 7, pp. 35–49.

—, 'Offensive Tactical Operations', *Military Review*, 1993, Vol. LXXIII, No. 12, pp. 48–56.

Holcomb, J.F., 'Soviet Forward Detachment: A Commander's Guide', *International Defense Review*, 1989, Vol. LXIX, No. 5, pp. 551–5.

Holley, I.B., 'Concepts, Doctrines, Principles', in Allen, R.L. (ed.), *The Operational Level of War – its Art* (US Army War College, Carlisle Barracks, PA, 28 Aug. 1985), pp. 2-8–2-10.

Holloway, D., 'Soviet Military Cybernetics: Social and Political Problems of Troop Control', *RUSI Journal*, 1971, Vol. 115, No. 4, pp. 59–64.

Hooker, R.D., 'Redefining Maneuver Warfare', *Military Review*, 1992, Vol. LXXII, No. 2, pp. 50–58.

—, 'Implementing Maneuver Warfare', in Hooker, R.D. (ed.), *Maneuver*

Warfare – An Anthology (Novato, CA, 1993), pp. 217–35.

House, J. 'Fire Support Tactics for Rear Operations', *Field Artillery Journal*, 1987, No. 2, pp. 21–5.

Howard, M., 'Men against Fire, Expectations of War in 1914', in Millet, S.E., Lynn-Jones, S.M. and Van Evera, S. (eds), *Military Strategy and the Origins of the First World War* (Princeton, 1990), pp. 3–19.

—, 'Military Science in the Age of Peace', *RUSI Journal*, 1974, Vol. 119, No. 1, pp. 1–6.

—, 'The Influence of Clausewitz', in Clausewitz, C. von, *On War*, ed. Howard, M. and Paret, P. (Princeton, 1976), pp. 27–44.

—, 'The Use and Abuse of Military History', *Parameters*, 1981, Vol. XI, No. 1, pp. 2–9.

—, 'The Forgotten Dimension of Strategy' in Allen, R.L. (ed.), *Operational Level of War – its Art* (US Army War College, Carlisle Barracks, PA, 28 Aug. 1985), pp. 3-28–3-38.

Ianovskii, A. Ia., 'Vozdushnyi desant i bor'ba s nim na zheleznykh dorogakh' (Air *Desant* and the Fighting against it on the Railways), *Voennaia mysl'*, 1938, No. 5, pp. 114–27.

Ilseman, C.G. von, 'Das Operative Denke des Alteren Moltke', in Boog, H. (ed.), *Operative Denken und Handeln in Deutschen Streitkräften im 19. und 20. Jahrhundert* (Bonn, 1988), pp. 17–44.

Isserson, G.S., 'Istoricheskie korni novykh form boia' (The Historical Roots of the New Forms of Combat), *Voennaia mysl'*, 1937, No. 1, pp. 3–27.

—, 'Kharakter upravleniia sovremennym boem' (The Character of Command of Contemporary Warfare), *Voina i revoliutsiia*, 1931, No. 5, pp. 56–62.

—, 'Razvitie teorii Sovetskogo operativnogo iskusstva v 30-e gody' (The Development of the Theory of Soviet Operational Art in the 1930s), *Voenno-istoricheskii zhurnal*, 1965, No. 1, pp. 36–46, No. 3, pp. 48–61.

—, 'Zapiski sovremennika o M.N. Tukhachevskom' (Observations of a contemporary on M.N. Tukhachevskii), *Voenno-istoricheskii zhurnal*, 1963, No. 4, pp. 64–78.

Ivanov, N., 'Udary po skhodiashchimsia napravleniiam' (Strikes along Converging Directions), *Voina i revoliutsiia*, 1935, No. 3, pp. 14–30.

Infantry School's Experts, 'New Clout for Mech Infantry: The M2 and Airland Battle 2000 Tactics', *Army*, 1983, No. 8, pp. 18–22, 25–27, 29.

Ivanov, I., 'Razvitie Sovetskogo operativnogo iskusstva' (The Development of Soviet Operational Art), *Voennaia mysl'*, 1967, No. 3, pp. 3–13.

Ivanov, S., 'Opyt nastupatel'nykh operatsii frontov v Velikoi otechestvennoi voine' (The Experience of Front Offensive Operations in the Great Patriotic War), *Voennaia mysl'*, 1967, No. 3, pp. 3–13.

Jablonsky, D., 'Strategy and the Operational Level of War', *Parameters*, 1987, Vol. XVII, No. 1, pp. 65–76, No. 2, pp. 52–67.

Johnson, W.P. and Russel, E.N., 'An Army Strategy and Structure', *Military Review*, 1986, Vol. LXVI, No. 8, pp. 69–77.

Jones, A., 'The New FM 100–5: A View from the Ivory Tower', *Military Review*, 1978, Vol. LVIII, No. 2, pp. 27–36.

—, 'FM 100–5: A View from the Ivory Tower', *Military Review*, 1984, Vol. LXIV, No. 5, pp. 17–22.

Kalinovskii, K.B., 'Tanki v gruppakh DD' (Tanks in the Long-Range Penetration Groups), *Mekhanizatsiia i motorizatsiia Armii*, 1931, No. 2, pp. 7–19.

—, 'Tanki v oborone' (Tanks in the Defensive), *Voina i revoliutsiia*, 1927, No. 8, pp. 117–127.

Karber, P.A., 'Anti-Tank Weapons and the Future of Armor', *Armed Forces Journal*, 1976, No. 11, pp. 52–3.

—, 'Dynamic Doctrine for Dynamic Defense', *Armed Forces Journal*, 1976, No. 9, p. 28.

—, 'Soviet Lessons of the Middle East War', *15th Annual Army Operations Research Symposium*, Army Research and Development, Nov.–Dec., 1976, pp. 11–15.

—, 'The Soviet Anti-Tank Debate', *Military Review*, 1976, Vol. LVI, No. 11, pp. 67–76.

—, 'The Tactical Revolution in Soviet Military Doctrine', *Military Review*, 1977, Vol. LVII, No. 11, pp. 83–5, No. 12, pp. 33–4.

Karipin, V.V. and Tatarchenko, E.I., 'Vozdushnaia voina' (The War in the Air), *Vestnik vozdushnogo flota*, 1934, No. 4, pp. 4–13.

Kazarnovskii, Iu., 'Sozdanie i ispol'zovanie udarnykh armii' (Creation and Employment of Strike Armies), *Voenno-istoricheskii zhurnal*, 1973, No. 9, pp. 54–60.

Kellerman, G. 'Nastuplenie tankov' (Tank attack), *Voina i revoliutsiia*, 1932, No. 8–9, pp. 64–75.

Kennedy, P., 'Military Effectiveness in the First World War', in Millett, A.R. and Murray, W. (eds), *Military Effectiveness in the First World War* (Boston, 1988), pp. 329–50.

Kindsvatter, P.S., 'VII Corps in the Gulf War: Deployment and Preparation for Desert Storm', *Military Review*, 1992, Vol. LXXII, No. 1, pp. 2–16.

—, 'VII Corps in the Gulf War: Ground Offensive', *Military Review*, 1992, Vol. LXXII, No. 2, pp. 16–37.

Kipp, J.W., 'Barbarossa, Soviet Covering Forces and the Initial Period of War: Military History and Airland Battle', *Journal of Soviet Military Studies*, 1988, No. 1, pp. 188–212.

—, 'Soviet Military Doctrine and the Origins of Operational Art, 1917–1936', in Frank, W.C. and Gillette, P.S. (eds), *Soviet Military Doctrine From Lenin to Gorbachev 1915–1991* (Westport, CT, 1991).

—, 'The Evolution of Soviet Operational Art: The Significance of "Strategic Defense" and "Premeditated Defense" in the Conduct of Theatre Strategic Operations', *Journal of Soviet Military Studies*, 1991, No. 4, pp. 322–6.

—, 'Where Is the Threat?', *Military Review*, 1990, Vol. LXX, No. 12, pp. 2–15.

Kiriev, N. and Dovbenko, N., 'Iz opyta boevogo primeneniia peredovykh otriadov tankovykh mekhanizirovannykh korpusov' (From the Experience of Combat Use of Tank and Mechanized Corps), *Voenno-istoricheskii zhurnal*, 1982, No. 9, pp. 20–27.

Kiselev, I., 'Motorizovanno-mekhanizirovannye soedineniia' (Motorized-mechanized Formations), *Voina i revoliutsiia*, 1930, No. 5, pp. 41–64.

Kobrin, N., 'Iz opyta vydvizheniia tankovykh armii iz raionov sosredotocheniia dlia vvoda v srazhenie' (On the Experience of the Forward Movement of Tank Armies from Concentration Areas to Commitment for Engagement), *Voenno-istoricheskii zhurnal*, 1976, No. 9, pp. 70–77.

Kokhanov, V., 'By Joint Efforts', *Soviet Military Review*, 1974, No. 12, pp. 20–21.

Kolenkovskii, A., 'Nastupatel'naia operatsiia protiv ostanovivshegosia protivnika' (The Offensive Operation against a Halting Enemy), *Voina i revoliutsiia*, 1931, No. 7, pp. 33–41.

Kolossovskii, V., 'Strategiia vozdushnoi voiny' (Strategy of Air War), *Voina i revoliutsiia*, 1928, No. 7–8, pp. 128–141.

Korkodinov, P.D., 'Operativnoe iskusstvo Krasnoi Armii' (The Operational Art of the Red Army), *Morskoi Sbornik*, 1946, No. 6, pp. 4–11.

Korotkov, I., 'Voprosy obshchei taktiki v Sovetskoi voennoi istoriografii 1918–1941' (Questions of General Tactics in Soviet Military Historiography), *Voenno-istoricheskii zhurnal*, 1977, No. 12, pp. 86–91.

Korzun, L., 'Razvitie taktiki vstrechnogo boia v poslevoennyi period' (The Development of Meeting Encounter Tactics in the Postwar Period), *Voenno-istoricheskii zhurnal*, 1982, No. 1, pp. 69–75.

Kosiba, L.M., 'Improving the Joint Doctrinal Process: Reinforcing Success', *Military Review*, 1984, Vol. LXIV, No. 1, pp. 46–57.

Kostylev, V., 'Stanovlenie i razvitie vozdushno-desantnykh voisk' (The Growth and Development of the Airborne *Desant* Force), *Voenno-istoricheskii zhurnal*, 1975, No. 9, pp. 80–85.

Kovalev, I., 'Zadachi bombardirovochnoi aviatsii' (Tasks of Bomber Aviation), *Voina i revoliutsiia*, 1928, No. 5, pp. 39–47.

Krasil'nikov, V., 'Nekotorye voprosy voenno-nauchnoi raboty' (Several Questions of Military Scientific Work), *Voina i revoliutsiia*, 1931, No. 12, pp. 45–9.

Krause, M.D., 'Moltke and the Origins of Operational Art', *Military Review*, 1990, Vol. LXX, No. 9, pp. 28–44.

Kravchenko, I., 'Kharakternye cherty nastupatel'nykh operatsii Krasnoi Armii v Grazhdanskoi voine' (Characteristic Features of Offensive Operations of the Red Army in the Civil War), *Voenno-istoricheskii zhurnal*, 1976, No. 3, pp. 95–100.

—, 'Vedenie oborony Krasnoi Armii v khode Grazhdanskoi voine' (The Conduct of Defence by the Red Army in the course of the Civil War), *Voenno-istoricheskii zhurnal*, 1977, No. 12, pp. 74–8.

— and Katukov, A., 'O metodakh podgotovki nastupatel'nykh operatsii tankovykh armii' (Methods of Preparing Tank Armies' Offensive Operations), *Voennaia mysl'*, 1970, No. 10, pp. 69–81.

Kravchenko, N., 'Rubezhi desantnikov' (Frontiers of the *Desant* Troops), *Voennyi vestnik*, 1986, No. 7, pp. 25–8.

Krupchenko, I.E., 'Battle for Berlin', in Zhilin, P.A. *et al.* (eds), *Revue*

Internationale d'Histoire Militaire (Moscow, 1979), pp. 128–38.

—, 'Kharakternye cherty razvitiia i primeneniia tankovykh voisk' (Characteristic Features of Development and Employment of Tank Forces), *Voenno-istoricheskii zhurnal*, 1979, No. 9, pp. 25–32.

—, 'Podgotovka i vedenie operatsii na okruzhenie i likvidatsiu gruppirovok protivnika' (The Preparation and Execution of Encirclement and Liquidation Operations of Enemy Groupings), *Voenno-istoricheskii zhurnal*, 1988, No. 2, pp. 58–66.

—, 'Razvitie tankovykh voisk v period mezhdu Pervoi i Vtoroi mirovymi voinami' (The Development of Tank Forces in the Intermediate Period between the First and the Second World Wars), *Voenno-istoricheskii zhurnal*, 1968, pp. 31–45.

—, 'Sposoby razvitiia uspekha v operativnoi glubine silami tankovykh armii, tankovykh i mekhanizirovannykh korpusov' (Problems of Exploiting Success at Operational Depth with the Forces of Tank Armies, and Tank and Mechanized Corps), *Voenno-istoricheskii zhurnal*, 1986, No. 6, pp. 12–20.

Kryzhanovskii, V., 'Legkie motomekhanizirovannye soedineniia v armeiskoi operatsii' (Light Moto-mechanized Formations in Army Operations), *Voina i revoliutsiia*, 1931, No. 10–11, pp. 45–75.

—, 'Samostoiatel'noe motomekhanizirovannoe soedinenie na otkrytom flange armii v nastupatel'noi operatsii' (The Independent Moto-mechanized Formation in the Army's Open Flank during Offensive Operation), *Voina i revoliutsiia*, 1932, No. 1, pp. 13–33.

Kuksha, A.I., 'Vzaimodeistvie tankov DPP i DD s aviatsiei i artilleriei pri proryve oboronitel'noi polosy protivnika v manevrennoi voine' (Synchronization of DPP and DD tanks with Aviation and Artillery in Penetration of Enemy Defensive Lines in a Manoeuvre War), *Voina i revoliutsiia*, 1932, No. 1, pp. 1–12.

Kunitskii, P., 'Razgrom protivnika v strategicheskikh nastupatel'nykh operatsiiakh' (Methods of Defeating the Enemy in Offensive Operations), *Voenno-istoricheskii zhurnal*, 1987, No. 10, pp. 25–31.

Kurasov, A., 'Vo vstrechnom boiu' (In an Encounter Battle), *Voennyi vestnik*, 1974, No. 8, pp. 29–32.

Kurochkin, P., 'Vozdushno-desantnym voiskam – 50 let' (Airborne *Desant* Forces – 50 Years), *Voenno-istoricheskii zhurnal*, 1980, No. 8, pp. 94–6.

Kush-Zharko, K., 'Oborona v khode nastupleniia po opytu Velikoi otechestvennoi voiny' (Defence in the Course of an Offensive Based on the Experience of the Great Patriotric War), *Voennaia mysl'*, 1972, No. 8, pp. 37–46.

Kutakhov, P., 'Primenenie VVS vo frontovykh nastupatel'nykh operatsiiakh' (The Employment of the Air Force in Front Level Offensive Operations), *Voenno-istoricheskii zhurnal*, 1977, No. 6, pp. 31–8.

Kutter, W.D., 'Deep behind Enemy Lines', *Military Review*, 1990, Vol. LXX, No. 6, pp. 38–49.

Lambeth, C.L. and Chen, N., 'C3I for Special Operations Forces: On War's

Threshold', *Army*, 1990, No. 4, pp. 49–52, 55–6.

Lancaster, M. 'The Armor Force in the Airland Battle', *Armor*, 1982, No. 1, pp. 26–32.

Lancaster, S. and Clemens, J., 'Airland Battle Defeat Mechanisms', *Armor*, 1982, No. 1, pp. 35–7.

Lanier Deal, C., 'BAI: The Key to the Deep Battle', *Military Review*, 1982, Vol. LXII, No. 3, pp. 51–4.

Lapchinskii, A.N., 'Osnovnye voprosy sovremennoi aviatsii' (Basic Questions of Contemporary Aviation), *Voennaia mysl'*, 1937, No. 3–4, pp 3–15.

—, 'Vozdushnye desanty' (Airborne *Desants*), *Voina i revoliutsiia*, 1930, No. 6, pp. 81–94.

—, 'Vozdushnaia voina budushchego' (The Future Air War), *Voina i revoliutsiia*, 1931, No. 3, pp. 3–15.

Leonhard, R.R., 'Maneuver Warfare and the United States', in Hooker, R.D. (ed.), *Maneuver Warfare – An Anthology* (Novato, CA, 1993), pp. 42–56.

Lewi, K.E. and Dellinger, J.D., 'Training the CSS', *Military Review*, 1989, Vol. LXIX, No. 11, pp. 34–42.

Lewis, K.N. and Wilson, P.A., 'A Follow-On US Echelon for NATO Defense', *Military Review*, 1986, Vol. LXVI, No. 6, pp. 12–25.

Lind, W.S., 'An Operational Doctrine for Intervention', *Parameters*, 1987, Vol. XVII, No. 4, pp. 30–36.

—, 'A Proposal for the Corps: Missions and Force Structure', *Marine Corps Gazette*, 1975, No. 12, pp. 12–16.

—, 'Debating Military Reform', *Marine Corps Gazette*, 1988, No. 11, pp. 20–22.

—, 'Defense Reform: A Reappraisal', in Clark, A.A., *et al.* (eds), *The Defense Reform Debate*, pp. 327–33.

—, 'Defining Maneuver Warfare for the Marine Corps', *Marine Corps Gazette*, 1980, No. 3, pp. 55–8.

—, 'FM 100–5: Some Doctrinal Questions', *Military Review*, 1977, Vol. LVII, No. 3, pp. 54–65.

—, 'Light Infantry: A Response', *Marine Corps Gazette*, 1991, No. 1, pp. 52–3.

—, 'Light Infantry Tactics', *Marine Corps Gazette*, 1990, No. 6, pp. 42–7.

—, 'Misconceptions of Maneuver Warfare', *Marine Corps Gazette*, 1988, No. 1, pp. 16–17.

—, 'The Case for Maneuver Doctrine', in Clark, A.A., *et al.* (eds), *The Defense Reform Debate*, pp. 88–100.

—, 'The Changing Face of War – Into the Fourth Generation', *Military Review*, 1989, Vol. LXIX, No. 10, pp. 2–11.

—, 'The Operational Art – Bridging the Doctrinal Gap', *Marine Corps Gazette*, 1988, No. 4, pp. 45–50.

—, 'The Theory and Practice of Maneuver Warfare', in Hooker, R.D. (ed.), *Maneuver Warfare – An Anthology* (Novato, CA, 1993), pp. 3–18.

—, 'Why the German Example?', *Marine Corps Gazette*, 1982, No. 6, pp. 59–63.

—, 'Holder, L.D. and Swain, R., 'A Dialogue on the Evolution of Doctrine',

Military Review, 1989, Vol. LXIX, No. 11, pp. 74–6.

Lobov, V.N., 'Aktual'nye voprosy teorii Sovetskoi strategii 20-kh serediny 30-kh godov' (Actual Problems Regarding Soviet Strategic Theory in the 1920s to the mid-1930s), *Voenno-istoricheskii zhurnal*, 1989, No. 2, pp. 41–50.

Lomov, N., 'Izbrannye proizvedeniia M.N. Tukhachevskogo' (M.N. Tukhachevskii's Selected Works – Review Article), *Voenno-istoricheskii zhurnal*, 1965, No. 7, pp. 69–76.

Loomis, D.G., 'FM 100–5 Operations: A Review', *Military Review*, 1977, vol. LVII, No. 3, pp. 66–9.

Losik, O., 'Sposoby vedeniia vysokomanevrennykh boevykh deistvii brone-tankovymi i mekhanizirovannymi voiskami po opytu Belorusskoi i Vislo–Oderskoi operatsii' (Questions Concerning the Conduct of High Tempo Manoeuvre Warfare Based on the Actions of Armoured and Mechanized Forces in the Belorussian and Vistula–Oder Operations), *Voenno-istoricheskii zhurnal*, 1980, No. 9, pp. 18–25.

Lossow, W. von, 'Mission Type Tactics versus Order Type Tactics', *Military Review*, 1977, Vol. LVII, No. 6, pp. 87–91.

Luck, G.E., 'The XVIII Airborne Corps: Puttin' Power on the Ground', *Military Review*, 1992, Vol. LXXII, No. 6, pp. 2–13.

Ludvigsen, E.C., 'Modernization: Readiness for Airland Battle 2000', *Army*, 1983, No. 5, pp. 38–44.

Lungerich, R., 'US Rapid Deployment Forces – US CENTCOM – What Is It? Can It Do the Job?', *Armed Forces Journal International*, 1984, Oct., pp. 88–103.

Luttwak, E.N., 'The Decline of American Military Leadership', *Parameters*, 1980, Vol. X, No. 4, pp. 82–8.

—, 'The Operational Level of War', *International Security*, 1980/81, No. 3, pp. 61–79.

Luvaas, J., 'Clausewitz, Fuller and Liddell Hart', in Handel, M. (ed.), *Clausewitz and Modern Strategy* (London, 1986), pp. 197–212.

—, 'European Military Thought and Doctrine 1870–1914', in Howard, M. (ed.), *The Theory and Practice of War* (London, 1965), pp. 70–95.

—, 'Thinking at the Operational Level', in Allen, R.L. (ed.), *Operational Level of War – its Art* (US Army War College, Carlisle Barracks, PA, 28 Aug. 1985), pp. 4-10–4-20.

MacGregor, D.A., 'Future Battle: The Merging Levels of War', *Parameters*, 1992, Vol. XXII, No. 4, pp. 33–46.

Machos, J.A., 'Airland Battles or Airland Battle?', *Military Review*, 1983, Vol. LXIII, No. 7, pp. 33–40.

—, 'Tacair Support for Airland Battle', *Air University Review*, 1984, Vol. LXIV, No. 4, pp. 16–24.

Maginnis, R.L., 'Harnessing Creativity', *Military Review*, 1986, Vol. LXVI, No. 3, pp. 12–20.

Malevskii, A., 'Mekhanizatsiia sovremennykh armii' (The Mechanization of Modern Armies), *Voennaia mysl'*, 1937, No. 3–4, pp. 117–27.

—, 'Osnovy upravleniia moto-mekhanizirovannymi soedineniiami' (The Fundamentals of Command of Moto-mechanized Formations), *Voennaia mysl'*, 1937, No. 2, pp. 87–101.

Malkhov, M., 'Boevoe primenenie operativnykh grupp voisk v Velikoi otechestvennoi voine' (The Combat Employment of Operational Groups of Forces in the Great Patriotic War), *Voennaia mysl'*, 1960, No. 11, pp. 62–71.

Mallory, G.C., 'Combat Training Center: Training the Force to Fight', *Military Review*, 1987, Vol. LXVII, No. 10, pp. 2–7.

Maramzin, V.A., 'Metody raboty komanduiushchikh i shtabov po upravleniiu voiskami v operatsiiakh Velikoi otechestvennoi voiny' (Methods of Work of Commanders and Staffs in Commanding Troops in Operations of the Great Patriotic War), *Voennaia mysl'*, 1988, No. 5, pp. 28–32.

—, 'Organizatsiia upravleniia voiskami fronta v nastuplenii' (The Organization of Command among Front Troops in the Offensive), *Voenno-istoricheskii zhurnal*, 1981, No. 2, pp. 20–27.

Margelov, V., Razvitie teorii primeneniia vozdushno-desantnykh voisk v poslevoennyi period' (Development of the Theory of Employing Airborne-*Desant* Troops in the Post-war Period), *Voenno istoricheskii zhurnal*, 1977, No. 1, pp. 53–9.

Marievskii, I., 'Stanovlenie i razvitie teorii operativnogo iskusstva' (The Birth and Development of the Theory of Operational Art), *Voenno-istoricheskii zhurnal*, 1962, No. 2, pp. 26–40.

Mariott, W.T., 'Force Integration's Next Big Challenge', *Military Review*, 1986, Vol. LXVI, No. 4, pp. 4–13.

Maryshev, A., 'Deistviia tankovykh voisk pri proryve oborony protivnika' (The Actions of Tank Forces in the Penetration of the Enemy's Defence) *Voenno-istoricheskii zhurnal*, 1982, No. 8, pp. 13–16.

Mastulenko, V., 'Razvitie operativnogo iskusstva v nastupatel'nykh operatsiiakh' (The Development of Operational Art in Offensive Operations), *Voenno-istoricheskii zhurnal*, 1967, No. 10, pp. 37–43.

—, 'Razvitie taktiki nastupatel'nogo boia' (The Development of Offensive Battle Tactics), *Voenno-istoricheskii zhurnal*, 1968, No. 2, pp. 28–46.

Matthews, L.J., 'Operational Mania', *Army*, 1987, No. 2, pp. 19–21, 24–5.

Matii, E., 'Presledovanie v sovremennykh usloviiakh' (Pursuit in Modern Conditions), *Voennaia mysl'*, 1972, No. 4, pp. 42–8.

Maynard, W.K., 'The New American Way of War', *Military Review*, 1993, Vol. LXXIII, No. 11, pp. 5–17.

McCaffrey, B.R., 'Infantry on the High Intensity Battlefield of Central Europe', *Military Review*, 1978, Vol. LVIII, No. 1, pp. 3–6.

Mccoy, T.W., 'Full Strike – The Myth and Realities of Airland Battle', *Armed Forces Journal*, 1984, No. 6, pp. 78–83.

McDonough, J., 'The Operational Art: Quo Vadis', in Hooker, R.D. (ed.), *Maneuver Warfare – An Anthology* (Novato, CA, 1993), pp. 106–18.

McLelland, C.A., 'Systems and History in International Relations – Some Perspective for Empirical Research and Theory', *General Systems*, 1958,

No. 3, pp. 221–47.

McNair, C.H. and Reinsprecht, J., 'Army Aviation Forces in the Airland Battle', *US Army Aviation Digest*, 1981, No. 7, pp. 6–13.

Meehan, J.F., 'The Operational Trilogy', *Parameters*, 1986, Vol. XVI, No. 3, pp. 9–18.

Meese, M.J., 'Institutionalizing Maneuver Warfare: The Process of Organizational Change', in Hooker, R.D. (ed.), *Maneuver Warfare – An Anthology* (Novato, CA, 1993), pp. 193–216.

Melikov, V., 'Konnye massy v Grazhdanskoi voine' (Massed Cavalry in the Civil War), *Voina i revoliutsiia*, 1933, No. 7–8, pp. 3–16.

—, 'Srazhenie na Visle v svete opyta maisko–avgustovskoi kampanii 1920g.' (The Engagement on the Vistula in the Light of the Experience of the May–August Campaign of 1920), *Voina i revoliutsiia*, 1930, No. 10, pp. 9–44.

—, 'Tvorcheskii voenno-nauchnyi put' V. Triandafillova i K. Kalinovskogo' (The Creative Military-scientific path of V. Triandafillov and K. Kalinovskii), *Voina i revoliutsiia*, 1931, No. 8, pp. 3–10.

Merimskii, V., 'BMP v boiu' (The BMP in Combat), *Voennyi vestnik*, 1976, No. 3, pp. 19–22.

Mesarovic, M.D., 'Foundations for a General System Theory', in Mesarovic, M.S. (ed.), *Views on General System Theory* (New York, 1964), pp. 1–24.

Messerschmidt, M., 'German Military Effectiveness Between 1919–1939', in Millett, A.R. and Murray, W. (eds), *Military Effectiveness in the Interwar Period* (Boston, 1988), pp. 218–54.

Metz, F., 'Airland Battle and Counterinsurgency', *Military Review*, 1990, Vol. LXX, No. 1, pp. 32–41.

Metz, S. and Downey, F.M., 'Centers of Gravity and Strategic Planning', *Military Review*, 1988, Vol. LXVIII, No. 4, pp. 22–33.

Mezheninov, S., 'Boevaia aviatsiia' (Combat Aviation), *Voina i revoliutsiia*, 1929, No. 1, pp. 14–31.

Miagkov, V., 'Boevoe primenenie aviatsii v armeiskoi nastupatel'noi operatsii' (Tactical Air Support in Army Offensive Operations), *Voenno-istoricheskii zhurnal*, 1976, No. 7, pp. 20–28.

Mialkovskii, A., 'Udarnaia armiia' (The Strike Army), *Voina i revoliutsiia*, 1930, No. 2, pp. 48–68.

Montcastle, J.W., 'On the Move: Command and Control of Armored Units in Combat', *Military Review*, 1985, Vol. LXV, No. 11, pp. 14–39.

Montero, M.F., 'Supporting Remote Operations', *Army Logistician*, 1984, No. 3, pp. 3–5.

Moore, W.B. and Harned, G.M., 'Air Assault in the Desert: How to Fight', *Military Review*, 1985, Vol. LXV, No. 1, pp. 43–60.

Morelli, D.R. and Ferguson, M.M., 'Low Intensity Conflict: An Operational Perspective', *Military Review* 1984, Vol. LXIV, No. 11, pp. 2–16.

Muller, K.J., 'The Army in the Third Reich: An Historical Interpretation', *Journal of Strategic Studies*, 1979, No. 2, pp. 123–52.

Murguizur, J.C., 'Some Thoughts on Operational Manoeuvre Group',

International Defense Review, 1984, No. 4, p. 380.

Naumov, N., 'Teoriia proryva oborony protivnika v predvoennye gody' (The theory of Penetration through the Enemy Defensive in the Prewar Years), *Voenno-istoricheskii zhurnal*, 1975, No. 1, pp. 57–63.

Newell, C.R., 'Balancing the Ends, Ways and Means', *Army*, 1986, No. 8, pp. 24–6, 31–2.

—, 'Exploring the Operational Perspective', *Parameters*, 1986, Vol. XVI, No. 3, pp. 19–25.

—, 'Operational Art in the Joint and Combined Arenas', *Parameters*, 1988, Vol. XVIII, No. 2, pp. 33–9.

—, 'What Is Operational Art?', *Military Review*, 1990, Vol. LXX, No. 9, pp. 2–16.

Neugbauer, K.V., 'Operatives Denken zwischen dem Ersten und Zweiten Weltkrieg', in Boog, H. (ed.), *Operatives Denken und Handeln im Deutschen Streitkräften im 19. und 20. Jahrhundert* (Bonn, 1988), pp. 97–122.

Nowak, L.G., 'Synchronizing Deep Attack Support – The Corps Troops' Operational Cell', *Military Review*, 1988, Vol. LXVIII, No. 7, pp. 20–26.

Oberer, W.F., 'The True Difference', *Military Review*, 1988, Vol. LXVIII, No. 4, pp. 74–81.

Oblinger, J.B., 'Air Defense in the Airland Battle', *Air Defense*, 1982, No. 1, pp. 35–38.

O'Connor, W.G., 'Heavy–Light Fire Support – Light Force Ops', *Field Artillery Journal*, 1991, No. 1, pp. 11–15.

Offley, R., 'Close Air Support for the Airland Battle', *Infantry*, 1985, No. 5, pp. 21–5.

Olson, W.J., 'Organizational Requirements for LIC', *Military Review*, 1988, Vol. LXVIII, No. 1, pp. 8–16.

O'Neill, R.J., 'Doctrine and Training in the German Army 1919–1939', in Howard, M. (ed.), *The Theory and Practice of War* (London, 1965), pp. 143–66.

Orlov, B., 'The High Command of the Red Army and the Terror of the 1930s in the USSR', Ph.D. diss. (Tel Aviv University, 1986).

Oseth, J.M., 'An Overview of the Reform Debate', in Clark, A.A., et al. (eds), *The Defense Reform Debate*, pp. 44–61.

Osipov, M., 'Vliianie chislennosti srazhaiushchikhsia i storon na ikh poteri' (The Influence of the Numerical Strength of Engaged Forces on the Casualty Rate), *Voennyi sbornik*, 1915, No. 6, pp. 59–74, No. 7, pp. 25–36, No. 8, pp. 31–40, No. 9, pp. 25–37, No. 10, pp. 93–6.

Ostovich, R., 'Airland Battle: Dramatic Changes in Emerging Aviation Doctrine', *US Army Aviation Digest*, 1986, No. 11, pp. 2–7.

—, 'Army Aviation in Airland Battle Future', *Military Review*, 1991, Vol. LXXI, No. 2, pp. 25–9.

Otstott, C.P., Hagan, C.A. and Richmond, M.E., 'Battle Rhythm – Division Command and Control', *Military Review*, 1990, Vol. LXX, No. 6, pp. 14–26.

Pavlenko, N., 'Nekotorye voprosy razvitiia teorii strategii v 1920-kh godakh'

(Some Questions Regarding the Development of Strategic Theory in the 1920s), *Voenno-istoricheskii zhurnal*, 1966, No. 5, pp. 10–26.

Pavlenko, P., 'Razvitie taktiki vozdushno-desantnykh voisk v poslevoennyi period' (The development of Airborne *Desant* Force Tactics in the Post-war Period), *Voenno-istoricheskii zhurnal*, 1980, No. 1, pp. 28–33.

Pavlovskii, I., 'Sovetskoe operativnoe iskusstvo v Velikoi otechestvennoi voine' (Soviet Operational Art in the Great Patriotic War), *Voennaia mysl'*, 1968, No. 5, pp. 18–32.

Pechenenko, S., 'Armeiskaia nastupatel'naia operatsiia v usloviiakh dal'nevostochnogo teatra voennykh deistvii' (Army Offensive Operations in the Conditions of the Far-eastern Theatre of War), *Voenno-istoricheskii zhurnal*, 1978, No. 8, pp. 42–9.

Peters, R., 'Attacking the Attacker', *Armor*, 1983, No. 3, pp. 31–3.

Petraeus, D.H., 'Light Infantry in Europe: Strategic Flexibility and Conventional Deterrence', *Military Review*, 1984, Vol. LXIV, No. 12, pp. 35–55.

Petrov, S., 'Organizatsiia i podderzhanie vzaimodeistviia voisk v nastu-patel'nom boiu' (Organization and Maintenance of Synchronization among Forces in Offensive Warfare), *Voenno-istoricheskii zhurnal*, 1975, No. 5, pp. 22–9.

Petrovskii, D., 'Edinaia voennaia doktrina v Akademii General'nogo Shtaba' (Unified Military Doctrine in the General Staff Academy), *Voennoe znanie*, 1921, Nos. 14–15, pp. 1–19.

Popov, M.G. and Mal'ginov, N.I., 'O nekotorykh tendentsiiakh razvitiia teorii frontovoi nastupatel'noi operatsii' (Certain Tendencies Concerning the Development of the Theory of Front Offensive Operations), *Voennaia mysl'*, 1982, No. 1, pp. 17–26.

Porch, D., 'Clausewitz and the French', in Handel, M. (ed.), *Clausewitz and Modern Strategy* (London, 1986), pp. 287–302.

Portugal'skii, R.M., 'K voprosy o perekhode ot oborony k nastupleniiu' (Concerning the Problems of Transition from Defense to Offence), *Voennaia mysl'*, 1990, No. 6, pp. 15–22.

'Prikaz NKO No. 325 ot 16 oktiab'ra 1942g.' (Order of the People's Defence Commissariat of 16 October 1942), *Voenno-istoricheskii zhurnal*, 1974, No. 10, pp. 68–73.

Raach, G.T., 'The Logistic Estimate – A New Approach', *Military Review*, 1985, Vol. LXV, No. 7, pp. 66–72.

Radzievskii, A.I., 'Razvitie taktiki obshchevoiskovykh soedinenii' (The Development of Tactics of All-Arms Formations), *Voenno-istoricheskii zhurnal*, 1978, No. 2, pp. 27–34.

—, 'Vvod tankovykh armii v proryv' (The Commitment of Tank Armies to the Break-in), *Voenno-istoricheskii zhurnal*, 1976, No. 2, pp. 19–26.

Ramanichev, N., 'Razvitie teorii i praktiki boevogo primeneniia vozdushno-desantnykh voisk v mezhvoennyi period' (The Development of the Theory and Practice of the Combat Use of Airborne *Desant* Forces in the Interwar Period), *Voenno-istoricheskii zhurnal*, 1982, No. 10, pp. 72–7.

Rampy, M.R., 'Campaign Planning – Paradox or Paradigm', *Military Review*, 1990, Vol. LXX, No. 8, pp. 42–9.

Rapoport, A., 'Lewis F. Richardson's Mathematical Theory of War', *General Systems*, 1957, No. 2, pp. 55–91.

Record, J., 'The Military Reform Caucus', *Washington Quarterly*, 1983, No. 6, pp. 125–9.

Reed, J.W., 'Congress and Politics of Defense Reform', in Clark, A.A., *et al.* (eds), *The Defense Reform Debate*, pp. 230–49.

Reinhardt, T.H., 'Der Vorstoss des XXXXI Panzerkorps im Sommer 1941', *Wehrkunde*, 1956, No. 3, pp. 122–36.

—, 'Die Panzergruppe 3 in der Schlacht vor Moskau und ihre Erfahrungen im Rückzug', *Wehrkunde*, 1953, No. 9, pp. 1–11.

Reznichenko, V.G., 'Podgotovka i provedenie armeiskikh operatsii' (Preparation and Execution of Army Operations), *Voennaia mysl'*, 1991, No. 1, pp. 19–27.

Rice, C., 'The Making of Soviet Strategy', in Paret, P. (ed.), *Makers of Modern Strategy* (Oxford, 1986), pp. 648–76.

Richardson, W.R., 'FM 100–5: The Airland Battle in 1986', *Military Review*, 1986, Vol. LXVI, No. 3, pp. 4–11.

—, 'Winning on the Extended Battlefield', *Army*, 1981, No. 6, pp. 35–42.

Richie, S.W., 'Auftragstaktik – Schwerpunkt – Aufrollen – The Philosophical Basis of the Airland Battle', *Military Review*, 1984, Vol. LXIV, No. 7, pp. 48–53.

Riscassi, R.W., 'Doctrine for Joint Operations in a Combined Environment – A Necessity', *Military Review*, 1993, Vol. LXXIII, No. 6, pp. 20–37.

Robel, M.K., 'Operational Mobility for the Light Division', *Military Review*, 1989, Vol. LXVII, No. 7, pp. 41–8.

Rodin, A., 'Razgrom kontrudarnykh gruppirovok v nastuplenii' (The Defeat of Counterstrike Groupings in the Offensive), *Voennaia mysl'*, 1974, No. 5, pp. 28–34.

Rogers, B.W., 'Follow on Forces Attack (FOFA) – Myths and Reality', *NATO Review*, 1984, No. 12, pp. 21–32.

—, 'ACE Attack of Warsaw Pact Follow-On Forces', *Military Technology*, 1983, No. 5, pp. 39–52.

Rogers, J.B., 'Synchronizing the Airland Battle', *Military Review*, 1986, Vol. LXVI, No. 4, pp. 61–5.

Romjue, J.L., 'Airland Battle: The Historical Background', *Military Review*, 1986, Vol. LXVI, No. 3, pp. 52–5.

Rostunov, I., 'Sovetskaia voennaia istoriografiia v mezhvoennyi period' (Soviet Military Historiography in the Interwar Period), *Voenno-istoricheskii zhurnal*, 1967, No. 11, pp. 86–93.

Rotmistrov, P., 'Bronetankovye voiska' (Armoured Forces), *Voenno-istoricheskii zhurnal*, 1982, No. 2, pp. 18–25.

Runals, S.E., 'A Different Approach', *Military Review*, 1987, Vol. LXVII, No. 10, pp. 44–9.

—, 'A Difference in Style', *Military Review*, 1987, Vol. LXVII, No. 4, pp.

46–50.

Rush, R.S., 'Comparing Light Divisions', *Military Review*, 1987, Vol. LXVII, No. 1, pp. 62–9.

Rybicki, J.F., 'Advanced Conventional Munitions and the Airland Battle', *Military Technology*, 1986, No. 10, pp. 32–41.

—, 'Surveillance and Reconnaissance for the Airland Battle', *Military Technology*, 1985, No. 2, pp. 59–60, 62.

Saint, C.E., 'A CINC's View of Operational Art', *Military Review*, 1990, Vol. LXX, No. 9, pp. 65–78.

—, 'Attack Helicopter Operations in the Airland Battle: Close Operations', *Military Review*, 1988, Vol. LXVIII, No. 6, pp. 2–15.

—, 'Attack Helicopter Operations in the Airland Battle: Deep Operations', *Military Review*, 1988, Vol. LXVIII, No. 7, pp. 2–9.

—, 'Attack Helicopter Operations in the Airland Battle: Rear Operations', *Military Review*, 1988, Vol. LXVIII, No. 10, pp. 2–10.

— and Franks, T.R., 'Fire Support in Mobile Armored Warfare', *Field Artillery Journal*, 1988, No. 3, pp. 12–14.

Salikov, V., 'V peredovom otriade' (In the Forward Detachment), *Voennyi vestnik*, 1987, No. 3, pp. 33–6.

Salitan, I., 'Operativnaia deiatel'nost' armeiskoi konnitsy po opytu voiny s Pol'shei 1920g.' (The Cavalry Operational Activity According to the Experience of the 1920 Polish War), *Voina i revoliutsiia*, 1928, No. 12, pp. 67–86.

Sandrat, H.H. von, 'Considerations of the Battle in Depth', *Military Review*, 1987, Vol. LXVII, No. 10, pp. 8–15.

—, 'Defense Concepts and the Application of New Military Thinking', *RUSI Journal*, 1989, Vol. 134, No. 2, pp. 23–7.

Saunders, R.T., 'Is Airland Battle a Paper Tiger?', *Armor*, 1983, Vol. XLII, No. 6, pp. 49–50.

Savinov, I., 'Operatsii okruzheniia' (Encirclement Operation), *Voina i revoliutsiia*, 1934, No. 7, pp. 15–25.

Savushkin, R., 'K voprosu zarozhdeniia teorii posledovatel'nykh nastupatel'nykh operatsii 1921–1929gg.' (Concerning Questions of Sources of the Theory of Successive Offensive Operations 1921–1929), *Voenno-istoricheskii zhurnal*, 1983, No. 5, pp. 77–83.

—, 'Evoliutsiia vzgliadov na oboronu v mezhvoennye gody' (The Evolution of Defensive Perceptions in the Interwar Years), *Voenno-istoricheskii zhurnal*, 1987, No. 1, pp. 37–42.

—, 'K voprosu o vozniknovenii i razvitii operatsii' (On Questions of Origin and Development of the Operation), *Voenno-istoricheskii zhurnal*, 1979, No. 5, pp. 78–82.

—, and Ramanichev, N., 'Razvitie taktiki obshchevoiskovogo boia v period mezhdu Grazhdanskoi i Velikoi otechestvennoi voinami' (The Development of All-Arms Combat Tactics between the Civil and the Great Patriotic Wars), *Voenno-istoricheskii zhurnal*, 1985, No. 11, pp. 60–64.

Schmidt, R.L., 'A Doctrine for Command', *Military Review*, 1985, Vol. LXV,

No. 11, pp. 45–7.

Schneider, J.J., 'Introduction', in Triandafillov, V.K., *The Nature of Operations of Modern Armies*, ed. Kipp, J.W. (London, 1992), pp. XXV–XLVI.

—, 'Theoretical Implications of Operational Art', *Military Review*, 1990, Vol. LXX, No. 9, pp. 17–27.

—, 'The Loose Marble and the Origins of Operational Art', *Parameters*, 1989, Vol. XIX, No. 1, pp. 85–99.

—, 'V.K. Triandafillov – Military Theorist', *Journal of Soviet Military Studies*, 1988, No. 3, pp. 287–306.

— and Izzo, L.L., 'Clausewitz's Elusive Center of Gravity', *Parameters*, 1987, Vol. XVII, No. 3, pp. 46–57.

Schreyach, J.C., 'Deep-Attack System of Systems', *Field Artillery Journal*, 1989, No. 6, pp. 48–54.

—, 'Fire Support for Deep Operations', *Military Review*, 1989, Vol. LXIX, No. 8, pp. 29–36.

Schultz, J., 'Airland Battle 2000: The Force Multiplier', *Defense Electronics*, 1983, No. 12, pp. 48–67.

Schwarzkopf, H.N., 'Ability to Fight–Surest Way Proving for the Common Defense', *Army*, 1987, No. 10, pp. 111–13, 116–18, 121–2.

Schweppenburg, Frhr. G. von, 'Elementen der Operativen und Taktischen Führung von Schnellen Verbänden des 2. Weltkrieges', *Wehrwissenschaftliche Rundschau*, 1962, No. 2, pp. 93–110.

Scott, J.T., 'Special Operations Forces: The Future is the Focus', *Army*, (1993–1994 Green Book), Oct. 1993, pp. 180–84.

Scott, N.F. and H.F., 'The Historical Development of the Soviet Forward Detachment', *Military Review*, 1987, Vol. LXVII, No. 11, pp. 27–34.

Sediakin, A., 'Blizhnii boi' (The Close Battle), *Voennyi vestnik*, 1936, No. 8, pp. 1–4.

—, 'Tanki i protivotankovaia oborona' (Tanks and Anti-tank Defence), *Voina i revoliutsiia*, 1933, No. 11, pp. 29–36.

Senger und Etterlin, F.M. von, 'New Operational Dimensions', *RUSI Journal*, 1983, Vol. 128, No. 2, pp. 11–15.

Sennewald, R., 'Tailoring "Airland" Doctrine to Theater in Korea', *Army*, 1983, No. 10, pp. 92–104.

Shaw, L., 'System Theory', *Science*, 1965, No. 149, p. 1005.

Shelton, H.H. and Benson, K.C., 'Depth and Simultaneity: Half the Battle', *Military Review*, 1993, Vol. LXXIII, No. 12, pp. 57–63.

Shields, H.S., 'Why the OMG?', *Military Review*, 1985, Vol. LXV, No. 11, pp. 5–13.

Shilovskii, E.A., 'Evoliutsiia akademicheskoi podgotovkii' (The Evolution of Academic Instruction), *Voina i revoliutsiia*, 1928, No. 11, pp. 15–28.

—, 'Podgotovka i vedenie operativnogo proryva' (The Preparation and Execution of Operational Penetration), *Voennaia mysl'*, 1939, No. 8, pp. 21–9.

Shimanskii, A.M., 'Evoliutsiia operativnogo postroeniia fronta i armii po opytu Velikoi otechestvennoi voiny' (The Evolution of Operational

Structuring of Front and Army According to the Experience of the Great Patriotic War), *Voennaia mysl'*, 1978, No. 11, pp. 67–75.

Shvarts, M., 'Nekotorye uroki Varshavskoi operatsii 1920g.' (Basic Lessons of the 1920 Warsaw Operation), *Voina i revoliutsiia*, 1931, No. 4, pp. 34–60.

Sickler, R.A., 'Mine Warfare for Airland Battle – Future', *Military Review*, 1989, Vol. LXIX, No. 10, pp. 42–51.

Sidorenko, A.A., 'Sozdanie udarnykh gruppirovok vo frontovykh nastupatel'nykh operatsiiakh' (The Formation of Strike Groupings in Front Offensive Operations), *Voennaia mysl'*, 1980, No. 12, pp. 22–32.

Silvasy, S., 'Airland Battle Future: The Tactical Battlefield', *Military Review*, 1991, Vol. LXXI, No. 2, pp. 2–12.

Simpkin, R., 'Countering the OMG', *Military Technology*, 1984, No. 3, pp. 82–92.

—, 'Flying Tanks – A Tactical Technical Analysis of the Main Battle Air Vehicle', *Military Technology*, 1984, No. 8, pp. 62–82.

Sims, D.R. and Shilling, A.M., 'The Achilles' Heel of Airland Battle Future', *Field Artillery Journal*, 1990, No. 5, pp. 4–6.

Sincere, C.J., 'Target Acquisition for the Deep Battle', *Military Review*, 1989, Vol. LXIX, No. 8, pp. 23–8.

Sinnreich, R.H., 'Tactical Doctrine or Dogma?', *Army*, 1979, No. 9, pp. 16–19.

Smichenko, I., 'Peredovoi otriad forsiruet reku' (The Forward Detachment Forces a River), *Voennyi vestnik*, 1985, No. 11, pp. 72–4.

Smirnov, A., 'K voprosu ob operativnom iskusstve v Grazhdanskuiu voine 1918–1920gg.' (Concerning Questions of Operational Art in the Civil War 1918–1920), *Voina i revoliutsiia*, 1933, No. 1, pp. 18–29.

Smith, D., 'The Roots and Future of Modern Day Military Reform', *Air University Review*, 1985, No. 9, pp. 29–36.

Smith, D.L., and Meier, A.L., 'Ogarkov's Revolution: Soviet Military Doctrine for the 1990s', *International Defense Review*, 1987, No. 7, pp. 869–73.

Smith, R., 'The Gulf War: The Land Battle', *RUSI Journal*, 1992, Vol. 137, No. 1, pp. 1–5.

Snow, J.J., 'Airland Battle Doctrine: Tenets in Opposition', *Military Review*, 1987, Vol. LXVII, No. 10, pp. 63–7.

Sokhorukov, D.S., 'Vozdushno-desantnye voiska' (Airborne *Desant* Forces), *Voenno-istoricheskii zhurnal*, 1982, No. 1, pp. 37–43.

Sokolov, S., 'Sovetskoe operativnoe iskusstvo v kampanii 1945g. v Evrope' (Soviet Operational Art in the 1945 Campaign in Europe), *Voenno-istoricheskii zhurnal*, 1975, No. 5, pp. 28–35.

Sokolov-Strakhov, K., 'K.E. Voroshilov o kharaktere sovremennoi voiny' (K.E. Voroshilov on the Character of Modern War), *Voina i revoliutsiia*, 1931, No. 2, pp. 3–8.

Sollinger, J.M., 'Airland Battle – Implications for the Infantry', *Infantry*, 1982, No. 2, pp. 22–5.

Sosnitskii, V., 'Desantniki v atake' (Airborne Troops in the Attack), *Voennyi vestnik*, 1985, No. 11, pp. 72–4.

Starner, S.G., 'Deep Attack – We Can Do It Now', *Field Artillery Journal*,

1986, No. 3, pp. 11–13.

Starry, D.A., 'A Perspective on American Military Thought', *Military Review*, 1989, Vol. LXIX, No. 7, pp. 2–11.

—, 'Armor Conference Keynote Address', *Armor*, 1978, No. 4, pp. 32–6.

—, 'A Tactical Evolution – FM 100–5', *Military Review*, 1978, Vol. LVIII, No. 8, pp. 2–11.

—, 'Extending the Battlefield', *Military Review*, 1981, Vol. LXI, No. 3, pp. 31–50.

—, 'Running Things', *Parameters*, 1987, Vol. XVII, No. 3, pp. 13–20.

—, 'To Change an Army', *Military Review*, 1983, Vol. LXIII, No. 3, pp. 20–27.

—, 'The Principles of War', *Military Review*, 1981, No. 9, pp. 2–12.

Steen, K.O.W., 'Airland Battle Future', *Marine Corps Gazette*, 1991, No. 3, pp. 44–6.

Steger, G.F., 'More Dilemmas in Studying Soviet Tactics', *Military Review*, 1978, Vol. LVIII, No. 2, pp. 88–91.

Steiner, C.W. 'Special Operations Forces', *Parameters*, 1992, Vol. XXII, No. 2, pp. 2–11.

—, 'The Strategic Employment of Special Operations Forces', *Military Review*, 1991, Vol. LXXI, No. 6, pp. 2–13.

Stepnoi, K., 'Tanki i operativnoe iskusstvo' (Tanks and Operational Art), *Voennaia mysl'*, 1937, No. 1, pp. 28–45.

Stewart, M., 'Second Echelon Attack: Is the Debate Joined?', *Armed Forces Journal*, 1982, No. 9, pp. 111–17.

Stouder, R.L., 'Airland Operations: Are Unit Changes Needed?', *Military Review*, 1991, Vol. LXXI, No. 10, pp. 72–7.

Stubbs, K.D., 'Beyond the Army of Excellence', *Military Review*, 1988, Vol. LXVIII, No. 8, pp. 24–41.

Stumpf, R., 'From Tobruk to El Alamein: The Operational Basis of the Decision in North Africa in the Summer and Fall of 1942', in Roth, G. (ed.), *Development, Planning and Realization of Operational Conceptions in World Wars I and II* (Bonn, 1989), pp. 45–70.

Sullivan, B.D., 'Logistical Support for the Airland Battle', *Military Review*, 1984, Vol. LXIV, No. 2, pp. 2–16.

Sullivan, G.R., 'Doctrine – A Guide to the Future', *Military Review*, 1992, Vol. LXXII, No. 2, pp. 2–9.

—, 'Learning to Decide at the Operational Level of War', *Military Review*, 1987, Vol. LXVII, No. 10, pp. 16–23.

Summers, H.S., 'Principles of War and Low Intensity Conflict', *Military Review*, 1985, Vol. LXV, No. 3, pp. 43–49.

Sutten, C.G., 'Command and Control at the Operational Level', *Parameters*, 1986, Vol. XVI, No. 4, pp. 15–22.

Svechin, A.A., 'Integral'noe ponimanie voennogo iskusstva' (The Integral Comprehension of Operational Art), *Krasnye zori* (Red Dawns), 1924, No. 11, pp. 15–23.

Swan, G.C., 'Countering the Daring Thrust', *Military Review*, 1986, Vol. LXVI, No. 9, pp. 42–53.

Swita, B., 'The OMG in the Offense', *Military Review*, 1993, Vol. LXXIII, No. 11, pp. 30–40.

Taran, I. and Kolesnik, V., 'Organizatsiia sviazi v bronetankovykh i mekhanizirovannykh voiskakh deistvuiushchikh na razobshchennykh napravleniiakh' (The Organization of Radio Communication in Armoured and Mechanized Forces Operating in Several Directions), *Voenno-istoricheskii zhurnal*, 1982, No. 6, pp. 12–17.

Tatarchenko, E., 'Operativno-strategicheskaia podvizhnost' vozdushnykh sil' (Operational-strategic Mobility of Air Forces), *Voina i revoliutsiia*, 1932, No. 7, pp. 30–35.

Tate, C.J. and Holder, L.D., 'New Doctrine for the Defense', *Military Review*, 1981, Vol. LXI, No. 3, pp. 2–9.

Thompson, J.E., 'Heavy-Light Operations in the Desert', *Military Review*, 1985, Vol. LXV, No. 5, pp. 53–62.

Thurman, M.R., 'TRADOC: Evolving to Meet the Threat', *Army*, 1987, No. 10, pp. 52–5, 58–60.

Tiagunov, M., 'Operativnost' v upravlenii voiskami' (Operational Quality in the Command of Troops), *Voennyi vestnik*, 1976, No. 8, pp. 49–53.

Tiberi, P., 'German versus Soviet Blitzkrieg', *Military Review*, 1985, Vol. LXV, No. 9, pp. 63–71.

Tilson, J.C.F., 'The Forward Defense of Europe', *Military Review*, 1981, Vol. LXI, No. 5, pp. 66–76.

'TRADOC's Reply', *Armed Forces Journal*, 1976, No. 9, p. 27.

Triandafillov, V.K., 'K voprosu ob ocherednykh zadachakh po usovershenstvovaniiu boevoi podgotovki vysshego komandnogo sostava' (Concerning Questions of Relevant Objectives through the Improvement of the Combat Training of Higher Command Staffs), *Voina i revoliutsiia*, 1927, No. 1, pp. 31–43.

—, 'O Volkovyskoi operatsii' (On the Volkovysk Operation), *Krasnaia Armiia: vestnik voenno-nauchnogo obshchestva pri Voennoi akademii* (The Red Army: Military Scientific Herald to the Audience of the Military Academy), 1922, No. 10–11, pp. 34–43.

—, 'Perekopskaia operatsiia Krasnoi Armii' (The Perekop Operation of the Red Army), in Bubnov, A.S., *et al.* (eds), *Grazhdanskaia voina 1918–1921: Voennoe iskusstvo Krasnoi Armii* (The Civil War 1918–1921: The Military Art of the Red Army) (Moscow, 1928–1930) pp. 339–57.

—, 'Vzaimodeistvie mezhdu Zapadnym i Iugo-zapadnym frontami vo vremia letnego nastupleniia Krasnoi Armii na Vislu v 1920g.' (Cooperation between the Western and South-western Fronts in the Course of the Red Army's Offensive towards the Vistula in 1920), *Voina i revoliutsiia*, 1925, No. 2, pp. 19–51.

Trotsky, L., 'Voennaia doktrina ili mnimo-voennoe doktrinerstvo' (Military Doctrine or Pseudo-military Doctrinairism), *Voennaia nauka i revoliutsiia*, 1921, No. 2, pp. 204–13.

Trukhin, F., 'Osnovy operativnogo presledovaniia' (The Fundamentals of Operational Pursuit), *Voennaia mysl'*, 1939, No. 11, pp. 92–107.

Tsiffer, R., 'Kharakteristika predstoiashchei voiny' (A Description of the Coming War), *Voina i revoliutsiia*, 1931, No. 10–11, pp. 3–19.

Tsirlin, A., 'Operativnaia maskirovka vo frontovoi nastupatel'noi operatsii po opytu Velikoi otechestvennoi voiny' (Operational Deception in Front Offensive Operations according to the Experience of the Great Patriotic War), *Voennaia mysl'*, 1966, No. 9, pp. 58–67.

Tukhachevskii, M.N., 'K voprosu sovremennoi strategii' (Questions of Contemporary Strategy), in *Voina i voennoe iskusstvo v svete istoricheskogo materializma* (War and Military Art in the Light of Historical Materialism) (Moscow, 1927), pp. 129–33.

'Novye voprosy voiny' (New Questions of War), *Voenno-istoricheskii zhurnal*, 1962, No. 2, pp. 62–77.

—, 'O strategicheskikh vzgliadakh prof. Svechina' (On the Strategic Views of Prof. Svechin), in Bocharov, K., Nizhechek, I. and Suslov, P. (eds), *Protiv reaktsionnykh teorii na voenno-nauchnom fronte: kritika strategicheskikh i voenno-isotricheskikh vzgliadov prof. Svechina* (Against Reactionary Theories on the Military-scientific Front: A Critique of Prof. Svechin's Strategic and Military-historical Views) (Moscow, 1931), pp. 3–16.

—, 'Pervaia armiia v 1918 godu' (The First Army in 1918), *Revoliutsiia i voina*, 1921, no. 4–5, pp. 190–206.

—, 'Upravlenie armiei i frontom' (Commanding Army and Front), *Voennyi vestnik*, 1922, No. 8, pp. 46–47 (a summary of a lecture given on 3 April 1922 in the military academy).

—, 'Voina' (War), in *Bol'shaia Sovetskaia Entsiklopediia*, Vol. 12, 1928, pp. 576–8.

Turlington, J.E., 'Truly Learning the Operational Art', *Parameters*, 1987, Vol. XVII, No. 1, pp. 51–64.

Ul'ianov, V., 'Razvitie teorii glubokogo nastupatel'nogo boia v predvoennye gody' (The Development of the Theory of the Deep Offensive Battle in the Prewar Years), *Voenno-istoricheskii zhurnal*, 1988, No. 3, pp. 26–33.

Usol'chev, N.G., 'Iz opyta reidovykh deistvii podvizhnykh grupp frontov i armii: operativnoe iskusstvo' (From the Experience of Front and Army Mobile Group Raiding Actions: Operational Art), *Voennaia mysl'*, 1980, No. 1, pp. 13–18.

Vakulich, P., 'Sovremennaia operatsiia' (The Contemporary Operation), in Levichev, V.N. (ed.), *Voina i voennoe delo* (Moscow, 1933), pp. 546–64.

Van der Vlis, A., 'Airland Battle in NATO: A European View', *Parameters*, 1984, Vol. XIV, No. 2, pp. 10–14.

Vann, J.M., 'The Forgotten Forces', *Military Review*, 1987, Vol. LXVII, No. 8, pp. 2–17.

Varfolomeev, N., 'Manevry na zapfronte' (Manoeuvres on the Western Front), *Revoliutsiia i voina*, 1923, No. 19, pp. 5–26, No. 20, pp. 77–104.

—, 'Operativnaia vnezapnost' i maskirovka (Operational Surprise and Deception), *Voina i revoliutsiia*, 1927, No. 3, pp. 96-11.

—, 'Podgotovka operatsii udarnykh armii' (The Preparation of a Strike Army Operation), *Voina i revoliutsiia*, 1932, No. 3, pp. 1–13.

—, 'Strategiia v akademicheskoi podgotovke' (Strategy in an Academic Setting), *Voina i revoliutsiia*, 1928, No. 11, pp. 78–93.

—, 'Vstrechnaia operatsiia' (The Meeting Operation), *Voina i revoliutsiia*, 1930, No. 7, pp. 11–42.

Velocci, T., 'Battle Doctrine for the 21st Century', *National Defense*, 1982, No. 11, pp. 11–14.

Vermillion, J.M., 'The Pillars of Generalship', *Parameters*, 1987, Vol. XVII, No. 2, pp. 2–17.

Vigor, P.H., 'Doubts and Difficulties Confronting a Would-Be Soviet Attacker', *RUSI Journal*, 1980, Vol. 125, No. 2, pp. 32–8.

—, 'Fighting in Built-Up Areas', *RUSI Journal*, 1977, Vol. 122, No. 2, pp. 39–47.

—, 'Soviet Army Wave Attack Philosophy', *International Defense Review*, 1979, No. 1, pp. 43–7.

—, 'Soviet Military Exercises', *RUSI Journal*, 1971, Vol. 116, No. 3, pp. 23–9.

—, 'Soviet Military Thought: A New American Venture', *RUSI Journal*, 1979, Vol. 124, No. 1, pp. 74–6.

—, 'Soviet Reconnaissance', *RUSI Journal*, 1975, Vol. 120, No. 4, pp. 41–5.

—, 'The Soviet View of Fuller and Liddell Hart', *RUSI Journal*, 1978, Vol. 123, No. 1, pp. 74–7.

— and Erickson, J., 'The Soviet View of the Theory and Strategy of War', *RUSI Journal*, 1970, Vol. 115, No. 2, pp. 3–13.

Vinnikov, V. 'O vstrechnom boe' (On the Encounter Battle), *Voennyi vestnik*, 1973, No. 1, pp. 20–25.

Vol'pe, A., 'Nekotorye mysli o dialektike voiny' (Some Thoughts on the Dialectics of War), *Voina i revoliutsiia*, 1929, No. 5, pp. 36–54.

—, 'Presledovanie v Grazhdanskoi voine' (Pursuit in the Civil War), in Bubnov, A.S., *et al.* (eds), *Grazhdanskaia voina, 1918–1921* (The Civil War, 1918–1921) (Moscow, 1928–1930), Vol. II, pp. 233–59.

Vorob'ev, I.N., 'Oruzhiia i taktika' (Arms and Tactics), *Krasnaia zvezda*, 12 Jan. 1982, p. 2.

Wagner, R.E., 'Active Defense and All That', *Military Review*, 1980, Vol. LX, No. 8, pp. 4–13.

Walker, J., 'The Conundrum of Airland Warfare', *RUSI Journal*, 1988, Vol. 133, No. 2, pp. 15–22.

Wallach, J., 'Misperception of Clausewitz's *On War* by the German Military', in Handel, M. (ed.), *Clausewitz and Modern Strategy* (London, 1986), pp. 213–39.

Wass de Czege, H., 'Army Doctrinal Reform', in Clark, A.A., *et al.* (eds), *The Defense Reform Debate*, pp. 101–22.

—, 'Toward a New American Approach to Warfare', in Franz, W.P. (ed.), *The Art of War Quarterly*, Vol. II (US Army War College, Carlisle Barracks, PA, Sep. 1983), pp. 31–62.

— and Holder, L.D., 'The New FM 100–5', *Military Review*, 1982, Vol. LXII, No. 7, pp. 53–70.

Watkins, S.H. and Barron, M.J., 'Air Maneuver on the Modern Battlefield',

Military Review, 1989, Vol. LXIX, No. 7, pp. 49–53.

Wertman, C., 'Attack – Soviet Style', *Marine Corps Gazette*, 1982, No. 7, pp. 46–9.

Westwood, J.T., 'Maneuver: A Broadened Concept', *Military Review*, 1983, Vol. LXIII, No. 3, pp. 15–19.

Wheeler, A.G., 'Operational Logistics in Support of the Deep Attack', *Military Review*, 1986, Vol. LXVI, No. 2, pp. 12–19.

Whelden, C.B., 'Light Cavalry: Strategic Force for the Future', *Military Review*, 1993, Vol. LXXIII, No. 4, pp. 13–20.

Woodmansee, J.W., 'Blitzkrieg and the Airland Battle', *Military Review*, 1984, Vol. LXIV, No. 8, pp. 21–39.

Wright, G.R., 'The 20×20 Threat', *Infantry*, 1981, No. 2, pp. 15–17.

Yeosock, J.J., 'Army Operations in the Gulf Theater', *Military Review*, 1991, Vol. LXXI, No. 9, pp. 2–15.

Zakharov, M.V., 'Teoriia glubokoi operatsii' (The Theory of Deep Operation), *Voenno-istoricheskii zhurnal*, 1970, No. 10, pp. 10–20.

Zheltoukhov, A., 'Vzaimodeistvie – osnova uspekha v boiu' (Synchronization – the Basis of Success in Combat), *Voennyi vestnik*, 1973, No. 9, pp. 46–50.

Zhigur, Iu., 'Operativnyi plan voiny Shliffena i sovremennaia deistvitel'nost'' (Schlieffen's Operational War Plan and Modern Reality), *Voina i revoliutsiia*, 1929, No. 6, pp. 3–16, No. 7, pp. 3–14.

—, 'Proryv oboronitel'noi sistemy po opytu Mirovoi voiny' (The Penetration of Defensive Systems according to the Experience of the World War), *Voina i revoliutsiia*, 1935, No. 1, pp. 74–89.

Zhilin, P., 'Diskussii o edinoi voennoi doktrine' (The Discussions of a Unified Military Doctrine), *Voenno-istoricheskii zhurnal*, 1961, No. 5, pp. 61–74.

Zhuravlev, N., 'Operativnoe sosredotochenie' (Operational Concentration), *Voina i revoliutsiia*, 1935, No. 11, pp. 41–47.

Ziemke, E.F., 'Franz Halder and Orsha: The German General Staff Seeks a Consensus', *Military Affairs*, 1975, No. 39, pp. 173–6.

Zlobin, A.B., 'K voprosu ob organizatsii manevra v operatsii' (Concerning Questions of Organization of Manoeuvre within Operations), *Voennaia mysl'*, 1987, No. 9, pp. 24–33.

Zoellner, A.D. von, 'Schlieffens Vermächtnis', *Militärwissenschaftliche Rundschau*, Sonderheft 1938, 4 Jan., pp. 48–52.

Zotov, A.Iu, 'Boi 1-oi Konnoi armii v raione Rovno v iiune 1920g.' (The Battle of the 1st Cavalry Army in the Region of Rovno in June 1920), *Voina i revoliutsiia*, 1929, No. 2, pp. 102–3.

Index

Printed in the United States
123146LV00001B/154-198/A